Thailand

Other Travellers' Wildlife Guides

Alaska
Australia: The East
Belize and Northern Guatemala
Brazil: Amazon and Pantanal
Costa Rica
Ecuador and the Galápagos Islands
Florida
Hawaii
Peru
Southern Africa
Southern Mexico

TRAVELLERS' WILDLIFE GUIDES

Thailand

by David L. Pearson and Les Beletsky

Contributors: Richard Francis, Peter Paul van Dijk

Illustrated by:
Marc Dando (mammals)
Kyoko Kurosawa (fish)
John Myers (plants)
Colin Newman (insects, fish)
David Nurney (birds)
Fernanda Oyarzun (marine invertebrates)
Andy Woodham (fish)
Additional animal art by: Linda Feltner, H. Douglas Pratt

Photographs by:
Peter Paul van Dijk (amphibians, reptiles, habitats)
John Moore (insects)
Nancy Pearson (insects, habitats)
Additional photographs by: Rhett Butler, Jannie Dusseau, Heike Feldhaar, William Schaedla, Harald Schillhammer, Uthai Treesucon

CHASTLETON TRAVEL
An imprint of Arris Publishing Ltd
Gloucestershire

First published in Great Britain 2008 by

Chastleton Travel
An imprint of Arris Publishing Ltd
12 Main Street
Adlestrop
Moreton-in-Marsh
Gloucestershire GL56 0YN
www.arrisbooks.com

Text copyright © David L. Pearson and Les Beletsky 2008
Illustrations © Marc Dando (Plates 61–75); Linda Feltner (Plates 14b, 19f); Kyoko Kurosawa (Plates 77b,e,f, 79a, 80a,b, 81a–c, 83b,d,e, 86b,c, 87a,d–f, 88a, 89a–c,e,f, 90a,e,f, 91a, 92b,d,f, 93a–e, 94b–f, 95c–e, 96a,b,d–f, 97a,b,e); John Myers (Figures 1–15); Colin Newman (Plates 1b,c, 2, 6c,e, 76c,e, 78b, 79c, 80d–f, 82a–d, f, 83a,c,f, 84a,b,d, 85, 86a,d–f, 87b,c, 88b–e 89d, 90b–d, 91c,d, 92a,c,e, 93f, 94a, 95a,b,f, 96c, 97c,d, 98b, 99a,b,g, 100a); David Nurney (Plates 23–60); Fernanda Oyarzun (Plates 101–108), H. Douglas Pratt (Plate 14a); Andy Woodham (Plates 76a,b,d,f, 77a,c,d, 78ac–f, 79b,d–f, 80c, 81d–f, 82e, 84c,e,f, 91b,e,f, 97f, 98a,c–f, 99c–f, 100b–g). Photos © Rhett Butler (Plate 6d); Jannie Dusseau (Habitat Photos 6,16); Heike Feldhaar (Plate 6b); John Moore (Plates 1a,d, 3, 4a–d, 5); Nancy Pearson (Plates 1e,f, 4e; Habitat Photos 1, 3–5, 7, 8, 10, 11, 17, 19, 20, 22); William Schaedla (Habitat Photo 2); Harald Schillhammer (Plate 6a); Uthai Treesucon (Habitat Photos 13–15, 18, 21) Peter Paul van Dijk (Plates 7–13, 14c,d, 15–18, 19a–e, 20–22; Habitat Photo 23)

The moral rights of David L. Pearson and Les Beletsky to be identified as copyright holders of this work have been asserted by them in accordance with the Copyright, Design, and Patents Act 1988.

ISBN 13: 978-1-905214-60-0

All rights reserved
British Library in Cataloguing Data
A catalogue record for this book is available from the British Library

Cover image: Great hornbill © Photographer: Chanyut Sribua-rawd/Agency: Dreamstime.com

Printed and bound in China

To request our complete catalogue, please call us on **01608 659328**,
visit our web site at: **www.arrisbooks.com**, or e-mail us at:
info@arrisbooks.com.

CONTENTS

Preface		**ix**
Chapter 1.	**Ecotourism: Travel for the Environmentally Concerned**	**1**
	What Ecotourism is and Why It's Important	1
	How Ecotourism Helps; Ecotravel Ethics	2
	Thailand: Environmental Threats and Conservation	4
Chapter 2.	**Thailand: Geography and Habitats**	**8**
	Geography and Climate	9
	Landform Regions	9
	Biogeographical Regions	11
	Vegetation Patterns	12
	Tree Shape and Forest Layering	12
	Large-leaved Understory Plants	14
	Tree Bases and Roots	14
	Climbers and Stranglers	14
	Epiphytes	14
	Palms	15
	Major Ecosystems and Common Plant Species	15
	Evergreen Forest	15
	Tropical Mixed Deciduous Forest	18
	Dry Deciduous Dipterocarp Forest	18
	Limestone Forest	19
	Pine Forest	20
	Marshes and Swamps	20
	Mangrove and Coastal Vegetation	21
	Pastures, Farms, and Plantations	22
	Coral Reefs	22
	Environmental Close-Up 1: Why Is Farming So Difficult in the Tropics?	37
Chapter 3.	**Parks and Reserves**	**40**
	Peninsular Thailand (PT)	41
	The Southeast (SE)	44
	The Central Plains (CP)	44
	The West (W)	44
	The Northeast (NE)	45
	The Far North (FN)	46
	Environmental Close-up 2: Brazilian Rubber in Thailand: Economic Boom or Environmental Disaster?	47
Chapter 4.	**How to Use This Book: Ecology and Natural History**	**50**
	What Is Natural History?	50
	What Is Ecology and What Are Ecological Interactions?	50
	How to Use This Book	52
	Information in the Family Profiles	52
	Information in the Color Plate Sections	56

Chapter 5. Insects and Other Terrestrial Arthropods — 59
Introduction — 59
General Characteristics and Classification — 61
Features of Tropical Arthropods — 61
Seeing Arthropods in Thailand — 63
Order and Family Profiles
    1. Dragonflies and Damselflies — 63
    2. Grasshoppers, Crickets, and Cockroaches — 64
    3. Termites — 65
    4. Cicadas — 66
    5. Antlions — 66
    6. Beetles — 67
    7. Butterflies and Moths — 69
    8. Flies — 70
    9. Ants, Wasps, and Bees — 71
    10. Spiders — 72

Chapter 6. Amphibians — 74
Introduction — 74
General Characteristics and Classification — 75
Seeing Amphibians in Thailand — 76
Family Profiles
    1. Salamanders — 77
    2. Caecilians — 79
    3. Leaf-litter Toads — 81
    4. True Toads — 82
    5. True Frogs — 83
    6. Narrow-mouthed Frogs — 84
    7. Treefrogs — 87
Environmental Close-Up 3: Frog Population Declines — 90

Chapter 7. Reptiles — 93
Introduction — 93
General Characteristics and Classification — 94
Seeing Reptiles in Thailand — 96
Family Profiles
    1. Crocodilians — 97
    2. Turtles — 99
    3. Geckos — 101
    4. Monitor and Agamid Lizards — 103
    5. Skinks and Grass Lizard — 105
    6. Venomous Snakes — 107
    7. Pythons and Miscellaneous Snakes — 111
    8. Colubrids: Your Regular, Everyday Snakes — 113
Environmental Close-up 4: Endemism and High Species Diversity: Why Thailand? — 115

Chapter 8. Birds — 118
Introduction — 119
General Characteristics and Classification — 120
Features of Tropical Birds — 121
Seeing Birds in Thailand — 122
Family Profiles
    1. Pelican Allies — 124
    2. Herons and Egrets — 125

Contents vii

    3. Marsh and Stream Birds   127
    4. Ducks   128
    5. Terns and Gulls   130
    6. Shorebirds (Waders)   131
    7. Pheasants and Buttonquail   133
    8. Hawks, Eagles, and Kites   135
    9. Falcons   137
    10. Pigeons and Doves   138
    11. Parrots   140
    12. Cuckoos   142
    13. Owls   143
    14. Nightjars and Frogmouths   145
    15. Trogons   146
    16. Kingfishers   147
    17. Bee-eaters and Rollers   148
    18. Hornbills   150
    19. Barbets   151
    20. Woodpeckers   152
    21. Broadbills and Pittas   154
    22. Swifts, Treeswifts, and Swallows   156
    23. Pipits and Cuckoo-shrikes   158
    24. Ioras and Leafbirds   159
    25. Bulbuls   160
    26. Drongos and Orioles   161
    27. Crows and Magpies   163
    28. Tits and Nuthatches   164
    29. Babblers   165
    30. Old World Warblers   166
    31. Thrushes   168
    32. Old World Flycatchers   169
    33. Shrikes and Starlings   170
    34. Sunbirds, Flowerpeckers, and White-eyes   171
    35. Sparrows, Munias, and Finches   173
    Environmental Close-Up 5: Frugivory: Animals That Eat Fruit and the Trees That Want Them To   175

Chapter 9. Mammals   **179**
    Introduction   179
    General Characteristics and Classification   180
    Features of Tropical Mammals   181
    Seeing Mammals in Thailand   182
    Family Profiles
        1. Treeshrews, Shrews, and Hedgehogs   183
        2. Flying Lemurs and Bats   185
        3. Primates   189
        4. Pangolins   192
        5. Rodents and Rabbits   194
        6. Carnivores   197
        7. Even-toed Ungulates   201
        8. Elephant, Tapir, and Rhinoceros   203
        9. Dolphins and Dugong   205

Chapter 10. Underwater Thailand (by Richard Francis)   **207**
    Introduction   207
    The Andaman Sea   208

Contents

The Gulf of Thailand	208
Monsoons	209
Reef Creatures	209
Invertebrate Life	210
Vertebrate Life	211
Final Remarks	216
Environmental Close-Up 6: Nosebleeds and the Nature of Light	217

References and Additional Reading   **218**

Habitat Photos   **221**

Identification Plates   **232**

Species Index   **450**

General Index   **465**

PREFACE

This book and others in the series are aimed at environmentally conscious travellers for whom some of the best parts of any trip are glimpses of wildlife in natural settings; at people who, when speaking of a journey, often remember days and locations by the wildlife they saw: "That was where we watched the monkeys," and "That was the day we saw the hawk catch a snake." The purpose of the book is to heighten enjoyment of a trip and enrich wildlife sightings by providing you with information to identify several hundred of the most frequently encountered animals and plants of Thailand, along with up-to-date information on their natural history, behavior, and conservation. Your skills at recognizing many of the species you see on your travels through Thailand will be greatly enhanced with this book's color illustrations of 31 species of insects and spiders, 94 amphibians and reptiles, 186 birds, 68 mammals, and 54 common plants that are characteristic of Thailand's major habitats. In addition, for you snorkelers and divers, there are color illustrations of 209 fish and marine invertebrates.

The idea to write this book grew out of our own travel experiences and frustrations. First and foremost, we found that we could not find a single book to take along on a trip that would help identify all the types of animals and plants that interested us. There are bird and mammal field guides and plant identification handbooks, but their number and weight quickly accumulate until you need an extra suitcase just to carry them. Thus, the idea: create a single guidebook that travellers could carry to help them identify and learn about the different kinds of animals and plants they were most likely to see. Also, in our experience with guided tours, we've found that guides vary tremendously in their knowledge of nature and wildlife. Many, of course, are fantastic sources of information on the ecology and behavior of animals and plants. Some, however, know only about certain kinds of animals, such as birds, for instance. Many others, we found, knew precious little about animals or plants, and what information they did tell their groups was often incorrect.

Last, like most ecotravellers, we are concerned about the threats to many species as their natural habitats are damaged or destroyed by people; when we traveled, we wanted current information on the conservation statuses of species we encountered. This book provides the traveller with conservation information on many of the species pictured or discussed in the book.

A few administrative notes: because this book has an international audience, we present measurements in both metric and English system units. The scientific classification of common species by now, you might think, would be pretty much established and unchanging, but you would be wrong. These days, what with molecular methods to compare species, classifications of various species groups that were first worked out during the 1800s and early 1900s are undergoing radical changes. Many bird groups, for instance, are being reclassified after comparative studies of their DNA. The research is so new that many biologists are still arguing about the results. We cannot guarantee that all the classifications that we use in the book are absolutely the last word on the subject, or that we have been wholly consistent in the classifications we used. However, for most users of this book, such minor transgressions are probably too esoteric to be of much significance.

Finally, we have tried to make the style of writing interesting and readable, but at the same time challenging and precise. We have tried to avoid terse, dry, textbook prose, sometimes with narratives that include anthropomorphisms— providing plants and animals with human characteristics. We do this for fun; hopefully, in so doing, we have not offended our professional colleagues. Plants and animals do not, of course, reason and think like humans. If you do not appreciate our sense of humor, please ignore those sections; you should still have remaining a solid natural history guide to Thailand.

We need to acknowledge the help of a large number of people in producing this book. First, much of the information we use is gleaned from published sources, and we owe the authors of these books and scientific papers a great deal of credit; their names and the titles of their publications are listed in the References and Additional Reading section. We are especially indebted to Richard Francis for his writing of the Underwater Thailand chapter and the marine life species accounts; to Peter Paul van Dijk for his writing of the amphibian and reptile species accounts, parts of the amphibian chapter, and for supplying the excellent photos of amphibians and reptiles; and to Martha L. Crump for contributions to the amphibian chapter. In addition, most sections were read and critiqued by at least one outside expert in that field, and their comments and corrections greatly increased the accuracy of the book. These experts include: Indraneil Das (University of Malaysia, Sarawak), Uthai Treesucon (Bangkok, Thailand); Bruce Gill (CPQP, Ottawa, Canada), Matjaz Kuntner (George Washington University), Steve Lingafelter (USDA-Smithsonian Institution), Tony Gill (Arizona State University), and Bill Schaedla (Arizona State University). Nancy Pearson cheerfully supported us at every step and critiqued chapters based on her travels in Thailand. The logistics of travel within the country were greatly facilitated by Anavaj "Wat" and Anuncha "Jeed" Chaimongkol (Green International Concepts, Co., Ltd., Bangkok; anavaj@anet.net.th), who also generously shared their knowledge of Thai culture and Thai wildlife. Rhett Butler, Jannie Dusseau, Heike Feldhaar, John Moore, Nancy Pearson, Bill Schaedla, Harald Schillhammer, and Uthai Treesucon provided the excellent habitat and insect photos. We wish also to thank our editors at Interlink Books, and the artists who produced the marvelous illustrations: Marc Dando (mammals), Kyoko Kurosawa (fish), John Myers (plants), Colin Newman (fish, insects), David Nurney (birds), Fernanda Oyarzun (marine invertebrates), and Andy Woodham (fish).

Please let us know of any errors, opinions on the book, and suggestions for future editions. Write care of the publisher or e-mail: ECOTRAVEL8@aol.com.

Chapter 1

ECOTOURISM: TRAVEL FOR THE ENVIRONMENTALLY CONCERNED

- What Ecotourism Is and Why It's Important
- How Ecotourism Helps; Ecotravel Ethics
- Thailand: Environmental Threats and Conservation

What Ecotourism Is and Why It's Important

Ecotourism or *ecotravel* is travel to (usually exotic) destinations specifically to admire and enjoy wildlife and undeveloped, relatively undisturbed natural areas, as well as indigenous cultures. The development and increasing popularity of ecotourism is a clear outgrowth of escalating concern for conservation of the world's natural resources and *biodiversity* (the different types of animals, plants, and other life forms found within a region). Owing mainly to peoples' actions, animal species and wild habitats are disappearing or deteriorating at an alarming rate. Because of the increasing emphasis on the importance of the natural environment by schools at all levels and the media's continuing exposure of environmental issues, people now have an enhanced appreciation of the natural world and an increased awareness of environmental problems globally. They also have the very human desire to see undisturbed habitats and wild animals before they are gone, and those with the time and resources are increasingly doing so.

But that is not the entire story. The purpose of ecotravel is actually twofold. Yes, people want to undertake exciting, challenging, educational trips to exotic locales—wet tropical forests, wind-blown deserts, high mountain passes, mid-ocean coral reefs—to enjoy the scenery, the animals, the nearby local cultures. But the second major goal of ecotourism is often as important: travellers want to help conserve the very places—habitats and wildlife—that they visit. That is, through a portion of their tour cost and spending into the local economy of destination countries—paying for park admissions, engaging local guides, staying at local hotels, eating at local restaurants, using local transportation services, etc.—ecotourists help to preserve natural areas. Ecotourism helps because local people benefit economically as much or more by preserving habitats and wildlife for continuing use by ecotravellers than they could by "harvesting" the habitats for short-term gain. Put another way, local people can sustain themselves better economically by participating in ecotourism than by, for instance, cutting down rainforests for lumber or hunting animals for meat or the pet trade.

Preservation of some of the Earth's remaining wild areas is important for a number of reasons. Aside from moral arguments—the acknowledgment that we share the planet with millions of other species and have some obligation not to be the continuing agent of their decline and extinction—increasingly we understand that conservation is in our own best interests. The example most often cited is that botanists and pharmaceutical researchers each year discover another wonder drug or two whose base chemicals come from plants that live, for instance, only in tropical rainforest. Fully one-fourth of all drugs sold in the US come from natural sources—plants and animals. About 50 important drugs now manufactured come from flowering plants found in rainforests, and, based on the number of plants that have yet to be cataloged and screened for their drug potential, it is estimated that at least 300 more major drugs remain to be discovered. The implication is that if the globe's rainforests are soon destroyed, we will never discover these future wonder drugs, and so will never enjoy their benefits. Also, the developing concept of *biophilia*, if true, dictates that, for our own mental health, we had better preserve much of the wildness that remains in the world. Biophilia, the word coined by Harvard biologist E. O. Wilson, suggests that because people evolved amid rich and constant interactions with other species and in natural habitats, we have deeply ingrained, innate tendencies to affiliate with other species and actual physical need to experience, at some level, natural habitats. This instinctive, emotional attachment to wildness means that if we eliminate species and habitats, we will harm ourselves because we will lose things essential to our mental well-being.

If ecotourism contributes in a significant way to conservation, then it is an especially fitting reprieve for rainforests and other natural habitats, because it is the very characteristic of the habitats that conservationists want to save, wildness, that provides the incentive for travellers to visit and for local people to preserve.

How Ecotourism Helps; Ecotravel Ethics

To the traveller, the benefits of ecotourism are substantial (exciting, adventurous trips to stunning wild areas; viewing never-before-seen wildlife); the disadvantages are minor (sometimes, less-than-deluxe transportation and accommodations that, to many ecotravellers, are actually an essential part of the experience). But what are the actual benefits of ecotourism to local economies and to helping preserve habitats and wildlife?

The pluses of ecotourism, in theory, are considerable:

1. Ecotourism benefits visited sites in a number of ways. Most importantly from the visitor's point of view, through park admission fees, guide fees, etc., ecotourism generates money locally that can be used directly to manage and protect wild areas. Ecotourism allows local people to earn livings from areas they live in or near that have been set aside for ecological protection. Allowing local participation is important because people will not want to protect the sites, and may even be hostile toward them, if the people formerly used the now-protected site to support themselves (by farming or hunting, for instance),

but are no longer allowed such use. Finally, most ecotour destinations are in rural areas, regions that ordinarily would not warrant much attention, much less development money, from central governments for services such as road building and maintenance. But all governments realize that a popular tourist site is a valuable commodity, one that it is smart to cater to and protect.

2   Ecotourism benefits education and research. As people, both local and foreign, visit wild areas, they learn more about the sites—from books, from guides, from exhibits, and from their own observations. They should come away with an enhanced appreciation of nature and ecology, an increased understanding of the need for preservation, and perhaps a greater likelihood of supporting conservation measures. Also, in many cases, a percentage of ecotourist dollars are funneled into research in ecology and conservation, work that will in the future lead to more and better conservation solutions.

3   Ecotourism can also be an attractive development option for developing countries. Investment costs to develop small, relatively rustic ecotourist facilities are minor compared with the costs involved in trying to develop traditional tourist facilities, such as beach resorts. Also, it has been estimated that, at least in some regions, ecotourists spend more per person in the destination countries than any other kind of tourists.

A conscientious ecotraveller can take several steps to maximize his or her positive impact on visited areas. First and foremost, if travelling with a tour group, is to select an ecologically-committed tour company. Basic guidelines for ecotourism have been established by various international conservation organizations. These are a set of ethics that tour operators should follow if they are truly concerned with conservation. Travellers wishing to adhere to ecotour ethics should ascertain whether tour operators conform to the guidelines (or at least to some of them), and choose a company accordingly. Some tour operators conspicuously trumpet their ecotour credentials and commitments in their brochures and sales pitches. A large, glossy brochure that fails to mention how a company fulfills some of the ecotour ethics may indicate an operator that is not especially environmentally concerned. Resorts, lodges, and travel agencies that specialize in ecotourism likewise can be evaluated for their dedication to eco-ethics.

Basic ecotour guidelines, as put forth by the United Nations Environmental Programme (UNEP), the International Union for Conservation of Nature (IUCN), and the World Resources Institute (WRI), are that tours and tour operators should:

1   Provide significant benefits for local residents; involve local communities in tour planning and implementation.
2   Contribute to the sustainable management of natural resources.
3   Incorporate environmental education for tourists and residents.
4   Manage tours to minimize negative impacts on the environment and local culture.

For example, tour companies could:

1   Make contributions to the parks or areas visited; support or sponsor small, local environmental projects.
2   Provide employment to local residents as tour assistants, local guides, or local naturalists.
3   Whenever possible, use local products, transportation, food, and locally owned lodging and other services.
4   Keep tour groups small to minimize negative impacts on visited sites; educate

ecotourists about local cultures as well as habitats and wildlife.
5   When possible, cooperate with researchers; for instance, Costa Rican researchers are now making good use of the elevated canopy walkways in tropical forests that several ecotour facility operators erected on their properties for the enjoyment and education of their guests.

Committed ecotravellers can also adhere to the ecotourism ethic by disturbing habitats and wildlife as little as possible, by staying on trails, by being informed about the historical and present conservation concerns of destination countries, by respecting local cultures and rules, and even by actions as simple as picking up litter on trails.

Ecotourism, of course, is not a perfect remedy for threatened habitats and wildlife. Some negatives are noteworthy, such as overuse of trails and the disruption of the natural behavior of wildlife when ecotourists intrude upon the animals' domains. However, most experts agree that in many situations, in most parts of the world, responsible ecotourism can have a positive role in conservation.

Thailand: Environmental Threats and Conservation

With nearly 65 million people and an economy that places it well beyond the Third World status of most of its neighbors, Thailand is faced with many problems familiar to Europeans and North Americans. Air pollution from vehicle emissions and agricultural burning is choking the life out of many cities. Water pollution from industrial and agricultural wastes, rampant development of land for construction, and conspicuous consumption of resources by a large and obvious middle class have a major impact on the environment. However, Third World problems are simultaneously common, especially in rural areas. Some of these are (1) soil erosion due to careless farming practices and lack of agricultural planning; (2) deforestation to the point that only 15% of Thailand's land area remains forested and virtually no forests remain outside of protected areas; and (3) wildlife populations threatened by poaching and unlicensed hunting. How did this set of environmental tragedies come about, and what is in store for the future of Thailand's wildlife and natural habitats?

Forty-five years ago, almost 60% of Thailand's land area was covered with forest. Tigers, elephants, and abundant wildlife occurred even near the major cities. Only about 11 million people lived in the country, and except for a few large population centers, such as Bangkok, Chiang Mai, and Khorat, most Thais lived in small villages scattered throughout the lowlands and surrounded by vast expanses of undeveloped areas. Hunting and foraging in nearby forest supplemented the harvest from small rice paddies. A tradition of dependence on the forest for housing materials, food, and medicine impacted the natural habitats very little. As long as human populations were small, any sense of conservation and logical use of natural resources was non-existent and unneeded.

After World War II, some minor changes in forestry practices and agricultural expansion began as the country's population grew. In the 1960s, however, a major change occurred as world politics sucked Thailand into the conflict in Vietnam. America used Thailand as a staging area for its military ventures, and this involvement meant new roads, airports, and electronic communications that opened up many parts of the country that had been isolated from the more developed parts of the country, to say nothing of the rest of the world. The increased interconnection of the country was enhanced by the Thai government's problems with home-grown communist insurgents and the need to quickly transport military to many parts of the country. On these new roads, movements of private citizens, products, and new ideas became possible. A desire for economic improvements along with a hard-work ethic brought a level of wealth that produced a strong middle class. A flood of foreign investment in the 1980s in turn produced even greater levels of wealth.

Up to this time prosperity and the heady fumes of economic success left little room for the environment and conservation. A few Thai conservation pioneers, such as Dr. Boonsong Lekagul and Seub Nakasathien, began lobbying the government for protected areas and control of rampant logging. Several important laws in the 1960s finally established a basis for the present day grid of national parks and reserves across Thailand. Not until the 1980s, however, did two dramatic events galvanize the environmental movement in Thailand. A huge hydroelectric dam was proposed for the Nam Choam area of western Thailand, smack in the middle of one of Thailand's most extensive and pristine forest areas. Arguments from conservation pioneers, growing publicity for the environment, a large and educated middle class, an empowered lower class, newly formed student NGOs (non-governmental organizations, such as Wildlife Fund Thailand), newspapers, and television coalesced to produce the first nationwide protest against a government-sponsored development project—and the dam project was abandoned.

With the success of this dissent, Thais developed enough confidence and experience to attack yet another environmental problem. The government had reinterpreted an old law to enable private logging concessionaires to drastically increase their logging efforts with little or no control of where and when, or of reforestation efforts. Now that the environmental coalition knew that the government could be held responsible and that public opinion could change things, they forced the government to declare a ban on all logging in Thailand (in 1989). The environmental movement in Thailand had come to maturity and would not turn back.

Thailand's environmental movement arose from a unique combination of western notions of wilderness, ancient animism, and Buddhist philosophy of limited wants and harmony between humans and their natural surroundings. Both a politically powerful middle class and an increasingly indignant lower class began to see the negative economic impacts of deforestation, chemically intensive agriculture, decline in water availability, soil erosion, air and water pollution, and congestion. Not just esthetics were being lost, but livelihoods were being threatened. The response was a powerful alliance that crossed economic and social class distinctions. The result was an environmental movement influenced from overseas but grounded in Thai society and culture.

Along with student activists, farmers, an educated middle class, and an often-contentious press, another vital factor in Thailand's environmental movement lies with its Buddhist monks. Much of the education of young Thais, especially in rural areas, is in schools run by monks. Their influence over curriculum, content, and extracurricular activities is pervasive in the country's school system. A small but increasing number of activist monks began a movement aimed specifically at village development and forest conservation that has grown into a broader forum for conservation. One forest monk, Phra Prajak, gained national attention in 1991 by taking a stand against a government-sponsored reforestation project that took land away from peasants and replanted degraded land with exotic eucalyptus trees, under the guise of forest restoration and expansion of protected areas. This attempt to provide fast-growing wood products to logging companies or more forest for foreign tourists to visit (and not for the local people) quickly became clear for what it really was. To pursue his protest, this monk and others like him have had to revisit Buddhist philosophy and regard it from a "green" point of view: that spiritual and material development must proceed together based on the principle of the good of the whole and the interdependence of society, culture, and nature; the principle of social equity and generosity; and the principle of respect for community.

This re-emphasis of Buddhist philosophy, when taught to more and more grade-schoolers, will eventually have an impact on national policies. Instead of a national environmental policy developed by the government and dictated to the people, in Thailand the grassroots origin of environmental ideas has had to work its way up democratically into the government echelons. One intriguing outcome of this environmental education program together with Thai cultural values is an enthusiasm for visiting their own national parks and reserves. In many national parks in Africa, Latin America, and Asia, you are likely to see few park visitors who are actually citizens of that country. Often the only nationals present are guides, drivers, and waiters; the vast majority of visitors are foreigners. Not so in Thailand, especially on holiday weekends. Thai visitors regularly outnumber foreigners in Thailand's national parks and reserves. Beyond that, NGOs, wildlife societies, and birdwatching clubs are very popular in Thailand. It is not unusual to see a group of Thai birdwatchers with their binoculars and telescopes focused on a rare bird species visiting near Bangkok from northern Asia, or searching for a certain resident species in the forest marsh of Doi Inthanon. Look carefully at these groups of enthusiastic, if not obsessed, Thai nature-lovers. Rarely do you see any of them over the age of 35 years. The changing influence of environmental education in the schools and the media began when these people were five or six years old, and it has been the single most important factor in changing the face of conservation in Thailand.

One of these changing conservation problems directly involves tourism. Along all of Thailand's coasts, the beaches and coral reefs are quickly being degraded. The very multitudes of tourists attracted to the diversity and beauty of coral reefs are destroying them. Increased problems of inadequate waste management, pollution runoff, and physical damage are then driving tourists to more pristine areas, which in turn are becoming degraded. Short-term economic returns are leading to long-term economic ruin, to say nothing of a natural history disaster.

As the environmental problems Thais face become more complicated, their solutions must become more sophisticated and less parochial. For instance, although the logging ban in Thailand stopped most tree-cutting within the country, national logging companies have simply moved their operations to neighboring areas of Myanmar, Laos, and Cambodia. Now Thai NGOs must develop international solutions to deforestation issues. The argument is that depleted sources of fresh water, climate change, and soil erosion caused by unbounded deforestation across the border also impact Thailand and its well-being. Solutions based on purely individual or national viewpoints in these cases are inadequate. Regional planning and international accommodation are a must. At the same time, forest reduction within the country has increased local problems. The available forest land in Thailand is now so cut back that little forest exists outside of protected areas. Conflicts over forest rights between local ethnic groups and the Thai government are clearly escalating. Community rights versus national security have led to many struggles that can be addressed only at a local level.

As Thailand continues its economic advance, its environmental movement must also grow to incorporate simultaneously a broad range of international, national, and local environmental challenges. As an informed and concerned ecotraveller, you can become part of the solution. As we outlined earlier, there are many thing you can do to be proactive about Thailand's environment. Your trip to experience Thailand's natural wonders is a statement in itself that can benefit Thailand's environment. If you want to be more than passively involved, however, use your influence to help Thailand and its environment actively. If you see tour agencies, lodge operators, or officials following procedures or policies that run counter to the principle of ecotourism as a sustainable use of resources, say something to them. Also, seek out and make contributions to the Thai NGOs that run on donations.

Chapter 2

THAILAND: GEOGRAPHY AND HABITATS

- Geography and Climate
  - Landform Regions
  - Biogeographical Regions
- Vegetation Patterns
  - Tree Shape and Forest Layering
  - Large-leaved Understory Plants
  - Tree Bases and Roots
  - Climbers and Stranglers
  - Epiphytes
  - Palms
- Major Ecosystems and Common Plant Species
  - Evergreen Forest
  - Tropical Mixed Deciduous Forest
  - Dry Deciduous Dipterocarp Forest
  - Limestone Forest
  - Pine Forest
  - Marshes and Swamps
  - Mangrove and Coastal Vegetation
  - Pastures, Farms, and Plantations
  - Coral Reefs
- Environmental Close-up 1: Why Is Farming So Difficult in the Tropics?

Geography and Climate

Thailand (Map 1, p. 10) is a Texas-sized country of 513,115 sq km (198,115 sq mi), or, if you are more familiar with European geography, about the size of France. It is shaped like the head of an elephant facing west, with its ears making up the bulk of the northern part of the country and its long slender trunk extending south along the narrow Malay Peninsula. This narrow peninsula is bordered on the east by the Gulf of Thailand and on the west by the Andaman Sea, with a total of 3,219 km (2,011 mi) of coastline. The country shares common boundaries with Myanmar (Burma), Malaysia, Cambodia, and Laos. It stretches 1,860 km (1,163 mi) from its northernmost border at 20 degrees North latitude (about the same latitude as Guadalajara, Mexico, and Mecca, Saudi Arabia) to its southernmost border at 5 degrees North latitude (about the same as Lagos, Nigeria, and Cayenne, French Guiana). In terms of geographic variety it is located entirely within the tropics, but with considerable elevational relief, especially in the north and west; the tops of the mountains have characteristics of temperate central Asia. Much of the rest of the country is relatively flat to rolling lowlands with some hills and low mountains (Map 2, p. 42). Biologists who study the global distribution patterns of plants and animals (biogeographers) consider Thailand part of the Oriental Region. This area includes all of southern Asia from India to Japan and has several unique families and groups of plants and animals not found in other parts of the world. Both the northern and peninsular regions of Thailand show distinct seasonality in rainfall (with rainy periods known as monsoons), and, to some extent, temperatures. In general this seasonality becomes more and more marked and the annual rainfall greater the farther south you go. Some average annual rainfall values are as follows (see Map 1, p. 10, for locations): For the city of Bangkok, average annual rainfall is 1,467 mm (58 in) and driest months are December to May; for Chiang Mai in the north, average annual rainfall is 1,197 mm (47 in) and driest months are November to April; for Phuket on the Malay Peninsula, average rainfall is 2,393 mm (94 in) and driest months are January to April. In the dry, winter months (November to February), the northern portions of the country occasionally receive cold weather fronts moving down from central Asia. At these times, the temperature in the lowland areas drops to 10o C (50o F) and even lower on the tops of the taller mountains, such as Doi Inthanon (doi = mountain peak), Thailand's highest peak. The effects of these winter cold fronts can sometimes be felt as far south as Bangkok where winter temperatures can stay below 30o C (85o F) for a week or more until they rebound to the normal year-round highs of 32o to 35o C (89o to 95o F). Humidity is generally high, especially during the monsoon seasons and in the peninsular region. The hottest time of the year is the pre-monsoon season (April to May), and the hottest part of Thailand is in the northeast, where temperatures can reach 44o C (111o F).

Landform Regions

Based on general land forms and their geological origins, Thailand can be divided into three zones. The north, west, and south are made up of folded mountain ranges running north–south. They were formed primarily by uplifting when the floating plate of the Indian subcontinent crashed into the underbelly of the Asian mainland

MAP 1.
Thailand and its surroundings, showing locations of main cities and towns, roads, and rivers.

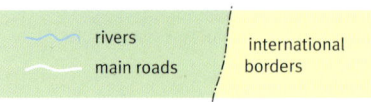

50 million years ago. The highest point in Thailand, Doi Inthanon (elevation 2,576 m, 8,500 ft), near the city of Chiang Mai, was forced up, along with these mountain chains and the Himalayas, by the action of the Indian Plate diving under the earth's crust as it pushed northward. In the peninsula, these mountain chains similarly have been pushed up from the Sunda Shelf, a landmass that links the islands of Sumatra and Borneo to the Southeast Asian mainland. This shelf is primarily underwater now, but many times in the past during worldwide lowering of sea levels, the shallow China Sea exposed land bridge connections between Malaysia and much of what is now these large Indonesian islands.

Thailand's second zone, the central region, lies in two flat basins divided by low hills running east–west. Low hills border these basins on the north, east, and west, and the sea lies to the south.

The third region, the northeast, has escaped the lifting forces of the Indian Plate, and the Khorat Plateau has been stable for more than 120 million years. It is drained by the Mekong River toward the southeast. Weathering over such a long period has left this region with the most infertile soils in the country.

Biogeographical Regions

When we consider animal and plant distributions and their geographical affinities (*biogeography*), more detailed regions become obvious than were found based solely on geological influences. Six principle biogeographical regions are recognized by most researchers in Thailand, and we follow them in this book (see Map 2, p. 42):

1   Peninsular Thailand: With only low mountains but high annual rainfall, the coastal mangroves and lowland evergreen forests dominate here. Many of the plants and animals of this region occur nowhere else within Thailand and come from the Indonesian–Malayan region to the south.
2   Central Plains: Formed by the flood plain of the Chao Phraya River and several other major rivers flowing south into the Gulf of Thailand, this low-lying area forms a habitat that serves as a barrier to many forest species trying to move from the higher ground to the west and to the east. Severely impacted by human population, most of the marshes and natural wetlands of this region have long since been drained and modified into rice paddies, but the region still remains the principle distribution for many aquatic species within Thailand.
3   Southeast: Primarily lowlands, this region receives very high rainfall and was entirely covered with forest in the recent past. Much of this forest, however, has been cleared. The few low mountains in this region harbor many species that are found nowhere else in Thailand and have their origins in southeastern Indochina.
4   West: Primarily mountainous, this region extends in a narrow strip along the southern boundary with Myanmar. It contains the largest intact forests in the country. Because these forests are often contiguous with extensive undeveloped areas in Myanmar, this region supports some of the few remaining populations of species otherwise exterminated from Thailand's more developed forest regions. This area is the northernmost extent of many Malaysian species and the southernmost extent of many western Indian and Myanmar species.
5   Northeast: A plateau with low annual and highly seasonal rainfall, this part of Thailand has the second-highest density of human population in the country (after the Central Plains). The natural habitats in this region have been severely impacted by human culture for centuries. Together with poor soils,

this impact best explains the relatively low diversity of species here.
6   Far North: Mainly mountainous, this region contains the highest elevations in the country. Many central Asian species of plants and animals reach the southern extremes of their distributions on these mountain tops. Surrounding lowlands are also the southern limits of many species more adapted to grasslands and flood plains.

Vegetation Patterns

The most striking thing about tropical habitats is their high degree of species diversity. Temperate forests in Europe or North America often consist of only a few tree species. The norm in tropical forests is to find between 100 and 300 tree species within the area of a few hectares or acres. Sometimes after appreciating a specific tree and then looking around for another of the same species, you have to walk several kilometers before finding the next one. Ecologists say tropical areas have a much higher *species richness* than temperate regions—for plant life, as well as for some animals such as insects and birds. Thailand, for instance, has more than 27,000 species of plants, 1,300 species of which are orchids.

During first visits to tropical forests, people from Europe, North America, and other temperate-zone areas are usually impressed with the richly varied plant forms, many of which are not found in temperate regions. Although not every kind of tropical forest includes all of them, you will usually see a number of highly typical plant forms and shapes.

Tree Shape and Forest Layering

Many tropical trees grow to great heights, straight trunks rising many meters (yards) before branching (in Thailand, most of these very tall and straight trees are in the dipterocarp plant family). Tropical forests often appear layered, or *stratified*, and several more or less distinct layers of vegetation can sometimes be seen. A typical tropical forest has a surface herb layer (*ground cover*), a low layer of shrubs and immature trees (*understory*), one or more levels of short trees (*subcanopy*), and a higher, or *canopy*, tree layer (Figure 1, p. 13). In reality, there are no formal layers—just various species of trees that grow to different, characteristic, maximum heights. Lone, very tall trees that soar high above their neighbors are sometimes referred to as *emergents* and are characteristic of tropical forests. Trees whose *crowns*, or high leafy sections, are in the often continuous upper layer are part of the canopy. Many of the crowns of tropical trees in the canopy are characteristically-shaped and look like umbrellas (Figure 1). The *leaf litter* on the forest floor is a variable layer that during the dry season accumulates many dry leaves, uneaten fruits, and fallen branches. However, it becomes very thin during the rainy season, when warm temperatures and moist humidity permit fungi, insects, and bacteria to quickly break down this organic material into chemicals and nutrients. This in turn is taken up immediately by the shallow root systems and fungal associates of the trees and shrubs.

Thailand: Geography and Habitats   13

Figure 2 Interior view of a typical tropical forest.

Figure 1 Exterior view of a typical tropical forest.

Large-leaved Understory Plants

Tropical forests often have dense concentrations of large-leaved understory herbs (Figures 1 and 2). In Thailand, two common plant families in the undergrowth include the gingers (family Zingiberaceae) and melastomes (family Melastomacea). The large leaves of these understory plants at least partially function to help gather the meager sunlight that makes its way though the canopy and subcanopy, so that adequate photosynthesis can take place to maintain these undergrowth plants. A famous forest floor plant is the huge and rare Rafflesia, several species of which occur in lowland Thailand (Figure 3, p. 24). Species of the undergrowth plant genus *Macaranga* (Figure 3) often have large leaves but grow in a clearing maintained by several species of ants.

Tree Bases and Roots

A visitor from the temperate zone visiting a tropical forest for the first time is likely to stop in his or her tracks and stare at the bottoms of the trees. The trunks of temperate zone trees may widen a bit at the base but they more or less descend straight into the ground. Not so in the tropics, where many trees are *buttressed*—huge ridges emerge and descend from the lower section of the trunk and spread out around the tree before entering the ground (Figure 2). The buttresses are the narrow vertical ridges attached to the sides of a trunk. In older trees they are big and deep enough to hide a person (or a coiled snake!). The function of buttresses is believed to be tree support, and indeed, buttressed trees are highly wind resistant and difficult to blow down. But whether increased support is the primary reason that buttressing evolved is an open question, one that plant biologists study and argue over (the "hypotenuse theory" of shorter distances between the major roots and the crown is another hotly argued possible explanation). Another unusual root structure associated with the tropics is *stilt,* or *prop roots*. These are roots that seem to raise the trunk of a tree off the ground. They come off the tree some distance from the bottom of the trunk and grow out and down, entering the ground at various distances from the trunk (Figure 2). Stilt roots are characteristic of many palms and of trees that occur in habitats that are covered with water during parts of the year, such as mangroves. Aside from anchoring a tree, functions of stilt roots are controversial.

Climbers and Stranglers

Tropical trees are often conspicuously loaded with climbing vines (Figures 1 and 2). Vines, also called *climbers, lianas,* and *bush-ropes,* are species from a number of plant families that spend their lives associated with trees. Some ascend or descend along a tree's trunk, perhaps loosely attached; others spread out within a tree's leafy canopy before descending toward the ground, free, from a branch. Vines are surprisingly strong and difficult to break; many older ones grow less flexible and more woody, sometime reaching the diameter of small trees.

Epiphytes

Epiphytes are plants that grow on other plants (usually trees) but do not harm their "hosts" (Figure 2). They are not parasites—they do not burrow into the trees to suck out nutrients; they simply take up space on trunks and branches. Ecologically, we would call the relationship between a tree and its epiphytes *commensal*: one party to the arrangement, the epiphyte, benefits—it gains growing space and access to sunlight—and the other party, the tree, is unaffected. Epiphytes harm trees probably only when an epiphyte load becomes so heavy that the branch bearing it breaks off. How do epiphytes grow if they are not rooted in the host tree or the ground? Epiphyte roots that grow along the tree's surface capture nutrients from the air—bits of dust, soil, and plant parts that breeze by. Eventually, by collecting debris, each epiphyte develops its own bit of soil, into which it is rooted. Epiphytes are especially numerous and diverse in middle- and higher-elevation evergreen forests, where persistent cloud cover and mist provide ideal growing conditions. *Orchids*, with their striking flowers that attract bees and wasps for pollination, are among the most famous kinds of epiphytes. Other plants that grow as epiphytes are mosses and ferns.

Palms

The trees most closely associated with the tropics worldwide are *palms*. Being greeted by palm trees upon exiting a jet is a sure sign that you have arrived in a warm climate. In fact, it is temperature that probably limits palms mainly to tropical and subtropical regions. They grow from a single point at the top of their stems, and so are very sensitive to frost; if that part of the plant freezes, the plant dies. Almost everyone recognizes palms because, for trees, they have unusual forms: they have no branches, but all leaves (which are quite large and called *fronds*) emerge from the top of the single trunk; and their trunks are usually of the same diameter from base to top. Many taller palms have stilt roots propping them up. Some palms have no trunks, but grow as small understory plants. More than 155 species of palms are found in Thailand. The most unusual palms in the country are the spiny and vine-like, climbing species known as *rattan*. They provide cane for basketry, cordage, and furniture.

Major Ecosystems and Common Plant Species

Using associations of particular plant species, several broad ecosystems and habitats can be distinguished in Thailand. Each ecosystem consists of large numbers of unique plant species that characterize and differentiate it from other ecosystems. Often, certain animal species are associated with each of these ecosystems. Below are brief descriptions of Thailand's major ecosystems and listings of some of the more abundant and recognizable types of vegetation that visitors are almost sure to see. Note that many plants occur in more than one ecosystem type. Some common plants do not have English names. Forests that are pristine and have not been cut down by humans are called *primary* or *old growth forests*. Forests that have grown up in areas where humans earlier cut down the primary forest are called *secondary forests*.

Evergreen Forest

The trees of evergreen forests have leaves all year. They can be divided into several categories:
Tropical Evergreen Forests occur from sea level to 1,000 m (3,300 ft) elevation

in areas with at least 2 m (6.6 ft) of rain spread evenly throughout the year. They are limited to the peninsula and characterized by a dominance of trees in the family Dipterocarpaceae, a family of Old World tropical hardwoods that reach amazing heights. Emergent trees regularly are 55 meters (182 ft) or more tall, and the dense and continuous canopy forms at 25 to 35 m (83 to 115 ft). Below the canopy are bamboos, palms, and small trees fighting for the little light that filters through. Canopy trees have broad crowns and subcanopy trees smaller and deeper crowns. Tree buttresses are very common and often extend high up on trunks. The ground in these forests is either mostly bare or sparsely covered with herbs, seedlings, ferns, and shrubs. Vines and epiphytes are usually abundant. Biologically, these kinds of forests are probably the richest ecosystems on Earth, supporting the most species of both plants and animals per unit area (more plant species probably support greater animal richness). This forest is made up of numerous patches of forest habitats, many often occurring within a small area. Tall, cathedral-like tree species grow on higher ground that is never flooded by rising rivers. Closer to rivers and swamps, the forests are flooded more regularly, and the vegetation is made up of species quite different from that found in unflooded forest.

Monsoon Evergreen Forest is drier (1 to 2 m, 3.3 to 6.6 ft, of annual rainfall) and some of the trees lose their leaves seasonally (*deciduous*), but even in the dry season, this forest is moist. During the monsoon season, it is as wet as any tropical forest you can imagine. This type of forest is most common north of the peninsula, in the lowlands and in the hill areas of the northeast (where it comprises half of the surviving forest cover now left in Thailand). Although similar to tropical evergreen forest, monsoon evergreen forest is not so tall and is dominated by different species of dipterocarps.

Hill Evergreen Forest is at elevations above 1,000 m (3,300 ft) where annual rainfall exceeds 2 m (3.3 ft), and winter temperatures fall below $10°C$ ($50°F$). Fog and clouds regularly cover the forest in the mornings. The dominant trees are oaks, chestnuts, magnolias, rhododendrons, and laurels, which produce a low (20 m, 65 ft) and open canopy. Their branches are thickly festooned with mosses, lichens, and other epiphytes.

Some recognizable trees and plants of Thailand's evergreen forests are:

Rafflesia (*Rafflesia* and *Sapria* sp.): Three species occur in Thailand. They are parasitic on roots of one genus (*Tetrastigma*) of vine in the grape family. For most of their lives these plants remain subterranean, inside the roots of their host plant. However, at infrequent intervals of several years, the huge (15 to 75 cm, 6 to 30 in), bright red and fleshy flower pushes up above the soil surface. It is covered with small yellow spots, and for a few days produces a smell said to be overpoweringly nauseating. This smell travels great distances and apparently attracts carrion flies to pollinate it. The fruit is fleshy with numerous hard seeds (Figure 3).

Wild Ginger (*Curcuma* sp.): More than a dozen species of wild ginger occur in Thailand. They are short forest undergrowth plants with broad oval-shaped leaves. The flower is made up of bright pink bracts that resemble a lotus blossom, within which hide the actual purple and yellow flowers, which are quite small (Figure 3).

White Costus (*Costus speciosus*): A tall herb, its long and slender stem spirals up from the forest floor. Its flower head and fruits are at the top of the stem and shaped like a spindle. The small white flowers bloom one at a time over a week or two and are protected by green and red bracts (Figure 3).

Macaranga (*Macaranga* sp.): An often large-leaved understory bush or tree (Figure 3). Many species of this genus have hollow stems and produce packets of starch to attract particular species of ants to live on the plant. The ants defend their home and food source against herbivorous insects that attack the plants. The ants also remove offending leaves and stems of neighboring plants that come into contact with the Macaranga plant as it grows up from the forest floor, reducing competition for light and space. This ant association has evolved so tightly for some species of plants and ants that neither species can survive without the other (*obligate mutualism*).

Thai Bauhinia (*Bauhinia pulla*): A thick vine, this member of the pea family (Legume) grows on trunks of other trees in forest light gaps and on the forest edge. Its peculiar bi-lobed leaf and greenish-white flowers are distinctive (Figure 4). Other bauhinia species grow as shrubs or small trees, but they share the distinctively shaped leaves.

Straits Melastome (*Melastoma normale*): This undergrowth bush grows in sunny patches and is distinguished by it long narrow leaf with numerous veins running its length and numerous parallel veins across its width. Its showy purple flowers are unmistakable (Figure 4).

Rattan Palm (*Calamus* spp.): About 40 species of this palm occur in Thailand. Generally they occur in moist forest undergrowth and near marshy forest areas. Most are vine-like or low undergrowth plants. All are armed with sharp spines (Figure 4). The heart of the young shoots is edible, and the plant fibers are used to make furniture and baskets.

Tropical Dipterocarp (*Anisoptera* sp.): These huge trees reach 40 m (130 ft) or more and a girth of 3 to 5 m (10 to 17 ft). Their long straight trunks (Figure 4) are distinctive and sought after for plywood and packing crates. They are restricted to tropical evergreen forest.

Upland Dipterocarp (*Dipterocarpus costatus*): This tree is usually among the tallest trees (30 to 35 m, 100 to 115 ft) in monsoon evergreen forest. Its smooth bark is brown with irregular flaking. Its flowers are conspicuous and often fill the forest air with pleasant scents (Figure 5).

Peninsular Dipterocarp (*Hopea* sp.): A huge tree often reaching 45 m (150 ft) or more in height. This tropical evergreen tree is a popular construction timber. Its flowers are small but numerous (Figure 5). Its resins (damar) are used as a varnish.

Riverine Bamboo (*Bambusa arundinacea*): The large, round stems of this oversized grass reach heights of 20 m (66 ft) (Figure 5). It grows rapidly in moist, shaded areas, and its feathery leaves are distinctive. The stems are used for scaffolding and as water pipes.

False Chestnut (*Castanopsis* sp.): This evergreen tree is a tropical cousin to the Horse Chestnuts of Europe and northern Asia. In Thailand it is easiest to find on the cool, moist mountain tops of the north. Individuals are usually covered with many layers of epiphytes. Their nuts, which are completely enclosed by a prickly covering (Figure 5), are dispersed by rodents.

Hill Oak (*Quercus* sp.): Related to the familiar oaks of the northern latitudes, the species in the mountains of Thailand are evergreen. Their nuts are familiar acorns with a hard cap covering the top of the nut (Figure 6).

Rhododendron (*Rhododendron* spp.): Numerous native rhododendrons grow in the hill forests of northern Thailand. Some are found in low brushy areas and have showy white flowers (*R. veitchianum*). Others are in moister and shadier forest, where they grow to be small trees 7 m (23 ft) or taller and with huge, bright red or lavender flowers in season (*R. arboreum*) (Figure 6).

Hill Bamboo (*Thyrostachys siamensis*): Growing commonly in disturbed areas, this bamboo species is often found in dense stands (Figure 6).

Magnolia (*Talauma* sp.): The huge and showy flowers of these evergreen shrubs and small trees vary from white to pink, depending on species (Figure 6). They produce intense but pleasant scents to attract pollinating insects.

Tropical Mixed Deciduous Forest

This highly seasonal forest grows in areas with less than 2 m (6.6 ft) of annual precipitation. With a very open canopy, light easily makes it to the forest floor, and bamboos dominate the lower levels. Few dipterocarp trees occur in it, and the forest instead is made up of 30-m (100-ft) high deciduous trees, all of which blossom with thick and brightly colored flowers during the late dry season. Because historically this forest type grew primarily on good soils in valleys and in the foothills of north, west, and central Thailand, it has been severely reduced by agriculture and human settlements. It is the most threatened forest type in Thailand.

Some common, recognizable trees and plants of Thailand's tropical mixed deciduous forests are:

Pride of India (*Lagerstroemia speciosa*): Deciduous tree whose bright pink blossoms are borne in bunches on tall stems. The trunk is covered with smooth, gray bark. Often grown in city parks and gardens (Figure 7).

Coral Tree (*Erythrina* sp.): This short tree has leaves in threes but loses them during the dry winter. The bright red flowers, which blossom at the ends of the branches, are waxy and curved like claws (Figure 7).

Red Silk Cotton Tree (*Bombax malabaricum*): A large tree (35 to 40 m, 115 to 132 ft). Its three to five large leaflets are attached to the ends of branches in the form of fingers on a hand (*palmate*). During the dry season, the leaves are lost and large red flowers with five separated petals replace the leaves in the same position (Figure 7). Young trees have short, stout spines on the trunk. The distinctive seeds are large, flattened, and oval in shape. They contain a fluffy cotton, called kapok, with seeds attached for wind dispersal.

Pink Shower Tree (*Cassia bakeriana*): A large tree of the pea family (Legume). Large clusters of small but spectacular pink-white flowers blossom during the dry season (Figure 7). Often grown in gardens and parks. Other species of *Cassia* produce yellow flowers.

Flame of the Forest (*Butea monosperma*): Often one of the largest trees in these forests, the large round leaves are distinctive during the rainy season. During the dry season the leaves are lost and large, curved orange-red flowers blossom (Figure 8).

Dry Deciduous Dipterocarp Forest

This forest type is also called *savannah forest*, and it is found in areas with less than 1.2 m (4 ft) of rain annually. It typically has a long and severe dry season and grows on quickly drained and nutrient-poor soils. Dry deciduous dipterocarp forest is the predominant forest type in the northeastern part of the country, and four dry-adapted (*xeric*) species of dipterocarps of the genera *Dipterocarpus* and *Shorea* make up the bulk of the trees in the forest. Individual trees rarely exceed 15 m (50 ft) in height, and they grow sufficiently far from each other that there is no continuous canopy. The ground usually has a thick cover of grasses, and fires are a common occurrence here. The dipterocarp trees and their seeds, however, are extremely fire-resistant. Human-set fires are extending the range of this forest type into adjacent mixed deciduous forests, which have little resistance to regular fires.

Some common, recognizable trees and plants of Thailand's dry deciduous dipterocarp forests are:

Dipterocarpus obtusifolius: This small (6 to 24 m, 20 to 80 ft) deciduous dipterocarp has rough, gray bark (reddish on the inside) and grows in dry areas up to 950 m (3,135 ft) elevation. Its reddish flowers appear in February to March, and they are pollinated by large moths at night and butterflies during the daytime (Figure 8). The thick bark helps it endure the frequent fires in these areas. It is usually outnumbered in these dry forests by its relative, *D. tuberculatus*.

Dipterocarpus tuberculatus: A medium-sized deciduous tree (25 to 35 m, 83 to 115 ft), this species often grows in pure stands on reddish laterite soil. Its thick gray bark is remarkably resistant to fire. Its large pinkish flowers appear in March (Figure 8).

Burmese Sal (*Shorea siamensis*): Leaves of the Burmese Sal (Figure 9) turn red just before being shed in late December. This widespread tree species (medium-sized; 20 to 25 m, 66 to 83 ft, tall) is pollinated primarily by Stingless Bees (Plate 6). The bees will not move long distances between flowering trees, however; they must have a relatively dense stand of Sal trees to successfully pollinate a large percentage of the flowers. If a forest of these trees is severely thinned by logging, the trees are unlikely to survive into the next generation because the pollinators will abandon the area.

Teak (*Tectona grandis*): The wood of this tall (35 to 45 m, 116 to 150 ft) tree is so durable and water resistant that it has been used in shipbuilding for centuries. Although native to dry areas of Thailand and southern Asia, it is often planted in large plantations. Its leaves are very large and the large bunches of flowers at the ends of small branches are creamy white (Figure 9). Older individuals have been used to retrace climate over the last few centuries by looking at tree-ring widths.

Fan Palm (*Licuala* sp.): Fifteen species of this palm occur in Thailand, mostly in moist, swampy, or mangrove areas. One species, *L. sponosa*, is widespread in disturbed and dry habitats. Some have spines, others are unarmed, but all are relatively small (3 m, 30 ft, tall), with large, fan-shaped fronds (Figure 9).

Limestone Forest

Limestone does not erode away as quickly as surrounding soil types, and often large outcroppings of limestone become isolated as monoliths or steep-sided hills, especially in western Thailand. Some of these outcroppings are actual islands along the coast. Because of their isolation and harsh soil type, the vegetation on them is often unique. Fig trees are common on many of them. Limestone also tends to produce many caves, and they are often the home to immense colonies of bats that pass the daylight hours in them.

Among the common, recognizable trees of Thailand's limestone forests are:

Fig Trees (*Ficus* sp.): Several hundred species of figs occur in Thailand, in most forest types. Several species seem to be fruiting at any given time of the year, and they are an important source of food for many birds and mammals. Most fig species are pollinated by specialized, tiny wasps that mate and lay their eggs within the fig fruits. Many species of figs are "strangler" figs, and start their lives in the canopy of a host tree (Figure 9). The fig quickly usurps the sunlight for photosynthesis and grows its crown, branches, and trunk down the sides of the host tree. Eventually it overgrows the host, plants its roots into the ground, and kills the host.

Euphorbia (*Euphorbia* sp.): Related to the rubber tree, these tall plants have green trunks and branches with no leaves but lots of spines (Figure 8). Some of the largest species grow to 3 m (10 ft) in height and grow out of the sides of steep cliffs, dry ledges, and sun-exposed slopes. They look for all the world like some small saguaro cactus from Arizona, but there are no native cacti in the Old World. This is most likely an example of *evolutionary convergence,* unrelated species that have evolved superficially similar appearances by coincidence—as adaptations to similar habitats in different geographical areas.

Pine Forest

Covering only a small area of Thailand (2,500 sq km, 1,000 sq mi), pine forests are found mainly on the tops of mountains (at 400 to 1,400 m, 1,320 to 4,620 ft) with sandy soils. A few groves also occur naturally on the plains and along the coast, but they all represent relic populations of an extensive pine forest that covered much of Thailand in the cooler and moister Pleistocene Era, 20,000 years ago. These pine forests consist mainly of two species of long-needled pines interspersed with oak trees (*Quercus*) and other deciduous species. In many areas, the pine forests are fire-maintained, and they tend to be open with considerable grass growing among them.

Some common, recognizable trees and plants of Thailand's pine forests are:

Two-needled Pine (*Pinus merkusii*): The most common of Thailand's pines (Figure 10), it often occurs in pure stands with the Three-needled Pine where fire is regular. At lower elevations it mixes with trees typical of mixed deciduous and dry dipterocarp forests.

Three-needled Pine (*Pinus kesiya*): More restricted to elevations above 500 m (1,600 ft), this species (Figure 10) is almost always associated with the Two-needled Pine and fire-resistant species of oaks.

Highland Morning Glory (*Argyreia splendens*): A common vine trailing on the ground or climbing other vegetation, its large funnel-shaped flowers are purple (Figure 10).

Chaen-daeng Lily (*Dracaena lourieri*): A species endemic to Thailand, it is often a meter (3.3 ft) tall with a stout, trunk-like, gray stem. Its long, thin leaves all emerge from top of the trunk, and its flowers are small, white, and tube-shaped (Figure 10).

Marshes and Swamps

Although much of the natural wetlands of Thailand has been altered or drained for rice farming, extensive areas of seasonal flooding still make this ecosystem an important one for many aquatic plants and animals. Fragments of swamp forest persist in some areas. Only a few natural lakes occur in Thailand, but many artificial reservoirs and holding ponds have been created for hydroelectric projects and flood control over the last few decades.

Red-stemmed Palm (*Eliodoxa conferta*): Confined to swamp forests in lowland areas of peninsular Thailand, this 8-m (25-ft) tall species is heavily armed with spines, grows thickly, and often forms impenetrable thickets. Its habitat, short stems, and long, upright fronds are distinctive (Figure 11).

Paper Bark (*Melaleuca leucadendron*): Because of its fire-resistance, this species has become very common and dominant in the few forested marshes remaining in Thailand. It is seldom over 20 m (65 ft) tall, and its whitish bark, lance-shaped leaves, and white bottle-brush flowers are diagnostic (Figure 11).

Phragmites Grass (*Phragmites* sp.): These tall grasses, often 3+ m (10+ ft) tall (Figure 11), grow in thick stands in shallow marshy areas.

Sacred Lotus (*Nelumbo nucifera*): A plant with large round leaves that are raised by a stem attached to the center; leaf margins are deeply cut in at several points. Its flashy flowers have broad pink or white petals and a yellow center (Figure 11). Its seeds are often eaten as a delicacy. The native lotus is often confused with the introduced water lily. Unlike the lotus, the lily leaves are rounded and always floating on the water. The leaf edges are fairly smooth to serrate with only a single indentation to one side for the attachment of the stem. The flowers are usually pink to red (sometimes white or bluish), with long pointed petals and a reddish or yellowish center.

Water Lettuce (*Pistia stratiotes*): This floating herb is common on canals, lakes, marshy areas, and ponds. Its green leaves form a rosette (Figure 12).

Mangrove and Coastal Vegetation

Along the coast of Thailand where fresh or brackish water is predictable, such as along estuaries, mangroves are common and form another floral region with distinct plants and animals.

Some common, recognizable trees of Thailand's coast are:

Mangroves: These are relatively short tree species of several unrelated plant families. They have in common the fact that they grow in areas exposed to salt water, usually around bays, lagoons, and other protected coastal areas, and they produce short, conical "breathing" roots. Along with the mangroves, these forests typically support several species of palms as well. Although they have relatively few plant species, mangrove forests have great ecological and economic importance. They act as a breakwater to control beach erosion when storms hit the coast. Their roots trap the silt and organic material carried in by the tides and accumulate nutrient-rich areas. These high amounts of nutrients support breeding grounds for many marine fish and invertebrates, that in turn, as adults, serve as the basis for much of Thailand's fisheries industry.

Beach vegetation: At the high-tide line, usually along sandy beaches, other plants typically grow to produce a narrow band of beach vegetation. Bushy trees of several species are common here. In the undergrowth grow grasses, many vine flowers, and palm-like cycads.

Red Mangrove (*Rhizophora apiculata*): The stilt roots and "breathing" roots of this tree are distinctive. It is the quintessential mangrove, and grows tall, usually in the interior of the mangrove forest. Its leaves are broad, its small flowers grow hanging on short stems, and its seeds are long, thin pods (Figure 12).

Black Mangrove (*Avicennia alba*): This mangrove dominates the vegetation at the ocean edge of the mudflats. Its leaves are long and thin. Its small flowers grow on upright stems, and its fruits are short, oval-shaped seeds (Figure 12).

Cork Tree (*Sonneratia caseolaris*): The leaves of this mangrove-like tree grow on stems opposite each other on the branch. The flowers are conspicuous and bell-shaped, and it does not have the stilt roots typical of the other mangroves (Figure 12).

Ironwood (*Casuarina equisetifolia*): This tall tree grows on the beach and inland margin of the mangroves. It looks like a pine but is instead a flowering plant. Its "needles" are actually long, scale-like leaves. The fruit is round and cone-like (Figure 13).

Pandanus (*Pandanus odoratissimus*): This palm-like tree has long, narrow leaves clustered at the tops of its trunk. Each leaf has sharp teeth along its edges. The fruit is brownish-yellow, large and pineapple-like, hanging from the base of the leaves (Figure 13). The leaves are used commonly for weaving mats.

Beach Cycad (*Cycas litoralis*): Only ten cycad species occur in Thailand. These low, primitive plants resemble palms but have no flowers. Instead, they have a huge cone that grows up vertically out of the base of the frond-like leaves (Figure 13). They are related to pine trees.

Spinifex Grass (*Spinifex littoreus*): This coarse grass grows by creeping along sandy beaches. It has silvery stems and long, lance-like leaves. The needle-like flowers grow up on tall stems in large clusters (Figure 13).

Pastures, Farms, and Plantations

Agriculture in Thailand is split between traditional, small, family farms of, usually, 5 to 10 hectares (12 to 25 acres), and large corporate plantations. Family farms generally grow several crops, and plantations, single crops. The biggest crops are rice, cassava (tapioca), rubber, corn, coconuts, soybeans and sugar cane (*Saccharum officinarum*) (Figure 14). Some cashews (*Anacardium occidentale*) (Figure 14), durian (*Durio zibethinus*) (Figure 14), breadfruit (*Artocarpus incisus*) (Figure 14), jackfruit (*Artocarpus heterophylla*) (Figure 14), Papaya (*Carica papaya*) (Figure 15), and bananas (*Musa* sp.) (Figure 15) are also commonly grown. Banana trees, with their large leaves and distinctive fruit, have an Asian origin. They occur in gardens, throughout the tropical lowlands. Sugar cane, grown in several regions of Thailand but particularly in the warmer lowlands, is a perennial grass that may have originated in the New Guinea region. Pineapple plants (*Ananas comosus*) (Figure 15) are bromeliads, and are Neotropical in origin. They are grown mainly in the moist lowlands. Forest plantations usually include Rubber Tree (*Hevea brasiliensis*) (Figure 15), which is native to Amazonian South America, Coconut Palm (*Cocos nucifera*) (Figure 15), and Teak (*Tectona grandis*) (Figure 9).

Coral Reefs

Although corals are animals and not plants, this ecosystem and its habitats are usually defined by the type of dominant coral life. In shallow tropical oceans, coral reefs produce some of the most complex and diverse communities in the world. The corals are colonies of invertebrate animals, each producing a calcium carbonate skeleton on the outside (*exoskeleton*). Different species of corals produce variously-shaped exoskeletons. Some are branched like trees or deer antlers; others are smooth and encrusting; some resemble an exposed brain; others are mushroom-shaped; while others are flexible and fan-shaped.

Thousands of individual *coral polyps* (the living portion of the coral that when feeding extend from the coral surface as small frilly fingers) of hundreds of species constantly grow and add to the hard calcium exoskeleton. The exoskeletons eventually become so dense they coalesce and produce the framework of a continuous reef. Coral polyps find some of their food by filtering plankton (microscopic plants and animals) from the water. Much of their food, however, comes from symbiotic algae (*zooxanthellae*) living inside the coral polyps, which produce sufficient food from photosynthesis to feed themselves as well as supply the corals with essential nutrients. These zooxanthellae also provide much of the rainbow of colors exhibited by the corals. The coral polyps themselves extend from their crusty exoskeleton primarily during the night to feed on the soup of plankton surrounding them.

Most coral species do best in warm, shallow and clear water that permits light to penetrate. Few corals grow below 60 m (200 ft) deep as most light cannot penetrate beyond this depth. The light is critical for the corals because without light, the zooxanthellae have no energy to drive photosynthesis and produce much of the food on which the corals depend. Corals grow, on average, about 1.25 cm (0.5 in) per year. Different types of reefs form depending on water depth, climate and the type of ocean bottom available. *Barrier reefs* generally occur offshore at continental margins; *fringing reefs* hug the coastline; and *patch reefs* are in shallow water near the shore.

The coral reefs provide a complex and diverse physical habitat for a myriad of marine invertebrates and vertebrates to find shelter and food. The most diverse coral reefs in the world are in the southern Philippines/Borneo area. The least diverse coral areas are in the western Atlantic and Caribbean Sea. The Andaman Sea off the west coast of Thailand is intermediate in diversity, and the Gulf of Thailand, due to water turbidity, is considered somewhat less diverse. As in the forests of Thailand, the coral reefs provide a refuge for organisms active at night, others during the daytime, and others most active just at sunset or sunrise.

Coral reef growth is most often slowed or stopped by wave action from storms, which breaks off coral branches and stirs up bottom sediments so that water turbidity reduces light availability. Natural enemies, such as Coral Boring Clams and Crown-of-thorns Starfish (Plate 107) can kill large numbers of coral in a short time. Increased pollution, such as dredging, can cause coral death as sediment settles out on top of the coral. Oil leakage from ecotravellers' boats and sewage from ecotravellers' hotels is an increasing problem. Even physical destruction of reefs by the anchors of ecotravellers' boats has ruined reefs in some areas. In other areas of Thailand, fisherman use dynamite to harvest fish, destroying large areas of reef at the same time. Some fisherman use liquid cyanide to kill crustaceans and fish hiding in hard to reach crevices of the coral. Unfortunately, the cyanide also kills the coral polyps. Even in areas little-impacted by humans, entire reefs of coral can turn pure white in a few weeks. This process is called bleaching and is caused by the rapid expulsion of zooxanthellae and resultant loss of coral color that leaves exposed only the pure white calcium carbonate. If the zooxanthellae are not quickly recovered, the corals begin to die and become overgrown by brownish fungi. Bleaching is caused by pollution but also apparently by rising water temperatures, which are perhaps the result of global warming phenomena.

With all these threats to coral, it is a wonder that any reefs remain. Obviously fast and drastic protective measures need to be implemented both by the Thai government and foreign ecotravellers visiting this habitat. Fortunately, several studies show that many reef species have wide-ranging larvae that can disperse quickly and recolonize into recovering areas in which pollution and destruction have been curtailed.

Rafflesia, *Rafflesia* sp.

Wild Ginger, *Curcuma* sp.

White Costus, *Costus speciosus*

Macaranga, *Macaranga* sp.

Figure 3

Thailand: Geography and Habitats

Thai Bauhinia, *Bauhinia pulla*

Straits Melastome, *Melastoma normale*

Tropical Dipterocarp, *Anisoptera* sp.

Rattan Palm, *Calamus* spp.

Figure 4

Upland Dipterocarp, *Dipterocarpus costatus*

Peninsular Dipterocarp, *Hopea* sp.

False Chestnut, *Castanopsis* sp.

Riverine Bamboo, *Bambusa arundinacea*

Figure 5

Thailand: Geography and Habitats

Hill Oak, *Quercus* sp.

Rhododendron, *Rhododendron* spp.

Hill Bamboo, *Thyrostachys siamensis*

Magnolia, *Talauma* sp.

Figure 6

Pride of India, *Lagerstroemia speciosa*

Coral Tree, *Erythrina* sp.

Red Silk Cotton Tree, *Bombax malabaricum*

Pink Shower Tree, *Cassia bakeriana*

Figure 7

Thailand: Geography and Habitats

Flame of the Forest, *Butea monosperma*

Dipterocarpus obtusifolius

Dipterocarpus tuberculatus

Euphorbia sp.

Figure 8

Burmese Sal, *Shorea siamensis*

Teak, *Tectona grandis*

Fan Palm, *Licuala* sp.

Fig Tree, *Ficus* sp.

Figure 9

Thailand: Geography and Habitats

Two-needled Pine, *Pinus merkusii*

Three-needled Pine, *Pinus kesiya*

Highland Morning Glory, *Argyreia splendens*

Chaen-daeng Lily, *Dracaena lourieri*

Figure 10

Red-stemmed Palm, *Eliodoxa conferta*

Paper Bark, *Melaleuca leucadendron*

Phragmites Grass, *Phragmites* sp.

Sacred Lotus, *Nelumbo nucifera*

Figure 11

Thailand: Geography and Habitats

Water Lettuce, *Pistia stratiotes*

Red Mangrove, *Rhizophora apiculata*

Black Mangrove, *Avicennia alba*

Cork Tree, *Sonneratia caseolaris*

Figure 12

Ironwood, *Casuarina equisetifolia*

Pandanus, *Pandanus odoratissimus*

Beach Cycad, *Cycas litoralis*

Spinifex Grass, *Spinifex littoreus*

Figure 13

Thailand: Geography and Habitats

Sugar Cane, *Saccharum officinarum*

Cashew, *Anarcardium occidentale*

Durian, *Durio zibethinus*

Breadfruit, *Artocarpus incisus*

Jackfruit, *Artocarpus heterophylla*

Figure 14

36 Travellers' Wildlife Guides: Thailand

Papaya, *Carica papaya*

Bananas, *Musa* sp.

Pineapple, *Ananas comosus*

Rubber Tree, *Hevea brasiliensis*

Coconut Palm, *Cocos nucifera*

Figure 15

Environmental Close-up 1:
Why Is Farming So Difficult in the Tropics?

An experienced farmer from the temperate zone, such as from Iowa or France, gazing for the first time at a tropical rainforest, could be excused if he thought he saw a farming bonanza before him. It would be natural for him to exclaim: "Just cut down the forest and plant the cleared fields with a more useful crop, a cash crop. If those dense, tall trees can grow there so luxuriantly, surely a field of alfalfa, corn, cotton, or soy beans should also grow wonderfully there! Why, with the perpetual warm weather and regular rain, you could even have three or four harvests a year!" But it is not as easy as that; indeed, this type of thinking has led many hopeful farmers in the tropics into an economic and ecological disaster.

The main problem is that tropical soils, in contrast to most temperate soils, are often very nutrient-poor. In fact, tropical rainforests themselves, and the soil in which they are rooted, are of such different designs when compared with temperate forests and soils, that many of the agricultural rules a farmer would have learned in North America and Europe don't even apply. For instance, in temperate zones, soils accumulate organic material in the form of dead leaves, fallen branches, dead animals, and so on—they are essentially a natural compost heap. This accumulation of organic chemicals, including many of the basic nutrients that plants need to grow (such as nitrogen-containing compounds and phosphates), is possible because there is only a relatively short period each year when it is warm and moist enough for fallen plant and animal material to decompose completely. The bacteria, fungi, and other soil organisms that make decomposition possible can't be active and break down dead tissues if it is too cold or dry. Thus, over time, organic materials build up in the soil and produce *humus* (rich black soil) and a large reservoir of nutrients sometimes 30 cm (a foot) or more deep. This is not the case in tropical forests. Here the forest floor is generally so warm and humid throughout the year that any organic material falling to the forest floor is quickly broken down completely by the abundant *decomposer* termites, fungi, and bacteria. There is little chance for a build-up of organic humus. The average depth of organic material below the floor of moist tropical forests is measured in millimeters (tenths of an inch) instead of centimeters (inches). In addition, most tropical soils are composed largely of old clay with a high content of aluminum and iron (thus the reddish soil visible in cleared areas); minerals in these soils that are useful to plants have long ago been weathered away.

How does the lush tropical vegetation of these forests exist if soils are so nutrient-poor? Actually, the plants do have access to nutrients; they just have to be ready to capture the nitrogen, phosphates, and other nutrients almost as soon as they become available via the action of the soil decomposers. Instead of having root systems that penetrate deep down into the soil, tropical trees tend to produce roots that grow sideways, close to the soil surface. Most roots in tropical forests are within 30 cm (1 ft) of the soil surface. Together with symbiotic fungi, called *mycorrhizae*, living in the roots, these trees (and other plants) with shallow roots are able to efficiently and quickly capture the nutrients as they are made available at the soil surface by the action of soil decomposers. Unlike temperate zone habitats, in which more than half of an area's nutrients are in the soil, tropical forest habitats often have only 1% of their nutrients in the soil at any one time. So where are the rest of the habitat's nutrients? They are stored in the cells of living plants. That means up to 99% of the nutrients in tropical forests are in the plants themselves. So if you cut tropical forest and burn off the dead vegetation, you lose much the habitat's nutrients—they disappear by logging truck and/or into the air with the smoke. When the rains begin, the few remaining nutrients are eroded (*leached*) out of the soil by the runoff of the water.

The main consequence of tropical forest clearing and burning for agriculture is obvious. After one or two crops of corn replace the luxuriant tropical forest, the few nutrients left in the soil are used up. Because commercial fertilizer is too expensive for most farmers in the tropics, the sad alternative is to move to the next patch of forest, cut or burn it down, and squeeze out another couple of years of crops before the soil there is also exhausted. This wasteful, destructive procedure is known as *slash-and-burn agriculture*—moving every two or three years to a new patch of forest and cutting and/or burning it to provide temporarily productive fields.

Even selective timber removal from tropical forests is a limited economic option. This is because the shallow root systems, seeds in the soil, and the decomposer community are easily disrupted or killed with the compacting action of heavy tractors and equipment. Also, if too many trees are removed for timber, the total amounts of nutrients in the system may fall below a critical minimum to maintain the rest of the uncut forest. In addition, large cleared areas (called *light gaps*) permit high levels of sunshine to strike the soil surface, and if the clay is of just the right composition, it can be baked into a stone-like adobe called *laterite*. Seeds and roots cannot penetrate the laterite, and the forest can only regenerate itself in these areas with great difficulty. If that weren't bad enough, it turns out that these trees with shallow root systems depend on dense stands of trees to protect themselves from high-wind storms. Large light gaps remove this protection on the edge of a gap, so the trees there are easy victims of the next storm. When they fall, their neighbors become unprotected, and so on. In fact, in one study in Indonesia, after 8% of trees were selectively extracted from an area, another 19% of trees in that area died and a further 27% were badly damaged.

Beyond these nutrient cycling problems of farming, precipitation cycles also have different rules in tropical rainforests. Although rainfall is generally high compared with that in most temperate zone forests, cutting tropical forest to produce agricultural fields actually reduces rainfall that crops need. Through a process that moves water and nutrients up from the roots to the leaves (called *evapotranspiration*), water vapor escapes from leaf surfaces in tropical rainforests and builds up over the canopy. As this vapor rises it eventually cools and condenses. Some tropical rainforests produce up to 70% of their own rainfall in this manner (though the amount in Thailand's rainforests has not been determined). Thus, if extensive areas of tropical forest are cleared and then burned off to create cattle pastures or for crop farming, most of the local nutrients and much rainfall are removed in one fell swoop.

What then are the alternatives for agriculture in rainforests? Theoretically, one plan would be to follow traditional agricultural practices. Indigenous peoples long ago developed a system that mimics natural processes, maintains soil nutrients, and so allows for continual use of the same fields (that is, permits "sustainable" agriculture). They clear only small areas of the forest and then plant a mixed cultivation of fast-growing food crops, such as corn and beans, interplanted with slower growing pepper and passion fruit, which are vines that grow up into trees such as cacao, rubber, and fruit palms. They also plant crops with high numbers of mycorrhizae in their roots, which pump nutrients into the soil, enriching it, and helping to recycle nutrients locally. Furthermore, rotation and succession of these crops helps reduce the occurrence of plant pests and diseases. But this kind of sustainable agricultural system is obviously labor intensive and involves careful, thoughtful planting. Tropical agriculture can work, but only with great care and substantial training.

New farmers and new settlers who push into rainforests to claim land and homestead usually do not have such skillful knowledge. With high hopes they burn and plant, only to discover after a few years that their fields' productivity has declined; they move and start over again. Large-scale commercial ranching and farming operations prefer to continually grow single crops over large areas (that is, *monocultures*), which quickly deplete soil nutrients and require ever-increasing amounts of artificial fertilizers and pesticides to maintain the crop. These agricultural forces—essentially mistreatment of tropical forests and soils for ill-informed farming—in combination have created what most consider to be an ecological disaster (disappearing tropical forests; increasingly poor soils for farming; increasing use of fertilizer and pesticides, which eventually enter local waterways to pollute them and downstream areas). Remedies, such as encouraging ecologically sustainable farming practices on large scales, are only beginning to be proposed. But until such practices are widely adopted, much farming in the tropics will continue to be difficult and ecologically damaging.

Chapter 3

PARKS AND RESERVES

- *Peninsular Thailand (PT)*
- *The Southeast (SE)*
- *The Central Plains (CP)*
- *The West (W)*
- *The Northeast (NE)*
- *The Far North (FN)*
- *Environmental Close-up 2: Brazilian Rubber in Thailand: Economic Boom or Environmental Disaster?*

Thailand has about 77 national parks, 24 marine parks, 48 wildlife sanctuaries, and more than 55 non-hunting areas. Combined they protect 16% of Thailand's total land area. Presently (2008) an additional 33 new national parks and 3 marine parks are in development. Additional protected areas are near Buddhist monasteries, and these sanctuaries often are small but critical areas for plants and animals that the government cannot or will not protect near developing areas or politically sensitive sites.

We chose to focus on some of these parks and natural areas, described below, for two reasons. Many of these areas are the ones most often visited by ecotravellers in Thailand—by people who come on organized tours and also those who travel independently. Others are more remote, and to see them takes additional planning and effort—although not so much that a major expedition has to be mounted. Because these latter areas are more remote, they are less likely to have the illegal colonization, poaching, and mining that have altered or severely affected the quality of habitats and wildlife in some parks that are more easily accessible. See Map 2 (p. 42) for park locations. Although some major wildlife sanctuaries have extensive forest habitat and protect many unique plants and animals, unlike the national parks they are not set up for ecotravellers and many are reserved primarily for conservation research and scientific studies. The animals profiled in the color plates are keyed to parks and reserves in the following way: the profiles list the Thai regions (see Chapter 2 for details) of Peninsular Thailand (PT), the Southeast (SE), the Central Plains (CP), the West (W), the Northeast (NE), and Far North (FN), in which each species is most likely to be found, and the parks and sanctuaries listed below are arranged by the regions. Visitors who stay at lodges or resorts in the same regions as the parks listed below can expect to encounter similar types of habitats and wildlife as described for these parks and preserves. Tips on increasing the likelihood of seeing mammals, birds, reptiles, amphibians, coral reef fish, or flashy insects are given in the introductions to each of those chapters. For more particulars on planning your trip to Thailand, choosing which areas to visit, places to stay, and transportation, we suggest you consult one of several ecotravel-friendly guides available at bookstores, such as those published by Lonely Planet and Insight Guides.

A powerful earthquake in December 2004 triggered a large, deadly tsunami that hit coastal areas of the west side of peninsular Thailand. Many resort and other tourist areas were damaged, especially parts of the Phuket, Krabi, and Khao Lak resort areas. Some coastal national parks and marine reserves were also damaged. However, major infrastructure (roads, bridges, airports) emerged largely intact, and by this book's publication date (2008), almost all tourist sites have been rebuilt and re-opened. Damage to coral reefs was moderate in some areas, but diving and snorkeling have resumed throughout the region.

Peninsular Thailand (PT)

Khao Sok National Park. Adjacent to two large wildlife sanctuaries, Khao Sok is the largest tropical evergreen forest area protected on the peninsula. Limestone outcroppings covered with vegetation rise to 1,000 m (3,300 ft). It is one of the best places in Thailand to find the rare Rafflesia flower (Figure 3), a parasitic species that produces a huge blossom on the forest floor. Rafting down forest rivers and hiking are exciting ways to see the views and wildlife in this park. Hiking trails begin from the headquarters in the southwestern part of the park. Access to the more remote parts of the park is via power boats across the huge reservoir formed by the Rajaprubbha Dam at the east end of the park. Bungalows and a privately run resort are available in or near the park, and regular daily tours run from Phuket, 50 km (30 mi) to the southwest.

Koh Samui and Koh Ang Thong National Park. An archipelago of more than 40 islands (koh = island) makes up this national park in the Gulf of Thailand. The limestone hills are covered with evergreen tropical forests. Some diving and snorkeling is done here, but the coral is not as extensive nor the water as clear as other areas. Passenger boats make regular runs to the islands from Surat Thani and Koh Samui. Guest houses and tent camping are available on Koh Wua Talab.

Krabi Area. The city of Krabi has a population of nearly 20,000 and is a handy base out of which to make excursions to islands in the Andaman Sea (Ko Phi-Phi Don, Ko Poda, Ko Hua Khwan), half-day boat trips to visit estuaries and mangrove forests, or visits to nearby tropical evergreen forest areas such as *Khao Nor Chuchi Lowland Forest Project* and *Khao Pra Bang Kram Wildlife Sanctuary.* Khao Pra Bang Kram is home to the highly endemic bird, Gurney's Pitta (Plate 43), only 25 of which probably still exist here together with perhaps 50 more at a few sites in Myanmar.

Phuket Island Area. This popular tourist island offers a wide array of entertainment and accommodations. For wildlife viewing, *Had Nai Yang National Park* offers some of the island's only coastal forest, an excellent coral reef, and one of the four beach-nesting sites of the Leatherback Sea Turtle (Plate 14) remaining in Thailand. In the northern interior of the island, the small *Khao Phra Thaw Royal Wildlife and Forest Reserve* offers hiking and wildlife viewing opportunities within its 2,333 hectares (5,762 acres) of monsoon evergreen forest. Numerous operators conduct

daily tours of several nearby national parks, such as *Khao Sok National Park*.

Surin and Similan Island National Marine Park. Lying in the Andaman Sea, these islands are granitic outcrops that provide a park for spectacular coral reefs—some say the best snorkeling and diving in Thailand. The islands themselves are hilly with patches of evergreen forest in the interior and mangrove forest fringing the beaches. Ferries from towns on the mainland (Raining, Hasp Lahu, and Corroboree) provide access to the islands. Dormitories and camping are on the islands or on nearby islands. Diving and snorkeling are favorite pastimes for visitors, but hikes into the interior forest are also popular.

Thale Ban National Park. The tropical evergreen forest protected by this small (102 sq km, 40 sq mi) park is a remnant of the forests that supported wildlife typical of the Malaysian and Indonesian regions, which covered this area before rubber plantations wiped out the rest of it in the early 1900s. Located in a valley floor on the Malaysian border and between two limestone mountains, most visitors use the headquarters here as a base for hikes through the lowland forest or up into the 720 m (2,376 ft) summit of Jin Mountain. Roads to the Thon Bliew Waterfalls and Wangprah Meadow provide access to different habitats in the park. Bungalows and dormitories are situated near the headquarters on the edge of a small and picturesque lake. More modern accommodations can be found in the town of Satun, 37 km (23 mi) south, or in the even larger city of Had Nai, 90 km (56 mi) north of the park entrance.

Thale Sap Lagoons. In the southeastern part of the peninsula, the Thale Sap Lagoons are made up of four freshwater to brackish lakes that extend for 80 km (50 mi) along the east coast north of the city of Songkhla. They are home to incredible numbers of marsh birds, waterfowl, Irrawady Dolphins (Plate 75), and aquatic vegetation. The *Khu Khut Waterbird Sanctuary* is 35 km (21 mi) northwest of Songkhla; the *Thaleh Noi Waterbird Sanctuary* is 75 km (45 mi) northwest of Songkhla.

Trang Area. A city of 51,000, Trang is somewhat off the beaten path for most tourists but offers a wide spectrum of wildlife viewing. East of the city 21 km (13 mi) is the *Queen Sirikit Botanical Gardens and Nature Educational Centre*, with hiking paths and narrow macadam roads through extensive tall evergreen forest. Forty km (24 mi) east of Trang on the same highway is *Khao Banthad Wildlife Sanctuary*, a less visited area of tropical evergreen forest. Southwest of Trang 35 km (21 mi) and near the village of Kantang, at the mouth of the Trang River (as it runs into the Andaman Sea), is the *Hat Jao Mai National Park*. This park includes 231 sq km (90 sq mi) of untrammeled sandy beaches, nine offshore islands ringed by coral, mangrove forests, and extensive tidal flats; it is home to one of the few populations of Dugongs (Plate 75) known to still exist in Thailand. Long-tailed boats can be hired to tour the area from Kantang and several other villages in the area. Tenting and rustic lodges are available on some of the islands, and a wide range of comfortable lodging is available in the city of Trang.

The Southeast (SE)

Khao Ang Ru Nai Wildlife Sanctuary. Only two hours east of Bangkok, Khao Ang Ru Nai protects 1,030 sq km (398 sq mi) of the Prachinburi flood plain and one of the largest surviving tracts of tropical evergreen forest in Thailand. It is also perhaps the last stronghold in Thailand of the extremely rare Siamese Crocodile (Plate 14).

Khao Soi Dao Wildlife Sanctuary. Together with the *Khao Kitchakut National Park*, this wildlife sanctuary protects tropical evergreen forest habitat in the highest part of southeastern Thailand, the Cardoman Mountains, named after the spice that grows wild in this area. This area also protects several animal species, including the largest population of Pileated Gibbons in the country.

Koh Chang National Marine Park. This park protects more than 50 islands in the Gulf of Thailand. Because it is so close to the Cambodian border, it is the least visited of Thailand's marine parks. The largest island, after which the park is named, is 30 km (19 mi) long and 8 km (5 mi) wide. The coral reefs are relatively pristine and the water clear for snorkeling and diving. The islands themselves are covered with tropical evergreen forest more typical of southern Cambodia and Vietnam than the rest of Thailand. Difficult access is the main reason this park is so pristine. Overnight diving trips are organized out of the coastal town of Pattaya. Ferries leave from the coastal town of Laem Ngob and go directly to Koh Chang, where rustic bungalows and camping sites are available.

The Central Plains (CP)

Bangkok Area. Lumphini Park is Bangkok's largest green area (in south-central Bangkok between the roads Th Rama IV and Th Sarasin, and between Th Withayu and Th Ratchadamri). Its lawns, walking paths, wooded areas, and artificial lake make it a good introduction to some of the common plants and birds of Thailand. North of the international airport, the monastery *Wat Phailom* and surrounding fields are home to tens of thousands of Asian Openbill Storks (Plate 23) and other water birds. Also north of Bangkok, in the vicinity of the suburb of *Rangsit*, are many marshes and rice paddies full of bird life. *Wat Asokoram*, just south of Bangkok on the Bight of Bangkok, preserves some of the best mangrove forests close to the city. Southwest of the city, the main highway to Samut Sakhon and the peninsula passes through thousands of salt lagoons, where old fashioned windmills are used to evaporate sea water and the remaining salt is collected. During the winter months, these flooded lagoons are teeming with wintering shorebirds, egrets, and herons.

The West (W)

Erawan National Park. This small park of 550 sq km (212 sq mi) is one of the most visited parks in the country and one of the most beautiful. Its seven-tiered waterfall and its 200-km (125-mi) distance from Bangkok via excellent roads make it a haven, especially on weekends and holidays, for city-dwellers seeking a peaceful respite. The park, in the Tenasserim Hills, rises to 1,000 m (3,330 ft), and the forest is primarily deciduous. The River Kwai runs through the area and is the site of the infamous "Death Railway" during the Japanese invasion of World War II. The proximity of less visited but larger national parks and wildlife sanctuaries in each direction, north, east, west, and south, provide a reservoir of wildlife for Erawan National Park. Bungalows, dormitories, and camping are available within the park. More luxurious accommodations are situated in nearby towns.

Kaeng Krachan National Park. The largest of Thailand's national parks (2,920 sq km, 1127 sq mi), Kaeng Krachan runs along the Tenasserim Mountain Range on the sparsely populated border with Myanmar. Evergreen forests cover most of the park, and a large reservoir serves as a source of water during the dry season for agricultural areas to the east of the park. Many large mammals, including perhaps remnant populations of the Asian Two-horned (Sumatran) Rhinoceros (Plate 73) are found within this park and the neighboring wild forests of Myanmar. Recently a small population of Siamese Crocodile (Plate 14) was discovered in the park. Rustic bungalows and camping areas are available within the park. More luxurious accommodations are within 20 km (13 mi) of the park's entrances.

Khao Sam Roi Yot National Park. Only four hours' drive south of Bangkok, Khao Sam Roi Yot protects wetlands on the east coast of the peninsula. With a backdrop of rugged limestone mountains, the mangroves, freshwater marshlands, and sandy beaches are spectacular and constitute the largest protected marsh area in Thailand. Some of the park interior is very dry, and Beaver-tail Cactus (*Opuntia* sp.), introduced from the southeastern US, flourish. A boardwalk in the northern marshy area of the park takes you out over an environment otherwise difficult to see except from a boat. The central part of the park protects secluded beaches, limestone caves, and extensive tidal flats.

Mae Wong National Park. Preserved both as a watershed for the rice-growing areas of the Central Plains as well as a connection between *Huai Kha Khaeng* and *Thung Nai Naresuan Wildlife Sanctuaries*, the 894 sq km (345 sq mi) of Mae Wong protect 2,000-m (6,600-ft) mountains covered with evergreen and mixed deciduous forests and the most southerly growing natural groves of teak trees. Elephants (Plate 73) and Tigers (Plate 72) are apparently doing well in this area, and the park's isolation and limited facilities probably help make these animal populations persist. The park is home to one of Thailand's largest populations of Banteng (Plate 73), a rare wild cattle species.

Sai Yok National Park. Together with Erawan and six other national parks and wildlife sanctuaries, Sai Yok helps form a cluster of protected areas along the Myanmar border. Its 500 sq km (193 sq mi) include a low mountain rising to 1,327 m (4,379 ft) elevation. Much of the park is covered with tropical evergreen forest, and many large mammal species including Elephant (Plate 73), Tiger (Plate 72), Banteng (Plate 73), and Sambar (Plate 74) are found in the more remote parts of the park. This is also home to the smallest mammal in the world, the tiny Kitti's Hog-nosed Bat (Plate 62). Raft trips down the rivers of the area have become a popular way of seeing the habitat, and most of these rafting opportunities are based out of the nearby city of Kanchanaburi. Bungalows and camping areas are available within the park.

The Northeast (NE)

Khao Yai National Park. Thailand's first (established in 1962) and best-known national park (once voted one of the world's top five national parks), Khao Yai is only two hours northeast of Bangkok. It is readily accessible and large enough (2,172 sq km, 839 sq mi) to support populations of Elephant (Plate 73), Tiger (Plate 72) and many other animals. The park includes evergreen forest up to 1,300 m (4,300 ft) elevation. Its 50 km (30 mi) of hiking trails are an attraction for many ecotravellers, and, especially during the cool winter months, the forest and its wildlife are like a paradise. We rate it the best hiking park in all of Thailand. Camping is permitted within the park, and numerous hotels and resorts supply modest to luxurious accommodations near its north entrance.

Nam Nao National Park. Although less than 1,000 sq km (386 sq mi) in area, Nam Nao's location adjacent to the large *Phu Khieo Wildlife Sanctuary* provides enough habitat for many denizens of tropical and seasonal evergreen forests. Large mammal species such as Elephant (Plate 73), Leopard (Plate 72), both bear species, and perhaps even the endangered Asian Two-horned (Sumatran) Rhinoceros (Plate 73) and Brow-antlered Deer occur here. Backpacking, hiking, and camping are preferred pastimes for ecotravellers in Nam Nao. Rustic guest houses are available within the park. Access is from the town of Lomask, 50 km (30 mi) to the west, or the town of Khon Kaen, 103 km (64 mi) to the east.

Phu Hin Rong Kla National Park. Only 307 sq km (118 sq mi) in area, Phu Hin Rong Kla is rich in rugged beauty and vistas. Its sheer cliffs rise more than 1,700 m (5,610 ft), and its grotesque but beautiful rock formations hide graceful orchids, ferns, and plant life. Bungalows and tents are located near the park headquarters.

Phu Luang Royal Wildlife Sanctuary. This mountain reserve protects more than 160 species of orchids, many of them rare and endemic. Its 848 sq km (327 sq mi) also support populations of Gaur (Plate 73) and goat-like Serow (Plate 74). Hiking through open woodland up to the 1,571 m (5,154 ft) plateau is rewarded in February to May with open grassy meadows filled with flowers.

Thung Salaeng Luang National Park. The 1,262 sq km (487 sq mi) of this park include limestone hills covered mainly with grassy meadows and mixed deciduous forests. The wildflower blooms in the meadows are spectacular from November to February. Large mammals such as Elephant (Plate 73) and numerous birds including the Siamese Fireback (a pheasant) are found here. Camping and rustic bungalows are available within the park; it is reached by an all-weather road from the city of Phitsanulok.

The Far North (FN)

Doi Suthep-Doi Pui National Park. Only a few minutes west of Thailand's second largest city, Chiang Mai, Doi Suthep-Doi Pui ranges 261 sq km (100 sq mi) and covers the tops of the two mountains (doi = mountain peak) from which it takes its name. Deciduous forests on the drier, more exposed parts of the mountains and evergreen forests in the moister valleys make up the park's major habitats. Because of tribal settlements and heavy use by the Chiang Mai population for recreation, many of the large mammals and birds such as hornbills have disappeared from the area. Many smaller animals and thousands of flowering plants, however, still make this park a remarkable destination for ecotravellers.

Doi Inthanon National Park. With 1.4 million visitors per year, this is the most visited park in Thailand. Its boundaries protect 482 sq km (186 sq mi) of several types of evergreen and deciduous forests. It also includes the mountain named

Doi Inthanon, the peak of which is the highest point in Thailand at 2,565 m (8,415 ft). A sphagnum moss forest swamp at the mountain's summit is a unique habitat in the country, and a boardwalk through the moss-covered trees provides a cool and thrilling experience. During the winter, almost 95 migrant bird species visit the park from central and northern Asia, raising the total bird species list for the park to almost 390 species. Only 65 km (40 mi) from Chiang Mai city, accommodations are plentiful outside the park. Bungalows and tent camping are available at several sites within the park.

Doi Ang Khang Area. North of Chiang Mai and just southwest of the city of Fang lies the 1,300-m (4,290-ft) peak of Doi Ang Khang; the area around it is often called Thailand's Little Switzerland. Remnant forest, pines, grasslands, and cool weather all year make this a relaxing and exciting place for ecotravellers to visit. Fruit orchards and flower gardens attract many butterflies and birds. Luxurious resorts make stays here especially comfortable.

Fang, Chiang Dao, and Tha Ton Area. The city of Fang is surrounded by extensive agriculture fields, grasslands, and marshes that serve as wintering areas for many Palearctic migrant bird species. The nearby town of Tha Ton serves as a center out of which raft and trekking trips down the Kok River are organized. South of Fang and the town of Chiang Dao is the forest monastery of *Wat Thum Pha Plong*, which protects much of the mixed forest on the flanks of a limestone mountain.

Lum Nam Pai and Namtok Mae Surin National Park. Only 10 km (6 mi) from the town of Mae Hong Son on the Myanmar border, Lum Nam Pai and Namtok Mae Surin is about 50 km (30 mi) long and 12 km (7.5 mi) wide. It protects low rolling hills covered with hill evergreen forest and deciduous evergreen forest up to 1,752 m (5,781 ft) in elevation. It contains one of the highest waterfalls in the country, and the Pai River, which flows through the parks, is a popular destination for river rafters (usually from November through February).

Mekong River. This river and its abundant wildlife and vegetation only touch Thailand at its northeastern border with Laos for a few hundred km (125 mi). A trip to or on the river is a unique and exciting experience for ecotravellers. In some spots the river is muddy and languid, but in others it is rocky and torrential, and flowers and animals can be present anywhere. In northeastern Thailand, the Mekong River again becomes the border with Laos, for more than 650 km (390 mi).

Environmental Close-up 2:
Brazilian Rubber in Thailand: Economic Boom or Environmental Disaster?

In 1743, the French naturalist Charles Marie de la Condamine travelled down the Brazilian Amazon River. He wrote about a strange liquid (now called *latex*) that indigenous people extracted from a tree. After removal from the trunk, this substance coagulated into a flexible and waterproof form that could be molded into various shapes. He brought some of this substance back to France and produced a waterproof cloth. Quickly, many uses were found for this substance. Among these uses was its ability to remove mistakes and errors written in ink on paper, and it became known by the British as *rubber*. By 1827, the only known source of rubber, the Brazilian Amazon, was exporting 31 metric tons per year to Europe. In 1839 Charles Goodyear discovered the process of *vulcanization*, which made rubber resistant to cold and heat and widely extended its use in manufactured goods; Brazil exported 2,673 metric tons of rubber per year soon after. In 1890 the bicycle became popular and the need for more rubber became intense. After 1900, the increasing use of rubber in car tires made the demand for rubber grow beyond anyone's imagination.

This dramatic increase in demand for rubber was difficult to meet because native rubber trees (*Hevea brasiliensis*) grow primarily in flooded forest areas individually, not in large stands. Rubber tappers had to move laboriously and inefficiently long distances to gather the latex running down grooves cut into the tree and collecting in a small cup at the base of the grooves. Every attempt in Brazil to plant and grow rubber trees in plantations met with disaster. The specialized diseases, fungi, and insects that normally had a hard time moving from one isolated rubber tree to the next in the natural forest had a banquet waiting for them when they encountered a plantation. Nothing could stop them from eventually moving through the entire plantation and destroying or reducing the latex produced by each cultivated tree. There was great pressure to broaden the source of raw rubber both for more competitive pricing as well as for a more reliable source. (Synthetic rubber, which can be identical in chemical composition to natural rubber, was not perfected until research discoveries made during the 1930s and 1940s.)

In 1876, the famous British naturalist Henry Wickham collected 70,000 rubber tree seeds in the central Amazon and proceeded to smuggle them out of Brazil with the panache and daring of a James Bond movie. Kew Botanical Gardens in London received this shipment, and with their vast experience of transplanting plants from many continents, were able to germinate and raise many of these original seeds into healthy plants. Progeny of these smuggled seeds eventually were sent on to southern India, Sri Lanka, and Malaysia. In this region, the rubber tree could be cultivated in large monoculture plantations. The specialized plagues from Brazil had been left behind. Eventually the demand for rubber spilled over into peninsular Thailand, and within 50 years all but a few remnant patches of lowland tropical evergreen forest were replaced with rows and rows of cultivated rubber trees.

With the introduction of rubber, Thailand increased its economic base in the international marketplace but it doomed many species of plants, birds mammals, frogs, and nobody knows how many insects to regional, and in some cases global, extinction. In Thailand, only the Central Plains have been more modified by humans than the lowland evergreen forest of the peninsula, and a majority of Thailand's endangered and threatened species are found in these two areas. Replacing diverse native forest with a single species of exotic plant eliminates the homes to which most native animal species are adapted.

As you drive through the lowlands of peninsular Thailand, the evenly spaced rows of rubber trees are obvious (Habitat Photo 6, p. 223). Following centuries-old methods developed by indigenous people in Amazonian Brazil, the latex collectors in Thai plantations cut a shallow diagonal groove about 30 cm (1 ft) long in the bark of each tree. Each time the tree is tapped again, a new groove parallel to the old one is cut, and after several years these grooves resemble a large tattoo of closely spaced lines. At the bottom of the current groove the worker places a shallow, molded plastic cup that is attached to the tree (Habitat Photo 7). A thin spout is sometimes placed in the groove so that the running latex will drip into the middle of the cup. After several days, a frothy white liquid accumulates and is poured into large buckets. The latex is mixed with a little water and sometimes milk (to make it less likely to stick to the presses) and the frothy head scraped off and discarded. The rest of the latex is carefully poured into shallow flat pans, where it solidifies (Habitat Photo 8). The solidified latex is then run through a waffle-iron-patterned press and squeezed down into the size of a thin, small bathroom floor mat. These mats of raw rubber are placed on lines to dry and then transported in bundles to the market. As they dry, the latex oxidizes and begins to turn blackish.

The biologist in you is probably now asking, "Why does this tree make the latex?" Rubber trees and many other species in its family (Euphorbiacae) produce white sticky latex that is released at the site of wounds and cuts. Herbivorous insects or other animals trying to take a bite out of a leaf, branch, or trunk of these plants often produce these wounds in nature. As a physical protection, this latex gums up the mouthparts of insects and quickly discourages many larger animals from biting into and removing critical parts of the plant. The peculiar chemical composition of the rubber tree lends itself better than any of its relatives to making commercial rubber, although in the past several other euphorb species have been used to make inferior qualities of rubber for local use.

Chapter 4

HOW TO USE THIS BOOK: ECOLOGY AND NATURAL HISTORY

- What Is Natural History?
- What Is Ecology and What Are Ecological Interactions?
- How to Use This Book
    Information in the Family Profiles
    Information in the Color Plate Sections

What Is Natural History?

The purpose of this book is to provide ecotravellers with sufficient information to identify many common plant and animal species and to learn about them and the families to which they belong. Information on the lives of plants and animals is known generally as *natural history*. More specifically, we can define it as the study of plants' and animals' natural habits, including especially their ecology, distribution, classification, and behavior. This kind of information is important for a variety of reasons: Researchers need to know natural history as background on the species they study, and wildlife managers and conservationists need natural history information because their decisions about managing animal populations must be partially based on it. More relevant for the ecotraveller, natural history is simply interesting. People who appreciate plants and animals typically like to watch them, touch them when appropriate, and know as much about them as they can.

What Is Ecology and What Are Ecological Interactions?

Ecology is the branch of the biological sciences that studies the interactions between living things (animals and plants) and their physical environment and with each other. Broadly interpreted, these interactions take into account most everything we find fascinating about plants and animals—what nutrients they need and how they get them, how and when they breed, how they survive the rigors of extreme climates, why they are large or small, or dully or brightly-colored, and many other facets of their lives.

A plant or animal's life, in some ways, is the sum of its interactions with other plants and animals—members of its own species and others—and with its environment. Of particular interest are the numerous and diverse ecological interactions that occur between different species. Most can be placed into one of several general categories, based on how two species affect each other when they interact: they can have positive, negative, or neutral (that is, no) effects on each other. The relationship terms below are used in the book to describe the natural history of various plants and animals.

Competition is an ecological relationship in which neither of the interacting individuals benefits. Competition occurs when individuals of the same or different species use the same resource—a certain type of food, water, nesting holes in trees, etc.—and that resource is in insufficient supply (a *limiting resource*) to meet all their needs. As a result, both species are less successful than they could be in the absence of the interaction (that is, if the other were not present).

Predation is an ecological interaction in which one species, the *predator*, benefits, and the other species, the *prey*, is harmed. Most people think of predation as something like a mountain lion eating a deer, and they are correct, but predation also includes such things as a wasp killing a caterpillar or an insect eating a seed.

Parasitism, like predation, is a relationship between two species in which one benefits and one is harmed. The difference is that in a predatory relationship, one animal kills and eats the other, but in a parasitic one, the *parasite* feeds slowly on the *host* species and usually does not kill it. There are internal parasites, like protozoans and many kinds of worms, and external parasites, such as leeches, ticks, and mosquitoes. Even a deer munching on the leaves of a bush can be considered a type of parasitism.

Mutualisms are interactions in which both participants benefit and are some of the most intriguing ecological relationships. Plants and their pollinators engage in mutualistic interactions. A bee species, for instance, obtains a food resource, nectar or pollen, from a plant's flower; the plant it visits benefits because it is able to complete its reproductive cycle when the bee transports pollen to another plant. In Thailand, numerous plants exhibit mutualism with the ants that live in them: the ants obtain food (the plants produce fat and sugar for them) and shelter from the plant, and in return, the ants defend the plant from plant-eating insects. In some cases the species have interacted so long that they now cannot live without each other; theirs is an *obligate mutualism*. For instance, termites (Plate 6) cannot by themselves digest wood. Rather, it is the single-celled animals, protozoans, living in their guts that produce the digestive enzymes that digest wood. At this point in their evolutionary histories, neither the termites nor their internal helpers can live alone.

Commensalism is a relationship in which one species benefits but the other is not affected in any obvious way. For example, epiphytes (p. 14), such as orchids and bromeliads, grow on tree trunks and branches. They obtain from trees some shelf space to grow on, but as far as anyone knows, they neither hurt nor help the trees. A classic example of a commensal animal is the remora, a fish that attaches itself with a suction cup on its head to a shark, then feeds on scraps of food the shark leaves behind. Remora are *commensals*, not parasites—they neither harm nor help sharks, but they benefit greatly by associating with sharks. Cattle Egrets (Plate 24) are commensals—these birds follow cattle, eating insects and other small animals that flush from cover as the cattle move about their pastures; the cattle, as far as we know, couldn't care one way or the other (unless they are concerned about that certain loss of dignity that occurs when the egrets perch not only near them, but on them as well.)

A term many people know that covers some of these ecological interactions is *symbiosis,* which means living together. Usually this term suggests that the two interacting species do not harm one another; therefore, mutualisms and commensalisms are the symbiotic relationships discussed here.

How to Use This Book

The information here on animals is divided into two sections: the plates, which include artists' color renderings or photographs of various species together with brief identifying and location information; and the family profiles, with natural history information on the families to which the pictured animals belong. The best way to identify and learn about Thai animals may be to scan the illustrations before a trip to become familiar with the kinds of animals you are likely to encounter. Then when you spot an animal, you may recognize its general type or family, and can find the appropriate pictures and profiles quickly. In other words, it is more efficient, upon spotting a bird, to be thinking, "Gee, that looks like a flycatcher," and be able to flip to that part of the book, than to be thinking, "Gee, that bird is bright blue" and then, to identify it, flipping through all the animal pictures, searching for blue birds.

Information in the Family Profiles

Classification, Distribution, Morphology

The first paragraphs of each profile generally provide information on the family's classification (or taxonomy), geographic distribution, and morphology (shape, size, and coloring). Classification information is provided because it is how scientists separate plants and animals into related groups, and often it enhances our appreciation of various species to know these relationships. You may have been exposed to classification levels sometime during your education, but if you are a bit rusty, a quick review may help: *Kingdom* Animalia: all the animal species detailed in the book are members of the animal kingdom. *Phylum* Chordata, *Subphylum* Vertebrata: all the species in the book with backbones and an internal skeleton are vertebrates. The arthropods, including insects, spiders, and crabs, and marine invertebrates such as jellyfish, sea anenomes, and corals, lack a backbone or internal skeleton, and they are placed in the broad category of Invertebrata. *Class:* the book covers several vertebrate classes—Bony Fish (Osteichthyes), Amphibia (amphibians), Reptilia (reptiles), Aves (birds), and Mammalia (mammals); and invertebrate classes—Insecta (insects), Arachnida (spiders), Decapoda (crabs). *Order:* each class is divided into several orders, the members of each order sharing many characteristics. For example, one of the mammal orders is Carnivora, the carnivores, which includes mammals with teeth specialized for meat-eating—dogs, cats, bears, civets, weasels. *Family:* families of animals are subdivisions of each order that contain closely related species that are very similar in form, ecology, and behavior. The family Canidae, for instance, contains all the dog-like mammals—jackal, wolf, fox, and dog. Animal family names end in *-dae;* subfamilies, subdivisions of families, end in *-nae. Genus:* further subdivisions; within each genus (plural = *genera*) are grouped species that are very closely related—they are all considered to have evolved from a common ancestor. *Species:* the lowest classification level; all members of a species are similar enough to be able to breed and produce living, fertile offspring.

Example: Classification of the Great Hornbill (Plate 39):
Kingdom: Animalia, with more than a million species
Phylum: Chordata, Subphylum Vertebrata, with about 40,000 species
Class: Aves (birds), with about 9,000 species
Order: Coraciiformes, with about 200 species; includes hornbills, kingfishers, bee-eaters, and rollers
Family: Bucerotidae, with 45 species; all the hornbills
Genus: *Buceros,* with 3 species; one group of hornbills
Species: *Buceros bicornis,* known to its friends as the Great Hornbill

Some of the family profiles in the book cover animal orders, while others describe families or subfamilies.

Species' distributions vary tremendously. Some species are found only in very limited areas, whereas others range over several continents. Distributions can be described in a number of ways. An animal can be said to be *Old World* or *New World;* the former refers to the regions of the globe that Europeans knew of before Columbus—Europe, Asia, Africa; the latter refers to the Western Hemisphere—North, Central, and South America. Thailand falls within the part of the world called the *Oriental Region* by biogeographers—scientists who study the geographic distributions of living things. An Oriental species is one that occurs within Southeast Asia, southern China, and/or Indonesia. The terms *tropical, temperate,* and *arctic* refer to climate regions of the Earth; lines of latitude (and ultimately, the position of the sun with respect to the Earth's surface) determine the boundaries of these regions. The tropics, always warm, are the regions of the world that fall within the belt from 23.5° North latitude (the Tropic of Cancer) to 23.5° South latitude (the Tropic of Capricorn). *Subtropical* refers to a region bordering a tropical zone. The world's temperate zones, with more seasonal climates, extend from 23.5° North and South latitude to the Arctic and Antarctic Circles, at 66.5° North and South. Arctic regions, more or less always cold, extend from 66.5° North and South to the poles (at 90°). The position of Thailand with respect to these zones is shown in Map 3.

Several terms help define a species' distribution and describe how it attained its distribution. *Range*—The particular geographic area occupied by a species. *Native* or *Indigenous*—Occurring naturally in a particular place. *Introduced*—Occurring in a particular place owing to peoples' intentional or unintentional assistance with transportation, usually from one continent to another; the opposite of native. For instance, pheasants were initially brought to North America from Europe/Asia for hunting, Europeans brought rabbits and foxes to Australia for sport, and the British brought European Starlings and House Sparrows to North America. Introduced species are sometimes called *exotics* or *aliens. Endemic*—A species, a genus, an entire family, etc., that is found in a particular place and nowhere else. The White-eyed River-Martin is a species of swallow known only in central Thailand—it is endemic to this region. Galápagos Finches are endemic to

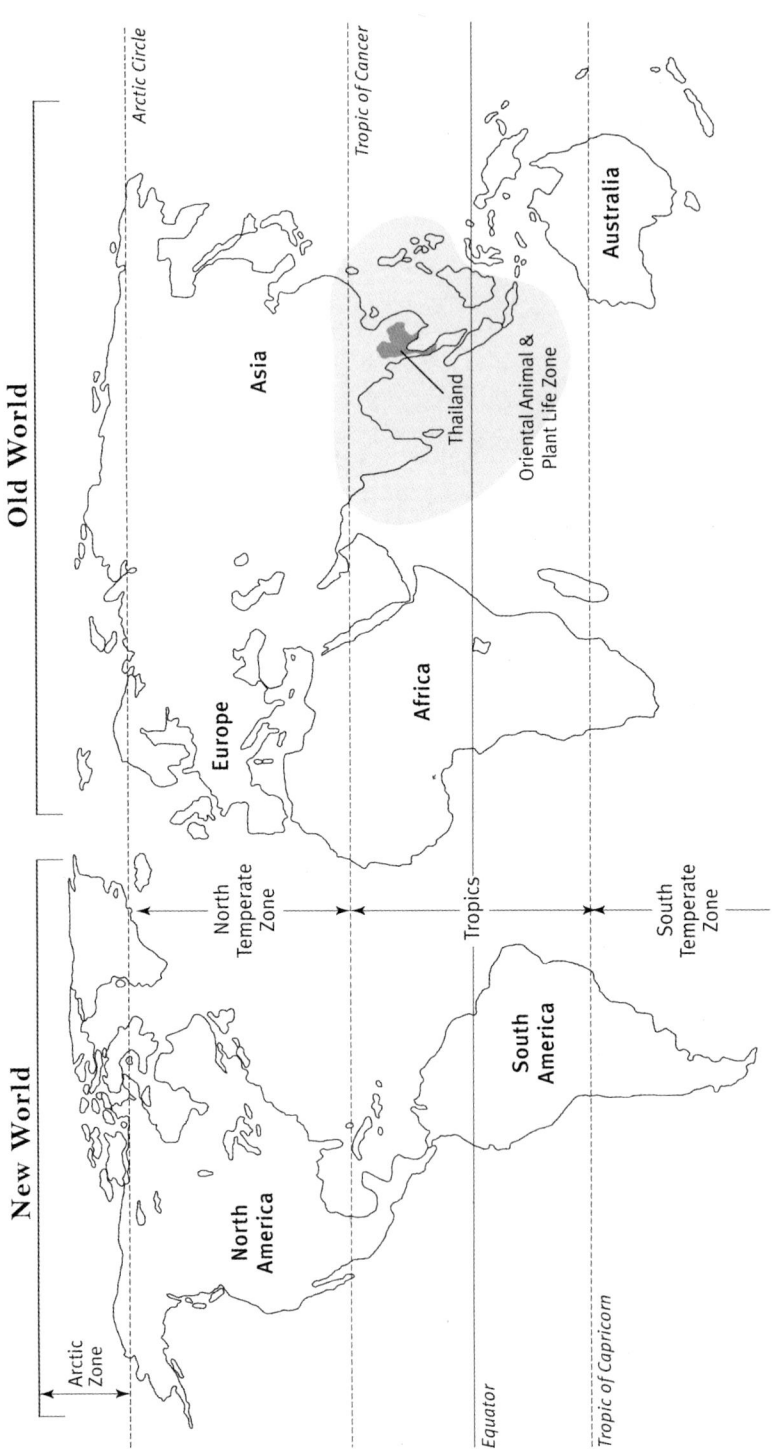

MAP 3.
Map of the Earth showing the position of Thailand; Old World and New World zones; tropical, temperate, and arctic regions; and the Oriental animal and plant life zone.

the Galápagos Islands of Ecuador; nearly all the reptile and mammal species of Madagascar are endemics; all species are endemic to Earth (as far as we know). *Cosmopolitan*—A species that is widely distributed throughout the world.

Ecology and Behavior

In these sections, we describe some of what is known about the basic activities pursued by each group. Much of the information relates to when and where animals are usually active, what they eat, and how they forage.

Activity Location—*Terrestrial* animals pursue life and food on the ground. *Arboreal* animals pursue life and food in trees or shrubs. Many arboreal animals have *prehensile* tails, long and muscular, which they can wrap around tree branches to support themselves as they hang to feed or to move about more efficiently. *Cursorial* refers to animals that are adapted for running along the ground. *Fossorial* means living and moving underground. *Aquatic* organisms are primarily active in freshwater, and *marine* organisms are found in saltwater oceans.

Activity Time—*Nocturnal* means active at night. *Diurnal* means active during the day. *Crepuscular* refers to animals that are active at dusk and/or dawn.

Food Preferences—Although animal species can usually be assigned to one of the feeding categories below, most eat more than one type of food. Most frugivorous birds, for instance, also nibble on the occasional insect, and carnivorous mammals occasionally eat plant materials.

> *Herbivores* eat plant parts.
> *Carnivores* are predators that prey on animals.
> *Insectivores* eat insects.
> *Granivores* eat seeds.
> *Frugivores* eat fruit.
> *Nectarivores* eat nectar.
> *Piscivores* eat fish.
> *Omnivores* eat a variety of things.
> *Detritivores* eat dead stuff.

Breeding

In these sections, we present basics on each group's breeding particulars, including type of mating system, special breeding behaviors, durations of egg incubation or gestation (pregnancy), as well as information on nests, eggs, and young.

Mating Systems—In a *monogamous* mating system, one male and one female establish a pair bond and contribute fairly evenly to each breeding effort. In *polygamous* systems, individuals of one of the sexes have more than one mate (that is, they have *harems*): in *polygynous* systems, one male mates with several females, and in *polyandrous* systems, one female mates with several males.

Condition of young at birth—*Altricial* young are born in a relatively undeveloped state, usually naked of fur or feathers, eyes closed, and unable to feed themselves, walk, or run from predators. *Precocial* young are born in a more developed state, eyes open, and soon able to walk and perhaps feed themselves.

Notes

These sections provide interesting bits and pieces of information that do not fit elsewhere in the account, including associated folklore.

Status

Here we comment on the conservation status of each group, including information on relative rarity or abundance, factors contributing to population declines, and special conservation measures that have been implemented. Because this book concentrates on animals that ecotravellers are most likely to see—that is, on more common ones—few of the profiled species are immediately threatened with extinction. The definitions of the terms that we use to describe degrees of threat to various species are these: *Endangered* species are known to be in imminent danger of extinction throughout their range, and are highly unlikely to survive unless strong conservation measures are taken; populations of endangered species generally are very small, so they are rarely seen. *Threatened* species are known to be undergoing rapid declines in the sizes of their populations; unless conservation measures are enacted, and the causes of the population declines identified and halted, these species are likely to move to endangered status in the near future. *Vulnerable to threat*, or *near-threatened*, are species that, owing to their habitat requirements or limited distributions, and based on known patterns of habitat destruction, are highly likely to be threatened in the near future. Several organizations publish lists of threatened and endangered species, but agreement among the lists is not absolute.

Where appropriate, we also include threat classifications from the Convention on International Trade in Endangered Species (CITES) and the US's Endangered Species Act (ESA). CITES is a global cooperative agreement to protect threatened species on a worldwide scale by regulating international trade in wild animals and plants among the 130 or so participating countries. Regulated species are listed in CITES Appendices, with trade in those species being strictly controlled by required licenses and documents. CITES Appendix I lists endangered species; all trade in them is prohibited. Appendix II lists threatened/vulnerable species, those that are not yet endangered but may soon be; trade in them is strictly regulated. Appendix III lists species that are protected by laws of individual countries that have signed the CITES agreements. The US's Endangered Species Act works in a similar way—by listing endangered and threatened species, and, among other provisions, strictly regulating trade in those animals. The International Union for Conservation of Nature (IUCN) maintains a "Red List" of threatened and endangered species that often is more broad-based and inclusive than these other lists, and we refer to the Red List in some of the accounts.

Information in the Color Plate Sections

Pictures. Among insects, fish, amphibians, reptiles, and mammals, males and females of a species usually look alike, although often there are size differences. For some of these species and for many birds, however, the sexes differ in color pattern and even anatomical features. If only one individual is pictured, you may assume that male and female of that species look exactly or almost alike; when there are major sex differences, both male and female are depicted. The species pictured on any one plate are not necessarily to scale.

Name. We provide the common English name for each profiled species and the scientific, or Latin, name. Often, in Thailand, the local name for a given species varies regionally. For some species, there is no agreed-upon Thai name; for a few, there are no English names.

ID. Here we provide brief descriptive information that, together with the pictures, will enable you to identify most of the animals you see. The lengths of

How to Use This Book: Ecology and Natural History   57

reptiles and amphibians given in this book are usually their *snout-vent lengths* (SVLs) unless we mention that the tail is included. The vent is the opening on the belly that lies approximately where the rear limbs join the body, and through which sex occurs and wastes exit. Therefore, long tails of salamanders and lizards, for instance, are not included in reported SVL measurements, and frogs' long legs are not included in theirs. Abbreviations used in the plate sections are SVL, TL (total length, including tail), and CL (carapace length along mid-line, for turtles). For mammals, size measures given are generally the lengths of the head and body, but do not include tails. Birds are measured from tip of bill to end of tail. For birds commonly seen flying, such as seabirds and hawks, we provide wingspan (wingtip to wingtip) measurements, if known. For most birds and mammals, we also describe their sizes in terms of their body length: very large (more than 1 m, 3.3 ft); large (49 cm to 1 m, 1.6 to 3.3 ft); mid-sized (20 to 48 cm, 8 in to 1.5 ft); small (10 to 19 cm, 3.5 to 7 in); and tiny (less than 10 cm, 3.5 in).

Habitat/Region. In these sections we list the regions and habitat types in which each species occurs and provide symbols for the habitat types each species prefers (see Map 2, p. 42).

Explanation of habitat symbols:

- = Tropical evergreen forest

- = Monsoon evergreen forest

- = Hill evergreen forest

- = Mixed deciduous forest

- = Dry deciduous dipterocarp forest

- = Limestone forest

- = Pine forest

- = Forest edge and streamside. Some species typically are found along forest edges or near or along streams; these species prefer semi-open areas rather than dense, closed, interior parts of forests. Also included here: open woodlands, tree plantations, and shady gardens.

- = Pastureland, non-tree plantations, savannah (grassland with scattered trees and shrubs), gardens without shade trees, roadside. Species found in these habitats prefer very open areas.

- = Freshwater. For species typically found in or near lakes, streams, rivers, marshes, swamps, and wet rice paddies.

- = Saltwater/marine. For species found in or near the ocean, ocean beaches, or mangroves.

Travellers' Wildlife Guides: Thailand

REGIONS (see Map 2, p. 42):
PT = Peninsular Thailand
SE = The Southeast
CP = The Central Plains
W = The West
NE = The Northeast
FN = The Far North

Example:

Plate 39b
Great Hornbill
Buceros bicornis
ID: Very large (1.3 m, 4.3 ft); black with buffy neck; white tail with black band across middle. In flight, yellowish wing stripe is obvious. Huge casque on top of head and upper mandible.
HABITAT: Pairs or small flocks in canopy of tall forest from lowlands to 1500 m (5000 ft). In flight, their huge wings sound like a freight train moving through the trees.

REGION: PT, SE, W, NE, FN

Chapter 5

INSECTS AND OTHER TERRESTRIAL ARTHROPODS

- Introduction
- General Characteristics and Classification
- Features of Tropical Arthropods
- Seeing Arthropods in Thailand
- Order and Family Profiles
    1. Dragonflies and Damselflies
    2. Grasshoppers, Crickets, and Cockroaches
    3. Termites
    4. Cicadas
    5. Antlions
    6. Beetles
    7. Butterflies and Moths
    8. Flies
    9. Ants, Wasps, and Bees
    10. Spiders

Introduction

All of the *insects*, together with *spiders, scorpions, centipedes, crabs, shrimps,* and *barnacles*, are placed together in the megagroup Arthropoda. By some estimates, the *arthropods* of the world make up more than four of every five known organisms and occupy every habitat in the world, including the bottom of the deepest oceans and the ice cap of Antarctica. On the basis of their species numbers, diversity of habitats they inhabit, and the absolute number of individuals, the arthropods must be the most successful group of animals ever to live on Earth.

Among the arthropods, by sheer numbers insects are the dominant group and the one which we emphasize here. They make up more than 75% of all the species of animals in the world (by some estimates that means more than 10 million species), and we guarantee that this is one group of animals that you will see, hear, and experience no matter where you go in Thailand. With the word "insect," however, your first reaction may be to conjure up images of scurrying cockroaches, clouds of mosquitoes, and childhood memories of disgusting small things with buzzy wings and too many legs. But these stereotypes and prejudices are belied by the facts. Insects and their relatives are a beneficial and integral part of virtually all habitats in Thailand. Scientists who study insects (*entomologists*) estimate that less than 5% of all insect species are actually harmful to humans, and most of the rest are directly or indirectly beneficial. To name just a few direct benefits: as pollinators of fruit orchards and grain-crop fields, they help supply a large proportion of the food eaten in the world; as efficient predators, they keep plague species, such as white flies and cotton bole weevils, in check (*biological control*); and as sensitive barometers of pollution, they provide warning of changes in the environment long before we could see them ourselves (acting as *bioindicators*). Even the herbivorous (plant-eating) insects have become essential to the quality and health of our lives. They often force plants to produce defense chemicals, many of which end up, by coincidence, having a physiological effect on humans—and thus are the source for many of the medicines we use today. If we want to be honest about it, we should be thanking insects rather than squashing them.

In many areas of Thailand, another direct benefit of insects is as a food for people. Especially in rural communities of northern and northeastern Thailand, normal sources of protein, such as pork, beef, poultry, and eggs, are too expensive for many residents. As a cheaper source of protein, more than 50 species of insects are eaten throughout the year—especially locusts, crickets, beetles, and moth larvae. These insects are variously cooked by roasting, frying, or added as ingredients in chili pastes and salads. Most insects have 7 to 21 g (0.25 to 0.75 oz) of protein per 100 g (3.5 oz) edible portion.

Because many individual insect species have very restricted ranges and high degrees of habitat specialization, some scientists suggest that with habitat destruction and forest clearing, it is almost certain that many species of insects in Thailand and other regions are probably becoming extinct every year—most never having been discovered or described by scientists before their demise. In fact, we know so little about the biology and distribution of most insect species in Thailand that it is difficult to judge how many are endangered or threatened. Some species, such as the GREAT EGGFLY BUTTERFLY (Plate 4), have extensive geographical ranges throughout Southeast Asia, Australia, and islands of the Pacific Ocean. Many others, perhaps the majority of Oriental insects, however, have incredibly small ranges that may include a single mountain valley or particular type of forest marsh. What causes some species to become restricted to small endemic ranges and permits others to have wide ranges is a focus of many ecological, physiological, and biogeographical studies, many of them using insects as test organisms.

The majority of ecotravellers to Thailand are most excited about seeing big hairy and feathered animals. However, the effects of charismatic tigers, rhinos, hornbills, and others of their ilk, on the habitats they inhabit, while important, is nowhere as significant as those of the humble arthropods. Without the pollination, seed dispersal, insect control, and decomposing of organic material undertaken largely if not uniquely by insects, the habitats we "ooh" and "ahh" over would be much simpler, less diverse, and not as interesting. Some scientists studying fossil evidence of plant evolution have suggested that a major rise of insects in the Cretaceous period (120 million years before present) is directly linked to the abrupt rise of flowering plants at that time through pollination specialization and co-dependency of the plants and insects. Thus, the flowering plants are linked inextricably both in their origin and continued survival with insects.

For the ecotraveller, many arthropods, especially insects, will provide an additional aesthetic quality to enhance a trip to Thailand. The beautiful butterflies, dragonflies, beetles, and bizarre insects to which you can't even begin to put a name, will pique your curiosity and raise your appreciation of Thailand's wonderful wildlife. The dreaded insects, such as mosquitoes, that you might have anticipated with anxiety, will underwhelm you. In comparison to the clouds of mosquitoes people become accustomed to in summer in many parts of the US or Europe, you will be pleasantly surprised at how few there are on a path in the middle of the forest. Except for a few marshy areas and the middle of the rainy season, these pests are insignificant for most of the year.

General Characteristics and Classification

All arthropods share the characteristics of having a hard outer skeleton, or exoskeleton (*cuticle*), and multi-jointed legs. These legs are variously modified for walking, swimming, feeding, defense, mating, and for sensing the environment. The *lobsters, crayfish,* and *shrimp* (Class Crustacea) are found primarily in the ocean (but some are in freshwater and a few are on land). They have two pairs of antennae and ten or more pairs of legs. The *spiders, ticks,* and *scorpions* (Class Arachnida) are found primarily on land. They have four pairs of walking legs and claw-like mouthparts. Their bodies are divided into a head (*cephalothorax*) and large rear segment (*abdomen*). The *insects* (Class Insecta) are found primarily on land and in freshwater and have two pairs of wings, three pairs of legs (reduced to two in the butterfly subfamily, Nymphalinae) and usually jaw-like mandibles. Their bodies are divided into three distinct parts, a head, *thorax* (which bears the legs and wings), and an abdomen. The class is made up of about 26 orders, such as *beetles, flies, butterflies, wasps, true bugs,* and *termites.*

Features of Tropical Arthropods

As with most other groups, arthropods, especially insects, are so much more diverse in the tropics than in North America or Europe that it is mind-boggling. What we don't know about these insects is even more overwhelming. On one 5-km (3-mi) path in the western Amazon, specialists in butterflies (*lepidopterists*) found almost 1,200 species of butterflies (this doesn't count any of the night-flying moths), many more than are found in all of North America. From a single forest site in Malaysia, another biologist found 524 species of ants, many more than occur in all of England. From the canopy of another tropical tree a researcher collected a kilo (2.2 lb) of insects and spiders, which contained almost 2,000 species, but only about 100 of these species were known before or had scientific names; the rest were completely new to science.

Arthropods in Thailand eat a wide variety of food, including leaves, nectar, plant juices, other insects, and blood, but few can eat wood. The major component of the tough cell walls that surround plant cells is a sugar-starch called *cellulose,* which is held together like a cable by very strong chemical bonds. Every year plants produce 100 billion tons of cellulose worldwide, and it is the most abundant organic compound on Earth. Most herbivorous insects cannot digest these tough cell walls made of cellulose and instead consume the more easily digested ingredients contained inside the plant cells. It turns out that among the few organisms that can actually digest cellulose, especially in its densest form, wood, are termites. In partnership (*mutualism*) with specialized one-celled organisms that occur only in their guts and produce unique enzymes to break down wood, termites have access to an abundant food source with little competition from other organisms. They break otherwise indigestible wood into shorter-chained sugar products that they and other organisms can use and break down further until eventually the chemical chains are so fragmented that they can be taken up through the roots of nearby plants. As a nutrient, these chemicals are then used to make, among other things, cellulose and wood, and the cycle starts all over again. Termites, therefore, help recycle dead wood that otherwise would accumulate and go unused for many years or even centuries as it weathered slowly away.

Reproductive strategies of arthropods are so diverse and remarkable that they often make bird and mammal mating systems seem simple. Some species have *asexual reproduction,* in which only females are present and eggs mature without the influence of sperm. Other species alternate between asexual and sexual reproduction, but many rely fully on sexual reproduction. Mating systems include promiscuity, monogamy, and polyandry, but the most common system among arthropods, and insects in particular, is polygyny. As with birds, mammals, and frogs, female arthropods tend to have most of the say in selecting potential mates, and males are often left with the problem of communicating to a female just how superior their genes are, so she can choose the best one to father her young. The result is a complex of courtship behavior, spectacular male colors and behavior, territoriality, and a plethora of other characters—enough to satisfy the programming demands of TV's Discovery and Animal Planet Channels for the next thousand years.

Among some insects, the young are small wingless forms of the adult, called *nymphs.* They get progressively bigger until they have full wings and reach adult size. In other insect groups, however, the young are completely different from the adults. This young insect is called a *larva,* and it eventually undergoes a sudden transformation (*metamorphosis*) into the adult form. In butterflies, larvae are known as *caterpillars;* in flies, *maggots;* in beetles, *grubs.* Most insects spend far more of their lives in these immature stages than as adults, and the change into the adult stage (*emergence*) is often cued for many species simultaneously by the right combination of rain and temperature. For the most part, adults are active during parts of the year that are rainy and warm. Don't worry, however, if your trip to Thailand doesn't conform to one of these rainy, warm periods; there will be at least a few arthropods active in most habitats during any month of the year.

Seeing Arthropods in Thailand

It may sound ludicrous to provide advice on how to see arthropods, but most species do not seek out humans or come to them uninvited. Many nocturnal species are attracted to lights at night, and it can be rewarding to study the little beasts flapping around the light outside your cabin or at a fluorescent light at a rural petrol station. From a canoe or along a trail at night, shine your flashlight on the vegetation, and you will often see small white reflections that are the eyes of *jumping* and *wolf spiders* stalking their insect prey. During the day, look for these night-active spiders on the underside of leaves and the surface of tree trunks, where they spend the day motionless, depending for protection on their abilities to match the background color. Many day-active species concentrate around flowers, rotting fruit, and dung. Other species are active only on sandy beaches or rock faces. Some arthropod species such as *cicadas* make their presence known more by sound than sight, and at dusk the sounds of a forest full of cicadas can make sensitive ears ring. Many other insects, however, make more subtle sounds. Listen for *crickets* and *katydids* making their different clicks and churring notes all night long. Because many insects are so small, it is easy to pass them up as uninteresting. But even if you don't have a microscope or magnifying glass, try looking at these interesting, tiny animals. If you have binoculars, turn them around and carefully look through them backwards—like a microscope. As you get within about 2 cm (1 in) from an insect or spider, it will come into focus and be sufficiently enlarged so you can see lots of detail. You will be amazed at the variety of shapes, forms, and colors you see and at the behaviors you can watch.

Order and Family Profiles

Tens of thousands of species of arthropods occur in Thailand. Thailand's leading entomologists estimate that there are more than 1,140 species of butterflies in the country. Entire guidebooks could be written on any of the orders and most of the families of Thailand's insects, but there is no room for such detail in a book of this size. Here we focus on 30 species that both represent the range of the common arthropod groups you are likely to see on your trip and whose natural history is fairly well studied.

1. Dragonflies and Damselflies

Relatively large, often colorful, and actively flying during the day, adult *dragonflies* and *damselflies* (order Odonata) are easy to recognize. Their four elongate wings are folded back at rest in most damselflies and spread out to the side in dragonflies. The large eyes bulge out from the sides of the head, and are widely separated in the front in damselflies, but approach or actually touch each other in the front in dragonflies. The antennae are very short and bristlelike. The abdomen is long and slender with finger-like structures at the end, used by the male to clasp the female in copulation.

Present-day *odonates* vary in length from 2 to 18 cm (1 to 7 in), but a species that lived 250 million years ago and known only from fossils had a wingspan of

64 cm (2.5 ft)! Adults catch small insects in the air using their legs like a basket. Unlike all other insects, which have their copulatory organs at the end of their abdomen, male odonates have theirs at the front of the abdomen. The two sexes spend considerable time flying together in "tandem," with the male clasping the female. The female may lay her eggs while in tandem with the male or alone, depending on the species, but she always deposits her eggs in or near water. Some species show considerable territoriality, with the male guarding the female while she deposits eggs in his territory. The nymphs live underwater using gills at the end of the abdomen to breathe. They use modified mouthparts to grab small prey items such as tadpoles, small fish, and larvae of other insects. When they eventually grow large enough, the last nymphal stage crawls out of the water on a blade of grass or detritus. The adult, winged form breaks out of the husk of hard exoskeleton that surrounded the nymph and sits quietly just above the surface of the water. Here its soft brown outer surface slowly hardens and takes on color. During this hardening stage, the young adult is especially vulnerable to predation because it cannot fly well.

You will see many dragonflies and damselflies in virtually every moist habitat in Thailand, and most will look and behave like ones you might have seen in North America or Europe.

Profile
Red Darter Dragonfly, *Neurothemis* sp., Plate 1a

2. Grasshoppers, Crickets, and Cockroaches

Most of the species of this order (Orthoptera) are large, from 2 to 18 cm (0.8 to 7 in) long. They have front wings that are elongated and thickened like leather. At rest, these thickened wings cover the membranous hindwings. The body is elongated and the antennae are very short to relatively long. Young develop gradually into adults. Some of the best songsters in the insect world are found in this order—especially *grasshoppers* and *crickets*. Sounds are produced by *stridulation:* rubbing a scraper over a file-like ridge that is variously placed on the legs, wings or other body parts. Each species produces a different song. Along with this sound-producing ability, most species have a large ear (*tympanum*) along the side of the thorax or abdomen. It is used to detect the sounds and distinguish specific rhythms in songs that are used, for instance, for mate attraction or to signal species identity. In some species many males will sing together in a synchronized chorus. Most species feed on plant material like leaves and seeds, but a few eat other insects and others, such as many *cockroaches,* are scavengers.

Many of the species of LEAF INSECTS (Plate 1) have wings so resembling leaves that you have to look twice to see it is an insect and not part of the plant on which it is resting. These herbivorous insects are night-active and eat leaves mainly from vegetation in the understory of forests. Quite often adults are attracted to lights at night. To make sounds at night, they have little bumps on the insides of their wings that they rub over each other by moving the closed wings back and forth. Usually males make most of these sounds to attract females, and the song of each species is different. The young nymphs also eat leaves. During the day you can find leaf insects sitting in among the leaves of undergrowth shrubs.

Profiles
Long-legged Katydid, *Macrolyristes corporalis*, Plate 1b
Leaf Insect, *Phyllium* sp., Plate 1c

3. Termites

The small insects in the order Isoptera, known as *termites*, are the oldest of all social insects and have the most complex societies in the insect world. Termite colonies usually have two or three different-sized and -shaped individuals (*castes*) within a single species, each having different jobs—such as workers, soldiers, or reproductives (Plate 6). Within the same colony, there can be individuals with wings (for seasonal dispersal) and those without wings. More subtly, there can be further specialization within each caste so that some workers do only one task and other workers a different task. Some colonies have "wild-card" nymphs, which, as they grow, perform a variety of tasks but transform into workers, soldiers or reproductives depending on the colony's needs. In many species, males and females also are different castes.

Most, but not all, termites are light-colored, with soft bodies, long and threadlike antennae, and a broad connection between the abdomen and thorax. They look somewhat like white ants, but are different in several respects. Ants have hard, dark bodies, short and bent antennae, and usually a narrow waist connecting the abdomen to the thorax. In ants, the castes are exclusively female except for a few male drones, and the young are white grubs that do not work. In termites, the various body forms or castes within a colony are made up of both sexes, and young nymphs are usually workers. Termites must eat each other's droppings to pass on one-celled organisms that live in their guts and carry the enzymes for breaking down wood (p. 51)—the main food of most termites. Without these tiny helpers, termites would starve. Termite nests can be completely underground (subterranean), sit on the ground in the form of a hard mud-like cone (*termitarium*), or, rarely in Asia, sit attached to the trunk or large branch of a tree (arboreal). The covered tunnels or runways running from these nests to feeding areas are constructed of termite feces; they function to protect the termites from predators and temperature fluctuations.

Spectacular mass flights of dispersing winged termites often follow a heavy rainfall. At this time they are easy pickings for many birds, even large and ungraceful hornbills. Evidently, however, the explosion of dispersing termites is so dense and short-lived that the predators in the area are never abundant enough to eat all of them. No matter how easy they are to catch, many termites survive to start new colonies. Some termite species frequently live with up to five other termite species in the same nest. Whether this togetherness is equally beneficial to all the species is not yet known for sure.

One common and very obvious termite in Thailand is the GIANT BLACK TERMITE (Plate 6). Its often enormous ground nests (termitaria) are made of sunbaked clay and rise from the floor of secondary forest and open dipterocarp forests. The conical nest can be up to 4 m (13 ft) high and 5 m (16.5 ft) in diameter at the base. The workers and soldiers are usually active at night, but their long sinuous columns sometimes continue moving across the forest floor into the morning hours as well. Unlike many other termite species they are darkcolored and do not use their excrement to make hollow tubes in which to walk. Species of this genus do not consume wood, but instead bring plant material to chambers in their dark, damp nest. Here they cultivate fungus gardens and consume the fungus.

Profile
Giant Black Termite, *Macrotermes carbonarius,* Plate 6e

4. Cicadas

Cicadas belong to the insect order Homoptera. This order includes species distinguished by mouthparts that have been modified for a piercing-sucking function; in fact, they cannot chew. They insert their beak into plants and suck juices from them. The wings at rest are held roof-like over the back.

The EVENING CICADA (Plate 1), as is typical of all cicadas, lives as an adult for only a month or so. Most of its life is spent as a nymph underground, sucking plant juices from roots. On the floor of some forests these larvae construct chimney-like turrets 2 cm (1 in) across and that extend 2 to 5 cm (1 to 2 in) above the soil surface (Plate 1). Nymphs develop gradually into adult forms, and the leftover brownish and hollow skin (*exuvium*) of the last stage before the adult is often left hanging on the side of a tree trunk or some other vertical surface. Because adult cicadas are mainly found in the canopy of the forest, you are most likely to see them only when they are attracted to lights at night. More often, however, your encounter with adult cicadas will be auditory. Male cicadas produce sounds, often painfully loud, and each species gives sounds at its own characteristic pitch, intensity, and timing. Some species sing in all-male choirs that can become very intense. The sound-producing organs are called *tymbals,* which are thin plates on the side of the abdomen; they are depressed inwards by a pair of large muscles attached to them and then spring back to make a noise. They are depressed and released with extreme rapidity to make the various sounds and pitches, much like the old metal clicker or "cricket" toys that mature ecotravellers will remember from their childhood. Strangely, these sound producers are located right at the opening of the ears on the side of the abdomen—how can you hear anything with such a noise next to your ear? Most species make their sounds in the late afternoon and early evening. These sounds, however, not only attract mates but enemies as well. A study of cicadas in Thale Ban National Park found that bats ate 70% of calling adults.

Profiles
Evening Cicada, *Tosena splendida,* Plate 1d
Larval cicada turret, Plate 1e

5. Antlions

As adults, all the members of this order (Neuroptera) have soft bodies, four membranous wings, and long antennae. They are relatively weak fliers. Most are predators on other insects, but some species do not feed at all as adults. Larvae of most species live in the ground, but a few live underwater. The representative of this order that you are most likely to see in Thailand is the ANTLION (Plate 2). The adults look like dragonflies but have long antennae with knobs on the end. They sometimes come to lights at night. It is the larval form, however, that you will see most commonly. The short, flat larva has enormous mandibles. It excavates a funnel-shaped pit in dry sand and lies in wait at the bottom, often completely buried except for its mandibles (Plate 2). When an insect comes strolling along and accidentally stumbles at the precipitous edge, the Antlion flicks sand grains out of the bottom to produce a constant avalanche of sand giving out under the hapless insect. This causes the insect to slide down into the waiting mandibles of the Antlion. Crunch!

Profile
Antlion, *Myrmeleon* sp., Plate 2a

6. Beetles

The *beetle* order (Coleoptera) has more species in it than any other insect order—some estimate more than a million. These species occur in virtually all habitats on land and in freshwater, but not in the ocean or in Antarctica. The trait shared by all these species is a front pair of wings hardened into shields (*elytra*) that when the insect is at rest covers the second pair of membranous flight wings and the top of the abdomen. The mandibles of the adults are usually large and variously used for catching small insect prey, crushing seeds, or chewing wood. The grub larvae often occur in habitats different from those of the adults or have very different behavior. Many beetle species are attracted to lights at night.

Along muddy and sandy river banks, the GOLDEN-SPOTTED TIGER BEETLE (Plate 2) runs actively at the water's edge or in the moist grassy upper beaches. On sunny days, you can see these medium-sized (1.7 cm, 0.7 in), maroon and gold-spotted beetles running on the mud. During cloudy or cool days of the winter they hide out under rocks or burrow in the mud. When scared, tiger beetles (family Cicindelidae) will fly short distances. They are predators on other arthropods and search for them using their large eyes. With their long legs, they run prey down, grab them in their monstrous and sharp mandibles, then puree them. If you catch one, watch out for the mandibles; the bite, together with an enzyme they spit up, can really sting. They lay their eggs in moist sand and mud, and when the larvae hatch they immediately burrow vertically down into the soil. Then the larva waits, its head just perfectly filling the mouth of the tunnel, for an ant or some other arthropod to come within striking distance. The larva, aided by hooks on its back, stretches quickly out of the tunnel backward to grab the prey in its large mandibles. If successful, the larva pulls the prey to the bottom of the tunnel and dismembers it, eventually tossing the inedible parts out of the tunnel. More than 120 species of tiger beetles have been found in Thailand, some of them on sandy river banks like the Golden-spotted Tiger Beetle, but most of them active during the day on moist soil surfaces, grassy fields, and on the forest floor or undergrowth leaves of evergreen forest.

The large and spectacular (9.5 cm, 3.7 in, long and 4.5 cm, 1.7 in, wide) GIANT FIDDLER BEETLE (Plate 2) is a member of the predaceous ground beetle family (Carabidae) and closely related to the tiger beetles. This huge beetle is so flattened that it is only a few millimeters (twentieths of an inch) high. Supposedly this shape allows it to pursue its insect prey into very flat areas. Alternatively, and probably more likely, its flat shape and dark color help it hide from its own predators by enhancing its camouflage against the trees of the dark forests in which it lives.

The GIANT ASIAN DUNG BEETLE (Plate 2) is conspicuous and intriguingly shaped, but its habits may at first be off-putting to more squeamish ecotravellers. The members of this part of family Scarabaeidae are some of the most intensely studied insects in Thailand. They are crucial in passing nutrients and vital chemicals to the rest of the ecosystem by helping decompose dung. They are also unusual among insects because so many of these species have complex behavior when it comes to constructing nests and caring for their young.

Some dung beetles, called *dwellers,* merely eat their way through dung and deposit their eggs below a dung pat in a superficial nest. Other species, the *tunnelers,* dig a vertical tunnel below the dung pat and carry, push, and drag dung down into the bottom of the tunnel to avoid competitors and predators. Here the dung is either used as food by the adults or stored as food for eggs laid here. Finally, a large number of dung beetles are *rollers.* Making a ball of dung, they stand on their fore legs, use their hind legs to push and steer the ball, and transport this resource away from the dung pat area before burying it in a suitable location. The female sometimes helps roll this ball, but more often than not she just rides on top of the ball, walking as the world turns under her. At some distance from the original site of the pat, the pair stops and buries the ball. They mate, and the female lays eggs on the section of dung they buried. When the eggs hatch, the larvae are protected underground from predators and competitors and have a dung banquet upon which they can feed and grow. Males of many species have a prominent horn on the tip of their snouts that curves back over the head. The horn is used to battle other males over the dung as well as to impress the females who wait to see who wins the dung fight.

Dung is located mainly by smell, and the beetles' feather-shaped antennae act as super sniffers. Particular types of dung, however, are so prized by some dung beetle species that they also apparently use their eyes to quickly locate this resource as it falls from the canopy. The beetles use a circling flight with ever-tighter loops to home in on the prize. Some species of dung beetles will use almost any type of dung they encounter, while others are highly specialized on bird dung, monkey dung, cat dung, and even snail and millipede dung. The dung of herbivorous animals tends to be rich in carbohydrates, whereas dung of carnivorous animals tends to be rich in nitrogen, and the different needs of various dung beetle species (during larval growth as well as for energy in adult phases) influence their choice of repast.

A huge and attractive insect, the BICOLORED METALLIC WOOD-BORING BEETLE (Plate 2) has beautiful metallic coloring typical of many species in the family Buprestidae, and many species characteristically have many grooves running the length of the elytra, or hard wing coverings. In the sunlight the colors of these beetles are incomparable. The big-headed larvae burrow into the wood of large softwood trees and form mazes, or *galleries,* of tunnels that can damage smaller trees or kill branches of larger trees. Both adults and larvae are roasted by indigenous people and eaten like popcorn. The elytra of the adults are often strung together as adornments.

The long-horned beetle family (Cerambycidae) is characterized by extremely long antennae and a propensity to bore into dead or living tree trunks and branches. Some members of this family are unusual in that they directly produce enzymes that break down plant cellulose. Unlike termites (p. 65) and other cellulose-eating insects, they do not rely on one-celled organisms in their gut to provide the proper enzymes. The contrasting gray and black coloring of the HIRSUTE LONG-HORNED BEETLE (Plate 2) may function to break up its shape visually, so predators do not notice it easily. The adults are primarily active during the day. After mating, the female chews a gash in the bark of a tree and places her eggs in it. The young hatch out and tunnel deeper into the tree, producing galleries of tunnels. Sometimes their damage can be so extensive that they kill the tree. Many species of the long-horned beetle genus (*Anoplophora*) in Asia are serious pests on tree plantation and orchards, especially poplar and citrus trees. The concentrations of larvae can kill up to twenty percent or more of a stand of trees, but are naturally controlled by parasitic insects and woodpeckers. Because poplar is a soft and fast-growing tree, its wood is often used for packing crates to ship produce and consumer products around the world. Apparently numerous larvae of this beetle genus were transported in packing-crate wood from China to New York. Here the larvae eventually emerged as adults and began in 1966 to infest many species of hardwood trees. Their spread has been phenomenal and difficult to control. The North American tree species have no defenses against the larvae of this beetle and draconian measures of cutting down entire stretches of trees around infections are being used in an attempt to stop the spread of this Asian beetle throughout North American forests.

Profiles
Golden-spotted Tiger Beetle, *Cicindela aurulenta*, Plate 2b
Giant Fiddler Beetle, *Mormolyce phyllodes*, Plate 2c
Bicolored Metallic Wood-boring Beetle, *Megaloxantha bicolor*, Plate 2d
Giant Asian Dung Beetle, *Catharsius molossus*, Plate 2e
Hirsute Long-horned Beetle, *Anoplophora longehirsuta*, Plate 2f

7. Butterflies and Moths

The *butterflies* and *moths* (order Lepidoptera) are perhaps the most easily recognized insect groups in the world. They have four wings, but the hindwing and forewing on each side often have a coupling mechanism that makes them look and act like a single huge wing. The characteristic shared by all members of this group, however, is the layer of tiny scales covering the wings. They come off easily, and if you handle the wings of a butterfly, look for the scales on your finger (the scales will look like dust). The adults either do not feed at all or feed on nectar, defecation, or rotting fruit juices. Their mouthparts are shaped into a long thin proboscis, which can be rolled up when not extended for feeding. This proboscis can be longer than the insect's body and is used to access nectar at the base of long flowers. While partaking of the flower's sweet reward, pollen falls onto the insect's body or head and is passed on to the next flower visited. Males often need extra sodium and other salts for producing sperm, and it is not unusual to see clouds of male butterflies fluttering near and landing on dung, urine, rotting fruit, or even the nose of a basking turtle, to suck up excretions containing these chemicals. Along beaches of watercourses, clouds of butterflies often assemble where large mammals have recently urinated or defecated. Even salt-laden human sweat can attract beautiful butterflies; so don't swat all the insects that come flying around you. (However, if you attract butterflies day after day, it may be time to take a shower.) This predilection to suck juices from skin surfaces may have led to the evolution of one species of moth in southeastern Asia, *Calpe eustrigata*, sucking blood from mammals by piercing their skin with its needle-like tongue.

In general, adult butterflies are active during the day and have thread-like antennae with knobs on the end. Butterflies usually rest with their wings folded together, vertically, over their backs. Male butterflies of many species are extremely territorial, and fights between neighboring males over females are common. Moths are usually active at night and rest with their wings held horizontally. They have either thread-like antennae without knobs or large feather-shaped antennae. These feather-like antennae are usually found in the males, and they can contain more than 60,000 minute structures called *sensilla*. These structures are used to detect molecules of a perfume (*pheromone*) released by a female ready to mate. Each female moth species releases a different scent, and the pheromone plume is carried by the wind. The male follows this plume upwind by zigzagging back and forth, moving toward higher concentrations of the molecules until he finds the female. Experiments have shown that males can follow this scent plume for more than 10 km (6 mi).

Larval *lepidopterans* are almost all plant eating and use large mandibles to chew holes out of the edges of leaves. Many of the major agricultural pests in the world are larval moths. Some lepidopteran species have their own specific food plant species on which they lay eggs and on which their caterpillars feed when they emerge. The ornate and often colorful chamber in which the larval butterfly metamorphoses into an adult is called a *chrysalis*. The brown silken chamber of the larval moth is called a *cocoon*. The protein (*fibroin*) used by many moth species to construct these cocoons is the product we weave into silk cloth. However, species of only four moth families are used for commercial production of silk, all of them in Asia.

Swallowtails and *birdwings* (Plates 3 and 4) are the largest and most spectacular of all butterflies in Thailand. Their beauty and large size make them desirable for collectors. For a very rare species, the value of a single specimen can rise into the hundreds and even thousands of dollars. As a result, in several countries species of spectacular and rare butterflies, such as birdwings, have been declared endangered and illegal to collect. In some cases they are reared in captivity and marketed under government control.

Profiles

Golden Birdwing, *Troides aeacus*, Plate 3a
Giant Atlas Moth, *Archaeoattacus edwardsii*, Plate 3b
Long-tailed Silk Moth, *Actias selene*, Plate 3c
Common Rose Swallowtail, *Atrophaneura aristolochiae*, Plate 3d
Lime Swallowtail, *Papilio demoleus*, Plate 3e
Great Eggfly Butterfly, *Hypolimnas bolina*, Plate 4a
Green Dragontail, *Meges virescens*, Plate 4b
Common Sailor, *Neptis hylas*, Plate 4c
Peacock Pansy, *Precis almana*, Plate 4d
Fivebar Swordtail, *Pathysa antiphates*, Plate 4e
Common Grass Yellow, *Eurema hecabe*, Plate 5a
Great Orange Tip, *Hebomoia glaucippe*, Plate 5b
The Wanderer, *Valeria valeria*, Plate 5c
The Peacock Royal, *Pratapa cippus*, Plate 5d
Common Nawab, *Polyura athamas*, Plate 5e

8. Flies

Another very large group of insects is the *flies* (Order Diptera). Their identifying characteristic is the presence of only the front pair of wings. The rear wings have been reduced to small knobs (*halteres*) used for balance in flight. Most adults are small and soft-bodied, and they include many of the biting insects we stereotype as "bad," such as mosquitoes, horseflies, "no-seeums," and black flies; only the females bite. Because of their roles in the spread of disease as well as in agricultural plagues, representatives of this group surely rank high as pests. However, many species of flies are critical for such functions as cleaning up rotted bodies, killing other insects, and pollinating flowers. Larvae are grub-like and most live in water, where they feed on dead vegetation, decaying animal matter, or other larvae.

One of the most spectacular flies in Thailand is the STALK-EYED FLY (Plate 6). Some male flies have eyestalks up to 1 cm (0.4 in) long. The placement of their functional eyes at such great distances from the head is though by some scientists to be a way of enhancing depth perception. Other scientists, however, think this bizarre development is to enhance courtship behavior. Some data show that males with longer eyes are more successful at attracting mates. In some parts of the world these stalk-eyed flies are considered pests on rice because they bore into rice plant stems to lay their eggs.

Profile
Stalk-eyed Fly, *Cyrtodiopsis* sp., Plate 6a

9. Ants, Wasps, and Bees

Although this group (order Hymenoptera) is perhaps best known for its stinging defensive behavior, it contains some of the most beneficial insect species in the world. *Ants* help turn over and aerate soil as well as disperse seeds. Many species of *wasps* are predators on herbivorous insects and function as a major biological control of numerous pest species. *Bees* are important pollinators of many native and agricultural plants. In Thailand, four native honeybee species contribute to a steadily rising market for honey. The *hymenopteran* species with wings have four membranous wings, in which the forewing and hindwing on each side are fastened together with tiny hooks. The mouthparts are either strong mandibles for chewing or modified into a long tongue for sucking up nectar and other liquid food. In most species the abdomen is attached to the thorax by a narrow waist. The larvae are grub-like and usually cared for in hives or nests. Many species are highly colonial. Sex of an egg is determined by whether or not it has been fertilized by male sperm. If it has been fertilized, it develops into a female, but if not, it develops into a male. Only females can sting, but we do not recommend using this difference to determine the sex of the bee or ant you are watching.

Many species of plants attract stinging ants to their leaves to protect against damage from herbivores that would eat important plant tissue. In Thailand, several species of the Macaranga plant (Figure 3, p. 24) have evolved this attraction of protective ants to such a degree that they can no longer survive without the ants (this relationship is called *obligate myrmecophily*). The Macaranga plants have hollow twig tips and leaf parts with cells that produce packets of starch. Ants of the genus *Crematogaster* are attracted to these starches as a ready source of food and to the hollow stems as a protected site for their nests. If a caterpillar or grasshopper lands on the plant, it is immediately attacked and driven off by the ants that are protecting their home and food source. Theses ants may also be important in helping the plant overcome competition for food, water, and sunlight from nearby plants. Apparently the ants snip away at leaves, twigs, and whatever parts of the neighboring plants come in contact with the Macaranga plant—thus producing an unobstructed space around the growing tree.

Several species of ants, including the SHEPHERD ANT (Plate 6), tend groups of other insects, such as aphids, scale insects, and membracid bugs. Herding them like shepherds, the ants keep these small flocks of insects protected from their numerous enemies. In turn, the herd of insects produces drops of liquid that contain sugar or other valuable chemicals, such as nitrogen, that are consumed by the ants. These insects that provide food in exchange for protection are called *trophobionts*.

Another species, the TONIC ANT (genus *Polyrhachis*), is high in zinc, and, when ground up into a medicinal powder, is widely believed to prevent symptoms of aging such as lumbago, memory loss, joint problems, fatigue, and cardiovascular disease.

ASIAN WEAVER ANTS (Plate 6) are obvious throughout Thailand, even in the middle of Bangkok. They weave a small football-sized nest by pulling leaves of a tree or bush together and using silk-spinning larvae to cement the leaves together. An entrance hole is left on the outside, from which defending ants pour if the tree is disturbed by herbivorous insects or careless ecotravellers. These ants are so diligent in their vigorous defense against intruders that people transplant them to plantations of cashews to construct their nests. There they serve as a bio-control against insect pests in lieu of expensive and unhealthy pesticides.

Tiny STINGLESS or SWEAT BEES (Plate 6) are common insects of the forest. They cannot sting but they are attracted to sweaty bodies and are extremely persistent in lapping up the sweat. If you swat and kill one, it gives off a distinctive chemical odor that may serve to attract and antagonize the other members of its hive. The entrance to their hive is a trumpet-like funnel made of wax leading to the nest in a tree hollow or a hole in the forest floor. Disturb this entrance, and the bees fly out in large numbers to bite with their mandibles—they especially like crawling into the hair of humans who have disturbed their lair.

Profiles
Shepherd Ant, *Anoplolepis* sp., Plate 6b
Asian Weaver Ant, *Oecophylla smaragdina*, Plate 6c
Stingless Bee, *Trigona* sp., Plate 6d

10. Spiders

Probably the most maligned arthropods are the *spiders*. Although almost all the 35,000 species in the world have venom glands that they use together with their fangs to kill prey, only a very few species are dangerous to humans. The benefits spiders provide by controlling populations of insects more than outweigh the problems of a few bites and extra duties for fastidious house-cleaners. Most spiders dwell on land, but a few hunt underwater. Many spiders build webs to catch flying insects. These webs can be sticky, ornate orbs, flat sheets, funnel-shaped, or combinations thereof. Some spiders even use webbing-like nets to throw onto prey. The common HOUSE SPIDER in Thailand, *Crossopriza lyoni*, throws webbing at flying mosquitoes, using its hind legs. Because it is very common in houses, specializes on capturing mosquitoes, and is immune from the Dengue fever virus carried by mosquitoes, it has been proposed as an important bio-control of the Dengue-carrying mosquito species *Aedes aegypti*.

Most spiders catch small- to medium-sized insect prey, but some species, like the GIANT WOOD SPIDER (Plate 1), are large enough to catch small birds in their webs. Waiting in a retreat at the side of the web, the spider detects a struggling prey by the vibrations transmitted along the strands of webbing. It then rushes out to inject the prey with poison and often wraps it in a cocoon of silk.

Several large groups of spiders, however, do not use webs to catch prey but instead rely on ambush, stealth, or stalking. All produce silk, however, which is a protein produced in the abdomen. It is released from the abdomen through finger-like holes called *spinnerets*. The silk threads of the Giant Wood Spider can stretch thirty percent before breaking and have such a high tensile strength that they are stronger per weight than steel. Venture capital companies as well as the US Army are studying the molecular composition and orientation of these proteins, and several patents of synthetic spider silk are now being pursued for obvious military use and economic gain.

Because they are all predators and cannibalism is common, most spiders are solitary. Only during courtship and mating do they socialize, and then often to the detriment of the male. Because males of many spider species are in such danger when approaching the voracious females to mate, they have evolved several adaptations to get close to her. One strategy is for the males to be so small that they do not attract the predatory attention of the female. For instance, male Giant Wood Spiders are almost one-tenth the size of the females. In some species, males tend to seek out females who have just finished their final molt and are thus physically exhausted. Finally, males walk carefully along the webbing and avoid producing vibrations that the female uses to detect a struggling prey item.

Eggs are laid in a silk pouch near the web, on the female, or in a crevice. The young hatch out looking like miniature spiders, and they grow gradually. Young spiders often go to a high point in the habitat, spin out a line of silk and then let the wind take them, the silk serving as a balloon or parachute. This method of transportation can disperse spiders over long distances.

Other small species of spiders also take advantage of their size to steal small prey items captured in the larger spider species' webs. These bandits are called *kleptoparasites,* and their impact on the owner of the web varies from little to great depending on the range of prey they steal and how common they become in the web of their host.

Profile
Giant Wood Spider, *Nephila* sp., Plate 1f

Chapter 6

AMPHIBIANS

- *Introduction*
- *General Characteristics and Classification*
- *Seeing Amphibians in Thailand*
- *Family Profiles*
    1. *Salamanders*
    2. *Caecilians*
    3. *Leaf-litter Toads*
    4. *True Toads*
    5. *True Frogs*
    6. *Narrow-mouthed Frogs*
    7. *Treefrogs*
- *Environmental Close-Up 3: Frog Population Declines*

Introduction

We know from the fossil record that during the middle of the Paleozoic Era (the Devonian period, about 380 million years ago), fish with lungs that could breathe air were common in freshwater lakes. These fish had fins in the shape of stubby lobes, which were probably used to support themselves on the bottoms of their ponds while waiting for prey to swim by, and to waddle about on land during times when their ponds dried. Both of these characteristics, lungs and lobed fins, allowed the fish to survive for brief periods on land. About 365 million years ago, these fish evolved into the first *tetrapods* (terrestrial vertebrates)—the amphibians. As you would expect, this evolution involved drastic changes in support and locomotor systems, feeding mechanisms, and breathing organs, to name but a few modifications.

The word amphibian comes from the Greek *amphibios,* meaning "living a double life," in reference to the fact that most amphibians spend part of their lives in water and part on land. Approximately 4,700 species of living amphibians are known today. Biologists separate amphibians into three main groups. The largest group, with about 4,100 species, is the *frogs* and *toads* (order Anura, "without tails"), followed by the *salamanders* (order Caudata, the "tailed" amphibians) with about 430 species, and a little-known group, the *caecilians* (suh-SEAL-ians, order Gymnophiona), with approximately 170 species.

General Characteristics and Classification

Most amphibians retain the reproductive pattern of their fish ancestors and return to water to breed because their eggs dry out easily. Most frogs and toads have *external fertilization;* that is, as the female releases her eggs, the male releases sperm onto them—outside the body. Only a few species have *internal fertilization*. In contrast, most salamanders and all caecilians have internal fertilization. Most amphibians pass through the aquatic phase of their "two-world" lifestyle only as eggs and free-swimming larvae (larval frogs and toads are called *tadpoles;* larval salamanders and caecilians are just called *larvae*). Some amphibians, however, are fully aquatic as adults. Still other species lay their eggs in moist areas on land and never enter standing water. Water is essential for all amphibians because, in addition to using lungs, they breathe through their skin. In order to do this, their skin must be kept moist. Thus, even species that are fully terrestrial in all phases of their lives require a humid environment.

Most salamanders look like lizards, with four limbs and a long tail. They are easily distinguished from lizards, however, by their skin. Salamanders have skin that is kept moist by mucus, whereas lizards have scales. A few aquatic species of salamanders have four tiny legs, and several have only the two front legs. Salamanders range in size from among the smallest known terrestrial vertebrates, with body lengths of less than 1.5 cm (0.6 in), to a giant Asian species that grows to 2 m (6.5 ft). Because their skin is susceptible to drying out, salamanders inhabit moist environments. Familiar salamanders of North America and Europe typically live on the ground, hidden under logs when they're not active. They forage for invertebrate prey such as insects, worms, and spiders in the leaf litter and under rocks or decaying logs. Many live near streams in moist forests. Some species, however, are completely aquatic, spending their entire lives in swamps, ponds, lakes, and rivers. Others live in trees (*arboreal*) or underground (*fossorial*). Most salamanders secrete poisons from glands in the skin as a defense against predators. Some of the most toxic species are brightly colored to warn potential predators of their toxicity. About 90% of salamanders have internal fertilization. In these species, males produce packets of sperm called *spermatophores*. In most species, during courtship, males deposit spermatophores onto the substrate. They lead the females over the spermatophores, at which point they are picked up into the females' bodies.

Salamanders are found mostly in North America and in northern Eurasia, where they are primarily aquatic but with several species occurring in leaf litter of moist forests. Salamanders are not known in tropical regions of the Old World, and only a single species occurs in Thailand, in the northern, cooler reaches.

Most people have never heard of *caecilians*, and fewer still have ever seen a live one. Caecilians resemble large earthworms with rings around their bodies. They lack limbs throughout their lives, and they either have short tails or none at all. Their bodies feel slimy because they are covered with mucus. In fact, it is very difficult to hold onto one! Caecilians are poorly known because they live only in tropical regions (in Africa, Asia, and Central and South America) and because they are difficult to find. Caecilians either live underground or in water. The only time you are likely to see the underground ones is following heavy rain, when the soil becomes saturated and they move to the surface. Because their eyes are covered with skin or bone, caecilians have severely reduced visual systems. They rely to a large degree on smell and perhaps electrical fields to detect prey, such as earthworms and insects, and enemies. They have sensory organs called *tentacles,* small fleshy projections located between the eyes and nostrils that are their smell receptors. Of the species for which the mode of reproduction is known, about 75% have internal fertilization of eggs that undergo development inside the mother's body; the young are born as tiny but fully formed baby caecilians. Although the other 25% of the species for which their reproductive pattern is known also have internal fertilization, they have aquatic larvae.

Frogs and toads are found just about everywhere in the world except in extremely dry deserts, on some islands, and near the North and South poles. All frogs and toads have four limbs as adults; their rear limbs are much larger than their front ones. Most of them are strong jumpers and can cover long distances. Some brightly colored species have poisonous skin secretions that protect them from predators. Others have toxins but are dull in color. Males use mating calls to attract females during the breeding season; each species has its own particular call, and females respond only to that call. Almost all adult frogs and toads eat insects, spiders, and other invertebrates; a few species eat other frogs and even small lizards, snakes, birds, and mammals. Presumably most if not all Thai species breed via external fertilization. During mating, the male mounts the back of the female and holds on to her tightly with his front legs either around the waist or in her armpits. This position is called *amplexus.* As she releases her eggs, he releases sperm over them. Although most species abandon their eggs, some have elaborate forms of parental care. Most species have aquatic tadpoles. In some species, however, the eggs develop directly into tiny froglets. The frogs and toads known in Thailand are diverse in body shape, size, color, and habits.

Seeing Amphibians in Thailand

It is almost impossible to visit Thailand without seeing and hearing amphibians. Several species are widespread and abundant even in cities, and the only places visited by ecotravellers that will not have amphibians are coral reefs.

Currently, 107 amphibian species are confirmed to inhabit Thailand. However, new species continue to be discovered, and as amphibian surveys continue, occurrences in Thailand of species previously known only in neighboring countries are found. An ecotraveller who makes a two-week trip to Thailand and visits the main habitat types should be able to encounter up to 30 species. To see anything more than an occasional toad, though, it is essential that you look for amphibians at the time that they are active—mainly at night. However, looking for amphibians after rain in the afternoon is often rewarding. In the north, the best period is during the rainy season (May to October), while the Peninsular region is good year-round.

There are different ways to find frogs and toads. Although many species spend much of their life in forest, it is slow and laborious to find individual frogs by walking forest trails at night. It is much more effective to visit their breeding sites. Depending on the species, these can be streams, pools, or puddles in forest, open areas, and gardens. The great advantage of looking for frogs at their breeding sites is that they are likely to call there as well, which makes it easier to find both the site and the individual frogs. During daytime walks, remember the location of streams and pools in the immediate vicinity of your accommodations. If you see tadpoles, chances are high that the adults will be there and visible during the hours of darkness. If you did not check for streams and ponds during the daytime, you can still let the sound of a frog chorus guide you to a good site. Use common sense, though, and do not go further than is safe. Getting lost in forest at night is not fun.

Essential equipment to find and identify frogs includes a flashlight and a notebook with pen or pencil (to write notes on frog descriptions). The flashlight, apart from helping you make your way in the dark, allows you to "freeze" frogs in the light; many frogs are reluctant to jump or move when illuminated and you can approach them closely. Capturing or otherwise disturbing animals including frogs is prohibited in protected areas in Thailand, and we do not recommend this even in unprotected areas. In captivity, few frogs die of suffocation, but dehydration kills many.

Finding a caecilian is a matter either of luck, encountering an animal crossing a trail or road at night, or of very hard labor—the animals spend nearly their entire life underground and finding them would require extensive digging (hardly appropriate for an ecotraveller!). Likewise, finding Thailand's only salamander is a matter of luck to encounter one in a small stream or pool high in the mountains of northern Thailand. The animals may be active at any time, day or night. Remember that the species is strictly protected.

In conclusion, please remember to minimize your impact on Thailand's amphibians and their habitat: disturb them as little as possible, do not damage their habitat, and do not accidentally introduce problems. In recent years, populations of amphibians have collapsed catastrophically, in some cases to extinction, in various places in tropical Central and South America, Australia, and elsewhere (see Close-up, p. 90). The cause of the declines remains unclear, but epidemic disease is a strong possibility. The amphibian decline phenomenon has not (yet) reached Thailand, but there is no guarantee that Thailand's amphibians are immune. If you have travelled in regions and habitats where amphibians are in catastrophic decline, please minimize the chance of spreading the problem further. Leave your boots and field pants that have been in contact with frog habitat behind, and buy new hiking shoes and field clothing before visiting Thailand or immediately after arrival.

Family Profiles

1. Salamanders

As a group of amphibians, *salamanders* are unmistakable: they have a long body, a long tail even as adults, and four legs of similar, small size. Nobody will confuse a salamander with a frog, toad, or caecilian, but confusion between a salamander and a lizard is easy. Salamanders have thin, moist skin (lizards have dry scaled or granular skin), a broad rounded head (lizards generally have pointed heads), move very slowly, and live underwater for a substantial part of the time. In addition, salamanders have an aquatic larval stage that emerges from a jelly-coated egg and breathes through external gills before it develops lungs for respiration (lizards typically lay shelled eggs on dry land and breathe through lungs from the moment of hatching as miniature replicas of the adult).

The 430 or so species of salamanders of the world are placed into ten generally recognized families. Nine of the families occur partly or exclusively in the New World; three of these also occur in the Mediterranean region. The tenth family, Hynobiidae, is restricted to temperate Asia, and, with about 40 species, is the most diverse Asian family of salamanders. In total, just over 100 salamander species occur in Eurasia, compared to about 330 species in the New World. Three salamander species occur in the northern parts of tropical southeast Asia, but only one of these reaches Thailand, the CROCODILE SALAMANDER (Plate 7), which belongs to family Salamandridae (containing 56 species that are distributed over North America, Europe, northwestern Africa, the Caucasus region, and Siberia, in addition to East Asia).

Natural History

Ecology and Behavior

The CROCODILE SALAMANDER, or Himalayan Newt, extends along the high slopes of the Himalayas into three or four mountaintops of northern Thailand, near Chiang Mai and in Loei Province. It occurs only above 1,500 m (4,900 ft) in shrubby forest full of mosses and epiphytes. Outside the breeding season, these salamanders live in forest, on damp surfaces but not in water. They are active at night and occasionally early in the morning during foggy weather. They forage on the forest floor and spend the daytime hidden in moist crevices among rocks, logs, and leaf litter. Adults feed on a variety of food items including worms and insects. Not much is known of natural predators on Crocodile Salamanders. The large glands on the head may secrete noxious or poisonous substances. When threatened, the animals raise their tail over their head to display its bright coloration to maximum effect.

Breeding

Adult CROCODILE SALAMANDERS make local migrations to breeding ponds or pools at the beginning of the rainy season, and remain there throughout the rainy season. Breeding pools can be rain pools but more often are deep quiet sections of small streams, usually with large boulders, in heath and scrub forest. Pools may be densely vegetated with algae and higher plants or may be in dark forest and devoid of vegetation. The main requirement for a breeding pool seems to be that the water be crystal clear. The presence of fish does not stop salamanders from using a particular pool, in contrast to many frogs, which can detect whether fish occur in a particular pool and will not deposit their eggs in the presence of these potential egg predators.

Courtship and mating occur in water. During courtship, the male salamander crawls under the female and grabs her front legs with his own; this is followed by a "piggy-back ride," which eventually leads to the male depositing a spermatophore, a gel-coated parcel of sperm, on the pond bottom. The female accepts this spermatophore into her cloaca and the eggs are fertilized internally. Eggs are large, about 0.6 to 1.0 cm (0.25 to 0.40 in). Emerging larvae have three pairs of external bushy gills, a crested tail, and a pair of *balancers*, rod-like structures that extend from the sides of the head and keep the young salamander from sinking into the sediment of the pond bottom. All four legs develop early, the front legs first (in contrast to frogs, where the hind legs develop first). The larvae are mainly predatory, feeding on aquatic insect larvae and other small prey; mosquito larvae are a favorite. The larvae *metamorphose* into the lung-breathing adult phase by the end of the rainy season, when they are 5.2 to 7.5 cm (2 to 3 in) long, resorbing the external gills, balancers, and tail crest in the process. After metamorphosis, the young of most salamander species move away from the water.

Notes
The CROCODILE SALAMANDER, the single salamander found in Thailand, is restricted to the upper slopes and summits of three or four northern mountains. It is likely that these populations are isolated relicts from a more widespread distribution that occurred at a time of cooler climate conditions. As the climate warmed after the last Ice Age, the cool, damp conditions favored by the salamanders became restricted to higher altitudes and northerly latitudes. The salamander populations retreated to the temperate conditions and became isolated in these high elevation areas.

Status
Salamanders in Thailand are restricted to a few scattered localities and also lead hidden lives, making population status assessments difficult. The effects of habitat degradation, particularly forest fires, are unknown but unlikely to be beneficial. There is a demand for these salamanders in the Thai domestic pet trade, which likely exerts some pressure on their populations. Nevertheless, it is encouraging that surveys in the 1990s had little trouble locating viable populations of the CROCODILE SALAMANDER in appropriate habitat.

Profile
Crocodile Salamander, *Tylototriton verrucosus*, Plate 7a

2. Caecilians

Ecotravellers are usually unfamiliar with *caecilians,* and most likely will be puzzled if they accidentally stumble across one. Although caecilians look like very large worms, complete with rings around the body, a close look will reveal that they are very different. The smooth head has a large mouth with numerous small, sharp, needle-like teeth, and careful examination will show odd organs, the *tentacles,* at each side of the snout tip. With some patience, you may see the animal's tiny eyes (even though they are rudimentary and set deep under the skin). While earthworms in Thailand may be large (up to 20 cm, 8 in, long and 1 cm, 0.4 in, wide), none match a caecilian's 30-cm (12-in) length and thumb-like thickness. Finally, the most common caecilian species in Thailand, the YELLOW-BANDED CAECILIAN (Plate 7), is grey or black with a bright yellow stripe along the body, a color pattern that no earthworms possess.

Caecilians (order Gymnophiona) form the third major group of amphibians, along with frogs and toads (order Anura) and salamanders (order Caudata). The world's 170 or so species of caecilians are currently assigned to six families. Caecilians inhabit the tropics of America, Africa, and Asia, but they are absent from Madagascar, the Australia–New Guinea region, and apparently from central, equatorial Africa. Some Caecilians are permanently aquatic, while others have only an aquatic larval stage and live a burrowing lifestyle during their adult years. Don't let the understated and often dull characteristics of a caecilian fool you—if you run across one during your trip to Thailand, savor the moment and know that hundreds of scientists would give almost anything to have that rare opportunity.

Natural History

Ecology and Behavior
Very little is known of the ecology of Asian caecilians. The adults have a burrowing lifestyle and are occasionally encountered on forest trails or roads during wet nights, or are found when overturning logs and rocks or while digging ditches. Such encounters are nearly always in proximity to intact or lightly degraded forest and may be near streams. The common feature is that the soil is damp, although the soil may be quite heavy and difficult to dig through. Caecilians are considered to be completely carnivorous, feeding on a variety of worms, insect larvae, slugs, and other invertebrates.

Breeding
Unlike frogs and toads, caecilians apparently do not court with songs and calls. Caecilians have internal fertilization, which occurs with the aid of the male's penis-like organ, which is a modified part of the gastrointestinal tract. The female places up to 50 large jelly-coated eggs in mud near shallow water of a stream or pond. The mother remains close to the eggs, often wrapping herself around them to protect them from predators and other dangers. Upon hatching, the young enter the water, where they spend a substantial period in their aquatic, gill-breathing, larval stage. The larvae look rather like the adults but have three pairs of large, bushy, external gills. These are resorbed as the internal gill chambers develop. Larvae bear a fin on the tail for improved swimming ability. Growth in the larval stage is extensive and may take up to two years. After development of the lungs is complete and the tail fin is resorbed, the animals assume a burrowing lifestyle on land. Depending on the species, the larvae metamorphose into a body length of 13 to 24 cm (5 to 10 in), representing two-fifths of adult size in some species and near full adult length in others.

Notes
Some biologists believe that up to five species of caecilians inhabit Thailand, but the identification problems are of such magnitude, the classifications so controversial, that other experts recognize only two species, and most, even professional amphibian biologists, fudge the identification issue and determine animals to genus level only. Not surprisingly for a group of animals with so few obvious external features, the characteristics used to recognize Asian caecilian species include very esoteric traits, such as the number and shape of annuli (rings) around the body, the number and placement of teeth, the number and arrangement of microscopic scales hidden in the body folds, and the presence and shape of the yellow body stripe. Precisely identifying the species of a living, squirming caecilian in the field is nearly impossible.

Status
Caecilians have a hidden lifestyle and are rarely encountered. When they are, they are usually mistaken for something else. Many end up as road kills. Data to indicate what are viable natural caecilian population numbers and how these numbers have changed over time are pretty much completely lacking. All we

know is that caecilians are usually encountered in areas of primary and secondary forest, and if these forests are disappearing, it is likely that the caecilians are, too.

Profile
Yellow-banded Caecilian, *Ichthyophis kohtaoensis*, Plate 7b

3. Leaf-litter Toads

Not to be confused with the "true" toads (p. 82), the *leaf-litter toads* (family Megophryidae; 74 species worldwide, 11 in Thailand) are confined to the Oriental Region, from central China to the Philippine islands. However, some experts consider them to be a subgroup within the north temperate family Pelobatidae (the spadefoot toads). They are short-legged with smooth skin and often have spade-like growths (tubercles) on their hind feet. In Thailand, many of the species have fleshy folds running along each side of the back. At night some species are noted by the reflection of light from their eyes.

Natural History

Ecology and Behavior
Adult leaf-litter toads spend most of their life in the leaf litter of forests, often along streams. They are active at night hunting insects and other small prey on the forest floor. The adult toads sit amazingly erect but slump down immediately into a crouch when disturbed. They spend the day under leaves or logs. Tadpoles live in forest streams, temporary pools, and swampy forest ponds, where they graze on algae attached to rocks, dead and decaying vegetation, or on floating vegetation (plankton).

Breeding
Adult male leaf-litter toads gather, often in large numbers, along the edges of clear, rocky streams, forested swamps, and temporary ponds. They call intensely from the leaf litter or climb up onto leaves of short bushes and herbs to broadcast their availability to females. Little is known of their breeding particulars.

Notes
Many indigenous people of Thailand's forests believe that frogs can call forth the rains. Actually this belief is not as far-fetched as you might think. Apparently the males of many forest frog species can detect decreases in barometric pressure that precede rainstorms. They begin to call, anticipating the formation of pools of water and females eager to breed at this time.

Status
Because so many species of leaf-litter toads are restricted to the floor of primary forest or along pristine streams flowing through uncut forest, these frogs have been especially susceptible to forest clearing. Good information on the population statuses of most species is lacking.

Profiles
Orange-eyed Leaf-litter Frog, *Leptobrachium smithi*, Plate 7c
Cascade Slender Leaf-litter Frog, *Leptolalax pelodytoides*, Plate 7d
Mountain Horned Frog, *Megophrys lateralis*, Plate 7e
Big-headed Horned Frog, *Megophrys carinensis*, Plate 7f

4. True Toads

Although many people think of *frogs* and *toads* as two distinct groups, all toads are frogs, just as all poodles are dogs. The common name "toad" is used for species in several families of frogs, but the main family of toads is Bufonidae, a worldwide group of about 380 species (11 in Thailand). Most bufonid toads, especially those in genus *Bufo,* have thick, dry skin that enables them to live in dry habitats. Toads typically have short, squat, heavy bodies with relatively short limbs and broad, rounded snouts. Many species have distinct bony crests between the eyes. *Bufonids* lack teeth, an unusual condition among frogs. The majority are colored dull olive to dark brown. Most toads have scattered wart-like bumps on the skin of the upper surface of the body. Most also have a pair of large, prominent *parotoid glands* on the shoulder area, one behind each eye. Toads range from tiny species less than 2 cm (0.8 in) in length as adults to other species that reach 25 cm (10 in). In Southeast Asia, one group of bufonids, the small *slender toads* (genus *Ansonia*), generally endemic to the region, are quite diverse in moist lowland and mid-elevation forest floors, but they are also usually quite rare.

Natural History

Ecology and Behavior

Most toads of the genus *Bufo* are nocturnal and terrestrial, spending much of their time foraging for invertebrate prey, such as insects, on the ground. Because of their thick dry skin, many species of toads are able to live much of their life away from water and often in very dry places. The dark tan or brown colors typical of most toads allow them to blend in with the soil and dead leaves on the forest floor. Toads can often be seen at night as they sit near lights, attracted by the insects flying into the light.

Many of the toads are masters at defending themselves from would-be predators. When harassed, these toads puff up by inflating their lungs with air. They also secrete a milky poison from their huge parotoid glands. When this substance is absorbed through a predator's mucous membranes, nausea and vomiting often result. In larger quantities, paralysis and death may occur. Because the poison is not absorbed through human skin, it's generally safe to handle these large toads as long as you don't have open cuts on your hands, don't rub your eyes or put your fingers in your mouth or nose, and wash your hands thoroughly afterward. Even better, overcome the temptation to pick up any toad you encounter.

Breeding

Most bufonid toads lay their eggs in water, and the eggs hatch into tadpoles. Males call from in or near the water to attract females. The male grasps the female (*amplexus*) and deposits sperm over the eggs she releases into the water. Bufonids are unique in their habit of laying eggs in two long strings, one from each ovary, as opposed to the clumps of eggs produced by most other frogs. Each egg is connected to the one before and after it, like beads in a necklace. Sometimes the strings of eggs sink to the bottom of the pond, but usually they get entwined around vegetation. Toads breed in a wide variety of temporary and permanent bodies of water, each female producing from 8,000 to 20,000 eggs and then abandoning them. Needless to say, there is considerable predation on the tadpoles... otherwise Thailand would be overrun with toads in no time!

Notes

People from many different cultures in the world use toads for medicines. Eighteenth-century physicians used powder made from dried toads to lower a patient's fever. The Chinese make a powder from *Bufo* parotoid secretion. Called *Ch'an Su*, this powder is used in treating heart ailments, for drying boils and abscesses, and for healing ulcers. It seems odd that *Bufo* secretion is so widely used as medicine—until you learn that the secretion contains epinephrine (adrenaline) and norepinephrine, chemicals known to stimulate the human heart and to help the human body deal with stress. Counter to a widespread myth, these chemicals from the toads' skin do NOT cause warts.

Other uses for parotoid secretions have been invented as well. The parotoid secretions of the MARINE TOAD (from Central and South America) are often one of the ingredients of a complex soup concocted by Haitian witch doctors to induce near-death comas and to create "zombies." The secretions of COLORADO RIVER TOADS in North America contain powerful hallucinogenic chemicals. Smoking dried parotoid secretions has become a popular pastime among some foolhardy people in Arizona and California! Anthropologists have speculated that the ancient cultures of Mesoamerica may have used toad parotoid secretions as hallucinogens during religious ceremonies, as abundant images of toads with prominent parotoid glands have been found on sculptures and engravings at archaeological sites.

Status

Although we know little about the population status of most toads in Thailand, several species of true toads are tentatively placed on the IUCN Red List of threatened and endangered species. Some toads, however, are only too abundant. The MARINE TOAD, mentioned above, becomes a pest when it is introduced into areas where it is not native. For example, this toad has been widely introduced into sugarcane-growing areas around the world to control insect pests (thus the alternate common name, Cane Toad). But the toads don't just feed on sugarcane pests. They also eat beneficial insects and other frogs. Among other places, it has become established in parts of Australia, New Guinea, and southern Florida (US), where it is abundant and threatens native amphibians due both to competition and direct predation. In addition, these large toads cause the death of pet dogs and cats, which, when they attack the toads, can receive a fatal mouthful of parotoid secretion.

Profiles

Asiatic Toad, *Bufo melanostictus*, Plate 8a
River Toad, *Bufo asper*, Plate 8b
Large-eared Toad, *Bufo macrotis*, Plate 8c
Dwarf Toad, *Bufo parvus*, Plate 8d

5. True Frogs

The *true frogs* (family Ranidae, with more than 700 species) have a nearly worldwide distribution. There are 45 species of true frogs, or *ranids*, in Thailand. These frogs are called "true frogs" not because they are better frogs than any other but because they are the most common frogs of Europe, where the early classification of animals took place. Ranids, which resemble North American *bullfrogs* and can grow to 13 cm (5.2 in) in length, are medium to dark green, often with scattered dark spots on the back and legs. They are powerfully built frogs usually with granular, rough skin, with many small to large bumps scattered on the back. Their hind feet are fully webbed, but the front feet lack webbing. They have prominent external ear discs and distinct folds of skin on the upper sides of the body. Ranid tadpoles are large, with heavy black beaks.

Natural History

Ecology and Behavior
Thailand's true frogs occupy a diverse range of habitats and show a broad range of behaviors. Some live along the banks of medium to large rivers, some in torrential mountain streams, some in swamps, some on the forest floor, and some in ponds, ditches, and rice paddies. Many species are terrestrial but some species climb on trees and shrubs.

Breeding
To attract females to mate, male ranids have characteristic calls that they give near to or in the water. Most species place their eggs in quiet water and have aquatic tadpoles. Some species that live in mountain streams, with rapidly flowing water, have tadpoles with suckers on their mouths for attaching to rocks in these streams.

Notes
The largest frog in the world belongs to family Ranidae, western Africa's GIANT SLIPPERY FROG, at 30 cm (12 in).

Status
Considerably more data are needed to determine the conservation statuses of Thai ranids. Some species are conspicuously rare, and they are likely victims of habitat destruction, but hunting for human consumption may also have had an impact on populations.

Profiles
Marsh Puddle Frog, *Occidozyga lima*, Plate 8e
Streamside Puddle Frog, *Phrynoglossus martensii*, Plate 8f
Field Frog, *Rana limnocharis*, Plate 9a
Oriental Bullfrog, *Rana rugulosa*, Plate 9b
Big-headed Frog, *Rana kuhlii*, Plate 9c
Giant River Frog, *Rana blythi*, Plate 9d
Crow Frog, *Rana hascheana*, Plate 9e
Flap-headed Stream Frog, *Rana pileata*, Plate 9f
Green Marsh Frog, *Rana erythraea*, Plate 10a
Copper-eared Frog, *Rana chalconota*, Plate 10b
Green Boulder Frog, *Rana livida*, Plate 10c
Dark-flanked Stream Frog, *Rana nigrovittata*, Plate 10d
Rough-sided Frog, *Rana glandulosa*, Plate 10e
Flank-ridged Cascade Frog, *Amolops larutensis*, Plate 10f

6. Narrow-mouthed Frogs

Narrow-mouthed frogs, family Microhylidae, contrary to what the family name suggests, are not all tiny frogs. There are about 315 species in the family, distributed nearly worldwide. Many narrow-mouthed frogs look ridiculous, with their rotund bodies, short stubby limbs, and tiny pointed heads. If you spot a small, dull gray to dark brown, smooth-skinned frog that resembles a mud-covered golf ball with legs and a pointed head, hopping about on the ground, you probably have found a narrow-mouthed frog. Lifestyle for *microhylids* is highly variable, including terrestrial, fossorial (burrowing), and arboreal. Many species in the family have tadpoles with a peculiar funnel-shaped mouth that opens upward. These frogs live in arid deserts, in wet rainforests, and in just about all habitats in between these extremes. They range in size from tiny (1 cm, 0.4 in) to medium-sized frogs (10 cm, 4 in).

The family has 19 species in Thailand. In general Thai microhylid frogs are very small, reaching no more than 2 cm (0.8 in) in length, but they have relatively long legs. Some Thai species, however, (in genera *Kaloula, Calluella,* and *Glyphoglossus*) are much stouter and larger (up to 7.5 cm, 3 in).

Natural History

Ecology and Behavior

Narrow-mouthed frogs inhabit probably all damp habitats in Thailand except salty coastal regions. Several species have adapted well to human land use and are abundant in wet rice paddies, gardens, bathrooms, and in other human landscapes. All species in Thailand are terrestrial, living on land among leaf litter and dense undergrowth. The species of the genera *Kaloula, Calluella,* and *Glyphoglossus* bury themselves in soil when at rest. All species are effectively nocturnal, although *Microhyla* species, such as the JEWEL NARROW-MOUTHED FROG (Plate 11), may occasionally be seen by day. Narrow-mouthed frogs clearly prefer damp areas, but the only time that they actually enter water is during breeding.

The diet of narrow-mouthed frogs is not well studied, but most likely all species feed on small insect prey, specifically ants and termites. Narrow-mouthed frogs rely primarily on camouflage and rapid escape to avoid predators. The large, slow *ox-frog* species secrete an apparently distasteful substance from their skin when molested. The species of genus *Kalophrynus* are called *sticky frogs* (such as the STRIPED STICKY FROG, Plate 11), and, as their name suggests, they take this secretion one step further—their skin chemicals dry into a sticky layer, effectively gluing up anything that comes in contact with the frog. To avoid getting themselves stuck and incapacitated with this glue, sticky frogs clean themselves carefully after any rough encounter that leads to glue secretion. The fascinating cleaning process involves the frog wiping much of its body with its hands, followed by the hind legs cleaning each other and the back while the frog balances on its hands only!

Breeding

The one constant feature among all narrow-mouthed frog species inhabiting Thailand is that they all breed in temporary bodies of standing water—rain puddles and pools. Some species have a main breeding period at the onset of the rainy season, while others call and breed after any heavy downpour anytime during the year. Males call while sitting near the edge of the pool; BANDED OX-FROG (Plate 11) males call while floating in the pool. Most species have a rattling, grating, or snoring call that is repeated over a long period; a few have bellowing calls that are spaced over time.

Mating (amplexus) in narrow-mouthed frogs is *axillary,* meaning that the male clamps onto the female by digging his hands into her armpits. Mating occurs in the water, typically a quick process in which a few hundred eggs are extruded and fertilized in a minute or so. The eggs generally form a floating loose raft at the water surface, and develop rapidly into tadpoles. Tadpoles of narrow-mouthed frogs have no teeth and generally feed by filtering fine particles from the water. These tadpoles are quite distinctive, tending to be transparent or translucent, with a large head and body, small eyes at the side, and a delicate tail. These tadpoles hover in mid-water, often in large schools. There are some specialized microhylid tadpoles, such as those of the Banded Ox-Frog, which may feed very little during their development and rely instead on the yolk nutrients of their eggs for their growth. The specialized tadpoles of the DARK-SIDED CHORUS FROG (*Microhyla heymonsi*) have slender, fish-like bodies and enlarged lips to collect food particles from the water's surface. Tadpole development is rapid to extremely rapid; some *Microhyla* species require little more than a week to develop from egg to metamorphosing froglet ready to leave the water. Clearly this is a valuable ability for species breeding in rain pools that may evaporate and disappear over short periods.

Notes

The BIG-LIPPED BURROWING FROG (Plate 11) is widespread in Thailand and commonly found in markets as food for humans. Three to five individuals are impaled whole on a wooden stick and roasted to a crisp over a fire—amphibian shish kabob!

Narrow-mouthed frogs clearly demonstrate how different call frequencies have different carrying ability. Loud, low-pitched calls, as given by the BANDED OX-FROG, carry for hundreds of meters (many hundreds of feet) but are *ventriloqual* (very difficult to pinpoint the precise source of the sounds). Such calls are perfect for attracting females from a wide area into a pool of modest size, where the animals are likely to locate each other by vibrations in the water or simply bumping into each other. High-pitched calls, such as that of the JEWEL NARROW-MOUTHED FROG, on the other hand, do not carry far but allow precise location of a calling male even if he is completely hidden under leaf litter well away from the water.

Status

While precise scientific data do not exist, subjective observations suggest that narrow-mouthed frogs are generally doing fine in Thailand. Their calls can be heard almost anywhere after heavy rain, and most species remain abundant and fairly easy to find. Nevertheless, local declines are known, probably as a result of pollution of breeding habitats. For instance, the call of the BANDED OX-FROG was a familiar sound in Bangkok but it gradually disappeared during the 1980s and 1990s. The hidden lifestyle and short breeding season of some species, mostly the large ox-frogs and *burrowing frogs,* make them more difficult to assess; because these species are exploited as food in remarkable quantities, a conservation assessment would be beneficial.

Profiles

Blotched Spadefoot Frog, *Calluella guttulata,* Plate 11a
Big-lipped Burrowing Frog, *Glyphoglossus molossus,* Plate 11b
Banded Ox-Frog, *Kaloula pulchra,* Plate 11c
Marbled Narrow-mouthed Frog, *Microhyla pulchra,* Plate 11d
Jewel Narrow-mouthed Frog, *Microhyla inornata,* Plate 11e
Striped Sticky Frog, *Kalophrynus interlineatus,* Plate 11f

7. Treefrogs

In much of the world, the name *treefrog* automatically refers to members of the family Hylidae, an extremely diverse and species-rich group of the Americas, New Guinea, and Australia, plus a few scattered species in temperate Eurasia. In a tropical Asian setting, however, as well as in Madagascar and tropical Africa, the treefrog niche is occupied by frogs of a different family, Rhacophoridae. About 20 of the world's 200 species of *rhacophorid* treefrogs occur in Thailand. The similarities between species of the two families can be amazing, having adapted to similar ecological niches with similar body plans: slender bodies; long slender legs ending in fingers and toes with large, rounded adhesion pads; cartilage discs between the last two phalange bones of the fingers and toes that allow extra flexibility; and a large, broad head with enormous eyes. Even though they are anatomically similar, the two families have very different origins, the rhacophorids being closely related to the true frogs (p. 83), and the hylids being related to bufonid toads (p. 82). This, at least superficial, resemblance between unrelated forms in geographically separated areas is called *convergent evolution*. It is thought to be the result of coincidental evolution in similar habitats, caused by common natural selective forces—such as similar predators, climates, etc.

Beyond the basic treefrog attributes of slender body, slender limbs, and big head, some groups of rhacophorids have developed a variety of remarkable physical characteristics. *Bush-frogs* of the genus *Chirixalus* have hands whose outer two fingers can oppose the inner two fingers, allowing the animals to grip around a leaf edge. The *gliding treefrogs* of genus *Rhacophorus* have large hands and feet with full skin webbing between the fingers and toes. When jumping down from a tree, these animals spread out their limbs, hands, and feet, in effect having a small parachute at all four corners of the body. This webbing effectively slows their fall, sufficiently reducing the impact of a fall of 10 to 20 m (33 to 66 ft) or more. The animals voluntarily use the parachuting method to descend rapidly to a breeding pool, but presumably it also works well to escape arboreal predators.

Not surprisingly for a group of frogs that rests during the day in a wide variety of conditions, their body coloration differs widely. Some species are simply dull brown, but others are spectacular, intense green, golden yellow, or orange with numerous white polka dots. The bush-frogs in genus *Theloderma* have superb camouflage that not only involves coloring resembling moss, lichen, tree bark, or bird droppings, but also remarkable skin surfaces and textures to reinforce the resemblance to coarse, inedible items.

Natural History

Ecology and Behavior

Species of rhacophorid treefrogs are likely to inhabit any given patch of vegetation in Thailand, but each species tends to occupy a different specialized forest type or a distinct part of the forest. Species of genus *Rhacophorus* are restricted to fairly undamaged evergreen forest, in lowlands as well as on mountain slopes. Bush-frogs of genus *Theloderma* are primarily inhabitants of open, scrubby, forest-edge habitats in locations that are damp throughout the year; thus they occur in rainforest climate regions of the Peninsula and Southeast as well as at higher elevations of the hill and mountain areas. *Philautus* bush-frogs likewise inhabit mainly montane scrub and rainforest regions. Most *Chirixalus* bush-frog species, in contrast, inhabit open, seasonally dry deciduous forest in lowland and at low altitudes. The species of *Polypedates*, particularly the WHITE-LIPPED TREEFROG (Plate 12) are more catholic in their habitat requirements, and they can be found almost anywhere, from village bathrooms in dry lowlands to dense evergreen hill forest and scrub forest on remote mountaintops.

All known rhacophorid treefrogs are active at night and rest by day in crevices, under leaf litter, or tightly pressed to the underside of a shaded leaf. Being treefrogs, virtually all their time is spent on vegetation or other structures off the ground, and most species only touch soil during breeding (and some species even manage to avoid that). All adult rhacophorid treefrogs feed on animal prey, and courtesy of their proportionally large heads and mouths their diet may include insects and spiders of quite substantial size. Obviously the frogs themselves are on the menu of a wide variety of predators, from large insects feeding on tadpoles and newly metamorphosed froglets to snakes, monitor lizards, herons, civets, mongooses, and small wild cats.

Breeding

Rhacophorid treefrogs are generally pool-breeders, using a wide variety of temporary and permanent, still water bodies for the development of their tadpoles. Such pools include rain puddles, isolated hollows along streams, rhino and buffalo wallows, and human water storage basins. As a result of the rain-dependent nature of most of these water bodies, treefrogs time their reproductive activity to occur at the onset or throughout the rainy season. Some species breed over long periods, while the entire mating activity of some species may be restricted each year to one or two nights after the first heavy downpours of the rainy season.

Rhacophorid treefrogs have the most diverse and variable call types of all Asian frogs. Males of many species have a repertoire of different calls. In the case of the WHITE-LIPPED TREEFROG, these include barking calls that are used to advertise the male's presence and (hopefully) fitness and desirability to any females within earshot, and clicking sounds that warn intruding males to stay out of a male's immediate vicinity. The frequencies and volumes of these species-specific sounds are apparently fixed, but the elements can be strung together creatively by a calling frog, yielding a wide variety of songs within each species. Advertisement calls of gliding frogs of genus *Rhacophorus* may consist of loud staccato rattles (FLANK-SPOTTED GLIDING TREEFROG, Plate 12), a soft buzz resembling an electric short-circuit (PHU KRADUNG GLIDING TREEFROG), or a soft, high-pitched warbling (BLACK-WEBBED GLIDING TREEFROG, Plate 12). The various *Theloderma* species have calls consisting of a whistle, whose inflection (up, down, or level) varies depending on the species. The repertoire of *Chirixalus* bush-frogs includes both single-note "ping" advertisement calls and a high-pitched staccato "RRRRIET" that may be an inter-male aggressive call. The DWARF BUSH-FROG (Plate 12) has a single-note "ping" call, but increases the number of notes as a call series progresses, so that what starts off as a spaced series of single "pings" is followed by a number of "ping-ping" calls, followed by "ping-ping-ping" calls and so on, up to calls with six or seven "ping" notes strung together.

Whereas most frogs place their eggs directly in the water, all known rhacophorid treefrog species in Thailand deposit their eggs out of water in a variety of ways and locations. Some, such as the STRIPED BUSH-FROG (Plate 12), produce a clump of eggs that is coated in a clear jelly and deposit the entire clump on a broad vertical reed blade at the edge of a pool. Individual frogs are frequently seen in the daytime sitting on the same leaf just above the egg mass, with their posterior in contact with the egg mass. If disturbed, the frog will jump off, but is likely to return within an hour or so. Whether this is a form of brood care, possibly keeping the clump moist or guarding it from small predators, or whether it is coincidence and the frogs find a damp object attractive to sit against, remains a fascinating topic for further study.

In some treefrog species the female secretes a liquid substance with the eggs and, apparently on her own, whips this mixture of egg and liquid into a foamy mass on top of a broad horizontal shrub leaf over the pool. In the White-lipped Treefrog, the male and the female in amplexus use their hind legs to whip the egg and liquid mass into a foam nest. The cooperative effort is taken one step further by some species of gliding treefrogs, including the Black-webbed Gliding Treefrog, when more than one female and up to half a dozen males may all be involved in the construction of a single foam nest. Foam nests of *Polypedates* and *Rhacophorus* species are preferentially constructed at the tips of tree branches overhanging water, often several meters above the water level. The nests hang free and need very little support; within hours of construction the outer surface of the foam begins to turn brown and rubbery, and after the first day of sunlight the entire outer surface will be dry and hard to the touch, feeling much like polyurethane foam used for home insulation. The outer coating seals in the moisture in the foam mass, within which the eggs develop. As the eggs hatch after a few days, the wriggling of the tadpoles weakens and helps to dissolve the bottom of the foam nest until it gives way. As the bottom falls out, the remaining foamy liquid and the young tadpoles drop from the nest into the pool below (if the pool has not dried up in the meantime). From there the development of the tadpoles follows the traditional pattern of feeding on algae, other vegetation, and detritus; growing; developing hind legs, front legs, and lungs; resorption of the tail and remodeling of the mouth and digestive system; and, eventually, emergence onto land. The foam nest keeps the eggs and earliest tadpole stages safe from aquatic predators. Given that the parent frogs select the nest site and construct the foam nest while balancing far above the water and in the dark, it is amazing that only very few nests are accidentally not located above water.

Few details are available about reproduction in bush-frogs of the genus *Philautus;* what is known indicates that many, perhaps all, *Philautus* species dispense with open water and a tadpole stage altogether. The Dwarf Bush-Frog produces only about ten eggs per clutch, and apparently places these in a damp crevice among moss on a tree trunk or branch. Here the eggs develop into a non-feeding tadpole inside the jelly-coated egg, which rapidly progresses through the normal tadpole development stages all the way up to small froglet. Thus these animals emerge from their egg as fully-formed little frogs.

The fact that each treefrog species has its own preferred time and place for breeding helps to reduce competition for breeding sites. Furthermore, because some species deposit their eggs on leaves above water and others are independent of water for reproduction, there is less demand on the available sites than there would be without this reproductive diversity. If all the frogs were to lay their eggs in temporary ponds at the same time, food would likely be severely limited for the tadpoles and mass starvation could ensue.

Notes

Adult treefrogs avoid or escape predators by rapid jumping; cryptic coloring that allows them to blend into their environment; loud, startling screams or squawks given when grabbed by predators; curling up and playing dead; and by poisons in their skin. Many treefrogs (and other types of frogs) have contrasting color patterns (such as bands of dark purple on an orange background) on surfaces of the limbs and the body that are usually hidden and that also assist with predator evasion. These colors are only visible when the limbs are extended. When a frog jumps to escape danger, these contrasting color patches, called *flash coloration*, attract the predator's attention. Then when the frog assumes a sitting position the predator loses the image because the frog is now cryptic once again.

Status

The WHITE-LIPPED TREEFROG is probably the most commonly seen frog in Thailand (especially by people visiting outside bathrooms at night), and it is widespread and fairly abundant in almost every habitat in Thailand. The other treefrog species are not so tolerant of regular human disturbance and tend to occur only in relatively intact forest areas. Where they occur, though, these species are generally quite abundant. Being slender with very little muscle, treefrogs are not eaten by the rural people. At present, no treefrog species in Thailand is considered threatened, although this more likely represents our general ignorance of frog population statuses than actual knowledge of wild populations.

Profiles

White-lipped Treefrog, *Polypedates leucomystax*, Plate 12a
Flank-spotted Gliding Treefrog, *Rhacophorus bipunctatus*, Plate 12b
Black-webbed Gliding Treefrog, *Rhacophorus nigropalmatus*, Plate 12c
Striped Bush-Frog, *Chirixalus vittatus*, Plate 12d
Dwarf Bush-Frog, *Philautus parvulus*, Plate 12e
Lichen Bush-Frog, *Theloderma asperum*, Plate 12f

Environmental Close-up 3:
Frog Population Declines

For more than two decades, scientists have reported that many populations of frogs, toads, and salamanders are declining in numbers. Some populations, and in fact entire species, have disappeared entirely. Several major questions are being asked: (1) How widespread is the problem? (2) Are amphibian population declines a special case, happening for reasons unrelated to the general loss of biodiversity? and (3) If there is a generalized worldwide amphibian decline, what are the causes?

The available data indicate a widespread pattern of amphibian declines. There are reports from low elevations and high elevations, from the US, Central America, the Amazon Basin, the Andes, Europe, and Australia. As of 2007, a few amphibian declines have been detected in Thailand and other parts of Southeast Asia, but the extent still appears to be much less in this part of the world than in other regions. Habitat loss almost certainly contributes to general declines in population sizes of amphibians, and in this sense, amphibian declines are part of the worldwide loss of biodiversity. But what is going on with amphibians seems to be more extreme than the declines seen in other animals. Why would amphibians be more vulnerable? One reason is that because amphibians have thin, moist skin that they use for breathing, chemical pollutants found in the water, soil, and air are able to enter their bodies easily. Secondly, many amphibians are exposed to double jeopardy: because they live both on land (usually in the adult stage) and in the water (usually the egg and larval stages), they are exposed to environmental contaminants, vagaries of the weather, and other potential factors affecting survivorship in both habitats.

So what could be causing the observed declines of amphibians? One possible cause is environmental pollution, for example *acid rain*—rain that is acidified by various atmospheric pollutants, leading to lake and river water being more acidic. Acidic water is known to decrease fertilization success because sperm become less active and often disintegrate. The eggs that are fertilized often develop abnormally. Another suggestion is that the increased levels of ultraviolet (UV) radiation, due to the thinning of the protective atmospheric ozone layer, might be damaging. Frogs often lay their eggs in shallow water directly exposed to the sun's rays, tadpoles often seek shallow water where the temperatures are warmer, and some juvenile and adult frogs bask for warmth. Studies have shown that increased levels of UV light kill some species of frog eggs and can interact chemically with diseases and acid rain to increase amphibian mortality rates.

Another possible cause is global warming. Some species of amphibians may not be able to adapt to the warmer, drier climate that some parts of the world are currently experiencing. For example, drought during a severe El Niño year in 1986–1987 has been implicated in the declines and disappearances of 40% (20 of 50 species) of the frog species (including the now likely extinct Golden Toad) that lived in the vicinity of Monteverde, Costa Rica. The frogs may have died directly from desiccation (drying out), or they may have been so stressed that they became more vulnerable to disease, fungus, or wind-borne environmental contaminants. Another cause of some population declines is a parasitic chytrid fungus that has been identified from Central and South America, the US, Europe, and Australia. The fungus seems to infest especially the victims' bellies—the area where frogs take up water through the skin. Thus, one speculation is that the frogs may be suffocating and drying out. Another possibility is that the fungus may release toxins that are lethal to the frogs when they are absorbed into the skin. Scientists are wondering where the killer fungus will show up next, and what is stressing amphibians to make them more vulnerable to pathogens such as fungus. They're also wondering if people (including researchers and ecotourists) could inadvertently be spreading the fungus on their shoes and boots. Perhaps non-human animals, such as insects, are spreading the fungus as well.

The fact that some areas of the world, such as Southeast Asia, may not be experiencing general amphibian declines, may aid scientists in their detective work—if they can identify ecological difference between these areas and those regions in which amphibian populations are crashing.

Not all biologists agree that amphibian declines are a phenomenon over and above the worldwide decline in biodiversity. Scientists who study natural fluctuations in sizes of animal populations point out that populations of many animals cycle between scarcity and abundance. Many insects are known for their wildly fluctuating population sizes. Population levels of vertebrates also fluctuate with environmental conditions such as food availability and density of prey. For example, voles and lemmings, small rodents of the arctic tundra, are well known for being at low population densities (a few per hectare or acre) one year, but being at very high densities (thousands per hectare or acre) several years later. Skeptics point out that, unless those sounding the alarm of amphibian declines can show that the declines are not part of natural cycles, it is too early to panic. They emphasize that the only way to document natural population cycles is to monitor amphibian populations during long-term field studies. Unfortunately, few such studies have been done.

Those scientists who believe that widespread amphibian declines are more than mere natural fluctuations argue that we need to act *now*. Although they agree that we need to initiate long-term studies, they believe we can't wait for the conclusions of such studies in 10 or 20 years before we try to reverse the situation. At that point, they argue, it will be too late to do anything but record extinctions.

The controversy will continue. The important consequence of the debate is that many investigators are working on the problem, considering many different possible causes, from climate change to a parasitic fungus. A major problem is that even if the scientific consensus right now were that disease, fungi, pollution, climate change, increased levels of UV radiation, or some combination thereof were causing worldwide amphibian declines, the interest and resources are currently lacking to do anything about it on the massive scale required. Because amphibians and reptiles are not uniformly liked and respected, preservation efforts for these animals, except for special cases like sea turtles, will always lag behind conservation efforts made on behalf of birds and mammals. Fortunately, however, because the current conservation emphasis is on preserving entire ecosystems, rather than particular species, amphibians will benefit even if they don't have feathers or fur.

Chapter 7

REPTILES

- Introduction
- General Characteristics and Classification
- Seeing Reptiles in Thailand
- Family Profiles
   1. Crocodilians
   2. Turtles
   3. Geckos
   4. Monitor and Agamid Lizards
   5. Skinks and Grass Lizard
   6. Venomous Snakes
   7. Pythons and Miscellaneous Snakes
   8. Colubrids: Your Regular, Everyday Snakes
- Environmental Close-up 4: Endemism and High Species Diversity: Why Thailand?

Introduction

Ecotravellers often have ambivalent feelings about reptiles. On one hand, many people react with surprise and rapid withdrawal when suddenly confronted with reptiles anywhere but the zoo. But on the other hand, these creatures, with their variety of colors, shapes, behaviors, and highly intriguing lifestyles, are fascinating to look at and contemplate. Most reptiles are harmless to people and, if discovered going about their daily business, are worth a look. Unfortunately, to avoid predation, most reptiles are inconspicuous both in their behavior and color patterns and often flee when alerted to people's presence; consequently most reptiles are never seen by people during a brief visit to a region. But there are some exceptions. For instance, crocodiles and monitor lizards, both very large reptiles, are *not* inconspicuous and *do not* always immediately flee from humans; small lizards can be quite common along forest trails, and geckos are often common in the lodges where ecotourists stay. To see many species of reptiles in the wild, you need to walk slowly and quietly and look closely—so keep a careful watch for reptiles and count yourself lucky for each one you see.

General Characteristics and Classification

Reptiles have been around for a long time, arising during the late Paleozoic Era, some 300 million years ago. Today more than 7,000 species live in almost all regions of the Earth, with a healthy contingent in Southeast Asia. Reptile skin is covered with tough scales, which cuts down significantly on water loss from the body surface. The development of this trait first permitted vertebrates to remain for extended periods on dry land. Most of today's reptiles are completely terrestrial. In contrast, most amphibians lack a tough skin and must remain in or near water or moist places. Reptiles have much more efficient heart and blood systems than those of amphibians. This increased efficiency allows for a high blood pressure and the sustained muscular activity required for living on land. The crocodilians (crocodiles and alligators) even have a completely four-chambered heart that is otherwise found only in birds and mammals. A reptile egg is covered with a shell that provides mechanical protection, but at the same time allows movement of respiratory gases and water vapor through the shell. One of the major differences between a reptile egg and an amphibian egg is that, in the egg, the reptile embryo is surrounded by a membrane called the *amnion*. This membrane provides the developing embryo with a fluid environment; thus, unlike most amphibians, reptiles do not have to return to the water to deposit their eggs. In addition, the developing young in reptile eggs are much better protected against predators and the elements than are amphibians at similar life stages.

Biologists recognize four major living groups of reptiles. The *turtles* and *tortoises* (land turtles) constitute one group, with about 260 species worldwide. Most turtles live in lakes and ponds, though some turtles live on land throughout their lives. The *sea turtles* live in the oceans, coming ashore only to lay eggs. Some eat plants, some are carnivorous, and others eat both plants and animals. Turtles are easily distinguished by their unique body armor of tough plates that cover their back and belly, creating wraparound shells into which head and limbs are retracted when danger looms. The *crocodiles* and their relatives, large predatory carnivores that live along the shores of swamps, rivers, and estuaries, constitute a small second group of 22 species. The third group is represented by two lizard-like species of *tuataras*, found only on small islands off the coast of New Zealand. The fourth group consists of the *squamates*, the 3,300 *lizard* species and 3,500 *snakes*. Lizards and snakes have very similar skeletal traits, indicating that they are closely related.

Lizards walk on all four limbs, except for a few that are legless. Many live on the ground, but a fair number spend much of their lives in trees. Almost all are capable of moving rapidly. Most lizards are insectivorous, but some, especially larger ones, eat plants, and several prey on amphibians, other lizards, mammals, birds, and even fish. The ecological success of lizards is likely due primarily to a combination of their efficient predation on insects and other small animals as well as their low daily energy requirements. Lizards rely primarily on external sources of heat such as the sun to raise their internal temperature enough to be active. When it gets too hot, they use behavior such as seeking shade to lower their internal temperature so they can again be active. However, when the external temperature falls too much, instead of burning up stored energy to maintain their body temperature, they just let their internal temperature drop and become inactive. Their cooled bodies go into a resting state that needs little energy. In some ways, this can be considered an advantage over birds and mammals, which must continually seek food to maintain constant high body temperatures.

Most Thai lizards eat insects, spiders, and mites, but a few eat leaves and plant material. Insectivorous lizards use two main foraging strategies. Some, such as the small grass lizards (p. 105), are *active searchers*. They move continually while looking for prey, nosing about in the leaf litter of the forest floor. *Sit-and-wait* predators are usually highly camouflaged; they remain motionless on the ground or on tree trunks or branches, waiting for prey to happen by. When they see a likely meal, they snatch it if it is close enough or dart out to chase it down. Many lizards are territorial, defending territories from other members of their species with displays such as bobbing up and down on their front legs, spreading out their *dewlaps* (throat fans), and raising their head crests. Lizards are especially common in open, dry areas, but they also can be numerous in lowland evergreen forests. They are active primarily during the day, except for many of the gecko species, which are nocturnal.

Snakes probably evolved from burrowing lizards, and all are limbless. Although all snakes are carnivores, their methods of capturing prey differ. Several groups of species have evolved glands that manufacture toxic venom, which is injected into prey through the teeth. The venom immobilizes and kills the prey, which is then swallowed whole. Other snakes strike out at and then wrap themselves around their prey, constricting the prey until it suffocates. Most snakes are nonvenomous; they seize prey with their mouths and rely on their size and strong jaws to subdue it. Snakes have no eardrums for hearing, but they can detect ground vibrations through their bodies. They generally rely most on vision and smell to locate prey, although members of two families have thermal sensor organs on their heads that detect the heat of prey animals.

The success of snakes is at least partially attributable to their ability to devour prey that is larger than their heads. Their jaw bones are highly mobile and can be moved easily out of their socket joints on the cranium to accommodate large prey as it is swallowed. Because they eat large items, they need to search for and capture prey only infrequently. For this reason, they can spend long periods hidden and secluded, safe from predators. Snakes use either active searching or sit-and-wait foraging strategies.

As is true for lizards, temperature regulates a snake's life, and is the key to understanding their ecology. Unlike birds and mammals, snakes' body temperatures are determined primarily by how much heat they obtain from the physical environment. Many can only be active when they gather sufficient warmth from the sun. They have some control over their body temperature, but it is behavioral rather than physiological. Snakes can lie in the sun or retreat to shade to raise or lower their internal temperatures to within a good operating range, but only up to a point. They must "sit out" hours or days in which the air temperature is either too high or too low. This dependence on air temperature affects most aspects of snakes' lives, from timing of birth, to food requirements, to the rapidity with which they can strike at prey.

Snakes are themselves prey for hawks and other predatory birds, other snakes, and for some mammals. Many snakes, with their bold and colorful skin patterns, are quite conspicuous against a solid color. But against their normal backdrops, such as a leaf-strewn forest floor, they are highly camouflaged. They rely on this *cryptic coloration,* and sometimes on speed, to evade predators. Within a species, male and female snakes usually look alike, although in some there are minor differences between the sexes in color patterns or the sizes of their scales.

Seeing Reptiles in Thailand

Most of the 317 or so species of reptiles that occur in Thailand are shy and often difficult to observe. They spend most of their time concealed or still. Few vocalize like birds or frogs, so you cannot use sound to find them. The superb cryptic coloration of many snakes means that they will probably see more of you than you will of them. Because of the difficulty people have seeing snakes before getting very close to them, the rule for exploring any area known to have venomous snakes or any area for which you are unsure, is NEVER to place your hand or foot anywhere that you cannot see first. Do not climb rocks or trees; do not clamber over rocks where your hands or feet sink into holes or crevices; do not reach into bushes or trees. Walk carefully along trails and try to watch your feet and where you are going. Don't be frightened, but be respectful.

If you want to see reptiles, there are a few ways to increase the chances. Knowing about activity periods helps. Lizards and many snakes are active during the day, but some snakes are active at night. Thus, a night walk with flashlights that is organized to find nocturnal birds, mammals, and amphibians may also yield reptile sightings. Also, many small lizards and some snakes sleep on leaves and branches above the ground, in the same places where treefrogs are active—so if you are out looking for active frogs, you may also locate some sleepy reptiles. In rainforest, many lizards are active by day on tree trunks and also in sunny areas near forest edges. Snakes and lizards are often more active in sunny, warm weather. If all else fails, look for small snakes and lizards by CAREFULLY moving aside rocks and logs with a robust stick or with your boots. Because there are some venomous snakes that are difficult to identify correctly, all snakes are best observed from a safe distance unless you are accompanied by someone who is very familiar with these animals.

Unfortunately, common names of reptiles are not standardized, as they are for birds. Common names for many Southeast Asian reptiles are especially troublesome. For example, some people call *Boiga dendrophila* (Plate 22) the YELLOW-RINGED CAT-SNAKE; others call it the MANGROVE CAT-SNAKE. The BANDED RAT-SNAKE (PLATE 21) is also called, by various reference books, BAND-TAILED RAT-SNAKE, COMMON RAT-SNAKE, and ASIAN RAT-SNAKE. How are the uninitiated supposed to know it's the same species? Also, some species have no generally accepted common names. For the sake of consistency, where possible we use the common names adopted by the renown herpetologist from the Field Museum of Natural History in Chicago, Robert Inger, and those that appear in previous Travellers' Wildlife Guides.

Unless otherwise indicated, reptile body lengths are given as total lengths (that is, tail included). For lizards, however, lengths reported in the plate section are from the tip of the snout to the vent (that is, excluding the tail; the vent is the opening on the belly that lies approximately where the rear limbs join the body, and through which sex occurs and wastes exit). The reason is that lizard tails in the same species vary considerably in length. This is because lizards often "lose" their tails when attacked by predators (p. 106), and when tails regenerate, they are usually smaller than they were initially.

Family Profiles

1. Crocodilians

Remnants of the age when reptiles ruled the world, today's 22 species of *crocodilians* (*alligators, caimans, gavials,* and *crocodiles*), generally inspire awe, respect, a bit of fear, and a great deal of curiosity. Crocodilians are distributed over most tropical and sub-tropical areas of the world. None of the three species of crocodilians known in Thailand are likely to be seen by casual ecotravellers on a two- or three-week visit to the country. Fifty to eighty years ago all three species, the SIAMESE CROCODILE (Plate 14), the ESTUARINE (or SALTWATER) CROCODILE, and even the slender-snouted FALSE GAVIAL (or FALSE GHARIAL), were fairly common in their respective habitats within Thailand. Coastal development, conversion of inland swamps to agriculture, and extensive hunting for their skins have now virtually exterminated them in the wild in Thailand.

Natural History

Ecology and Behavior

Although crocodilians usually move slowly over land, they can cover ground rapidly in short bursts. They are easiest to see as they bask in the sunshine along banks of rivers, streams, lakes, and ponds. Most of their time is spent in the water, however, where they are largely hidden and can resemble floating logs. This unassuming appearance allows them to move close to shore and seize animals that come to the water to drink. Crocodilians are meat-eaters, but they also eat carrion. Juveniles primarily eat aquatic insects, while adults often prey on fish and amphibians, and on birds and small mammals when they have the opportunity.

Crocodilians have some of the most developed parental care behaviors of any reptile. Nests are guarded, and one or both parents often help hatchlings free themselves from the nest. In some species, parents carry hatchlings to water. Females may remain with and protect the young for up to two years. Juveniles give alarm calls when threatened, and parents respond by coming quickly to their rescue. This complex parental care in crocodilians is sometimes used by scientists who study dinosaurs to support the idea that dinosaurs may have exhibited complex social and parental behaviors. Crocodilians are long-lived animals, many surviving 60+ years in the wild.

Breeding

During courtship, male crocodilians often defend aquatic territories, giving displays with their tails—up-and-down and side-to-side movements—that probably serve both to defend the territory from other males and to court females. Typically the female makes the nest by scraping together grass, leaves, twigs, and sand or soil, into a pile near the water's edge. She then buries 20 to 30 eggs in the pile that she, and sometimes the male, guard for about 70 days until hatching. As with turtles and some lizards, the sex of developing crocodilians is determined largely by the temperature of the ground around the eggs (p. 100); males develop at relatively high temperatures, females at lower ones. Today crocodiles are bred in Thailand on farms, where the freshwater SIAMESE CROCODILE often hybridizes with the saltwater ESTUARINE CROCODILE.

Notes

ESTUARINE CROCODILES are notoriously dangerous to people, and in some parts of their range, such as Australia, they are particularly aggressive and large enough to eat large land mammals. Because of their predatory nature and large size, crocodilians play important roles—both positive and negative—in the history and folklore of many cultures, going back at least to ancient Egypt and a crocodile-headed god known as Sebek. Egyptians even built and named the holy city of Crocodilopolis in honor of crocodiles. The Egyptians apparently welcomed crocodiles into their canals, possibly as a defense from human invaders. On the other hand, because this reptile is often nocturnal, Egyptians and other African peoples associated it with darkness and believed that crocodiles caused blindness. Blindness was a very real fear for these people because of the prevalence of a disease called *river blindness,* actually caused by a river-borne parasitic roundworm. To appease the crocodiles during canal construction, a virgin was sacrificed to the reptiles. Indeed, providing crocodiles with virgins seems to have been a fairly common practice among several early cultures, showing a preoccupation with these animals (and with virgins). Crocodilians were also important in the cultures of many early South American peoples. For example, the ancient Olmecs of eastern Mexico had a crocodile deity. The Mayans had a god, a symbol of death, shaped like a crocodile. The Aztecs had a crocodilian image that symbolized agricultural fertility and another that brought the rain. Potions made from crocodilians were, and still are, used in both the Old and New Worlds as traditional cures for various ailments and diseases.

Status

Most crocodilian species worldwide were severely reduced in numbers during the twentieth century. Several were hunted almost to extinction for their skins. For instance, in the US, hunting almost caused AMERICAN ALLIGATORS to go extinct. In 1961 hunting alligators was declared illegal, but poaching continued. Thanks to the US's 1973 Endangered Species Act, which gave protection to alligators, they have returned to most of the areas from which they were eliminated. Crocodile and alligator farms (with captive-bred stock) and ranches (wild-caught stock) in many areas of the world now provide skins, leaving wild populations relatively unmolested. All crocodilians are listed by the international CITES agreements, preventing or highly regulating trade, and their numbers have been steadily rising during the past 20 years. Nevertheless, most of the 22 crocodilian species are still threatened or endangered. The ESTUARINE CROCODILE is CITES Appendix II listed for Australia, Indonesia, and New Guinea, but Appendix I listed (endangered) for elsewhere in its range, including Thailand. The FALSE GAVIAL and SIAMESE CROCODILE are endangered, the latter critically so; both are included in CITES Appendix I and the IUCN Red List. Many experts believed the Siamese Crocodile was extinct in Thailand, but researchers have found several small populations recently in Kaeng Krachan National Park and Khao Ang Ru Nai Wildlife Sanctuary.

Profile
Siamese Crocodile, *Crocodylus siamensis*, Plate 14c

2. Turtles

It is a shame that *turtles* are rarely encountered in the wild at close range because they are such intriguing animals. It is always a pleasant surprise stumbling across a turtle on land, perhaps laying eggs, or discovering a group of them basking in the sunshine on rocks or logs along a river's edge or in the middle of a pond. The world's 260 living turtle species are grouped into 12 families that can be divided into three types by their typical habits. There are two families of *sea turtles*, ocean-going animals whose females come to shore only to lay eggs. The members of nine families, containing most of the turtle species, live in freshwater habitats—lakes and ponds—except for the *box turtles*, which live on land (*terrestrial*). Finally, one family contains the *land tortoises*, which, as their name suggests, are all terrestrial. Nearly 30 species of turtles are found in Thailand.

Turtles all have the same basic anatomy: bodies encased in tough shells (made up of two layers—an inner layer of bone and an outer layer of scale-like plates); four limbs, sometimes modified into flippers; highly mobile necks; toothless jaws; and small tails. This body plan must be among nature's best, because it has survived unchanged for a long time; turtles have looked more or less the same for at least 200 million years. Enclosing the body in heavy armor above and below apparently was an early solution to the problems vertebrates faced when they moved onto land. It provides rigid support when outside of buoyant water and protection from predators and desiccation (drying out).

Turtles range in color from brown to black to green, with many being olive-green. They range in size from tiny *terrapins* 11.5 cm (4.6 in) long to giant LEATHERBACK SEA TURTLES (Plate 14) that can grow to more than 2 m (6.5 ft) long, 3.6 m (11.8 ft) across (flipper to flipper), and that weigh 600+ kg (1,300+ lb). Leatherbacks are the heaviest turtles. In many turtle species, females are larger than males.

Natural History

Ecology and Behavior
Some turtle species scavenge carrion, some are specialized to eat snails, and others eat water weeds, including, in Thailand, the introduced water hyacinth. The diet of many freshwater turtles changes as they develop. Early in life they are carnivorous, eating almost anything they can get their jaws on—snails, insects, fish, frogs, salamanders, reptiles. As they grow, the diet of many species changes to herbivory. Turtles are slow-moving on land, but they can retract their heads, tails, and limbs into their shells, rendering them almost impregnable to predators—unless they are swallowed whole, such as by crocodiles. Long-lived animals, individuals of many turtle species typically live 25 to 60 years in the wild. As is typical of most, if not all, reptiles, turtles grow throughout their lives.

The turtles of Thailand occupy a variety of habitats. Sea turtles live in the open oceans off the coast of Thailand, except when females come onto beaches to lay their eggs. Some of the aquatic freshwater species spend most of their time in lakes and ponds, but a few leave the water to forage on land. Tortoises, including Thailand's huge ASIAN BROWN TORTOISE (up to 40 kg, 88 lb) are almost exclusively terrestrial. In Thailand, ponds and pools associated with temples often serve as refuges for many species of freshwater turtles.

If turtles can survive the dangerous juvenile stage, when they are small and soft enough for a variety of predators to eat them, they enjoy very high year-to-year survival; up to 80% or more of an adult population usually survives from one year to the next. However, there is very high mortality in the egg and juvenile stages. Nests are not guarded, and many kinds of predators, such as crocodiles, lizards, and rats, dig up turtle eggs or eat the hatchlings.

Breeding

Courtship in turtles can be quite complex. In some, the male swims backward in front of the female, stroking her face with his clawed feet. Males of some species nibble at the edge of the female's upper shell. Courtship in land tortoises often involves butting and nipping. When a male turtle is ready to copulate, he climbs onto a female's shell and grabs the rim with all four feet. All turtles lay their leathery eggs on land. The female digs a hole in the earth or sand, deposits the eggs into the hole, then covers them and leaves. It is up to the hatchlings to dig their way out of the nest and navigate to water. Many tropical turtles breed at any time of year.

Although the numbers of eggs laid per nest varies extensively among Thai freshwater turtles (from 1 to about 100), in general these turtles lay small clutches. The reason seems to be that, because of the continuous warm weather, they need not breed in haste like their northern cousins, putting all their eggs in one nest. The danger with a single nest is that if a predator finds it, a year's breeding is lost. Tropical turtles, by placing only one or a few eggs in each of several nests spread throughout the year, are less likely to have predators destroy their total annual breeding production. Also, it may pay to lay a few big eggs rather than many small ones because bigger hatchlings may be less vulnerable to predators.

Notes

There is an intriguing relationship between turtle reproduction and temperature that nicely illustrates the intimate connection between animals and the physical environment. For many vertebrates, the sex of an individual is determined by the kinds of sex chromosomes it has. In people, if each cell has an X and a Y chromosome, the person is male, and if two Xs, female. In birds, it is the opposite. But in most turtles, it is not the chromosomes that matter, but the temperature at which an egg develops. In most turtles studied to date, eggs incubated at constant temperatures above $30°C$ ($86°F$) all develop as females, whereas those incubated at 24 to $28°C$ (75 to $82°F$) become males. At 28 to $30°C$ (82 to $86°F$), both males and females are produced. In some species, a second temperature threshold exists—eggs that develop below $24°C$ ($75°F$) again become females. (In the crocodiles and lizards, the situation reverses, with males developing at relatively high temperatures and females at low temperatures.) The exact way that temperature determines sex is not clear, although it is suspected that temperature directly influences a turtle's developing brain. Scientists haven't yet figured out *why* this system of sex determination exists. Is there some advantage of this system to the animals that we as yet fail to appreciate? Or is it simply a consequence of reptile structure and function, some fundamental constraint of their biology?

In Thailand, turtles, unlike other reptiles, are considered propitious and signs of good luck. In both Hindu and Chinese mythology, the turtle symbolizes the universe. The top of the domed shell represents the vastness of the sky and the bottom of the shell represents the Earth, which moves upon the water. Because turtles live long lives, the Chinese consider them symbols of old age and endurance. Many people in Thailand release turtles as a form of the Theraveda Buddhist practice of merit-making, especially around temples.

Status

The ecology and status of populations of most Southeast Asian freshwater and land turtles are poorly known, making it difficult to determine whether population numbers are stable or changing. Several species of large turtles have virtually disappeared from all but the most remote streams and lakes. This rapid decline is due largely to over-harvesting of their eggs, which are buried in river sandbars. These nests are easily found by local people who then sell them to food markets in regional cities. Worldwide, sea turtles are heavily exploited by people, and almost all of them are threatened or endangered. Sea turtle eggs are harvested illegally for food in many parts of the world, including Thailand, and adults of some species are taken for meat and for their shells. The HAWKSBILL SEA TURTLE (Plate 14), for instance, is the chief provider of tortoiseshell, which is carved for decorative purposes. The IUCN Red List includes two Thailand species of freshwater turtles as being critically threatened, the PAINTED TERRAPIN and the NARROW-HEADED SOFTSHELL TURTLE; another species, the RIVER TERRAPIN, is considered endangered. Six additional Thai species of freshwater turtles are listed as vulnerable. All sea turtles are listed as threatened or endangered (IUCN Red List and CITES Appendix I).

Profiles

Elongated Tortoise, *Indotestudo elongata*, Plate 13a
Asian Box Turtle, *Cuora amboinensis*, Plate 13b
Stream Terrapin, *Cyclemys dentata*, Plate 13c
Ricefield Terrapin, *Malayemys subtrijuga*, Plate 13d
Big-headed Turtle, *Platysternon megacephalum*, Plate 13e
Stream Softshell Turtle, *Dogania subplana*, Plate 13f
Hawksbill Sea Turtle, *Eretmochelys imbricata*, Plate 14a
Leatherback Sea Turtle, *Dermochelys coriacea*, Plate 14b

3. Geckos

Geckos are fascinating organisms because, of their own volition, they have become "house lizards." The family, Gekkonidae, is spread throughout tropical and subtropical areas of the world, with about 870 species (40 in Thailand). In many regions, geckos have invaded houses and buildings, becoming ubiquitous adornments of walls and ceilings. Ignored by human residents, they move around dwellings chiefly at night, munching insects.

Thai geckos are fairly small lizards, usually gray or brown, with large eyes (they lack eyelids). They have thin, soft skin, usually covered with small, granular scales that produce a slightly lumpy appearance. Many have large fingers and toes with well-developed claws and broad specialized pads that allow them to cling to vertical surfaces and even upside-down on ceilings. The way geckos manage these feats has engendered a fair amount of scientific detective work. Various forces have been implicated in explaining the gecko's anti-gravity performance, from the ability of their claws to dig into tiny irregularities on man-made surfaces, to their large toes acting as suction cups, to an adhesive quality of friction. The real explanation appears to lie in the series of minuscule hair-like structures on the bottoms of the finger and toe pads, which provide attachment to walls and ceilings by something akin to surface tension—the same property that allows some insects to walk on water. Most adult geckos are only 5 to 10 cm (2 to 4 in) in length, tail excluded; tails can double the length. Because lizard tails frequently break off and regenerate (p. 106), their length varies tremendously; gecko tails are particularly fragile.

Natural History

Ecology and Behavior

Although most lizards are active during the day and inactive at night, many gecko species, including most of Thailand's, are nocturnal. In natural settings, many species are primarily ground dwellers, but, as their behavior in buildings suggests, they are also excellent climbers. For instance, the beautiful TOCKAY GECKO (Plate 15) is often found on the ground or on roads, but is also seen on hotel walls. It is often easy to watch geckos forage for insects around lights at night, both in and outside of buildings. In the canopy of lowland evergreen forest, Thailand is home of two species of *flying geckos* (including KUHL'S FLYING GECKO, Plate 15), which are sometimes seen during daylight hours, clinging to their primary home, tree trunks. These amazing lizards can spread the fleshy skin folds they have on their sides between their legs and body to form a gliding membrane. They use the gliding membrane, enhanced by their webbed feet, to leap from tree trunk to tree trunk, or to the ground, covering aerial distances of 10 m (33 ft) or more. When they are chased by a predator, they leap to another tree or to the ground to escape. (Some agamid lizards in Thailand, known as *flying dragons* or *gliding lizards,* also glide; p. 104.)

Unlike most lizards, which do not vocalize, geckos at night are avid little chirpers and squeakers. They communicate with each other with loud calls—surprisingly loud for such small animals; some bark as loud as small dogs. Various species sound differently. The word "gecko" approximates the sound of calls from some of the Asian species.

Geckos feed chiefly on insects. In fact, it is their ravenous appetite for cockroaches and other insect undesirables that render them welcome house guests in many parts of the world. Geckos are *sit-and-wait* predators. Instead of wasting energy actively searching for prey that is usually highly alert and able to flee, they sit still for long periods, waiting for unsuspecting insects that venture a bit too near, then lunge, grab, and swallow. Geckos rely chiefly on their *cryptic coloration* and their ability to flee rapidly for escape from predators, which include snakes and birds during the day and snakes, owls, and bats at night. When cornered, geckos give threat displays; when seized, they give loud calls to distract predators, and they bite. Should the gecko be seized by its tail, it breaks off as a last resort, allowing the gecko time to escape, albeit tail-less (p. 106). Although it causes considerable stress to the animal, the tail usually regenerates. Some geckos when seized also secrete thick, noxious fluids from their tails; these secretions presumably discourage predators.

Breeding

Almost all geckos are egg-layers. Mating occurs after courtship, which involves a male displaying to a female by waving his tail around, followed by some mutual nosing and nibbling. Clutches usually contain only one to a few eggs, but a female may lay several clutches per year. There is no parental care; after eggs are deposited, they and the tiny geckos that hatch from them are on their own.

Status
Some of Thailand's forest gecko species are listed as rare, vulnerable, threatened, or endangered, but the actual conservation status of most is very poorly known.

Profiles
Flat-tailed House Gecko, *Cosymbotus platyurus*, Plate 15a
Spiny-tailed House Gecko, *Hemidactylus frenatus*, Plate 15b
Kuhl's Flying Gecko, *Ptychozoon kuhlii*, Plate 15c
Tockay Gecko, *Gekko gecko*, Plate 15d
Siamese Leaf-toed Gecko, *Dixonius siamensis*, Plate 15e
Cardamom Slender-toed Gecko, *Cyrtodactylus intermedius*, Plate 15f

4. Monitor and Agamid Lizards

For convenience we group together here two distantly related families of lizards—*monitor lizards* (family Varanidae, about 48 species total, four in Thailand) and *agamid lizards* (family Agamidae, 340 species total, 34 species in Thailand). Both families contain many species that are large to very large in size, and both are restricted to the Old World. About half the species of monitors occur in Australia (where they are known as *goannas*).

Monitor lizards are dinosaur-like, and they are often arrogantly obvious in many habitats as they lumber along a forest floor, bask on rocks, or swim across rivers. All species in this family are similar in shape and form, with a long, flattened body, long tail, long neck, and an extremely long forked tongue similar to that of snakes. Their eyes have well-developed eyelids, and their feet have long, curved claws. The smallest monitor, a pygmy species, is only about 20 cm (8 in) in total length, and occurs in Australia. The largest member of the family, the KOMODO DRAGON of eastern Indonesia, is the world's largest lizard, growing to a length of more than 3 m (10 ft) and weighing 70 to 100 kg (150 to 220 lb). The BENGAL MONITOR (Plate 14), the species most often observed by travellers in Thailand, often reaches 2 m (6.6 ft) in length (including the long tail) and 50 kg (110 lb) in weight. One of Thailand's other monitors, the WATER MONITOR, which inhabits not only wetlands but also agricultural areas and some forests, is one of the world's largest lizards, reaching total lengths of 2.6 m (8.5 ft).

Agamid lizards (often called *dragons*) reach their greatest diversity in the Oriental Region, which includes Thailand. They closely resemble the *iguanas* of the New World, not only in their great variation of sizes and shapes but also in the diversity of habitats they occupy. Arboreal species are flattened side to side and terrestrial species are flattened top to bottom; the head in all species is held off the ground by a distinct neck. Many in the family, especially males during reproductive seasons, are brightly colored and have adornments such as crests, spines, or throat fans (*dewlaps*). The smallest agamids are only a few centimeters in total length and a few grams in weight; the largest member of the family is the INDO-CHINESE WATERDRAGON (Plate 16), which reaches 70+ cm (2.3+ ft) in total length. Some species of small agamids are very common in and around human habitations.

Natural History

Ecology and Behavior

Monitor lizards are diurnal but usually most active in the morning and late afternoon. They forage on the ground by moving slowly with their forked tongues flicking in and out; the tongue transfers odors to sense organs located in the roof of the mouth, and so helps to locate prey. Monitors readily climb trees and swim well, some species being able to remain submerged for several minutes. At night and often to escape danger, monitors seek burrows in the ground. If danger approaches before they can get to their burrows, they will usually lie motionless, flat against the ground. If prodded, they will run quickly and noisily with the tail cocked up at an angle. When cornered, they can attack viciously, hissing and biting. Monitor lizards are carnivorous, eating any animal they can catch or dig out of the ground, including mammals, birds, eggs, reptiles, scorpions, fish, and crabs. They are not above eating carrion. Our personal experiences suggest they also have a deep fondness for canned corned beef—especially Australian brands that say "for export only."

The majority of agamid lizards climb vegetation agilely using their sharp claws, but some, such as the BUTTERFLY LIZARD (Plate 16), live in burrows in the ground and hunt prey on the soil surface. Most agamids eat insects and other small animals, but a few agamids are herbivorous. One of the truly exceptional adaptations within the family is found among a small group of species that have evolved the ability to glide between trees. These *flying dragons,* or more accurately, *gliding lizards* (such as the BLACK-THROATED GLIDING LIZARD, Plate 16), have developed false ribs that spread a flap of highly colored, loose skin on the flanks into a gliding membrane (*patagium*). With this "parachute" they can glide up to 30 m (100 ft)—usually covering a distance of about 5 m (16 ft) for every 1 m (3.3 ft) they lose in altitude. These lizards are primarily active during the day and spend the night sleeping on tree trunks, tips of slender twigs, or underground in burrows. (Some geckos, known as *flying geckos,* also glide; p. 102.)

Breeding

Male monitor lizards are territorial during the breeding season, and combat between rival males is fairly regular at this time. After mating, females dig deep holes in the soil and lay 8 to 20 eggs, which are then covered by refilling the hole. The eggs take 9 month to hatch, the young usually emerging at the beginning of the rainy season.

Almost all agamid lizards lay soft-shelled eggs that are deposited in holes in the soil. Even the females of otherwise purely arboreal species, such as the gliding lizards, descend to the ground to lay their eggs. The males of most species are highly territorial during the breeding period and chase away other males that intrude into their territories.

Notes

Monitor lizards and agamids are not venomous, and they will not bite unless given no other choice. Large agamids are hunted by local people for food. Many people say they are delicious, the meat tasting, of course, like chicken. Monitor lizards have a very bad reputation in Thailand, and are believed to bring bad luck. To call someone a monitor lizard, *hia* in Thai, is considered an obscenity, and it is one sure way to see normally mild-mannered Thais become very angry.

Via interactions between the external environment and their hormonal and nervous systems, many agamids can change their body color. Some color changes are seasonal. For instance, territorial males often become brighter for a month or so during the breeding period, presumably helpful for attracting mates and repelling male competitors. Other color changes, in both males and females, take place over a much shorter timespan, seconds to a few minutes. Such color changes may be adaptations that allow them to be more *cryptic*, to blend into their surroundings, and hence, to be less detectable to predators. Alterations in color throughout the day may also aid in temperature regulation. Lizards must obtain their body heat from the sun, and darker colors absorb more heat. The feat is accomplished by moving pigment granules within individual skin cells either to a central clump (causing that color to diminish) or spreading them evenly about the cell (enhancing the color). It is now thought that the stimulus to change colors arises with the physiology of the animal rather than with the color of its surroundings.

Status

All monitors are listed by the CITES agreements (Appendix II), considered vulnerable or threatened; four species, including Indonesia's KOMODO DRAGON, are considered endangered (CITES Appendix I). Another of the four is Thailand's BENGAL MONITOR, which has a broad distribution in southern Asia; it is listed as endangered because of the demand for its skin. Thailand's WATER MONITOR is also often sought for its skin. Monitor lizard skin is used in the international fashion industry. For instance, 220,000 Bengal Monitor skins were exported from Indonesia in 1980. Most skins are destined for Europe, but Japan is also a big importer, especially for Asian monitor skin. In addition, in southern and Southeast Asia, monitors have historically been exploited for food, for traditional medicines, and for other uses (such as skin being used as drum heads). Monitor eggs are also dug up and eaten by people. Most monitor species occur in Australia, and they are fairly secure there, protected by state and federal laws; but six species are categorized as rare, vulnerable, or threatened by Australian conservation authorities. Several agamid lizard species are known to be threatened—for example, in Australia, where the GRASSLANDS EARLESS DRAGON has been in decline since its native grasslands were altered with introduced pasture grasses. The ecology and population statuses of most of Thailand's agamid lizards are too poorly known to comment on the state of their conservation.

Profiles

Bengal Monitor, *Varanus bengalensis,* Plate 14d
Garden Fence Lizard, *Calotes versicolor,* Plate 16a
Blue Crested Lizard, *Calotes mystaceus,* Plate 16b
Cross-bearing Tree Lizard, *Acanthosaura crucigera,* Plate 16c
Black-throated Gliding Lizard, *Draco melanopogon,* Plate 16d
Butterfly Lizard, *Leiolepis belliana,* Plate 16e
Indo-Chinese Waterdragon, *Physignathus cocincinus,* Plate 16f

5. Skinks and Grass Lizard

The *skinks* are a large family (Scincidae, with nearly 1,100 species, 43 species in Thailand) of small and medium-sized lizards with a worldwide distribution. Skinks are easily recognized because they look different from other lizards, being slim-bodied with relatively short limbs, and having smooth, shiny scales that produce a satiny look. Many are in the 5 to 9 cm (2 to 3.6 in) range, not including the tail, which can easily double an adult's length; some skinks, though, are as long as 50 cm (20 in).

Grass lizards constitute a relatively small family, Lacertidae (about 200 species total), which is distributed throughout the Old World (except Australia and Madagascar). Europe's COMMON WALL LIZARD is a member of this family. Only a single species of this family occurs in Thailand, the LONG-TAILED GRASS LIZARD (Plate 17). It is small, long-tailed, and agile.

Natural History

Ecology and Behavior

Many terrestrial skinks are found in moist habitats such as near streams and springs or under wet leaf litter. A few species are arboreal, and some are burrowers. Terrestrial and arboreal skinks tend to be day-active while the burrowing species tend to be crepuscular or nocturnal. Skinks use their limbs to walk but when the need arises for speed, they move by making rapid wriggling movements with their bodies, snake-fashion, with little leg assistance. Through evolutionary change, in fact, some species have lost limbs entirely, all movement being snake-like. Diurnal skinks in the tropics tend to be most active in the morning hours; they spend the heat of midday in sheltered, insulated hiding places, such as deep beneath the leaf litter. Some skinks are sit-and-wait foragers, whereas others actively seek their food. They consume many kinds of insects, which they grab, crush with their jaws or beat against the ground, then swallow whole. Predators of Thai skinks include snakes, larger lizards, birds, and mammals. Skinks generally are not seen unless searched for. Most species are quite secretive, spending most of their time hidden under rocks, vegetation, or leaf litter.

Grass Lizards, active during the day, are almost exclusively terrestrial and are usually found in sandy or grassy areas. They feed primarily on insects and other small invertebrates and apparently rely on smell to a considerable degree to locate their prey.

Breeding

Skinks are either egg-layers or live-bearers. Live-bearing skinks give birth to 3 to 8 young; the eggs are protected within the mother's body throughout development. Egg-laying species have clutches of 2 to 18 soft-shelled eggs that grow in size during incubation. The eggs are deposited in rotten wood or loose soil 5 to 8 cm (2 to 3 in) below the surface.

Grass lizards are egg-layers. The female places 6 to 13 soft-shelled eggs under stones or in shallow holes dug in the ground, and then covers them. The eggs hatch in 7 to 12 weeks. Males do not actively defend territories. Several species of this family in southwest Asia are *parthenogenic;* that is, there are no males, and eggs initiate development without male sperm.

Notes

Many lizards, including skinks and geckos, have a drastic predator escape mechanism: they leave their tails behind for the predator to attack and eat while they make their escape. The process is known as *tail autotomy*—"self removal." Owing to some unusual anatomical features of the tail vertebrae, the tail is only tenuously attached to the rest of the body; when the animal is grasped forcefully by its tail, the tail breaks off. The shed tail then wriggles vigorously for a while, diverting a predator's attention for the instant it takes the lizard to find shelter. A new tail can grow to replace the lost one (but this regeneration requires a lot of energy, so other growth and reproduction are usually curtailed for some period of time). New tails are often shorter or different shapes than original tails.

Is autotomy successful as a lifesaving tactic? Some snakes that have been dissected have had nothing but lizard tails in their stomachs. Also, a very common finding when a field biologist surveys any population of small lizards (catching as many as possible in a given area to count and examine them) is that often 50% or more have regenerating tails. This indicates that tail autotomy is common and successful in preventing predation.

Status

None of Thailand's skinks or its grass lizard are known to be threatened. As is the case for many reptiles, however, especially smaller ones, many species have not been sufficiently monitored to ascertain the health of populations. In other parts of the world, where research on skink populations has been conducted, some species have been found to be in trouble—many skinks of Australia and New Zealand, for instance, regularly make lists of vulnerable and threatened animals, and several Caribbean skinks are endangered. A main threat to skinks is alteration of their natural habitats for agriculture and development. Skinks and grass lizards fortunately do not encounter one hazard faced by other reptiles such as monitor lizards, tortoises, chameleons, and many kinds of snakes—they are not usually targets of the illicit international trade in exotic pets. On a worldwide list of the hundred or so wild-caught reptiles most often sold as exotic pets, there are only two skink species—huge ones that occur naturally in the Solomon Islands (PREHENSILE-TAILED SKINK) and Australia (BLUE-TONGUED SKINK).

Profiles

Long-tailed Grass Lizard, *Takydromus sexlineatus*, Plate 17a
Fire-tailed Tree-Skink, *Lipinia vittigera*, Plate 17b
Streamside Skink, *Sphenomorphus maculatus*, Plate 17c
Bowring's Supple Skink, *Lygosoma bowringii*, Plate 17d
Speckled Forest Skink, *Mabuya macularia*, Plate 17e
Many-lined Sun-Skink, *Mabuya multifasciata*, Plate 17f

6. Venomous Snakes

Many people think that all snakes, particularly tropical species, are venomous, and hence, must be avoided. Unfortunately, this "reptile anxiety" prevents some people from enjoying tropical forests. In Thailand about a third of snakes are very venomous, a third are only mildly venomous, and the remaining third are not venomous. Venomous snakes in Thailand's wild areas tend to be secretive and hard to find, even if you are looking for them. Therefore, with appropriate caution, you can enjoy your days in Thailand without worrying unduly about venomous snakes. If you do find one, you will likely discover that it is a beautiful animal and worth a look.

For convenience, we group together in this section what are usually considered the most highly venomous snakes, and so the most dangerous. Many of these snakes are well camouflaged, secretive in their habits, and/or nocturnal. Others, however, are highly colorful and out and about during the day.

Vipers, of family Viperidae (230 species total, 17 in Thailand), comprise the kingdom's most commonly seen venomous snakes. If you are trying to capture and eat a large animal without the benefit of hands and feet, any way of quickly stopping the prey from wriggling free of your grasp would be advantageous. Some groups of snakes have evolved just such a method—a venom-injection mechanism consisting of long, hollow fangs that introduce poison into the prey. Among the vipers, these poison-injecting fangs reach their greatest complexity. When not being used, the fangs lie flat, folded back against the upper jaw. When striking, the fangs are brought forward into position, pierce the prey, and then are withdrawn quickly from the victim after a fast injection of venom. Typically vipers coil prior to striking. They vary considerably in size, shape, color pattern, and lifestyle. Many viper species are referred to as *pit-vipers* because they have thermal-sensitive pits, or depressions, between their nostrils and eyes that are sensory organs. In Thailand, all but one of the viper species, RUSSELL'S VIPER, is a pit-viper. The familiar venomous snakes of North America—*rattlesnakes, copperheads,* and *water moccasins* —are all pit-vipers. Many of Thailand's vipers are brightly colored.

Family Elapidae (270 species total, 13 species in Thailand) contains what are regarded as the world's deadliest snakes, the Old World *cobras, kraits,* and *mambas.* In the Western Hemisphere, the group is represented by *coral snakes*—slender snakes that are usually quite gaily attired in rings of red, yellow, and black. *Elapids* have a very powerful venom. Unlike vipers, the fangs of elapids are held permanently erect at the front of the jaws. When the snake's mouth is closed, the fangs fit into a pocket in the gum tissue inside the lower lip. Some of the cobras spit their venom into the eyes of enemies. This thin stream of venom can be sprayed with great force up to almost 2 m (6.6 ft) with extreme accuracy. Washed out immediately, the venom usually has minimal long-term effect on the eye, but if left in, can cause blindness. The KING COBRA (Plate 19) is usually considered the world's longest venomous snake. It reaches lengths of more than 5 m (16.5 ft), although in Thailand a King Cobra longer than 4 m (13 ft) would be very rare. Although of great length, they are usually quite slender—one that was 4.7 m (15.4 ft) long weighed only 12 kg (26.5 lb).

The world's 55 or so species of sea snakes, which inhabit most regions of tropical and subtropical oceans, are sometimes considered members of family Elapidae, but other experts place them in their own group, family Hydrophidae. They are represented in Thailand by 26 species, but most of these occur in Thai waters only very rarely. They differ from elapids in their adaptations for living in tropical oceans. Their tails and lower bodies are flattened side to side into the shape of a narrow paddle, and their nostrils can be closed tightly like a valve when swimming underwater. Many, such as the YELLOW-BELLIED SEA SNAKE (Plate 19), are brightly colored with splashes of yellow against dark bodies.

Natural History

Ecology and Behavior

A majority of Thai vipers are primarily arboreal. After striking a victim for food, the viper follows the prey's scent trail using its long, forked tongue as a chemical (odor) sensing device. Perhaps to avoid being bitten, scratched, or stung, the snake waits until the victim dies before swallowing it. Food varies from small birds, mammals, and reptiles, to large insects and scorpions. Pit-vipers (and some other snakes) can sense the heat radiated by prey animals, which assists their foraging. Searching by heat detection probably works for both warm-blooded prey (birds, mammals) and cold-blooded (insects, lizards, frogs), as long as the prey is at a higher temperature than its surroundings. Two terrestrial vipers, the MALAYAN PIT-VIPER (Plate 18) and RUSSELL'S VIPER, are widely distributed in the Thai lowlands and account for the vast majority of venomous snakebites in the kingdom.

Cobras occur in a wide range of habitats, from forest floor, termite nests, and agricultural fields to human habitations. They are frequently found near water and are good swimmers. Normally docile and shy, they can be notoriously fierce when disturbed, their peculiarly flattened necks (hoods) projecting a warning that few will ignore. Cobras are generally nocturnal and crepuscular, but they can also be seen foraging during the day. They feed on rats, frogs, birds, lizards, other snakes, and eggs. KING COBRAS mainly feed on other snakes, and have even been known to take large Reticulated Pythons; they also eat monitor lizards.

Kraits are usually secretive and difficult to observe; consequently relatively little is known about their ecology and behavior in the wild. They apparently forage by crawling along slowly on the ground, intermittently poking their heads into the leaf litter. They eat lizards, caecilians (p. 79), and small snakes, which they kill with their powerful venom. They are often found under rocks and logs, and many probably burrow into the soil for protection, and while foraging. They can be day- or night-active.

Some sea snakes can spend considerable time out of water, but they tend to be awkward on land and at these times are restricted to mangrove areas. Other species are entirely or almost entirely restricted to the ocean. At sea they seldom occur far from shallow coastal shelf waters. They feed primarily on fish, and are often found in fishermen's nets. Following major storms, numerous sea snakes become washed up on Thailand's beaches. (If you find one on a beach, leave it alone—these snakes are dangerous.) Sea eagles (Plate 27) are major predators on these snakes. Although very poisonous, sea snakes are generally docile around humans swimming or wading in their habitat.

Breeding

Details of the breeding in the wild of most tropical vipers are not well known. Many may follow the general system of North American rattlesnakes, which have been much studied. Female rattlesnakes attract males when they are ready to mate by releasing *pheromones* (odor chemicals) into the air and also, through the skin of their sides and back, onto the ground. Males search for females. When one is located, the male accompanies and courts her for several days before mating occurs. Although North American rattlers have distinct breeding periods, many tropical vipers may breed at almost any time of year. Most of the vipers give birth to live young.

Cobras form pairs that stay together from courtship to hatching of the young. The nest of up to 25 eggs is guarded by both parents, and at this time they can be quite aggressive. Incubation of the eggs takes from 70 to 80 days. Kraits also lay eggs, but little is known of their breeding biology.

Some sea snake species come to shore to lay their eggs, but most of the species give birth to live young. The young are born on shore in tide pools or at sea, depending on the species.

Notes

All of the venomous snakes discussed in this section, if encountered, should be given a wide berth. Watch them only from a distance. Very few visitors to the tropics, even those that spend their days tramping through forests, are bitten by venomous snakes. Remember that their venom-delivery system is a highly evolved prey-capture strategy, and only secondarily a defensive mechanism. Venom is energetically costly to produce, and venomous snakes can bite without injecting any venom. They can also vary the amount of venom injected, so even if a person is bitten, he or she does not necessarily receive a fatal dose. Within the same species, the toxicity of a snake's venom can vary geographically, seasonally, and from individual to individual.

Venom is not a single substance but rather a complex mixture of components containing a variety of proteins designed to destroy specific targets, such as nerves or blood. Venom is stored in glands situated behind a snake's eyes and is carried to the front of the head, where it enters a duct or groove in a fang and travels down to the tip to be injected into prey. Because snake venoms are such complex mixtures of poisons that have varying physiological effects on the prey (or person) that is injected, generalities about the effects of a certain type of snake's venom are often misleading. From a practical standpoint, what is important for treatment of snakebite is that if at all possible, the snake involved be correctly identified. This is because there are usually different types of pharmaceuticals (anti-venoms) to treat bites of different snake species. (However, some new anti-venoms, in Australia for instance, can be used to treat bites of multiple species, so in some regions of the world, identification of the offending snake is no longer so important.) Hospitals sometimes have test kits to determine the species of snake responsible.

If someone is bitten, do not bother about washing the site of the bite and do not cut the site. Apply a broad constrictive bandage as soon as possible, working from the site of the bite toward the heart. Most bites occur on a limb, and as much of the limb as possible should be bound. Wind the bandage firmly but not too tightly. Immobilize the limb with a splint or sling. Keep the bitten person calm, do not administer alcohol, and keep movement to a minimum. Transport the person to the nearest hospital.

Status

Because the snakes detailed in this section can be deadly, there is fascination with them from keepers of exotic pets worldwide, but also concerns about safety. They are traded on the illicit international market in exotic pets, but in relatively small numbers. Some Asian species, however, are hunted for their skins, which are shipped to Europe, Japan, or the US for the fashion industry (shoes, boots, belts, handbags, etc.). Two Thai species, which are also widely distributed over southern Asia, are taken frequently for this purpose, the KING COBRA and COMMON COBRA; these species are considered threatened by this hunting pressure on their populations, so are listed in CITES Appendix II. The biology of most sea snake species is poorly known, so evaluating the statuses of their populations is difficult. Although no sea snakes are known to be presently threatened, these snakes are used for food, leather, and medicines in various parts of the world (several species, for example, are caught in the Philippines, processed, and exported as "sea snake leather"), and large numbers of them are sometimes caught accidentally in nets used in the fisheries industry.

Profiles

White-lipped Pit-Viper, *Trimeresurus albolabris,* Plate 18d
Malayan Pit-Viper, *Calloselasma rhodostoma,* Plate 18e
Small-spotted Coral Snake, *Calliophis maculiceps,* Plate 19a
Blue Krait, *Bungarus candidus,* Plate 19b
Banded Krait, *Bungarus fasciatus,* Plate 19c
Monocellate Cobra, *Naja kaouthia,* Plate 19d

King Cobra, *Ophiophagus hannah*, Plate 19e
Yellow-bellied Sea Snake, *Pelamis platurus*, Plate 19f

7. Pythons and Miscellaneous Snakes

Members of the snake family Boidae kill their prey by constriction. The family encompasses 63 species (three in Thailand) distributed throughout the world's tropical and subtropical regions. *Boids* (BOH-ids) include the Old World *pythons* and the New World *boas* and *anacondas*. Pythons and anacondas are the world's largest snakes. Thailand's most common python, the RETICULATED PYTHON (Plate 18), often reaches lengths of about 5 m (16.5 ft), but typically individuals are only 1.5 to 2.5 m (5 to 8 ft) long. One specimen from Borneo was reportedly 10 m (33 ft) long! The other species that occur regularly in Thailand are the BURMESE PYTHON, which ranges up to 6 m (19.5 ft) long (most, of course, being much shorter), and the uncommon brown or reddish BLOOD PYTHON, which only reaches about 2.75 m (9 ft) at its maximum length. Pythons have shiny, smooth scales and most species exhibit patterns of dark, squarish shapes that provide good camouflage against an array of backgrounds.

Several other families of non-venomous snakes also are represented in Thailand. *Blind snakes* (also called *worm snakes*; family Typhlopidae) have characteristics intermediate between snakes and lizards and have been classified as both at one time or another. There are a total of about 40 species of these worm-like snakes distributed in South/Central America, Africa, southern Asia, and Australia. Eight occur in Thailand, including MUELLER'S BLIND SNAKE (Plate 18). Blind snakes are dark and shiny, with blunt heads, cylindrical bodies, and short tails that end in a spine; they range from 20 to 80 cm (8 to 31 in) long.

Pipe snakes (family Anilidae; 10 species total, occurring only in South America and southern Asia) are represented by a single species in Thailand, the RED-TAILED PIPE SNAKE (Plate 18). It is cylindrical, with a short, thick tail that is peculiarly red on the underside. The SUNBEAM SNAKE (Plate 18) is the sole member of another family, Xenopeltidae. This species, restricted to Southeast Asia, is characterized by iridescent scales that reflect light and appear bright blue, green, red, or purple, depending on the angle between the snake and observer. The body is cylindrical and the tail short.

Natural History

Ecology and Behavior

Some pythons burrow in the soil, others are arboreal, and others are frequently found in the water. They feed on large birds and mammals, which they suffocate in their coils. RETICULATED PYTHONS, terrestrial and arboreal, occur mainly in moister forests from lowland areas up to about 1,500 m (4,900 ft) elevation, but are also seen in agricultural areas and even around towns and villages. They eat mammals up to the size of pigs and deer.

Blind snakes are usually found burrowing in the soil of fields, gardens, and even flower pots, where they eat soil invertebrates. They are one of the most common kinds of snakes in Thailand, but are rarely seen, or if seen, typically mistaken for earthworms. RED-TAILED PIPE SNAKES frequent swampy areas and often swim. They feed primarily at night on other snakes, eels, and worms, and have been known to consume eels that weigh almost as much as themselves. When one of these snakes is threatened, it lifts its colorful tail off the ground and displays its pattern much as many venomous snakes do. The SUNBEAM SNAKE burrows in soft soil and is often found underneath logs and stones in rice paddies and gardens. It feeds at night on other snakes, small mammals, and frogs.

Breeding
Some members of the python family give birth to live young, but the RETICULATED PYTHON lays as many as 100 eggs in a shallow pit in the forest floor. Here the mother broods the eggs for as long as 75 days. With her coils wrapped protectively around the eggs, and by flexing her muscles and so generating heat, evidently she can raise the temperature in the nest by 3 or 4° C (6 or 7° F). She can also be fairly aggressive toward intruders at this time.

Blind snake reproductive behavior is very poorly known. Some species lay 2 to 7 tiny oval eggs, but other species give birth to live young. The RED-TAILED PIPE SNAKE gives birth to 2 to 3 live young, each about 13 cm (5 in) long. The secretive SUNBEAM SNAKE'S reproductive behavior is almost completely unknown.

Notes
RETICULATED PYTHONS are amazingly adaptable, and they often occur near or in human habitation. The old sewage system of Bangkok, with its protected sites and unlimited rat population, is apparently a favorite haunt of pythons. Following heavy rains that overload the sewage system, it is not unusual to find pythons that are 5 m (16.5 ft) long appearing in flooded streets, gardens, and homes. Unfortunately these beautiful snakes are captured in large numbers for a variety of reasons: to be kept locally as pets or to be sold for the illicit international trade in exotic pets; for export to zoos; or for their skin, meat, or other body parts (see below). In Thailand, a drink of python blood in the morning is considered a good way to stimulate yourself when you are tired.

Python personalities vary; some are docile, while others are very willing to defend themselves. Pythons may hiss loudly at people, draw their heads back with mouths open in a threat posture, and bite. They have large, sharp teeth that can cause deep puncture wounds. Also, there are stories and even some photos of giant RETICULATED PYTHONS killing and eating people. Therefore, even though pythons, even large ones, present little threat to adult people, keeping a respectful distance is strongly advised.

Status
Worldwide, all members of family Boidae (pythons and boas) are CITES Appendix II listed, considered vulnerable or threatened, mainly because they are frequent victims of the illicit international trade in exotic "pet" animals and the trade in reptile skins for the fashion industry. Four pythons, three of which occur in Thailand, are killed in large numbers and traded for their skins: AFRICAN ROCK PYTHON, BURMESE PYTHON (also called Asian Rock Python and, in India, Indian Python; the Indian Python is considered endangered, CITES Appendix I listed), BLOOD PYTHON, and RETICULATED PYTHON. The Reticulated Python is the most often traded member of the group. For instance, four million skins were traded from 1983 to 1989; most come from Indonesia, but many come from other countries, including Thailand. The skins eventually reach Europe, Japan, or the US. These four species, along with several other pythons, are also popular as exotic pets, frequently sold in pet stores around the globe. Constrictors, such as pythons, are sometimes positively regarded in Asia,

permitted to roam villages and agricultural districts because of their rodent-catching ways.

Many blind snake species are listed by various conservation authorities as being of concern, mainly because they are known from only a few specimens. Pipe snakes and the SUNBEAM SNAKE are common and probably not threatened.

Profiles

Mueller's Blind Snake, *Typhlops muelleri*, Plate 18a
Red-tailed Pipe Snake, *Cylindrophis ruffus*, Plate 18b
Sunbeam Snake, *Xenopeltis unicolor*, Plate 18c
Reticulated Python, *Python reticulatus*, Plate 18f

8. Colubrids: Your Regular, Everyday Snakes

The largest group of snakes is the family Colubridae—the *colubrid* snakes. Most of these are nonvenomous or, if venomous, dangerous only to small prey such as lizards and rodents. This is a worldwide group comprising more than 1,700 species, of which 103 occur in Thailand. Most of the snakes with which people are familiar, such as *water, brown, garter, whip, green, rat,* and *wolf snakes,* are colubrids, and the family has a wide variety of habits and lifestyles. It is not possible here to provide a general physical description of all colubrid snakes because of the great variety of shapes and colors associated with their respective lifestyles. Most people will not get close enough to notice, but an expert could identify colubrids by their anatomy. Colubrids have rows of teeth on the upper and lower jaws but they do not have hollow, venom-injecting fangs in front on the upper jaw. If they have venom, it is usually weak and administered by somewhat longer teeth in the back of the mouth, by the so-called *rear-fanged* snakes.

Natural History

Ecology and Behavior

Because colubrids vary so much in their natural history, we will concentrate on the habits of some of the representative species profiled in the color plates, grouped by habitat: arboreal, terrestrial, and aquatic. Arboreal snakes spend most of their time in trees and shrubs. The PAINTED BRONZEBACK (Plate 22), for example, is a slender arboreal snake that feeds on lizards and frogs. Their thin, long bodies resemble vines, and if not moving, these snakes are very difficult to see. They rely on camouflage for both hunting and protection, freezing in place when alerted to danger. MANGROVE CAT-SNAKES (Plate 22), also arboreal, have broad, triangular heads, long, stout bodies, and short tails. They forage at night in mangroves and shrubs of coastal forests for small frogs, birds, lizards, rodents, and other snakes. Another group of arboreal tree snakes are the so-called *flying snakes,* which includes the GOLDEN TREE-SNAKE (Plate 22). These slender, meter-long (3 ft) snakes have a long tail that makes up a quarter of the body length. They can launch themselves into the air from a branch, straightening out the body and drawing in the belly scales to form a concave gliding parachute that enables them to fall great distances at controlled speed. They are active during the day, and with their rear fangs and a mild venom, they move very quickly to catch and subdue their main prey, arboreal lizards.

Typical of terrestrial colubrids in Thailand are the *racers* in genus *Elaphe* (Plate 21). They are long, slender, and as their name suggests, very fast-moving. They are active mainly during the day, searching for rats and birds. Although they are nonvenomous, they often act very aggressive when cornered and can bite. The small *slug-eating snakes* (such as the WHITE-SPOTTED SLUG-SNAKE; Plate 21) have a blunt head and short tail. They crawl at night on the forest floor, searching for their namesake food, slugs. Looking and acting very much like a viper, the COMMON MOCK VIPER (Plate 21) is active at night on the forest floor. Its bite, although painful, is not dangerous.

Most aquatic colubrids are rear-fanged and mildly venomous. The YELLOW-BELLY WATERSNAKE (Plate 20) is typical of this group of snakes. It is common in swampy areas, drainage ditches, rice paddies, and buffalo wallows, where it moves in and out of the aquatic environment from one wet area to another. It actively pursues fish and frogs in the shallow water during the day and at night. At the other end of the spectrum of aquatic colubrids is the bizarre TENTACLED SNAKE (Plate 20), which is restricted almost exclusively to living in lakes and ponds. Its adaptations for underwater feeding and respiration are the focus of research by physiologists as well as behavioral ecologists. The unique worm-like tentacles extending from the side of its mouth are evidently used as lures to attract fish as the snake lies motionless on the bottom of a lake or pond.

Breeding

Relatively little is known of the breeding patterns of Thai colubrids. The typical number of eggs per clutch varies from species to species, but some lay small clutches of 1 to 3 eggs. Most colubrids that lay eggs deposit them in a suitable location and depart; the parents provide no care of the eggs or young. Female BANDED RAT-SNAKES (Plate 21) are unusual in that they apparently guard their clutch of eggs. Some species, especially among the watersnakes, give birth to live young.

Notes

Snakes' limbless condition, their manner of movement, and the venomous nature of some of them have engendered fear in people stretching back thousands of years. Myths about the evil power and intentions of snakes are ubiquitous, though one need go no farther than the Old Testament, in which the snake plays the pivotal role as Eve's corrupt enticer, responsible for humans' expulsion from the Garden of Eden. Because these myths cross so many cultures, sociobiologists have hypothesized that fear of snakes may be instinctive. Some studies of monkey behavior seem to support this possibility. But another school of thought is that in humans, at least, the fear response to snakes is largely learned. We lean toward the latter argument, based primarily on our visits to grade schools with live snakes in hand—most young children seem to lack the fear of snakes often exhibited by their parents.

Although snakes are feared by many people, they are also a source of fascination for those same people. Snakes are despised in many cultures, but are worshiped by some; they symbolize disease and danger in some cases, but health in others. No doubt because of their ability to throw off their old skins and acquire fresh ones, snakes also represent rejuvenation and immortality in diverse cultures around the world.

Status

Worldwide, about 30 colubrid species are listed as vulnerable, threatened, or endangered. The leading threats are habitat destruction and the introduction by people of exotic animals that prey on snakes at some point in their lifecycles. In

Thailand, the population levels of most colubrids are so poorly known that their conservation status is difficult to determine.

The nonvenomous BANDED RAT-SNAKE (Plate 21), which resembles the KING COBRA in size and coloration, is a special case. It is often considered the largest colubrid snake in the world, reaching lengths of 3.5 m (11.5 ft) in parts of its range (which is most of southern Asia), and it is (still) fairly common. Because of its size and abundance, this species (and another closely related Thai species, the INDO-CHINESE RAT-SNAKE) has become one of the most sought-after reptiles for its skin. Snake skins are used in the fashion industry; they are exported in large quantities from many Asian countries, including Thailand, and shipped to Europe, Japan, and the US. In 1984 alone, for example, 734,000 skins of the Banded Rat-Snake were imported into the USA. Because of the huge demand for its skin, the Banded Rat-Snake is one of only a few colubrid snakes listed (Appendix II) in the international CITES trade agreements.

Profiles

Yellowbelly Watersnake, *Enhydris plumbea*, Plate 20a
Dog-faced Watersnake, *Cerberus rynchops*, Plate 20b
Puff-faced Watersnake, *Homalopsis buccata*, Plate 20c
Tentacled Snake, *Erpeton tentaculatum*, Plate 20d
Checkered Keelback, *Xenochrophis piscator*, Plate 20e
Red-necked Keelback, *Rhabdophis subminiatus*, Plate 20f
White-spotted Slug-Snake, *Pareas margaritophorus*, Plate 21a
Common Mock Viper, *Psammodynastes pulverulentus*, Plate 21b
Striped Kukri Snake, *Oligodon taeniatus*, Plate 21c
Green Tree Racer, *Elaphe prasina*, Plate 21d
Southern Stripe-tailed Racer, *Elaphe taeniura ridleyi*, Plate 21e
Banded Rat-Snake, *Ptyas mucosus*, Plate 21f
Golden Tree-Snake, *Chrysopelea ornata*, Plate 22a
Painted Bronzeback, *Dendrelaphis pictus*, Plate 22b
Oriental Whip-Snake, *Ahaetulla prasina*, Plate 22c
House Wolf-Snake, *Lycodon aulicus*, Plate 22d
Spotted Cat-Snake, *Boiga multomaculata*, Plate 22e
Mangrove Cat-Snake, *Boiga dendrophila*, Plate 22f

Environmental Close-up 4.
Endemism and High Species Diversity: Why Thailand?

An organism is *endemic* to a place when it is found only in that place. But the size or type of place referred to is variable: a given species of frog, for example, may be endemic to the Eastern Hemisphere, to a single continent such as Asia, to a mountainous region of Thailand, or to a speck of an island off Thailand's coast.

A species' history dictates much of its present distribution. When it's confined to a certain or small area, the reason may be that: (1) there are one or more barriers to stop further spread (an ocean, a mountain range, a thousand kilometers or miles of tropical rainforest in the way), (2) the species evolved only recently and has not yet had time to spread, or (3) the species evolved long ago, spread long ago, and now has become extinct over all but a remnant part of its prior range. A history of isolation also matters: the longer a group of animals or plants is isolated from its close relatives, the more time it has to evolve by itself and to change into new, different, and unique groups. The best examples are on islands. Some islands once were attached to mainland areas, but continental drift and/or changing sea levels led to their isolation in the middle of the ocean; other islands arose suddenly via volcanic activity beneath the seas. Take the island of Madagascar, for example. Once attached to Africa and India, the organisms stranded on its shores when it became an island had probably 100 million years in isolation to develop into the highly endemic fauna and flora we see today. It's thought that about 80% of the island's plants and animals are endemic—half the bird species, about 800 butterflies, 8,000 flowering plants, and essentially all the mammals and reptiles. Most of the species of lemurs of the world—small, primitive but cute primates—occur only on Madagascar, and an entire nature tourism industry has been built there around the idea of endemism: if you want to see wild lemurs, you must go there. Other examples of islands with high concentrations of endemic animals abound: Indonesia, where about 15% of the world's bird species occur, a quarter of them endemic; Papua New Guinea, where half the birds are endemic; the Philippines, where half the mammals are endemic; and the Galápagos Islands, where 42% of the resident bird species occur nowhere else in the world.

Recent biological surveys of Thailand show that it supports a surprising number of species (some of which are endemic but most of which are not). Thailand is, in fact, considered one of the 15 or so most bio-diverse countries in the world—meaning it has more species of animals and plants than most other regions (see Table 1). Thailand's high biodiversity is due to several factors:

(1) Virtually all groups of animals and plants, such as lizards, insects, trees, and birds, show a pattern of species number related to latitude. The higher latitudes (the north and south poles are at 90° E latitude and the equator is at 0° E latitude) have few species, and at lower and lower latitudes toward the equator, the number of species increases. This pattern is called a *latitudinal gradient in species diversity* and is likely caused by an increasing availability of sunlight energy, photosynthetic rates, and thus food availability as you move toward the equator. Thailand is close to the equator, where the world's greatest species diversity occurs.

(2) Due to Thailand's *topography* (land surface configuration and altitudinal relief), there are a multitude of habitat types, and some highly isolated habitats that act as "biological islands" (for example, mountain tops surrounded by lower lying regions). These isolated areas support several endemics, and the wide range of habitat types, especially at different altitudes, makes room for lots of species, endemic and non-endemic, to exist in a relatively small area.

(3) The country's central location places it at a crossroads of dispersal routes that have brought in, over many thousands of years, Indonesian–Malayan plant and animal species from the south, Indian species from the west, and Central Asian species from the north. Thailand shares a different set of species with each of its neighboring countries, but not all the species with any single country.

Group	Total Number of Species in US	Total Number of Species in Thailand	Number of Species Endemic to Thailand (% Endemic)	Approx. No. of Species Worldwide (% in Thailand)
Mammals	428	297	5 (2)	4629 (6)
Birds	700	970	2 (0.2)	9040 (11)
Reptiles	261	317	31 (10)	7000 (5)
Amphibians	517	107	10 (10)	4700 (2)
Butterflies	678	1140	2 (0.2)	24,000 (5)
Tiger Beetles	108	123	29 (24)	2600 (5)

Table 1 Number of species of selected animal groups in Thailand (513,115 sq km, 198,115 sq mi, in area) and in the US (9.4 million sq km, 3.6 million sq mi), the number of those that are endemic to Thailand, and a comparison to the worldwide number of species.

Chapter 8

BIRDS

- *Introduction*
- *General Characteristics and Classification*
- *Features of Tropical Birds*
- *Seeing Birds in Thailand*
- *Family Profiles*
    1. *Pelican Allies*
    2. *Herons and Egrets*
    3. *Marsh and Stream Birds*
    4. *Ducks*
    5. *Terns and Gulls*
    6. *Shorebirds (Waders)*
    7. *Pheasants and Buttonquail*
    8. *Hawks, Eagles, and Kites*
    9. *Falcons*
    10. *Pigeons and Doves*
    11. *Parrots*
    12. *Cuckoos*
    13. *Owls*
    14. *Nightjars and Frogmouths*
    15. *Trogons*
    16. *Kingfishers*
    17. *Bee-eaters and Rollers*
    18. *Hornbills*
    19. *Barbets*
    20. *Woodpeckers*

21. *Broadbills and Pittas*

22. *Swifts, Treeswifts, and Swallows*

23. *Pipits and Cuckoo-shrikes*

24. *Ioras and Leafbirds*

25. *Bulbuls*

26. *Drongos and Orioles*

27. *Crows and Magpies*

28. *Tits and Nuthatches*

29. *Babblers*

30. *Old World Warblers*

31. *Thrushes*

32. *Old World Flycatchers*

33. *Shrikes and Starlings*

34. *Sunbirds, Flowerpeckers, and White-eyes*

35. *Sparrows, Munias, and Finches*

- *Environmental Close-Up 5: Frugivory: Animals That Eat Fruit and the Trees That Want Them To*

Introduction

By far the most common vertebrate animals you will see on a visit to Thailand are birds. Unlike many other terrestrial vertebrates, birds are most often active during the day, visually conspicuous and usually quite vocal as they pursue their daily activities. But why are birds so much more conspicuous than other vertebrates? The reason goes to the essential nature of birds: they fly. The ability to fly is one of nature's premier anti-predator escape mechanisms, and animals that can fly well are released from the danger of being stalked by a large proportion of the predators in an area. Most mortality from predators among tropical birds comes while they are eggs or helpless young in the nest. Once they reach adulthood, their mortality rate by predation falls to very low levels. By being able to escape most predation, they are released from much of the tyranny of natural selection that places a premium on camouflage, unobtrusiveness, and shyness. Thus they can be both reasonably conspicuous in their behavior and also reasonably certain of daily survival. Most flightless land vertebrates, tied by gravity to moving in or over the ground or on plants, are easy prey unless they are quiet, concealed, and careful or, alternatively, very large or fierce; many smaller ones, in fact, have evolved special defense mechanisms, such as poisons or nocturnal behavior.

Not only are birds among the easiest animals to watch, but they are among the most beautiful. Experiences with Thailand's birds will almost certainly provide some of your trip's most memorable naturalistic moments. Your first view of a pair of huge and noisy Great Hornbills flying over the forest tops in a southern national park or of a flock of thousands of nesting Asian Openbill Storks near Bangkok will be highlights you will want to share with everyone.

General Characteristics and Classification

Birds have one trait that they share with no other vertebrates—they have *feathers*. Feathers evidently evolved from reptilian scales, and they, together with most everything else in and on the bird body, serve to lighten the load and provide the power to make flight possible. The feathers provide an ultra-light but durable protective covering. The hollow bones of the skeleton provide a light but sturdy framework to attach powerful flight muscles, especially on the breast. The teeth are replaced by an expanded part of the digestive tract, the *gizzard*, which, along with the reduction and rearrangement of many internal organs, makes the center of gravity more aerodynamically positioned. A four-chambered heart together with warm-bloodedness and a super-efficient lung system make possible an accelerated use of energy to sustain the physiologically expensive costs of flight. Finally, the forelimbs have evolved to become sublime wings, with spoilers to overcome wing-tip air turbulence, ailerons for maneuvering, and such a host of detailed adaptations for flight control that engineers at the Boeing Company can only marvel with envy.

Birds began evolving from reptiles during the Jurassic Period of the Mesozoic Era, perhaps 150 million years ago, and then there was an explosive development of new species during the last 50 million years or so. The development of flight is the key factor behind birds' evolution, their historical spread throughout the globe, and their current ecological success. Flight, as mentioned above, is a fantastic predator evasion technique, but it also permits birds to move over long distances in search of particular foods or habitats, and its development opened up an entirely new and vast theater of operations for vertebrate exploration and exploitation—the atmosphere.

At first glance, birds appear to be highly variable beasts, ranging in size from 135-kg (300-lb) ostriches to 4-kg (10-lb) eagles to 3-gram (a tenth of an ounce) hummingbirds. However, when compared to other types of vertebrates, birds are remarkably standardized physically. The reason is that, whereas mammals or reptiles can be quite diverse in form and still function as mammals or reptiles (think how different in form are lizards, snakes, and turtles), if birds are going to fly, the physics of aerodynamics narrowly dictates which shape and form will most efficiently stay in the air. Thus, all flying birds have a similar gestalt, or body plan. (The flying mammals, bats, also follow these dictates.) Only birds such as ostriches, which have lost the ability to fly, developed very un-birdlike body shapes.

Bird classification is one of those areas of science that continually undergoes revision. Currently more than 9,000 separate species are recognized worldwide, and they are placed in 2,040 genera. These genera are grouped into 170 families, which in turn are grouped into 28 to 30 orders, depending on whose classification scheme you want to follow. The orders are roughly divided into two major groups, the perching ("dickie bird") species such as robins, sparrows, and jays (passerines) and all the rest (non-passerines), including everything from penguins, ducks, and herons to parrots, kingfishers, and hawks. For this book we divide birds into various groups: those that are unrelated but occur together in broad habitat types; those that are similar in appearance and might be confused easily; and finally, those that are closely related (and thus often found in similar habitats and also often similar in appearance).

Features of Tropical Birds

The first thing to know about tropical birds is that they are exceedingly diverse. There are many more species of birds in the tropics than in temperate or arctic regions (see Close-up, p. 115). For instance, somewhat fewer than 700 bird species occur regularly in North America north of Mexico, but more than 950 species are found in the relatively small area of Thailand.

Tropical birds, like their temperate zone brethren, eat insects, seeds, nectar, fruits, and, for the predaceous species, meat. A big difference, however, is the degree of specialization in tropical species. In temperate areas fruit is such a temporary resource that few species can afford to make their living as confirmed *frugivores,* but in many tropical areas fruit is available throughout much of the year, so bird species have evolved bills, digestive systems, and behavior that make them experts on finding and eating fruits. Similarly, species that eat insects (*insectivores*), seeds (*granivores*), flower nectar (*nectarivores*), and, to some degree, even the meat-eaters (*carnivores*), have high degrees of specialization.

Mating systems of birds show a pattern of inequality between the sexes. Females generally have the most power to choose mates. Each male is thus left with the task of convincing these picky females that he and he alone is the most appropriate one to father their young. A male can scream this message with louder or prettier songs, longer and more colorful tail feathers, or a combination of sounds, colors, and behavioral antics that increase his chances of convincing a female of his gene superiority.

Mating systems range from single territorial males with one female (*monogamy*) to one male having numerous female mates (*polygyny*) and even some cases of a female having numerous male mates (*polyandry*). Among tropical birds, monogamy is apparently the most common form of mating, although we now know that a lot of extracurricular sneaking around goes on. Monogamous mating is perhaps made most obvious when the males sing on the boundaries of their territories to declare to all the world, but especially to other males of the same species, "Stay out. This is my home and you are not welcome to tarry here." Polygyny is less common but often made obvious by the many bizarre behaviors associated with this mating system. In some polygynous species, males congregate together, each male in the group strutting his gene superiority so that a female can compare them side by side and make her choice—a kind of beauty contest. This type of congregated male courting is called a *lek*. Females in this type of society are usually single working mothers because the father, after mating, has no further contact with his mate or his eventual offspring. Polyandry is the rarest type of mating system, and it is practiced primarily by only three groups of birds in Thailand: painted snipe, buttonquail, and jacanas. In these cases, males guard nests and females lay eggs in each of several males' nests after mating with them.

Breeding seasons in the tropics tend to be longer than in temperate areas but are usually closely tied to the wet season and the abundance of food associated with it, especially heavy concentrations of insect life and ripening fruit. In Thailand, birds breed primarily at the beginning of the wet season, from February to July. One notable aspect of bird breeding in the tropics that has long puzzled biologists is that clutches of the small land birds (passerines) are usually small, most species typically laying only two eggs per nest. Similar birds that breed in temperate zone areas usually have clutches of three to five eggs. Possible explanations are that (1) small broods attract fewer nest predators; (2) because such a high percentage of nests in the tropics are destroyed by predators, it is not worth putting too much energy and effort into any one nest; and (3) with the increased hours of daylight during the summer breeding season in northern areas, temperate zone birds have more time each day to gather enough food for extra nestlings.

Finally, tropical birds include some of the most gorgeously attired birds in the world. Many have bright, flashy colors and vivid plumage patterns, with some of Thailand's pittas, barbets, trogons, leafbirds, and minivets claiming top honors. Why so many tropical birds possess highly colored plumages is unknown, but it may be at least partially explained by the presence of a large number of species in which males are under natural selection pressures by female mating choices to have gaudy plumage. Also, although people take more notice of birds with bright, striking plumage colors and patterns, we should point out that, actually, most species in the tropics are dull-colored and visually unremarkable. In addition, nearly one quarter of Thailand's bird species are visitors that migrate south from their nesting grounds in Central Asia to spend a warm winter. Many of these species have drab winter plumages that are changed into brighter colors just before they return in the spring (March–May) to their nesting areas in the north.

In Thailand, many bird species are experiencing declining population sizes because of deforestation, poaching, and unlicensed hunting. The IUCN Red List for Thailand includes 90 bird species that are considered near-threatened, 26 that are vulnerable, five that are endangered (Storm's Stork, Greater Adjutant, White-winged Duck, Chestnut-headed Partridge, Nordmann's Greenshank), and four that are critically endangered (White-rumped Vulture, Chinese Crested-tern, Gurney's Pitta, White-eyed River-Martin); the latter two critically endangered species are endemic to Thailand (although Gurney's Pitta was recently found in Myanmar for the first time since 1914).

Seeing Birds in Thailand

We chose for illustration and profiling below 187 species that are among Thailand's most frequently seen birds, or, in a few cases, rare species that are representative of some of Thailand's vanishing habitats. The best way to spot these birds is to follow three easy steps: (1) Look for them at the correct time. You can see birds at any time of the day, but your best chance of seeing them is when they are most active and singing frequently, during early morning and late afternoon. Some species of owls, frogmouths, and nightjars are strictly nocturnal, and the best way to see them is to follow their calls at night and find them in the beam of your flashlight. (2) Be quiet as you walk along trails or roads, and stop periodically to look around carefully. Not all birds are noisy, and some, even brightly-colored ones, can be quite inconspicuous when they are skulking through thick grass or are directly above you in the forest canopy. Trogons, for instance, beautiful medium-sized birds with green backs and bright red or orange bellies, are notoriously difficult to see among branches and leaves. Sometimes sitting or standing quietly, especially along a stream, is the best way to see otherwise shy denizens. (3) BRING BINOCULARS on your trip. You would be surprised at the number of people who visit tropical areas with the purpose of viewing wildlife and don't bother to bring binoculars. They need not be an expensive pair, but binoculars are essential to bird viewing. If you become excited about wildlife in the middle of your trip and have no binoculars, many eco-lodges rent them out by the day.

A surprise to many people during their first trip to the tropics, especially to a habitat like tropical evergreen forest, is that they do not immediately see or hear hordes of birds upon entering a trail. During large portions of the day, in fact, most habitats are mainly quiet, with few birds noticeably active. The birds are there, but many are inconspicuous—small brownish birds near to the ground, and greenish, brownish, or grayish birds in the tops of the vegetation. A frequent, at first discombobulating experience, is that you will be walking along a trail, seeing few birds, and then, suddenly, a *mixed-species foraging flock* with many species swooshes into view, filling the bushes and trees around you at all levels—some hopping along the ground, some moving through the brush, some clinging to tree trunks, others in the canopy—more birds than you can easily count or identify—and then, just as suddenly, the flock is gone, moved on in its meandering path through the forest. If the trail system is extensive, sometimes you can move quietly ahead of the flock and let it pass by you again and again. This works especially well for low-moving flocks of babblers, warblers, woodpeckers, and flycatchers. High-moving flocks, with birds such as cuckoos and drongos, are much harder to follow and are often best seen from nearby mountain- or hillsides that overlook the canopy.

Throughout Thailand, but especially in the central and northern regions, many migrants escaping the cold winter in central and northern Asia seasonally augment the resident species. Some of these winter visitors join up with resident species in forest flocks; others find room in shrubby areas and grasslands. Others, such as shorebirds, form immense flocks of their own on mudflats and saltpans near the ocean.

It would be a shame to leave Thailand without seeing at least some of its spectacular birds, such as parrots, pittas, hornbills, trogons, and starlings. If you have trouble locating such birds, be sure and let people around you know of your interest—tour guides, resort employees, park personnel. Everyone involved in Thailand's tourist industry wants to share the country's richness of natural beauty, and they can either tell you the best places to go for particular birds or send you to someone who knows.

Family Profiles

1. Pelican Allies

Pelicans (8 species worldwide, one in Thailand), *cormorants* (39 species worldwide, 3 in Thailand), and *anhingas* (2 species worldwide, one in Thailand) are all families in the order Pelicaniformes. The members of this order are fairly large and have webbing that extends between four toes (ducks, for instance, only have webbing between three toes). They are marine or aquatic and have bodies and behavior modified to feed on fish caught underwater. The only species of this order you are likely to see in Thailand is one of the cormorants that is common along portions of the coast, the LITTLE CORMORANT (Plate 23).

Natural History

Ecology and Behavior
Although these pelican relatives all feed mainly on fish, they catch fish in quite different ways. Thailand's only pelican, the SPOT-BILLED PELICAN, scoops fish out of the water as it swims on the surface. The only anhinga in the country, the ORIENTAL DARTER, catches fish underwater by spearing them with its long, sharply pointed bill. LITTLE CORMORANTS dive from the surface of lakes, rivers, lagoons, and coastal saltwater areas to pursue fish underwater. Using their large webbed feet for propulsion, cormorants catch fish (and occasionally crustaceans like crabs) in their hooked bills. They often feed in large groups, especially when fish are concentrated in a small area. They roost together in large numbers, usually on island peaks or in the tops of tall trees, and they move between roosting and feeding areas in large "V"-shaped flocks.

Breeding
The LITTLE CORMORANT nests in large colonies either on isolated islands or in groves of trees surrounded by water, both of which are relatively predator-free. All of these pelican relatives are monogamous, and both mates share in nest-building, incubation, and feeding young. In some groups like the pelicans, the male gathers sticks and stones for the nest, but the female actually constructs the nest. Individuals keep the same mate for several seasons and tend to return to the same site to nest. Little Cormorants begin breeding when they are 3 or 4 years old. Two to 4 eggs are incubated for about 4 weeks, and the young fledge 5 to 8 weeks after hatching. The helpless young of cormorants push their head and bill deep into the gullet of the returning parent birds to get at the food awaiting them there.

Notes
Anhingas are also known as *darters*, the name derived from the way the birds underwater swiftly thrust their necks forward to spear fish on the points of their bills. Because they often swim with their bodies submerged and only the long necks and heads above water, they are also often called *snake-birds*. Cormorants have been used for centuries by people in China, Japan, and Central Europe as fishing birds. A ring is placed around a cormorant's neck so that it cannot swallow its catch. Then, usually on a long leash, it is permitted to swim underwater to pursue fish. When the bird returns to the surface, it is reeled in, usually with an unswallowable fish clenched in its bill.

Status

At the turn of the century, the SPOT-BILLED PELICAN nested in large numbers in the swamps of Thailand's Central Plains. Changing these swamps into rice paddies eliminated this species as a nesting bird in Thailand, and now fewer than 20 are seen every year in the country. It is listed as globally threatened by the IUCN Red List. The ORIENTAL DARTER evidently was at one time a regular nester in the country but is now only a rare, non-breeding visitor.

Profile

Little Cormorant, *Phalacrocorax niger*, Plate 23b

2. Herons and Egrets

Herons and *egrets* are beautiful medium- to large-sized wading birds that enjoy broad distributions throughout temperate and tropical regions around the world. Herons, egrets, and the more elusive *bitterns* constitute the heron family, Ardeidae, which includes about 62 species. Nineteen species occur in Thailand, most of which breed there. Herons frequent all sorts of aquatic habitats: along rivers and streams, in marshes and swamps, and along lake and ocean shorelines. The difference between what is called an egret and what is called a heron is arbitrary and inconsistent. Generally, however, the term egret is reserved for species that are all white. Most herons and egrets are easy to identify. They are the tallish birds standing upright and still in shallow water or along the shore, staring intently into the water. They have slender bodies, long necks (usually folded back in a flattened "S" in flight and sometimes when perched or resting, producing a short-necked, hunched appearance), long, pointed bills, and long legs with long toes. Thai species range in height from 38 cm to 1.1 m (1.3 to 3.6 ft). Most are attired in soft shades of gray, brown, blue, or green, and black and white (but some, as we said, are all white). Close-up, many are exquisitely marked with small colored patches of facial skin or broad areas of spots or streaks. During the breeding season both sexes of some species acquire long back and head plumes, and leg and bill color become brighter.

Natural History

Ecology and Behavior

The CATTLE EGRET (Plate 24) makes its living following herds of large grazing mammals. Unlike all the other herons and egrets, it rarely enters the water but, instead, in upland areas, eats insects flushed by tractors crossing rice paddies and by the feet of elephants, Gaurs, and cows. The other herons are mainly sit-and-wait hunters along water edges. Some species wait with infinite patience for prey to move and then strike out in a flash with their bill to grab the fish, frog, or crab. The LITTLE EGRET (Plate 24), however, often staggers around in the shallows like a drunken sailor, trying to scare up prey that are then easy targets for its bill. The STRIATED HERON, which occurs in several areas of the world but not in Thailand, is known to use bait, such as bread stolen from a picnic area, to swish in the water and attract fish to within striking range of its bill. The BLACK-CROWNED NIGHT-HERON (Plate 23) and MALAYAN NIGHT-HERON are denizens of vegetated edges of forest swamps and small streams. They are often so well camouflaged that you can pass close by them in your canoe without noticing them. At daybreak and again just before sunset they are more likely to be out in the open. As their names suggest, these herons are nocturnal and your best chance of seeing them is by shining a flashlight in the tangled foliage along waterways at night or finding a small group in a protected roost within dense thickets during the day.

Breeding
Most herons are social birds, roosting and breeding in colonies, often several species together. Some, however, like the YELLOW BITTERN (Plate 24), are predominantly solitary. Herons are known for their often elaborate courtship displays and ceremonies, which continue through pair formation and nest-building. Generally the female constructs the nest from sticks presented to her by the male. The nests are in trees, reeds, or occasionally on the ground. Both sexes incubate the 3 to 7 eggs for 16 to 30 days, and both feed the young for another 35 to 50 days until they fledge.

Herons and egrets often lay more eggs than the number of chicks they can successfully feed. This seems contrary to our usual view of nature, which we regard as finely tuned through natural selection so that behaviors avoid waste. The likely answer to this puzzle is that this behavior allows a pair to raise the maximum number of offspring every year even if food levels are unpredictable from year to year. Females lay eggs one or two days apart, and start incubating with the first egg. Chicks hatch out at the same intervals, and so the young in a single nest are of different ages and quite different sizes. The largest chicks receive the most food, probably because they can more easily attract the adults and get to the food they regurgitate. The larger chicks on occasion will also kill their smaller siblings (*siblicide*), especially if food is scarce. If there is sufficient food, the next biggest chicks will also be able to eat often enough to survive. In years of super-abundant food, even the smallest chicks will be able to eat enough. Thus, laying more eggs than can be reared as chicks most years may be to insure that many chicks are raised in the years of abundance.

Notes
All herons have a distinctive comb on the flattened middle toe of each foot. They use it to groom themselves and spread bits of specialized feathers, called *powder down*, throughout their body surface. Powder down is found in only a very few other birds in the world; its function appears to be to help clean the large body feathers when they become full of fish scales and grime.

Status
Some of Thailand's herons and egrets are fairly rare, but perhaps except for the CHINESE EGRET, a rare wintering visitor on the mud flats near Krabi and a few other coastal locations, they are not considered threatened species because they are common in other parts of their ranges, outside the country.

Profiles
Gray Heron, *Ardea cinerea*, Plate 23c
Purple Heron, *Ardea purpurea*, Plate 23d
Black-crowned Night-Heron, *Nycticorax nycticorax*, Plate 23e
Pacific Reef-Egret, *Egretta sacra*, Plate 24a
Chinese Pond Heron, *Ardeola bacchus*, Plate 24b
Little Egret, *Egretta garzetta*, Plate 24c
Yellow Bittern, *Ixobrychus sinensis*, Plate 24d
Cattle Egret, *Bubulcus ibis*, Plate 24e
Great Egret, *Ardea alba*, Plate 24f

3. Marsh and Stream Birds

Marsh and stream birds are a collection of unrelated species that share a habitat of standing and running water surrounded by grasses, bushes, trees, and other relatively thick vegetation. They do not rely heavily on flight but instead swim in the water or walk on and through vegetation near the water. They tend to be shy and retiring, and they often slink away from danger before a predator (or an approaching canoe with tourists) has a chance to see them.

Storks (family Ciconiidae) are large, heron-like birds usually placed together in the same order as herons. They differ by flying with the neck outstretched and often soaring high in the sky on broad wings. Most species of storks are predominantly white with black patches on the wings (19 species worldwide, 7 of which occur in Thailand). In Thailand, you are likely to see only the ASIAN OPENBILL STORK (Plate 23). The *jacanas* (jha-SAH-nahs) form a worldwide family, Jacanidae (8 species worldwide), only two species of which are found in Thailand. They have incredibly long toes for walking on floating vegetation without sinking. Female jacanas are larger than males, and immatures are lighter and streaked. The *rails*, family Rallidae (135 species worldwide, 15 in Thailand), are often shy and difficult-to-see inhabitants of swampy areas. The medium-sized WHITE-BREASTED WATERHEN (Plate 29) is common in marshy areas and mangroves of Thailand and is the rail you are most likely to encounter; the COMMON MOORHEN (Plate 29) is another common species. The MASKED FINFOOT (Plate 29), in family Heliornithidae, is a small duck-like species that is usually seen swimming. The LITTLE GREBE (Plate 25), in family Podicipedidae (20 species worldwide, 2 in Thailand), is a small duck-like species found in Thailand only in marshy lakes. Its small size and thin bill immediately separate it from any of the true ducks that also occur in these marshes.

Natural History

Ecology and Behavior

Storks use their long bills to probe for food in shallow water, grass, and mud. They eat small mammals, frogs, and insects. The BRONZE-WINGED (Plate 29) and PHEASANT-TAILED JACANAS are common and easy to see in flooded grasslands and open marshy areas. They use their immensely long toes to walk on floating vegetation and lily pads. The MASKED FINFOOT swims in among the roots and overhanging leaves of thick vegetation along lakes and streams, where it feeds on frogs, worms, crustaceans, and insects. It runs across the surface of the water and flies low to escape predation, and your best view will probably be as it skitters away from your canoe into the dense vegetation.

Breeding

Storks are monogamous and most nest colonially in trees or in reeds near the water. Nests are made of sticks and contain up to 5 eggs. Chicks take food regurgitated from the adults' mouths and throats. Rails build their nests in moist areas either in reeds or grass. Moorhens, waterhens, and grebes construct large nests on small islands of floating vegetation. Egg numbers per nest are often high and range from 2 to 16 for moorhens and waterhens, and 2 to 8 for grebes. Jacanas are unusual in that they are often *polyandrous* (one female mates with numerous males). Males each defend small territories from other males, but each female has a larger territory that encompasses 2 to 4 male territories. Males build nests of floating, compacted aquatic vegetation, into which the female deposits 3 or 4 eggs. The male incubates the nest for 21 to 24 days and then cares for the chicks by himself. Jacanas also are able to move their young chicks in case of flooding or danger by holding them under their closed wings and running to safety. The MASKED FINFOOT makes a flat nest of sticks and reeds, often on branches of dead trees low over the water. Both parents incubate the 2 to 5 eggs.

Grebes are monogamous and build a floating nest of aquatic material. Because the nest floats, a rise or fall in the water level of the marshy lake does not affect the safety of the 2 to 6 eggs or young. When both adults are away from the nest at the same time, they cover the eggs or chicks with vegetation to keep them warm and camouflaged from potential enemies. Both mates are equally involved in incubation and guarding the striped chicks, which soon leave the nest. The young continue to be dependent on the adults for 3 to 4 weeks as they swim around the pond and hide in vegetation at night.

Notes

The term "skinny as a rail" refers originally not to a railroad track but to the bird. Rails are extremely flattened from side to side so they can fit into narrow spaces—thus the saying.

Status

Because of draining of marshes and swampy areas, especially in the Central Plains, several species of storks have become rare or virtually extinct in Thailand, such as WOOLLY-NECKED STORK, BLACK-NECKED STORK, PAINTED STORK, GREATER ADJUTANT, and LESSER ADJUTANT; the last two of these are also globally threatened. The MILKY STORK, another globally threatened species, is now extinct in Thailand. Many other marsh and wetland birds have met similar fates in Thailand. The former resident SARUS CRANE is now extinct in Thailand due to the destruction of wetlands (cranes, often confused with herons and storks, are actually large relatives of rails and buttonquail). The BLACK-FACED SPOONBILL, WHITE-SHOULDERED IBIS, and GIANT IBIS, all large waterbirds and relatives of herons and storks, are on the IUCN Red list of threatened species and are almost extinct in Thailand. The MASKED FINFOOT is also listed on the IUCN Red List.

Profiles

Asian Openbill Stork, *Anastomus oscitans*, Plate 23a
Little Grebe, *Tachybaptus ruficollis*, Plate 25b
White-breasted Waterhen, *Amaurornis phoenicurus*, Plate 29a
Common Moorhen, *Gallinula chloropus*, Plate 29c
Bronze-winged Jacana, *Metopidius indicus*, Plate 29d
Masked Finfoot, *Heliopais personata*, Plate 29e

4. Ducks

Members of family Anatidae, which includes about 150 species of *ducks, geese,* and *swans,* are all associated with water. They are distributed throughout the world in habitats ranging from open sea to high mountain lakes. Although abundant and diverse in temperate regions, relatively few species migrate to or reside in the tropics. Ducks vary quite a bit in size and coloring, but most share the same major traits: duck bills, webbed toes, short tails, and long, slim necks. Plumage color and patterning vary, but there is a preponderance within the group of grays and browns and black and white, although many species have at least small patches of brighter colors. In some species male and female look alike, but in others there is a high degree of difference between the sexes. About 19 species occur in Thailand.

Natural History

Ecology and Behavior
Ducks eat aquatic plants, small fish, and invertebrates, but some, such as the LESSER WHISTLING DUCKS (Plate 25), regularly graze on grasses, moist upland vegetation, and terrestrial insects. More typical is the dabbling feeding behavior of the GARGANEY (Plate 25), which finds food by dipping its bill into the water while swimming. Sometimes it will tip its rear end into the air trying to reach a bit deeper into the water for a morsel, but this species does not dive underwater.

Breeding
Most ducks nest on the ground in protective vegetation near their feeding areas. However, whistling ducks nest in tree cavities often more than 15 m (50 ft) above the ground. Typically, duck nests are lined with downy feathers that the female plucks from her breast. In most species of ducks the female alone performs the duties dealing with nesting and caring for the young. In larger species, such as geese and swans, the pair typically mates for life, and both parents are more equally involved in raising the young. The young are precocial—they hatch feathered and able to run within a few minutes and can swim and feed themselves soon after. The parents' main role is to guard them against predators and teach them how to find food.

Notes
Ducks, geese, and swans have been objects of people's attention since ancient times, chiefly as a food source. These birds typically have tasty flesh, are fairly large and thus economical to hunt, and usually easier and less dangerous to catch than many other animals, particularly large mammals. Owing to their frequent use as food, several wild ducks and geese have been domesticated for thousands of years; Thailand's MUSCOVY DUCK, in fact, is a domesticated form imported from South and Central America. Wild ducks also adjust well to the proximity of people, to the point of taking food from them—a practice that surviving artworks show has been occurring for at least 2,000 years. Hunting ducks and geese for sport is also a long-practiced tradition. As a consequence of these long interactions between ducks and people, and the research on these animals stimulated by their use in agriculture and sport, a large amount of scientific information has been collected on the group; many ducks and geese are among the most well-known birds. The close association between ducks and people has even led to a long contractual agreement between certain individual ducks and the Walt Disney Company.

Status
The populations of all the species profiled here have been affected to some degree by hunting pressures. Although drainage of marshes and wetlands has probably affected populations of most ducks and geese in Thailand, many species are still relatively common in their appropriate habitats. The only ducks in Thailand that are considered endangered are the WHITE-WINGED DUCK, which now has a world population of about 300 individuals and in Thailand is resident in only a few isolated areas of the central part of the country, and the BAER'S POCHARD, which is a rare winter visitor.

Profiles

Cotton Pygmy-Goose, *Nettapus coromandelianus*, Plate 25a
Garganey, *Anas querquedula*, Plate 25c
Lesser Whistling Duck, *Dendrocygna javanica*, Plate 25d
Northern Pintail, *Anas acuta*, Plate 25e

5. Terns and Gulls

On the open ocean, over coastal estuaries, and along inland rivers, *terns* and *gulls* are often present and obvious. They dive, swoop, and soar through the air in a spellbinding search for their food on the water's surface or in noisy encounters with each other. At rest they swim together in tight clusters on the water's surface or perch on sandy beaches and mudflats almost always in flocks of single or mixed species.

Terns and gulls are members of order Charadriiformes, which also includes the shorebirds (p. 131). The gulls and terns are sometimes placed in the same family, Laridae (88 species worldwide, 23 in Thailand). Terns are smaller, more streamlined forms of gulls. On the coast of Thailand, several species of terns winter or are transient in migration. Four species nest along isolated parts of the coastline and two species, at least formerly, nested along inland rivers. The wintering flocks of terns in estuaries, sewage effluents, and marshy areas near the coast are often numerous and noisy. These flocks are made up mainly of the WHISKERED TERN (Plate 32). No gull species nest in Thailand, and of the six species wintering, all but the BROWN-HEADED GULL (Plate 32) are rare.

Natural History

Ecology and Behavior

Terns feed primarily on small fish, which they catch by hovering high over the water and then diving below the surface. Terns on inland rivers are sparsely encountered, probably because the fish are generally not concentrated. Gulls are mainly scavengers, but they will do some hunting of fish and crustaceans when these prey items are abundant and easy to catch. Gulls do not dive into the water but instead pick food off its surface.

Breeding

As with most seabirds, terns and gulls breed in noisy colonies, usually on an isolated island or remote sand spit. Generally they are monogamous, the male and female sharing brooding and feeding the young. Males often present food to prospective mates in a ritual feeding that apparently provides clues to a female of the male's ability to catch quality prey and to be a good provider for their offspring. Because they nest on the ground, they have little protection from predators, although they will vigorously dive-bomb, peck, and defecate on intruders into their nesting colony, human or otherwise. They lay up to 4 eggs, which are incubated for about 30 days. Young are fed when they push their bills down into their parents' throats, in effect forcing the parents to regurgitate food stored in their crops—enlargements of the top part of the esophagus.

Notes

Because their nesting colonies are so obvious and concentrated, tern eggs are often collected by humans for food. In some parts of the world, large colonies of these fast-flying birds roost or nest in the vicinity of airports, where there are lots of suitable open areas and protection from most intruding humans.

Status

The RIVER TERN and BLACK-BELLIED TERN were at one time resident along inland rivers and in marshy areas of the Far North and Central Plains of Thailand. As with many other freshwater-nesting birds, draining of wetlands for rice paddies and agriculture is likely the main cause of their elimination in the country over the last fifty years. The limited ranges and specialized habitats for the nesting colonies of the ROSEATE, BLACK-NAPED, and GREAT CRESTED TERN on Thailand's coastal islands make them susceptible to disturbance from humans (mainly tourists) and pollution.

Profiles

Whiskered Tern, *Chlidonias hybridus*, Plate 32a
Brown-headed Gull, *Larus brunnicephalus*, Plate 32b

6. Shorebirds (Waders)

Spotting *shorebirds* is usually a priority only for visitors to the tropics who are rabid birdwatchers. The reason for the lack of interest is that most shorebirds in Thailand are wintering visitors and are in their dull non-breeding plumages. Mostly brown and lacking in reasonably distinguishing characteristics, they are frustratingly difficult to identify. Nevertheless, it can be a treat watching these fellow travellers in their tropical wintering areas as they forage in meadows, along streams, on mudflats, and on sandy ocean beaches. When a large flock, often of several species, rises from a sandbar, it is fun to follow its progress until out of sight. The resident species of shorebirds in Thailand are intriguing for their combination of similarities to and frequently jarring differences from their migratory cousins. Shorebirds are traditionally placed along with the gulls and terns in the avian order Charadriiformes. They are global in distribution, and we profile species from four families found in Thailand. Most shorebirds, regardless of size, have a characteristic look. They are usually drably-colored birds (especially during the nonbreeding months), darker above, lighter below, with long, thin legs for wading through wet meadows, mud, sand, or surf. Depending on feeding habits, bill length varies from short to very long.

The *sandpipers*, family Scolopacidae, are a worldwide group of approximately 85 species. About 32 species occur in Thailand, some being quite abundant during the winter months, especially along the coasts. All of these sandpipers are migrants that nest in the Arctic or central plateau of Asia. Most of these sandpipers range from 15 to 59 cm (6 to 23 in) long. They are generally slender birds with straight or curved bills of various lengths and live on sandy beaches or mudflats along rivers, lakes, and the coast.

Plovers, in family Charadriidae, are small to medium-sized (15 to 33 cm, 6 to 13 in) shorebirds with short tails and straight, relatively stout, dove-like bills. They are mostly shades of gray and brown but some have bold color patterns such as a broad white or dark band on the head or chest. Worldwide, there are more than 60 species. Twelve species occur regularly in Thailand, three of which are resident non-migratory species on the coast or on inland rivers and marshy areas.

The family of *stilts*, Recurvirostridae, has 10 species worldwide but only one species in Thailand. The BLACK-WINGED STILT (Plate 31) congregates in flocks of 5 to 100 birds in shallow ponds and muddy areas along the coast and in inland marshy areas. The flocks are so noisy you often hear them before you can see them.

Pratincoles make up a bizarre family (Glareolidae) of nine species in Africa, Asia, and Australia. On a river beach they at first look like a strange tern, but they run like plovers. When they fly, however, it is usually in flocks, and their forked tail and long pointed wings make them look like large swallows. Two species occur in Thailand.

Natural History

Ecology and Behavior
Even though shorebirds are all excellent fliers, they spend a lot of time on the ground foraging and resting. When pursued, they often prefer running to flying away. Sandpipers tend to use their bills to probe into the soil or mud for small invertebrates, and different shapes and lengths of bills help the various sandpiper species find different prey even when they are feeding side by side. The plovers use their bills to take prey or even seeds off the soil surface and never probe. Stilts take advantage of their long legs and bills to probe mud in deeper water, sometimes feeding with their heads entirely underwater. Pratincoles pursue prey on sand and mud beaches by running, but more commonly they pursue flying insects on the wing, usually at dusk and in flocks. Many shorebirds, especially the sandpipers, establish winter feeding territories along stretches of beach; they use the area for feeding for a few hours or for the day, defending it aggressively from other members of their species. Many of the sandpipers and plovers are gregarious birds, often seen in large groups especially when travelling. Several species make long migrations over large expanses of open ocean.

Breeding
Most shorebird nests are simple, small depressions in the ground in which eggs are placed; some of these are in sand, on gravel, or on a grass hummock. Seldom do the adults prepare the nest with more than a few pebbles. In almost all these shorebird families monogamy is the rule, and both parents incubate the eggs. Shorebird young are precocial, able to run and feed themselves soon after hatching. Parents usually stay with the young to guard them until they can fly, 3 to 5 weeks after hatching. Adults of many ground-nesting species, such as these shorebirds, protect their nests and young by performing a "broken wing" display. At the approach of a predator, the adult runs in front of the danger, calling and dragging one of its wings on the ground as if it is severely injured. The predator sees an easy meal and follows after the adult, which is able to keep just out of the striking range of the predator and leads it away from the young hidden in the nest or in the grass. If this fails, species like stilts and RED-WATTLED LAPWINGS (Plate 30) fly close to the predator and hassle it until it leaves. The ORIENTAL PRATINCOLE (Plate 31) nests in colonies in fallow rice paddies, marshes, and grassy uplands.

Notes
The manner in which flocks of thousands of birds, particularly shorebirds, fly in such closely regimented order, executing abrupt maneuvers with precise coordination, such as when all individuals turn together in a split second in the same direction, has puzzled biologists and engendered some research. The questions include: What is the stimulus for the flock to turn—is it one individual within the flock, a "leader," from which all the others take their "orders" and follow into turns? Or is it some stimulus from outside the flock that all members respond to in the same way? And how are the turns coordinated? Everything from "thought transference" to electromagnetic communication among the flock members has

been advanced as an explanation. After studying films of DUNLIN, a North American and Eurasian sandpiper that occasionally winters in Thailand, flying and turning in large flocks, one biologist has suggested that the method birds within these flocks use to coordinate their turns is similar to how the people in a chorus-line know the precise moment to raise their legs in sequence or how "the wave" in a sports stadium is coordinated. That is, one bird, perhaps one that has detected some danger, like a predatory falcon, starts a turn, and the other birds, seeing the start of the flock's turning, can then anticipate when it is their turn to make the turn—the result being a quick wave of turning coursing through the flock.

Status

The resident MALAYSIAN PLOVER occurs on remote sandy beaches of the peninsular coast and is threatened in Thailand by disturbance and habitat destruction. Three very rare and poorly known shorebirds pass through or winter in Thailand's coastal estuaries—ASIAN DOWITCHER, NORDMANN'S GREENSHANK, and SPOON-BILLED SANDPIPER. The global population of these three species is likely in the thousands or less, and they all nest in high latitudes of Siberia. A major goal for conservation of shorebirds is the need to preserve critical wintering and migratory stopover points—pieces of habitat, sometimes fairly small, that hundreds of thousands of shorebirds settle into midway during their long migrations to stock up on food. These staging areas are vital for shorebird populations, and several such areas likely exist in Thailand. These very sites, however, usually flat and near the ocean, are also heavily threatened from construction and pollution.

Profiles

Red-wattled Lapwing, *Vanellus indicus*, Plate 30a
Little Ringed Plover, *Charadrius dubius*, Plate 30b
Pacific Golden Plover, *Pluvialis fulva*, Plate 30c
Common Redshank, *Tringa totanus*, Plate 30d
Whimbrel, *Numenius phaeopus*, Plate 30e
Black-winged Stilt, *Himantopus himantopus*, Plate 31a
Marsh Sandpiper, *Tringa stagnatilis*, Plate 31b
Wood Sandpiper, *Tringa glareola*, Plate 31c
Common Sandpiper, *Actitis hypoleucos*, Plate 31d
Oriental Pratincole, *Glareola maldivarum*, Plate 31e

7. Pheasants and Buttonquail

Chicken-like birds strutting about the forest floor are bound to be members of the *pheasant* family, Phasianidae. This family is distributed in North America, Europe, Africa, and Asia. Twenty-three species are found in Thailand, one of which is *the* chicken from which all domestic chicken have descended, the RED JUNGLE FOWL (Plate 28). The largest in Thailand are the huge peafowl (peahens and peacocks; males, with their huge tails, grow up to 2.45 m, 8 ft long). The smallest are *quail* (only 15 cm, 6 in long). All species have long legs and long, heavy toes. Many have conspicuous crests and tails—especially in males. The colors of the smaller members of the family, the quail, *partridges*, and *francolins*, are generally drab—gray, brown, olive, or black and white; some appear glossy in the right light. Males of the peafowl and pheasants, however, are among the most spectacularly colored birds anywhere in the world. Spotting a pair of SILVER PHEASANTS (Plate 29), for instance, at roadside in some national park, is an experience you will not soon forget.

Buttonquail are similar in appearance to small quail but differ in several key characteristics. Most obvious, they lack a hind toe, their wings are more pointed in flight than are the rounded wings of regular quail, and males are considerably smaller than females. Related instead to the rails and cranes, buttonquail are placed in their own small family (Turnicidae), of which three species occur in Thailand. Although common on the ground in open grasslands and scrubby areas, the small BARRED BUTTONQUAIL (Plate 29) is very shy and hides easily in even the barest vegetation. You will be lucky to see this bird slinking away into thicker grass or occasionally flying up in a whirr of wings from underfoot.

Natural History

Ecology and Behavior

Pheasants are birds of the forest, and the larger the species, the more it is limited to denser forest. Partridges and some quail tend to be in forest undergrowth but regularly venture out into nearby open areas—especially in the early morning and evening. Francolins and other quail are usually in open grasslands and scrub forest. All members of this family prefer to eat fruits, seeds, and insects from the ground, often scratching vigorously with their large feet and bills to expose food under the soil surface or in leaf litter. In the non-breeding season, family parties often remain together and even combine with other family parties to form large flocks. Buttonquail are often inconspicuous as they slink around in grassy areas eating grass seeds and small insects from the ground. They also often scratch the soil surface to expose seeds.

Breeding

Species that show extreme difference in size and color between the sexes, such as pheasants, peafowl, and junglefowl, tend to be polygynous (one male mates with several females), and in the case of these chicken-like birds, the males defend huge territories. The males use their flashy colors, long tail and neck feathers, noisy wing-whirring, and crowing displays to intimidate other males away from the territory. The smaller species of quail and partridges, in which males and females are similar in size and dull coloration, tend to be monogamous. In many of these plainer species, both sexes help defend the territory. All species in this family make a nest of dead leaves or twigs, constructed by the female alone and usually on the ground. The GREAT ARGUS (Plate 28), larger pheasants, and peafowl lay only two eggs per nest. Partridges, francolins, and quail lay up to 15 per nest. Eggs are incubated for 17 days among the smaller species and 28 or more days by the larger species. The young in a nest hatch within a few hours of each other, apparently using peeping calls within the unhatched eggs as a cue. This synchronization of hatching means they can all leave the nest at the same time and over a short period to avoid nest predators. The newly hatched chicks can run and feed themselves within minutes of hatching. They generally need the care of only one parent (usually the female) to watch for predators and point out feeding areas.

Breeding behavior of buttonquail is peculiar in that many of the roles of the sexes are reversed. One female mates with several males (polyandry). She is larger than the males, with brighter colors, and she defends her territory by singing a low booming note. The nest is secreted under a tussock of grass or in a well-covered grassy depression. Usually 4 eggs are laid, and then the female takes on her duties of defending the territory against other females while the male incubates the eggs for less than two weeks—one of the shortest incubation periods for any bird species. Young are able to run almost immediately and within two weeks are flying and independent of the parents.

Notes
The members of the pheasant family probably have more economic impact around the world than any other bird group. The chicken is the most widely domesticated animal in the world. Because they are more efficient at converting their food into meat than domesticated mammals, chickens are easier to raise for profit and can be kept in much greater numbers. Many species in this family are also commonly hunted, both as a hobby and for food.

Female buttonquail are so aggressive toward each other during the breeding season that in India they are frequently caught and used as entertainment in "hen fights."

Status
A variety of factors converge to ensure that the large and showy species of pheasants will remain a problem group into the foreseeable future. They are chiefly birds of the forests at a time when Oriental forests are increasingly being cleared. They are desirable game birds, hunted by local people for food. In the face of these unrelenting pressures on their populations, pheasants are among the birds thought most likely to survive in the future only in protected areas, such as national parks. In Thailand, seven pheasant species are listed as threatened or endangered: CHESTNUT-HEADED PARTRIDGE, CHESTNUT-NECKLACED PARTRIDGE, SIAMESE FIREBACK, CRESTED FIREBACK, GREEN PEAFOWL, MALAYAN PEACOCK PHEASANT, and HUME'S PHEASANT.

Profiles
Scaly-breasted Partridge, *Arborophila chloropus,* Plate 28a
Chinese Francolin, *Francolinus pintadeanus,* Plate 28b
Red Junglefowl, *Gallus gallus,* Plate 28c
Silver Pheasant, *Lophura nycthemera,* Plate 28d
Great Argus, *Argusianus argus,* Plate 28e
Barred Buttonquail, *Turnix suscitator,* Plate 29b

8. Hawks, Eagles, and Kites

The raptor family, Accipitridae, is an immense group that includes about 240 species (40 in Thailand) of *hawks, eagles,* and *kites* worldwide. Species in this family vary considerably in size and in patterns of their generally subdued color schemes, but all are similar in overall form—we know them when we see them. They are fierce-looking birds with strong feet, hooked, sharp claws, or *talons,* and strongly hooked bills. The plumages of the two sexes are usually similar, but females are larger than males, in some species extremely so. Juvenile raptors often spend several years in subadult plumages that differ in pattern and brightness from the adults.

Natural History

Ecology and Behavior
Although many raptors are common birds, typically they spread themselves out thinly over large areas, as is the case for all *top predators* (a predator at the pinnacle of the food chain and thus having too few prey available to support large populations of the predator). Some large eagles that feed on large prey, such as the ASIAN BLACK EAGLE, may need a territory of 500 sq km (190 sq mi) or

more to ensure sufficient food for itself and its nestlings. Most species have developed unique hunting techniques to increase efficiency of prey capture. Among the kites, for instance, the BLACK-SHOULDERED KITE (Plate 26) soars over open fields and shrubby areas searching for small mammals. It often quarters into the wind and hovers over an especially productive site for minutes at a time. Upon spotting a juicy rodent, lizard, or grasshopper, it swoops down, captures the prey, and carries it off to a perch to devour. The BRAHMINY KITE soars high over mangroves and coastal forests searching for dead fish and other animals floating on the water, which it deftly scoops up with its talons and takes to a nearby perch to consume (yum!). The PIED HARRIER (Plate 27) also soars, but low over grassy and marshy areas, tacking back and forth on wings lifted at their tips to enable slow flight without losing lift, the aerodynamic force that keeps flying objects aloft.

Among the hawks, The BLACK BAZA (Plate 26) is a generalist, and eats everything from insects, lizards, and snakes to small birds, bats and other mammals. On the other hand, the CRESTED HONEY BUZZARD is extremely and narrowly specialized to eat honey and larvae of bees, although it occasionally grabs an unsuspecting bird or mouse. The CRESTED SERPENT-EAGLE (Plate 27), despite its name, is intermediate in its tastes. It eats many lizards and snakes, but it doesn't pass up a rat or wounded bird if it finds one.

Breeding

Many raptors are territorial, a solitary individual or a breeding pair defending an area for feeding and, during the breeding season, for reproduction. Displays that advertise a territory and that also may be used in courtship consist of spectacular aerial twists, loops, and other acrobatic maneuvers. Hawk, eagle, and kite nests in general are constructed of sticks that both sexes place in a tree or on a rocky ledge. Some nests are lined with leaves. Usually only the female incubates the 1 to 6 eggs for about a month. The male hunts prey for the female while she sits on the eggs, and after the first chicks hatch out, he continues to give prey to the female, which she then tears up to give in turn to the chicks. When the chicks are a little bigger and the demand for food rises, both mates hunt and feed the chicks directly. The young can fly at 28 to 120 days, bigger species taking longer to fledge than the smaller species.

Notes

Large, predatory raptors have doubtless always attracted people's attention, respect, and awe. Wherever eagles occur, they are chronicled in the history of civilizations. Early Anglo-Saxons were known to hang an eagle on the gate of any city they conquered. Some Native American tribes and also Australian Aboriginal peoples deified large hawks or eagles. Several states have used likenesses of eagles as national symbols, among them Turkey, Austria, Germany, Poland, Russia, Mexico, and the US.

Status

Due to habitat destruction, several of Thailand's hawks and eagles are considered threatened or endangered within the country, such as the WHITE-BELLIED (Plate 27) and GRAY-HEADED SEA-EAGLES. Three eagle species found in Thailand are listed as globally threatened: GREATER SPOTTED EAGLE, IMPERIAL EAGLE, and WALLACE'S HAWK-EAGLE. The RED-HEADED VULTURE is dependent on dead large mammals, and, together with most large wild mammals, it is now confined to the most remote and isolated areas of its former range in Thailand. The BAT HAWK population in Thailand has been reduced to a few individuals in the southern part of the peninsula due to forest destruction. Conservation measures aimed at raptors are bound to be difficult to formulate and enforce because the birds are often persecuted for a number of reasons (hunting, pet and feather trade, farmers protecting livestock) and they roam very large areas. Also, some breed and winter on different continents and thus need to be protected in all parts of their ranges, including along migration routes. Further complicating population assessments and conservation proposals, there are still plenty of Oriental raptor species about which very little is known. Breeding behavior and typical prey taken for many species remain unknown.

Profiles

Black-shouldered Kite, *Elanus caeruleus*, Plate 26a
Black Baza, *Aviceda leuphotes*, Plate 26b
Black Kite, *Milvus migrans*, Plate 26c
Crested Goshawk, *Accipiter trivirgatus*, Plate 26d
Shikra, *Accipiter badius*, Plate 26e
White-bellied Sea-Eagle, *Haliaeetus leucogaster*, Plate 27a
Crested Serpent-Eagle, *Spilornis cheela*, Plate 27b
Pied Harrier, *Circus melanoleucos*, Plate 27d

9. Falcons

Closely related to the hawks, eagles, and kites, the *falcons* are placed in their own family, Falconidae. The family has about 60 species worldwide, 8 in Thailand. Externally they look like kites and other hawks. The main differences are found in subtle but consistent divergences in internal structures of the skeleton that indicate separate evolutionary branches.

Natural History

Ecology and Behavior

Typical falcons are best known for their remarkable eyesight and fast, aerial pursuit and capture of moving prey such as flying birds. Falcons hit perched or flying birds with their talons, stunning the prey and sometimes killing it outright. The PEREGRINE FALCON, one of Earth's most wide-ranging and broadly distributed birds, migrates through Thailand and a few even nest here. It is considered to be the fastest bird in the world, achieving more than 192 kph (120 mph) in a steep stoop on prey. For a prey item to be able to avoid or escape this speed of attack seems impossible, yet many if not most potential prey do escape. The success rate of attack is low, and the falcon must often try numerous times before finally catching something to eat or feed to its young.

The hunting behavior of falcons has, over evolutionary time, shaped the behavior of their prey animals. An individual bird caught unawares has little chance of escaping the rapid, acrobatic falcons. But birds in groups have two defenses. First, each individual in a group benefits because the group, with so many eyes and ears, is more likely to spot a falcon at a distance than is a lone individual, thus providing all in the group opportunities to watch the predator as it approaches and so evade it. This sort of anti-predation advantage may be why some animals stay in groups. Second, some flocks of small birds, such as starlings, which usually fly in loose formations, immediately tighten their formation upon detecting a flying falcon. The effect is to decrease the distance between each bird, so much so that a falcon flying into the group at a fast speed and trying to capture one of the small birds risks injuring itself—the "block" of starlings is almost a solid wall of bird; the close formation also makes a single victim more difficult to target. Biologists believe that the flock tightens when a falcon is detected because the behavior reduces the likelihood of an attack.

Breeding
Falcons nest in vegetation, in tree and rock cavities, or on ledges. Some make stick nests, but others make no obvious nest preparation. Incubation of the eggs takes 25 to 35 days, and in most species is performed only by the female. The male feeds the female until the chicks hatch, and then both sexes feed the chicks. The nestlings fledge after 25 to 49 days in the nest, but the parents continue to feed the young for several weeks after they fledge, until they are proficient hunters.

Notes
People have had a close relationship with falcons for thousands of years. Falconry, in which captive falcons are trained to hunt and kill game at a person's command, may be the oldest sport, with evidence of it being practiced in China 4,000 years ago and in Iran 3,700 years ago. One of the oldest known books on a sport is "The Art of Falconry," written by the King of Sicily in 1248. Although falconry is not as widely practiced today, many countries have aficionados who continue the tradition.

Status
None of Thailand's falcons is considered threatened.

Profiles
Eurasian Kestrel, *Falco tinnunculus*, Plate 27c
Collared Falconet, *Microhierax caerulescens*, Plate 27e

10. Pigeons and Doves

The *pigeon* family, Columbidae, includes about 308 species worldwide, 28 in Thailand. It is a diverse group with representatives on every continent except Antarctica. In Thailand, pigeons inhabit environments from coastal islands to grasslands and evergreen forest. In general the smaller species are called *doves* and the larger species pigeons, but there is considerable inconsistency.

All pigeons are generally recognized as such by almost everyone, a legacy of people's familiarity with domestic and feral pigeons. Pigeons worldwide vary in size from the dimensions of a sparrow to those of a small turkey; Thailand's species range in body length from 21 to 47 cm (8 to 19 in). Doves and pigeons are plump-looking birds with compact bodies, short necks, and small heads. Legs are usually fairly short. Bills are small, straight, and slender. Typically there is a swollen bulge (*cere*) at the base of the bill. Body colors are generally soft and understated grays and browns with an occasional splash of bolder black or white. Some have subtle patches of iridescence, usually on the neck or wings. The female tends to have similar, if somewhat duller, plumage than the male.

Natural History

Ecology and Behavior
Most pigeons and doves are at least partially arboreal, but several spend most of

their time on the ground. They eat seeds, ripe and unripe fruits, berries, and very rarely an insect. They do not have hard bills for seed cracking and thus swallow their food whole. Their chewing is accomplished in the gizzard, a muscular portion of the stomach in which food is smashed against small pebbles and other grit eaten from the soil. As they walk on the ground, all pigeons characteristically bob their heads. Camouflage and rapid flight are the two most important anti-predator tactics used by these birds. Many species are gregarious to some degree, and some form large flocks during the non-breeding season.

Breeding
Doves and pigeons are monogamous breeders. Nests are shallow, open affairs of loose twigs, plant stems, and roots placed on the ground, rock ledges, or in shrubs and trees. Reproductive duties shared by the male and female include nest-building, incubating the 1 or 2 eggs, and feeding the young. All doves and pigeons feed their young regurgitated *pigeon's milk,* a protein-rich fluid produced by sloughing off cells lining the *crop,* an enlarged portion of the esophagus otherwise used for food storage. As the chicks grow older, the proportion of solid food fed them increases until no more pigeon's milk is supplied. Incubation time ranges from 11 to 28 days, depending on species size.

Notes
Although many pigeons today are very common, some species met extinction within the recent past. There are two particularly famous cases. The DODO was a large, flightless pigeon, the size of turkey, with a large head and strong, robust bill and feet. Until the 17th century Dodos lived on the island of Mauritius in the Indian Ocean, east of Madagascar. Reported to be clumsy and stupid (hence the expression, "dumb as a dodo"), but probably just unfamiliar with and unafraid of predatory animals, such as people, they were killed by the thousands by sailors who stopped at the island to stock their ships with food. This caused population numbers to plunge; the birds were then finished off by the pigs, monkeys, and cats introduced by people to the previously predator-free island—animals that ate the Dodos' eggs and young. The only stuffed Dodo in existence was destroyed by fire in Oxford, England, in 1755.

North America's PASSENGER PIGEON, a medium-sized, long-tailed member of the family, suffered extinction because of over-hunting and because of its habits of roosting, breeding, and migrating in huge flocks. People were able to kill many thousands of them at a time on the Great Plains in the central part of the US, shipping the bodies to markets and restaurants in large cities through the mid-1800s. It is estimated that when Europeans first settled in the New World, there were three billion Passenger Pigeons, a population size perhaps never equaled by any other bird, and that they may have accounted for up to 25% or more of all the birds in what is now the US. It took only a little more than 100 years to kill them all; the last one died in the Cincinnati Zoo in 1914.

The common ROCK DOVE, the urban pigeon with which everyone who has visited a city or town is familiar, is a native of the Old World. Domesticated for thousands of years and transported around the world by people, feral populations have colonized all settled and many unsettled areas of the Earth. In the wild, they breed and roost in cliffs and caves.

Status

In Thailand, the PALE-CAPPED PIGEON is listed as globally threatened. The NICOBAR PIGEON, restricted to island habitats, and the LARGE GREEN PIGEON and the GREEN IMPERIAL PIGEON are threatened within Thailand due to forest destruction.

Profiles

Thick-billed Pigeon, *Treron curvirostra*, Plate 32c
Pied Imperial Pigeon, *Ducula bicolor*, Plate 32d
Red Turtle-Dove, *Streptopelia tranquebarica*, 32e
Zebra Dove, *Geopelia striata*, Plate 33a
Spotted Dove, *Streptopelia chinensis*, Plate 33b
Emerald Dove, *Chalcophaps indica*, Plate 33c

11. Parrots

Everyone knows *parrots* as caged pets, so discovering them for the first time in their natural surroundings is often a strange but somehow familiar experience (like a dog owner's first sighting of a wild coyote). One has knowledge and expectations of the birds' behavior and antics in captivity, but how do they act in the wild? Along with hornbills, parrots are probably the birds most commonly symbolic of the Old World tropics. The 300+ parrot species that comprise the family Psittacidae (the "P" is silent; try referring to parrots as psittacids to impress your friends and tour guide!) are globally distributed across the tropics with a few species spilling over into the temperate zones. Seven different species are found in Thailand, occupying forest habitats from mixed deciduous to tropical evergreen forest. Parrot fanciers have their own lexicon of common names that often bear no resemblance to the common names used by ornithologists. In Thailand the common names most widely used divide this family mainly by size: the smaller and short-tailed *parrots* (14 to 19 cm, 6 to 8 in, long), and the larger, long-tailed *parakeets* (33 to 51 cm, 13 to 20 in).

Parrots, regardless of size, share a set of distinctive traits that set them apart from all other birds. They are short-necked with a compact and stocky body. All have a short, hooked bill with a hinge on the upper half that provides great mobility for handling food and for clambering around branches and vegetation. Legs are short, and feet, with toes that are very dexterous, are highly adapted for grasping. Although most species are green, many depart from this scheme, often in a spectacular fashion, with gaudy blues, reds, and yellows. Their raucous calls in flight, usually in flocks, make them easy to see, but when they land in a tree overhead, they can virtually disappear instantaneously. Only the steady rain of discarded fruit parts gives away their presence. Your best view will probably be when a flock suddenly departs a feeding tree, or when a flock is located loafing and squabbling the afternoon away in an isolated, open tree. To distinguish the various species, listen for differences in their voices and look for the length of the tail.

Natural History

Ecology and Behavior

Parrots are incredibly noisy, highly social seed and fruit eaters. Some species give their assortment of harsh, often screeching vocalizations throughout the day, others only in flight, and others call from communal roosts mainly before leaving and when arriving. Many species roost in groups for the night, sometimes in the hundreds in more protected parts of the forest or on islands. Often several species roost together. During early morning, flocks of parrots leave the roost, moving out to cover the forest in search of fruiting trees. They may travel up to 75 km (45 mi) or more in a day. In the afternoon the flocks begin to head back from all directions to the same roosting site.

Parrots use their special locomotory talent to clamber methodically through trees in search of fruits and flowers, using their powerful feet to grasp branches and their bills as, essentially, a third foot. Just like caged parrots, they will hang at odd angles and even upside down, the better to reach some delicious morsel. Parrot feet also function as hands, delicately manipulating food and bringing it to the bill. Parrots feed mostly on fruits and nuts, buds of leaves and flowers, and on flower parts and nectar. Although they are usually considered frugivores, careful study reveals that when they attack fruit, it is often to get at the seeds within. The powerful bill slices open fruit and crushes seeds. As one bird book colorfully put it, "adapted for opening hard nuts, biting chunks out of fruit, and grinding small seeds into meal, the short, thick, hooked parrot bill combines the destructive powers of an ice pick (the sharp-pointed upper mandible), a chisel (the sharp-edged lower mandible), a file (ridged inner surface of the upper mandible), and a vise." Thick, muscular parrot tongues are also specialized for feeding, used to scoop out pulp from fruit and nectar from flowers. Thus parrots, unlike most frugivorous birds, are not ingesting seeds to eventually disperse them when they defecate. They are, more technically, seed predators. However, some studies suggest that because of the large amount of uneaten fruit that they drop to the ground, they make available fruits and their seeds to be dispersed by ground frugivores such as pheasants and rodents. These ground-dwelling species are more properly seed dispersers because they eat the pulp and do not regularly destroy the seeds contained within.

Breeding
In most Thai parrots, the sexes are very similar or identical in appearance. Breeding is monogamous and pairing is often for life. Nesting is carried out during the dry season and, for some, into the early wet season. Most species breed in cavities in dead trees, although a few build nests. A female parrot lays 2 to 8 eggs, which she incubates alone for 17 to 35 days while being periodically fed regurgitated food by her mate. The helpless young of small parrots are nest-bound for 3 to 4 weeks. Both parents feed nestlings and fledglings.

Notes
Parrots have been captured for people's pleasure as pets for thousands of years; Greek records exist from 400 BC describing parrot pets. The fascination stems from the birds' bright coloring, their ability to imitate human speech and other sounds (strangely enough, they do not appear to mimic sounds in the wild), their individualistic personalities (captive parrots definitely like some people while disliking others), and their long lifespans (up to 80 years in captivity). Likewise, parrots have been hunted and killed for food for thousands of years, and, historically, people have killed parrots to protect crops—Charles Darwin noted during his travels that in Uruguay in the early 1800s, thousands of parakeets were killed to prevent crop damage.

Status

Seventy or more parrot species are threatened or endangered worldwide, but within Thailand, only the BLUE-RUMPED PARROT is currently considered threatened. Many Thai parrot species still enjoy healthy populations and are frequently seen. Unfortunately, however, parrots are subject to three powerful forces that in combination take heavy tolls on their numbers: Parrots are primarily forest birds, and forests are increasingly under attack by farmers and developers; parrots are considered agricultural pests by farmers and orchardists owing to their seed- and fruit-eating, and are persecuted for this reason; and parrots are among the world's most popular cage birds. Several Thai species are prized as pets, and nests of these parrots are often robbed of young for local sale as pets or to international dealers. To get to the young birds, the nest tree, often a dead palm, is cut down. Few of the chicks survive the tree fall, and, with each tree cut, another of the few cavity nest sites around has been eliminated for renesting. For every parrot that reaches the marketplace, perhaps 20 to 50 die in the process. Without fast, additional protection, more Thai parrots could soon be threatened.

Profiles

Red-breasted Parakeet, *Psittacula alexandri,* Plate 33d
Vernal Hanging Parrot, *Loriculus vernalis,* Plate 33e

12. Cuckoos

Many of the *cuckoos* are physically rather plain but behaviorally rather extraordinary. As a group they employ some of the most bizarre breeding practices known among birds. Cuckoos, *ground-cuckoos, malkohas,* and *coucals* are considered by some to be in the same family, Cuculidae, which, with a total of 141 species, enjoys a worldwide distribution that includes both temperate and tropical areas; 17 species occur in Thailand. While the cuckoos are shy and solitary birds of woodlands, forests, and dense thickets, coucals are bold, obvious birds of savannahs, brushy scrub, and river edges. Ground-cuckoos are generally shy inhabitants of dense forest floor and thick grassy areas. They are difficult to see under the best of circumstances but tend to make their presence known by loud and often persistent calls and songs. Malkohas are a group of largish, very long-tailed cuckoos.

Most cuckoos are medium-sized, slender, long-tailed birds. Males and females mostly look alike, attired in plain browns, tans, and grays, often with streaked or spotted patches. Several have alternating white and black bands on their tail undersides, and a few cuckoos in Thailand are decorated with green, red, and violet. They have short legs and bills that curve downward at the end. The GREATER COUCAL (Plate 34) is found commonly in open and recently cleared brushlands throughout Thailand. Occasionally it will fly up from the ground or low vegetation and sit motionless on a fence post for many minutes. More often, however, you will be made aware of its presence by its persistent and booming, hooting notes.

Natural History

Ecology and Behavior

Most of the cuckoos are arboreal, but the coucals and ground-cuckoos spend considerable time on the ground. They eat insects, apparently having a special affinity for caterpillars. They even safely consume hairy caterpillars, which are avoided by most other predators because they have painful stinging hairs or even toxic poisons. Cuckoos have been seen snipping off one end of a hairy caterpillar, squeezing the body with the bill and beating it against a branch until the toxic entrails fall out. They can then swallow the remains safely. How they get around the hairs is still a mystery, however. A few cuckoos, such as the GROUND CUCKOO, are ground-dwellers. They are most often seen on the floor of evergreen forest, where they eat large insects and occasionally small lizards and birds.

Breeding

Most of the cuckoos in Thailand are highly evolved brood parasites. They build no nests of their own, and the females lay their eggs in the nests of other species (the hosts). Immediately after hatching, the young cuckoo nestlings push the rightful heirs out of the nest, and the host adults then raise the young cuckoos as their own offspring. Ground-cuckoos, coucals, and malkohas, however, are typical monogamous breeders. The male feeds the female in courtship, especially during her egg-laying period. Both sexes of the malkohas build a plain platform nest that is made of twigs and leaves and placed low in a tree or shrub. The coucals and CORAL-BILLED GROUND-CUCKOO build a domed nest low in bushes. Both sexes incubate the 2 to 6 eggs for about 10 days, and both parents feed the young.

Notes

The name cuckoo comes from the calls made by a common species in Europe, which is also the source of the sounds for cuckoo clocks.

Status

None of Thailand's cuckoos is considered threatened or endangered.

Profiles

Plaintive Cuckoo, *Cacomantis merulinus*, Plate 34a
Common Koel, *Eudynamys scolopacea*, Plate 34b
Green-billed Malkoha, *Phaenicophaeus tristis*, Plate 34c
Greater Coucal, *Centropus sinensis*, Plate 34d

13. Owls

Most *owls* are members of family Strigidae, with about 200 species worldwide, 19 in Thailand. Almost all species are nocturnal, and they share distinctive features such as large heads with forward-facing eyes, hooked bills, plumpish bodies, and sharp claws (talons). They tend to be camouflaged in colors of gray, brown, and black. The group includes species that range in size from 16 to 61 cm (6 to 24 in). The sexes are similar in color pattern, but females tend to be considerably larger. Because it is frequently active near human habitation, the SPOTTED OWLET (Plate 35) is the owl species that you are most likely to see in Thailand. For owls active at night, try locating them by their call notes and songs. When you locate an owl this way, shine a flashlight on it to see it well. Often owls will sit for a long time on the same perch calling and looking around, even in the bright beam of your flashlight. Note the body size and facial patterns to identify them. Also, watch for the "ear" tufts, which are usually evident on species that have them; but they can also be flattened and difficult to see.

Natural History

Ecology and Behavior

In general, owls occupy a variety of habitats: forests, clearings, fields, grasslands, mountains, and marshes. They are considered the nocturnal replacements of the day-active hawks, eagles, and falcons. Although most owls hunt at night, some hunt at twilight (*crepuscular* activity) and a few during the day. Owls eat a broad range of animals, from small mammals, birds, and reptiles to insects and earthworms. Fishing owls are almost exclusively associated with the forested edges of rivers and lakes, where they hunt fish from the water's surface. Some larger owls often develop a taste for smaller owls.

Owl vision is good in low light (mainly in black and white, as they are considered to be largely color-blind). In the absence of moonlight and under the cloak of a forest canopy, however, owls hunt using their ears to locate prey. Not only are the ears themselves extremely sensitive, but the two ears have different-sized openings. The effect of this asymmetry is comparable to the way you turn your head back and forth to better locate a sound. The owl can locate sounds without turning its head, especially important in flight. In addition, owls have soft flight feathers and a sound baffle of fringed feathers on the leading edge of the wings that provide a cloak of silence during flight; few prey can hear them coming. They swallow small prey whole, but instead of digesting or defecating the hard bones, fur, and feathers, they regurgitate these parts in compact *owl pellets*. These gray oblong pellets often accumulate beneath an owl's perch. If you come across some of these pellets, pull them apart to see what the owl has been dining on.

Breeding

Most owls are monogamous breeders. They do not build nests themselves, but either take over nests abandoned by other birds or nest in cavities such as a tree or rock hole. The female alone usually incubates the 1 to 10 eggs for 4 to 5 weeks, but she is fed regularly by her mate. Upon hatching, the female broods the young while the male continues to hunt for her and the young. The chicks fledge after 4 to 6 weeks in the nest.

Notes

The forward-facing eyes of owls are a trait shared with only a few other animals: humans, most other primates, and to a degree, cats. Eyes arranged in this way allow for almost complete binocular vision (both eyes can see the same object but from a slightly different angle), a prerequisite for good depth perception, which, in turn, is important for quickly judging distances when catching prey. However, owl eyes cannot move much, so owls swivel their heads to look left or right. Owls in many parts of the world, including Thailand, are considered an omen of bad luck, or even worse, death. Many indigenous people kill owls when they encounter them to avoid any future visits and bad news brought by the owl.

Status

Owls in Thailand are under attack primarily from forest clearing, but only the WHITE-FRONTED SCOPS OWL is considered threatened throughout its range; in Thailand its range is restricted to the peninsular evergreen forest. A new species of scops owl, not previously known to science, was identified in Malaysia in 2001.

Profiles
Asian Barred Owlet, *Glaucidium cuculoides*, Plate 35a
Spotted Owlet, *Athene brama*, Plate 35b
Brown Hawk-Owl, *Ninox scutulata*, Plate 35d
Brown Fish-Owl, *Ketupa zeylonensis*, Plate 35e

14. Nightjars and Frogmouths

Species of birds known as *nightjars* are in family Caprimulgidae, which has about 70 species worldwide, six species in Thailand. Like their closest relatives, the owls, nightjars are primarily nocturnal. They have a very characteristic appearance. Most range in size from 16 to 32 cm (6 to 12 in) long. They have long wings, medium or long tails, and big eyes. Their small, stubby bills enclose big, wide mouths that they open in flight to scoop up flying insects. Many species have bristles around the mouth area, which act as a food funnel. With their short legs and weak feet, they are poor walkers—flying is their usual mode of locomotion. The plumage of these birds is uniformly cryptic: mottled, spotted, and barred mixtures of browns, grays, tans, and black. They often have white patches on their wings or tails that can be seen only in flight.

The closely related *frogmouths* are placed in family Batrachostomidae, with a total of 12 species that occur from Southeast Asia south into Australia. In Thailand there are 4 species, but only one of them, the JAVAN FROGMOUTH (Plate 35), is found regularly. During the day, frogmouths sit on branches, usually out in the open, and with their camouflaged coloring and their bills pointed into the air, they look like dead branches.

Natural History

Ecology and Behavior
Most nightjars are nocturnal birds, with some becoming active at twilight (*crepuscular* activity). They feed on flying insects, which they catch on the wing, either by forays out from a perched location on the ground or from tree branches, or with continuous circling flight. You can see some species feeding on insects drawn to lights at night. Others you will see only as you flush them from their daytime roost on the ground or in low vegetation. Their camouflage coloring makes them difficult to see, even when you are close to them. The frogmouths are solitary species that hunt at night for large insects and small birds, lizards, and occasionally mammals, mainly on the ground of deep forest. A frogmouth's immense mouth opens like a cavern to catch prey as they pounce on them from a perch in the mid-story.

Breeding
Nightjars breed monogamously. No nest is built, but instead the female lays her 1 or 2 eggs on the ground in a small depression, usually under a bush or a rock. Either the female alone or both sexes incubate the eggs for 18 to 20 days, and both parents feed the young once they hatch. As is typical of many ground-nesting species, regardless of family, nightjars engage in *broken-wing displays* to distract predators away from the nest and young. They flop around on the ground, often with one or both wings held down as if injured, making gargling or hissing sounds, all the while moving away from the nest. Frogmouths build an open-cup nest of twigs in a tree fork or on a horizontal branch, and they lay a single white

egg. Their breeding biology is poorly known, but apparently both sexes are involved with incubation.

Notes
Other names for nightjars are *goatsuckers* and *nighthawks,* both of which are misleading monikers. At twilight some species fly low over the ground near grazing animals, such as goats. The birds often fly right next to the mammals to catch insects being scared up as the goats walk through the grass. Evidently the assumption was that these birds were after the goats' milk, and a legend was born. These often pointed-winged species of birds were also mistaken for hawks flying around at dusk and at night, when accurate identification was difficult, and the name "nighthawk" has stuck ever since. One of the nightjars, North America's COMMON POORWILL, may be the only bird known actually to hibernate, as some mammals do, during very cold weather. During their dormant state, poorwills save energy by reducing their metabolic rate and their body temperature, the latter by about $22°$ C ($40°$ F).

Status
None of Thailand's nightjars or frogmouths is listed as threatened, although the LARGE FROGMOUTH and GOULD'S FROGMOUTH are extremely rare in the country.

Profiles
Javan Frogmouth, *Batrachostomus javensis,* Plate 35c
Great Eared Nightjar, *Eurostopodus macrotis,* Plate 36c
Large-tailed Nightjar, *Caprimulgus macrurus,* Plate 36d

15. Trogons

Although not as familiar to most people as other gaudy birds such as hornbills and parrots, *trogons* are generally regarded by wildlife enthusiasts as among the globe's most visually impressive and glamorous birds. Family Trogonidae inhabits tropical and semitropical regions throughout South and Central America, Africa, and southern Asia. It consists of about 40 species (6 in Thailand), all of them colorful, medium-sized birds with compact bodies, short necks, and short, almost parrot-like bills. Considering the broad and widely separated geographical areas over which the species of this family are spread, the uniformity of the family's body plan and plumage pattern is striking. Males are consistently more colorful than the females. Their breasts and undersides are bright red, buffy, or orange. The duller females usually have the bright back and head colors replaced with brown or gray, but they share the males' brightly colored breasts and bellies. The characteristic tail is long and squared off, with horizontal black and white stripes on the underside. Trogons usually sit erect with their distinctive tails pointing straight down to the ground. Some of Thailand's trogons, such as the RED-HEADED TROGON (Plate 36), are among the region's most stunning birds— seeing them close up, with binoculars or a spotting telescope, can be a treat.

Natural History

Ecology and Behavior
You usually see trogons by themselves or occasionally in pairs. In spite of their persistent calls, they are often difficult to locate and see. Their bright colors meld into the colors of the foliage, and except during their fast and darting flight, they tend

to sit still for long periods. At a fruiting tree they will fly up to a fruit and grab it in the bill without landing. They take big insects and occasionally small lizards in much the same way. They are probably most easily seen as part of a mixed species feeding flock in the mid- to upper levels of closed-canopy forests. At these times they move around more and tend to sit out in the open for short periods.

Breeding
Trogons are monogamous, nesting in tree cavities and occasionally in excavations in arboreal ant nests. Generally the female incubates the 2 or 3 eggs overnight, and the male takes over during the day. Incubation is 17 to 19 days. Both parents tend the young, and fledging is at 14 to 30 days.

Notes
The skin of trogons is so thin that it has been described as being like wet toilet paper. Why is a question no one yet has been able to answer satisfactorily, but it does mean that you are unlikely to ever see trogons fighting with each other; the slightest cut would be severe.

Status
The trogons of Thailand are fairly common, and apparently none is threatened. However, the RED-NAPED TROGON is becoming increasingly rare because of the continuing destruction of the peat swamp forest habitat it occupies in the peninsula.

Profiles
Orange-breasted Trogon, *Harpactes oreskios*, Plate 36a
Red-headed Trogon, *Harpactes erythrocephalus*, Plate 36b

16. Kingfishers

Kingfishers are handsome, bright birds, and most of Thailand's are easy to see. Although generally found along forest streams, canals, mangroves, large rivers, and lakes, several species occur in forests and upland areas. Kingfishers are included in the worldwide family Alcedinidae (but the New World species are sometimes split into their own family, Cerylidae). Nearly 100 species occur throughout the world in temperate and tropical areas, 15 of which are found in Thailand. They range in size from 16 to 43 cm (6 to 17 in), but all are similar in form: large heads with very long, robust, straight bills, short necks, and short legs. Their colors range from black to turquoise and maroon above with white or chestnut breasts.

Natural History

Ecology and Behavior
Some of Thailand's kingfishers are true to their name and feed largely on fish (*piscivores*) and other aquatic animals by diving on them from perches over the water's surface. Some species, however, hunt in forests and gardens for insects and small vertebrates running or hopping on the ground. Usually seen hunting alone, a kingfisher sits quietly on a low branch over water or the forest floor, attentively scanning below. When it sees a prey item, it swoops down and catches it in its bill. If hunting for fish over water, the kingfisher often dives headfirst into the water, sometimes as deep as 60 cm (24 in) to catch the unwary fish in its bill. If successful, the kingfisher returns to its perch, beats the hapless prey item several times on the branch, and then swallows it head first. The PIED KINGFISHER, a largish black and white species that occurs in many parts of Thailand, will also hover over the

water several seconds before making its plunge. Kingfishers have a buzzy and fast flight when moving low through vegetation or over the water's surface.

Breeding
Kingfishers are monogamous breeders that nest in tunnels excavated from vertical or near vertical banks. Both mates help defend their territory, and both also help dig the nest tunnel, which can be 0.75 to 1.5 m (2 to 5 ft) deep. Both parents incubate the 3 to 8 eggs for a total of 19 to 26 days. They feed their young increasingly large prey until they fledge at 25 to 38 days old. Fledglings continue to be fed outside the nest by the parents for up to 10 weeks. Eventually the parents expel the young from the territory, and the young must then establish their own. Kingfishers are notoriously bad housekeepers, and the stench of decaying prey and droppings is often your first clue that a nest tunnel is nearby. This very stench, however, may be so overpowering that it overwhelms the delicate olfactory senses of predators and discourages them from entering to eat what would otherwise be easy prey.

Notes
Kingfishers are the subject of a particularly rich mythology, a sign of the bird's conspicuousness and its association throughout history with oceans, lakes, and rivers. The power over wind and waves that was attributed by sailors to the god Halcyon was passed on to the Halcyon bird, or kingfisher, which became credited with protecting sailors and calming storms. The seven days before and after the winter solstice were thought to be the days when this kingfisher nested and were thus days of peace and calm, the "halcyon" days. Several of Thailand's kingfisher species are in the genus *Halcyon*.

Status
BLYTH'S KINGFISHER, a rare winter visitor to extreme northern Thailand, is considered threatened (IUCN Red List) throughout its range in southern Asia. Among Thailand's resident kingfisher species, the RUFOUS-COLLARED KINGFISHER has become extremely rare in the last few decades, probably owing to destruction of its tropical evergreen forest habitat in the peninsula.

Profiles
Banded Kingfisher, *Lacedo pulchella*, Plate 37a
Common Kingfisher, *Alcedo atthis*, Plate 37b
Black-capped Kingfisher, *Halcyon pileata*, Plate 37c
Collared Kingfisher, *Halcyon chloris*, Plate 37d
White-throated Kingfisher, *Halcyon smyrnensis*, Plate 37e

17. Bee-eaters and Rollers

Bee-eaters and *rollers* are among the Old World's glamour birds—handsome and colorful. They are closely related to each other and, more distantly, to kingfishers, and range over Africa, Asia, and the Australian region. The bee-eater family (Meropidae) includes 24 species, with six in Thailand, and the roller family (Coraciidae) includes 11 species, with two in Thailand. Species of both families are generally flashy, and sometimes dazzling, with bright blues, reds, and greens and raucous and noisy vocalizations. Bee-eaters, 16 to 38 cm (6 to 15 in) long, have long, slender, sharply pointed bills that they use to catch bees and wasps, among other insects; often they have a thick black stripe passing through each eye and very long tails. Rollers, 27 to 38 cm (10.5 to 15 in) long, overall larger and stouter than the slim and streamlined bee-eaters, have large heads, broad bills, short necks, and fairly short legs.

Natural History

Ecology and Behavior

You are most likely to see bee-eaters on treetops, telephone wires, and other high perches in open areas—they are not shy birds. They sit, usually in pairs and family groups, or during the winter in large flocks chattering away, moving their heads back and forth and waiting for a large and tasty insect to fly by. Almost 80% of the diet of some species is made up of bees. A bee-eater darts out and deftly snatches an insect out of the air with the tip of its long bill and then celebrates success with a soaring flourish that returns the bird to a perch, often the same one from which it launched the aerial attack. After slamming the insect against the perch a couple of times, the bee-eater removes the insect's wings and swallows the body. Rollers also perch on high vantage points in open areas, but they are more solitary, and they are as likely to drop to the ground to grab a large insect or frog as they are to sally out to grab an insect in the air.

Breeding

Bee-eaters nest in horizontal burrows (some up to 2.4 m, 8 ft, long) that they dig in steep hillsides or in riverbanks. Both parents incubate the 2 to 4 eggs for a total of 20 to 22 days. They feed insects to the young for 19 to 26 days until fledging. In several bee-eater species nesting is colonial, with non-breeding adults (called "helpers-at-the-nest") aiding in bringing food to the nestlings. Other species, especially the forest-nesting species, such as the RED-BEARDED BEE-EATER (Plate 38), nest solitarily. In these species, the 2 to 6 white eggs are incubated for 10 days. The young must quickly learn to shuffle to the tunnel mouth every time they hear their parents arrive with food. The young fledge about a month later, but the adults continue to feed the juveniles outside the nest for two more weeks. Rollers nest in tree cavities or occasionally in rock crevices. The 3 to 6 eggs are incubated by both parents for almost three weeks. After fledging, the young are fed outside the nest by the adults for about 4 weeks.

Notes

The base of the forward-facing toes of bee-eaters and rollers is fused, apparently to provide a better digging tool for constructing or deepening their nest sites.

Rollers get their name from display flights in which they fly to high altitudes and then swoop down, rolling 360 degrees, and cackling their raucous call. The INDIAN ROLLER (Plate 38), a beautiful brownish and blue bird, is Thailand's most widely distributed roller. Thailand's other roller, the DOLLARBIRD, is named for the white patch on its wing, which is seen only in flight and very loosely resembles a dollar coin.

Much of what we know about the ecology and social behavior of bee-eaters comes from a long-term study of Africa's striking WHITE-FRONTED BEE-EATER, researched in Kenya by a biologist headquartered at New York's Cornell University.

Status

None of the bee-eater or roller species of Thailand is considered threatened or endangered.

Profiles

Indian Roller, *Coracias benghalensis*, Plate 38a
Chestnut-headed Bee-eater, *Merops leschenaulti*, Plate 38b
Blue-bearded Bee-eater, *Nyctyornis athertoni*, Plate 38c
Red-bearded Bee-eater, *Nyctyornis amictus*, Plate 38d
Green Bee-eater, *Merops orientalis*, Plate 38e

18. Hornbills

With their huge bills and often bold body color patterns, the *hornbills* are hard to mistake. The 57 species of family Bucerotidae occur in Africa and across southern Asia to New Guinea. The 12 species found in Thailand live mainly in evergreen and mixed deciduous forest. They are large birds (70 to 127 cm, 2.3 to 4 ft, long), and both sexes of many species have gaudy projections and ornamentation that enhance the size of their already long bills. Furthering their distinctiveness, hornbills have long tails, shortish legs, conspicuous eyelashes, and patches of bare skin on their face and throat that are often brightly colored. In flight, the larger species make a loud whooshing noise with their wings that sounds like a small freight train moving over the canopy of the forest.

Natural History

Ecology and Behavior

Loud and showy, hornbills produce all manner of croaks, creaks, hisses, and squeals. Often seen singly or in pairs during the day, some species form nightly communal roosts during the non-breeding season. Their choice of food is quite broad, and ranges from lizards, snakes, and small birds to insects and fruit. Thai hornbills spend most of their time in the canopy of forests, but many can be coaxed to lower levels by fruiting trees and mass emergence of flying termites.

Breeding

Hornbills have one of the most extraordinary breeding behaviors in the avian world. After a pair selects a tree cavity in a large emergent tree, the female enters it and, with the help of the male, begins to add mud, droppings, and whatever detritus they can find to make the opening to the cavity smaller and smaller. Eventually the female is completely walled in save for a tiny vertical slit. She lays her 2 to 4 eggs and incubates them for several weeks while imprisoned in her self-made cell. She is completely dependent on the male to bring her food. When the young hatch, the male adds to his duty by bringing food for them as well. The BROWN HORNBILL (Plate 39) is unusual in that several extra adults line up to help feed the female and her young inside their prison. After several more weeks, the female chips her way out of the tree cavity and escapes to help feed the young (and regain strength after so much inactive time). The young birds instinctively begin to replaster the hole shut, and they continue to be fed through the slit until they are ready to fledge and face the world on their own. At this time they chip away at the plastered hole, usually with no help from the parents, and squeeze out. The function of the plastered-shut hole may be a protection from predators. Others suggest that it serves as a "chastity belt" on the female so the male knows he is raising and feeding his own young—meaning that, while she is imprisoned in the tree cavity, a female hornbill cannot possibly copulate with other males, as the females of many other supposedly monogamous bird species are now known to do.

Notes

The humongous bills of most hornbills, together with their casques, horns, and other accouterment, appear massive and heavy. Actually they are constructed of a sponge-like tissue covered by a thin horn-like material and are very light. Only the HELMETED HORNBILL (of peninsular Thailand and Malaysia) has a solid casque on top of its bill. This casque is red on the outside, yellow on the inside, and has the texture of heavy plastic. The Chinese call this casque "hornbill ivory" and it is quite valuable when sold in the illicit market. Hornbills can become quite bold, and if not persecuted can even make pests of themselves.

Many campers in Kaeng Krachan National Park have learned the hard way not to leave food in a tent or even covered in the back of a pickup truck. GREAT HORNBILLS (Plate 39) have mastered the complexities of untying tent flaps and opening cardboard boxes, and use their dexterous bill tips to devour unattended food. We worked once at a scientific research station in Papua New Guinea, where one BLYTH'S HORNBILL (New Guinea's sole species) apparently owned the place—it flapped around the station each day, keeping an eye on things when it wasn't rifling through the trash bins or begging food outside the dining hut.

Not surprisingly, hornbills figure prominently in the indigenous cultures in the areas in which they occur. Many Asian groups use hornbill tail feathers in their ceremonial robes and headdresses. In parts of Borneo, the RHINOCEROS HORNBILL, which occurs in Thailand only in the extreme southern portion of the peninsula, and which has a huge reddish casque atop its bill, is imbued with mystical powers; the coat-of-arms of Sarawak, one of the Malaysian provinces on the island of Borneo, features this species.

Status

The WRINKLED, RUFOUS-NECKED, and PLAIN-POUCHED HORNBILLS are considered by the IUCN Red List to be threatened throughout their range, including in Thailand.

Profiles

Oriental Pied Hornbill, *Anthracoceros albirostris*, Plate 39a
Great Hornbill, *Buceros bicornis*, Plate 39b
Brown Hornbill, *Ptilolaemus tickelli*, Plate 39c
Wreathed Hornbill, *Rhyticeros undulatus*, Plate 39d
Bushy-crested Hornbill, *Anorrhinus galeritus*, Plate 39e

19. Barbets

Cousins to the woodpeckers, *barbets* (family Capitonidae) have a broad distribution in the tropics of Africa, southern Asia, and South and Central America, with a total of 83 species (some experts separate the Old World barbets into their own family, Megalaimidae); 13 species are found in Thailand. Barbets are colorful, mainly green with patches of red, orange, yellow, black, and white. Males are somewhat brighter than females. Ranging in size from 16 to 32 cm (6 to 13 in), barbets are stocky birds with largish heads and stout but not long bills.

Thailand's barbets are most common in primary forest, but a fruiting tree in secondary (recently cut) forest nearby can easily tempt them. They also regularly join mixed-species feeding flocks, often high in the canopy.

Natural History

Ecology and Behavior

Most Thai barbets live in evergreen forests, but some species are easily seen in cities and near human habitation. You often see barbets in mated pairs among large mixed-species foraging flocks in the subcanopy. They commonly eat fruits and seeds, but they also take insects and even small lizards. Many barbet species, particularly some of the African species, are known for their loud, raucous duets. A pair perches close together and bursts into cackling song—sometimes alternating notes, sometimes singing simultaneously, but in such a coordinated and spirited racket that it's impossible to tell which bird is producing which sounds.

Breeding

Barbets are apparently monogamous. They nest in tree cavities, either natural cavities or those built originally by woodpeckers; they occasionally use their bills to enlarge holes in softer or dead wood. Nests can be any height above ground up to 30 m (100 ft) or more. Both sexes incubate and feed the 2 to 4 young. Frugivorous birds such as barbets are critical for dispersing seeds away from the parent trees and helping maintain the healthy plant diversity of these forests (see Close-up, p. 175).

Notes

The COPPERSMITH BARBET (Plate 40), is readily seen in city parks and in vegetation near hotels. It gets its name from its monotonous ringing call, which sounds like a worker tapping a piece of metal with a small hammer—on and on, all day long without stopping. The word "barbet" refers to the beard of heavy tufts of modified hair-like feathers that these birds have around the base of their bills.

Status

None of the species of barbets in Thailand is regionally threatened, but the RED-CROWNED BARBET has recently become extremely rare in the peninsular region due to over-cutting of its habitat, tropical evergreen forests. It may soon be eliminated from the country; however, it is somewhat more common in Malaysia.

Profiles

Great Barbet, *Megalaima virens*, Plate 40a
Lineated Barbet, *Megalaima lineata*, Plate 40b
Blue-eared Barbet, *Megalaima australis*, Plate 40c
Red-throated Barbet, *Megalaima mystacophanos*, Plate 40d
Coppersmith Barbet, *Megalaima haemacephala*, Plate 40e

20. Woodpeckers

Everyone knows what a *woodpecker* is, at least by name and perhaps by their cartoon incarnations. They are highly specialized forest birds that occur almost everywhere in the world (even in some places without trees) except Australia, New Zealand, and Antarctica. The family, Picidae, includes more than 200 species that range in size from the tiny *piculets* (9 cm, 3.5 in, long) to the largest woodpeckers (50 cm, 1.7 ft). Thirty-six species of various sizes occur throughout Thailand's diverse habitats. They all share strong, straight, and chisel-like bills, very long and barbed tongues, and sharp toes that spread widely for clinging to tree trunks. All but the small piculets also have stiffly reinforced tail feathers that support them as they climb on vertical surfaces. To accommodate the constant banging and drumming with their bills on wood surfaces, they have extra-spongy bone at the base of the bill to absorb shock waves. They come in mostly subdued shades of gray, green, black, and white, frequently with bars and streaks. Most, however, have bright patches of crimson, especially males.

Natural History

Ecology and Behavior

Woodpeckers are adapted to cling to a tree's bark and move lightly over its surface, listening and looking for insects. They drill holes into bark where they hear insects chewing on the wood and then use their long, often sticky tongues to extract the juicy morsels, which include both adult insects and grubs. Many species also eat fruit, nuts, and nectar from flowers. The piculets forage on the smallest branches of trees, bushes, and bamboo, usually low in the forest; lacking a long stiff tail like the other woodpeckers, they clamber about on horizontal branches. In flight, woodpeckers typically undulate up and down with an alternating short burst of rapid wing beating; this causes a rise in altitude that is followed by a short period of folded-wing gliding in which altitude is lost. They sleep and rest in cavities they excavate from trees. Woodpeckers use their bills and their pecking ability in three ways: for drilling holes to get insect food; for excavating holes for roosting and nesting; and for *drumming*—extra rapid beats, usually on a hollow surface that amplifies the sound, for communication with other woodpeckers.

The holes that woodpeckers excavate for their own nests are used over and over again by a plethora of birds and mammals that cannot excavate their own cavities. Some of these interlopers use abandoned woodpecker holes, but others, such as some barbets (p. 151), will at times evict woodpeckers from their active cavity. These cavities are vital for protection from nest predators and are thus at a premium. Their availability may affect the population sizes of the many species that are dependent on them. A species or group of species whose presence or absence directly affects the ability of many other species to persist in a habitat is called a keystone species. In this case, the protection of woodpeckers, which can be considered keystone species, is important because their absence, and the resulting reduction in the number of tree holes, would harm a large number of other bird species.

Breeding

Woodpeckers are monogamous, and some live in family groups. Tropical woodpeckers usually remain paired throughout the year. Both mates are involved with the nest excavation, and line the interior of the nest with wood chips. Both sexes incubate the 2 to 4 eggs for 11 to 18 days, males typically taking the night shift. They feed the young for 20 to 35 days until fledging. Juveniles remain with the parents outside the nest for several months.

Notes

Woodpeckers often damage trees and buildings in their quest for food and nest sites. They also eat fruits from orchards and gardens and so are considered to be pests in some parts of the tropics.

Status

The PALE-HEADED WOODPECKER, which historically occurred in Thailand only in the extreme north along the Mekong River, is likely now extinct in the country due to destruction of river forest, its only habitat. Thailand's other woodpeckers are not considered threatened.

Profiles

Speckled Piculet, *Picumnus innominatus,* Plate 40f
Rufous Woodpecker, *Celeus brachyurus,* Plate 41a
Common Flameback, *Dinopium javanense,* Plate 41b
Laced Woodpecker, *Picus vittatus,* Plate 41c
Gray-capped Woodpecker, *Picoides canicapillus,* Plate 41d
Heart-spotted Woodpecker, *Hemicircus canente,* Plate 41e
White-bellied Woodpecker, *Dryocopus javensis,* Plate 42a
Great Slaty Woodpecker, *Muelleripicus pulverulentus,* Plate 42b
Crimson-winged Woodpecker, *Picus puniceus,* Plate 42c
Greater Yellownape, *Picus flavinucha,* Plate 42d

All of the birds considered below (except the swifts and treeswifts) are *passerine,* or *perching birds,* members of the order Passeriformes (see p. 121).

---

21. Broadbills and Pittas

Broadbills and *pittas* are two Old World families made up of extremely colorful and attractive forest species. Ranging from Africa to southern Asia and the Philippines, the 15 species of broadbills form the most ancient of all the passerine families, the Eurylamidae. Seven species occur in Thailand, and as their name suggests, they share a broad, heavy bill, almost grotesquely so in some species. They range in color from maroon with yellow spots to all emerald green, and in size from 13 to 30 cm (5 to 11 in). Most species show little difference in coloring between the sexes. In the wild they appear big-headed and sluggish, often sitting in one place for long periods.

Pittas are in family Pittidae, and the 32 species in the family occur primarily in tropical forests from west Africa to India and Australia (12 species in Thailand). Their often brilliant plumages range from bright red to blue, green, and yellow but are often difficult to appreciate in the dark shadows of the deep forest floor they inhabit. They range in size from 18 to 29 cm (7 to 11 in) and appear almost tailless with stout legs. Shy and easily overlooked, they would be almost invisible except for their haunting call notes and whistles. Occasionally, however, they hop out into the brilliant sunshine of an open forest path and make themselves breathtakingly noticeable to even the most jaded of ecotravellers.

Natural History

Ecology and Behavior
Confined to the canopy and subcanopy of evergreen and mixed deciduous forests, broadbills feed primarily on insects taken from leaves and branches or in flight. They occasionally eat small frogs, seeds, and fruits. Most species forage silently in pairs or small family parties, but some species, such as the LONG-TAILED BROADBILL (Plate 43), form large and noisy single-species flocks in the non-breeding season.

Pittas, in contrast, are restricted to the forest floor, where they hop about, turning over dry leaves with their bills. When they are alarmed, they bound away like a rat or fly up to a low branch or a fallen trunk to get a better look at a noisy ecotraveller invading their territory. Usually found in pairs, pittas feed on the ground searching for spiders, insects, snails, earthworms, lizards, and crabs. At times they can be quite noisy as they scratch at the leaf litter with their bills and powerful feet and legs, sending vegetation flying. At night they roost in trees. Most species in Thailand are resident year-round, but several are present only during the summer rainy season for breeding.

Breeding

Although courtship behavior is still poorly known among most broadbill species, some male broadbills give croaking and other unmusical calls during short display flights. The nests are long pendant affairs constructed by both sexes from leaves, roots, stems, and grass and ordinarily suspended low over a forest stream. The entrance hole is on the side toward the bottom and usually has a narrow overhang above it. Both parents incubate the 2 to 8 eggs. Feeding of the young is augmented in some species by adults (known as "helpers-at-the-nest") that are not the parents.

The timid pittas are so difficult to observe that little is known about their courtship and breeding biology. The nest is a large dome of sticks and vegetation shaped like a rugby football and with the entrance to one side. It is lined with fibers and leaves and built on the ground next to a tree base or occasionally low off the ground in a vine tangle or on a fallen trunk. The 2 to 7 eggs are very glossy and incubated by both parents.

Notes

Broadbills are such an ancient group that their closest relatives are difficult to figure out. It appears that because of the shape of their feet and voice box, they are most likely akin to the New World cotingas (mid-sized, colorful fruit-eaters). Because pittas feed in a manner reminiscent to that of the thrushes in Europe, and because of their spectacular colors, the early name for this family was "jewel thrushes."

Status

The BLACK-AND-RED BROADBILL has become extremely rare in Thailand over the last two decades, largely due to cutting of lowland evergreen forest. It is more common in Malaysia and Indonesia, but even there deforestation is affecting it. Four species of pittas are endangered within Thailand, the BAR-BELLIED PITTA, GIANT PITTA, GARNET PITTA, and GURNEY'S PITTA (Plate 43). However, all of these species, except Gurney's Pitta, are found more commonly in neighboring countries. Gurney's Pitta is now restricted to a single forest reserve in peninsular Thailand, and four sites in neighboring Myanmar. There may be no more than a hundred pairs total that make up the entire species. The cause of its demise is undoubtedly habitat destruction of the lowland forest to which it is restricted, compounded by trapping for the cage-bird trade.

Profiles

Dusky Broadbill, *Corydon sumatranus,* Plate 43a
Black-and-yellow Broadbill, *Eurylaimus ochromalus,* Plate 43b
Long-tailed Broadbill, *Psarisomus dalhousiae,* Plate 43c
Blue Pitta, *Pitta cyanea,* Plate 43d
Gurney's Pitta, *Pitta gurneyi,* Plate 43e

22. Swifts, Treeswifts, and Swallows

Swifts, treeswifts, and *swallows* are remarkably similar in appearance and behavior, but only the treeswifts and swifts are in closely related families. All three of these groups rely on the same feeding technique, catching insects on the wing during long periods of sustained flight. Treeswifts and swifts, although superficially resembling swallows, are instead closely related to hummingbirds. There are 100 or so species of swifts (family Apodidae) worldwide in temperate and tropical areas; 12 species are found in Thailand, albeit some only rarely. The similar treeswifts (family Hemiprocnidae) differ by having a crest on top of the head and being more brightly colored. The four species in this family range from Southeast Asia to Australia, and three of these species occur in Thailand. Swifts and treeswifts, like swallows, are slender, streamlined birds, with long, pointed wings. They are 17 to 33 cm (6.5 to 13 in) long and have very short legs, short tails or long, forked tails, and very short but broad bills. Swifts' tails are stiffened to support the birds as they cling to vertical surfaces. Treeswifts have softer but long and forked tails for maneuvering in the air. The sexes of swifts and treeswifts look alike: sooty-gray or brown, with white or grayish rumps or flanks. Many are glossily iridescent. Five of the swift species found in Thailand are migrants from northern nesting areas. The rest of the Thai swift species and all of the treeswifts are resident year-round, several species commonly living on or near human habitation.

The swallow family, Hirundinidae, is related to perching birds such as flycatchers, warblers, and thrushes. There are 80 species of swallows worldwide and 11 species in Thailand, five of which winter here or pass through on their way to or from northern Asian breeding grounds. Swallows are small, streamlined birds, 11.5 to 21.5 cm (4.5 to 8.5 in) long, with short necks, bills, and legs. They have long, pointed wings and often forked tails, wonderfully adapted for fast and sustained flight; they have amazing maneuverability in the air as they pursue flying insects or chase each other for competitive or amorous intentions. Some are colored in shades of blue, green, or black, but many are gray or brown. The sexes generally look alike, at least to us.

Natural History

Ecology and Behavior
Among the birds, swifts, treeswifts, and swallows represent the pinnacle of flying prowess and aerial pursuit of insects. It seems as if they fly effortlessly all day, circling low over water and land, or flying in seemingly erratic patterns high overhead. Swifts especially are perpetual fliers, rarely roosting except at night, when they come together in large groups to spend the non-flying hours gathered on a vertical cliff face behind a waterfall, inside a hollow tree, or among the fronds of a palm tree. They roost on these vertical surfaces clinging with their tiny but sharply clawed feet and bracing themselves against the sides of the roost with their stiff tail feathers. A swift spends more time airborne than any other type of bird, even copulating in the air in a death-defying tailspin that gives real meaning to the concept of sexual thrills. The name swift is apt, as these are the fastest flying birds in level flight, moving along at up to 160 kph (100 mph). Treeswifts also frequently show off their flying prowess high overhead, but just as often they sally out after flying insects from an exposed perch in a tree. Swifts and treeswifts can be distinguished from swallows by their faster, more twittering wing beats, made possible by an exceptionally short arm bone (the humerus). Some species

of swifts hunt every day for insects hundreds of miles from the nesting area. The chicks of swifts have the ability to go into short-term physiological inactivity (*torpor*) during extended periods of inclement weather, when no insects are flying. They can endure the lack of food for up to a week by lowering their body temperatures and energy requirements (and thus their need for food).

Swallows also take insects on the wing as they fly back and forth over water and open areas. Some also eat berries. Swallows perch more frequently than swifts, often resting during the hottest parts of the day on tree branches over water or open areas. Directly after dawn, however, and at dusk, swallows are always airborne. Because swallows depend each day on capturing enough insects, their daily habits are largely tied to the prevailing weather. Flying insects are thick in the atmosphere on warm, sunny days, but they are relatively scarce on cold, wet ones. Therefore, on good days, swallows can catch their fill of bugs virtually anywhere in only a few hours of flying. But on cool, wet days, they may need to forage all day to find enough food, and they tend to do so over water or low to the ground, where under such conditions bugs are more available.

Breeding

Swifts and treeswifts are monogamous, and while most swifts are colonial breeders, treeswifts nest solitarily. The sexes share nesting chores. Swift nests are usually attached to vertical surfaces of rocks, tree cavities, or palm fronds, depending on the species of swift. The nests consist of plant pieces, twigs, and feathers glued together with the birds' saliva. One to 6 eggs are incubated for 16 to 28 days, with young fledging at 25 to 65 days of age. Treeswifts construct a tiny cup nest out of bark and feathers and attach it to the side of a tree branch, often in a fork. They lay a single large, blue-gray egg. Swallows are also monogamous; many species breed in dense colonies of hundreds to thousands of pairs. They make nests of mud and some plant material that they attach to vertical surfaces, or they nest in cavities of trees or tunnel into vertical banks. Both sexes or the female alone incubates the 3 to 7 eggs for 13 to 16 days. Both parents help feed the young for 18 to 28 days, until the young fledge.

Notes

Although almost all species of swifts and treeswifts use some of their sticky saliva to hold their nests together, nests of EDIBLE-NEST SWIFTLETS (from India and Indonesia) are almost totally made of saliva. These nests are harvested to make bird's nest soup. Swallows have a long history of beneficial association with people. People's alterations of natural habitats, harmful to so many species, are often helpful to swallows (and swifts), which adopt buildings, bridges, road culverts, road banks, and quarry walls as nesting and roosting areas. BARN SWALLOWS (Plate 44) in some areas of Eurasia have for the most part given up nesting in anything other than human-crafted structures. In downtown Bangkok near Silom Road, wintering Barn Swallows roost together each night for half the year. Nearly a half-million swallows sit side by side on wires, buildings, and trees despite the traffic and pollution. Perhaps here they escape predators too timid to enter the concrete jungle. The result of this close association with humans is that, going back as far as ancient Rome, swallows have been considered good luck. Superstitions attached to the relationship abound; for example, it is said that the cows of a farmer who destroys a swallow's nest will give bloody milk. Arrival of the first migratory Barn Swallows in Europe is considered a welcoming sign of approaching spring.

Status

So little is known of many species of swifts, treeswifts, and swallows that we are uncertain of their populations' sizes or vulnerabilities. One of Thailand's only two endemic bird species is a swallow called the WHITE-EYED RIVER-MARTIN (the other is Deignan's Babbler; p. 166), and its history presents the mother of all mysteries. In 1968, while netting and marking immense numbers of roosting Barn Swallows in the reeds of a 100 sq-km (38 sq-mi) lake named Bung Boraphet in central Thailand, Thai biologists netted eight specimens of a bizarre black swallow completely new to science. Since then, this species has been seen only three more times, all in the same area, but not since 1980. Is this part of Thailand its wintering area? Where does it nest? Is it now extinct? No one knows the answers to these questions.

Profiles

House Swift, *Apus affinis,* Plate 44a
Asian Palm-Swift, *Cypsiurus balasiensis,* Plate 44b
Crested Treeswift, *Hemiprocne coronata,* Plate 44c
Barn Swallow, *Hirundo rustica,* Plate 44d
Striated Swallow, *Hirundo striolata,* Plate 44e

23. Pipits and Cuckoo-shrikes

The globally distributed family Motacillidae (66 species worldwide, 9 in Thailand) is made up of the *pipits* and *wagtails,* and the Old World tropical family Campephagidae (82 species worldwide, 18 in Thailand) is made up of *cuckoo-shrikes* and *minivets.* All the species of pipits and wagtails are small birds (13 to 22 cm, 5 to 9 in) with thin, slender bills and long legs that they use to run and walk on the ground. The sexes are similar, brownish with stripes or streaks among the pipits and bold patterns of black and white, yellow, or gray among the wagtails. The wagtails constantly bob their tails up and down as they walk along or even when sitting perched on a low branch or rooftop. The family is distributed from temperate to tropical areas around the world, although wagtails are limited to the Old World.

Cuckoo-shrikes and minivets vary considerably in size (13 to 31 cm, 5 to 12 in). The stockier cuckoo-shrikes are all some shade of gray, black, and white and the sexes appear similar. The slender minivets, however, are flashy black and red (males) or gray and yellow (females). Most members of this family have stiff feathers on the lower back that can be raised like porcupine quills.

Natural History

Ecology and Behavior

Pipits and wagtails pursue their insect prey on the ground with short sprints but sometimes fly up off the ground a short distance to capture an escaping bug. Wagtails are almost always seen near wet meadows, pond edges, and river beaches. Some wagtails will associate with large mammals, such as cows, and capture the insects that are scared up by the bovine feet. Pipits tend to be in drier grasslands, but several species commonly occur on paddy dikes and in wet meadows. Pipits are also more catholic in their diets, eating seeds as well as insects.

Cuckoo-shrikes and minivets primarily eat insects, especially caterpillars. The cuckoo-shrikes often form small parties and sit high in the tops of isolated trees.

Minivets are usually in large mixed-species feeding flocks high in the trees. Cuckoo-shrikes forage for large insects from the branches and outer leaves, and the minivets sally out to catch insects scared up by other members of their bird party. Both Cuckoo-shrikes and minivets occasionally also eat fruits.

Breeding
Pipits and wagtails nest on the ground or in rock crevices. The well-concealed nest is cup-like and constructed of grasses and vegetative fibers. Tropical species lay 2 to 3 eggs and take about 2 weeks to hatch. The young are fed by both parents in some species and by only the female in others. Male pipits have a short flight display in which they fly up quickly into the air and flutter slowly down, all the time singing a long tinkling song. Wagtails use courtship displays that remain on the ground and involve considerable tail and wing spreading.

Among cuckoo-shrikes, both parents build the cup-like nest high in a tall tree. They cover its outside with lichens and spider webbing for camouflage. Although in many species the female alone incubates the 2 to 3 eggs, the male shares in feeding duties when the young hatch. Minivets build cup nests, made of twigs, roots, and grass stems, usually placed on a horizontal tree branch.

Notes
Pipits and wagtails are so at home on the ground because they don't need to hop around. Instead they have relatively long, powerful legs for running swiftly in pursuit of their prey as well as for avoiding enemies. Some pipits have a claw on the hind toe that is curved, sharp, and almost as long as the toe itself. The function of this extra long claw is still not known.

Status
Eight species of Thailand's pipits and wagtails are winter visitors, some coming from nesting grounds in northern Siberia. Only the PADDYFIELD PIPIT (Plate 45) is resident year-round. None of the species of this family or that of the cuckoo-shrikes found in Thailand is considered threatened.

Profiles
Gray Wagtail, *Motacilla cinerea*, Plate 45a
White Wagtail, *Motacilla alba*, Plate 45b
Paddyfield Pipit, *Anthus rufulus*, Plate 45c
Scarlet Minivet, *Pericrocotus flammeus*, Plate 45d
Large Cuckoo-Shrike, *Coracina macei*, Plate 45e

24. Ioras and Leafbirds

Considerable controversy surrounds the family status of the *ioras* and *leafbirds*. Some ornithologists place all 14 species (9 in Thailand) together into a single family, Chloropseidae. Others separate out the ioras (3 Thai species) and place them in the crow family, Corvidae (p. 163), and put the leafbirds and *fairy-bluebirds* in the family Irenidae (6 Thai species). Whatever their relationships, ioras and leafbirds do share many similarities, and we will treat them here as one group. If they are indeed in a single family, it is the only bird family unique to the Oriental region of the world. They vary in length from 12 to 24 cm (5 to 9 in) and share a relatively long and somewhat down-curved bill. Greens, blues, and yellow predominate in these tree-loving species. The males of some of the species are more colorful than the females, most dramatically in the fairy-bluebirds.

Natural History

Ecology and Behavior
Found primarily in the midlevels and canopy of primary and secondary forests, most of the food of leafbirds and ioras is fruit and seeds eaten from large fruit such as guavas and figs. Some insects are eaten from leaves and fruit, more so by the ioras than other species in this group. The leafbirds also commonly suck nectar from flowers. In the non-breeding season many leafbirds and ioras form flocks of their own species or participate in large mixed-species foraging flocks that move through the canopy of forests.

Breeding
The nests of leafbirds and ioras are cup-shaped and placed in the crotch of two small branches high in the foliage. The fairy-bluebirds make a much larger nest out of sticks and moss. The 2 to 4 eggs are incubated for about two weeks by the female leafbirds and fairy-bluebirds and by both parents in the ioras.

Notes
Leafbirds are accomplished mimics of other birds' songs. Sometimes a pair of leafbirds hidden from view in the canopy can sound like an entire mixed-species flock. Why some birds have this ability to mimic is not clear. Perhaps if song serves as a way of marking a bird's territory, it is a way of keeping out other species as well as your own in a competitive free-for-all.

Status
None of Thailand's leafbirds or ioras is considered threatened or endangered, although by many reports the ASIAN FAIRY-BLUEBIRD (Plate 46) is eagerly sought-after as a cage-bird in some areas.

Profiles
Common Iora, *Aegithina tiphia*, Plate 46a
Golden-fronted Leafbird, *Chloropsis aurifrons*, Plate 46b
Blue-winged Leafbird, *Chloropsis cochinchinensis*, 46c
Asian Fairy-bluebird, *Irena puella*, Plate 46d

25. Bulbuls

The bulbuls, family Pycnonotidae, are a large Old World tropical group of about 125 species, with 36 in Thailand. They are medium-sized but slender passerine birds, 14 to 29 cm (5.5 to 11 in) long, with moderately long tails and bills. The sexes usually share a similar plumage and color pattern. Bulbuls are often abundant birds, and the beginning birdwatcher in Thailand will likely see more bulbuls than any other kind of bird.

Natural History

Ecology and Behavior
This large family has spread into many habitats, but generally most species are found either in open, scrubby vegetation or in forest interiors and forest edges. Most species are gregarious, travelling in small to large family groups or with starlings and babblers. Many species have loud songs and some can mimic other species. Fruit is the main food of bulbuls, but some species also regularly take insects from leaves or probe flowers for nectar.

Breeding

Both parents share in nest building, incubation, and feeding the young. Nests are either cup-shaped or suspended in the crotch of two small branches. Most are bulky with twigs, stems, and dry grass held together with spider webbing. Some species nest low in the undergrowth and others in the canopy of tall trees. The 2 to 5 eggs take about 2 weeks to hatch and then the young spend another 2 weeks in the nest.

Notes

Because of their often flashy colors, bold behavior, and rich song repertoire, several species of bulbuls have been introduced outside their ranges to other parts of the world. The RED-WHISKERED BULBUL (Plate 47), for instance, is a regular visitor to fruiting trees and feeding stations in southern parts of Miami, Florida. Often, however, these introductions of "exotic" species can have a detrimental impact on native species of animals and plants. The Miami population of Red-whiskered Bulbuls has barely held its own over the last few decades, however, and has not expanded its range to other areas. It could easily have become a pest on fruiting trees. The Red-whiskered Bulbul and the RED-VENTED BULBUL, both native to India and Southeast Asia, were introduced to Hawaii during the 1950s and 1960s and are now fairly common birds on the island of Oahu.

Status

The STRAW-HEADED BULBUL is likely extinct now in Thailand, probably due to a combination of forest destruction and capture for the cage-bird industry. It is on the IUCN Red List as threatened throughout its range in southeastern Asia. Even one of the most common bulbuls in the country, the RED-WHISKERED BULBUL, is now difficult to find in many parts of its range due to capturing for the cage bird industry.

Profiles

Black-crested Bulbul, *Pycnonotus melanicterus,* Plate 47a
Red-whiskered Bulbul, *Pycnontus jocosus,* Plate 47b
Sooty-headed Bulbul, *Pycnonotus aurigaster,* Plate 47c
Black Bulbul, *Hypsipetes madagascariensis,* Plate 47d
Streak-eared Bulbul, *Pycnonotus blanfordi,* Plate 47e

26. Drongos and Orioles

The all-black *drongos* are noisy and conspicuous. They range in size from 18 to 38 cm (7 to 15 in), not including the extra-long tail shafts of species such as the GREATER RACKET-TAILED DRONGO (Plate 48). Sittin g boldly at the tops of trees, bushes, and telephone poles, drongos are hard to ignore. They tend toward long, forked tails, and some species are ornamented with crests and wire-like tail extensions. The sexes are similar in color and shape. This Old World tropical family (Dicruridae) has 24 species, but only seven occur in Thailand. The closely related Old World *oriole* family (Oriolidae) has 29 species worldwide and six species in Thailand. They are relatively uniform in size, 20 to 28 cm (8 to 11 in) long. Although they are not as bold or conspicuous as the drongos, the flashy black and bright yellow plumage of the males of most oriole species, together with their flute-like whistles, make them easy to notice. The females tend to be duller with streaked breasts. Even though they share a common name and superficially look alike, the New World orioles are only distantly related to Thailand's orioles.

Natural History

Ecology and Behavior

The drongos feed primarily on insects they capture by sallying out from their exposed perch and grabbing them in the air. Their wings are long and pointed so that together with their long tails they can maneuver better to make spectacular pursuits of insects, changing direction in a heartbeat. Most species of drongos are solitary or found in pairs. They are aggressive, quick to chase other birds, even large hawks and eagles, that approach their feeding territories or nest sites. In some areas, small birds will nest close to a drongo nest as an umbrella of security—the drongo, in chasing every potential enemy from its nest area, also ends up protecting the smaller nesting birds nearby. Some species, such as the HAIR-CRESTED DRONGO (Plate 48), often gather in large flocks to feed on the nectar of a flowering tree. Other drongos regularly perch on the back of large herbivorous mammals or near them to catch insects scared up from the ground and vegetation by the mammals' feet. Forest species are often found in large mixed-species foraging parties.

Orioles eat insects from leaves in trees, but they also eat fruit when it is available. Usually seen alone or in pairs, orioles will occasionally join large mixed-species foraging parties. Three of Thailand's oriole species are present only as winter residents; the others show local movements within the country or are resident year-round.

Breeding

The small nest of drongos is hung in the fork of narrow branches high in the crown of a tree or in the base of tall palm tree fronds. It is made of small twigs and grass fibers and in many species is held together with spider webbing. Both parents help construct the nest, incubate the eggs, and feed the young. Orioles make a much more elaborate nest, woven from grass and bark strips and hung like a hammock from a forked branch. They frequently add moss and lichens to camouflage their handiwork. The female constructs the nest, and she is largely in charge of incubating the 3 to 5 eggs for almost 2 weeks. The male, however, does find some time to feed the brooding female as well as help feed the young after they are hatched.

Notes

Because of their pugnacious behavior, drongos are called "King Crows" in some parts of the world. The word oriole is derived from the Latin word for golden, *aureolus*, the predominant color in many species. Migrating GOLDEN ORIOLES can become pests in orchards as they consume fruits on their passage from European breeding areas to Asian and African wintering grounds.

Status

No drongo species is considered threatened or endangered. The SILVER ORIOLE, which nests in southern China and winters rarely in Thailand, is a threatened species throughout its range (IUCN Red List). No other Thai orioles are considered threatened or endangered.

Profiles

Greater Racket-tailed Drongo, *Dicrurus paradiseus*, Plate 48a
Black-naped Oriole, *Oriolus chinensis*, Plate 48b
Hair-crested Drongo, *Dicrurus hottentotus*, Plate 48c
Black Drongo, *Dicrurus macrocercus*, Plate 48d

27. Crows and Magpies

Crows, magpies, treepies, and *jays* are members of the Corvidae, a passerine family of 119 species that occurs just about everywhere in the world—or, as ecologists would say, corvid distribution is *cosmopolitan.* Twelve species occur in Thailand. Crows prefer open habitats, but treepies, magpies, and jays are primarily woodland or forest birds. Members of this family, aside from being strikingly handsome birds, are known for their versatility, adaptability, and for their seeming intelligence. In several ways, the group is considered by ornithologists to be one of the most highly developed of birds. They are also usually quite noisy.

Members of the family range in length from 18 to 77 cm (7 in to 2.5 ft), many near the higher end—large for passerine birds. *Corvids* have robust, fairly long bills and strong legs and feet. Many of them (crows, ravens, rooks, jackdaws) are all or mostly black, but the jays, magpies, and treepies are different, being attired in bright blues, purples, greens, yellows, and white. In corvids, the sexes generally look alike. The COMMON RAVEN is the largest passerine bird in the world, but although its range encompasses several continents, it does not extend to Thailand. There are 11 corvid species in Thailand, most of which you will see in small family groups (theirs, not yours).

Natural History

Ecology and Behavior
Corvids eat a variety of foods (and try to eat many others) and so are considered *omnivores.* They feed on the ground but also in trees, eating carrion, insects (including some in flight), fruits, and nuts, and also bird eggs and nestlings. They are considered to be responsible for a significant percentage of the nest predation on many songbird species, particularly those with open-cup nests. Bright and versatile, they are quick to take advantage of new food sources and to find food in agricultural and other human-altered environments. Jays use their feet to hold food down while tearing it with their bills. Hiding food for later consumption, *caching,* is practiced widely by the group.

Most corvids are quite social, Thai species being no exception. Many of these species remain all year in small groups of relatives, 5 to 10 individuals strong. They forage together within a restricted area, or *home range,* and at the appropriate time, breed together on a group-defended territory. Corvids are usually raucous and noisy, giving varieties of harsh, grating, loud calls as the foraging flock straggles from tree to tree, but at times they can be amazingly quiet and unobtrusive, especially during the breeding season.

Breeding
Several species of jays raise young cooperatively. Generally the oldest pair in the group breeds and the other members serve only as *helpers,* assisting in nest construction and feeding the young. Courtship feeding is common, the male feeding the female before and during incubation, which she performs alone. Bulky, open nests, constructed primarily of twigs, are placed in trees or rock crevices. Two to 7 eggs are incubated for 16 to 21 days, the young then being fed in the nest by parents and helpers for 20 to 24 days.

Notes
Although considered by many to be among the most intelligent of birds, and by ornithologists as among the most highly evolved, corvid folklore is rife with tales

of crows, ravens, and magpies as symbols of ill omen. This undoubtedly traces to the group's frequent all-black plumage and habit of eating carrion, both seen as sinister traits. COMMON RAVENS in particular have long been associated in many northern cultures with evil or death, although these large, powerful birds also figure more benignly in Nordic and Middle Eastern mythology. Several groups of indigenous peoples of northwestern North America consider the Raven sacred and sometimes, indeed, as a god.

Status
Some of Thailand's corvid species are fairly rare, but none is considered globally threatened. The HOUSE CROW is apparently extinct in Thailand, but it is common in many other parts of its extensive range. Many corvids adjust well to people's activities, often expanding their ranges when they can feed on agricultural crops. The RACHET-TAILED TREEPIE occurs in Thailand only as a single small population in Kaeng Krachan National Park. The nearest neighboring population is in Vietnam. Only recently discovered in Thailand, no one knows if the Kaeng Krachan population is somehow new or was there all the time, if it is a remnant of a formerly more continuous range, or if there are other undiscovered pockets of this species in between there and Vietnam.

Profiles
Large-billed Crow, *Corvus macrorhynchos*, Plate 49a
Blue Magpie, *Urocissa erythrorhyncha*, Plate 49b
Green Magpie, *Cissa chinensis*, Plate 49c
Rufous Treepie, *Dendrocitta vagabunda*, Plate 49d

28. Tits and Nuthatches

Two families that are mainly found in cold northern climes reach their southern extremes here in tropical Thailand, the *tits* (family Paridae), with 58 species worldwide (6 in Thailand), and the *nuthatches* (family Sittidae), with 23 species worldwide (5 in Thailand). Tits are small arboreal birds (11 to 20 cm, 4.5 to 8 in) with short bills and long, strong feet for hanging like acrobats from small branches. Nuthatches are also arboreal and about the same size, but the similarities end there. The portly, short-tailed nuthatches have stout, pointed bills and short legs used for climbing up and down vertical surfaces, mainly tree trunks.

Natural History

Ecology and Behavior
Both tits and nuthatches are fond of insects, but they also eat seeds. In the non-breeding season, birds from both these families commonly join mixed-species foraging flocks—the nuthatches prizing insects from cracks in bark and the tits gleaning them from small twigs and leaves. Both also handle seeds in a similar way—they take a seed and either wedge it into a crevice or hold it in their toes, and then hammer it relentlessly with their bills until it breaks open.

Breeding
Members of both families are cavity-nesters, usually occupying an old woodpecker hole or a rotted area of wood that they can easily excavate. Many nuthatches add mud and other debris to the nest hole entrance to make it smaller. Tits are notorious for their large clutches of eggs, in which a single pair will have 6 to 15 eggs. Incubation takes about 12 days, but the young are fed in the cavity for almost three

weeks before fledging. Each pair of nuthatches will lay 6 to 10 eggs in a nest; the young take 2 weeks to hatch and are then fed in the cavity for almost a month. Both tits and nuthatches are solitary breeders and rigorously defend their territories against other individuals of their own species. However, when the breeding season is over, they change their ways and become almost exclusively gregarious.

Notes
Nuthatches are among the few birds in the world that have been recorded using tools. Some species break off small twigs to hold in their bills and use them to draw insect grubs out of holes that are beyond the reach of their unaided bills.

Status
Both the BEAUTIFUL NUTHATCH and GIANT NUTHATCH are on the IUCN's Red List of threatened species. These two Asian species barely range into the extreme northern parts of Thailand in highland pine forests.

Profiles
Yellow-cheeked Tit, *Parus spilonotus,* Plate 50a
Sultan Tit, *Melanochlora sultanea,* Plate 50b
Velvet-fronted Nuthatch, *Sitta frontalis,* Plate 50c
Chestnut-bellied Nuthatch, *Sitta castanea,* Plate 50d

29. Babblers

The *babblers* make up an immense family (Timaliidae) of 274 species, 70 of which live in Thailand. Occurring throughout the Old World tropics, they reach the zenith of their diversity in southeastern Asia. With such a large number of species, you might expect a tremendous range in forms, shapes, and adaptations to different habitats—and you would be right. They vary in length from 9 to 30 cm (3.5 to 12 in) and mainly occupy habitats in evergreen forest, although a few species can be found in scrubby grasslands. Most species have camouflage colors of brown, gray, and white, but a few are boldly colored in reds, yellows, and oranges.

Natural History

Ecology and Behavior
Generally found in the undergrowth and lower levels of forest, these species are not strong fliers. They often are found together in family groups of 3 to 30 individuals, or in mixed-species foraging flocks. On the ground they use their bills to turn over leaves, looking for invertebrates to eat. Species that forage for insects at higher levels in the forest glean them off leaves and vegetation. Many species also eat fruits.

Breeding
Babblers employ a variety of mating systems, and cooperative breeding is common in the family. In these systems, only 1 or perhaps 2 pairs in a family group breed; the other members of the group participate as "helpers," assisting the breeding pair with feeding young and sometimes even with incubation of eggs. Most species build domed nests out of moss and dead leaves with a hole on the side for an entrance. Some nests are placed on or near the ground, while other species build cup-like nests high in bushes or trees. Both parents incubate the 2 to 5 eggs and share in feeding of the young.

Notes

The strange compound names of some of these birds, such as tit-babbler, shrike-babbler, rail-babbler, and laughingthrush, arose partially because, to the naturalists who first named them, there were obvious parallels in size and, at least superficially, appearance, of these various species to European and Asian tits, shrikes, rails, and thrushes. Further confusing the issue has been the long tendency of scientists who classify birds to place bird species that lack obvious relatives into the babbler family; the result is a "catch-all" family whose members may or may not really belong together.

The "handicap principle" of evolutionary biology was first proposed by an ornithologist who spent many years observing the breeding antics and courtship displays of male Arabian Babblers, *Turdoides squamiceps*, in Israel. The theory suggests that many "flashy" breeding characteristics of male animals, such as exaggerated tails of peacocks and elaborate courtship flight or "dancing" displays, which all make males more conspicuous to predators, evolved because they permit males to "show off" to females, to demonstrate that even with these "handicaps" against concealment, they are of sufficient quality to survive and prosper. Therefore, they are "high quality" individuals that females should choose to mate with and make the fathers of their offspring.

Status

Due to destruction of lowland evergreen forest, especially in the peninsula, several species of babblers recently have become very rare in Thailand: WHITE-CHESTED BABBLER, SOOTY-CAPPED BABBLER, STRIPED WREN-BABBLER, LARGE WREN-BABBLER, and BLACK-THROATED BABBLER. All these species, however, occur more commonly in Malaysia and Indonesia. In the north, the SHORT-TAILED PARROTBILL barely enters Thailand, but it is on the IUCN Red List as threatened throughout its range. Also in the north, one of Thailand's two endemic bird species, DEIGNAN'S BABBLER (the other is the White-eyed River-Martin; p. 158), is restricted to one mountaintop, Doi Chiang Dao. It has not been seen for several years.

Profiles

White-bellied Yuhina, *Yuhina zantholeuca*, Plate 50e
Lesser Necklaced Laughingthrush, *Garrulax monileger*, Plate 51a
White-crested Laughingthrush, *Garrulax leucolophus*, Plate 51b
White-browed Shrike-Babbler, *Pteruthius flaviscapis*, Plate 51c
Puff-throated Babbler, *Pellorneum ruficeps*, Plate 51d
White-browed Scimitar-Babbler, *Pomatorhinus schisticeps*, Plate 51e
Pygmy Wren-Babbler, *Pnoepyga pusilla*, Plate 51f
Gray-headed Parrotbill, *Paradoxornis gularis*, Plate 52b

30. Old World Warblers

The huge and worldwide family of *Old World warblers*, Sylviidae (361 species), is well represented in Thailand with 58 species. Unfortunately for ease of identifying and watching, many (some would say most) are small (10 to 20 cm, 4 to 8 in), brownish or olive, and lacking overtly distinctive characteristics. The 33 species of this family that escape the cold Siberian winter to spend this time in Thailand's warm forests tend to be among the most difficult species to distinguish in the family. Unlike the New World warblers (family Parulidae), which have nine long flight (primary) feathers in each wing, Old World warblers have 10; of course, only a journeyman birdwatcher or ornithologist would consider counting feathers, but it is a distinctive if not readily seen trait. Many of these species make up in voice what they lack in visual attractiveness, and the epithet of "warbler" is wonderfully appropriate.

Natural History

Ecology and Behavior
Primarily insectivores, some Old World warbler species, especially the migrant species, also eat fruits as a way to lay on fat for energy during their long flights north and south. Many species of Old World warblers occupy forests from the floor to the canopy. During the winter both resident and winter visitors join mixed-species foraging parties in the forest. Some species are restricted to marsh edges and mangrove areas. Others are found in scrubby uplands and dry grassy areas.

Breeding
Almost all species of Old World warblers are monogamous, and pairs defend breeding territories. Nests are usually elaborately built with fine grasses, spider webbing, mosses, and loose mammal hair. Most species construct cup-shaped nests suspended from reeds or a fork in the branches of a bush or tree. Some species build domed nests near to or on the ground. The most elaborate, however, are constructed by *tailorbirds*, such as the DARK-NECKED TAILORBIRD (Plate 52). These birds make their nests by sewing together the edges of large leaves like teak (p. 30). Vegetable down is used as the thread and the bird's bill as the sewing needle. The nest itself is placed in the cone formed by the stitched leaf and consists of plant down, spider webbing, and bark fiber. In general, both sexes of Old World warblers help in nest construction and in incubation of the 2 to 4 eggs, which lasts about two weeks. Both parents also feed the young for an additional two weeks. Old World warblers of many species are commonly used as host parents for brood parasitic cuckoos (p. 143) of several species.

Notes
People in several Mediterranean countries seek these tiny birds as food. During their intercontinental migrations, the birds fly all night. At dawn they seek a secure grove of trees in which to rest and feed during the day. In many areas these stopover sites are few and far between, and the local people put out "roosting sticks" in the trees that are covered with a sticky lime mixture, in which the birds become trapped. Even today, pickled birds are available in many parts of Europe, and many of these small birds are eaten as delicacies.

Status
None of Thailand's Old World warblers is considered endangered or threatened.

Profiles
Flyeater, *Gerygone sulphurea*, Plate 52a
Dark-necked Tailorbird, *Orthotomus atrogularis*, Plate 52c
Inornate Warbler, *Phylloscopus inornatus*, Plate 52d
Gray-breasted Prinia, *Prinia hodgsonii*, Plate 52e
Chestnut-crowned Warbler, *Seicercus castaniceps*, Plate 52f

31. Thrushes

Depending on which expert's definition of the family you follow, more than 300 species of *thrushes* inhabit most terrestrial regions of the world and include some of the most familiar park and garden birds. The family, Turdidae, has few defining, common features that set its members apart from other groups, as perhaps could be expected; so large an assemblage of species is sure to include a significant amount of variation in appearance, ecology, and behavior. Thrushes, *robins, redstarts, forktails,* and *chats* are slender-billed birds that range from 13 to 28 cm (5 to 11 in) in length. In Thailand there are 49 species of this family, some of which are migrants from nesting grounds in central and northern Asia. Generally they are not brightly colored; instead, they come in drab browns, grays, brown-reds, olive, and black and white, although a few species sport shades of blue and orange. The sexes are very similar in appearance. During their first months of life, young thrushes have distinctive spotting on the breast.

Many species of thrushes have adapted to living near humans and benefiting from their environmental modifications. On five continents, a thrush is among the most common and recognizable of garden birds, including North America's AMERICAN ROBIN, Europe's REDWING and BLACKBIRD, and Thailand's ORIENTAL MAGPIE-ROBIN (Plate 53). Thrushes in general are famous for their rich and musical vocalizations, and one of the champion singers of the world is the WHITE-RUMPED SHAMA (Plate 53). It is easily overlooked in the forests of Thailand, but it is one of the most remarkable songsters in Asia. Its rich, melodious notes come from low in the forest all day long, and the song of a single individual may include song phrases of other species; with some patience, this songster supreme can usually be found on its favorite perch day after day.

Natural History

Ecology and Behavior
Many thrushes eat fruits, some are primarily *insectivorous,* and most are at least moderately *omnivorous.* Many thrushes frequently forage on the ground for insects, other arthropods, and a particular favorite, delicious earthworms, although some are more arboreal. Thrushes are residents of many kinds of habitats—deep forest, forest edges, clearings, and other open areas such as shrub areas and grasslands, gardens, parks, suburban lawns, and agricultural areas. Many thrushes are quite social, spending their time during the nonbreeding season in flocks of the same species, feeding and roosting together. More than half (31 species) of Thailand's thrush species are migratory and spend only the winter months enjoying the warmth of southeastern Asia before returning to central and northern Asia to nest during summer.

Breeding
Thrushes breed monogamously, males and females together defending exclusive territories during the breeding season; pairs may associate year-round. Nests, usually built by the female and placed in tree branches, shrubs, or crevices, are open and cup-shaped, made of grass, moss, or other similar materials, and often lined with mud. The female incubates 2 to 6 eggs (usually 2 or 3) for 12 to 14 days. Both parents feed the young for 12 to 16 days prior to their fledging.

Notes
English colonists in the New World gave the AMERICAN ROBIN, a thrush, its name because it resembled England's common ROBIN, an Old World flycatcher—

both birds have reddish breasts. The New World bird, however, is more closely related to Europe's BLACKBIRD, also a common garden bird and a true thrush—and you wonder why common names of birds can be so confusing. The WHITE-RUMPED SHAMA, native only to Asia but imported into Hawaii in about 1940, is now a naturalized citizen on the tourist islands of Oahu and Kauai.

Status
Only two of Thailand's thrushes are considered threatened, BLACK-THROATED ROBIN and GRAY-SIDED THRUSH, both of which are irregular and unusual winter visitors from the far north of Asia.

Profiles
Siberian Blue Robin, *Luscinia cyane*, Plate 53a
Siberian Rubythroat, *Luscinia calliope*, Plate 53b
Slaty-backed Forktail, *Enicurus schistaceus*, Plate 53c
White-rumped Shama, *Copsychus malabaricus*, Plate 53d
Oriental Magpie-Robin, *Copsychus saularis*, Plate 53e
Blue Rock Thrush, *Monticola solitarius*, Plate 54a
Stonechat, *Saxicola torquata*, Plate 54b
Eye-browed Thrush, *Turdus obscurus*, Plate 54e

32. Old World Flycatchers

The more than 200 species of *Old World flycatchers* (Muscicapidae) vary considerably in shape, color, and size (10 to 21 cm, 4 to 8 in), but almost all of them catch insects as their main food. Members of the family occur from Europe and Africa to Australia, and Thailand has 39 representatives. They have short, flat bills, broad at the base with hair-like feathers sticking out from the hinge of their bills. Most experts now think that this huge conglomeration of species probably is made up of several unrelated families. Rather than going into the often contradictory and boring details, we will, for convenience, group them together here and let professional ornithologists fight over the minutiae in their scientific publications.

Natural History

Ecology and Behavior
Many species of Old World flycatchers sit conspicuously on an elevated perch and wait for a juicy insect to fly close by. The bird then launches itself into the air and, with some maneuvering, snaps the insect out of the air with its wide bill. The hair-like feathers around the base of the bill serve both to know when the insect is near the bill, by sense of touch, and as a funnel to help scoop the insect out of the air. Other species catch insects on leaf surfaces in the dark undergrowth of forests and are thus much less conspicuous. If fruits are available, several species often gather together at a tree to indulge themselves. Nineteen of Thailand's species are present in the country only during the winter or when passing en route to or from wintering grounds farther south. Most species are solitary, but a few participate in mixed-species foraging flocks, especially in the winter.

Breeding
Old World flycatchers have a wide variety of nest types (probably because, as we said above, the group is likely composed of several different families). Some nest in tree holes, others in crevices among boulders. Some construct elaborate cup-like nests in the crotches of small branches, yet others delicately balance a firmly woven

nest on the top of a small branch. Both parents help in nest construction, and both also incubate the 3 to 5 eggs as well as feed the young after hatching. Courtship tends to be simple, and their songs are not notable for length or resonance.

Status

The only Thai species of Old World flycatcher listed as threatened by the IUCN is the BROWN-CHESTED FLYCATCHER, which only stops over occasionally in peninsular Thailand on the way between its wintering grounds in Malaysia and nesting area in central and southeastern China.

Profiles

Red-throated Flycatcher, *Ficedula parva*, Plate 54c
Asian Brown Flycatcher, *Muscicapa dauurica*, Plate 54d
Verditer Flycatcher, *Eumyias thalassina*, Plate 55a
Gray-headed Canary Flycatcher, *Culicicapa ceylonensis*, Plate 55b
Asian Paradise Flycatcher, *Terpsiphone paradisi*, Plate 55c
Hill Blue Flycatcher, *Cyornis banyumas*, Plate 55d
Pied Fantail, *Rhipidura javanica*, Plate 55e

33. Shrikes and Starlings

Although not closely related, members of the *shrike* family (Laniidae) and the *starling* family (Sturnidae) are conspicuous, bold, and readily seen by even casual ecotravellers in Thailand. Shrikes are thrush-sized, with hooked bills that resemble those of miniature hawks. The bill, together with strong, sharp claws, is used to capture small to large prey items. The 30 species in family Laniidae occur throughout the Old Word and in North America and range in size from 16 to 37 cm (6 to 15 in). Five species are found in Thailand and all are clad in somber shades of gray, brown, and buff with a black mask or head.

The 112 species of starlings (including *mynas*) are native only to the Old World. They range in size from 18 to 43 cm (7 to 17 in) and are rather stocky, with a sharp, pointed bill and stout, strong legs. Most species are predominantly black, but many also have patches of white. Most of the 16 species in Thailand have relatively short, square tails. Starlings are renowned for their loud, ringing voices that vary, depending on the species, from a whistle to a croak to a screech.

Natural History

Ecology and Behavior

Shrikes hunt solitarily from an exposed perch in open habitats, and they prey on large insects, mice, small lizards, and birds. Upon spotting an appropriate prey item, a shrike swoops down from its elevated perch and kills with its hooked bill and sharp toenails. On occasion, when the prey are abundant and the shrike is satiated, it will continue to hunt but store its extra rations impaled on thorns, stalks, or even the sharp metal points of barbed wire. This peculiar habit has earned them the common name of "butcherbird." The LONG-TAILED SHRIKE (Plate 56) is unusual in its behavior of hunting in small groups.

Most starlings are decidedly opportunistic and catholic in their food, although a few prefer insects or flower nectar. Many species are common near human habitation, and a few species have expanded their ranges with the clearing of forest for human agriculture; these latter species often occur in large flocks.

Forest species tend to be shier and appear in small groups. They also are more likely to eat fruits.

Breeding
Shrikes are solitary nesters and aggressively defend their territories against many other bird species as well as other shrikes. The cup-shaped nest is built by both mates and is usually placed in the fork of a tall bush or short tree. It is made of dry leaves, twigs, and plant fibers and lined with feathers, grass, and cobwebs. The 2 to 5 eggs are incubated mainly by the female, but both parents participate in feeding the young.

Starlings nest in tree holes, usually a cavity originally excavated by a woodpecker or barbet. Some species, however, such as the ASIAN PIED STARLING (Plate 57), construct massive domed nests made of straw, roots, and twigs that they place in the outer branches of isolated trees. The 3 to 4 eggs are incubated by the female for two weeks but then fed by both parents for up to 25 days, at which time the young leave the nest.

Notes
In Thailand, as in other parts of the world, several species of starlings and mynas that occur in or around agricultural areas are of great economic significance as crop pests. Large flocks of COMMON MYNA (Plate 56) and other starlings can cause serious damage to fruit and seed crops. Large urban roosts at night attract tens of thousands of starlings in some areas, and their droppings can become a health hazard as well as corrode stone and brickwork of buildings. The EUROPEAN or COMMON STARLING, native to Europe and Asia, was spread by people from the Old World to the New, and to Australia/New Zealand, during the nineteenth century, and is now probably one of the most numerous birds on Earth.

Status
No shrike or starling species is considered threatened in Thailand, although the populations of HILL MYNA (Plate 57) have become severely reduced over many parts of the country owing to overcapture for the cage bird industry.

Profiles
Long-tailed Shrike, *Lanius schach*, Plate 56a
Brown Shrike, *Lanius cristatus*, Plate 56b
Asian Glossy Starling, *Aplonis panayensis*, Plate 56c
White-shouldered Starling, *Sturnus sinensis*, Plate 56d
Common Myna, *Acridotheres tristis*, Plate 56e
Asian Pied Starling, *Sturnus contra*, Plate 57a
Black-collared Starling, *Sturnus nigricollis*, Plate 57b
Hill Myna, *Gracula religiosa*, Plate 57c
White-vented Myna, *Acridotheres javanicus*, Plate 57d
Golden-crested Myna, *Ampeliceps coronatus*, Plate 57e

34. Sunbirds, Flowerpeckers, and White-eyes

Sunbirds, flowerpeckers, and *white-eyes* comprise three families of the Old World tropics that all contain small arboreal birds; the three groups share some superficial traits but are only distantly related to each other. The sunbirds are brightly colored members of family Nectariniidae, with 131 species that are distributed from Africa to Australia, 22 of which are found in Thailand. Ranging in size from

9 to 22 cm (3.5 to 8.5 in), the colorful males of most sunbird species have metallic green or blue iridescence mixed with spectacular reds, blues, and yellows. Females are much duller in shades of olive to yellow. Relatively thin and downcurved bills are characteristic of all species, but the large *spiderhunters* have extremely long, curved bills. In some species the male reverts each winter to a plumage that resembles that of the female.

Flowerpeckers are small (9 to 13 cm, 3.5 to 5 in) species in family Dicaeidae (44 species from India to Australia and 10 in Thailand). Their stout bodies, short tails, and short, down-curved bills are distinctive. Males of most species have splashes of brilliant scarlet, yellow, or orange; females are olive to dull yellow.

The 96 species of white-eyes (family Zostreopidae) are all very similar, with yellow-green color and a distinctive white ring around each eye. These small birds (7 to 14 cm, 3 to 5.5 in) occur from Africa to Australia, with many endemic species restricted to small areas and oceanic islands. In Thailand there are only four species, but they are often common and easily seen. The Thai species all have relatively short tails and short, thin bills. The sexes are similar in appearance.

Natural History

Ecology and Behavior

Sunbirds feed on insects and flower nectar. They have a long tongue that is tubular for most of its length and aids in sucking up the nectar. Their long, curved bills are perfect for reaching inside a long flower for the nectar there. During such reaching, the flower pollen sticks to the feathers of the bird's head and throat. At the next flower of the same species the pollen is rubbed from the feathers onto the female parts of the plant, and *pollination* has been accomplished. At the end of the sunbird's bill there are fine, sawtooth edges that help the bird hold onto struggling insects or a large fruit. This specialized bill also helps some sunbird species cheat by poking a hole at the base of a flower to get at the nectar, thereby escaping their duties as pollinators. Some sunbirds, especially the larger species called spiderhunters, hover in front of spiderwebs and pluck struggling insects or the spider itself from the webbing. This behavior must be done carefully because small birds can accidentally become entangled in the spiderweb (see GIANT WOOD SPIDER, Plate 1). There is another group of large spider species in southeastern Asia (genus *Euathlus*) called "bird-eating spiders," which make their living by capturing birds. Sunbirds are often easiest to observe when they are defending a group of flowers. Singing their buzzy little song while sitting conspicuously over the flowering plants, these sunbirds will chase any other sunbird, butterfly, or even bee that tries to get at the nectar.

The flowerpeckers also have specialized tongues and bills for eating nectar. They balance their diet of nectar with the juicy pulp of berries, especially mistletoe, and an occasional insect or spider. Most species are found in the canopy of forests or forest edges. Occasionally small flocks will form around a nectar or fruit supply.

The brush-tipped tongue of white-eyes is used to eat pulp and juice from fruits. The short, curved bill is also useful for getting at nectar in small flowers and for catching small insects. White-eyes almost always roam through the mid- to upper levels of the forest in large family groups or as part of an even larger mixed-species party. Their constant piping sounds keep the flock together and also make it easy for ecotravellers to notice them.

Breeding
The large hanging nests of sunbirds are often mistaken for masses of dead vegetation. The purse-like nest is woven from grass, plant fibers, and spider webbing, with a "trailer" of rubbish hanging from the bottom. The entrance hole is on the side near the top, and often a porch-like extension is built over the top of the hole. The female constructs the nest and incubates the 2 to 3 eggs alone for two weeks. The male, however, helps with feeding the hatched young for the next 16 days.

Flowerpeckers build an oval, bag-like nest suspended from a small twig. Both sexes contribute to nest building; the nest is made of vegetable down, grass, rootlets, moss, and spider webbing. Both parents incubate the 2 or 3 eggs as well as feed the young.

Female white-eyes use plant fibers, down, and spider webbing to build their cup-shaped nests, which are suspended by the rim in the fork of small branches. Both parents incubate the 2 to 3 eggs for 12 days and feed the young an insect diet for 10 more days.

Notes
Because of their iridescent colors, bill shape, nectar-feeding behavior, and aggressiveness in defending feeding territories, sunbirds are considered by many biologists to be the Old World equivalent of the New World hummingbirds. Of course, the similarities are superficial, but ecologically they do seem to stand in for each other in these different parts of the tropics. This replacement of unrelated species that end up looking and acting like each other in geographically different parts of the world is called *convergent evolution*. It is a coincidence of similarity brought about by similar habitats and ecological needs.

Status
None of Thailand's sunbird, flowerpecker, or white-eye species is considered threatened.

Profiles
Brown-throated Sunbird, *Anthreptes malacensis,* Plate 58a
Ruby-cheeked Sunbird, *Anthreptes singalensis,* Plate 58b
Olive-backed Sunbird, *Nectarinia jugularis,* Plate 58c
Gould's Sunbird, *Aethopyga gouldiae,* Plate 58d
Little Spiderhunter, *Arachnothera longirostra,* Plate 59a
Buff-bellied Flowerpecker, *Dicaeum ignipectus,* Plate 59b
Scarlet-backed Flowerpecker, *Dicaeum cruentatum,* Plate 59c
Crimson Sunbird, *Aethopyga siparaja,* Plate 59d
Oriental White-eye, *Zosterops palpebrosus,* Plate 59e

35. Sparrows, Munias, and Finches

The organization of this group of *sparrows, munias,* and *finches* into distinct and widely accepted families is currently in a state of flux. Superficially all these birds share stout conical bills, strong skulls, large jaw muscles, and well-developed gizzards for seed crushing and eating. But no two ornithologists seem to agree on which species belong to which group, or how many groups there actually are. Classically, however, the sparrows, munias, and *weavers* are placed in the Old World family Ploceidae (278 species worldwide, 15 of which occur in Thailand). These species are sexually different in appearance, and almost all of them build elaborate and relatively large nests. They range in size from 11 to 50 cm (4.5 to

20 in) and most are colored in browns, grays, black, and white, although blues and reds brighten a few species. The finches (traditionally placed in family Fringillidae) are generally brightly colored, especially the males, and range in size from 13 to 24 cm (5 to 10 in). More than 125 species of this family occur around the world, but only 8 are found in Thailand.

Natural History

Ecology and Behavior

The species in both the sparrow and finch families eat seeds year-round but supplement their diet with insects, especially when feeding their young. Evidently the chicks need the protein in insects for rapid growth. The size of the bill of the adults is often related to the size of the seed they can eat. The finches have a special groove on the roof of the mouth into which they can wedge a seed on its edge. Then, using their powerful jaw muscles to break the husk and their tongue to extract the seed, they efficiently ingest the nutritious part of the seed and spit out the indigestible outer covering. Many species feed on the ground in open fields, though others are more inclined to forage in forested areas. In the non-breeding season, species of both these families often form large foraging flocks that stay together all winter. In Thailand, all of the sparrows are permanent residents, but among the finches all but the resident SPOT-WINGED GROSBEAK of the far northern mountains are winter visitors from central and northern Asia.

Breeding

Courtship among the finches usually involves complicated displays and beautiful songs. The female finch builds a neat, cup-like nest and each pair defends a large breeding territory. The female alone incubates the 3 to 6 eggs, but the male helps feed the young after they hatch. In contrast the sparrows build large, domed nests, often intricately woven using species-specific knots that are tied with the bill and feet. Many species nest colonially, and courtship displays and dissonant songs are elaborate. The 2 to 4 eggs are incubated by the female alone in some species and by both parents in others. Both parents help feed the young for about two weeks until they leave the nest.

Notes

Because of the large flocks they form, both finches and sparrows can have major impacts on grain harvests. They are considered a plague in many parts of Asia. The singing ability of many finches have made them desirable as cage-birds. Some finches breed readily in captivity, such as the wild SERIN of the Canary Islands, from which all the strains of domestic canaries were derived.

Status

None of the finch or sparrow species in Thailand is considered threatened or endangered.

Profiles

Scaly-breasted Munia, *Lonchura punctulata*, Plate 60a
White-rumped Munia, *Lonchura striata*, Plate 60b
Eurasian Tree-Sparrow, *Passer montanus*, Plate 60c
Plain-backed Sparrow, *Passer flaveolus*, Plate 60d
Common Rosefinch, *Carpodacus erythrinus*, Plate 60e

Environmental Close-up 5:
Frugivory: Animals That Eat Fruit and the Trees That Want Them To

Frugivory from the Animal's Point of View

A key feature of tropical forests, and of the animal communities that inhabit them, is the large number of birds (parrots, hornbills, trogons, orioles, bulbuls, starlings, and flowerpeckers make up a partial list), mammals, and even some fish that rely on fruit as a diet staple. Frugivory represents a trade-off, each participant—the fruit-bearing tree and the fruit-eating animal—offering the other something of great value (and therefore it is a kind of mutualism—see p. 51). The complex web of relationships between fruit-eaters and fruit-producing trees is particularly interesting because it nicely demonstrates ecological interactions between plant and animal, between food producer and food consumer, between predator and prey, and the mutual dependence sometimes engendered by such relationships.

Benefits of frugivory for animals

Most small and medium-sized tropical forest birds, many mammals (especially bats), and some fish eat either fruits or animals such as insects, or they eat both. However, it is the fruit-eating habit that accounts for much of the incredible ecological success of animals in the tropics. For birds, many more species occupy the Earth's tropical areas than temperate zones, and ecologists believe that about twenty percent of the difference is directly attributable to the tropical birds' superior abilities to exploit fruit resources. In fact, probably fifty percent of tropical bird biomass (the summed weight of all tropical birds alive at one time) is supported by fruit-eating. You would think, therefore, that fruit must be tremendously profitable "prey" for birds, and in several ways it is:

1. Fruit is conspicuous. First consider insects as food. Palatable insects are often small and/or inconspicuous; they hide or blend in extremely well with their surroundings. Finding such insects is a chore that takes a lot of time. Ripe fruit, on the other hand, usually attracts attention to itself, being sweet smelling, brightly colored, and displayed out in the open.
2. Fruit is easy to stalk, run down, catch, kill, and devour. Insects, as far as we can tell, are absolutely loath to be eaten—they run, hide, and resist to the end; some even spray noxious chemicals at their attackers. Fruit, however, never attempts escape, and in fact, when it is ripe and most attractive to frugivores, it is most easily separated from the tree that bears it.

The underlying reason for points (1) and (2), which becomes clearer when considering frugivory from the trees' point of view (see below), is that fruits are made to be consumed by animals. It is their *raison d'etre*. Owing to this, trees could hardly be expected to make their fruit difficult to locate or pluck. Thus we have a major ecological insight: insects benefit by not being eaten, but unless a fruit is eaten, the plant gains nothing from the effort to produce it.

3. Fruit is abundant. When a bird or bat locates a tree with fruit, there is often a large amount available for consumption. Thus, meeting a day's or night's nutritional requirements means finding one or, at most, a few, fruit-bearing trees.

4   Fruit in the tropics is usually available year-round. There are wide-ranging consequences of points (3) and (4) for avian and bat frugivores. That fruit is always available and abundant means that birds and bats can safely specialize on it—evolve special ways to pluck, eat, and digest it—without encountering times of the year when no fruit is available, forcing the birds and bats to search for food that they are ill-equipped to handle. Owing to its abundance, species that concentrate on fruit often are quite successful, meaning that within a given area the numbers of individuals of these species can be quite large. But the greatest influence of frugivory on the lives of birds and bats is that, because fruit is abundant and easy to locate and eat, they can fulfill nutritional needs in only a few hours, leaving many hours each day available to pursue other activities. In contrast, an avian or bat insectivore or piscivore (specializing on insects or fish, respectively), may have to hunt most of each day or night to survive.

Problems of frugivory

Have birds encountered difficulties in the process of specializing on fruit? Yes, there are some associated problems:

1   Fruits, although providing plentiful carbohydrates and fats, are relatively low in protein, so frugivorous species, although easily meeting their daily calorie needs, sometimes have "protein deficits" that they must ease by feeding occasionally on insects or other animals (snails or frogs, or the odd lizard). Few bird species eat fruit exclusively.
2   Eating liquidy fruit pulp means that frugivores consume a lot of water, which is both bulky and heavy, and which must be transported for a time (using up energy) and disposed of regularly.
3   The frugivores' nutrition comes from the fleshy fruit pulp. The seeds that are eaten incidentally are usually indigestible or even poisonous and must be, like water, carried for a while and then disposed of—either by regurgitation or after being passed through the digestive tract.
4   When a species specializes on a particular type of fruit, it becomes vulnerable to any temporary or permanent decline in the fruit's availability. (It appears that most avian and bat frugivores avoid such vulnerability by not being overly specialized: in an observational study that followed the feeding habits of seventy fruit-eating birds species in the tropics, researchers discovered that each bird consumed, on average, ten species of fruits.)

Frugivory from the Tree's Point of View

It is clear what frugivores get from fruits, but what of the trees, which are picked clean of the fruit that they spend so much time and energy producing? The answer is that the trees, by having birds and bats eat, transport, and then drop their seeds, achieve efficient reproduction—something well worth their investment in fruit. The trees make use of frugivores as seed dispersal agents.

Why don't trees just let their seeds drop to the ground? It turns out that seeds dropped near the parent most often do NOT survive. They die because they must compete with the much larger parent plant for sun and other nutrients. Also, specialized insects that eat seeds can more easily find and destroy seeds that are in large accumulations, like under the mother tree. Seeds carried some distance from the parent tree have a better chance of germination and survival, and they will not compete with the parent tree (also, because in the tropics trees of the same species often do not grow near each other, seeds dropped by birds are unlikely to be regularly competing with any trees of the same species). Furthermore, because they are more spread out, seed predators are less likely to find them. Thus, seed dispersal by birds enhances a parent tree's prospects for successful reproduction and also allows the tree to colonize new sites.

The tree's use of animal power for seed dispersal is exquisitely fine-tuned. As seeds are being readied, fruit is green, hard, and bitter-tasting—unappealing fare to birds (and to people!). When the seeds mature and are ready for dispersal and germination, the surrounding fruit brightens in color, becomes softer and easier to pluck from the tree, and in a coup de grâce, trees inject sugars into fruits, making them sweet and very attractive.

Not all animals attracted to fruits are good seed dispersers. Some, notably parrots and squirrels, eat and digest seeds, acting as predators rather than dispersers (see below). These seed destroyers, however, in the course of their movements from branch to branch often knock many fruits out of the canopy that fall to the forest floor. Here, frugivorous animals that can't climb trees well, such as pheasants and rats, await this largesse. They eat the fruit, dispersing seeds later when they defecate, or cache it in the ground for later consumption, where seeds may later germinate.

Ecological Consequences of Frugivory for Birds, Trees, and Ecosystems

As tropical birds and bats have benefited in several ways by specialization on fruit, so too have trees. In fact, ecologists now suspect that together with pollination by insects, bats, and birds, seed dispersal by vertebrate animals was and is responsible for the initial spread and current domination of the Earth by flowering plants. They estimate that upwards of eighty percent of trees and shrubs in tropical evergreen forests have their seeds dispersed by animals. These plants provide the nutrients to support large, healthy populations of frugivorous birds and bats. Moreover, the great species diversity of plants in the tropics may be largely linked to frugivorous animals continually eating fruits and spreading seeds into new areas. Such constant dispersal, which also allows continual, healthy genetic mixing, is beneficial for plant populations, always working to decrease the chances that individual species will go extinct. In fact, the more successful a tree species is at being "preyed upon" by birds, the more its seeds will be dropped over a wide area, and the more abundant it will become.

One potential problem for trees, though, is that if their fruit is eaten by only one or two bird species, that strict dependence for seed dispersal brings vulnerability. If the bird that disperses such a specialist tree for some reason declines in abundance and becomes extinct, so too, in short order, will the tree species. Most tree species, however, enjoy the seed dispersal services of at least several bird and bat species.

The trade-offs that the frugivores and trees make, the conflicting strategies to survive and complete their lifecycles, are fascinating. Think about it from one evolutionary perspective: the beneficial aspect of the interaction for the tree—having an animal transport its seeds—is the negative aspect for the animal, which has no "desire" to carry seeds from which it gets no benefit. The beneficial aspect for the frugivore—the fruit pulp that the plant manufactures to attract animals—is the negative part of the interaction for the plant, which loses the energy and nutrients required to make the fruit. Frugivory is one of the tropic's most important and compelling ecological interactions, and one that currently attracts strong interest from ecological researchers. Frugivory may even have been a causative factor in the early evolution of color vision, as the first fruit-eaters that could easily distinguish ripe and unripe fruit plainly would have had advantages over those that could not.

Dipterocarp Mast Fruiting

Some animals have become enemies of plants by eating their seeds or otherwise destroying the seeds' abilities to germinate. These types of animal are called *seed predators,* and they include parrots, pigs, and some beetle larvae. These seed predators can cause tremendous mortality among seeds. In tropical evergreen forests of southeastern Asia, one apparent strategy to protect tree seeds from seed predators is *gregarious,* or *mast,* fruiting. This is when many species of dipterocarp trees (p. 17) fruit simultaneously and fruit becomes superabundant for a short period, but at intervals of several years. Seed predators cannot predict or wait for this fruiting, so they cannot specialize on the fruit of these tree species. If the seed predators were able to time their arrival in the area to correspond to this largesse of fruit, the trees would gain little protection.

The dipterocarp trees in question have developed a mechanism by which many species in these tropical evergreen forests fruit at exactly the same time but only once or twice a decade. Because the interval between mast fruiting is also highly variable, sometimes three years, sometime four or seven years, none of the seed predators can anticipate when to build up their populations to be able to eat all the seeds that appear at one time. In other words, the trees overwhelm, or "saturate," the available seed predators. More seeds will survive because the seed predators are never abundant enough to eat all the seeds. Any trees that fruit in the "off years" will do so in such relatively small numbers that the available seed predators can wipe out most if not all the crop of their seeds. So to ensure that most of their seeds survive, somehow trees of the same and different species have evolved mechanisms to recognize the same year and date to fruit. In Southeast Asia, dipterocarp trees apparently use an early and extreme dry season as a cue to synchronize especially heavy fruiting within and among tree species. Many species of bamboos also have mast fruiting (at intervals of twenty-five years or more!), and in Europe and North America, oak trees have mast fruiting at unpredictable intervals of several years.

Chapter 9

MAMMALS

- *Introduction*
- *General Characteristics and Classification*
- *Features of Tropical Mammals*
- *Seeing Mammals in Thailand*
- *Family Profiles*
    1. *Treeshrews, Shrews, and Hedgehogs*
    2. *Flying Lemurs and Bats*
    3. *Primates*
    4. *Pangolins*
    5. *Rodents and Rabbits*
    6. *Carnivores*
    7. *Even-toed Ungulates*
    8. *Elephant, Tapir, and Rhinoceros*
    9. *Dolphins and Dugong*

Introduction

Leafing through this book, you may have noticed that there are many more profiles of birds than mammals. At first glance you might think this odd, especially because people themselves are mammals and, because of that direct kinship, might often be keenly interested and motivated to see and learn about mammals. What's going on? Aren't mammals as good as birds? Why not include more of them? There are several reasons for the discrepancy—good biological reasons. One is that, even though the tropics generally have more species of mammals than temperate or Arctic regions, the total number of mammal species worldwide, and the number in any region, is almost always much less than the number of birds. In fact, there are only 4,629 mammal species in the world, as compared with 9,040 birds, and that relative difference is reflected in Thailand's fauna. Another compelling reason not to include more mammals in a book on commonly sighted wildlife is that throughout Thailand you will rarely see mammals—especially if you are a short-term visitor. Mammals are delicious fare for any number of predatory beasts (eaten in good numbers by reptiles, birds, other mammals, and even the odd amphibian), but most mammals lack a basic protection from predators that birds possess, the power of flight. Consequently, most have been forced into being active nocturnally, or, if active during daylight hours, they are highly secretive. Birds often show themselves with abandon; mammals do not. An exception is monkeys. They are fairly large and primarily arboreal, which keeps them safe from a number of predators, and thus permits them to be noisy and relatively conspicuous. A final reason for not including more mammals in the book is that about 92 (35%) of the 263 mammal species that occur in Thailand are bats. They are for the most part nocturnal animals that, even if you are lucky enough to get good looks at them, are very difficult for anyone other than an expert to identify to species.

General Characteristics and Classification

Mammals as a group first arose, so fossils tell us, approximately 245 million years ago, splitting off from the primitive reptiles during the late Triassic Period of the Mesozoic Era, somewhat before the birds did the same thing. Four main traits distinguish mammals from other vertebrates, and each of these traits helped mammals spread into most of the habitats around the world: hair on their bodies, which insulates and helps maintain constant internal temperatures as well as protects the skin from injuries; milk production for the young, freeing mothers from having to search for specific foods for their offspring; the bearing of live young instead of eggs, allowing breeding females to be mobile and hence, safer than if they had to guard eggs for several weeks; and advanced brains, with highly integrated sensory systems that contribute to mammals' breadth of survival mechanisms.

Mammals are quite variable in size and form, many being highly adapted—changed through evolution—to specialized habitats and lifestyles: bats specialized to fly, marine mammals specialized for their aquatic world, deer to run swiftly, etc. The smallest mammals are the *shrews,* tiny insect eaters that weigh as little as 2.5 grams (a tenth of an ounce). The largest are the *whales,* weighing in at up to 160,000 kg (350,000 lb, half the weight of a loaded Boeing 747)—as far as anyone knows, the largest animals that have ever lived.

Mammals are divided into three major groups, primarily according to reproductive methods. The *monotremes* are an ancient group that actually lays eggs and still retains some other reptile-like characteristics. Only four species of them survive, 1 platypus and 3 spiny anteaters, and they are found only in Australia and New Guinea. The *marsupials* give birth to live young that are relatively undeveloped. When born, the young crawl along mom's fur to attach themselves to her nipples, usually inside her pouch, where they find milk supplies and finish their development. There are about 240 marsupial species, including kangaroos, koalas, wombats, and opossum, and they are limited in distribution to Australia and South and Central America. The majority of mammal species are *eutherians*. These animals are distinguished from the other groups by having a well-developed placenta, which efficiently connects a mother to her developing babies, allowing for long internal development. This trait, which allows embryos to develop to a fairly mature form in safety, and for the female to be mobile until birth, has helped allow these mammals to colonize successfully and prosper in many habitats. Placental mammals include those with which most people are intimately familiar: rodents, rabbits, cats, dogs, bats, primates, elephants, horses, whales—everything from house mice to ecotravellers. The 4,600 species of living mammals are grouped into about 115 families, which are in turn categorized into about 20 orders.

Features of Tropical Mammals

There are several important features of tropical mammals and their habitats that differentiate them from temperate zone mammals. First, tropical mammals face different environmental stresses than do temperate zone mammals, and they respond to stresses in different ways. Many temperate zone mammals, of course, must endure extreme variation within a year, from cold winters with snow and low winter food supplies to hot summers with dry weather and abundant food. Many of them respond with *hibernation,* staying more or less dormant for several months until conditions improve. Tropical mammals, except in the higher altitude mountains, do not encounter such extreme annual changes, but they do face dry seasons, up to five months long, that sometimes severely reduce food supplies. For some surprising reasons, they cannot alleviate this stress by hibernating, waiting for the rainy season to arrive with its increased food supplies. When a mammal in Russia or Alaska hibernates, many of its predators leave the area. This is not the case in the tropics. A mammal sleeping away the dry season in a burrow would be easy prey for snakes and other predators. Also, external parasites, such as ticks and mites, which are inactive in extreme cold, would continue to be very active on sleeping tropical mammals, sucking blood and doing considerable damage. Last, the great energy reserves needed to be able to sleep for an extended period through warm weather may be more than any mammal can physically accumulate. Therefore, tropical mammals need to stay active throughout the year. One way they counter the dry season's reduction in their normal foods is to switch food types seasonally. For instance, some rodents that eat mostly insects during the rainy season switch to seeds during the dry; some bats that feed on insects switch to dry-season fruits.

The abundance of tropical fruit brings up another interesting difference between temperate and tropical mammals: a surprising number of tropical mammals eat a lot of fruit, even among the carnivore group, which, as its name implies, should be eating meat. All the carnivores in Thailand, save otters and the big cats, are known to eat fruit on occasion. Upon reflection, it makes sense that these mammals consume fruit. Fruit is very abundant in the tropics, available throughout much of the year, and, at least when it is ripe, easily digested by mammalian digestive systems. A consequence of such *frugivory* (fruit-eating) is that many mammals have become, together with frugivorous birds, major dispersal agents of fruit seeds, which they spit out or which travel unharmed through their digestive tracts to be deposited in feces far from the mother tree in defecation (see Close-Up, p. 175). Some biologists believe that even though carnivores plainly are specialized for hunting down, killing, and eating animal prey, it is likely that fruit has always been a major part of their diet.

Finally, there are some differences in the kinds of mammals inhabiting tropical and temperate regions. For instance, the tropics have few social rodents like beavers and prairie dogs and very few rabbit species. On the other hand, some groups occur solely in the tropics and do fabulously there. There are about 70 to 80 species of Old World monkeys (depending on which primate specialist you consult), almost all of which occur in tropical areas. Arboreal mammals such as monkeys are often plentiful in tropical forests, probably because there is a rich, resource-filled, dense canopy to occupy and feed in. Also, the closed canopy blocks light to the ground, which allows only an undergrowth that is sparse and poor in resources, and consequently permits few opportunities for mammals to live and feed there. Bats thrive in the tropics, being very successful both in terms of number of species and in their abundances. Ten families of bats occur in Thailand, including 92 species; only 4 families and 40 species occur in the entire US, an area almost 20 times greater than that of Thailand. While most of the North American bats are insect-eaters, the Thai bats are quite varied in lifestyle, among them being fruit-eaters, nectar-eaters, fish-eaters, and insect-eaters.

The social and breeding behaviors of various mammals are quite diverse. Some are predominantly solitary animals, males and females coming together occasionally only to mate. Others live in family groups. Like birds, female mammals have most of the say in choosing a mate. Unlike most bird species, where both mates are necessary to raise the young and thus monogamy (one male mates with one female) is common, milk production among female mammals usually frees the male from caring for the young. He is more likely to get more of his genes into the next generation by convincing additional females to mate with him. This leads to polygyny (one male mates with a harem of several females) or promiscuity (a sexual free-for-all in which dominant males tend to mate with a mind-blurring array of females) as the most common mating systems among mammals. Monogamy is uncommon but polyandry (one female mates with several males) is even rarer among mammals than birds. Depending on resources like food availability and access to mates, some mammal species are rigorously territorial, while others are not.

Seeing Mammals in Thailand

No doubt about it, mammals are tough to see. You could go for two weeks and, if in the wrong places at the wrong times, see very few of them. A lot of luck is involved—a civet, a small barking deer, or a porcupine happens to cross the trail just a bit ahead of you, or by chance someone in your group spots a squirrel in a tree. We can offer three pieces of mammal-spotting advice: first, if you have time and are a patient sort, stake out a likely spot near a stream or watering hole, be quiet, and wait to see what approaches. Second, try taking quiet strolls along paths and trails very early in the morning. At this time, many nocturnal mammals are quickly scurrying to their day shelters. Third, although only for the stout-hearted, try searching with a flashlight at night around field stations or campgrounds. After scanning the ground (for safety's sake as well as for mammals), shine the light toward the middle regions of trees and look for bright, shiny eyes reflecting the light. You will certainly stumble across some kind of mammal or another; then it is simply a matter of whether you scare them more than they scare you. Doing the same thing at night from a vehicle or canoe can also be a good way to spot eye-shine of mammals on the road or in the vegetation along the edge of a lake or mangrove forest. At night, slowly drive the main road through Khao Yai National Park and look for huge gray boulders sticking out of the roadside vegetation, especially at several natural salt licks; this road is arguably the most reliable place to see Asian Elephants in the country. Be sure to keep your vehicle's engine running, and do not drive close to these "boulders with trunks." Being hassled does not amuse them, especially when young elephants are present.

Some mammals, of course, you can see more reliably. Monkeys, for instance, are often easy to see in many of Thailand's national parks, and squirrels and deer are frequently sighted in forests. Banish all thoughts right now of ever encountering the Tiger, which is found regularly now only in isolated regions. Even in such locales, however, your chances of encountering one are slim, although their tracks (Plate 72) on river beaches and muddy roads are a regular sight in some areas.

Family Profiles

1. Treeshrews, Shrews, and Hedgehogs

The *treeshrews, shrews,* and *hedgehogs* belong to order Insectivora, the insect-eating mammals. This order has about 350 species and occurs worldwide except for Australia and much of southern South America. Most of these mammals have long thin snouts, are hyperactive, and feed mainly on insects and other invertebrates.

The treeshrews form a distinctive family of 17 species (family Tupaiidae). Males and females of each species are similar, except the male is larger. The body lengths of treeshrews ranges from 10 to 22 cm (4 to 8.5 in), and the tail is about equally as long as the body. The members of this family are characterized by a long, low head and pointed nose, five flexible toes including a moveable thumblike toe, and prominent eyes. Resembling thin, long-nosed squirrels, treeshrews lack the large, gnawing front teeth of squirrels. The treeshrews occur only in the Oriental Region (p. 53) of the world, and they are thought by many scientists to be primitive primates, or at least to be closely related to the most primitive, extinct primates. Unfortunately there are no fossils of treeshrews, which could help prove relatedness. Yet other scientists say that the superficial similarities between present-day treeshrews and ancient primates are coincidence and do not indicate relatedness. Four species occur in Thailand, only one of which, the COMMON TREESHREW (Plate 61), is found throughout the country.

The *true shrews* (family Soricidae) are the smallest insectivores, and almost 300 species occur worldwide, except in Australia and much of South America. Only nine species occur in Thailand, and all except the HOUSE SHREW (Plate 61) are rare. Shrews' small ears, tiny eyes, long pointed snouts, long tail, and high-energy movements make them distinctive. They can have heart rates between 800 and 1,200 beats per minute and breathe 800 times per minute.

The family of hedgehogs (Erinaceidae) has 17 species, all restricted to the Old World. In Thailand there are only two species, the MOONRAT (Plate 61) and the

GYMNURE. The fur of hedgehogs typically is thick and filled with shaggy bristles. The Thai species both have long, naked tails and resemble opossums. Beside the spiny hairs for defense, the Thai species produce a disgusting smell variously described as like rotten garlic or garbage.

Natural History

Ecology and Behavior

Despite their name, treeshrews spend as much time on the ground as they do in trees. They usually travel in pairs, and males can be quite belligerent towards one another when they meet at the edges of their territories. Treeshrews often run quickly through the forest canopy or across a gravel road. Most active during the day, they spend a lot of time drinking water and bathing in forest streams. They eat a lot of insects, but also indulge themselves with lizards, small rodents, seeds, and buds. At night they sleep in a nest made of vegetation, but this nest is not used for raising the young.

Active almost continuously night and day, true shrews must eat many insects and small animals, sometime 2 to 3 times their body weight per day. The smallest shrews can starve to death within 12 hours. The saliva of many shrews contains a toxin that is used in defense and to dispatch prey items. The only common species in Thailand, the HOUSE SHREW, was probably introduced by humans and is limited to urban and agricultural areas.

Inhabiting moist lowlands and forested hilly areas, Thailand's representatives of the hedgehog family are nocturnal and terrestrial, usually in primary or secondary forest. They spend the day sleeping in hollow logs or in the roots of trees. They eat everything from earthworms and insects to frogs, fish, and the bark of young trees.

Breeding

Unique among mammals, the male treeshrew constructs a "maternal nest" of leaves in a tree hollow or cavity and then abandons the area and his family until a month later, when the young are ready to leave the nest. The female nurses the 1 to 4 young in the nest but only for 10 to 15 minutes at two-day intervals. The rest of the time she stays away from the nest, mostly feeding herself. If the young are threatened by a predator during the mother's absence from the nest, the babies make loud sounds and stick all their legs out of the nest, apparently a startling display meant to discourage overconfident predators.

Most true shrews breed twice a year, and the 1 to 5 pink, naked young nurse for 18 days. Most species make nests on the ground in grassy areas; however, the young of the HOUSE SHREW use their teeth to hold onto the hair of the mother's rump and travel with her for long distances.

The sex life of Thailand's hedgehogs is poorly known, but they apparently breed year-round and have 2 young at a time.

Notes

The anatomy and behavior of the COMMON TREESHREW is extremely well known because this species is used commonly in medical studies.

Status

None of Thailand's insectivora species is considered threatened or endangered. However, several species of shrews barely reach the southern extreme of their Asian distribution in Thailand, and they are quite rare in the country.

Profiles
Common Treeshrew, *Tupaia glis*, Plate 61a
Moonrat, *Echinosorex gymnurus*, Plate 61c
House Shrew, *Crocidura murina*, Plate 61d

2. Flying Lemurs and Bats

Thailand has two groups of mammals that can fly, the *flying lemurs* (often called *colugos*) and the *bats*. Both types of mammals are mainly nocturnal and spend the day hanging upside down in a protected roost. Here the similarities end. There are only two species of flying lemurs (family Cynocephalidae) in the world, one in southeastern Asia and the other in the Philippines. About 40 cm (16 in) long, flying lemurs have a broad band of skin that connects the neck, wrists of the forelegs, wrists of the hind legs and the tail. Only the head and the claws of the feet extend beyond this furry cloak. This parachute-like gliding membrane functions as an airfoil used to glide between trees, as far as 136 m (449 ft) in a single "flight." Bats, like birds, flap their wings to gain altitude and maintain sustained flight, but the flying lemurs can only glide. To do so, they extend their legs and tail and the membrane between their appendages is then spread in a relatively fixed position. Apparently they can steer by shifting their weight around, but they never flap this membrane and they always lose altitude as they swoop from one tree to the next. To land, the flying lemur disrupts the airfoil function of its gliding membrane by lifting its head and tail and extending its feet out in front of itself.

The flying lemurs also differ from bats and most other mammals in that they lack teeth in the front part of the jaw. Their extreme modifications for gliding make it difficult to establish which other mammal groups are their close relatives. Currently many mammalogists believe they are either related to the insectivores (p. 183) or to primitive primates.

Because they are so hard to see or hear, bats have always been considered foreign, exotic, and mysterious, even in our own backyards. Unlike any other mammals, they engage in sustained, powered flight ("rats with wings," in the memorable phrasing of an unappreciative acquaintance). Bats are active mainly at night and navigate the dark skies chiefly using "sonar," or *echolocation:* by broadcasting ultrasonic sounds—extremely high-pitched chirps and clicks—and then gaining information about their environment by "reading" the echoes. They also use this sonar to locate prey such as flying insects and surfacing fish. Although foreign to people's primate sensibilities, bats, precisely because their lives are so very different from our own, are increasingly of interest to us. In the past, of course, bats' exotic behavior, particularly their nocturnal habits, engendered in most societies not ecological curiosity but fear and superstition.

Bats are widely distributed, inhabiting most of the world's tropical and temperate regions, except for some oceanic islands. With a worldwide total of about 980 species, the bats are second in diversity among mammals only to the rodents. Ecologically, they can be thought of as nighttime replacements for birds, which dominate the daytime skies. Bats of southeastern Asia, except for the roosts of huge *flying foxes* in open trees, are often hard to see and, in most cases, difficult for anyone other than experts to identify to species. But owing to their diversity and abundance, bats are tremendously important mammals. Their numbers tell the story: 37% of all non-marine Thai mammal species are bats, and there are often more species of bats in some forests than of all other mammal species combined. Researchers estimate that bats make up most of the mammalian biomass (the total amount of living tissue, by weight) in any given tropical region. Of the 249 species of non-marine mammals that occur in Thailand, more than 92 are bats. We profile 10 species that represent a spectrum of the types of bats you are most likely to encounter.

Bats have true wings that are made of thin, strong, highly elastic membranes that extend from the sides of the body and legs to cover and be supported by the elongated fingers of the arms. (The name of the order of bats, Chiroptera, refers to the wings: *chiro,* meaning hand, and *ptera,* wing.) Other distinctive anatomical features include bodies covered with silky, longish hair (except for the bizarre HAIRLESS BAT of Indonesia, Malaysia, and extreme southern peninsular Thailand); toes with sharp, curved claws that allow the bats to hang upside down and are used by some to catch food; scent glands that produce strong, musky odors; and, in many, very odd-shaped folds of skin on their noses (*nose-leaves*) and prominent ears that aid in echolocation. Like birds, bats' bodies have been modified through evolution to conform to the needs of energy-demanding flight: they have relatively large hearts, low body weights, and high metabolisms.

Bats, although they come in a variety of sizes, are sufficiently standardized in form such that all species are easily recognized by everyone as bats. Females in most species are larger than males, presumably so they can fly when pregnant. Thailand is home to the largest and smallest bat species in the world. The COMMON FLYING FOX (Plate 62) weighs up to 1.1 kg (2.4 lb) and has a wingspan of 1.5 m (5 ft); the tiny KITTI'S HOG-NOSED BAT (Plate 62) weighs only 2 g (0.07 oz) and has a body length of 3 cm (1.2 in). At night in almost any Thai habitat, this group of mammals takes over. At dusk, when it is not yet too dark to see them, some species are already flying over streams and forests. During the night, as you walk along a closed forested path, bats frequently will fly past the light beam of your flashlight. They may even brush your body with their wings as they swiftly fly by in hot pursuit of a scrumptious insect. Don't panic. They are harmless, unless you act like an insect. Contrary to folklore, bats absolutely do NOT make nests in your hair.

Natural History

Ecology and Behavior

Flying lemurs are arboreal and feed exclusively on leaves, shoots, buds, and fruits. They feed while hanging upside down, much like the Central and South American sloths. They move from tree to tree by gliding from the top of one to the lower levels of the next and then climbing clumsily up the trunk to its highest branches. During the day, they sleep in a tree hollow or hanging from the base of a palm frond.

Most tropical bat species specialize in eating insects (a single individual has been estimated to eat up to 1,200 insects per hour!). They use their sonar not just to navigate the night, but also to detect insects, which they catch on the wing, pick off leaves, or scoop off the ground. Bats use several methods to catch flying insects. Small insects may be captured directly in the mouth; some bats use their wings as nets and spoons to trap insects and pull them to the mouth; and others scoop bugs into the fold of skin membrane that connects the tail and legs, then somersault in midair to move the catch to the mouth. Small bugs are eaten immediately on the wing, while larger ones, such as big beetles, are taken to a perch and dismembered. However, not all species are insectivores. Tropical bats have also expanded ecologically into a variety of other feeding niches: some specialize in eating fruit, feeding on nectar and pollen at flowers, or eating fish.

Bats are highly gregarious animals, roosting and often foraging in groups. They spend the daylight hours in day roosts, usually tree cavities, shady sides of trees, caves, rock crevices, or, these days, in buildings or under bridges. More than one species of bat may inhabit the same roost, although some species will associate only with their own kind. For most species, the normal resting position in a roost is hanging by their feet, heads down, which makes taking flight as easy as letting go and spreading their wings. Many bats leave roosts around dusk and then move to foraging sites at various distances from the roost. Night activity patterns vary, perhaps serving to reduce food competition among species. Some tend to fly and forage intensely in the early evening, become less active in the middle of the night, then resume intense foraging near dawn; others are relatively inactive early in the evening, but more active later on. Bats do not fly continuously after leaving their day roosts, but group together at a *night roost,* a tree for instance, where they rest and bring food. Fruit-eaters do not rest in the tree at which they have discovered ripe fruit, where predators might find them, but they make several trips per night from the fruit tree to their night roost.

If you see any bats on your trip to Thailand, they likely will be one of two obvious types. The huge *fruit bats,* such as the LESSER LONG-TONGUED FRUIT BAT (Plate 62), many of which roost in large groups during the day at the tops of isolated trees, slowly wrap and unwrap their wings around their bodies to offset heat from the direct sunlight. When they fly out from the treetop, they look like large broad-winged hawks. These fruit bats include the largest species of bats in the world. The other bat you are likely to see is equally if not even more astonishing. From cave openings late in the afternoon, up to a quarter-million individual WRINKLE-LIPPED BATS (Plate 63) can take more than an hour to emerge. Look for what appears to be a narrow plume of smoke coming from the side of a limestone mountain or hill. Many hawks and falcons await this feast and pluck hapless individual bats from the edge of the column over and over. The location of these bat caves is well known, and it is a sight you must see while in Thailand.

Bats are beneficial to forests and to people in a number of ways. Many tropical plants have bats, instead of bees or birds, as their main pollinators. These species generally have flowers that open at night and are white, making them easy for bats to find. They also give off a pungent aroma that bats can home in on. Nectar-feeding bats use long tongues to poke into flowers to feed on nectar—a sugary solution—and pollen. As a bat brushes against a flower, pollen adheres to its body and is then carried to other plants, where it falls off and leads to cross-pollination. Fruit-eating bats, owing to their high numbers, are important seed dispersers (see Close-Up, p. 175), helping to regenerate forests by transporting and dropping fruit seeds onto the forest floor. Also, particularly helpful to humans, bats consume enormous numbers of annoying insects each night.

Relatively little is known about which predators prey on bats. The list, however, includes birds of prey (owls, hawks), snakes, other mammals such as civets, cats, and (yes) people. Tiny bats are even captured and eaten by large spiders and cockroaches. Bats, logically, are usually captured in or near their roosts, where predators can reliably find and corner them. One strong indication that predation is a real problem for bats is that many species reduce their flying in bright moonlight, a "lunar phobia." On the other hand, other species do not decrease their activity levels under a full moon, perhaps because they hunt mostly in the darker understory of forests. Because of the crowded conditions in their roosts, however, the most prevalent enemies of bats are parasitic invertebrates that can move freely from bat to bat, including bat flies (a specialized family of wingless flies), fleas, mites, and ticks. In addition to the body fluids and blood these parasites eat, they can also spread diseases. To rid themselves of these parasites, bats spend considerable time grooming themselves and each other with their claws and tongue.

Breeding

Little is known of the breeding biology of flying lemurs. The single young (rarely twins) is born in a very undeveloped stage after a gestation of only 8 weeks. The young is carried in a folded part of the flight membrane near the mother's tail, much like the marsupial opossums of Australia and South America.

Bat mating systems are diverse. The males of some species have harems of 2 to 5 females, but various species employ monogamy, polygyny, and/or promiscuity; the breeding behavior of many species has yet to be studied in detail. Some Thai species breed at particular times of the year, but others have no regular breeding seasons. Most bats produce a single pup at a time. Females of many species of bats, both in temperate areas and the tropics, store sperm and can delay fertilization or the beginning of the development of the embryo. This ability is apparently so that the time of birth for the young bats can be more finely coordinated with delayed rainy seasons and the appearance of insects and fruits.

Notes

Bats have frightened people for a long time. The result, of course, is that there is a large body of folklore that portrays bats as evil, associated with or incarnations of death, devils, witches, or vampires. Undeniably, it was the bats' alien lives—their activity in the darkness, flying ability, and strange form—and people's ignorance of bats, that were the sources of these myriad superstitions. Many cultures worldwide have evil bat legends, from Japan and the Philippines to Europe, the Middle East, Australia, and Central and South America. Many ancient legends tell of how bats came to be creatures of the night. But the association of bats with vampires—blood-sucking monsters—may have originated in recent times with Bram Stoker, the English author who in 1897 published *Dracula* (the title character, a vampire, could metamorphose into a bat). Vampire bats are native only to Central and South America. Stoker may have heard stories of their blood-lapping ways from travellers, and, for his book, melded the behavior of these bats with legends of vampires from India and from Slavic Gypsy culture.

The large fruit bats of Thailand are considered pests in banana, mango, and palm fruit orchards. A colony of fruit bats can descend on an orchard and completely wipe out the crop in one night. Some people eat the larger flying foxes. The peculiar odor of these bats gives them a rabbit-like flavor when curried (or so we have been told).

Status

Determining the statuses of bat populations is difficult because of their nocturnal behavior and habit of roosting in places that are hard to census. With some exceptions, all that is known for most Thai species is that they are common or not common, widely or narrowly distributed. Some species are known from only a few museum specimens, or from their discovery in a single cave, but that does not mean that there are not healthy but largely hidden wild populations. Because many forest bats roost in hollow trees, deforestation is obviously a primary threat. Four species of Thai bats are considered threatened in the IUCN Red List of Threatened Animals, including the tiny and recently discovered KITTI'S HOG-NOSED BAT, which is presently known from a single cave in western Thailand. Many bat populations in temperate regions in Europe and the US are known to be declining and under continued threat by a number of agricultural, forestry, and architectural practices. Traditional roost sites have been lost on large scales by mining and quarrying, by the destruction of old buildings, and by changing architectural styles that eliminate many building overhangs, church belfries, etc. Many forestry practices advocate the removal of hollow, dead trees, which otherwise frequently provide bats with roosting space. Additionally, farm pesticides are ingested by insects, which are then eaten by bats, leading to death or reduced reproductive success. Flying foxes sometimes feed on fruit crops, and because of this, they are sometimes killed in large numbers by farmers. Some flying fox species, particularly those on some Pacific Ocean islands, are threatened or endangered (several are CITES Appendix I listed) because of destruction of their forest habitat, local hunting for food, and hunting for commercial trade. On Guam, for instance, flying foxes and other fruit bats are considered delicacies, so huge numbers of these bats during the 1970s and 1980s were killed on other islands, frozen, and shipped to Guam.

Profiles

Malayan Flying Lemur, *Cynocephalus variegatus*, Plate 61b
Common Flying Fox, *Pteropus vampyrus*, Plate 62a
Kitti's Hog-nosed Bat, *Craeseonycteris thonglongyai*, Plate 62b
Lesser Long-tongued Fruit Bat, *Macroglossus minimus*, Plate 62c
Lyle's Flying Fox, *Pteropus lyeli*, Plate 62d
Greater Short-nosed Bat, *Cynopterus sphinx*, Plate 62e
Blyth's Tomb Bat, *Taphozous saccolaimus*, Plate 63a
Long-winged Tomb Bat, *Taphozous longimanus*, Plate 63b
Greater Yellow Bat, *Scotophilus heathi*, Plate 63c
Wrinkle-lipped Bat, *Tadarida plicata*, Plate 63d
Greater Bent-winged Bat, *Miniopterus schreibersi*, Plate 63e

3. Primates

Most people, it seems, find *monkeys* striking, even transfixing, when first encountered, but then responses diverge. Some people adore the little primates and can watch them for hours, whether it be in the wild or at zoos. Others, however, find them a bit, for want of a better word, unalluring—even to the point of making people slightly uncomfortable. It is probably the same characteristic of monkeys that both so attracts people and turns them off, and that is their quasi-humanness. Whether or not we acknowledge it consciously, it is this trait that is the source of all the attention and importance attached to monkeys and apes. They look like us, and, truth be told, they act like us, in a startlingly large number of ways. Aristotle, 2,300 years ago, noted similarities between human and nonhuman primates, and Linnaeus, the Swedish originator of our current system for naming plants and animals, working more than 100 years pre-Darwin, classed people together in the same group with monkeys. Therefore, even before Darwin's ideas provided a possible mechanism for people and monkeys to be distantly related, we strongly suspected there was a link; the resemblance was too close to be accidental. Given this bond between people and other primates, it is not surprising that visitors to parts of the world that support nonhuman primates are eager to see them and very curious about their lives. Fortunately, Thailand provides homes for several monkey species, some of them still sufficiently abundant in protected areas to be readily located and observed.

Primates are distinguished by several anatomical and ecological traits. They are primarily arboreal animals. Most are fairly large, very smart, and highly social—they live in permanent social groups. Most have five very flexible fingers and toes per limb. Primates' eyes are in the front of the skull, facing forward (eyes in the front instead of on the sides of the head are required for binocular vision and good depth perception, without which swinging about in trees would be an extremely hazardous and problematic affair), and primates have, for their sizes, relatively large brains. Unlike most other mammals, primates have color vision. Female primates give birth usually to a single, very helpless infant.

The globe's 180 species of primates are distributed mainly throughout tropical areas and some subtropical ones, save for the New Guinea/Australian region. The primate order is divided into four groups, three of which occur in Thailand: (1) *Prosimians* include several families of primitive primates from the Old World. They look the least like people, are mainly small and nocturnal, and include lemurs, lorises, galago (bushbaby), and tarsiers. (2) *Old World monkeys* (family Cercopithecidae) include baboons, mandrills, and various monkeys such as rhesus and proboscis monkeys. (3) *New World monkeys* (families Callitrichidae and Cebidae) include many kinds of monkeys, marmosets, and tamarins. (4) The *Hominoidea,* or ape group, contains the gibbons, orangutans, chimpanzees, gorillas, and ecotravellers.

Natural History

Ecology and Behavior

Eleven species of *loris* (family Lorisidae) make up one of the very un-monkey-like groups of Prosimians. They occur in Africa, southern India, and southeastern Asia. The two Asian species in this family are slow-moving and large-eyed. Only the SLOW LORIS (Plate 64) is found in Thailand, and it lives up to its name. It lacks a tail and has a large thumb and first toe for grasping. It is entirely arboreal, and when it climbs, it is with slow and deliberate changes of position from one branch to the next, never leaping. Lorises also walk hand over hand along a branch with a peculiar snake-like bending of the back. Typical of many nocturnal animals, the Slow Loris has an extra layer of pigment on the retina of the eye for concentrating low light. This layer is also highly reflective, and in the beam of a flashlight, the eyes "glow" brightly. Loris have little or no color vision, unlike their diurnal primate cousins. They eat snails, insects, birds, small mammals, and lizards, which they grab with both hands in an extremely fast motion. They also eat fruit. During the day, the male and female usually sleep close together, curled up in the crotch of a tree or in a clump of bamboo. The recorded life span of the Slow Loris in the wild is 12 to 14 years.

The family of Old World monkeys (Cercopithecidae) includes 70 species in Africa and Asia, nine of which occur in Thailand. All of them are diurnal and have prominent muzzles, heavy jaws, rounded ears, and nostrils set close together and facing forward and downward. Many members have cheek pouches for temporary storage of food, and all have hands and feet with grasping fingers and toes. All the digits have flat nails, and the tail is never prehensile. Most species are either leaf-eating or omnivorous. The leaf-eating *langurs* have specialized stomachs divided into three compartments for breaking down hard-to-digest plant material through fermentation. They have long tails and tend to be arboreal. The *macaques* are more terrestrial and catholic in their tastes; they will eat almost anything, from fruit, seeds, insects, and small animals to potato chips and cookies. The CRAB-EATING MACAQUE (Plate 65) has become specialized on crabs, crustaceans, and shellfish that are exposed at low tide in the mangrove swamps it inhabits.

Gibbons are representatives of the apes and form the family Hylobatidae, which has nine species distributed from western India to Borneo. In Thailand there are three species. They are all tailless, and have short snouts and amazingly long arm bones. The long arms are used for swinging (*brachiating*) through the canopy of evergreen forests, as well as for reaching fruits on the ends of small branches that other monkey species cannot get to. Gibbons will also eat leaves, insects, nestling birds, and lizards. The loud, whooping vocalizations of Thailand's gibbons are a dazzling part of the ecotraveller's visit to national parks in the west and peninsular parts of the country that have tall trees.

Primates are especially crucial elements of forest ecosystems because they are seed dispersers for many hundreds of plant species, particularly of the larger canopy trees. Seeds of some plant species have velcro-like coverings that stick to hair until they eventually fall off days later. Mammals that are *frugivores* (fruit-eaters) often carry fruit away from a tree, then eat the soft parts and drop the seeds, which may later germinate; or they eat the fruit whole and transport the seeds in their digestive tracts. The seeds eventually fall, unharmed, to the ground and germinate (see Close-Up, p. 175). One primate species that was studied was found to disperse more than 300,000 tiny seeds of a single tree species each day; up to two-thirds of the seeds that passed through the monkeys' digestive systems later germinated (a proportion that was actually higher than seeds that made it to the ground without passing through an animal gut). However, monkeys at times are also seed predators. They extract seeds from fruit and chew them, destroying them, and also eat young fruits and nuts that contain seeds too undeveloped ever to germinate.

Breeding

Male SLOW LORIS are extremely territorial and mark the boundaries of their defended area with urine. Pairs or small family groups occupy each territory. The female gives birth to a single young after a relatively long gestation period of 193 days. Young are born with their eyes open and well-developed. The mother and father share duties of carrying the young around on their backs for up to 6 months.

Macaques and langurs form troops of 10 to 100 individuals, usually with many females and immatures but only a few adult males. These troops roam over large areas, and the females advertise their readiness to breed (ovulation) with distinctive brightening of skin colors in their face and on their rumps. Dominant males chase each other and vie for the females' acceptance of them as fathers. The single young is born after 7 months of gestation and suckles milk from the mother for three to ten months. Several species give birth only every other year.

The gibbons are unique among the apes in forming small family groups of six or fewer individuals that are highly territorial. They actively declare the boundaries of their areas against intruding family groups with their loud vocalizations, each species with a distinctly different set of calls. The male and female calls of each species are also distinct, and sometimes males and females chorus together. A single young is born after 7 months' gestation. The baby gibbon is carried around the mother's waist for about a year. It clings to the hairs of her sides as she swings from one branch to the next. The mother will breed again when the first young is about 18 months old and able to feed itself.

Notes

Considerable local folklore has arisen around primates, especially the gibbons. Indigenous people such as those of the Karen and Meo Hill Tribes in northern Thailand believe that gibbon calls help crops grow, and thus the gibbons are welcomed in the forests near the fields. The whooping calls of female WHITE-HANDED GIBBONS (Plate 65) are thought by some Thai villagers to be saying *pua, pua,* the Thai word for "husband." In Khao Yai National Park, the White-handed and PILEATED GIBBONS interbreed to produce hybrids that look like a different species. The RHESUS MACAQUE (Plate 64), because of its adaptability to captivity and its extreme similarity to human beings in physiology and anatomy, has been used extensively in medical testing. For instance, an important part of the typing of red blood corpuscles in humans is based on the presence of an Rh marker (Rh- or Rh+), so-named because it was first identified in the blood of the Rhesus Macaque.

Status

All non-human primates are listed in CITES Appendix II as species that, although they may not be currently threatened, need to be highly regulated in trade or else they could soon become threatened. The IUCN Red List includes four species of Thai primates that are considered threatened or endangered—STUMP-TAILED MACAQUE (Plate 64), ASSAMESE MACAQUE, PIG-TAILED MACAQUE (Plate 64), and PILEATED GIBBON. Main menaces to monkeys are deforestation—elimination of their natural habitats—and poaching. The larger monkeys are often hunted for their meat, and therefore are usually rare near human settlements.

Profiles

Slow Loris, *Nycticebus coucang,* Plate 64a
Pig-tailed Macaque, *Macaca nemestrina,* Plate 64b
Stump-tailed Macaque, *Macaca arctoides,* Plate 64c
Rhesus Macaque, *Macaca mulatta,* Plate 64d
Crab-eating Macaque, *Macaca fascicularis,* Plate 65a
Banded Langur, *Presbytis melalophus,* Plate 65b
Dusky Langur, *Presbytis obscura,* Plate 65c
White-handed Gibbon, *Hylobates lar,* Plate 65d

4. Pangolins

Without a doubt, the most bizarre mammals in Thailand are *pangolins* (family Manidae), which are more similar to an animal drawing from some child's imagination than to something from the real world. Covered with large, sharp-edged scales, their long tail sticking out one end and their long thin snout at the other end, your first sighting of this enigmatic mammal will be memorable.

Not only are the pangolins enigmatic for ecotravellers, they have confused many scientists trying to figure out who their relatives are and where they came from. For a long time, the seven species (two of which occur in Thailand), all found in sub-Saharan Africa and southern Asia, were thought to be Old World replacements of their New World cousins, the armadillos and anteaters. The latest thinking, however, places the pangolins far from the armadillos and anteaters, alone in an ancient mammalian branch, with no close relatives among living mammals.

In addition to the peculiar overlapping scales covering their bodies (made of combined stiff hairs), pangolins have short legs, long tapering tails and snout, tiny or no ears, no teeth, and a tongue that is half as long as its head and body combined! They have long claws on the feet, especially long and powerful on the front feet, and the tails of the Asian species are prehensile. Males tend to be considerably larger than females.

Natural History

Ecology and Behavior

Found solitarily or occasionally in pairs, pangolins are almost completely nocturnal. They feed exclusively on ants and termites using their powerful front legs and claws to excavate the insects' mounds and nests. When the interior of an insect nest is exposed, the pangolin's long tongue flicks in and out, and its sticky surfaces capture adults, eggs, and larval insects, which are hungrily lapped up. The pangolin's nostrils and ear openings can be closed to avoid painful stings and bites from the defending insects.

Although often active on the ground, Asian pangolins also readily climb trees, which they do using their feet and tail to hitch their way up the trunk. During the day they rest curled up in a burrow dug deep into the ground. When threatened by a predator, a pangolin immediately curls up into a ball with the sharp scales sticking out. The tail can also be flayed about like a spiked mace.

Breeding

Little is known of the breeding biology of pangolins. A single young is born in the underground nest after a gestation period of 2 to 3 months. While travelling, until about 3 or 4 months of age, the young rides on the mother's back at the base of the tail. In its defense posture, the mother transfers the young to its chest, in effect providing a protective chamber.

Notes

The word "pangolin" comes from the Malay language and refers to a cushion that has the scaly appearance of a pangolin rolled into a ball.

Status

Although not listed as threatened or endangered, pangolin populations are under severe pressure because of the purported medicinal value of their scales. The Chinese use these scales, ground into a powder and mixed with herbs and water, to treat skin diseases and sexually transmitted diseases.

Profile

Malayan Pangolin, *Manis javanica*, Plate 66a

5. Rodents and Rabbits

Rodents and *rabbits* superficially resemble each other with their large, front incisor teeth. They are, however, only distantly related. Rodents (order Rodentia) are distributed worldwide from the Arctic to the tropics, and they include *mice, rats, squirrels, chipmunks, marmots, gophers, beavers,* and *porcupines.* Worldwide there are more than 2,000 species, representing 44% of the approximately 4,629 known mammalian species. More individual rodents are estimated to be alive at any one time than individuals of all other types of mammals combined. Nevertheless, many ecotravellers will discover among rodents a paradox: although diverse and abundant, rodents are, with a few obvious exceptions in any region, relatively inconspicuous and rarely encountered. Rodents' near-invisibility to people, particularly in the tropics, can be explained best by the facts that most rodents are very small, secretive or nocturnal, and many of them live in subterranean burrows. Of course, many people do not consider it a hardship that rodents are so rarely encountered.

High rodent abundance and diversity are likely related to their efficient, specialized teeth and associated jaw muscles, as well as to their broad, nearly omnivorous, diets. Rodents are characterized by having four large incisor teeth, one pair front-and-center in the upper jaw, one pair in the lower (other teeth, separated from the incisors, are located farther back in the mouth). With these strong, sharp, chisel-like front teeth, rodents "make their living": gnawing (*rodent* is from the Latin *rodere,* to gnaw), cutting, and slicing vegetation, fruit, and nuts, killing and eating small animals, digging burrows, and even, in the case of beavers, imitating lumberjacks.

More than 70 species occur in Thailand. However, visitors commonly spot only a few representatives of 4 families, and we profile 12 species from these families. Squirrels are members of family Sciuridae, a worldwide group of 273 species that occur on all continents except Australia and Antarctica. The family includes *ground, tree,* and *flying squirrels;* an amazing 27 species occur in Thailand. Family Hystricidae contains the 8 species of Old World porcupines, which are distributed throughout southern Asia and Africa. Three species of these sharp-spined mammals are native to Thailand. The 4 species of *bamboo rats* are placed in family Rhizomyidae and are restricted to dense bamboo forests. Three species occur in Thailand. By far the most diverse family of rodents in Thailand are the Old World rats and mice in family Muridae. Of the almost 400 species in this family, 36 are found in Thailand.

Porcupines generally are fairly large (up to 27 kg, 60 lb), heavyset rodents (although Thailand has one small species, the BUSH-TAILED PORCUPINE, Plate 68, which is half that size) with many sharp spines covering their bodies and often the tail. The spines easily break off to embed themselves in the skin of a predator unfortunate or naive enough to try to bite a porcupine.

The bamboo rats are short, pudgy, animals with short tails, small eyes and ears, short, stout claws, and soft, thick fur. Unlike many other rodents, they lack cheek pouches for temporarily storing food.

Nobody has to describe what Old World mice and rats look like, but just for the record they are the most numerous kind of mammal in the world, both in numbers of species and probably numbers of individuals. They tend to have long, naked, scaly tails, large eyes, and pointed snouts. On the hand, the thumb has a flat nail, and the other four fingers are clawed. Many species, such as NOR-

WAY and BLACK RATS and the HOUSE MOUSE, have become involved with humans, some to the point of dependency, and have spread with them all over the world.

Rabbits, even though they look like rodents, are in a separate order, the Lagamorpha. The group is differentiated from rodents by four instead of two front incisor teeth on the upper jaw, large hind legs, and long ears. Only one species occurs in Thailand, the SIAMESE HARE (Plate 66), and it looks similar to rabbits and small hares common throughout North America and Europe.

Natural History

Ecology and Behavior

Rodents are important ecologically primarily because of their great abundance. They are so common that they make up a large proportion of the diets of many carnivores. In addition, rodents, owing to their ubiquitousness and numbers, are themselves important predators on seeds and fruit. That is, they eat seeds and seed-containing fruit, digesting or damaging the seeds so that they cannot germinate. Of course, not every seed is damaged (some fall to the ground as rodents eat, others pass unscathed through their digestive tracts), and so rodents, at least occasionally, also act as seed dispersers (see Close-Up, p. 175). Burrowing is another aspect of rodent behavior that has significant ecological implications because of the sheer numbers of individuals that participate. When so many animals move soil around (rats, mice, and bamboo rats especially), the effect is that over several years the entire topsoil of an area is turned, keeping soil loose and aerated, and therefore more suitable for plant growth.

Squirrels are all bushy-tailed, solitary species, generally seen in trees and occasionally foraging on the ground. However, three species of Thailand squirrels are found only on the ground. Most tend to be diurnal in activity. The larger squirrels typically feed on fruits and large nuts, and they are usually found at many levels in the forest and often on the ground or in the understory, where they frequently hide (cache) food for later meals by burying it or placing it in tree cavities. In contrast, the smaller squirrels' diet is largely made up of insects, spiders, and other arthropods they search out on branches, tangles, and other vegetation, from high in the canopy to the forest floor. Some of these smaller species are quickly and reliably attracted to squeaking noises that mimic a bird or small mammal in distress. This behavior may indicate that insectivorous squirrel species are also partially carnivorous.

Ten species of flying squirrels also occur in Thailand. They all have a flat sheet of skin between the fore and hind legs that can be spread out to form a gliding membrane when they leap from one tree to the next. As with flying lemurs (p. 185), this movement through the air is not proper flying but gliding, in which they lose elevation from one point to the next. Flying squirrels, unlike most other non-flying squirrels, are nocturnal and limited to the canopy of tall forest. When not flying and running along branches, the gliding membrane is difficult to see. Flying squirrels spend the day in tree hollows or cavities.

Thailand's porcupines are solitary, nocturnal animals, almost always found on the ground. They move slowly along paths, secure in their spiny defense. When challenged, they raise the hairs and spines on their backs, shake their tails to rattle the hollow quills, and may even charge backward at an intruder to run it through with the sharp spines. They feed on leaves, green tree shoots, and fruit. During the day they sleep in burrows in the ground. Quite often piles of bones appear in or around their burrows. These bones, as well as remnants of old elephant tusks, are chewed for the calcium in them. All three Thai species are found in secondary and primary forests.

Bamboo rats are active only at night and spend the daytime resting in burrows below thick tangles of vegetation, usually in or near bamboo thickets. They are adapted for burrowing in the ground and feed underground mainly on leaves, shoots, and stems.

Old World rats and mice include species that are in houses, farms and cities as well as species that occur only in the deepest forests and natural habitats. It is the human-associated species, however, that are the best studied. Rats and mice eat nearly twenty percent of Thailand's annual rice crop. Bandicoots eat sewn seeds in the paddies; other rats burrow through irrigation dikes and canals that divert water for irrigation. After harvest, many species eat through bags in storage areas to eat the rice kernels. Several rats are reservoirs for human diseases, such as scrub typhus, plague, and rabies.

Hares feed on many types of vegetation. Commonly hares eat their own fecal pellets, apparently as a way of breaking down the difficult-to-digest plant chemicals. The hares spend much of the day hiding alone in dense ground vegetation and feeding in open, grassy areas during the night. They use their long hind legs to run and dodge their many predator enemies.

Breeding

Relatively little is known of the breeding behavior of most tropical tree squirrels and of many other rodents. Tree squirrel nests consist of a bed of leaves placed in a tree cavity or a ball of leaves on a branch or in a tangle of vegetation or tree cavity. One to 4 young are born per litter, although 2 is the norm.

Porcupines usually have 2 young per litter. Pregnancy is relatively long, and as a result the young are *precocial*—born eyes open and in an advanced state of development. They are therefore mobile and quickly able to follow the mother.

Bamboo rats give birth to 3 to 5 young in an underground nest. The young are born naked and helpless, and suckle milk from the mother for 3 months. Similarly, Old World rats and mice have 3 to 6 young, usually in a protected burrow, mound of grass, or, for some species, the hollow space within a giant bamboo stalk.

Hares have several litters of 3 to 4 young each year. The gestation period, following an often physically active courtship by the male, is 40 days. Unlike the rodents (and the closely related rabbits), young hares are born fully furred and active, with their eyes wide open. They are suckled for about a month and then are on their own.

Notes

Through the animals' constant gnawing, rodents' chisel-like incisors wear down rapidly. Fortunately for the rodents, their incisors, owing to some ingenious anatomy and physiology, continue to grow throughout their lives, unlike those of most other mammals.

Contrary to folk wisdom, porcupines cannot "throw" their quills, or spines, at people or predators. Rather, the spines detach quite easily when touched, such that a predator snatching a porcupine in its mouth will be impaled with spines and hence rendered very unhappy. The spines have barbed ends, like fishhooks, which anchor them securely into the flesh of the offending predator.

The meat of rats, especially bamboo rats, is considered a delicacy by many hill tribes in Thailand and elsewhere.

Status

Five of Thailand's rodents are listed as threatened or endangered by the IUCN Red List. Of these, two are rats (NEILL'S RAT, a limestone mountain specialist, and SIKKIM RAT), two are squirrels (RED-RUMPED SQUIRREL and PARTICOLORED FLYING SQUIRREL), and one is a porcupine (MALAYAN PORCUPINE, Plate 68). The BUSH-TAILED PORCUPINE is endangered in part of its range (but not in Thailand). Habitat destruction and hunting for food by people are the main threats to all of these rodents.

Profiles

Siamese Hare, *Lepus peguensis*, Plate 66b
Black Giant Squirrel, *Ratufa bicolor*, Plate 66c
Red Giant Flying Squirrel, *Petaurista petaurista*, Plate 66d
Red-cheeked Squirrel, *Dremomys rufigenis*, Plate 66e
Gray-bellied Squirrel, *Callosciurus caniceps*, Plate 67a
Variable Squirrel, *Callosciurus finlaysoni*, Plate 67b
Striped Tree Squirrel, *Tamiops macclellandi*, Plate 67c
Belly-banded Squirrel, *Callosciurus flavimanus*, Plate 67d
Malayan Porcupine, *Hystrix brachyura*, Plate 68a
Bush-tailed Porcupine, *Atherurus marourus*, Plate 68b
Great Bandicoot, *Bandicota indica*, Plate 68c
Ryukyu Mouse, *Mus caroli*, Plate 68d
Yellow Rajah Rat, *Rattus surifer*, Plate 68e

6. Carnivores

Carnivores are ferocious mammals—including the cat that sleeps on your pillow and the dog that takes table scraps from your hand—that are specialized to kill and eat other vertebrate animals. They all share clawed toes and teeth customized to grasp, rip, and tear flesh—witness their large, cone-shaped canines. Most are meat-eaters, but many are at least somewhat omnivorous, taking fruits and other plant materials. Carnivore populations tend to be sparse and individuals notoriously difficult to see at any time. They range in size from weasels 9 cm (3.5 in) long to bears 3 m (10 ft) long. Five families within the Order Carnivora have Thai representatives: *dogs, bears, weasels, civets,* and *cats*. Of these, only the civet family is unique to the Old World; the others are widely represented throughout the New World as well.

The 36 species in the worldwide dog family (Canidae) include wolves, jackals, foxes, and wild dogs. They are all highly adapted for running, their feet arranged so that they bear weight on the toes, and they tend to be highly vocal. The bear family (Ursidae) is made up of 8 species of large and robust animals. They have poor eyesight but excellent powers of hearing and smell, and they tend to be highly omnivorous as well as scavengers. The civet family (Viverridae) includes 75 medium-sized species (including genets and mongooses) that carry their full weight on the soles of the feet and have long tails, both of which help with maneuverability and balance in their largely arboreal habitats. Several *viverrid* species are very cat-like, including possessing retractable claws, but the presence of five, not four, toes on all feet distinguishes the viverrids. Civets and genets, in general, resemble spotted, long-nosed cats with long slender bodies and pointed ears. Most viverrids are nocturnal and carnivorous but some are omnivorous.

Many species have well-developed scent glands under the tail, which produce an often vile-smelling musk. The weasel family (Mustelidae) includes 70 species of weasels, stoats, skunks, minks, wolverines, and badgers and is characterized by relatively long bodies, short legs, and walking on the soles of the feet. Most *mustelids* have dense, soft fur and a gland that produces chemicals with powerful odors. Their extremely powerful jaws and sharp teeth can kill large prey quickly. The 36 members of the cat family (Felidae) bear weight on their toes and have retractable claws. They are completely carnivorous and use their extremely sharp, long teeth to dispatch prey with a bite to the back of the head or neck. They tend to have excellent vision, including color vision. They have short noses and their eyes are set at the front of the head to maximize depth perception.

Natural History

Ecology and Behavior

Dogs. The dogs have two representatives in Thailand. If you encounter either, it will probably be in the form of tracks or *scat* (droppings). The ASIAN WILD DOG (Plate 69), or DHOLE, hunts in packs early in the morning and late in the afternoon. Using both sight and smell to run down their prey in a relentless and steady pursuit, they often hunt animals much larger than themselves. In contrast, the ASIATIC JACKAL (Plate 69) hunts alone or in pairs, feeding on small animals, fruits, and carrion. It is nocturnal and often found near human habitation.

Bears. Only two species of bear occur in Thailand, the ASIATIC BLACK BEAR and MALAYAN SUN BEAR (Plate 69). Both species are primarily nocturnal and occur in forested areas. They tend to be solitary and extremely shy. The bears eat tubers, buds, fruits, and other vegetable matter dug out with their powerful claws, and invertebrates. But if given the opportunity, they will not turn down a juicy rodent or the chance to scavenge a dead deer or cow. They usually remain on the ground but are also amazingly agile tree climbers.

Civets. Thirteen species of civets, genets, and mongooses occur in Thailand, many of them secretive and arboreal. You are only likely to see a few of the more terrestrial viverrid species. The most visible ones are some of the larger civets, which you are likely to see only at night in the headlights of your vehicle or with a flashlight along a forest path. The JAVAN MONGOOSE (Plate 71), however, often runs across roads in open areas during the daytime, and you likely will get a glance of several during your visit as they flash in front of you, rarely stopping for a better look. These animals eat rats, snakes, and birds, including domestic chickens.

Weasels. In Thailand, the mustelid family is represented by 10 species of weasels, badgers, and otters. These species include some of the most ferocious and intrepid predators in the world. They prey mainly on rodents, birds, and insects, but often attack prey many times their own size. Many species in this group have anal scent glands used for marking territory boundaries or as a defensive chemical against enemies. Mustelids generally are solitary and terrestrial, occasionally arboreal. Only the otters have evolved an aquatic lifestyle, feeding on fish, crustaceans, and frogs. This life of swimming has also led to a social life that revolves around small family groups. In western Thailand, three species of otters occur together in the same waterways. Apparently to reduce competition for food, each species feeds on different prey. COMMON OTTERS feast on similar percentages of fish and crab (35% of the diet for each), SMOOTH-COATED OTTERS (Plate 70) primarily on fish (86%), and SMALL-CLAWED OTTERS (Plate 70) mainly on crabs (91%).

Cats. Because all nine species of cats that occur in Thailand are fairly rare, some to the point of being endangered, and because of their mainly nocturnal habits, your chances are slim of seeing even a single wild cat on any brief trip. More than likely, all that you will see of cats are traces; some tracks in the mud near a stream or scratch marks on a tree trunk or log. (Although some communication is vocal, cats also signal each other by making scratch marks on vegetation and by leaving urine and feces to scent-mark areas.)

Thai cat species can be placed into two groups—those with spots or stripes and those that are wholly or mostly unmarked. The six marked species generally are yellowish, tan, or cinnamon on top and white below, with black spots and stripes on their heads, bodies, and legs. The smallest and perhaps most common is the LEOPARD CAT (Plate 72), the size of a large house cat. The largest is the TIGER (Plate 72), which is also the largest cat in the world and the region's largest carnivore, males weighing up to 300 kg (660 lb). Three other spotted cats are shown in Plate 72; the only spotted cat not illustrated is the small MARBLED CAT. The unspotted cats are the small and very rare FLAT-HEADED CAT, and the medium-sized JUNGLE CAT and ASIAN GOLDEN CAT. Female cats of most species are smaller than males, up to a third smaller in the Tiger. The cats are finely adapted to prey on vertebrate animals, and hunting methods are extremely similar among the various species. They do not run to chase prey for long distances. Rather, cats slowly stalk their prey or wait in ambush, then capture the prey after pouncing on it or after a very brief, fast chase. Biologists are often impressed by the consistency in the manner that cats kill their prey. Almost always it is with a sharp bite to the neck or head, breaking the neck or crushing the skull. Retractile claws, in addition to their use in grabbing and holding prey, give cats good abilities to climb trees, and some of them are partially arboreal animals, foraging and even sleeping in trees.

Aside from some highly social large cats of Africa, most cats are solitary animals, foraging alone, individuals coming together only to mate. Some species are territorial, but in others individuals overlap in the areas in which they hunt. Cats, with their big eyes to gather light, are often nocturnal, especially those of forests, but some are also active by day. When inactive, they shelter in rock crevices or burrows dug by other animals, and often spend daylight hours asleep in trees. Cats are the most carnivorous of the carnivores; that is, their diets are more centered on meat than any of the other families. They also tend to be the most adaptable to human presence, especially if a chicken coop is involved. Thai cats inhabit low and middle elevation forests, savannahs, and grasslands, hunting for large prey such as WILD PIGS (Plate 74) and deer, but also monkeys, birds, and lizards.

Breeding

Most dogs are monogamous, and although they often dig their own dens in which to have young, they are not above taking over a hole made by a porcupine or some other burrowing animal, enlarging and modifying it for their own use. The large litter of young is born naked and blind, and is fed by both parents even after emergence from the den.

After mating, the fertilized egg of female bears in most tropical species does not implant in the uterus for several months (delayed implantation), a trait apparently held over from their northern cousins, whose semi-hibernation forces them to extend pregnancy so that the young aren't born too early. Bears give birth in a den to 1 to 2 naked and helpless young. They are cared for by only the mother for the next 3 years or until the next litter is born.

Among all the Thai viverrids, females raise the 2 to 3 young without help from males. Young are born in nests made in tree holes or burrows in the ground. Duration of pregnancy varies from about 56 days in mongooses, to about 65 days in civets, to about 77 days in genets.

Female mustelids give birth in dens under rocks or in crevices, or in burrows under trees. As with bears, a female's eggs are often not implanted in the uterus until several months after mating. Pregnancy usually lasts about 60 to 70 days, and they produce 2 to 4 young per litter. As is true for many of the carnivores, mustelid young are born blind and helpless, but both parents help care for them. Several species of mustelids in Thailand are thought to pair for life.

In contrast, male and female cats in Thailand come together only to mate; the female bears and raises her young alone. She gives birth in a den that is a burrow, rock cave, or tree cavity. The young are sheltered in the den while the female forages; she returns periodically to nurse and bring the kittens prey to eat. Most of the cats have 1 or 2 young at a time, although some species may have up to 4. Pregnancy is about 75 days in the smaller cats, about 100 in the large ones. Juvenile Tigers remain with their mother for up to 18 months, learning to be efficient hunters, before they go off on their own.

Notes

TIGERS rarely attack people, who normally are given a wide berth. Cats in Thailand are sometimes seen walking at night along forest trails or roads. General advice if you happen to stumble across a large cat: do not run because that often stimulates a cat to chase. Face the cat, make yourself large by raising your arms, and make as much loud noise as you can.

One facet of mustelid natural history that is particularly helpful to people, though not universally appreciated, is that these carnivores eat a staggering number of rodents. For instance, it has been calculated that weasels each year in New York State eat some 60 million mice and millions of rats.

The mustelids and the viverrids both produce a volatile chemical given off as a glandular secretion that is used to deter enemies as well as mark territorial boundaries. Paradoxically, these chemical are also used as a base to produce extremely high quality and expensive perfumes.

Status

Nine carnivore species that occur in Thailand are considered threatened or endangered by the IUCN Red List: ASIAN WILD DOG, ASIATIC BLACK BEAR, OTTER CIVET, SMOOTH-COATED OTTER, HAIRY-NOSED OTTER, BACK-STRIPED WEASEL, CLOUDED LEOPARD, FLAT-HEADED CAT, and TIGER. Their habitats are increasingly cleared for agricultural purposes; they were, and still are to a limited extent, hunted for their skins; and large cats are killed to avoid potential predation on livestock and pets. Tigers face a special threat: they are hunted in Thailand and indeed throughout their range in Asia, mainly to supply body parts to the illicit Chinese pharmaceutical trade. Tigers have been eliminated from much of Thailand and are present only in small numbers in protected areas; probably fewer than 300 remain. Many mustelids in the past were trapped intensively for their fur, which is often soft, dense, and glossy, just the ticket, in fact, to create coats of otter or weasel, mink or marten, sable or fisher.

Profiles

Asiatic Jackal, *Canis aureus*, Plate 69a
Asian Wild Dog, *Cuon alpinus*, Plate 69b

Malayan Sun Bear, *Helarctos malayanus,* Plate 69c
Yellow-throated Marten, *Martes flavigula,* Plate 69d
Hog Badger, *Arctonyx collaris,* Plate 70a
Smooth-coated Otter, *Lutra perspicillata,* Plate 70b
Small-clawed Otter, *Aonyx cinerea,* Plate 70c
Small Indian Civet, *Viverricula malaccensis,* Plate 70d
Large Indian Civet, *Viverra zibetha,* Plate 70e
Common Palm Civet, *Paradoxurus hermaphroditus,* Plate 71a
Masked Palm Civet, *Paguma larvata,* Plate 71b
Binturong, *Arctictis binturong,* Plate 71c
Javan Mongoose, *Herpestes javanicus,* Plate 71d
Clouded Leopard, *Neofelis nebulosa,* Plate 72a
Leopard Cat, *Felis bengalensis,* Plate 72b
Leopard, *Panthera pardus,* Plate 72c
Tiger, *Panthera tigris,* Plate 72d
Fishing Cat, *Felis viverrina,* Plate 72e

7. Even-toed Ungulates

Wild species of *pigs, mouse deer, deer,* and *cattle* represent the four families of the order Artiodactyla found in Thailand. This order of large hoofed mammals (*ungulates*) is distributed globally and is distinguished by an even numbers of toes on each foot. Other *artiodactyls* are hippos, giraffes, antelope, bison, buffalo, gazelles, goats, and sheep. In general, the group is specialized to feed on leaves, grass, and fallen fruit.

The pig family (Suidae) has seven species found in Europe, Africa, and Asia. One species, the widespread WILD PIG (Plate 74), occurs in Thailand. Pigs are stocky animals with a flat, disklike muzzle that is used for plowing through soil litter to find buried food. The upper canine teeth turn upward to form external curved tusks. They have long, coarse guard hairs on the back. Internally they have a simple stomach and are not cud chewers.

About the size of a large hare, the mouse deer, or chevrotains (family Tragulidae), are the smallest hoofed animals in the world. Two species, the LESSER (Plate 74) and GREATER MOUSE DEER, occur in the forests of Thailand, and they are probably the most common ungulates in the country. More closely related to camels or pigs than they are to deer, they lack antlers or horns. Their legs are slender, and the upper canine teeth of males are elongated and curved to extend below the upper lip. They have a primitive three-chambered stomach to facilitate cud-chewing.

The deer family (Cervidae) has about 40 species worldwide, six in Thailand (one of which is now extinct). Deer are large mammals with long, thin legs, short tails, and big ears. Males have antlers that they shed each year and regrow. They have a complex, four-chambered stomach and are cud-chewers.

Nearly 50 species of wild cattle and goats (family Bovidae) occur worldwide, except in South America, Australia, and Antarctica. The members of this family have horns (unlike antlers, horns are not shed) on the males and, in many species, also on the females. Most bovids are large with long legs. They have well-developed four-chambered stomachs for cud-chewing. Four species of wild cattle at one time occurred in Thailand, but only the BANTENG (Plate 73) and GAUR (Plate 73) still have significant populations in the country. Two species of wild goats, the SEROW (Plate 74) and GORAL, occur on precipitous cliff faces and limestone hills in Thailand.

Natural History

Ecology and Behavior

Pigs are typically diurnal, but under hunting pressure they often become nocturnal. They are highly social animals, rarely encountered singly. The boars (males), however, tend to be solitary. The herds travel noisily along narrow forest paths, spreading out when good foraging sites are found. These animals are omnivores, but mainly they dig into the ground with their snouts, *rooting* for vegetation. Pigs feed on roots, underground stems, and bulbs, but also on leaves, fruit, insects, and even small vertebrates that they stumble across. Pigs often wallow in mud and shallow water, and there is usually a customary wallowing spot within their home range, the area within which a group lives and forages. During dry seasons, pigs may gather in large numbers near lakes or streams. Because pigs are hunted by people, the approach of humans causes them to become quiet, wary, and therefore, sometimes hard to notice or approach. Besides their tracks, you can detect that a group has just passed by a cloyingly sweaty smell that lingers after them for a half-hour or more in the undergrowth of a forest. Large snakes such as pythons as well as Leopards and Tigers prey upon pigs.

Almost completely nocturnal, the tiny mouse deer are solitary and make tunnels through the dense undergrowth of forests, through which they wander in search of grass, leaves, fallen fruit, and occasionally a small bird or lizard. They spend the day in a protected site, such as a tree hollow or a crevice in a rock.

Deer eat grass (*grazing*) as well as leaves and twigs from trees and shrubs that they can reach from the ground (*browsing*). The COMMON BARKING DEER (Plate 74), in particular, also eats fruit and flowers, chiefly those that have already fallen to the ground. Thai deer are almost always solitary or in small groups. They are active during daylight hours but also often at night, although they are most commonly seen during early mornings and at dusk. Deer are *cud-chewers*. After foraging and filling a special chamber of their stomach, they find a sheltered area, rest, regurgitate the meal into their mouths and chew it well so that it can be digested. Predators on deer include the big cats—Leopard and Tiger.

In Thailand, wild cattle (BANTENG, GAUR) stay during the day in open forests and venture into open grassland areas during the night. Gregarious animals, they usually occur in herds of 5 to 20. However, the bulls are often solitary. These wild cattle both graze and browse on grass and leaves. Stalked by large cats and humans, the herds of cattle are often joined by WILD PIGS so that their combined senses of smell, vision, and hearing can be shared. Cattle Egrets (p. 125) and several species of drongos (p. 161) regularly associate with these grazing herds during the daytime. As the cattle walk they scare up large insects that are quickly and conveniently captured by the birds. Often the birds ride on the backs of the cattle to have better access to their insect banquet. Thailand's wild goats, GORAL and SEROW, feed in the early morning and late afternoon on twigs, grass, and nuts along steep mountainsides. The Serow is usually solitary, but the Goral occurs in family groups of 4 to 12.

Breeding

Female pigs have up to 10 young at a time, born about 115 days after mating. The black-and-white-striped young are *precocial*, meaning that they can walk and follow their mother within a few days of birth. The rest of the ungulates generally give birth to a single or occasionally a pair of precocial young—mouse deer after a gestation period of 5 months, deer after 6 months, cattle after 10 months, and goats after 8 months. Within a week or two, the young are strong enough to follow the mother. Until that time, they stay in a sheltered spot while their mother forages, returning at intervals to nurse them. The fawns of most deer species have small white spots on their flanks and back.

Notes
The WILD PIG was first domesticated in China about 5000 BC There is some evidence that it was independently domesticated in Thailand even earlier. Because they grow quickly, have large litters, are resistant to many diseases, feed on garbage, and herds are led by a dominant individual (human beings can take over as the dominant individual), pigs have become one of the most important domesticated animals throughout the world. For similar reasons, wild species of cattle, goats, and sheep have also lent themselves to domestication and helped change human culture over the last few thousand years.

Status
Thailand's only endemic ungulate, SCHOMBURGK'S DEER, became extinct in 1938, owing to over-hunting and habitat destruction. The BROW-ANTLERED or ELD'S DEER has been reduced by over-hunting in Thailand to a few herds along the northeast border. It is listed as endangered by the IUCN Red List. Three species of wild cattle in Thailand are endangered (GAUR, BANTENG, and WILD WATER BUFFALO). Only 900 Gaur, 470 Banteng, and about 40 Wild Water Buffalo remain in Thailand, and all of them are in protected areas. The KOUPREY, a Southeast Asian wild ox first known to science in 1937, is probably extinct in Thailand and nearly so in neighboring Cambodia. Both wild goats, the GORAL and SEROW, are listed as threatened or endangered.

Profiles
Gaur, *Bos gaurus*, Plate 73c
Banteng, *Bos javanicus*, Plate 73d
Lesser Mouse Deer, *Tragulus javanicus*, Plate 74a
Common Barking Deer, *Muntiacus muntjak*, Plate 74b
Sambar, *Cervus unicolor*, Plate 74c
Serow, *Capricornis sumatrensis*, Plate 74d
Wild Pig, *Sus scrofa*, Plate 74e

8. Elephant, Tapir, and Rhinoceros

The largest terrestrial mammals in Thailand belong to two somewhat related groups. The *elephants* (family Elephantidae) were once a diverse group that roamed much of the world. During the last 10,000 years or so, however, the family has been reduced to two species, one in Africa and one in Asia. The long trunk, thick, pillar-like legs, huge ears, flattened feet, and immense size make them unmistakable.

The *tapirs* and *rhinoceros* belong to a group distantly related to the even-toed ungulates (p. 201), called the *odd-toed ungulates* (order Perissodactyla). They have three or four toes on each foot and are stocky with relatively short and thick legs. They have long snouts and a prehensile upper lip. The four species of tapirs (family Tapiridae) are smaller than rhinoceros and have bodies covered with short, bristly hairs. Only one species, the ASIAN TAPIR (Plate 69), occurs in the Old World. The five species of rhinoceros are much larger and are found only in Africa and southeastern Asia. Their huge heads support one or two horns that extend up from the snout.

In Thailand, elephants and tapirs are now relegated to isolated areas of protected forest. Your encounter is most likely to consist of distinctive footprints on muddy paths and along sandy river beaches.

Natural History

Ecology and Behavior

Usually found in extended family groups, the ASIAN ELEPHANT (Plate 73) herd is usually led by an old female who knows where all the best sites for food, water, and salt are. Elephants usually avoid open sunny areas, and spend much of the day in cool shady areas sleeping while standing up. They frequently visit ponds, lakes, and rivers to bathe, drink, and cool off. Elephants feed on leaves, bamboo, and other vegetation, and each adult needs 200 kg (440 lb) of food each day. The daily output of huge log-like droppings reflects this major input of food.

Tapirs are active primarily at night and hide in dense thickets of undergrowth during the day. They browse on leaves and vegetation as well as fruits fallen to the ground. Tapirs follow habitual trails through vegetation and routinely cross rivers at the same place, thus forming obvious tunnels through the undergrowth and gulleys at river banks, where they are most likely to be seen (and shot if being hunted). Individuals use established wallowing areas in which they apply a layer of mud to their skin to help protect them from horseflies and other biting insects that plague them throughout the year. Although generally solitary, tapirs, by using these habitual trails and wallowing areas together with communal defecation sites, at least loosely associate and communicate with each other. They are shy and retiring, and except for grunts of alarm and high whistles during the mating season, are quiet.

Two species of rhinoceros occurred until recently in Thailand. The JAVAN or LESSER ONE-HORNED RHINOCEROS is probably extinct now in Thailand. A few individuals may survive in Myanmar and cross into Thailand (in Kanchanburi Province) during the rainy season, but there have been no confirmed records of this species in Thailand for several decades. There may be only 20 to 30 individuals left in the world, mostly on the island of Java. The ASIAN TWO-HORNED RHINOCEROS (Plate 73) is a bit more common, with a total world population of fewer than 200. As recently as the late 1970s, confirmed sightings, tracks, and droppings indicated that fewer than 10 individuals remained in Thailand, along the Malay and Myanmar borders. Both species inhabit dense evergreen forests with marshy areas. They are solitary and eat shoots, twigs, and fallen fruit.

Breeding

A dominant male, who constantly monitors the smells and behavior of the females, usually tracks a herd of elephants. When one comes into heat, he mates with her. Sometimes younger bulls challenge the dominant male at this time, and serious injuries can result from the battle. Gestation is 20 months and one young is born at a time, very rarely two. A calf at birth can weigh up to 90 kg (198 lb). The calf is suckled for up to two years and remains with the mother several years more. Sexual maturity takes 12 years.

Tapirs remain together as mated pairs for only a few weeks of courtship and then separate. Occasionally males will fight to the death over a sexually receptive female. Females are entirely responsible for rearing the young, which have peculiar horizontal stripes and spots. Usually a single but rarely two calves are born after a gestation period of 13 months. The calf remains with the mother for 8 months. The long gestation period and extended care of the young means a female can reproduce only every two years.

The single rhinoceros calf is born after a gestation period of 10 to 16 months. The calf suckles the mother for at least a year and stays with her for another year beyond that. A mature female probably gives birth every 4 or 5 years.

Notes
In addition to a declining population of wild elephants, there is a large population of "domestic" elephants in Thailand. In the past they earned their keep by working in the logging industry, but they were largely thrown out of work by the 1989 nationwide ban on logging. Now one of their major uses is in the tourism industry—giving rides in cities and towns and taking the adventurous for treks into forests and mountains.

The tusks of elephants grow throughout their lives. Long tusks in the ASIAN ELEPHANT are usually found only in males. The tusks of wild elephants are kept pointed by constant sharpening on trees, gravel, and riverbanks. Tusks of domestic elephants become rounded at the point because of inactivity.

Status
Habitat destruction and isolation of forest habitat has led to the reduction of populations of these large mammals. Fewer than 2,000 elephants remain wild now in Thailand, and tapir populations have become severely reduced in the last two decades. Because they are so heavily hunted, tapirs are very shy and cautious animals. This hunting pressure may be forcing them more and more into nocturnal activity, and, together with low population sizes, may explain why they are so rarely seen. Both rhinoceros species are probably extinct now in Thailand and may be so globally within a decade or two. The IUCN Red List includes the rhinoceros species and the elephant as endangered. The tapir is considered severely threatened.

Profiles
Asian Tapir, *Tapirus indicus,* Plate 69e
Asian Elephant, *Elephas maximus,* Plate 73a
Asian Two-horned Rhinoceros, *Dicerorhinus sumatrensis,* Plate 73b

9. Dolphins and Dugong

Along with the three species of *manatees* of tropical America and Africa, the single species of DUGONG (Plate 75), or *sea cow,* forms the tropical order Sirenia. Despite their similarities to cetaceans (whales and dolphins) and seals, they are unrelated to either group (more related to elephants). Dugongs live in warm coastal waters of the tropics from Africa to Australia. Except for bristles on the snout, they are basically hairless and look like walruses. They have tiny eyes and back molar teeth that resemble those of elephants. As adaptations for their marine life, they have evolved streamlined bodies; their hind feet have developed into a horizontal, crescent-shaped *fluke* and their forelegs into flippers.

All *dolphins, porpoises,* and *whales* belong to order Cetacea, and all but a few freshwater forms are restricted to the *marine* environment (sea water). They never leave the water and generally come to the surface only to breathe. Their hind legs have been lost through evolution and their forelegs modified into paddle-like flippers. Their tails have become flattened into broad flukes. A single or double nostril, called a *blowhole,* is on top of the head. Although cetacean eyes are relatively small, hearing is well developed. Cetaceans are often divided into two broad categories, *baleen* and *toothed whales*. The baleen group consists of large whale species that have mouths that look like immense radiator grills, filled with long, vertical, brownish strands of baleen, or whalebone. The largest mammal, and probably the largest animal ever, the BLUE WHALE, is a member of this group. It reaches 30+ m (100 ft) in length and 150 tons in weight. Members of the other group have mouths with short, sharp teeth instead of baleen. In the same group as the toothed whales are the dolphins and porpoises.

Natural History

Ecology and Behavior

DUGONGS in Thailand feed mainly at night on aquatic vegetation like floating grasses. During the day they retreat to deeper waters, rising to breathe at the surface every few minutes. The marine vegetation on which they feed grows primarily in rocky areas, so Dugongs are seldom seen along muddy shores. Generally this species is seen solitarily or in small groups.

Dolphins feed chiefly on fish as well as other marine organisms such as crabs. They use their excellent eyesight to locate prey in clear water, but in turbid water they emit a series of clicking noises, 30 to 80 per second, which they then use as sonar by listening for them to bounce off potential prey items. They use their ability to flex their necks back and forth to broadcast and scan these clicking sounds over a large area. They also emit numerous other sounds including a screeching alarm call. Most species live in small to large schools.

Breeding

DUGONGS give birth to a single calf after a gestation period of 12 months. The calf is dependent on the mother and accompanies her closely for two or more years. Thus, a female gives birth only every three and a half years or more.

Dolphins reproduce seasonally. The gestation period is 9 to 11 months and a single young is produced every two years. The mother cares for the calf for almost a year.

Notes

DUGONGS and manatees are probably the source of the mermaid myth. Sailors at sea for far too long saw these large aquatic mammals floating in shallow coastal waters and imagined beautiful maidens with fish tails.

Status

All cetaceans are CITES Appendix I or Appendix II listed. The DUGONG is considered threatened or endangered over its entire range. In Thailand, the shallow coastal waters of the peninsula formerly supported thousands of Dugongs. Now the entire population in Thailand has been reduced to about 40 individuals, almost all of them in one area at the mouth of the Trang River, on the southwestern coast.

Profiles

Irrawaddy Dolphin, *Orcaella brevirostris,* Plate 75a
Common Dolphin, *Delphinus delphis,* Plate 75b
Bottle-nosed Dolphin, *Tursiops truncatus,* Plate 75c
Dugong, *Dugong dugon,* Plate 75d

Chapter 10

UNDERWATER THAILAND

by Richard Francis

- *Introduction*
- *The Andaman Sea*
- *The Gulf of Thailand*
- *Monsoons*
- *Reef Creatures*
    Invertebrate Life
    Vertebrate Life
- *Final Remarks*
- *Environmental Close-Up 6: Nosebleeds and the Nature of Light*

Introduction

The waters of Thailand's extensive coastline and numerous offshore islands provide rich and varied habitats that will reward both the casual and careful observer. Thailand is especially blessed in encompassing two quite distinct biogeographical regions, the Andaman Sea and the Gulf of Thailand. The Andaman Sea comprises the northwesternmost portion of the Indian Ocean, while the Gulf of Thailand represents the northeasternmost portion of the tropical Western Pacific. Though currently separated only by the narrow Isthmus of Kra (the narrowest part of the Malay Peninsula), the faunas of these two regions have been isolated from one another for extensive periods, especially when sea levels were lowered by glaciation in the northern hemisphere. As a result, a number of species that are common in the Gulf are absent from the Andaman sea, and vice versa.

On the other hand, as a result of the recent contact between the Indian Ocean and Western Pacific faunas, a number of Indian Ocean species have made their way to the Gulf of Thailand, and a number of Western Pacific species have expanded their range into the Andaman Sea. In fact, you will find in the

Andaman Sea more Western Pacific fishes than you would observe throughout most of the rest of the Indian Ocean, and you will find more Indian Ocean fishes in the Gulf of Thailand than you would observe throughout most of the rest of the tropical Western Pacific. For these reasons, the warm waters off southern Thailand are of great interest to ecologists, evolutionary biologists, and biogeographers.

The Andaman Sea

The deep waters of the Andaman Sea are bounded by Sri Lanka and Southern India to the west, and Southern Myanmar (Burma), Southern Thailand (Isthmus of Kra) and the Malay Peninsula to the east. There are many areas to explore along the mainland coastline of Thailand's Andaman Sea, but the best sites are on reefs around offshore islands. The Surin and Similan Islands (comprising Surin and Similan Island National Marine Park; p. 43) in particular, are world-renowned dive destinations, famous for their gorgeous underwater scenery and abundant marine life. These densely forested granitic outcrops lie in deep, clear water, and the large boulders on their underwater slopes provide perfect anchorage for hard corals and other reef-building invertebrates. The best reefs occur on the eastern side of these islands, which are protected from the ravages of the southwest monsoon. However, the western slopes, which are covered with large boulders, are also worth exploring. This is where you are most likely to encounter Manta Rays (Plate 100) and other pelagic (open-ocean) fishes.

Northwest of the Surin Islands lies a series of open-ocean seamounts (underwater mountain peaks) known as the Burma Banks, which provide an underwater wilderness experience for advanced divers. The Burma Banks are especially renowned for their large pelagic fishes. Sharks, which are not common in most Thai waters, are abundant here.

The coastline south of Phuket, around Krabi, provides some of the best snorkeling in Thailand. Numerous shallow fringing reefs, surrounding impressive limestone formations, support rich coral growth and abundant fish life. Offshore from the Krabi area, the Phi Phi Islands, famous for their palm-fringed white sand beaches, have become increasingly popular with snorkelers and divers as well.

Farther south, in the vicinity of Koh Lanta, lie some of the most pristine reefs and best dive sites in Thai waters. For example, Hi Moung contains the deepest dropoff in Thailand, while Hin Daeng provides one of the best opportunities to see large schools of Grey Reef Sharks (Plate 100). The rare Dugong (Plate 75) can be observed in the coastal waters of Koh Lipong.

The Gulf of Thailand

The Gulf of Thailand is a huge shallow depression on the continental slope. Maximum depth is generally around 60 m (200 ft). The Gulf coastline, which extends in an arc from the Malay border to Kampuchea and the southern tip of South Vietnam, is twice as long as the Andaman Sea coastline. The Gulf is generally more turbid than the Andaman Sea, owing to runoff from large rivers. Suspended soil and other particles get trapped in the Gulf by an underwater shelf that runs across its mouth from Malaysia to Vietnam. This turbidity limits the development of true coral reefs to areas south of Chumphon (about the point of the narrowest part of the Malay Peninsula). There are numerous islands in the Gulf waters, and the fringing reefs surrounding their shorelines are generally better developed than those found off the mainland coastline. Marine life, though somewhat less diverse than on Andaman Sea reefs, is nonetheless impressive and includes species that will not be found on the other side of the Isthmus of Kra.

The reefs around Koh Tao include some of the best dive and snorkeling sites in all of Thailand. Shallow reef gardens, easily accessible from the beach, are perfect for snorkeling. Divers can explore submerged pinnacles and arches blanketed with exuberantly colored soft corals. A bit further south lies Koh Phangan, which provides magnificent wall dives and a chance to view large schools of pelagic fishes, as well as sharks. Adjacent to Koh Phangan lies Koh Samui, which has lately become a tourist magnet. The fringing reefs lie especially close to shore here, so it is possible to conduct beach dives. For the more adventurous, Koh Chang, in the eastern Gulf, provides excellent opportunities for underwater exploration, including superb wreck dives, far from the madding crowd.

Monsoons

The underwater conditions in Thailand are largely determined by two monsoon seasons. From November through April, the northeast monsoon boils out of the Western Pacific, bringing heavy rains and strong winds to the Gulf of Thailand. Underwater visibility is drastically reduced in the Gulf during these months and strong currents make diving rather treacherous. But the Andaman Sea, on the other side of the Isthmus of Kra, is largely protected from the northeast monsoon, and the conditions are optimal for underwater exploration during this period, when underwater visibility can approach 30 m (100 ft). The situation is reversed during the southwest monsoon (from May to October), which originates in the Indian Ocean. During this period the waters of the Andaman Sea are roiled, while the Gulf waters are calm and underwater visibility is at its maximum. Because of these alternating conditions, throughout the year there will be ideal conditions for underwater exploration somewhere in Thailand.

Reef Creatures

The diversity of living things you will see on even a single visit to a particular reef can be overwhelming. In order to make some sense of this variety it helps to focus first on learning to distinguish some of the more common types of animals, for example, what makes a crab a crab and a shrimp a shrimp. Then work your way down to the species level. With respect to the fishes, it helps to first focus at the family level, on what makes a parrotfish a parrotfish, a wrasse a wrasse, or a butterflyfish a butterflyfish. Then, once you have learned these fish types, look for the diversity within them. Notice that most butterflyfish tend to have yellow, black. and white coloration, but some don't. Notice too that butterflyfish color patterns vary, sometimes subtly, sometimes markedly, among different species. Once you are attuned to these differences, you will be able to distinguish different species of butterflyfishes. But that is just the beginning. The really fun part comes from noticing, for example, the similarities and differences in the way these different butterflyfish species behave; what they eat and how their diet relates to their snout length; whether or not they are territorial; whether they occur singly, in pairs, or in larger groups; and how they interact with other members of their species or members of other species. Remember, the ability to recognize different reef creatures is important, but it is just a means to an end—in this case, furthering your aquatic enjoyment.

Invertebrate Life

The majority of reef inhabitants are not fish but an extremely varied assortment of animals that are collectively referred to as *invertebrates*. The corals themselves are the most prominent invertebrates and they are the foundation of any coral reef. The corals from which coral reefs get their name are known as *hard corals*. Hard coral is hard because the actual coral creature, which is soft, secretes a covering of calcium carbonate within which it resides. These stony secretions accrete and grow along with the coral colony, upward and outward, with each succeeding generation. There are more than 200 kinds of hard corals in Thai waters, many of which cannot be distinguished by the untutored eye. But anyone can quickly learn some of the more common hard coral types because of basic differences in growth patterns and/or colony size, which result in characteristic colony shapes. Among the common types of hard coral are the *Pocillopora* (Plate 102) which tend to form dense heads that look like cauliflowers. *Porites* (Plate 102) are encrusting corals that form domes of various sorts. Corals of the genus *Fungia* (Plate 102) are named for their mushroom shapes, and those of the genus *Favia* are often referred to as brain corals (as are corals of some other genera, such as *Platygyra;* Plate 102). *Acropora* (Plate 102) coral heads have characteristic branching patterns and provide shelter for numerous reef creatures, including Humbug Damselfishes (Plate 81). Each coral species can have quite variable growth patterns, which complicates identification. Local environmental conditions largely determine these growth patterns. For instance, *Acropora* corals tend to be more deeply branched in protected areas than in exposed areas.

While the hard corals provide much of the reef structure, the *soft corals* and *gorgonians* provide much of the texture and color. The soft corals include some of the most brilliantly colored creatures on Thai reefs, while gorgonians, such as *sea whips* and *sea fans* (Plate 101), provide both color and dramatic shapes. The corals, hard and soft, comprise but one large group of an animal phylum known as cnidarians, which includes the jellyfish (Plate 103) and sea anemones (Plate 101). All cnidarians possess stinging elements known as *nematocysts*, by means of which they capture prey and ward off predators. One group of damselfishes, called *anemonefishes* (Plate 82), has evolved a close symbiotic relationship with certain anemones, and are able to take advantage of the anemones' stinging elements for their own protection. *Sponges* (Plate 101) comprise another important group of sessile (non-mobile) reef creatures. They add much of the color to the reef environments and provide homes for many reef inhabitants. Some form large barrel-like structures, others form amorphous mats, and still others look like incredibly colorful puffs of velvet.

The so-called flatworms, such as *Pseudoceros dimidiatus* (Plate 103), are among the most beautiful reef inhabitants. They are sometime confused with nudibranchs (see below) but they are not even closely related. *Polychaete worms,* also called marine worms, (such as *Phercardia striata,* Plate 103), including feather dusters (such as the Christmas Tree Worm, Plate 103) and tube worms, are another important element in the reef community.

The *mollusks* comprise perhaps the largest marine group. One sub-group, the gastropods (*snails* and *slugs*), are particularly bountiful. These include, in addition to the cone shells (Plate 105), cowries (Plate 104), olives (Plate 105), tritons (Plate 104), volutes, helmets (Plate 103), turbans, limpets, and sea hares, the incredibly gorgeous *nudibranchs,* or *sea slugs* (Plates 105, 106). The Spanish Dancer (Plate 106), which comes in varying shades of red, is one of the largest and most commonly seen. It is named for the flamenco-like undulatory movements it makes while swimming. The observant diver will spy a number of other beautiful nudibranchs as well. Another important group of mollusks includes the cockles, clams, scallops, and oysters. These so-called *bivalves* (Plate 106) can be found under sand or attached to rocks. Also belonging to the mollusk phylum are the squids and octopuses (Plate 106), collectively referred to as *cephalopods.* These are among the most intelligent creatures in the sea, and well worth looking for.

Phylum Arthropoda (p. 59) includes many inhabitants of both land and sea. The *crustaceans* are the largest group of marine arthropods. This group includes all the shrimp and crabs, as well as lobsters (Plate 107). These can be further subdivided into several families each. Among the more interesting shrimp species are those that serve as *cleaners,* several of which are illustrated in the plates. They set up *cleaning stations* in much the same way as the cleaner wrasses (p. 214; Plate 84).

Finally, the *echinoderms* comprise a large and diverse phylum of marine animals, the most famous of which are the sea stars (Plates 107, 108). Another large group of echinoderms consists of sea urchins (Plate 108) and their relatives, the sand dollars. The sea cucumbers (Plate 108) are perhaps the oddest members of this group—they look like caterpillars on steroids.

Vertebrate Life

The most obvious coral denizens are the fishes. Their staggering variety and abundance are what underwater explorers first notice upon entering the water. The following accounts of some of the major fish families are intended to provide a way to begin to appreciate their biodiversity.

Surgeonfishes (family Acanthuridae)
This family is well-represented in both the Gulf of Thailand and the Andaman Sea. Surgeonfishes are so-called because of the scalpel-like projections at the base of their tails, which they use to slash at other fishes. They are primarily algae grazers and they have exceptionally long intestines that are essential for the digestion of this food. The POWDER-BLUE SURGEONFISH (Plate 94), one of the most beautiful members of this family, is common in the Andaman Sea, sometimes forming huge aggregations, a breathtaking sight. Among the most spectacular reef inhabitants are the subgroup of surgeonfishes known as unicornfish, so-called because

of the oryx-like projections extending forward from their heads. The BLUESPINE UNICORNFISH (Plate 94) is typical; the horn-like projections give it a somewhat sinister look.

The MOORISH IDOL (Plate 94) is on everyone's list of the top five most gorgeous reef creatures. This species is closely related to surgeonfishes but comprises its own distinct family (Zanclidae). You will usually find these beauties in pairs or small groups, probing the nooks and crannies with their long snouts. Notice how much more deliberately they move compared to the more skittish surgeonfishes. Their grace only enhances their spectacular coloration.

Rabbitfishes (family Siganidae)

Rabbitfishes, which are often referred to as "spinefeet" in Australia, are closely related to surgeonfishes. They generally have ovoid, compressed bodies and small mouths. They feed primarily on benthic algae and seaweed, but some species also feed on benthic invertebrates. Their spines are venomous and can inflict painful—though not life-threatening—wounds to the unwary diver. The beautiful CORAL RABBITFISH (Plate 94) can be found in clear lagoons and seaward reefs of both the Andaman Sea and the Gulf of Thailand, while the aptly named MAGNIFICENT RABBITFISH (Plate 95) is confined to the Similan Islands and adjacent waters.

Butterflyfishes (family Chaetodontidae)

Butterflyfishes are among the most celebrated reef inhabitants. Their graceful movements and striking color patterns have long delighted aquarists and divers alike. They have high and thin bodies, narrow snouts, and very small mouths. Some butterflyfishes feed on live coral polyps, for which activity their narrow snouts are ideally suited. In the LONGNOSE BUTTERFLYFISH (*Forcipiger longirostris*) the snout extends into needle-shaped pincers, ideal for probing the reef's recesses. Most butterflyfishes, especially the larger species, can be found in mated pairs. Interestingly, they pair up as juveniles, long before they become sexually mature. It is suspected that they can change sex during the early part of the association, if they both happen to be females. Alternatively, both may have the capacity to mature as either males or females, so that they must decide this matter among themselves. Once paired, they remain paired for life—which can exceed 20 years—with a degree of fidelity unrivaled among mammals.

If you visit both sides of the Isthmus of Kra you will have a chance to observe a phenomenon known as *species pairs,* or *sibling species,* among butterflyfish that diverged recently (in evolutionary time), during the last period of lowered sea levels. For instance, the COLLARED BUTTERFLYFISH (*Chaetodon collare;* Plate 76) on the Andaman Sea side, is the Indian Ocean equivalent of (and very similar in form and coloration to) the RETICULATED BUTTERFLYFISH (*Chaetodon reticulata*) found in the Gulf of Thailand and throughout the Western Pacific. The same is true of the TRIANGULAR BUTTERFLYFISH (*Chaetodon triangulum;* Plate 76) and the EASTERN TRIANGULAR BUTTERFLYFISH (*Chaetodon baronessa*), respectively. Look for other species pairs among butterflyfishes and other reef fishes as well.

Angelfishes (family Pomacanthidae)

These beauties are closely related to the butterflyfishes. They too have deeply compressed bodies and small mouths. They can be distinguished from butterflyfishes, however, by a prominent cheek spine. Most are territorial, but there is marked variation in diet. The EMPEROR ANGELFISH (Plate 79) and other members of its genus feed primarily on sponges, while EIBL'S ANGELFISH (Plate 78) eat only algae and detritus. Many, and perhaps most, angelfish undergo sex change. They begin life as females; those that live long enough to attain a large size then change into males. This is referred to as *protogynous* (female first) *sex change*.

Damselfishes (family Pomacentridae)

These small fishes comprise another important component of the reef community. They are not nearly as colorful as the butterflyfishes or angelfishes, but behaviorally damselfishes are among the most interesting reef inhabitants. Those species that feed on benthic (bottom-dwelling) algae, such as the WESTERN GREGORY (Plate 80) and the BENGAL SERGEANT (Plate 80), are highly territorial. Among the most pugnacious reef inhabitants, they strike out at any fish that dares enter their territories, even much larger surgeonfish and butterflyfish. When in breeding mode they will even attack divers.

Unlike most reef fishes, damselfishes lay their eggs on the substrate. They then carefully guard them against marauding wrasses and surgeonfishes for one to two weeks. The males tend the eggs. When the larvae hatch they become planktonic, but they enter the plankton (the ocean's huge population of tiny floating organisms) at a much more advanced state of development and for a shorter period of time than most reef fishes. Since they have fairly short planktonic stages, damselfishes tend to have smaller geographic ranges than, say, butterflyfishes or surgeonfishes.

Many damselfishes, including the INDIAN HUMBUG (Plate 81) and the RETICULATED DAMSELFISH (*Dascyllus reticulata*), are *protogynous sex changers*, beginning their lives as females and becoming males only after reaching a large size. The anemonefishes however, which are a type of damselfish, are *protandous* (male-to-female) *sex changers*. The largest fish in the anemone is always a female. Anemonefishes have a commensal or mutualistic (p. 51) relationship with tropical sea anemones, always staying within or near to the anemones' protective tentacles; the anemonefishes are not stung by the anemone's stinging nematocyst cells because they have a mucous coating that prevents the nematocysts from discharging. Among the anemonefishes in Thai waters are the beautiful TOMATO ANEMONEFISH (Plate 82) and the FALSE CLOWNFISH (Plate 82), an aquarium favorite. Other anemonefishes worth looking for are the SADDLEBACK ANEMONEFISH (Plate 812), which is confined to the Gulf of Thailand, and the SKUNK ANEMONEFISH (Plate 82), which occurs in the Andaman Sea.

Wrasses (family Labridae)

This is one of the largest families of fishes. Though they vary greatly in size, shape, and habits, wrasses all have a single, continuous dorsal fin and they tend to stay close to the bottom. Many wrasses move in a distinctive jerky manner as they explore the substrate for food. They primarily use their pectoral fins to swim, bringing their tails into play only when rapid movement is required.

Many wrasse species undergo dramatic color changes as they mature, and this is often accompanied by a sex change as well. Formerly these different developmental stages were often mistakenly identified as distinct species. A convention has arisen in which the first color pattern in a sexually mature fish is referred to as the "initial phase," and the second color pattern as the "terminal phase." Some species, such as the AFRICAN CORIS (Plate 84), have a distinct juvenile coloration as well. Juveniles of the aptly named ROCKMOVER WRASSE (Plate 85) mimic drifting algae and do not remotely resemble the adults in color or shape.

In some species, such as the CLEANER WRASSE (Plate 84), all of the initial phase fish are females. In these species the color change is accompanied by sex change to male (protogynous sex change). In other species, such as the MOON WRASSE (Plate 85), the initial phase fish may be either male or female. Some initial phase males eventually undergo a color change to become terminal phase males. In addition, some females subsequently undergo both a color change and a sex change to become terminal phase males. The two male types in these "diandric" species exhibit completely different reproductive behavior. The terminal phase males defend a territory to which they attract females with their vigorous courtship displays. The much smaller initial phase males, however, use their female-like appearance to get close to the courting couple, which they then shower with their own sperm, a deceitfully effective way for a small male to compete with its larger counterparts. In addition, initial phase males sometimes form marauding gangs that overwhelm the territorial defense of the terminal phase males.

All wrasses are fascinating to watch and brimming with personality. One of the most famous in this regard is the Cleaner Wrasse (Plate 84). The male Cleaner Wrasse stakes out a territory to which he attracts several females to form a harem. His territory attracts more than mates, however; it attracts his *clients* as well. And his clients include such large predatory fish as jacks and snappers. They come here in order to have their external parasites removed, and the Cleaner Wrasses are happy to oblige, systematically probing the surface, and, in what looks initially like suicide, inside the mouth as well. The cleaner completely disappears into the maw of larger fish, often emerging through the gills. When one client is done, the next fish, which has been patiently waiting in the queue, steps up for his ministrations. *Cleaning stations*, as these territories are called, can usually be found in fairly prominent locations on the reef such as outcrops. They are well worth seeking out. Some other wrasse species, in addition to the Cleaner Wrasse, also act as cleaners.

Parrotfishes (family Scaridae)

Parrotfishes are closely related to the wrasses and share their complex life histories, including the color and sex changes. Parrotfishes are distinguished by their beak, formed by the fusion of several front teeth. Further back in the mouth are powerful molars formed of bony plates, the lower convex, the upper concave. They put both their beak and pharyngeal molars to good use in first removing and then grinding chunks of hard coral in order to extract the algae. The sounds they make in the process are quite audible underwater. Parrotfishes manage to digest their food without the aid of a stomach. Instead they have an exceptionally long intestine. When the coral residue reaches the end of the line (intestine), the parrotfish excretes it in wispy clouds of fine sand, destined someday for one of Thailand's famous beaches.

The initial phase fish form aggregations that seem to swarm over the reef with the rising tide, taking their bites of coral on the move. The terminal phase males, however, tend to be highly territorial. In general, the terminal phase parrotfishes are brightly colored, while the initial phase fish (both female and male) are some shade of red or brown, and often mottled.

Gobies (family Gobeidae)

Gobies comprise the largest fish family and are particularly abundant in tropical marine environments. Because of their diminutive size, gobies, such as the ORNATE GOBY (Plate 92), are generally overlooked by snorkelers and all but the more observant divers. They are, however, fascinating creatures. Like damselfishes, they lay eggs on the substrate that are tended by the father. Some gobies have fascinating relationships with alpheid shrimp. The fish lives in the shrimp's burrow; in return the goby keeps a lookout for predators while the none-too-keen-sighted shrimp goes about its labors. At the first sign of danger the goby darts into the burrow along with the alerted shrimp. This is a nice example of inter-species symbiosis of the sort known as mutualism (p. 51): "if you scratch my back, I'll scratch yours."

Blennies (family Blenniidae)

This is another large family of small bottom-dwelling fishes. Like the gobies, blennies lay eggs on the substrate that the male tends. They are highly territorial and pugnacious. Blennies have scaleless, elongate bodies; the head is typically blunt, with fleshy tentacles, or cirri, on the upper surface; the dorsal fin extends along the entire body. The mouth is generally low on the head and replete with numerous slender teeth. Most blennies are herbivorous, but the so-called *fang blennies,* which are named for their large canine teeth, feed on the scales and flesh of live fish. One of these, the MIMIC BLENNY (Plate 91), secures its meals by mimicking the Cleaner Wrasse (Plate 84), which enables it to get close to unsuspecting large fish, which it then rudely robs of fin or scales (often called *aggressive mimicry*). The MIDAS BLENNY (Plate 91) mimics a species of fairy basslet for less sinister ends.

Triggerfishes (family Balistidae)

The name triggerfish derives from a mechanism by which these fishes erect their stout first dorsal spine by means of the movement of the second dorsal spine. Presumably this helps discourage any would-be predators. They swim by undulating the dorsal and anal fins. Triggerfishes have somewhat compressed bodies and long tapering snouts equipped with chisel-like teeth that they employ while feeding on a variety of hard-shelled benthic animals, including crabs, mollusks and sea urchins. Female triggerfish also deploy their teeth while guarding their eggs. Divers should take care not to swim too close to some of the larger triggers, such as the TITAN TRIGGERFISH (Plate 95), while so engaged, as they can inflict a nasty wound.

Puffers (family Tetradontidae) and Porcupinefishes (family Diodontidae)

No survey of reef fishes would be complete without mentioning these two closely related groups of unique reef fishes. Puffers (Plate 97) are so-called because of their ability to inflate themselves in the presence of predators. Porcupinefishes (Plate 97) add to this defense mechanism an array of spines that are erected in the process. When they are inflated, the pectoral fins, by means of which they propel themselves, become ineffective, so they tend to list and roll in a comical manner. Though comical looking, both groups should be treated with respect—especially the larger individuals—because they can inflict a nasty bite. Like the triggerfishes, puffers and porcupinefishes feed on invertebrates with hard exoskeletons. The puffers tend to be diurnal, but the larger-eyed porcupinefish are nocturnal.

Groupers (family Serranidae)

This family contains some of the most important reef predators. Groupers prey primarily on other fish and crustaceans but they are not at all finicky. Some species, including the GIANT GROUPER (Plate 88) achieve truly massive sizes and are among the largest fish on the reef. The family includes a number of diminutive species as well, including the basslets of subfamily Anthiinae. Fairy basslets (genus *Pseudanthias*), such as the SCALEFIN and FLAME ANTHIAS (both Plate 87), are spectacularly beautiful fish that form large aggregations above the reefs. Many groupers and basslets are haremic (one male maintains a harem of females) and protogynous sex changers (p. 213).

Sharks and Rays

Several shark species can be found on or around the reefs. Of these, the BLACKTIP REEF SHARK (Plate 100) is most likely to be encountered by day in shallow water. These slender and sleek creatures are quite timid but they have been known to bite the legs of wading humans. The WHITETIP REEF SHARK (Plate 100) is nocturnal, but can be found in the caves where they rest during the day. The HAMMERHEAD is more of an open water species that you are most likely to see off reef walls. TIGER SHARKS are rarely seen but they represent the greatest threat to divers. It is extremely rare, however, for an encounter with a Tiger Shark to result in an attack. The SILVERTIP SHARK and GRAY REEF SHARK (Plate 100) should also be treated with respect.

The shark most frequently encountered in Thai waters is called the LEOPARD SHARK (Plate 100), which you will generally find by day resting in the sand. By far the most spectacular shark in Thai waters, and the largest, is the WHALE SHARK (Plate 99). These peaceful giants are often seen off the Similan Islands during March and April.

A number of stingrays inhabit Thai waters, including the striking BLUE-SPOTTED STINGRAY (Plate 100). Stingrays are bottom-dwellers, but other rays, such as the SPOTTED EAGLE RAY (Plate 100) are active swimmers. These enchanting animals often perform acrobatics both underwater and above. I have noticed that they seem particularly prone to leap out of the water when they are in pairs but I don't know what to make of this. The ray equivalent of the Whale Shark is the MANTA RAY (Plate 100). These are among the most impressive and awe-inspiring creatures on land or sea. A group of Mantas, gracefully winging their way through the water with their entourages of remoras (smaller fish that have commensal relationships with sharks and rays; p. 51) is a sight you will remember for the rest of your life.

Final Remarks

Don't just be dazzled. The reefs reward those who can appreciate the subtle as well as the dramatic. When you enter the water you will encounter an environment that differs dramatically from that of your everyday life. Let yourself be dazzled, but also seek to look beyond the surface spectacle. When you enter the water, schools of fusiliers (such as LUNAR FUSILIERS and YELLOWTOP FUSILIERS, both Plate 90) and fairy basslets will first attract your attention, and closer to the reef, butterflyfishes and damselfishes. As you explore further, you will encounter surgeonfishes, angelfishes, and rabbitfishes. You will need to look much closer to find the anemonefishes—which never stray far from the shelter of their anemones—or the sweetlips and groupers. Once you have familiarized yourself with these more obvious reef denizens, begin to look for the more recondite inhabitants, the squirrelfishes under the ledges, the puffers and porcupinefishes. And, for a real challenge, try to find some of the small gobies in the reef's nooks and crannies. When you are good at finding gobies, you can consider yourself a true reef connoisseur.

Environmental Close-Up 6:
Nosebleeds and the Nature of Light.

If you dive regularly, you have likely had a nosebleed underwater at some time or another. If you were deeper than 10 meters (33 ft), your blood in the bottom of the mask appeared bright green. The plants, animals and rocks at this depth were also greenish or bluish. But turn on a portable spotlight or rise toward the surface, and your blood turns bright red and flecks of red, orange, and yellow appear in the objects around you. Why? The answer is in the nature of light. In the 1800s, Sir William Herschel discovered that visible light was made up of a continuous spectrum of colors: red, orange, yellow, green, blue, indigo, and violet (ROY G BIV). This is the same sequence of light colors you see in a rainbow or in light separated out through a prism. Herschel also discovered that each color of the spectrum heats surfaces to different temperatures, and the amount of heat increases in the same order as the colors. From these experiments, he deduced that each wavelength of light not only produced a different color but also carried a different amount of energy (what Einstein later described as *photons*). Red light waves are the weakest in energy and blue to violet the strongest.

We also know that light passes through air with more ease than it passes through dense water. As light hits the surface of the water and penetrates down into its depths, the weak red light waves are stopped within a few meters. Then the orange and yellow light waves are stopped a bit deeper. Light in high-energy green and blue wavelengths goes as deep as light can in water. Your blood and the surfaces of the rocks, plants, and animals below 10 meters have only green and blue light to reflect. Because of this nature of light, some fish at great depths have bright red pigments, and with no red light to reflect, they become invisible to their visual predators.

REFERENCES AND ADDITIONAL READING

If, in the course of your travels through Thailand, you find yourself becoming more and more interested in the wildlife and plants around you, one of our major goals in writing this book will have been achieved. If you would like to satisfy your heightened natural history interest with additional reading, perhaps to find out about Thailand's other wildlife (the 80% of it that we had not the space to cover in this book), we list below some of the best and most detailed reference books and articles that would assist you in these goals. We used these references ourselves as we wrote this book.

Allen, G. R. 1997. *Tropical Marine Life of Thailand.* Bangkok: Asia Books Co. Ltd.
Allen, G. R. 1997. *Tropical Reef Fishes of Thailand.* Bangkok: Asia Books Co. Ltd.
Allen, G. R. and R. C. Steene. 1987. *Reef Fishes of the Indian Ocean.* Neptune City, NJ: T. F. H. Publications, Inc.
Braack, L. E. O. 2000. *Fascinating Insects of Southeast Asia.* Singapore: Times Editions.
Carwardine, M. 1995. *Whales, Dolphins and Porpoises: The Visual Guide to All the World's Cetaceans.* New York: DK Publishing, Inc.
Colin, P. L. and C. Arenson. 1995. *Tropical Pacific Invertebrates: A Field Guide to the Marine Invertebrates Occurring on Tropical Pacific Coral Reefs, Seagrass Beds, and Mangroves.* Beverly Hills, CA: Coral Reef Press.
Cox, M. J., P. P. van Dijk, J. Nabhitabhata, and K. Thirakhupt. 1998. *A Photographic Guide to Snakes and Other Reptiles of Thailand and Southeast Asia.* London: New Holland Publishers, Ltd.
Cummings, J. 1999. *Lonely Planet Thailand,* 8th ed. Hawthorn, Australia: Lonely Planet Publications, Ltd.
Duellman, W. E., ed. 1999. *Patterns of distribution of amphibians: A global perspective.* Baltimore, MD: John Hopkins University Press.
Duellman, W. E. and L. Treub. 1994. *Biology of amphibians.* Baltimore, MD: John Hopkins University Press.
Ernst, C. H. and R. W. Barbour. 1989. *Turtles of the World.* Washington, DC: Smithsonian Institution Press.
Gill, F. B. 1994. *Ornithology,* 2nd ed. San Francisco, CA: W. H. Freeman.
Graham, M. and P. D. Round. 1994. *Thailand's Vanishing Flora and Fauna.* Bangkok: Finance On Public Co., Ltd.
Hairston, N. G. 1994. *Vertebrate Zoology: An Experimental Field Approach.* Cambridge: Cambridge University Press.
Henley, T. 1999. *Waterfalls and Gibbon Calls: Exploring Khao Sok National Park,* 2nd ed. Phuket, Thailand: Linmark Advertising and Printing.
Hirsch, P., ed. 1998. *Seeing Forests for Trees: Environment and Environmentalism in*

Thailand. Chiang Mai, Thailand: Silkworm Books.
Hodel, D. R. 1998. *The Palms and Cycads of Thailand*. Nong Nooch Garden, Thailand: Kampon Tansacha.
IUCN 2000. 2000. IUCN Red List of threatened animals. Compiled by C. Hilton-Taylor, The World Conservation Union (IUCN), Gland, Switzerland.
Lekagul, B., K. Askins, J. Nabhitabhata, and A. Samruadkit. 1977. *Field Guide to the Butterflies of Thailand*. Bangkok: Association for the Conservation of Wildlife.
Lekagul, B. and J. A. McNeely. 1988. *Mammals of Thailand*. Bangkok: Saha Karn Bhaet, Ltd.
Lekagul, B. and P. D. Round. 1991. *A Guide to the Birds of Thailand*. Bangkok: Saha Karn Bhaet, Ltd.
McMakin, P. D. 1988. *A Field Guide to the Flowering Plants of Thailand*. Bangkok: Saha Karn Bhaet, Ltd.
Perrins, C. M. and A. L. A. Middleton. 1985. *The Encyclopedia of Birds*. New York: Facts on File Publications.
Pough, F. H., R. M. Andrews, J. E. Cadle, M. L. Crump, A. H. Savitzky, and K. D. Wells. 1998. *Herpetology*. Upper Saddle River, NJ: Prentice Hall.
Rabinowitz, A. 1991. *Chasing the Dragon's Tail*. New York: Doubleday Publishing.
Robson, C. 2005. *A Field Guide to the Birds of Thailand*. London: New Holland Publishers, Ltd.
Stores, A. and J. Stores. 1997. *Discovering Trees and Shrubs in Thailand and Southeast Asia*. Bangkok: Craftsman Press, Ltd.
Stewart-Cox, B. 1997. *Wild Thailand*. London: New Holland Publishers, Ltd.
Vaughn, T. A. 1997. *Mammalogy*, 3rd ed. Philadelphia, PA: Saunders.
Whitmore, T. C. 1975. *Tropical Rain Forests of the Far East*. Oxford: Clarendon Press.

HABITAT PHOTOS

1. Mist rises above tropical evergreen forest after an afternoon downpour, Khao Sok National Park in peninsular Thailand. © N. Pearson

2. Tropical evergreen forest meets ocean beach on the island of Koh Tarutao off the west coast of peninsular Thailand. © W. Schaedla

3. A shaded stream runs through tropical evergreen forest in Khao Phanon Bencha National Park near the city of Krabi, peninsular Thailand. © N. Pearson

4. Swamp forest in the Khao Pra Bang Kram Wildlife Sanctuary south of Krabi in peninsular Thailand, the only known home of Gurney's Pitta, an endangered bird species. © N. Pearson

Habitat Photos

5. Picturesque lake at the base of limestone hills covered with tropical evergreen forest, Thale Ban National Park, peninsular Thailand, near the Maylasian border. © N. Pearson

6. Rubber tree plantation (p. 47) south of the city of Chumphon in peninsular Thailand. © J. Dusseau

7. Rubber latex creeps down grooves carved in the trunk of a rubber tree to collect in a cup suspended at the base of the grooves (p. 47), peninsular Thailand. © N. Pearson

8. Rubber latex is poured into flat pans to solidify (p. 49), peninsular Thailand south of the city of Chumphon. Note the press in the upper left through which the solidified latex will be passed to flatten it into rubber mats for drying and transportation to market. © N. Pearson

9. Monsoon clouds build up in the early afternoon over monsoon evergreen forest near Mae Hong Son in northern Thailand. © U. Treesucon

Habitat Photos

10. Monsoon evergreen forest at the edge of a forest lake in Khao Yai National Park, northeastern Thailand. © N. Pearson

11. Spiny trunks and leaves of Rattan Palms make some parts of monsoon evergreen forest impenetrable, Khao Yai National Park in northeastern Thailand. © N. Pearson

12. The monstrous buttress roots of a huge tree in the monsoon evergreen forest of Khao Yai National Park engulf an intrepid ecotraveller. © W. Schaedla

13. Fog settles on epiphyte-covered trees in hill evergreen forest at the summit of Thailand's tallest mountain, Doi Inthanon, at 2,565 m (8,415 ft), far northern Thailand. © U. Treesucon

Habitat Photos

14. The bare trees of a tropical mixed deciduous forest in the midst of the dry season. Huay Kha Khaeng, western Thailand. © U. Treesucon

15. At the beginning of the dry season, leaves of the Sal trees in dry dipterocarp forest turn bright red and yellow. Huay Kha Khaeng, western Thailand. © U. Treesucon

16. Limestone karst monolith emerging from the ocean, north of the city of Krabi on the west coast of peninsular Thailand. © J. Dusseau

17. Desert-adapted vegetation, including cactus-like euphorbs, cling to vertical surfaces of a limestone karst near the city of Krabi, peninsular Thailand. © N. Pearson

18. Pine and oak forest near the summit of Dai Chiang Dao, in far northern Thailand. © N. Pearson

Habitat Photos

19. Much of the formerly extensive wetlands and marshes of the Central Plains is now confined to canals, such as this one in southern Bangkok. © N. Pearson

20. Coastal limestone hills rise above the largest marshland remaining in peninsular Thailand, at Khao Sam Roi Yot National Park on the east coast. © N. Pearson

21. *Phragmites* grass, growing 3 m (10 ft) tall, borders rice fields near the city of Fang in northern Thailand. © U. Treesucon

22. Stilt roots of mangroves near the city of Krabi exposed at low tide, peninsular Thailand. © N. Pearson

Habitat Photos

23. Paperbark (*Melaleuca*) trees in swamp forest area of peninsular Thailand, near Thale Noi. © P. VanDijk

IDENTIFICATION PLATES

Explanation of Symbols Used in the Plate Section

HABITAT SYMBOLS

= Tropical evergreen forest

= Monsoon evergreen forest

= Hill evergreen forest

= Mixed deciduous forest

= Dry deciduous dipterocarp forest

= Limestone forest

= Pine forest

= Forest edge and streamside. Some species typically are found along forest edges or near or along streams; these species prefer semi-open areas rather than dense, closed, interior parts of forests. Also included here: open woodlands, tree plantations, and shady gardens.

= Pastureland, non-tree plantations, savannah (grassland with scattered trees and shrubs), gardens without shade trees, roadside. Species found in these habitats prefer very open areas.

= Freshwater. For species typically found in or near lakes, streams, rivers, marshes, swamps, and wet rice paddies.

= Saltwater/marine. For species found in or near the ocean, ocean beaches, or mangroves.

REGIONS (see Map 2, p. 42):

PT = Peninsular Thailand
SE = The Southeast
CP = The Central Plains
W = The West
NE = The Northeast
FN = The Far North

Abbreviations on the Identification Plates are as follows:

M   male
F   female
A   adult
IM immature

The species pictured on any one plate are not necessarily to scale.

Plate 1 (*See also:* Dragonflies, p. 63, etc.)

Plate 1a
Red Darter Dragonfly
Neurothemis sp.
ID: Long (5 cm, 2 in), thin body; males with bright maroon body and wings; females usually duller.
HABITAT: Flying low over puddles, lakes, or slow streams; often perched with wings horizontal on vegetation at the water's edge.
REGION: PT, CP, SE, W, NE, FN
Photo by J. Moore

Plate 1b
Long-legged Katydid
Macrolyristes corporalis
ID: Long (10 cm, 4 in) and narrow-bodied; green with wings resembling leaves and legs looking like twigs; sharp spines on legs are used for defense. The largest katydid in the world.
HABITAT: Rests on vegetation during the day and feeds on vegetation at night; makes creaking noises by rubbing its legs together.
REGION: PT, W

Plate 1c
Leaf Insect
Phyllium sp.
ID: Long (15 cm, 6 in), broad, and flat; green with wings resembling leaves and legs looking like twigs.
HABITAT: These are among the best camouflaged insects in the world. They live on undergrowth bushes in tropical lowland forests and feed on leaves. Some species are thought to reproduce without males.
REGION: PT, CP, SE, W, NE, FN

Plate 1d
Evening Cicada
Tosena splendida
ID: Delicate colors; wings held over back tent-like; large (5 cm, 2 in), and often conspicuous when resting on vertical trunks of moist forest, usually during the day.
HABITAT: Active at night feeding; begins loud trilling calls at sundown, although other similar-sounding species call during the day.
REGION: PT, CP, SE, W, NE, FN
Photo by J. Moore

Plate 1e
Larval cicada turret
ID: Tower-like structure built of clay in moist areas of forest floor, usually 5–10 cm high.
HABITAT: The larval cicada spends most of its time in a deep vertical tunnel in the ground below the turret, sometimes 1 m down, where it feeds on roots.
REGION: PT, CP, SE, W, NE, FN
Photo by N. Pearson

Plate 1f
Giant Wood Spider
Nephila sp.
ID: Large (body length 5 cm, 2 in; legs 10 cm, 4 in); black and yellow color make it obvious to spot.
HABITAT: Sits often head down, in the middle of its immense silken orb; the orb is usually placed in a forest edge or small clearing, 2 to 4 m (6.5 to 13 ft) above the ground.
REGION: PT, CP, SE, W, NE, FN
Photo by N. Pearson

Plate 1

a Red Darter Dragonfly

b Long-legged Katydid

c Leaf Insect

d Evening Cicada

e Larval cicada turret

f Giant Wood Spider

Plate 2a
Antlion
Myrmeleon sp.
ID: Small (5 to 10 mm, 0.2 to 0.4 in) larvae at the bottom of inverted cones (1 to 2.5 cm, 0.4 to 1 in, across at their tops); dragonfly-like adult (3 to 4 cm, 1.6 to 1.7 in length); long antennae with clubbed ends.

HABITAT: Larvae in dry sandy areas, adults often attracted to lights at night.

REGION: PT, CP, SE, W, NE, FN

Plate 2b
Golden-spotted Tiger Beetle
Cicindela aurulenta
ID: Iridescent maroon and dark green with 4 bright gold spots on each wing covering (1.5 cm, 0.6 in); long legs and large, bulging eyes.

HABITAT: Runs quickly across moist sand and rock beaches of forested streams; flies quickly to escape danger but lands only a few meters away; active only on warm sunny days; larvae make vertical tunnels in the sand in which they await their insect prey.

REGION: PT, CP, SE, W, NE, FN

Plate 2c
Giant Fiddler Beetle
Mormolyce phyllodes
ID: Large (body length 9.5 cm, 3.7 in; width 4.5 cm, 1.7 in) beetle with extremely broad and flattened body; overall brown-black color.

HABITAT: Under loose bark and on tree trunks in moist forest.

REGION: PT, CP, SE, W, NE

Plate 2d
Bicolored Metallic Wood-boring Beetle
Megaloxantha bicolor
ID: Large (7 cm, 2.8 in) beetle, dark metallic greenish blue; orange spots on each side of the thorax; wing coverings (elytra) long, narrow and tapered at their ends, with two large, bright yellow spots.

HABITAT: Active during the day and obvious as it flies slowly and noisily at mid levels through moist forest; often seen on the trunks of trees on which it lays its eggs.

REGION: PT, CP, SE, W, NE

Plate 2e
Giant Asian Dung Beetle
Catharsius molossus
ID: Large (body length 2.6 cm, 1 in), massive blackish brown beetle; males with three short horns on head; female similar but lacks horns.

HABITAT: Dung of a large range of vertebrate species; commonly attracted to lights at night.

REGION: PT, CP, SE, W, NE, FN

Plate 2f
Hirsute Long-horned Beetle
Anoplophora longehirsuta
ID: Large (4 cm, 1.6 in) and black with broad blue-gray bands on head and body; extremely long (8 cm, 3 in) antennae.

HABITAT: Active during the day; conspicuous on tree trunks and freshly-cut wood in secondary and primary forests, orchards, and plantations.

REGION: PT, CP, SE, W, NE, FN

Plate 2

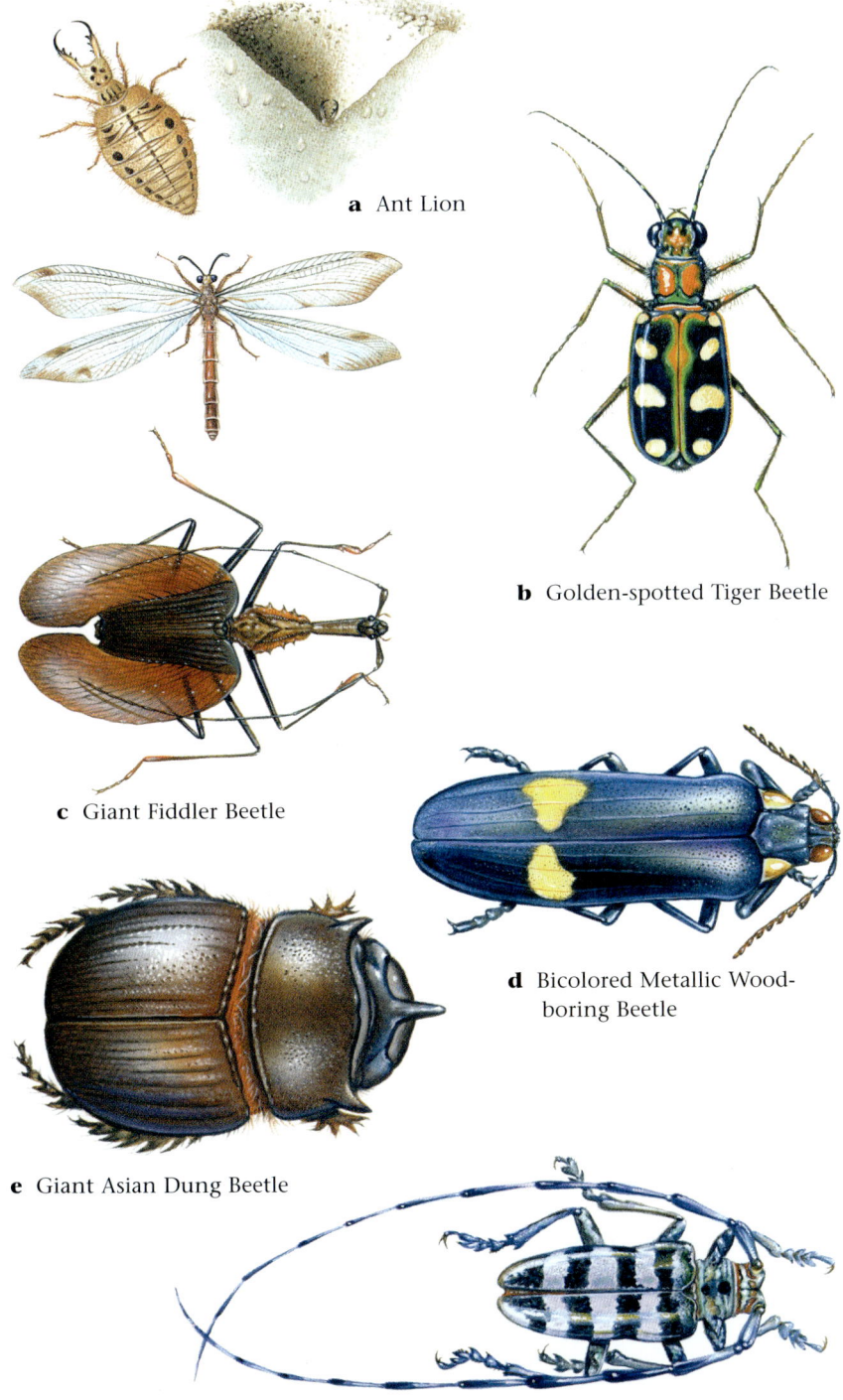

a Ant Lion

b Golden-spotted Tiger Beetle

c Giant Fiddler Beetle

d Bicolored Metallic Wood-boring Beetle

e Giant Asian Dung Beetle

f Hirsute Long-horned Beetle

Plate 3 (*See also:* Butterflies and Moths, p. 69)

Plate 3a
Golden Birdwing
Troides aeacus
ID: Large (wingspan 16 cm, 6 in); golden hindwings and brownish forewings.
HABITAT: Common in mid to high levels of forest clearings, forest edges, and gardens from lowlands to 2500 m (8250 ft) elevation.
REGION: PT, CP, SE, W, NE, FN
Photo by J. Moore

Plate 3b
Giant Atlas Moth
Archaeoattacus edwardsii
ID: Large (wingspan 20 cm, 8 in); chestnut brown wings with gray and black patches; forewings with peculiar bend at their front tips.
HABITAT: Nocturnal and often attracted to lights at night in a wide range of secondary and primary forests.
REGION: PT, CP, SE, W, NE, FN
Photo by J. Moore

Plate 3c
Long-tailed Silk Moth
Actias selene
ID: Large (wingspan 13 cm, 5 in); wings brown to pale yellow with conspicuously long "tail" (10 cm, 4 in) on each hindwing ends in an expanded racquet.
HABITAT: Nocturnal; often attracted to lights at night in a wide range of secondary to open primary forests.
REGION: PT, CP, SE, W, NE, FN
Photo by J. Moore

Plate 3d
Common Rose Swallowtail
Atrophaneura (Pachliopta) aristolochiae
ID: Large (wingspan 10 cm, 4 in); dark brown to black with orangish spots on hindwing; short tail (1.5 cm, 0.6 in) extending from each hindwing; female lighter colored than male.
HABITAT: Broad range of open habitats, from lowlands to 2500 m (8250 ft) elevation.
REGION: PT, CP, SE, W, NE, FN
Photo by J. Moore

Plate 3e
Lime Swallowtail
Papilio demoleus
ID: Large (wingspan 9 cm, 3.5 in); black with diffusion of yellow spots on both fore- and hindwings; red and blue spot on leading edge of hindwing.
HABITAT: Gardens, open forests, and citrus trees in the lowlands.
REGION: PT, CP, SE, W, NE, FN
Photo by J. Moore

Plate 3

a Golden Birdwing

b Giant Atlas Moth

c Long-tailed Silk Moth

d Common Rose Swallowtail

e Lime Swallowtail

Plate 4a
Great Eggfly Butterfly
Hypolimnas bolina
ID: Large (male wingspan 7 cm, 2.8 in; female 10 cm, 4 in); all black with single pale blue spot in each wing (male) or a yellow band along edge of fore- and hindwings (female).

HABITAT: Secondary forest, open fields, gardens of lowlands, and coastal vegetation; often seen flying high overhead in migratory flights.

REGION: PT, CP, SE, W, NE, FN

Photo by J. Moore

Plate 4b
Green Dragontail
Meges (Lamproptera) virescens
ID: Medium-sized (wingspan 5 cm, 2 in); black with pale green patch on inner wing; white tip on forewings; long (4 cm, 1.6 in) black tail extending from each hindwing.

HABITAT: Along sunlit spots near forested streams of lowlands to 1000 m (3300 ft) elevation; wings in flight and when settled on the ground vibrate rapidly.

REGION: PT, CP, SE, W, NE, FN

Photo by J. Moore

Plate 4c
Common Sailor
Neptis hylas
ID: Medium-sized (wingspan 5 cm, 2 in); black with pale yellow bands and spots on wings.

HABITAT: Common in open fields, secondary forests, gardens, forest clearings, and coastal vegetation, from lowlands to 2500 m (8250 ft) elevation.

REGION: PT, CP, SE, W, NE, FN

Photo by J. Moore

Plate 4d
Peacock Pansy
Precis (Junonia) almana
ID: Medium-sized (wingspan 6 cm, 2.3 in); rusty with black margin on wings and a large eye-like ocellus on the outer part of each wing.

HABITAT: Open fields, scrub vegetation, and gardens of the lowlands, especially around the Sensitive Plant, *Mimosa pudica*.

REGION: PT, CP, SE, W, NE, FN

Photo by J. Moore

Plate 4e
Fivebar Swordtail
Pathysa antiphates
ID: Large (wingspan 9 cm, 3.5 in); lime green and pale yellow with black patches on wing tips; long black tails extend from hindwings.

HABITAT: Lowland forest; this species of swallowtail is a swift flier but is most often seen congregating at moist places on the forest floor or on the beaches of forest streams.

REGION: PT, CP, SE, W, NE, FN

Photo by N. Pearson

Plate 4

a Great Eggfly Butterfly

b Green Dragontail

c Common Sailor

d Peacock Pansy

e Fivebar Swordtail

Plate 5 (See also: Butterflies and Moths, p. 69)

Plate 5a
Common Grass Yellow
Eurema hecabe
ID: Medium-sized (wingspan 4 cm, 1.5 in); bright yellow with black wing edges and body.

HABITAT: Open fields, gardens, riverbanks, scrubby vegetation, from coast to 2500 m (8250 ft); often gathers in large numbers at moist areas on roads and in fields.

REGION: PT, CP, SE, W, NE, FN

Photo by J. Moore

Plate 5b
Great Orange Tip
Hebomoia glaucippe
ID: Large (wingspan 10 cm, 4 in); white with bright orange tips on forewings; female with black spots along edge of hindwings; at rest on the ground the buffy-brown color of the underside of the closed wings makes it well camouflaged.

HABITAT: Gardens, parks, open fields, scrubby vegetation in lowlands to 1000 m (3300 ft) elevation.

REGION: PT, CP, SE, W, NE, FN

Photo by J. Moore

Plate 5c
The Wanderer
Pareronia (Valeria) valeria
ID: Medium-sized (wingspan 7 cm, 2.7 in); white with thin black stripes and broad wing edges.

HABITAT: Forest edges and forest clearings, from lowlands to 2500 m (8250 ft) elevation.

REGION: PT, CP, SE, W, NE, FN

Photo by J. Moore

Plate 5d
Peacock Royal
Pratapa (Tajuria) cippus
ID: Small (wingspan 3 cm, 1.2 in); male bright metallic blue with broad black edges on forewings; two thread-like tails on each hindwing; female similar but blue-gray.

HABITAT: Open vegetation, parks, gardens, and forest edges in lowlands.

REGION: PT, CP, SE, W, NE, FN

Photo by J. Moore

Plate 5e
Common Nawab
Polyura athamas
ID: Medium-sized (wingspan 7 cm, 2.7 in); black with pale yellow patches on inner wings; two short tails on hindwings.

HABITAT: Forest edge, forest clearings and open secondary forest of lowlands to 1000 m (3300 m) elevation; especially along streams and near decaying organic matter.

REGION: PT, CP, SE, W, NE, FN

Photo by J. Moore

Plate 5

a Common Grass Yellow

b Great Orange Tip

c The Wanderer

d Peacock Royal

e Common Nawab

Plate 6 (*See also:* Flies, p. 70; Ants, Wasps, and Bees, p. 71)

Plate 6a
Stalk-eyed Fly
Cyrtodiopsis sp.
ID: Tiny (body length 0.5 cm, 0.2 in); black with brown head and long, stalked eyes that look like antennae.
HABITAT: Resting on leaves of low undergrowth vegetation, usually near water in forests or wet rice paddies.
REGION: PT, CP, SE, W, NE, FN
Photo by H. Schillhammer

Plate 6b
Shepherd Ant
Anoplolepis sp.
ID: Colonies inhabit undergrowth foliage and canopy areas. They often tend groups of young membracid bugs, such as pictured here.
HABITAT: Secondary and open primary forest of lowlands to 1000 m (3300 ft) elevation.
REGION: PT, CP, SE, W, NE, FN
Photo by H. Feldhaar

Plate 6c
Asian Weaver Ant
Oecophylla smaragdina
ID: Large colonies of reddish ants with greenish abdomens; nest of living leaves in bush or tree crown glued together and shaped like a small football.
HABITAT: Wide range of open forest, forest edge, parks and gardens, from lowlands to 1500 m (5000 ft) elevation.
REGION: PT, CP, SE, W, NE, FN

Plate 6d
Stingless Bee
Trigona sp.
ID: Tiny (body length 0.5 cm, 0.2 in); blackish bees in large colonies; the waxy funnel-like opening to their nest in a tree trunk or on the forest floor is characteristic.
Habitat: In a wide range of forests; often attracted to sweat and their persistent aggregations around the head, back, and arms of hikers in the forest can be annoying.
REGION: PT, CP, SE, W, NE, FN
Photo by R. Butler

Plate 6e
Giant Black Termite
Macrotermes carbonarius
ID: Large (2 cm, 0.8 in) blackish termites; soldiers with immense and powerful mandibles.
HABITAT: Nocturnal; secondary and open primary forest floor; in columns on the forest floor; when disturbed they slam their abdomens against the ground to produce a beating sound of warning. Their ground nests are conical and often made of dried clay. CAUTION: the soldiers can bite mightily.
REGION: PT, CP, SE, W, NE, FN

Plate 6

a Stalk-eyed Fly

b Shepherd Ant

c Asian Weaver Ant

d Stingless Bee

e Giant Black Termite

Plate 7 (*See also:* Salamanders, p. 77; Caecilians, p. 79; Leaf-litter Toads, p. 81)

Plate 7a
Crocodile Salamander
Tylototriton verrucosus
ID: SVL 7.5 cm (3.0 in), TL 18 cm (7.1 in); blackish brown salamander with orange bony ridges on head and spine; underside black.

HABITAT: Higher-elevation forest above 1200 m (3900 ft); adults forage among leaf litter; mainly nocturnal; breeds in quiet pools of small streams.

REGION: NE, FN

Plate 7b
Yellow-banded Caecilian
Ichthyophis kohtaoensis
ID: TL to 35 cm (14 in); purplish black body with uninterrupted yellow flank band that forks at mouth angle; 355 to 375 body skin folds.

HABITAT: Evergreen forest of hills and lower mountain slopes, usually near streams and pools; burrowing, occasionally on surface at night; larvae inhabit small streams.

REGION: PT, SE, W, NE, FN

Plate 7c
Orange-eyed Leaf-litter Frog
Leptobrachium smithi
ID: SVL to 5.6 cm (2.2 in); proportionally enormous head; upper part of eye orange; slender limbs; loud barking call.

HABITAT: Evergreen and dense mixed deciduous forest of hills and lower mountain slopes, usually near streams; among leaf litter; nocturnal; breeds in deep muddy pools of streams.

REGION: PT, W, NE, FN

Plate 7d
Cascade Slender Leaf-litter Frog
Leptolalax pelodytoides
ID: SVL to 3.7 cm (1.5 in); small marbled grayish brown frog; skin smoothly granular; large silvery eyes with slight orange tint in upper part and vertical pupil; cream-colored glands on chest, thighs, and flanks; harsh chirping call.

HABITAT: Fast-flowing boulder streams in evergreen forest above 500 m (1600 ft); on rocks, floating material in water, forest floor, and low vegetation; nocturnal; breeds in streams.

REGION: W, NE, FN

Plate 7e
Mountain Horned Frog
Megophrys lateralis
ID: SVL to 9.4 cm (3.7 in); sides of head dark brown with cream upper lip; long slender legs, tarsus (ankle) reaches snout; groin region and under thighs yellowish; small soft spine above eye; soft grating call.

HABITAT: Evergreen forest at lower to mid-elevations (100 to 500 m, 300 to 1600 ft), usually near fast-flowing boulder and gravel streams; on forest floor and among streambed boulders; nocturnal; breeds in streams.

REGION: PT, W, FN

Plate 7f
Big-headed Horned Frog
Megophrys carinensis
ID: SVL to 15 cm (5.9 in); enormous broad flat head; several soft spines above eye; short stubby legs; pair of skin ridges diverging from neck toward flanks; loud raucous call.

HABITAT: Evergreen forest at mid-elevations (150 to 1050 m, 500 to 3400 ft), usually near streams; on forest floor; nocturnal; breeds in streams.

REGION: W, FN

Plate 7

a Crocodile Salamander

b Yellow-banded Caecilian

c Orange-eyed Leaf-litter Frog

d Cascade Slender Leaf-litter Frog

e Mountain Horned Frog

f Big-headed Horned Frog

Plate 8a
Asiatic Toad
Bufo melanostictus
ID: SVL to 11.5 cm (4.5 in), mostly smaller; large, elongate paratoid gland; narrow, black, raised bony ridges from snout to eye and surrounding upper orbit and tympanum (eardrum); monotonous, pulsing, rasping call.

HABITAT: Any habitat, from city gardens to hill forest; terrestrial; nocturnal and crepuscular; breeds in large pools.

REGION: PT, SE, CP, W, NE, FN

Plate 8b
River Toad
Bufo asper
ID: SVL to 17.0 cm (6.7 in); large, coarse-skinned toad without bony ridges on head; rounded, rather small paratoid gland; tympanum (eardrum) small and indistinct; call moderately loud "Ouik-ook-oohk," descending in tone.

HABITAT: Stream banks and adjacent forest floor along large streams and small rivers in lowland evergreen forest; terrestrial; nocturnal; breeds in small tributary streams.

REGION: PT, W

Plate 8c
Large-eared Toad
Bufo macrotis
ID: SVL to 5.5 cm (2.2 in); large tympanum (eardrum); small, round paratoid gland; no bony ridges on head; brown, but male turns mustard yellow when breeding.

HABITAT: Deciduous forests between 200 and 2100 m (600 to 6900 ft); terrestrial; diurnal; breeds in large rainpools.

REGION: PT, W, FN

Plate 8d
Dwarf Toad
Bufo parvus
ID: SVL to 4.7 cm (1.9 in); a single pair of curved bony ridges between eyes; small, round paratoid gland; series of distinct warts along flank; call an irregular series of loud grating pulses.

HABITAT: Lowland evergreen forest; on forest floor and low vegetation; nocturnal; breeds in streamside puddles.

REGION: PT, SE, W

Plate 8e
Marsh Puddle Frog
Occidozyga lima
ID: SVL to 4.0 cm (1.6 in); plump little frog; small eyes on top of head; finely granular skin; large, fully-webbed feet; call a short rapid series of squeaks.

HABITAT: Widespread and common in lowland wetlands with dense vegetation, including ponds and agricultural landscapes; aquatic; active throughout the day; breeds in ponds and pools.

REGION: PT, SE, CP, W, NE, FN

Plate 8f
Streamside Puddle Frog
Phrynoglossus martensii
(formerly *Occidozyga martensii*)
ID: SVL to 3.2 cm (1.3 in); small frog with small, short head; back skin coarsely granular; feet partly webbed; olive-gray color with or without brown neck patch or orange mid-back line; calls in drawn-out single squeaks or running together into a rapid series.

HABITAT: Common in swampy areas along slow-flowing streams and in wetlands, where it occurs at the water's edge and in shallow seepage areas; nocturnal; breeds in rainpools.

REGION: PT, SE, CP, W, NE, FN

Plate 8

a Asiatic Toad

b River Toad

c Large-eared Toad

d Dwarf Toad

e Marsh Puddle Frog

f Streamside Puddle Frog

Plate 9 (See also: True Frogs, p. 83)

Plate 9a
Field Frog
Rana limnocharis
(formerly *Fejervarya limnocharis*)
ID: SVL to 6.0 cm (2.4 in); head narrow and pointed; dorsal skin with granules and short longitudinal ridges; feet less than half webbed; outer metatarsal tubercle (bump on outer part of ankle) present; color very variable, with or without yellow, green, or orange mid-back stripe and blotches; irregular rasping call with squeaking overtones.

HABITAT: Most abundant Thai frog, inhabiting nearly all damp habitats except evergreen forest; active at night and overcast daytime; breeds in rainpuddles and pools.

REGION: PT, SE, CP, W, NE, FN

Plate 9b
Oriental Bullfrog
Rana rugulosa
(formerly *Hoplobatrachus rugulosus*)
ID: SVL to 16 cm (6.3 in), mostly much smaller; back skin with short longitudinal ridges; feet fully webbed; throat and chest cream with gray spots.

HABITAT: Lowland wetlands; semi-aquatic; nocturnal; breeds in large pools. Commercially bred and traded in most markets.

REGION: PT, SE, CP, W, NE, FN

Plate 9c
Big-headed Frog
Rana kuhlii
(formerly *Limnonectes kuhlii*)
ID: SVL to 9.3 cm (3.7 in); enormous head, particularly in adult males; short stubby legs; coarse tubercles (bumps) on flank and thigh; feet almost fully webbed; orange-brown band from eye to jaw angle; tympanum (eardrum) hidden.

HABITAT: Small and mid-sized streams in hill and lower montane forests, 200 to 1500 m (650 to 4900 ft); aquatic, among boulders and tree roots; nocturnal; breeds in small tributary streams.

REGION: PT, W, NE, FN

Plate 9d
Giant River Frog
Rana blythii
(formerly *Limnonectes blythii*)
ID: SVL to 18 cm (7.1 in), usually smaller; large, robust, yet graceful frog; long powerful legs; slender feet almost fully webbed; snout pointed; lips black, usually with cream bars.

HABITAT: Streams with gravel or sand bottom in lowland and hill areas; semi-aquatic; nocturnal; builds nests in sandy stream areas.

REGION: PT, W

Plate 9e
Crow Frog
Rana hascheana
(formerly *Taylorana hascheana*)
ID: SVL to 4.0 cm (1.6 in); large robust head; top of head tan, sides brown; long slender toes only partly webbed; call perfectly like a crow.

HABITAT: Areas in evergreen forest that slope toward streams; lowlands to 1000 m (3300 ft); terrestrial, cryptic; calls by day and early evening; males construct mud-cup nests under leaf litter, in which eggs develop directly into small frogs.

REGION: PT, W, FN

Plate 9f
Flap-headed Stream Frog
Rana pileata
(formerly *Limnonectes pileatus*)
ID: SVL to 6.0 cm (2.4 in); male with greatly enlarged head and free, round skin flap (indistinct in female); tympanum (eardrum) visible; skin coarsely granular.

HABITAT: Streams with boulder, gravel, or sandy bed in hill and montane evergreen forest (200 to 2200 m, 650 to 7200 ft); aquatic; nocturnal; breeds in streams.

REGION: SE, W, NE, FN

Plate 9

a Field Frog

c Big-headed Frog

b Oriental Bullfrog

d Giant River Frog

e Crow Frog

f Flap-headed Stream Frog

Plate 10a
Green Marsh Frog
Rana erythraea
(formerly *Hylarana erythraea*)
ID: SVL to 7.5 cm (3.0 in); green frog with broad cream bands at upper and lower flanks, usually black-edged; calls with soft irregular squeaks and whistles.

HABITAT: Lowland wetlands including rice paddies, occasionally along streams and rivers; usually among dense waterside and aquatic vegetation; diurnal and nocturnal; breeds in standing water.

REGION: PT, SE, CP, W, NE, FN

Plate 10b
Copper-eared Frog
Rana chalconota
(formerly *Chalcorana chalconota, C.raniceps*)
ID: SVL to 6.0 cm (2.4 in); slender frog with pointed head; long toes almost fully webbed, tips expanded into discs; tympanum (eardrum) large; upper lip cream, at least from eye to jaw angle; back green by day, brown at night; call irregular soft squeaks and staccato clicks.

HABITAT: Primary and secondary forest and other vegetated areas, mainly in lowlands; usually seen perched on undergrowth or in stream beds; mainly nocturnal; breeds in streamside pools.

REGION: PT

Plate 10c
Green Boulder Frog
Rana livida
(formerly *Odorrana livida*)
ID: SVL to 12 cm (4.7 in); large, slender green frog with rounded snout; back usually with brown spots; flanks usually brown; feet fully webbed; no outer metatarsal tubercle (bump on outer part of ankle); calls with irregular chirps.

HABITAT: Fast-flowing streams with boulders in evergreen forest at mid-altitudes (300 to 700 m, 1000 to 2300 ft); usually perched on mid-stream rocks and logs; nocturnal; breeds in streams.

REGION: W, NE, FN

Plate 10d
Dark-flanked Stream Frog
Rana nigrovittata
(formerly *Sylvirana nigrovittata*)
ID: SVL to 6.0 cm (2.4 in); broad skin ridge on upper flank separates rich brown back from dark brown flank; gland on upper arm; dark reticulation on back of thighs; regular barking call.

HABITAT: Streams with sand or mud bottom and occasionally pools in lowland and low-altitude forest; usually seen at water's edge, rarely on undergrowth; nocturnal; breeds in stream pools.

REGION: PT, SE, W, NE, FN

Plate 10e
Rough-sided Frog
(also called Waterdog)
Rana glandulosa
(formerly *Pulchrana glandulosa*)
ID: SVL to 9.2 cm (3.6 in); plump frog with coarsely granular skin; iris coppery red; tympanum (eardrum) modest-sized; throat a uniform cream; large gland on upper arm; calls loud, low-pitched whooping barks.

HABITAT: Vegetated muddy swampy areas near streams and ponds mainly in lowlands; terrestrial; crepuscular and nocturnal; breeds in standing water.

REGION: PT

Plate 10f
Flank-ridged Cascade Frog
Amolops larutensis
ID: SVL to 5.3 cm (2.1 in); finger and toe tips expanded into large discs; raised skin ridge along upper flank and scattered rugosities on back and flanks; back always densely mottled green and dark brown; soft warbling call.

HABITAT: Waterfalls, cascades, and rapids in forest streams at 40 to 1800 m (140 to 5900 ft); always perched on rocks; nocturnal; breeds in fast flowing water.

REGION: PT

Plate 10

a Green Marsh Frog

b Copper-eared Frog

c Green Boulder Frog

d Dark-flanked Stream Frog

e Rough-sided Frog

f Flank-ridged Cascade Frog

Plate 11 (*See also:* Narrow-mouthed Frogs, p. 84)

Plate 11a
Blotched Spadefoot Frog
Calluella guttulata
ID: SVL to 5.0 cm (2.0 in); plump frog with eyes set high atop broad head; intricate pattern of yellows, greens, reds, and browns; large spade-like inner metatarsal tubercle (bump on inner part of ankle); call an irregular continuous loud rattle

HABITAT: Deciduous forest and disturbed habitats up to 1000 m (3300 ft); terrestrial, burrowing; nocturnal; breeds in rain pools.

REGION: PT, SE, CP, W, NE, FN

Plate 11b
Big-lipped Burrowing Frog
Glyphoglossus molossus
ID: SVL to 6.0 cm (2.4 in); lower lip greatly expanded; eyes set high atop small head; color highly variable; call of single notes.

HABITAT: Deciduous lowland forest and scrub areas; terrestrial, burrowing; nocturnal; breeds in rain pools.

REGION: NSE, CP, W, NE

Plate 11c
Banded Ox-Frog
Kaloula pulchra
ID: SVL to 7.5 cm (3.0 in); broad, pale band around blunt snout and over flanks; no central yellow stripe on rear part of back; loud, low bellowing call.

HABITAT: Open forest, scrublands, gardens, and wetlands in lowlands up to 450 m (1500 ft); terrestrial, burrowing; nocturnal; breeds in rain pools.

REGION: PT, SE, CP, W, NE, FN

Plate 11d
Marbled Narrow-mouthed Frog
Microhyla pulchra
ID: SVL to 2.9 cm (1.1 in); distinct "woodgrain" pattern around dark lower back; groin area deep yellow; call a rapid pulsing rattle.

HABITAT: Open forest, scrublands, and wetlands from sea level to 1000 m (3300 ft); terrestrial; nocturnal; breeds in rain pools.

REGION: SE, CP, W, NE, FN

Plate 11e
Jewel Narrow-mouthed Frog
Microhyla inornata
ID: SVL to 3.1 cm (1.2 in); bold pattern of black spots on iridescent pink or yellow back; feet not webbed; shrill cricket-like call.

HABITAT: Deciduous forest and scrub in low hills to 600 m (2000 ft); terrestrial; nocturnal; breeds in small rain pools.

REGION: PT, SE, W, NE, FN

Plate 11f
Striped Sticky Frog
Kalophrynus interlineatus
ID: SVL to 6.0 cm (2.4 in); pointed snout; striped or net-like back pattern; dark flanks; black spot just before hind leg; snoring call.

HABITAT: Forests and scrublands from lowlands to 900 m (3000 ft); terrestrial; nocturnal; breeds in grassy, swampy pools.

REGION: SE, NE, FN

Plate 11

a Blotched Spadefoot Frog

b Big-lipped Burrowing Frog

c Banded Ox-Frog

d Marbled Narrow-mouthed Frog

e Jewel Narrow-mouthed Frog

f Striped Sticky Frog

Plate 12a
White-lipped Treefrog
Polypedates leucomystax
ID: SVL to 7.5 cm (3.0 in); fingers lack webbing; skin fused to skull bones; snout rounded; color and pattern very variable; no skin fringe along forearm, no heel tubercle (bump), no broad flank stripe covering tympanum (eardrum); various cackling and staccato calls.

HABITAT: Nearly all open forests, scrublands, gardens, and wetlands, mainly in lowlands but occasionally in montane areas; usually perched on low vegetation, solid objects, or on ground near water; mainly nocturnal; constructs foam nest just above or at edge of small pools.

REGION: PT, SE, CP, W, NE, FN

Plate 12b
Flank-spotted Gliding Treefrog
Rhacophorus bipunctatus
ID: SVL to 5.4 cm (2.1 in); dark blue or black spots on lower flank behind arm; hands and feet with extensive yellow to red web; loud rattling call.

HABITAT: Hill forest between 400 and 1500 m (1300 and 4900 ft); arboreal; nocturnal; breeds at temporary forest pools.

REGION: PT, NE, FN

Plate 12c
Black-webbed Gliding Treefrog
Rhacophorus nigropalmatus
ID: SVL to 8.3 cm (3.3 in); hands and feet with full black webbing with yellow margin; body green, usually with white dots; soft warbling call.

HABITAT: Hill forest between 200 and 1500 m (600 and 4900 ft); found in tree canopy; nocturnal; constructs foam nest above temporary forest pools.

REGION: PT, FN

Plate 12d
Striped Bush-Frog
Chirixalus vittatus
ID: SVL to 3.2 cm (1.3 in); small, slender frog with large head; dark-edged pale flank band; inner two fingers opposable to outer two; call a single loud, glassy "chink."

HABITAT: Deciduous forests up to 850 m (2800 ft); among grassy undergrowth; nocturnal; breeds in vegetated rain pools.

REGION: SE, W, NE, FN

Plate 12e
Dwarf Bush-Frog
Philautus parvulus
ID: SVL to 2.1 cm (0.8 in); tiny plump froglet; fingers barely webbed; call a clear glassy "ping," single or in increasing series.

HABITAT: Hill forests between 900 and 1500 m (3000 and 4900 ft); usually perched on trees trunks and branches and among undergrowth, rarely near water; nocturnal; breeding sites unknown.

REGION: SE, NE, FN

Plate 12f
Lichen Bush-Frog
Theloderma asperum
ID: SVL to 3.5 cm (1.4 in); skin coarsely granular; fingers with only remnant of webbing; color pattern imitates bird droppings; call a short upward-inflected whistle.

HABITAT: Evergreen forest in hills at 700 to 1000 m (2300 to 3300 ft); on vegetation; nocturnal; breeds in small pools.

REGION: PT, W, NE, FN

Plate 12

a White-lipped Treefrog

b Flank-spotted Gliding Treefrog

c Black-webbed Gliding Treefrog

d Striped Bush-Frog

e Dwarf Bush-Frog

f Lichen Bush-Frog

Plate 13a
Elongated Tortoise
Indotestudo elongata
ID: CL to 30 cm (12 in); typical tortoise; yellow shell with extensive black areas; a single, enlarged scute (plate) above the tail.

HABITAT: Inhabits deciduous forests and scrub of low hill regions, 50 to 500 m (150 to 1600 ft); feeds mainly on leafy vegetation and fruits; terrestrial, most active in early morning and late afternoon.

REGION: PT, SE, W, NE, FN

Plate 13b
Asian Box Turtle
Cuora amboinensis
ID: CL to 21 cm (8.3 in); dark olive to black head with straight yellow stripes; hinge on underside of high domed shell permits complete closing of shell; underside of shell pale yellow with a black spot on each scute (plate).

HABITAT: Inhabits mainly lowland wetlands but also occurs in streams and ponds up to 400 m (1300 ft); feeds on a variety of plant and small animal food; semi-aquatic, equally at ease on land and in water; mainly active at dusk and night.

REGION: PT, CP, W

Plate 13c
Stream Terrapin
(also called Asian Leaf Turtle)
Cyclemys dentata
ID: CL to 22 cm (8.7 in); proportionally low rounded shell, with 5 large vertebral scutes (plates) over its midline; indistinct hinge in underside of shell permits some closure of shell in adults (not developed in juveniles); each scute (plate) on underside with a dark radiating pattern; anal scutes curve far forward.

HABITAT: Streams in lowland and hill regions to 1000 m (3300 ft), rarely in still water; feeds on vegetable and small animal food; mainly aquatic, but may bask on logs or make overland journeys through forest; mainly nocturnal.

REGION: PT, SE, W, NE, FN

Plate 13d
Ricefield Terrapin
Malayemys subtrijuga
ID: CL to 21 cm (8.3 in), usually much smaller; shell with three longitudinal ridges, dark brown with yellow marks around the edge; large gray head with complex white lines and marks; underside of shell completely rigid.

HABITAT: Lowland wetlands including irrigation canals and rice paddies, never in flowing water; feeds exclusively on snails and freshwater mussels; active mainly in late afternoon and evening.

REGION: PT, SE, CP, W, NE

Plate 13e
Big-headed Turtle
Platysternon megacephalum
ID: CL to 17 cm (6.7 in); unmistakable: enormous triangular head ending in pointed upper jaw; flat shell; tail almost as long as shell.

HABITAT: Inhabits small cascading streams flowing through gulleys on steep mountain flanks, rarely in boulder streams, between 600 and 1500 m (2000 and 4900 ft); natural diet unknown; nocturnal, spending the day hidden in rock crevices.

REGION: NE, FN

Plate 13f
Stream Softshell Turtle
Dogania subplana
ID: CL to 31 cm (12 in); a soft-shelled turtle (lacking a rigid shell covered with scutes, or plates); front edge of shell completely smooth, without tubercles (bumps); head large, usually with orange on the cheeks; underside uniform white or with vague gray pigmentation, never forming sharply defined symmetrical markings.

HABITAT: Streams in forested areas and plantations in lowlands and foothills, also on offshore islands; feeds on various small animal prey and carrion; nocturnal, spending the day buried in sand or hidden under rocks.

REGION: PT, W

Plate 13

a Elongated Tortoise

b Asian Box Turtle

c Stream Terrapin

d Ricefield Terrapin

e Big-headed Turtle

f Stream Softshell Turtle

Plate 14 (See also: Turtles, p. 99; Crocodilians, p. 97; Monitor Lizards, p. 103)

Plate 14a
Hawksbill Sea Turtle
Eretmochelys imbricata

ID: CL to 90 cm (3 ft); shell heart-shaped, serrated at back and with overlapping scutes (plates) in all but very old individuals; two pairs of scales on forehead between eyes.

HABITAT: Coral reefs and rocky coastal areas; feeds mainly on sponges as well as other marine invertebrates; lays eggs at night on coarse sandy beaches, often at small offshore islands.

REGION: PT, SE

Note: this species is endangered, CITES Appendix I and IUCN Red List.

Plate 14b
Leatherback Sea Turtle
Dermochelys coriacea

ID: CL to 1.8 m (6 ft); shell with longitudinal ridges and covered with skin or with fine scales in young animals.

HABITAT: Open ocean, feeds in deep water down to 970 m (3200 ft), eating mainly jellyfish and some other marine invertebrates; lays eggs at night on steep sandy beaches directly facing open sea.

REGION: PT

Note: this species is endangered, CITES Appendix I and IUCN Red List.

Plate 14c
Siamese Crocodile
Crocodylus siamensis

ID: TL to 4 m (13 ft); broad head with distinct bony crests behind eyes in adults; 6 large scales on neck; bony ridges in front of eyes point inward to form a broad triangle; longitudinal bony ridge between eyes.

HABITAT: Rivers and large wetlands, lowlands up to 200 m (650 ft); aquatic, basks on banks; crepuscular and nocturnal, resting by day.

REGION: SE; extinct from PT, CP, W, NE, FN

Note: this species is endangered, CITES Appendix I and IUCN Red List.

Plate 14d
Bengal Monitor
Varanus bengalensis

ID: SVL to 75 cm (2.5 ft), TL 1.75 m (5.7 ft); blunt, compressed snout; nostril halfway between snout tip and eye; neck scales regular, not enlarged; uniform dark or finely dotted with yellow, no distinct light bands across body. (The Water Monitor, *Varanus salvator,* is often larger, up to TL 3.2 m, 10.5 ft; it has a longer, flattened snout with nostrils close to the tip and is dark gray, often with yellowish bands across its body.)

HABITAT: Deciduous forests and open areas of evergreen forest up to 1,000 m (3300 ft); forages usually on ground, basks high up trees, and sleeps in hollow trees or burrows; diurnal. (The Water Monitor is more aquatic, occurring mainly at riverbanks and in marshy and mangrove areas, from coastal zones up to 1200 m, 3900 ft, elevation.)

REGION: PT, SE, CP, W, NE, FN

Note: this species is endangered in parts of its range, CITES Appendix I listed.

Plate 14

a Hawksbill Sea Turtle

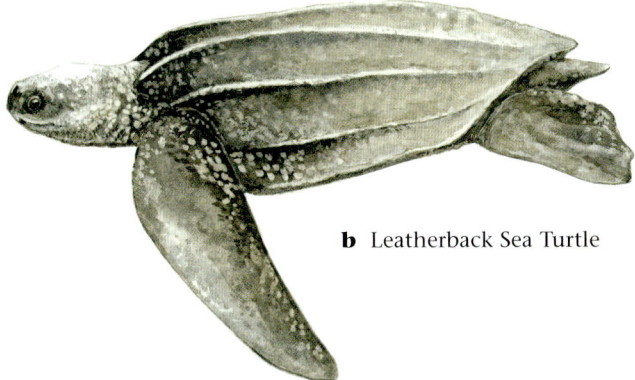

b Leatherback Sea Turtle

c Siamese Crocodile

d Bengal Monitor

Plate 15a
Flat-tailed House Gecko
Cosymbotus platyurus
ID: SVL to 6.0 cm (2.4 in), TL 13 cm (5.1 in); flattened tail without spines; fingers and toes webbed at base; fringe of skin along body; color varies from uniform pale gray to patterned dark brown.

HABITAT: Common on houses and other human structures as well as in dry open forest; mainly nocturnal, willing to feed near electric lights.

REGION: PT, SE, CP, W, NE, FN

Plate 15b
Spiny-tailed House Gecko
Hemidactylus frenatus
ID: SVL to 6.0 cm (2.4 in), TL 13 cm (5.1 in); original tail with regular whorls of spines; inner digit reduced in size but bearing a claw.

HABITAT: Abundant around human habitations but also inhabits dry open forests; mainly nocturnal, usually forages at street and porch lights.

REGION: PT, SE, CP, W, NE, FN

Plate 15c
Kuhl's Flying Gecko
(also called Kuhl's Gliding Gecko)
Ptychozoon kuhlii
ID: SVL to 9.5 cm (3.7 in), TL 19 cm (7.5 in); relatively large gecko with very wide skin flaps along head, body, limbs, and tail; tail scallops at right angles to tail; back bears large tubercles (bumps) among small granules.

HABITAT: Evergreen rainforest; usually seen at night on tree trunks, rarely on houses.

REGION: PT

Plate 15d
Tockay Gecko
Gekko gecko
ID: SVL to 18 cm (7.1 in), TL 35 cm (14 in); enormous gecko with large head and coarse, bumpy skin, gray with orange-red spots; unmistakable loud "Toc-kay" call.

HABITAT: Usually seen in or on houses, sheds, and other human structures, but also inhabits forest trees with adequate hiding places; mainly nocturnal but sometimes seen resting in a crevice by daytime; feeds on insects ranging from winged termites to large beetles.

REGION: PT, SE, CP, W, NE, FN

Plate 15e
Siamese Leaf-toed Gecko
Dixonius siamensis
(formerly *Phyllodactylus siamensis*)
ID: SVL to 5.0 cm (2.0 in), TL 11 cm (4.3 in); coarsely granular skin; digits slender, slightly widened at the tips; coloration varies from black with white dots in juveniles to marbled brown-gray in adults.

HABITAT: Deciduous and disturbed monsoon evergreen forest, scrublands; forages at night on ground and low on tree trunks, logs, woodpiles, etc.

REGION: PT, SE, CP, W, NE, FN

Plate 15f
Cardamom Slender-toed Gecko
Cyrtodactylus intermedius
ID: SVL to 8.5 cm (3.4 in), TL 19 cm (7.5 in); bold pattern of light-edged dark bands; digits not widened; 6 to 8 small holes in the large scales before the anus but no lengthwise groove in that region.

HABITAT: Evergreen forest and higher-elevation scrub areas (500 to 1000 m, 1600 to 3300 ft), usually low on tree trunks but also on rocks and earth banks; strictly nocturnal.

REGION: SE

Plate 15

a Flat-tailed House Gecko

b Spiny-tailed House Gecko

c Kuhl's Flying Gecko

d Tockay Gecko

e Siamese Leaf-toed Gecko

f Cardamom Slender-toed Gecko

Plate 16a
Garden Fence Lizard
Calotes versicolor
ID: SVL to 9.5 cm (3.7 in), TL 38 cm (15 in); body scales large, keeled, and regular; two spines above the tympanum (eardrum), none behind the eye; no skin fold at shoulder.

HABITAT: Most habitats in closed forest areas, particularly common in rural areas and along waterways; often on branches and undergrowth but also at ease on the ground; active throughout the day.

REGION: PT, SE, CP, W, NE, FN

Plate 16b
Blue Crested Lizard
Calotes mystaceus
ID: SVL to 14 cm (5.5 in), TL 42 cm (16.5 in); body scales large, keeled, and regular; head and part of body bright blue; upper lip white; reddish brown diamond marks on flanks; skin fold with fine granular scales before shoulder.

HABITAT: Monsoon evergreen and deciduous forest and rural areas with trees, mainly in lowlands; usually on tree trunks, occasionally on ground; active by day.

REGION: SE, CP, W, NE, FN

Plate 16c
Cross-bearing Tree Lizard
Acanthosaura crucigera
ID: SVL to 10 cm (3.9 in), TL 25 cm (9.8 in); body scales small with scattered large tubercles (bumps); low spiny crest on neck and body; spines behind eye and above tympanum (eardrum). NOTE: more than one species of lizard may be included under this name.

HABITAT: Evergreen forest at moderate altitudes (200 to 600 m, 650 to 2000 ft); lives in undergrowth and on the forest floor, often near streams; active by day, sleeping in vegetation at night.

REGION: PT, SE?, W, NE

Plate 16d
Black-throated Gliding Lizard
Draco melanopogon
ID: SVL to 8.5 cm (3.4 in), TL 24 cm (9.5 in); broad wing along body containing 5 ribs; long, narrow, black dewlap (skin sac) under throat; back marbled green, wing black with yellow spots.

HABITAT: Primary and tall secondary rainforest, lowlands to mid-elevations (800 m, 2600 ft); usually seen on tree trunks from ground to canopy level; feeds mainly on small ants and termites by day.

REGION: PT

Plate 16e
Butterfly Lizard
Leiolepis belliana
ID: SVL to 17 cm (6.7 in), TL 49 cm (19.3 in); large, rather flattened, long-tailed lizard; bold orange and triangular black markings on flanks that can be emphasised by spreading the ribs; back with scattered dark-edged pale spots. (The similar Reeve's Butterfly Lizard, *Leiolepis reevesii*, with black net-like pattern on back and reduced black flank markings, occurs in NE.)

HABITAT: Sandy areas with open vegetation, often in coastal areas but also inland up to 450 m (1500 ft); digs burrows for rest and refuge; actively forages for insects and soft vegetation only during the heat of the day.

REGION: PT, CP, W, FN

Plate 16f
Indo-Chinese Waterdragon
Physignathus cocincinus
ID: SVL to 25 cm (10 in), TL 90 cm (3 ft); large green lizard with tall spiny crest on neck, back, and tail; juveniles brown with green cross-bars and lacking crests; no bony crest over eye or spines in eye or tympanum (eardrum) region.

HABITAT: Lives in streamside vegetation in evergreen forest areas of lowland and moderate altitude; active by day.

REGION: SE

Plate 16

a Garden Fence Lizard

b Blue Crested Lizard

c Cross-bearing Tree Lizard

d Black-throated Gliding Lizard

e Butterfly Lizard

f Indo-Chinese Waterdragon

Plate 17a
Long-tailed Grass Lizard
Takydromus sexlineatus
ID: SVL to 6.5 cm (2.6 in), TL 36 cm (14 in); slender lizard with proportionally enormous tail; back covered by 6 rows of large keeled scales, flanks with fine granular scales.

HABITAT: Open deciduous forests, scrublands, and riverbanks; lives among dense grass and other undergrowth; active by day.

REGION: PT, SE, CP, W, NE, FN

Plate 17b
Fire-tailed Tree-Skink
Lipinia vittigera
ID: SVL to 4.5 cm (1.8 in), TL 10 cm (3.9 in); small skink with bold lengthwise black and silvery white stripes and a blazing orange tail.

HABITAT: Inhabits evergreen forest from lowlands to 1500 m (4900 ft); actively forages by day on tree trunks, logs, and occasionally wooden buildings in forest, from tree-root to canopy level.

REGION: PT, SE, W, NE, FN

Plate 17c
Streamside Skink
Sphenomorphus maculatus
ID: SVL to 6.0 cm (2.4 in), TL 16 cm (6.3 in); slender, long-tailed skink; bronze back with small black spots; brown band with cream spots along flank and side of tail; lower flank yellow with white and dark gray spots; rostral (head-top) scale concave.

HABITAT: Always close to streams in evergreen forest; forages by day among rocks and leaf litter for small insects.

REGION: PT, SE, W, NE, FN

Plate 17d
Bowring's Supple Skink
Lygosoma bowringii
(formerly *Riopa bowringii*)
ID: SVL to 5.0 cm (2.0 in), TL 11 cm (4.3 in); small, slender skink with small limbs; black band along upper flank; reddish area behind arm; white and black spots on lower flanks; yellow underside.

HABITAT: Deciduous forest, stream edges, and gardens, mainly in lowlands but occasionally up to 1500 m (4900 ft); lives mainly among leaf litter and loose sand; active by day, especially during overcast weather.

REGION: PT, SE, CP, W, NE, FN

Plate 17e
Speckled Forest Skink
Mabuya macularia
ID: SVL to 6.5 cm (2.6 in), TL 16 cm (6.3 in); broad, somewhat flattened skink; body scales strongly keeled; cream lines extend from eye back along upper flank and from lips to lower flank; flanks and limbs with numerous cream spots.

HABITAT: Occurs mainly in deciduous forest but also occasionally in evergreen forest; forages by day on ground and among leaf litter; occasionally seen basking on fallen logs.

REGION: PT, SE, W, NE, FN

Plate 17f
Many-lined Sun-Skink
Mabuya multifasciata
ID: SVL to 13 cm (5.1 in), TL 35 cm (14 in); large, heavy-bodied skink; distinct keels on each body scale; flank usually brown, often with black-edged white spots, sometimes a large orange blotch; usually dark longitudinal lines on the back.

HABITAT: Open grassy areas, including human habitation, river banks, and forest edges; mainly terrestrial but also climbs on logs, tree trunks, and other structures; active by day.

REGION: PT, SE, CP, W, NE, FN

Plate 17

a Long-tailed Grass Lizard

b Fire-tailed Tree-Skink

c Streamside Skink

d Bowring's Supple Skink

e Speckled Forest Skink

f Many-lined Sun-Skink

Plate 18a
Mueller's Blind Snake
Typhlops muelleri
ID: TL to 45 cm (18 in); blunt head with barely visible eye; scales on underside are the same size as on the rest of the body; underside creamy white, sharply set off from blackish upper surface.
HABITAT: Forest, scrublands, and water's edge in lowlands and low hills; burrows in soil and leaf litter; occasionally seen on the surface at night after heavy rain.

REGION: PT

Plate 18b
Red-tailed Pipe Snake
Cylindrophis ruffus
ID: TL to 1 m (3.3 ft); stocky snake with blunt head and short blunt tail; black above, irregular white and black blotches below, underside of tail black and orange-red.
HABITAT: Lowland wetlands, living hidden under logs and planks, among leaf litter and aquatic vegetation, both on the shore and in water; occasionally seen at night.

REGION: PT, SE, CP, W, NE, FN

Plate 18c
Sunbeam Snake
Xenopeltis unicolor
ID: TL to 1.25 m (4.1 ft); stout snake with broad, depressed snout; uniform brown upper surfaces have iridescent rainbow reflections; ventral scales slightly enlarged.
HABITAT: Inhabits forest and scrublands, generally near water, from lowlands to 1350 m (4400 ft); terrestrial, nocturnal, and usually stays under cover or buried in leaf litter or mud.

REGION: PT, SE, CP, W, NE, FN

Plate 18d
White-lipped Pit-Viper
Trimeresurus albolabris
ID: TL to 1 m (3.3 ft); large triangular head; strongly keeled scales; green above, yellow underside, male with white line along lower flank, no red head or flank lines. VENOMOUS.
HABITAT: Open deciduous forest and scrublands up to 400 m (1300 ft); mainly on shrubby vegetation, sometimes on ground; nocturnal.

REGION: PT, SE, CP, W, NE, FN

Plate 18e
Malayan Pit-Viper
Calloselasma rhodostoma
ID: TL to 1 m (3.3 ft); brown, with dark triangular pattern on back; pointed triangular head dark brown with pale stripe behind eye. VENOMOUS.
HABITAT: Open forests, scrublands, and tree plantations from lowlands to 2000 m (6600 ft); terrestrial, not likely to move if disturbed while resting; nocturnal.

REGION: PT, SE, CP, W, NE, FN

Plate 18f
Reticulated Python
Python reticulatus
ID: TL to 7 m (23 ft), occasionally more; heavy-bodied snake with distinctive tapering head and blunt snout; regular geometric body color pattern enclosing pure white areas on flanks. POTENTIALLY DANGEROUS CONSTRICTOR.
HABITAT: Forests, river banks, agricultural areas, and towns, from coastal areas to 1500 m (4900 ft); juveniles are arboreal, becoming increasingly terrestrial as they grow; nocturnal.

REGION: PT, SE, CP, W, NE, FN

Plate 18

a Mueller's Blind Snake

b Red-tailed Pipe Snake

c Sunbeam Snake

d White-lipped Pit-Viper

e Malayan Pit-Viper

f Reticulated Python

Plate 19 (See also: Venomous Snakes, p. 107)

Plate 19a
Small-spotted Coral Snake
Calliophis maculiceps
ID: TL to 47 cm (19 in); slender body brown or reddish with fine black spots; black head and two black tail bands; orange below, black and white under tail. VENOMOUS.

HABITAT: Deciduous forest from lowlands to 1000 m (3300 ft); terrestrial to fossorial; active at night and after rain.

REGION: PT, SE, CP, W, NE, FN

Plate 19b
Blue Krait
Bungarus candidus
ID: TL to 1.55 m (5.1 ft); black and white bands, usually black spots within white bands, underside uniform white; scales smooth, vertebral scales (along mid-back) enlarged. VENOMOUS.

HABITAT: Forests up to 1525 m (5000 ft), often near water; terrestrial; nocturnal.

REGION: PT, SE, CP, W, NE, FN

Plate 19c
Banded Krait
Bungarus fasciatus
ID: TL to 2 m (6.6 ft); bold yellow and black banded pattern; triangular body profile. VENOMOUS.

HABITAT: Forest, scrublands, and agricultural areas from lowlands to 2300 m (7500 ft); terrestrial, in both damp and dry areas; nocturnal and secretive.

REGION: PT, SE, CP, W, NE, FN

Plate 19d
Monocellate Cobra
Naja kaouthia
(formerly *Naja naja kaouthia*)
ID: TL to 2 m (6.6 ft); neck can be flattened wide, showing usually a ring-shaped pale mark on the back and paired black spots and a black band on the cream underside. VENOMOUS.

HABITAT: Widespread from forests to wetlands, agricultural lands, and towns, from sea level to 700 m (2300 ft); terrestrial or in low vegetation; nocturnal.

REGION: PT, SE, CP, W, NE

Plate 19e
King Cobra
Ophiophagus hannah
ID: TL 4 m (13 ft) or more; large; broad, fairly triangular body profile; body scales large and distinct; eyes proportionally small; neck can spread to narrow hood; juveniles black with narrow cream bands, adults fairly uniform gray, brown, or black. VENOMOUS.

HABITAT: Forest of all types including plantations, occasionally in cultivated areas, from lowlands to 2100 m (7000 ft); terrestrial, often near water; swift, alert, active by day and at night.

REGION: PT, SE, CP?, W, NE, FN

Plate 19f
Yellow-bellied Sea Snake
Pelamis platurus
ID: Long narrow head, distinct from neck; black or dark brown above with yellow or light tan lower sides and belly; flattened paddle-shaped tail; to 1 m (3.3 ft) but averages 70 cm (28 in). VENOMOUS.

HABITAT: Indian and Pacific Oceans; this deep-water sea snake occurs in the open sea; those found washed up on beaches are there because of strong currents or storms.

REGION: PT, SE

Plate 19

a Small-spotted Coral Snake

b Blue Krait

c Banded Krait

d Monocellate Cobra

juvenile

e King Cobra

adult

f Yellow-bellied Sea Snake

Plate 20a
Yellowbelly Watersnake
Enhydris plumbea
ID: TL to 56 cm (22 in); grayish above, sharply distinct from cream or yellow underside; a black line on underside of tail; distinct broad, flat head with small eyes on top.
HABITAT: Inhabits almost any type of water body, from estuaries and muddy lowland pools to swift-flowing streams at 1500 m (4900 ft); mainly aquatic, sometimes found on land at night.

REGION: PT, SE, CP?, W, NE, FN

Plate 20b
Dog-faced Watersnake
Cerberus rynchops
ID: TL to 1.20 m (3.9 ft); head rather distinct with eyes far forward; body scales strongly keeled; vague dark body markings.
HABITAT: Mainly a species of coastal lagoons, estuaries, and mangroves, occasionally found inland in rivers; almost purely aquatic and nocturnal.

REGION: PT, SE, CP

Plate 20c
Puff-faced Watersnake
Homalopsis buccata
ID: TL to 1.37 m (4.5 ft); distinct broad head; body scales keeled; distinctive banded pattern and masked face.
HABITAT: Various water bodies from coastal lowlands to 550 m (1800 ft); mainly aquatic but sometimes moves onto dry land; nocturnal.

REGION: PT, SE, CP, W, NE

Plate 20d
Tentacled Snake
Erpeton tentaculatum
ID: TL to 70 cm (2.3 ft); distinct broad, flat body; small head with pair of appendages; pattern either triangular marks or lengthwise lines.
HABITAT: Lowland still waters including open wetlands, canals, and flooded forest; aquatic, almost helpless on land; rarely active at any time.

REGION: PT, CP

Plate 20e
Checkered Keelback
Xenochrophis piscator
ID: TL to 1.1 m (3.6 ft); gray body with more or less distinct checkered pattern; creamy white area from eye to jaw angle; many individuals with yellow at side of neck.
HABITAT: Wetlands, ponds, streams, and riverbanks in lowlands and lower altitudes; mainly aquatic but regularly on dry land at water's edge; mainly nocturnal but also active by day.

REGION: PT, SE, CP, W, NE, FN

Plate 20f
Red-necked Keelback
Rhabdophis subminiatus
ID: TL to 1.3 m (4.3 ft); bright yellow and red color at sides of neck, often preceded by black neck patch; gray body with faint checker pattern.
HABITAT: Forest, in hill areas up to 1800 m (5900 ft), but uncommon in lowlands; usually near rivers, streams, or ponds, mostly on land but comfortable in water; active mainly by day.

REGION: PT, SE, CP?, W, NE, FN

Plate 20

a Yellowbelly Watersnake

b Dog-faced Watersnake

c Puff-faced Watersnake

d Tentacled Snake

e Checkered Keelback

f Red-necked Keelback

Plate 21 (*See also*: Colubrid Snakes, p. 113)

Plate 21a
White-spotted Slug-snake
Pareas margaritophorus
ID: TL to 47 cm (19 in); plump proportions and blunt snout; body with distinctive black and white spots; white, yellow, or pink neck collar.

HABITAT: Evergreen forest from foothills to 1640 m (5400 ft); terrestrial; crepuscular and nocturnal.

REGION: PT, SE, CP, W, NE, FN

Plate 21b
Common Mock Viper
Psammodynastes pulverulentus
ID: TL to 44 cm (17 in); distinct head with large eyes topped by "eyebrow" scale; fine pattern on head including central stripe; scales not keeled.

HABITAT: Open forests and scrub from lowlands to about 2000 m (6600 ft), with preference for hill areas; terrestrial and in vegetation, usually near water; active by day and night.

REGION: PT, SE, W, NE, FN

Plate 21c
Striped Kukri Snake
Oligodon taeniatus
ID: TL to 44 cm (17 in); pair of narrow brown stripes flanking yellowish body midline; underside orange with black markings; no black bands on upper side of tail.

HABITAT: Inhabits deciduous forests; terrestrial; diurnal.

REGION: PT, SE, CP, W, NE

Plate 21d
Green Tree Racer
Elaphe prasina
ID: TL to 1.2 m (3.9 ft); body and tail bright green, underside paler; slender head with large scales on top; round pupils.

HABITAT: Evergreen and bamboo forest at mid-altitudes but may range to lowlands and mountainous areas; terrestrial and arboreal; may be active at any time.

REGION: NE, FN

Plate 21e
Southern Stripe-tailed Racer
Elaphe taeniura ridleyi
ID: TL to 2.5 m (8.2 ft); front of body creamy yellow, grading to black and cream-striped tail; head gray with black eye mask. (The subspecies *Elaphe taeniura yunnanensis*, which has a dark gray body, occurs in FN.)

HABITAT: Limestone caves and cliffs, generally near bat roosts, sea level to 2000 m (6600 ft); good climber; feeds mainly on bats; mainly nocturnal.

REGION: PT

Plate 21f
Banded Rat-snake
(also called Common or Asian Rat-snake)
Ptyas mucosus
ID: TL to 3.2 m (10.5 ft); rounded body with distinct large scales; eye proportionally large; rear body and tail with black crossbars. (Often strongly resembles King Cobra (Plate 19) in size, coloration, and defensive behavior.)

HABITAT: Open forest, scrub, and agricultural areas from lowlands to 1300 m (4300 ft); terrestrial and in low vegetation, including in very dry areas; active mainly by day.

REGION: PT, SE, CP, W, NE, FN

Plate 21

a White-spotted Slug-snake

b Common Mock Viper

c Striped Kukri Snake

d Green Tree Racer

e Southern Stripe-tailed Racer

f Banded Rat-snake

Plate 22a
Golden Tree-Snake
Chrysopelea ornata
ID: TL to 1.3 m (4.3 ft); olive body color proves to consist of pale green scales with black edge and midline; lips and underside pure white; distinctive head pattern.

HABITAT: Can be found in almost any habitat, from dense forest to inner cities, coasts to hills (to 550 m, 1800 ft); arboreal, occasionally on ground; mainly active by day.

REGION: PT, SE, CP, W, NE, FN

Plate 22b
Painted Bronzeback
Dendrelaphis pictus
ID: TL to 1.43 m (4.7 ft); slender; rich brown back with turquoise skin between scales; black-edged cream band extends from lips along lower flank to tail; underside creamy yellow.

HABITAT: Forest, scrub, and gardens from sea level to 1350 m (4400 ft); comfortable on ground, among dense vegetation and climbing trees; active by day and at night.

REGION: PT, SE, CP, W, NE, FN

Plate 22c
Oriental Whip-Snake
Ahaetulla prasina
ID: TL to 1.97 m (6.5 ft); very slender, with long pointed head; snout blunt when seen from above; no speckling on top of head; anal scale divided; 194 or more ventral (mid-back) scales.

HABITAT: Forest, scrub, agricultural areas, and gardens from coast to 2100 m (6900 ft); normally in any kind of dense vegetation, occasionally on ground; diurnal.

REGION: PT, SE, CP, W, NE, FN

Plate 22d
House Wolf-Snake
Lycodon aulicus
ID: TL to 76 cm (2.5 ft); brick-red body with fine yellow markings and yellow neck collar; head flattened, tapering to fairly blunt snout.

HABITAT: Open forest, scrub, agricultural areas, and gardens, mainly in lowlands; a good climber which can be seen on the ground or on any object; active during twilight and at night.

REGION: PT, SE, CP, W, NE, FN

Plate 22e
Spotted Cat-Snake
Boiga multomaculata
ID: TL to 1.87 m (6.1 ft), usually much smaller; distinctive pattern of round, dark brown spots on tan body; body proportionally slender; head with large scales on top; body scales not keeled.

HABITAT: Open forest, forest edges, and scrub from lowlands to 1400 m (4600 ft); mainly arboreal, sometimes on ground; active at dusk, night, and early morning.

REGION: SE, CP, W, NE, FN

Plate 22f
Mangrove Cat-Snake
Boiga dendrophila
ID: TL to 2.5 m (8.2 ft); relatively slender, with distinct head; pure black with narrow yellow bars on flank that do not meet on the back.

HABITAT: Lowland evergreen forest, mangrove and scrub up to 600 m (2000 ft), usually near water; mainly arboreal, sometimes on ground, swims well; nocturnal.

REGION: PT

Plate 22

a Golden Tree-Snake

b Painted Bronzeback

c Oriental Whip-Snake

d House Wolf-Snake

e Spotted Cat-Snake

f Mangrove Cat-Snake

Plate 23a
Asian Openbill Stork
Anastomus oscitans
ID: Large (81 cm, 2.7 ft); white with black wings; peculiarly bowed bill with gap in it.
HABITAT: Marshes and rice paddies. Nests in CP November to April and a few individuals spend the rest of the year in inland areas.

REGION: PT, CP, NE, FN

Plate 23b
Little Cormorant
Phalacrocorax niger
ID: Large (52 cm, 1.7 ft); all black; long neck.
HABITAT: Swimming duck-like in water, sitting upright on dead branches in or near the water, or flying over inland reservoirs, rivers, and lakes or along the coast. Resident in CP but a wintering migrant in the rest of the country.

REGION: PT, CP, FN

Plate 23c
Gray Heron
Ardea cinerea
ID: Very large (1.2 m, 4 ft); white neck and head, grayish body, black crest on head.
HABITAT: Solitary in coastal estuaries, mangroves, and inland river banks, marshes, and rice paddies. Common wintering visitor.

REGION: PT, CP, W, NE, FN

Plate 23d
Purple Heron
Ardea purpurea
ID: Large (97 cm, 3.2 ft); gray wings and back, striped maroon neck, breast, and head; white throat; black crown.
HABITAT: Inland freshwater marshes, lakes, and river edges and coastal estuaries. Resident population augmented in winter by northern migrants.

REGION: PT, CP, SE, W, NE, FN

Plate 23e
Black-crowned Night-Heron
Nycticorax nycticorax
ID: Large (61 cm, 2 ft); bill relatively short but slender; adults with black crown and back; gray wings; whitish gray underparts; immature streaked brown and tan.
HABITAT: Coastal mangroves, river mouths, edges of lakes, marshes, and rivers; usually roosts in dense vegetation near water during the day in small groups; most easily seen flying overhead at dusk and giving a loud and harsh squawk; mainly active at night; nests in CP, winter visitor elsewhere.

REGION: PT, CP, NE, FN

Plate 23

a Asian Openbill Stork
b Little Cormorant
c Gray Heron
d Purple Heron
e Black-crowned Night-Heron

Plate 24a
Pacific Reef-Egret
Egretta sacra
ID: Large (58 cm, 1.9 ft); either all white with yellowish bill and green legs or all dark gray with dark bill and green legs.

HABITAT: Coastal beaches and rocky outcroppings; usually solitary.

REGION: PT, CP, SE, W

Plate 24b
Chinese Pond Heron
Ardeola bacchus
ID: Medium-sized (46 cm, 1.5 ft); chunky, with brown back and streaked breast in winter; maroon head and breast with black back in late spring plumage; startlingly white wings and tail in flight.

HABITAT: Common winter visitor in coastal sites and agricultural areas with standing water. Absent during the summer. (The very similar Javan Pond-Heron, *Ardeola speciosa,* is resident in CP and indistinguishable from the Chinese Pond Heron in the winter. In breeding plumage, February to July, it has a buffy head and black back.)

REGION: PT, CP, SE, W, NE, FN

Plate 24c
Little Egret
Egretta garzetta
ID: Large (61 cm, 2 ft); adults all white with black bill and legs and bright yellow feet.

HABITAT: Coastal estuaries, river mouths, inland lakes, marshes, rice paddies, and rivers, usually in small flocks. Resident in SE and CP but a winter visitor elsewhere.

REGION: PT, CP, SE, W, NE, FN

Plate 24d
Yellow Bittern
Ixobrychus sinensis
ID: Medium-sized (38 cm, 1.2 ft); buffy yellow; crown black; in flight wings black with distinctive buffy patches on inner half.

HABITAT: Solitary or in pairs in small marshes and wet grassy areas.

REGION: PT, CP, W, NE, FN

Plate 24e
Cattle Egret
Bubulcus ibis
ID: Large (51 cm, 1.7 ft); adults all white with orange-yellow bill and greenish legs. During the breeding season the back, head, neck, and breast become pinkish orange and the legs and bill reddish.

HABITAT: Marshes, rice paddies, pastures, and open areas along rivers and lakes, often in flocks; regularly associated with cattle and large herbivores. Nests in CP, winter visitor elsewhere.

REGION: PT, CP, NE, FN

Plate 24f
Great Egret
(also called Common Egret)
Ardea alba
ID: Large (1 m, 3.3 ft); all white with yellow bill and black legs.

HABITAT: Coastal estuaries, river mouths, inland lakes, marshes, and rivers; usually solitary. Resident in CP but a winter visitor elsewhere.

REGION: PT, CP, W, NE, FN

Plate 25 (*See also:* Ducks, p. 128; Marsh and Stream Birds, p. 127)

Plate 25a
Cotton Pygmy-Goose
Nettapus coromandelianus
ID: Medium-sized (32 cm, 1 ft); male white with black crown, neck band, and back; female similar but tan rather than white.

HABITAT: Freshwater marshes, lakes, and vegetated reservoirs.

REGION: PT, CP, SE, W, NE, FN

Plate 25b
Little Grebe
Tachybaptus ruficollis
ID: Medium-sized (25 cm, 10 in); duck-like with short, slender pointed bill; grayish brown in non-breeding plumage and reddish brown neck and face in breeding plumage.

HABITAT: Standing water on inland lakes, reservoirs, and marshes.

REGION: PT, CP, SE, W, NE, FN

Plate 25c
Garganey
Anas querquedula
ID: Medium-sized (41 cm, 1.4 ft); male brown with gray sides and a white crescent over the eye; female all brown with dark crown and two stripes through the face.

HABITAT: Winter visitor to freshwater marshes, reservoirs, vegetated lake edges, and coastal estuaries.

REGION: PT, CP, SE, W, NE, FN

Plate 25d
Lesser Whistling Duck
Dendrocygna javanica
ID: Medium-sized (41 cm, 1.3 ft); chestnut brown with buffy throat and breast; dark crown.

HABITAT: Small to immense flocks in ponds, marshes, rice paddies, and wooded lakes.

REGION: PT, CP, SE, W, NE, FN

Plate 25e
Northern Pintail
Anas acuta
ID: Large (56 cm, 1.8 ft); male with brown head, long white neck, and long, pointed tail; female all brown with long slender neck.

HABITAT: Inland lakes, marshes, and reservoirs and coastal estuaries; small flocks or pairs.

REGION: CP, W, NE, FN

Plate 25

b Little Grebe
non-breeding
breeding

a Cotton Pygmy-Goose

M

F

c Garganey

d Lesser Whistling Duck

F

M

e Northern Pintail

Plate 26 (*See also:* Hawks, Eagles, and Kites, p. 135)

Plate 26a
Black-shouldered Kite
Elanus caeruleus
ID: Medium-sized (32 cm, 1 ft); light gray upperparts and white underparts; black line through eye, on shoulder, and in flight on wing tips

HABITAT: Open country of lowlands; often sitting on telephone wires and poles; hovers in flight searching for prey.

REGION: PT, CP, SE, W, NE, FN

Plate 26b
Black Baza
Aviceda leuphotes
ID: Medium-sized (32 cm, 1 ft); black with white breast, barred dark brown; long narrow crest.

HABITAT: Sits on branches in mid-level to canopy of secondary and primary forest; nests in north and west, winters throughout.

REGION: PT, CP, SE, W, NE, FN

Plate 26c
Black Kite
Milvus migrans
ID: Large (63 cm, 2 ft); dark brown with forked tail; in flight with white patches at base of wing; rare resident population in CP with bright yellow legs and base of bill; more common wintering population with blue-gray legs and base of bill.

HABITAT: Open country of lowlands and coast.

REGION: PT, CP, SE, W, NE, FN

Plate 26d
Crested Goshawk
Accipiter trivirgatus
ID: Medium-sized (43 cm, 1.4 ft); upperparts all brown with short crest; underparts white with boldly barred breast and streaked throat; in flight short broad wings and long tail with four distinct dark bands.

HABITAT: Sits in canopy of trees but often soars alone or in pairs high over the forest; permanent resident.

REGION: PT, SE, W, NE, FN

Plate 26e
Shikra
Accipiter badius
ID: Medium-sized (32 cm, 1 ft); underparts white with rusty barring; male upperparts and cheeks blue-gray; female upperparts and cheeks grayish brown.

HABITAT: Open forests and agricultural areas; ambushes prey from leafy tree crown; normal flight alternates wingbeats with gliding; winter visitor to peninsula, resident elsewhere.

REGION: PT, CP, SE, W, NE, FN

Plate 26

a Black-shouldered Kite
b Black Baza
c Black Kite
d Crested Goshawk
e Shikra

Plate 27 (*See also:* Hawks, Eagles, and Kites, p. 135; Falcons, p. 137)

Plate 27a
White-bellied Sea-Eagle
Haliaeetus leucogaster
ID: Large (69 cm, 2.3 ft); upperparts slate-gray; underparts and head whitish gray; in flight tail white with broad black band at base and black trailing half of wings.

HABITAT: Soaring high over coastal limestone outcroppings, cliffs, and along the seashore; often perches upright on poles, rocks, and tall trees in or near the ocean; occasionally found inland on large lakes or rivers.

REGION: PT, SE

Plate 27b
Crested Serpent-Eagle
Spilornis cheela
ID: Large (60 cm, 1.9 ft); brown with black and white crest and white spots on breast.

HABITAT: Perched, often conspicuously, at the tops of dead trees in forest, from lowlands to 1500 m (5000 ft) elevation.

REGION: PT, CP, SE, W, NE, FN

Plate 27c
Eurasian Kestrel
Falco tinnunculus
ID: Medium-sized (33 cm, 1 ft); brown above and below with dark spotting and barring; male with pale gray head and white throat; female with brown streaked head, white throat, and black moustache; long pointed wings in flight with narrow black band on tail.

HABITAT: Common winter visitor in open habitats, rice paddies, towns, and parks.

REGION: SE, CP, W, NE, FN

Plate 27d
Pied Harrier
Circus melanoleucos
ID: Large (45 cm, 1.5 ft); male head, back, and wing tips black; rest of underparts and upperparts whitish gray; female upperparts gray and brown with white "V" on rump; underparts white streaked brown.

HABITAT: Winter visitor to marshes and open agricultural areas in the lowlands; soars low over grassy areas with wings held in a broad "V."

REGION: PT, CP, NE, FN

Plate 27e
Collared Falconet
Microhierax caerulescens
ID: Small (19 cm, 1.8 ft); black crown, line through eye, back, and tail; underparts white with rusty lower belly.

HABITAT: Resident in forest edges and clearings up to 1800 m (5900 ft); often perches in pairs or small groups on exposed dead branches high in the canopy. (Replaced in peninsular Thailand by the similar Black-thighed Falconet, *Microhierax fringillarius*.)

REGION: SE, W, NE, FN

Plate 27

a White-bellied Sea-Eagle

b Crested Serpent-Eagle

c Eurasian Kestrel

d Pied Harrier

e Collared Falconet

Plate 28 (See also: Pheasants, p. 133)

Plate 28a
Scaly-breasted Partridge
Arborophila chloropus
ID: Medium-sized (29 cm, 10 in); upperparts and breast brown, barred black; belly rusty; legs green.
HABITAT: Thick undergrowth of forest from lowlands up to 1000 m (3300 ft) elevation.

REGION: SE, W, NE, FN

Plate 28b
Chinese Francolin
Francolinus pintadeanus
ID: Medium-sized (33 cm, 1.1 ft); white cheek and throat divided by black moustache; rest of body black and brown with distinctive white spotting and barring.
HABITAT: Grasslands and open dry deciduous forest up to 1500 m (5000 ft) elevation.

REGION: CP, SE, W, NE, FN

Plate 28c
Red Junglefowl
Gallus gallus
ID: Male large (76 cm, 2.5 ft), female medium-sized (43 cm, 1.4 ft); male with orange-red upperparts, long, dark green tail, red wattle and comb, dark green underparts; female upperparts brownish, underparts golden-brown.
HABITAT: Floor of primary and tall secondary forest up to 1800 m (5900 ft). This ancestor of the domestic chicken should be familiar to everyone, especially when the male crows its "cock-a-doodle-do" from the undergrowth.

REGION: PT, SE, W, NE, FN

Plate 28d
Silver Pheasant
Lophura nycthemera
ID: Male very large (1.2 m, 4 ft), female large (51 cm, 1.7 ft); male with silver gray upperparts, long white tail, black crest, black underparts, bright red legs, and bare face; female upperparts brown, underparts black, scaled white.
HABITAT: Primary and tall secondary forest floor from 700 to 2000 m (2100 to 6600 ft) elevation.

REGION: SE, W, NE, FN

Plate 28e
Great Argus
Argusianus argus
ID: Male very large (2 m, 6.6 ft), female large (76 cm, 2.5 ft); male brownish gray with extremely long wing and tail feathers, gray head; female similar but with normal-length wing and tail feathers.
HABITAT: Floor of evergreen primary forests of lowland peninsula up to 900 m (3000 ft) elevation.

REGION: PT

a Scaly-breasted Partridge
b Chinese Francolin
c Red Junglefowl
d Silver Pheasant
e Great Argus

Plate 29a
White-breasted Waterhen
Amaurornis phoenicurus
ID: Medium-sized (33 cm, 1.1 ft); dark slaty gray upperparts, white face and breast, rusty lower belly; short tail; long green legs.

HABITAT: Skulks at the edge of wet vegetation in marshes, flooded rice paddies, ponds, roadside ditches, and mangroves. Resident population, especially in peninsular Thailand, greatly supplemented in winter by migrant individuals from central and northern Asia.

REGION: PT, CP, SE, W, NE, FN

Plate 29b
Barred Buttonquail
Turnix suscitator
ID: Small (17 cm, 7 in); short tail, dark legs; body brown with dark barring; male with white throat and female with black throat.

HABITAT: Solitary or pairs skulking in agricultural areas and dry grassland with shrubs, from lowlands to 1500 m (5000 ft) elevation. (Replaced in moister grasslands and marsh edges by similar Yellow-legged Buttonquail, *Turnix tanki*, which is absent from the peninsula.)

REGION: PT, CP, SE, W, NE, FN

Plate 29c
Common Moorhen
Gallinula chloropus
ID: Medium-sized (33 cm, 1.1 ft); all dark slaty gray with white streak on side and undertail; bill bright red with yellow tip.

HABITAT: Pairs swimming among floating vegetation of marshes and ponds. Resident population greatly supplemented in winter by migrant individuals from central and northern Asia.

REGION: PT, CP, SE, W, NE, FN

Plate 29d
Bronze-winged Jacana
Metopidius indicus
ID: Medium-sized (28 cm, 11 in); head, neck, and breast glossy black with bold white eye-line; back and wings bronze-olive; tail rusty; long green legs with huge toes.

HABITAT: Walks boldly on floating lily pads and water vegetation.

REGION: PT, CP, W, NE, FN

Plate 29e
Masked Finfoot
Heliopais personata
ID: Large (56 cm, 1.8 ft); olive-brown and white with a black mask and bright yellow bill; throat black in male and white in female.

HABITAT: Shy and secretive, swimming duck-like in forest ponds and streams and among mangroves; when frightened, often runs like a rail across the muddy shore to hide in dense vegetation. A winter visitor to Thailand, primarily in the peninsula.

REGION: PT, SE, W, NE, FN

Plate 29

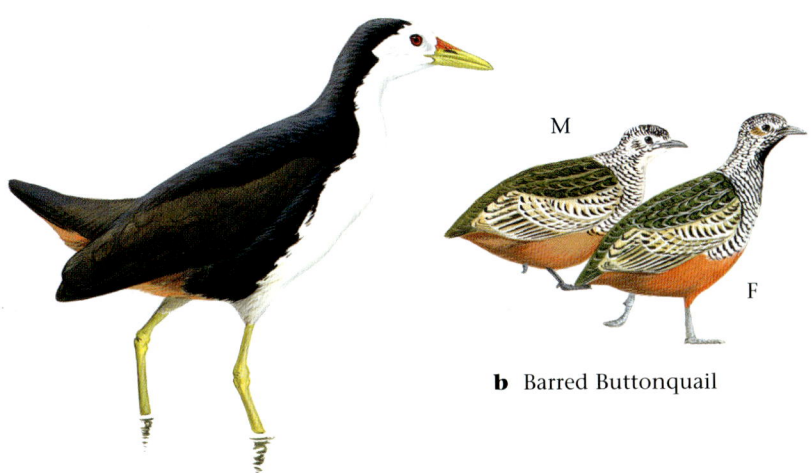

a White-breasted Waterhen

b Barred Buttonquail

c Common Moorhen

d Bronze-winged Jacana

e Masked Finfoot

Plate 30 (*See also:* Shorebirds (Waders), p. 131)

Plate 30a
Red-wattled Lapwing
Vanellus indicus
ID: Medium-sized (33 cm, 1.1 ft); black breast, throat, and head; large white ear patch; brown back and wings; white breast; white tail with black band on end.

HABITAT: Noisy resident of wet grassy areas, rice paddies, and upland grasslands.

REGION: PT, CP, SE, W, NE, FN

Plate 30b
Little Ringed Plover
Charadrius dubius
ID: Small (18 cm, 1.1 ft); upperparts brown; underparts white with brown (winter) or black (breeding) breast band and black mask; yellowish legs.

HABITAT: Muddy areas inland and along the coast; primarily a winter visitor but a few nest along riverbanks in the north.

REGION: PT, CP, SE, W, NE, FN

Plate 30c
Pacific Golden Plover
Pluvialis fulva
ID: Medium-sized (25 cm, 10 in); in non-breeding plumage, golden brown body and tail with dark spotting; in flight with pale brown underwings; in breeding plumage, breast black with broad white line running from above the eye along its flank. (Similar Gray [Black-bellied] Plover, *Pluvialis squatarola,* has a whitish rump and, in flight, pale gray underwings with black "wing pits.")

HABITAT: Both these plover species are common winter visitors to mudflats and grassy fields, but the Gray Plover is more restricted to the coast.

REGION: PT, CP, SE, W, NE, FN

Plate 30d
Common Redshank
Tringa totanus
ID: Small (28 cm, 11 in); upperparts and breast brownish, belly white with brown streaks; legs reddish; in flight a white back and trailing edge of wing. (Similar Spotted Redshank, *Tringa erythropus,* is a winter visitor mainly to northern Thailand, and in its winter plumage lacks the trailing edge of white in the wings.)

HABITAT: Muddy areas inland and along the coast; both species are winter visitors.

REGION: PT, CP, SE, W, NE

Plate 30e
Whimbrel
Numenius phaeopus
ID: Medium-sized (43 cm, 1.4 ft); upperparts dark brown with distinct dark crown stripes; underparts buffy brown; bill distinctly down-curved. (Similar Eurasian Curlew, *Numenius arquata,* is larger (58 cm, 1.8 ft), with all-brown head and longer down-curved bill.)

HABITAT: Muddy areas and sandy beaches along the coast and occasionally inland during migration; winter visitor.

REGION: PT, CP, SE

Plate 30

a Red-wattled Lapwing
b Little Ringed Plover
c Pacific Golden Plover
non-breeding
d Common Redshank
e Whimbrel

Plate 31a
Black-winged Stilt
Himantopus himantopus
ID: Medium-sized (37 cm, 1.2 ft); tall, slender with striking black back and wings; white head, breast, and tail; long thin legs pinkish red.

HABITAT: Primarily a winter visitor, but a small number nest south of Bangkok. Inland ponds, coastal estuaries, and mangrove swamps.

REGION: PT, CP, SE, NE, FN

Plate 31b
Marsh Sandpiper
Tringa stagnatilis
ID: Medium-sized (25 cm, 10 in); upperparts gray to dark gray; underparts whitish; legs green; bill thin and straight; in flight, white of tail extends as a wedge up the back.

HABITAT: A northern migrant wintering in Thailand. Solitary on stream sides, forested swamps, rice paddies, and coastal mudflats.

REGION: PT, CP, SE, NE

Plate 31c
Wood Sandpiper
Tringa glareola
ID: Medium-sized (23 cm, 9 in); upperparts and upper breast grayish brown with brown streaks; rest of underparts white; legs pinkish and eye-line white; in flight white confined to tail, which is barred black; underwings mottled white and brown; often bounces up and down as it walks. (The similar Green Sandpiper, *Tringa ochropus*, has green legs, a faint eye-ring, and in flight, dark underwings.)

HABITAT: A northern migrant wintering in Thailand. Usually in mixed-species flocks in freshwater mudflats and coastal estuaries.

REGION: PT, CP, SE, W, NE, FN

Plate 31d
Common Sandpiper
Actitis hypoleucos
ID: Medium-sized (20 cm, 8 in); upperparts brown; underparts white except for brown streaked neck; faint eye-line; legs pinkish; in flight brown tail has white bars on sides and the upper wings have a bold white stripe; bounces up and down while walking or resting; flies with a twittering, stiff-winged beat low over the water's surface.

HABITAT: A northern migrant wintering in Thailand. Solitary on muddy rivers, sandy beaches along lakes, roadside ditches, and rice paddy berms.

REGION: PT, CP, SE, W, NE, FN

Plate 31e
Oriental Pratincole
Glareola maldivarum
ID: Medium-sized (24 cm, 9 in); upperparts grayish brown; underparts tan to white; bold black and white crescent looping around throat; short red bill tipped black; on the ground resembles a plover, but in flight looks like a tern with black forked tail and white rump; wings long and pointed, underwings rusty colored.

HABITAT: A southern migrant nesting in Thailand during the summer. Small to large flocks on river beaches and rice paddies; flies like a swallow hawking insects out of the air, over marshes and moist grasslands, pastures, and rivers.

REGION: PT, CP, SE, W, NE, FN

Plate 31

a Black-winged Silt

b Marsh Sandpiper

c Wood Sandpiper

d Common Sandpiper

e Oriental Pratincole

Plate 32 (*See also:* Terns and Gulls, p. 130; Pigeons and Doves, p. 138)

Plate 32a
Whiskered Tern
Chlidonias hybridus
ID: Medium-sized (26 cm, 10 in); whitish gray; in non-breeding and immature plumage with a black line in back of eye and on extreme wingtips; in breeding plumage, breast light gray, cap black, and bill red.

HABITAT: Winter visitor to Thailand. Large flocks swoop and hover over estuaries and coastal waterways, and occasionally inland over freshwater ponds, lakes, and reservoirs.

REGION: PT, CP, SE, W, NE, FN

Plate 32b
Brown-headed Gull
Larus brunnicephalus
ID: Medium-sized (46 cm, 1.5 ft); back and wings light gray, wingtips black; rest of body white; bill red with black tip; legs reddish; in non-breeding plumage, head white with small black crescent in back of eye; in breeding plumage, head blackish brown.

HABITAT: Common winter visitor along the coast and occasionally on inland lakes and rivers.

REGION: PT, CP, SE, W, NE, FN

Plate 32c
Thick-billed Pigeon
Treron curvirostra
ID: Medium-sized (27 cm, 10 in); greenish except for maroon (male) or olive (female) back and yellow wing stripe; bill yellow with red base. Eleven other species of green pigeons in Thailand are similar but none is as common or widespread, and all of them lack a yellow bill.

HABITAT: Flocks of 5 to 40 individuals in fruiting trees of primary, tall secondary forest, and mangroves, from coast to 1200 m (4000 ft) elevation.

REGION: PT, SE, W, NE, FN

Plate 32d
Pied Imperial Pigeon
Ducula bicolor
ID: Medium-sized (41 cm, 1.3 ft); all white with black wing tips and tail.

HABITAT: Locally common in small to large flocks in treetops of coast and on coastal islands.

REGION: PT, SE

Plate 32e
Red Turtle-Dove
Streptopelia tranquebarica
ID: Medium-sized (23 cm, 9 in); male with gray head, reddish back, black wing tips and collar on neck; underparts pinkish; female brownish gray with black tail, wing tips, and collar on neck; both sexes in flight show the black tail with a conspicuous but incomplete white band at its tip.

HABITAT: Open forest, agricultural areas, and city parks.

REGION: CP, SE, W, NE, FN

Plate 32

a Whiskered Tern
breeding
non-breeding
non-breeding
b Brown-headed Gull
breeding
c Thick-billed Pigeon
d Pied Imperial Pigeon
e Red Turtle-Dove

Plate 33 (*See also:* Pigeons and Doves, p. 138; Parrots, p. 140)

Plate 33a
Zebra Dove
Geopelia striata
ID: Medium-sized (21 cm, 8 in); upperparts dark brown; gray face; nape of neck and flanks boldly barred black and white.
HABITAT: Pairs on ground and in low trees of open forest, tree plantations, gardens, parks, and agricultural areas in the lowlands.

REGION: PT, CP, SE, W, NE, FN

Plate 33b
Spotted Dove
Streptopelia chinensis
ID: Medium-sized (30 cm, 11 in); back and wings brown with black and white patches; tip of wings and tail black; broad black collar spotted white; head and underparts pinkish; in flight, long wedge-shaped tail with outer corners broadly tipped white.
HABITAT: Pairs or small family groups on ground and in low trees of open forest, tree plantations, gardens, parks, and agricultural areas, from lowlands up to 1800 m (6000 ft) elevation.

REGION: PT, CP, SE, W, NE, FN

Plate 33c
Emerald Dove
Chalcophaps indica
ID: Medium-sized (27 cm, 10 in); back and wings emerald green; crown and neck gray with white forehead and eye-line; rump banded black and white; underparts dark pinkish; bright red bill.
HABITAT: Solitary or in pairs on ground of evergreen and moist deciduous forest from lowlands up to 1500 m (5000 ft) elevation.

REGION: PT, SE, W, NE, FN

Plate 33d
Red-breasted Parakeet
Psittacula alexandri
ID: Medium-sized (38 cm, 1.3 ft); back, wings and long, pointed tail grass green; head blue-gray with black throat and forehead; upper breast pink; lower breast gray; bill bright red (male) or black (female).
HABITAT: Small flocks in fruiting trees of open forest, and agricultural areas of lowlands to 1200 m (5000 ft) elevation; often raid orchards and fields where they waddle across the ground eating fallen grain. (The similar Blossom-headed Parakeet, *Psittacula roseata,* occurs in similar habitats below 900 m (3000 ft) elevation, but it has an all green breast and a bill yellow above and black below.)

REGION: PT, CP, SE, W, NE, FN

Plate 33e
Vernal Hanging Parrot
Loriculus vernalis
ID: Small (14 cm, 5 in); all green except for a bright red rump and bill; very short square tail.
HABITAT: Pairs or small family groups high in canopy of deciduous and evergreen forest, from lowlands up to 1500 m (4000 ft) elevation. Their name comes from the peculiar habit of sleeping upside down while hanging from a small branch like a bat. (Replaced in extreme southern peninsular Thailand by the similar Blue-crowned Hanging Parrot, *Loriculus galgulus,* which has a black bill and the male has a bright red triangle on the upper breast.)

REGION: PT, SE, W, NE, FN

Plate 33

a Zebra Dove

b Spotted Dove

c Emerald Dove

d Red-breasted Parakeet

e Vernal Hanging Parrot

Plate 34 (See also: Cuckoos, p. 142)

Plate 34a
Plaintive Cuckoo
Cacomantis merulinus
ID: Medium-sized (23 cm, 9 in); upperparts charcoal brown; throat and upper breast gray; rest of breast and belly rusty.

HABITAT: Singly in open forest, secondary growth, parks, and cultivated areas up to 1800 m (6000 ft) elevation.

REGION: PT, CP, SE, W, NE, FN

Plate 34b
Common Koel
Eudynamys scolopacea
ID: Medium-sized (43 cm, 1.4 ft); long-tailed with red eye; male all black; female boldly spotted and barred brown and buffy-white.

HABITAT: Often silent and unobtrusive, this is a common species in open forest, parklands, gardens, and mangroves. During the breeding season, however, when it lays its eggs in the nests of Large-billed Crows, *Corvus macrorhyncos,* the males scream their name, "ko-EL," in progressively louder calls day and night.)

REGION: PT, CP, SE, W, NE, FN

Plate 34c
Green-billed Malkoha
Phaenicophaeus tristis
ID: Large (51 cm, 2 ft); extremely long tail tipped white; red patch around eye; upperparts gray-green; underparts gray.

HABITAT: Skulks in thick tangles and forest canopy; flies clumsily and slowly across openings in secondary and primary forests of lowlands up to 1500 m (5000 ft) elevation.

REGION: PT, CP, SE, W, NE, FN

Plate 34d
Greater Coucal
Centropus sinensis
ID: Large (53 cm, 1.7 ft); all black with rusty back and wings.

HABITAT: Tall grass and shrubby areas, savannah, mangroves, and agricultural fields up to 1500 m (5000 ft) elevation; usually on or near the ground. (Replaced in marshier areas by similar Lesser Coucal, *Centropus bengalensis,* which is smaller (38 cm, 1.3 ft) and has a streaked back in breeding plumage; all brown with buffy steaks in non-breeding plumage.)

REGION: PT, CP, SE, W, NE, FN

Plate 34

a Plaintive Cuckoo

b Common Koel

M

F

c Green-billed Malkoha

d Greater Coucal

Plate 35 (See also: Owls, p. 143; Frogmouths, p. 145)

Plate 35a
Asian Barred Owlet
Glaucidium cuculoides
ID: Medium-sized (23 cm, 9 in); upperparts brown, barred black; underparts brown with barring and streaks; white throat patch.

HABITAT: Primarily diurnal, often found sitting in the open on bare branches or dead tree stumps hunting for large insects, lizards, and small birds; often noticed by the alarm calls and mobbing behavior of flocks of small birds; forest edge from lowlands to pine forests at 1800 m (6000 ft).

REGION: PT, CP, SE, W, NE, FN

Plate 35b
Spotted Owlet
Athene brama
ID: Medium-sized (21 cm, 8 in); upperparts gray-brown, spotted white; underparts gray brown, barred white; prominent white line over eye and on throat.

HABITAT: Generally crepuscular and nocturnal but also often active during the daytime in open scrub and agricultural areas of the lowlands. When not roosting, perches in obvious sites such as fence posts, telephone wires, and bare branch tips. In the daytime, often noticed by the mobbing behavior of small birds around it.

REGION: SE, CP, NE, FN

Plate 35c
Javan Frogmouth
Batrachostomus javensis
ID: Medium-sized (25 cm, 10 in); rusty brown with silver spots on wings and breast; huge head; short, broad bill.

HABITAT: Active nocturnally in moist lowland forest, dense secondary vegetation, and bamboo areas. During the day roosts immobile and upright on a thin branch in lower parts of dark forest. Three other frogmouth species occur in Thailand, but they are rarer and have very restricted ranges within the country.

REGION: PT, SE, W, FN

Plate 35d
Brown Hawk-Owl
Ninox scutulata
ID: Medium-sized (32 cm, 1 ft); upperparts dark grayish brown with white forehead; underparts buffy with broad brown stripes; resembles a large, round-headed hawk, but generally not active during the day.

HABITAT: Solitary or in pairs roosting during the daytime in shaded vegetation; active at dusk and during the night in open forest, especially in the vicinity of water, from lowlands up to 1200 m (4000 ft) elevation. Winter visitor to CP and resident elsewhere.

REGION: PT, CP, SE, W, NE, FN

Plate 35e
Brown Fish-Owl
Ketupa zeylonensis
ID: Large (53 cm, 1.7 ft); rusty brown breast with narrow dark streaks; rusty-colored feather tufts extend from top of head like ears; legs unfeathered.

HABITAT: Solitary or in pairs roosting in sheltered vegetation near water; often active during the day but more commonly crepuscular and nocturnal when it sits on a stump or rock above the water, scooping fish, crabs, and frogs from the surface with its talons.

REGION: PT, W, NE, FN

Plate 35

a Asian Barred Owlet
b Spotted Owlet
c Javan Frogmouth
d Brown Hawk-Owl
e Brown Fish-Owl

Plate 36 (See also: Trogons, p. 146; Nightjars, p. 145)

Plate 36a
Orange-breasted Trogon
Harpactes oreskios
ID: Medium-sized (31 cm, 1 ft); male upperparts reddish brown with olive head; underparts orangish; female upperparts olive-brown; underparts orange with gray throat.

HABITAT: Low to mid levels of secondary and primary forest from lowlands to 1100 m (3300 ft) elevation.

REGION: PT, SE, W, NE, FN

Plate 36b
Red-headed Trogon
Harpactes erythrocephalus
ID: Medium-sized (35 cm, 1.1 ft); male upperparts rusty brown with bright red head and underparts; female similar but with an all-brown head; white crescent on breast in both sexes.

HABITAT: Singly or in pairs sitting upright below the forest canopy from lowlands to 2000 m (6600 ft) elevation; most noticed when they suddenly fly out to catch insects.

REGION: PT, SE, W, NE, FN

Plate 36c
Great Eared Nightjar
Eurostopodus macrotis
ID: Medium-sized (41 cm, 1.3 ft); bill short and wide; upperparts mottled gray, buff, and rusty; underparts buffy-white, barred black.

HABITAT: Crepuscular and nocturnal, when it circles high over forests and low over clearings with deep wing beats and gliding, often in pairs or small flocks; sharp whistled notes given in flight make it apparent. Spends the day roosting on the ground in undergrowth vegetation.

REGION: PT, SE, W, NE, FN

Plate 36d
Large-tailed Nightjar
Caprimulgus macrurus
ID: Medium-sized (33 cm, 1 ft); upperparts mottled brown, buffy, and rusty; underparts brown, finely barred dark; buffy line over eye; white moustache and throat patch.

HABITAT: Singly or in pairs hawking low over clearings and open forest, from lowlands to 2000 m (6600 ft) elevation; crepuscular and nocturnal. Often seen at night sitting on a path or road, its eyes reflecting bright red.

REGION: PT, CP, SE, W, NE, FN

Plate 36

a Orange-breasted Trogon

b Red-headed Trogon

c Great Eared Nightjar

d Large-tailed Nightjar

Plate 37a
Banded Kingfisher
Lacedo pulchella
ID: Medium-sized (23 cm, 9 in); male upperparts blue with black and white bars, underparts rusty with white throat and belly; female upperparts rusty barred black, underparts white with sparse black spots; both sexes with bright red bill.
HABITAT: In pairs or singly in mid to low parts of moist forest from lowlands to 1100 m (3300 ft) elevation.

REGION: PT, SE, W, NE, FN

Plate 37b
Common Kingfisher
Alcedo atthis
ID: Small (18 cm, 7 in); upperparts blue with a lighter blue back and rump; underparts rusty; white throat and ear patch; short tail.
HABITAT: Common winter visitor and rare summer resident along lowland streams, canals, ponds, and roadside ditches. Usually seen on branch, fence post, or some open perch over water, waiting to dive for a fish.

REGION: PT, CP, SE, W, NE, FN

Plate 37c
Black-capped Kingfisher
Halcyon pileata
ID: Medium-sized (30 cm, 1 ft); head black; back, wings, and tail dark blue; underparts buff white; large bill and legs coral red; conspicuous white wing patches in flight.
HABITAT: Winter visitor to lowland streams and lakes, but especially common in mangroves along the coast.

REGION: PT, CP, SE, W, NE, FN

Plate 37d
Collared Kingfisher
Halcyon chloris
ID: Medium-sized (24 cm, 9.5 in); upperparts greenish blue; underparts white; line in front of eye and collar white; bill blackish.
HABITAT: Resident along large inland rivers but most common in mangrove areas and rice paddies near the coast; occasionally in moist parklands and gardens.

REGION: PT, CP, SE, W, NE

Plate 37e
White-throated Kingfisher
Halcyon smyrnensis
ID: Medium-sized (28 cm, 11 in); back, wings, and tail bright turquoise blue; head and lower belly chestnut; throat white; large bill and legs coral red; large white wing patch obvious in flight.
HABITAT: In pairs or singly perched conspicuously on a fence post, telephone wire, or branch in a wide variety of habitats, often away from water.

REGION: PT, CP, SE, W, NE, FN

Plate 37

a Banded Kingfisher

M

F

b Common Kingfisher

c Black-capped Kingfisher

d Collared Kingfisher

e White-throated Kingfisher

Plate 38 (See also: Bee-eaters and Rollers, p. 148)

Plate 38a
Indian Roller
Coracias benghalensis
ID: Medium-sized (33 cm, 1.1 ft); large head, all dark olive and blue when perched; in flight, reveals spectacular flashes of blue and purple in the broad wings and tail.

HABITAT: Singly or in pairs perched on telephone wires, fence posts, plowed fields, and tall dead trees in open areas, lowlands to 1500 m (5000 ft) elevation.

REGION: PT, CP, SE, W, NE, FN

Plate 38b
Chestnut-headed Bee-eater
Merops leschenaulti
ID: Medium-sized (21 cm, 9 in); head and back rusty; face yellow; rump in flight pale blue; rest of body lime green.

HABITAT: Flocks of 5 to 30 perched in tops of bare tree branches or telephone wires. Flies out to catch insects and makes swooping glides back to the perch; very noisy. Resident in open forest and agricultural areas from coast to 1800 m (6000 ft) elevation.

REGION: PT, CP, SE, W, NE, FN

Plate 38c
Blue-bearded Bee-eater
Nyctyornis athertoni
ID: Medium-sized (35 cm, 1.2 ft); green with blue throat and crown; yellow belly streaked green.

HABITAT: Singly or in pairs perched high in forests from low plains to 900 m (3000 ft) elevation.

REGION: SE, W, NE, FN

Plate 38d
Red-bearded Bee-eater
Nyctyornis amictus
ID: Medium-sized (32 cm, 1 ft); green with brilliant red forehead, face, and throat; violet crown.

HABITAT: Singly or in pairs perched high in moist forests from low plains to 1500 m (5000 ft) elevation.

REGION: PT, W

Plate 38e
Green Bee-eater
Merops orientalis
ID: Medium-sized (21 cm, 8 in); green with rust on head and neck; black eye-line and crescent on upper chest; peculiar central tail feathers extend well beyond rest of tail.

HABITAT: Small flocks or singly in open habitats, from coast to 1500 m (5000 ft). Often associated with grazing cattle, on which they perch to capture insects scared up from the grass.

REGION: SE, CP, W, NE, FN

Plate 38

a Indian Roller

b Chestnut-headed Bee-eater

c Blue-bearded Bee-eater

d Red-bearded Bee-eater

e Green Bee-eater

Plate 39 (*See also:* Hornbills, p. 150)

Plate 39a
Oriental Pied Hornbill
Anthracoceros albirostris
ID: Large (70 cm, 2.3 ft); black with white belly and tail tip; banana-shaped casque on top of upper mandible. Tail completely white in peninsular part of range.

HABITAT: Open primary and tall secondary forest usually near water, from coast to 1400 m (4600 ft) elevation.

REGION: PT, SE, W, NE, FN

Plate 39b
Great Hornbill
Buceros bicornis
ID: Very large (1.3 m, 4.3 ft); black with buffy neck; white tail with black band across middle. In flight, yellowish wing stripe is obvious. Huge casque on top of head and upper mandible.

HABITAT: Pairs or small flocks in canopy of tall forest from lowlands to 1500 m (5000 ft). In flight, their huge wings sound like a freight train moving through the trees.

REGION: PT, SE, W, NE, FN

Plate 39c
Brown Hornbill
Ptilolaemus tickelli
ID: Large (76 cm, 2.5 ft); upperparts brown; underparts rusty. In flight, all dark with tip of wings and tail white.

HABITAT: Small flocks of 5 to 10 in the canopy of tall forest between 500 and 1500 m (1650 and 5000 ft) elevation.

REGION: SE, W, NE, FN

Plate 39d
Wreathed Hornbill
Rhyticeros undulatus
ID: Large (1 m, 3.3 ft); all black except for the entirely white tail and white face, throat, and neck of male; both sexes with peculiar yellowish (male) or bluish (female) pouch on throat.

HABITAT: Pairs and small flocks in canopy of tall forest between 200 and 1800 m (660 and 6000 ft) elevation.

REGION: PT, SE, W, NE, FN

Plate 39e
Bushy-crested Hornbill
Anorrhinus galeritus
ID: Large (89 cm, 2.9 ft); almost entirely blackish with small white spot at base of mandible and pale gray base of tail.

HABITAT: Small groups in canopy of peninsular evergreen forest.

REGION: PT

Plate 39

a Oriental Pied Hornbill

b Great Hornbill

c Brown Hornbill

d Wreathed Hornbill

e Bushy-crested Hornbill

Plate 40 (See also: Barbets, p. 151; Woodpeckers, p. 152)

Plate 40a
Great Barbet
Megalaima virens
ID: Medium-sized (33 cm, 1.1 ft); large yellow bill; blue-black head; maroon-brown back; green tail; brown breast that grades into yellow belly with gray stripes; bright patch of red undertail.

HABITAT: Singly or in small flocks in tall trees of mountain forests, from 600 to 2500 m (2000 to 8250 ft) elevation.

REGION: W, NE, FN

Plate 40b
Lineated Barbet
Megalaima lineata
ID: Medium-sized (28 cm, 11 in); grass green with head broadly streaked light buff; large yellowish bill.

HABITAT: Singly or in pairs in moist forest, tall secondary forest, gardens, and parklands, from lowlands to 800 m (2640 ft) elevation; primarily along the coast on the peninsula.

REGION: PT, CP, SE, W, NE, FN

Plate 40c
Blue-eared Barbet
Megalaima australis
ID: Small (17 cm, 7 in); green with blue throat and crown; red patches above and below blue ear patch.

HABITAT: Solitary or in flocks at fruiting trees at the tops of primary and tall secondary forest, from lowlands to 1500 m (5000 ft) elevation.

REGION: PT, SE, W, NE, FN

Plate 40d
Red-throated Barbet
Megalaima mystacophanos
ID: Medium-sized (23 cm, 9 in), green; male with red and yellow crown and red throat; female with blue and red crown and blue and white throat.

HABITAT: Pairs and small family groups at fruiting trees in lowland evergreen forest.

REGION: PT, W

Plate 40e
Coppersmith Barbet
Megalaima haemacephala
ID: Medium-sized (15 cm, 6 in); upperparts green; forehead and breast band red; throat and small patches above and below eye bright yellow; underparts streaked green; short tail. Most often noticed by its monotonous song, like a small hammer hitting metal over and over again in the middle of the day.

HABITAT: Singly or in pairs in open lowland habitats, mangroves, gardens, and parklands in large cities.

REGION: PT, CP, SE, W, NE, FN

Plate 40f
Speckled Piculet
Picumnus innominatus
ID: Small (10 cm, 4 in); yellow-olive back and wings; head black with white stripes over and under eye; underparts yellowish white with black spots and bars; tail very short.

HABITAT: Singly or in pairs in mixed-species foraging flocks creeping on small branches in mid to low parts of moist secondary forest and bamboo, from 300 to 1800 m (1000 to 6000 ft) elevation.

REGION: W, NE, FN

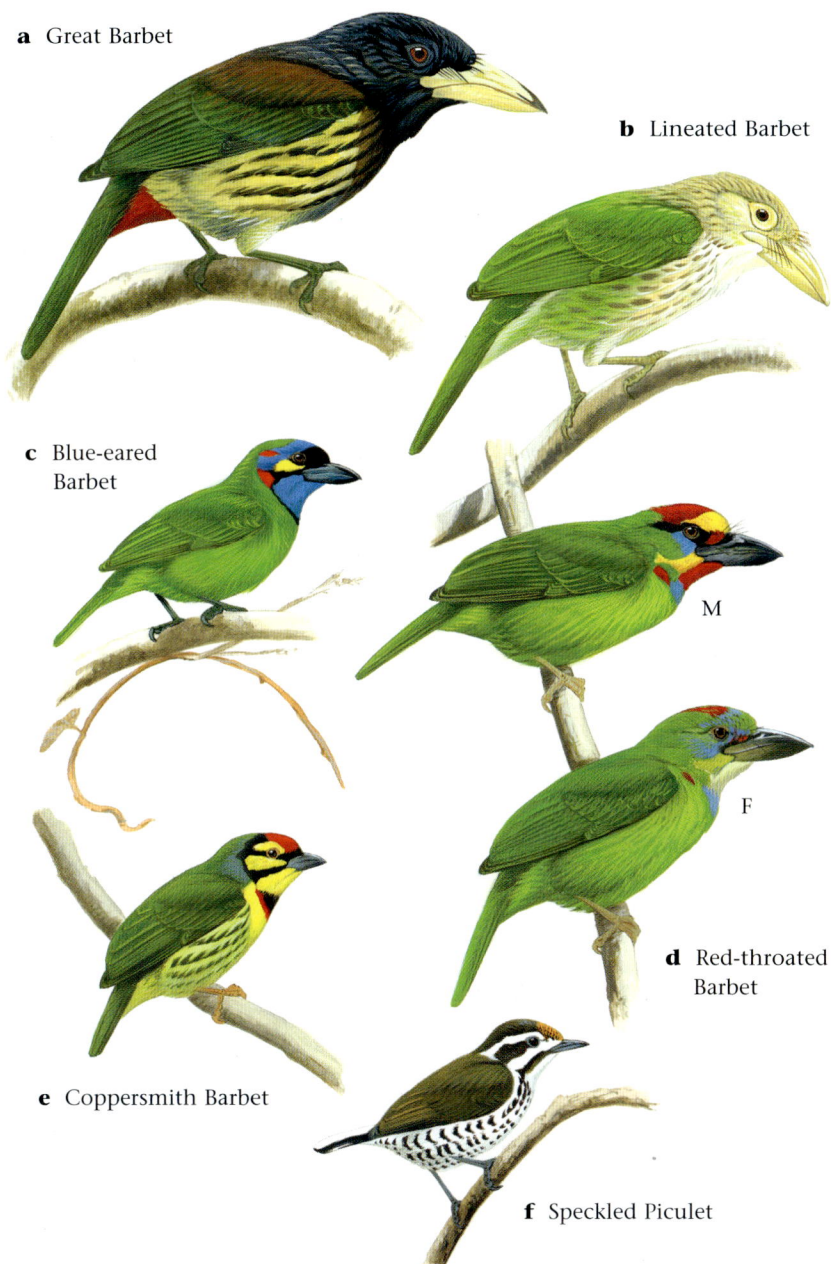

a Great Barbet
b Lineated Barbet
c Blue-eared Barbet
d Red-throated Barbet
e Coppersmith Barbet
f Speckled Piculet

Plate 41a
Rufous Woodpecker
Celeus brachyurus
ID: Medium-sized (25 cm, 10 in); dark chestnut, heavily barred black.

HABITAT: Pairs in primary and secondary forest, plantations, and mangroves; often associated with tree ant nests, in which it regularly constructs its own nest cavity.

REGION: PT, CP, SE, W, NE, FN

Plate 41b
Common Flameback
Dinopium javanense
ID: Medium-sized (30 cm, 1 ft); golden back and wings, crimson rump; boldly striped black and white on head and neck; underparts white, scalloped black; crested head red (male) or black, streaked white (female).

HABITAT: Pairs on tree trunks in open lowland forest, gardens, parklands, and mangroves.

REGION: PT, CP, SE, W, NE, FN

Plate 41c
Laced Woodpecker
Picus vittatus
ID: Medium-sized (31 cm, 1 ft); upperparts olive-green; breast yellowish and rest of underparts white, scaled black; crown red (male) or black (female).

HABITAT: Tree trunks in a wide range of primary and secondary forests, gardens, bamboo, and parklands, from coastal lowlands to 1500 m (5000 ft) elevation. Often feeds on the ground.

REGION: CP, SE, W, NE, FN

Plate 41d
Gray-capped Woodpecker
Picoides canicapillus
ID: Small (15 cm, 6 in); upperparts black with white spots; underparts white with fine dark streaks; crown gray (female) or gray and red (male).

HABITAT: Active on outer twigs and small branches of treetops and forest edge, from lowlands to 1800 m (6000 ft) elevation.

REGION: PT, SE, W, NE, FN

Plate 41e
Heart-spotted Woodpecker
Hemicircus canente
ID: Small (15 cm, 6 in); short rounded tail; black with white wing stripes and underparts; black markings on white wing stripes are heart-shaped; female with white forehead.

HABITAT: Moist, dense lowland forest up to 900 m (2700 ft) elevation.

REGION: PT, SE, W, NE, FN

Plate 41

a Rufous Woodpecker

b Common Flameback

c Laced Woodpecker

d Gray-capped Woodpecker

e Heart-spotted Woodpecker

Plate 42a
White-bellied Woodpecker
Dryocopus javensis
ID: Medium-sized (46 cm, 1.5 ft); black with white rump (black rump in peninsula) and lower belly; crest red.

HABITAT: Solitarily or in pairs, noisy and conspicuous in lowland forests and mangroves, usually in dead trees.

REGION: PT, SE, W, NE, FN

Plate 42b
Great Slaty Woodpecker
Muelleripicus pulverulentus
ID: Large (50 cm, 1.7 ft); all gray with a buffy throat patch and orange (male) whisker; the largest Old World woodpecker.

HABITAT: Pairs are noisy and conspicuous as they forage high on the trunks of large trees in lowlands up to 1000 m (3300 ft) elevation. Usually flies long distances to the next large tree.

REGION: PT, SE, W, NE, FN

Plate 42c
Crimson-winged Woodpecker
Picus puniceus
ID: Medium-sized (25 cm, 10 in); back, breast, and face olive-green; wings, moustache (male), and crown bright red; tip of crest yellow.

HABITAT: Pairs on tall emergent trees in lowland forest, often in mixed-species foraging flocks.

REGION: PT, W

Plate 42d
Greater Yellownape
Picus flavinucha
ID: Medium-sized (34 cm, 1.1 ft); back and wings bright green; crest bright yellow and throat buffy; rest of underparts gray; in flight, wings rusty with black barring.

HABITAT: Pairs in open forest from lowlands to 2000 m (6600 ft) elevation. Often found in mixed-species foraging flocks of drongos and babblers.

REGION: SE, W, NE, FN

Plate 42

a White-bellied Woodpecker

b Great Slaty Woodpecker

c Crimson-winged Woodpecker

d Greater Yellownape

Plate 43a
Dusky Broadbill
Corydon sumatranus
ID: Medium-sized (28 cm, 11 in); black with large pink bill and bare patch around eye, buffy throat patch.
HABITAT: Moist forest from lowlands to 1000 m (3300 ft) elevation.

REGION: PT, SE, W, NE, FN

Plate 43b
Black-and-yellow Broadbill
Eurylaimus ochromalus
ID: Small (17 cm, 7 in); upperparts black with yellow rump and wing stripe and white collar; underparts pinkish yellow with black and white bands on throat.
HABITAT: Moist lowland forest to 700 m (2300 ft) elevation.

REGION: PT, W

Plate 43c
Long-tailed Broadbill
Psarisomus dalhousiae
ID: Medium-sized (27 cm, 11 in); grass-green with long blue tail, black head and bright yellow chin and throat.
HABITAT: In loose flocks of 15 to 30 birds overhead in moist forest, from 300 to 2000 m (1000 to 6600 ft) elevation; often so tame they are easily approached.

REGION: PT, SE, W, NE, FN

Plate 43d
Blue Pitta
Pitta cyanea
ID: Medium-sized (23 cm, 9 in); upperparts cobalt blue (male) or olive (female) with orange crown, black eye-stripe, and buffy cheek; underparts blue with fine black barring; short tail and long legs.
HABITAT: Singly on ground in dark undergrowth of moist forests, from lowlands to 1500 m (5000 ft) elevation.

REGION: PT, SE, W, NE, FN

Plate 43e
Gurney's Pitta
Pitta gurneyi
ID: Medium-sized (22 cm, 9 in); back and wings brown, tail blue; black mask; crown blue (male) or orange (female); underparts black with yellow barring (male) or buffy (female).
HABITAT: Floor of moist bamboo and dense lowland forest of peninsular Thailand.

REGION: PT

Note: this species is endangered, CITES Appendix I listed.

Plate 43

a Dusky Broadbill
b Black-and-yellow Broadbill
c Long-tailed Broadbill
d Blue Pitta
e Gurney's Pitta

Plate 44 (See also: Swifts, Treeswifts, and Swallows, p. 156)

Plate 44a
House Swift
Apus affinis
ID: Small (15 cm, 6 in); blackish with conspicuous white rump, white throat, and short squared tail.

HABITAT: Loose flocks flying rapidly over agricultural areas and buildings hawking insects from the air. Nests in colonies under the eaves of houses, under bridges, and in temples. Primarily in lowlands but often seen up to 2000 m (6600 ft) elevation during warm months.

REGION: PT, CP, SE, W, NE, FN

Plate 44b
Asian Palm-Swift
Cypsiurus balasiensis
ID: Small (13 cm, 5 in); grayish brown; tail often spread in flight to reveal deep fork, otherwise appears pointed.

HABITAT: Loose groups twittering as they hawk insects from the air over open country and agricultural areas with palm trees, but also over forests; mainly in lowlands but often up to 1000 m (3300 ft) elevation.

REGION: PT, CP, SE, W, NE, FN

Plate 44c
Crested Treeswift
Hemiprocne coronata
ID: Medium-sized (23 cm, 9 in); blue-gray with dark wings and a long needle-like tail often spread in flight to show a deep fork; when perched, its backward-curving crest is raised and the rusty cheeks of the male become obvious. (Replaced in peninsula by smaller, bronzy-colored Whiskered Treeswift, *Hemiprocne comata*, which has two obvious white stripes on the head, one above and the other below the eye.)

HABITAT: Small family groups hawking insects high over treetops of open forests; often perches upright on tips of treetops, telephone poles, and other exposed points.

REGION: W, NE, FN

Plate 44d
Barn Swallow
Hirundo rustica
ID: Small (15 cm, 6 in); upperparts dark blue; underparts white (non-breeding) to pinkish (breeding) with rusty throat; long tail deeply forked. (Supplemented in coastal areas by the similar Pacific Swallow, *Hirundo tahitica*, which is a nesting resident and has a shorter tail, gray underwings, and a rusty forehead.)

HABITAT: Winter visitor to Thailand, but may breed rarely in the northern mountains. Usually seen flying low over open fields, water, and grassy areas. At night, often roosts together in large numbers, especially in reed beds and cane fields.

REGION: PT, CP, SE, W, NE, FN

Plate 44e
Striated Swallow
Hirundo striolata
ID: Small (18 cm, 7 in); upperparts dark blue with a conspicuous rusty rump; underparts buffy white with heavy streaks except for black undertail (underparts uniformly chestnut in the southern peninsula); deeply forked tail.

HABITAT: Pairs and family groups hawking insects overhead, often near water.

REGION: PT, CP, SE, W, NE, FN

Plate 45 (*See also:* Pipits and Cuckoo-shrikes, p. 158)

Plate 45a
Gray Wagtail
Motacilla cinerea
ID: Small (18 cm, 7 in); upperparts gray with yellow rump conspicuous in flight; black wings and tail; underparts yellowish. (The similar Yellow Wagtail, *Motacilla flava,* has an olive back and lacks the yellow rump.)

HABITAT: Common winter visitor to open grassy areas, usually near water, from lowlands to mountaintops. The Yellow Wagtail is also a common winter visitor, but more often encountered in coastal areas near mangroves and reed beds.

REGION: PT, CP, SE, W, NE, FN

Plate 45b
White Wagtail
Motacilla alba
ID: Small (18 cm, 7 in); upperparts black and dark gray with conspicuous white patches in wing and tail; underparts white with black crescent on chest.

HABITAT: Common winter visitor in open grasslands, river edges, marshes, and rice paddies. Singly or in small flocks walking or running on the ground, wagging tail up and down.

REGION: PT, CP, SE, W, NE, FN

Plate 45c
Paddyfield Pipit
(also called Paddy Pipit)
Anthus rufulus
ID: Small (15 cm, 6 in); upperparts dark brown streaked buffy; underparts buffy streaked brown; pinkish legs.

HABITAT: Walks and runs on the ground in dry grassy areas, lawns, city parks, and rice paddies, from lowlands to 1800 m (6000 ft) elevation.

REGION: PT, CP, SE, W, NE, FN

Plate 45d
Scarlet Minivet
Pericrocotus flammeus
ID: Small (21 cm, 8 in); male head and back black; breast, rump, and wing and tail patches brilliant red; female grayish with yellow underparts, rump, and patches in wing and tail. (Six additional species of similarly colored minivets occur in Thailand, but they are less common and more restricted in their distributions.)

HABITAT: Pairs or small groups in mixed-species foraging flocks in canopy of primary and secondary forests, from lowlands to 1700 m (5600 ft) elevation.

REGION: PT, SE, W, NE, FN

Plate 45e
Large Cuckoo-Shrike
Coracina macei
ID: Medium-sized (28 cm, 11 in); entirely bluish gray with black mask, wings, and tail and white lower belly; white rump obvious only in flight.

HABITAT: Noisy pairs sitting conspicuously in tops of trees in open forests, from lowlands to 1800 m (6000 ft) elevation.

REGION: SE, W, NE, FN

a Gray Wagtail
nonbreeding
breeding
b White Wagtail
c Paddyfield Pipit
d Scarlet Minivet
e Large Cuckoo-Shrike

Plate 46 (See also: Ioras and Leafbirds, p. 159)

Plate 46a
Common Iora
Aegithina tiphia
ID: Small (14 cm, 5 in); upperparts olive and black with two conspicuous white wing bars, tail black (male) or olive (female); underparts bright yellow. (Largely replaced in denser lowland forests by the similar Great Iora, *Aegithina lafresnayei,* which is somewhat larger (17 cm, 6.5 in) and lacks the wing bars.)

HABITAT: Pairs in mixed-species foraging flocks of open forest, gardens, mangroves, and secondary growth from lowlands to 1500 m (5000 ft) elevation.

REGION: PT, CP, SE, W, NE, FN

Plate 46b
Golden-fronted Leafbird
Chloropsis aurifrons
ID: Small (19 cm, 7 in); bright grass-green with orange forehead, black chin and throat, and blue shoulder patch.

HABITAT: Pairs or small flocks in mid to upper branches of secondary lowland forests.

REGION: SE, W, NE, FN

Plate 46c
Blue-winged Leafbird
Chloropsis cochinchinensis
ID: Small (18 cm, 7 in); grass-green with blue patches in wing and tail, male with black throat surrounded by yellow ring.

HABITAT: Secondary forest, forest edges, plantations, isolated trees in agricultural areas, and gardens, from lowland to 1200 m (4000 ft) elevation. Often aggressively protects flowering tree nectar sources from other birds.

REGION: PT, SE, W, NE, FN

Plate 46d
Asian Fairy-bluebird
Irena puella
ID: Medium-sized (27 cm, 11 in); male upperparts deep cobalt blue with black wings and tail, underparts and face black; female dark blue-green.

HABITAT: Pairs or family groups in treetops of dense moist forests from lowlands to 1500 m (5000 ft) elevation.

REGION: PT, SE, W, NE, FN

Plate 46

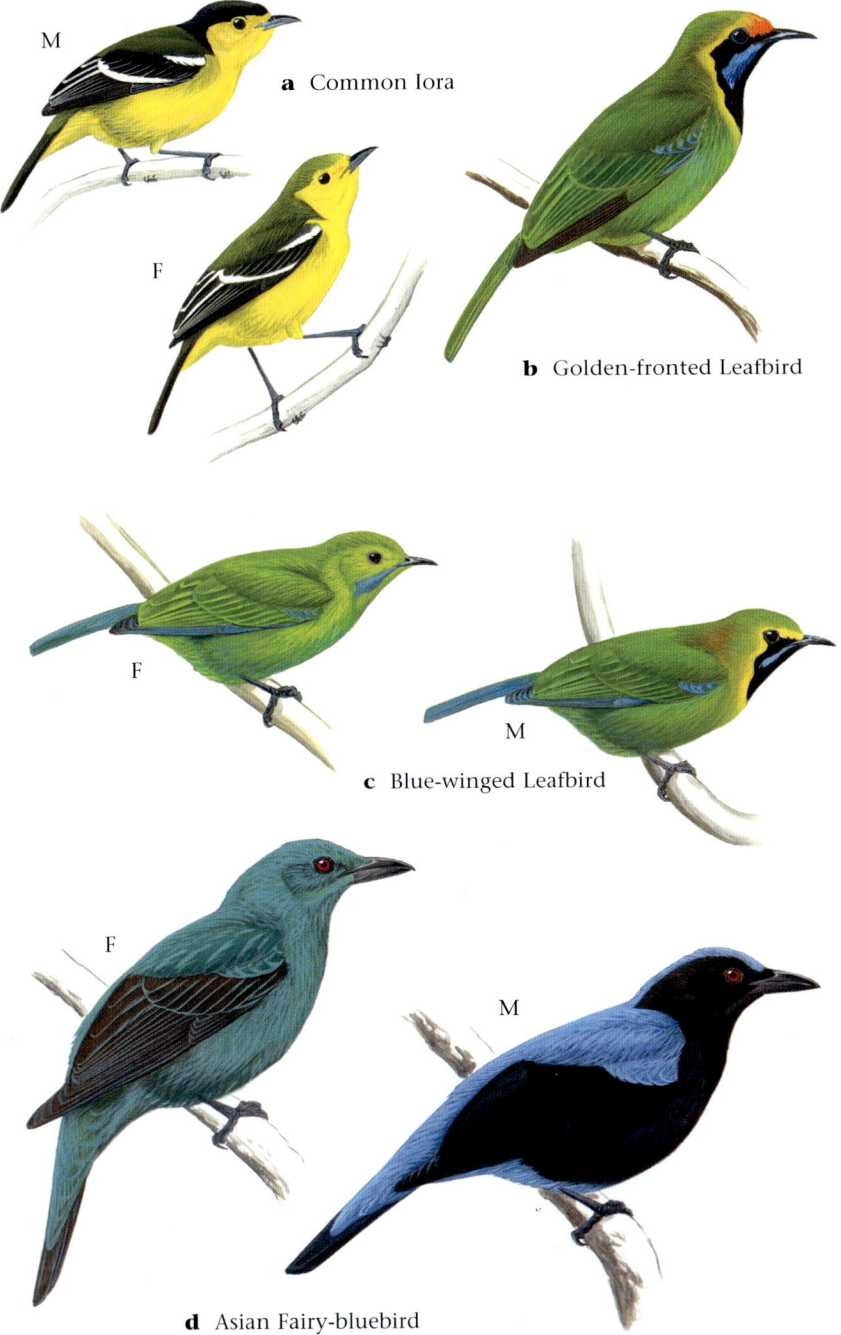

a Common Iora

b Golden-fronted Leafbird

c Blue-winged Leafbird

d Asian Fairy-bluebird

Plate 47 (See also: Bulbuls, p. 160)

Plate 47a
Black-crested Bulbul
Pycnonotus melanicterus
ID: Small (19 cm, 7.5 in); upperparts olive green; underparts bright yellow; head and short crest black; eye white.

HABITAT: Pairs or small flocks in the tops of fruiting trees in secondary and primary forest, from lowlands to 2000 m (6600 ft) elevation. (Similar Black-headed Bulbul, *Pycnonotus atriceps*, of scrubby lowland forest lacks crest, has an olive breast and a yellow band on the tail tip.)

REGION: PT, CP, SE, W, NE, FN

Plate 47b
Red-whiskered Bulbul
Pycnonotus jocosus
ID: Medium-sized (20 cm, 8 in); long, thin black crest, black crown and side of neck; back and tail olive-brown; underparts white except for bright red undertail and patch in back of eye.

HABITAT: Secondary forest, shrubby fields, gardens, and open agricultural areas, from lowlands to 1800 m (6000 ft) elevation.

REGION: PT, CP, SE, W, NE, FN

Plate 47c
Sooty-headed Bulbul
Pycnonotus aurigaster
ID: Medium-sized (20 cm, 8 in); black face and crown with short crest; upperparts grayish brown with pale gray rump; underparts pale gray with either a bright red or bright yellow undertail patch.

HABITAT: Secondary forest, shrubby fields, gardens, and open agricultural areas, from lowlands to 1800 m (6000 ft) elevation.

REGION: CP, SE, W, NE, FN

Plate 47d
Black Bulbul
Hypsipetes madagascariensis
ID: Medium-sized (25 cm, 10 in); all black with coral red bill and legs.

HABITAT: Noisy family groups in treetops of mountain forests.

REGION: W, NE, FN

Plate 47e
Streak-eared Bulbul
Pycnonotus blanfordi
ID: Medium-sized (20 cm, 8 in); brownish with gray streaked ear patches, yellowish lower belly, and gray eye.

HABITAT: Secondary forest, gardens, and open agricultural areas in lowlands; common in Bangkok city parks.

REGION: PT, CP, SE, W, NE, FN

Plate 47

a Black-crested Bulbul

b Red-whiskered Bulbul

c Sooty-headed Bulbul

d Black Bulbul

e Streak-eared Bulbul

Plate 48a
Greater Racket-tailed Drongo
Dicrurus paradiseus
ID: Medium-sized (32 cm, 1.1 ft) with a tail that adds 35 cm (1.2 ft) to its overall length; glossy black with a conspicuous crest and an even more conspicuous tail with two wire-like extensions with feathered flags at their ends.

HABITAT: Moist forest edge, plantations, and broken canopy in lowlands.

REGION: PT, CP, SE, W, NE, FN

Plate 48c
Hair-crested Drongo
Dicrurus hottentottus
ID: Medium-sized (32 cm, 1.1 ft); glossy black; tail long and squared but distinctly curled up at the corners of the tip.

HABITAT: Often in flocks eating nectar from the tops of tall flowering trees in moist forests, from lowlands to 1400 m (4600 ft) elevation.

REGION: CP, SE, W, NE, FN

Plate 48b
Black-naped Oriole
Oriolus chinensis
ID: Medium-sized (27 cm, 11 in); adult golden yellow with black line through eye and onto nape of neck; wing and tail with black patches; immature similar but greenish yellow and with streaks on breast.

HABITAT: Winter visitor to open secondary forest, forest edges, mangroves, and even parks of large cities such as Bangkok, from lowland to 1500 m (6000 ft) elevation. (The similar Black-hooded Oriole, *Oriolus xanthornus,* is a permanent resident in lowland dry forests and mangroves; it has an all-black head.)

REGION: PT, CP, SE, W, NE, FN

Plate 48d
Black Drongo
Dicrurus macrocercus
ID: Medium-sized (28 cm, 11 in); glossy black; tail long and flaring into a fork.

HABITAT: Conspicuous in lowland savannah and open agricultural areas; often sitting on telephone wires, fence posts, and riding on the backs of cattle, from which they sally out to catch insects in the air. Aggressively and noisily chases other birds, especially hawks and eagles. Winter visitor to peninsula, permanent resident throughout the rest of the country.

REGION: PT, CP, SE, W, NE, FN

Plate 48

a Greater Racket-tailed Drongo

b Black-naped Oriole

IM

c Hair-crested Drongo

d Black Drongo

Plate 49 (*See also:* Crows and Magpies, p. 163)

Plate 49a
Large-billed Crow
Corvus macrorhynchos
ID: Large (50 cm, 1.6 ft); black with heavy black bill.

HABITAT: Singly, in pairs, or in large flocks in open agricultural areas, scrubby vegetation, mangroves, towns, and cities, from lowlands to tops of tallest mountains.

REGION: PT, CP, SE, W, NE, FN

Plate 49b
Blue Magpie
(also called Red-billed Blue Magpie)
Urocissa erythrorhyncha
ID: Large (70 cm, 2.3 ft); upperparts spectacular bluish purple, extending to long white-tipped tail; head black with white nape; underparts grayish white; bill and legs bright coral red.

HABITAT: Pairs or small family groups in open forest, forest edges, and scrubby vegetation of lowlands to 1500 m (5000 ft) elevation.

REGION: CP, SE, W, NE, FN

Plate 49c
Green Magpie
Cissa chinensis
ID: Medium-sized (38 cm, 1.3 ft); bright yellowish green with long tail; rusty wings and bold black line through eye.

HABITAT: Notoriously shy in pairs, often associated with noisy mixed-species foraging flocks of laughingthrushes and drongos; mid to lower levels of dense moist forest of lowlands to 1800 m (6000 ft) elevation.

REGION: PT, SE, W, NE, FN

Plate 49d
Rufous Treepie
Dendrocitta vagabunda
ID: Large (50 cm, 1.6 ft); rusty with sooty gray head, gray tail, and black and white wings.

HABITAT: Noisy pairs or small family groups in open forest, scrubby vegetation, and gardens of lowlands; often associated with foraging flocks of drongos and woodpeckers.

REGION: SE, W, NE, FN

Plate 49

a Large-billed Crow

b Blue Magpie

c Green Magpie

d Rufous Treepie

Plate 50 (*See also:* Tits and Nuthatches, p. 164; Babblers, p. 165)

Plate 50a
Yellow-cheeked Tit
Parus spilonotus
ID: Small (14 cm, 5.5 in); upperparts black with white spots and short black crest; cheek and underparts golden yellow, with black down center of breast.

HABITAT: Often moves with mixed-species bird flocks in open oak, pine, rhododendron, and evergreen forest above 900 m (3000 ft) elevation; very active and frequently hangs acrobatically from thin branches in search of food.

REGION: W, NE, FN

Plate 50b
Sultan Tit
Melanochlora sultanea
ID: Medium-sized (20 cm, 8 in); forehead, long crest, and belly bright yellow; rest of body blackish (dark olive in females).

HABITAT: Pairs or small family groups often in mixed-species foraging flocks on forest edge and middle and lower parts of secondary and open primary forests, from lowlands to 1000 m (3300 ft) elevation.

REGION: PT, SE, W, NE, FN

Plate 50c
Velvet-fronted Nuthatch
Sitta frontalis
ID: Medium-sized (11 cm, 4 in); upperparts purplish blue with black forehead; underparts pinkish white; bill coral red.

HABITAT: Broad range of secondary and open primary forest, from lowlands to 1800 m (6000 ft) elevation.

REGION: PT, SE, W, NE, FN

Plate 50d
Chestnut-bellied Nuthatch
Sitta castanea
ID: Small (12 cm, 4.5 in); upperparts bluish gray with black eye-line; underparts chestnut with white chin and cheeks.

HABITAT: Pairs or small family groups often associated with mixed-species foraging flocks; clings to side of tree and spirals up or down, head first, hunting for food in nooks and crannies in dry deciduous forests up to 1200 m (4000 ft) elevation. (Replaced in evergreen hill forests above 1300 m (4300 ft) elevation by the similar Chestnut-vented Nuthatch, *Sitta nagaensis,* which has a white throat and gray breast.)

REGION: W, NE, FN

Plate 50e
White-bellied Yuhina
Yuhina zantholeuca
ID: Small (12 cm, 5 in); upperparts and short crest yellow-green; underparts whitish with yellow undertail patch.

HABITAT: Solitary or in pairs often associated with mixed-species foraging flocks in mid to lower levels of moist secondary and open primary forest; lowlands to 1800 m (6000 ft) elevation; hangs tit-like from small branches.

REGION: PT, SE, W, NE, FN

Plate 50

a Yellow-cheeked Tit

b Sultan Tit

c Velvet-fronted Nuthatch

d Chestnut-bellied Nuthatch

e White-bellied Yuhina

Plate 51a
Lesser Necklaced Laughingthrush
Garrulax monileger
ID: Medium-sized (27 cm, 11 in); upperparts olive-brown with rusty nape and white line over eye; underparts buffy white with black necklace on breast continuing up through eye.

HABITAT: Flocks feeding on the ground and dense undergrowth of evergreen and deciduous forest from lowlands to 2000 m (6600 ft) elevation; often joined by large flocks of laughingthrushes of several species.

REGION: SE, W, NE, FN

Plate 51b
White-crested Laughingthrush
Garrulax leucolophus
ID: Medium-sized (28 cm, 11 in); white head, bushy crest, and breast with conspicuous black eye-line; back and wings rusty.

HABITAT: Noisy flocks of 6 to 20 moving through the undergrowth of secondary forest, open primary forest, and bamboo stands; often in the company of other species of laughingthrushes and Green Magpies; shouting calls are often synchronized with other family members to keep in contact and produce a constant cacophony; lowlands to 1200 m (4000 ft) elevation.

REGION: SE, W, NE, FN

Plate 51c
White-browed Shrike-Babbler
Pteruthius flaviscapis
ID: Small (17 cm, 11 in); upperparts black (male) or olive-green (female) with bold white line over eye and rusty patches on wing; underparts grayish white.

HABITAT: Pairs or small family groups often associated with large mixed-species foraging flocks in treetops of evergreen forests above 800 m (2600 ft) elevation.

REGION: PT, SE, W, NE, FN

Plate 51d
Puff-throated Babbler
Pellorneum ruficeps
ID: Small (16 cm, 6 in); upperparts brown with rusty cap; thin white eye-line; underparts buff with bold brown streaks and spots; throat white.

HABITAT: Pairs or small family groups in thick undergrowth near or on the ground of moist forest and bamboo, from lowlands to 1800 m (6000 ft).

REGION: PT, SE, W, NE, FN

Plate 51e
White-browed Scimitar-Babbler
Pomatorhinus schisticeps
ID: Medium-sized (23 cm, 9 in); upperparts olive-brown with rusty neck, white eye-line and black mask; underparts white; long curved bill bright yellow.

HABITAT: Pairs or small family groups skulking in heavy undergrowth of moist secondary forest, ravines, and bamboo stands, from lowlands to 2000 m (6600 m) elevation.

REGION: PT, W, NE, FN

Plate 51f
Pygmy Wren-Babbler
Pnoepyga pusilla
ID: Tiny (9 cm, 3.5 in); tail so short it appears missing; upperparts brown with small buffy spots; underparts dark brown with white scaling.

HABITAT: Scuttles among moss and nettles on or near the ground of moist hill evergreen forests, often near streams or forest marshes; rarely flies; most easily noticed by its song, three evenly spaced whistles descending in tone. Note: On the forest marsh boardwalk at the summit of Doi Inthanon, individuals of this species often walk on or under the boardwalk, seemingly oblivious to the thumping human feet.

REGION: PT, W, FN

Plate 51

a Lesser Necklaced Laughingthrush

b White-crested Laughingthrush

c White-browed Shrike-Babbler

d Puff-throated Babbler

e White-browed Scimitar-Babbler

f Pygmy Wren-Babbler

Plate 52 (See also: Old World Warblers, p. 166; Babblers, p. 165)

Plate 52a
Flyeater
Gerygone sulphurea
ID: Tiny (9 cm, 3.5 in); upperparts gray-brown, underparts pale yellow.

HABITAT: Pairs in lowland secondary forests, plantations, gardens, mangroves, and scrubby coastal vegetation.

REGION: PT, CP, SE

Plate 52b
Gray-headed Parrotbill
Paradoxornis gularis
ID: Small (18 cm, 7 in); upperparts rusty brown with gray and black crown and white eye-ring; underparts white with a black chin; yellow-orange bill.

HABITAT: Small family groups of 6 to 8 in open forest, bushes, and bamboo of northern mountains, between 600 and 1800 m (2000 and 6000 ft) elevation.

REGION: FN

Plate 52c
Dark-necked Tailorbird
Orthotomus atrogularis
ID: Medium-sized (11 cm, 4 in); upperparts greenish with chestnut (male) or buffy (female) crown; underparts whitish but male with streaked black patch on breast.

HABITAT: Tail often cocked up while foraging in undergrowth of moist forest and mangroves from coast to 1200 m (4000 ft) elevation. (Replaced in dry open forests and scrub by similar Common Tailorbird, *Orthotomus sutorius*, which has a rusty forehead and all white breast; and in moist northern highland forests by Mountain Tailorbird, *Orthotomus cuculatus*, which has a black eye-line, gray breast, and bright yellow belly.)

REGION: PT, CP, SE, W, NE, FN

Plate 52d
Inornate Warbler
Phylloscopus inornatus
ID: Small (10 cm, 4 in) upperparts greenish olive with prominent buffy eye-line and two whitish wing bars; underparts white tinged yellow.

HABITAT: Winter visitor to wide range of open and secondary vegetation, gardens, city parks, and orchards as well as primary forest, from lowlands to 2000 m (6600 ft) elevation; usually in mixed-species foraging flocks but also often singly.

REGION: PT, CP, SE, W, NE, FN

Plate 52e
Gray-breasted Prinia
Prinia hodgsonii
ID: Small (11 cm, 4 in); long tail black-and-white tipped; upperparts brownish gray; white throat, gray breast, and buffy belly.

HABITAT: Tail often flicked up while foraging in scrubby vegetation with tall grass, thorn bushes, gardens, bamboo, reeds, and mangroves, from coast to 1500 m (5000 ft) elevation. (Replaced in lowland open forests by similar Rufescent Prinia, *Prinia rufescens*, which has a distinct white eye-line; and in lowland grassy marshes by Yellow-bellied Prinia, *Prinia flaviventris*, which has a yellow belly and white throat.)

REGION: SE, CP, W, NE, FN

Plate 52f
Chestnut-crowned Warbler
Seicercus castaniceps
ID: Small (10 cm, 4 in); crown chestnut; back olive, rump bright yellow; olive wing with two yellow bars; white eye-ring; throat and cheeks gray, belly yellow.

HABITAT: Often associated with large mixed-species foraging flocks in upper levels of moist oak, chestnut, and rhododendron forest of northern mountains, above 1200 m (4000 ft) elevation.

REGION: PT, W, FN

Plate 52

a Flyeater
b Gray-headed Parrotbill
c Dark-necked Tailorbird
d Inornate Warbler
e Gray-breasted Prinia
f Chestnut-crowned Warbler

Plate 53 (*See also:* Thrushes, p. 168)

Plate 53a
Siberian Blue Robin
Luscinia cyane

ID: Medium-sized (15 cm, 6 in); male with slaty blue upperparts, black cheeks; underparts snowy-white; female upperparts olive-brown tinged bluish on rump and tail; underparts whitish in the center and buffy-brown toward the sides.

HABITAT: Common winter visitor to floor of moist secondary forest and open primary forest of lowlands up to 600 m (2000 ft) elevation. Solitary or in pairs hopping quietly along the forest floor, quivering their tails up and down; best seen when one emerges onto a forest path in front of you.

REGION: PT, CP, SE, W, NE, FN

Plate 53b
Siberian Rubythroat
Luscinia calliope

ID: Medium-sized (15 cm, 6 in); upperparts olive-brown with white line over eye and on cheek; underparts buffy gray with red (male) or whitish (female) throat patch.

HABITAT: Common but often elusive winter visitor; singly low in dense shrubby tangles, tall thick grass, underbrush along roads, and reed beds of lowlands to 1800 m (6000 ft) elevation. Often cocks and flicks its tail up over its back and runs on the ground in short bursts.

REGION: SE, CP, W, NE, FN

Plate 53c
Slaty-backed Forktail
Enicurus schistaceus

ID: Medium-sized (25 cm, 10 in); upperparts slaty gray; bold white patch in front of eye, white rump and white patches in wings and long, forked tail; underparts white with black throat and chin.

HABITAT: Solitary or in pairs on large and forest-shaded rocky streams from 400 to 1800 m (1320 to 6000 ft) elevation; walks daintily on moss-covered and bare wet rocks. (Replaced along smaller forest streams with more closed vegetation by the similar White-crowned Forktail, *Enicurus leschenaluti,* which has a white forehead and more extensive black on the breast.)

REGION: PT, SE, W, NE, FN

Plate 53d
White-rumped Shama
Copsychus malabaricus

ID: Medium-sized (25 cm, 10 in); head, back, and long tail black (male) or gray (female), large rump patch white; breast and belly rusty (male) or pale orange (female).

HABITAT: Pairs in undergrowth of moist scrub forest, bamboo, and open primary forest, from lowlands to 1500 m (5000 ft) elevation; shy and retiring at times, bold and easily seen at other times; its loud melodic song is a quintessential part of the morning and dusk chorus in these forests.

REGION: PT, CP, SE, W, NE, FN

Plate 53e
Oriental Magpie-Robin
Copsychus saularis

ID: Medium-sized (20 cm, 8 in); upperparts glossy black (male) or slaty gray (female) with bold white patches on wing and longish tail; underparts snowy white except for black (male) or gray (female) chest and throat.

HABITAT: Pairs common and conspicuous in open habitats, gardens, city parks, and around human habitation, from lowlands to 1800 m (6000 ft) elevation. Hops on ground often flicking its wings and tail; perches upright on low bushes, fence tops, and buildings.

REGION: PT, CP, SE, W, NE, FN

Plate 53

a Siberian Blue Robin

b Siberian Rubythroat

c Slaty-backed Forktail

d White-rumped Shama

e Oriental Magpie-Robin

Plate 54a
Blue Rock Thrush
Monticola solitarius
ID: Medium-sized (23 cm, 9 in); male dark blue with brown and white scalloping; female upperparts gray-brown, barred black and underparts whitish, barred brown. (The larger (33 cm, 1 ft) but similar resident Blue Whistling Thrush, *Myiophoneus caeruleus,* has a yellow bill and occurs along forested streams.)

HABITAT: Winter visitor to bare open areas from the rocky coast to 1600 m (5280 ft) elevation; often on ledges and roofs of buildings.

REGION: PT, CP, SE, W, NE, FN

Plate 54b
Stonechat
Saxicola torquata
ID: Medium-sized (13 cm, 5 in); male with black head, white collar, buffy rump, and orangish breast; female similar but with grayish back and head.

HABITAT: Common winter visitor to dry scrubby hillsides, meadows, pastures, and fallow rice paddies, from lowlands to 2000 m (6600 ft) elevation; perches conspicuously a meter (3.3 ft) or less above the ground at the top of open bushes, stakes, and fence posts, fanning its tail open and shut.

REGION: PT, CP, SE, W, NE, FN

Plate 54c
Red-throated Flycatcher
Ficedula parva
ID: Small (13 cm, 5 in); upperparts brownish gray; underparts grayish white; tail black with white patches at base; bill all black; in breeding season male has a rusty throat patch.

HABITAT: Common winter visitor perched upright low or on the ground in open vegetation of secondary forest, scrub, and gardens, from lowlands to 2000 m (6600 ft) elevation; often cocks its tail open to reveal contrasting white patches.

REGION: PT, CP, SE, W, NE, FN

Plate 54d
Asian Brown Flycatcher
Muscicapa dauurica
ID: Small (14 cm, 5.5 in); upperparts grayish brown, underparts grayish white, eye-ring whitish; bill dark with orangish base.

HABITAT: Common winter visitor perched upright low in open forest, forest edge, gardens, and mangroves, from coast to 1500 m (5000 ft) elevation; small resident population in mountain evergreen and pine forests.

REGION: PT, CP, SE, W, NE, FN

Plate 54e
Eye-browed Thrush
Turdus obscurus
ID: Medium-sized (24 cm, 9 in); upperparts olive-brown with gray head and short white line over and under eye; underparts rusty with white central belly.

HABITAT: Winter visitor usually in small flocks at fruiting trees, but also seen running on the floor of open forest, gardens, and mangroves, from coast to 2000 m (6600 ft) elevation.

REGION: PT, CP, SE, W, NE, FN

Plate 54

a Blue Rock Thrush

b Stonechat

c Red-throated Flycatcher

d Asian Brown Flycatcher

e Eye-browed Thrush

Plate 55a
Verditer Flycatcher
Eumyias thalassina
ID: Small (16 cm, 6 in); male blue-green with black through eye; female similar but duller and grayer.

HABITAT: Singly or in pairs often in mixed-species foraging flocks in the upper to mid levels of open forest, especially in bushes along streams; nesting resident in higher elevations and winter visitor to mangroves and forests at lower elevations.

REGION: PT, CP, SE, W, NE, FN

Plate 55b
Gray-headed Canary Flycatcher
Culicicapa ceylonensis
ID: Small (body 13 cm, 5 in); head and short crest gray; rest of upperparts olive-green; lower breast and belly yellow.

HABITAT: Pairs or small family groups often in large mixed-species foraging flocks in mid to lower parts of open primary and secondary forest, gardens, and mangroves, from lowlands to 2200 m (7260 ft) elevation.

REGION: PT, CP, SE, W, NE, FN

Plate 55c
Asian Paradise Flycatcher
Terpsiphone paradisi
ID: Medium-sized (21 cm, 8 in, with long tail of male extending an additional 30 cm, 1 ft); male crown and short crest black, rest of head black (white form) or gray (rufous form); rest of body white or rufous back, wings, and tail with grayish white breast; extremely long tail of breeding adult; female similar to rufous form but lacks the long tail streamers.

HABITAT: Alone or in pairs frequently associated with mixed-species foraging flocks in the mid to upper levels of open primary forest, secondary forest, scrub, and mangroves, from lowlands to 1500 m (6000 ft) elevation; more common and widespread in lowlands during winter.

REGION: PT, CP, SE, W, NE, FN

Plate 55d
Hill Blue Flycatcher
Cyornis banyumas
ID: Small (15 cm, 6 in); male upperparts deep blue with black mask; underparts orange on throat and breast, white on lower belly; female upperparts olive-brown with orangish eye-ring, underparts similar to male.

HABITAT: Resident of dense undergrowth of moist forest from 400 to 2100 m (1320 to 7000 ft) elevation; migrants in winter at lower elevations and along the coast.

REGION: PT, CP, SE, W, NE, FN

Plate 55e
Pied Fantail
Rhipidura javanica
ID: Small (18 cm, 7 in); upperparts slate gray with white eye-line and long, white-tipped tail; underparts white with black breast band.

HABITAT: Tail often held fanned out and cocked up over back; pairs in mid to lower levels of open lowland forest, scrub, gardens, and mangroves; often associated with mixed-species foraging flocks. (Replaced in higher elevation forests by the similar White-throated Fantail, *Rhipidura albicollis*, which has all-gray underparts except for a white throat).

REGION: PT, CP, SE, W, NE

Plate 55

a Verditer Flycatcher

b Gray-headed Canary Flycatcher

c Asian Paradise Flycatcher
M white form
M rufous form

d Hill Blue Flycatcher
M
F

e Pied Fantail

Plate 56a
Long-tailed Shrike
Lanius schach
ID: Medium-sized (25 cm, 10 in); head, wings, and tail black, rest of upperparts rusty; underparts white to pinkish.

HABITAT: Permanent resident in open scrub, agricultural areas, marshes, gardens, and plantations, from lowlands to 1800 m (6000 ft) elevation; usually in pairs sitting on exposed perches.

REGION: CP, SE, NE, FN

Plate 56b
Brown Shrike
Lanius cristatus
ID: Small (19 cm, 7 in); upperparts rusty brown with black mask; underparts buffy; some forms have a gray crown and nape of neck.

HABITAT: Winter visitor; sits conspicuously by itself on the top of exposed perches in forest edge, clearings, scrubby secondary forest, grass hillsides with scattered bushes, marshes, farmland, rice paddies, and open secondary forest, from lowlands to 2000 m (6600 ft) elevation.

REGION: PT, CP, SE, W, NE, FN

Plate 56c
Asian Glossy Starling
(also called Philippine Glossy Starling)
Aplonis panayensis
ID: Medium-sized (20 cm, 8 in); dark glossy green with bright red eye.

HABITAT: Noisy flocks in treetops of coconut groves, forest edges, and agricultural areas with fruiting trees in lowlands of peninsula.

REGION: PT

Plate 56d
White-shouldered Starling
Sturnus sinensis
ID: Medium-sized (20 cm, 8 in); gray with black wings and tail; white shoulder and (male only) forehead.

HABITAT: Winter visitor to moist agricultural fields with trees in the open lowlands and mangroves on the coast.

REGION: PT, CP, SE, W, NE, FN

Plate 56e
Common Myna
Acridotheres tristis
ID: Medium-sized (25 cm, 10 in); brown with black head and white lower belly; bill, legs, and bare skin around eye yellow; large white patch in wing conspicuous in flight.

HABITAT: Cultivated areas, open fields, city parks, towns, and villages from lowlands to 1500 m (5000 ft) elevation; usually walking on the ground in pairs or small flocks.

REGION: PT, CP, SE, W, NE, FN

Plate 56

a Long-tailed Shrike

b Brown Shrike

c Asian Glossy Starling

d White-shouldered Starling

breeding M

nonbreeding M

e Common Myna

Plate 57 (*See also:* Starlings, p. 170)

Plate 57a
Asian Pied Starling
Sturnus contra
ID: Medium-sized (23 cm, 9 in); black with white crown, cheeks, and belly; red-orange bill and bare skin around eye.
HABITAT: Small flocks on ground in open agricultural areas of lowlands, usually near water.

REGION: CP, SE, W, NE, FN

Plate 57b
Black-collared Starling
Sturnus nigricollis
ID: Medium-sized (28 cm, 11 in); black with buffy white head; white belly and tail tip; black bill.
HABITAT: Small flocks in open agricultural areas; usually in bushes or small trees in the lowlands to 1500 m (5000 ft) elevation.

REGION: PT, CP, SE, W, NE, FN

Plate 57c
Hill Myna
Gracula religiosa
ID: Medium-sized (30 cm, 1 ft); black with bright yellow patches of bare skin on nape of neck and under eye; white patch in wing conspicuous in flight.
HABITAT: Small flocks in treetops of closed forest or isolated trees in open country, from lowlands to 1300 m (4300 ft) elevation.

REGION: PT, SE, W, NE, FN

Plate 57d
White-vented Myna
Acridotheres javanicus
ID: Medium-sized (25 cm, 10 in); all black with bold white patches under tail, on tail tip, and in flight on wings; yellow bill with short crest.
HABITAT: Small flocks in lowland rice paddies, moist grasslands, city parks and cattle fields.

REGION: CP, SE, W, NE, FN

Plate 57e
Golden-crested Myna
Ampeliceps coronatus
ID: Medium-sized (21 cm, 8 in); black with golden head and throat; yellow and white wing patch conspicuous in flight; female with gold limited to crown and patch around eye.
HABITAT: Pairs or small family groups in treetops of closed to open moist forest, from lowlands to 800 m (2640 ft) elevation.

REGION: PT, SE, W, NE, FN

Plate 57

a Asian Pied Starling

b Black-collared Starling

c Hill Myna

d White-vented Myna

e Golden-crested Myna

Plate 58a
Brown-throated Sunbird
Anthreptes malacensis
ID: Small (14 cm, 5 in); male upperparts metallic purple and blue with brown cheeks, underparts yellow with brown throat; female upperparts olive with faint yellow eye-ring, underparts yellowish.

HABITAT: Lowland secondary forest, gardens, coconut plantations, and mangroves.

REGION: PT, CP, SE

Plate 58b
Ruby-cheeked Sunbird
Anthreptes singalensis
ID: Small (11 cm, 4 in); male upperparts dark metallic green with coppery cheeks, underparts yellow with rusty throat patch; female upperparts olive-green, underparts yellowish with rusty throat.

HABITAT: Open primary forest, secondary forest, gardens, and mangroves, from coast to 900 m (3000 ft) elevation.

REGION: PT, SE, W, NE, FN

Plate 58c
Olive-backed Sunbird
Nectarinia jugularis
ID: Small (11 cm, 4 in); male upperparts olive with black and white tail, underparts bright yellow with dark purple throat and upper breast (breeding) or small purple throat patch (non-breeding); female upperparts olive, underparts yellow with black and white tail.

HABITAT: Open secondary forest, scrub vegetation, gardens, and mangroves, from coast to 900 m (3000 ft) elevation.

REGION: PT, CP, SE, W, NE, FN

Plate 58d
Gould's Sunbird
Aethopyga gouldiae
ID: Small (11 cm, 4 in); male bright scarlet with yellow rump and lower belly, metallic blue tail, crown, and throat, long central tail feathers; female olive with bright yellow rump and lower belly.

HABITAT: Winter visitor to flowering bushes and trees in openings and forest edges of moist primary and tall secondary forest above 1200 m (4000 ft) elevation in the mountains of the far north.

REGION: FN

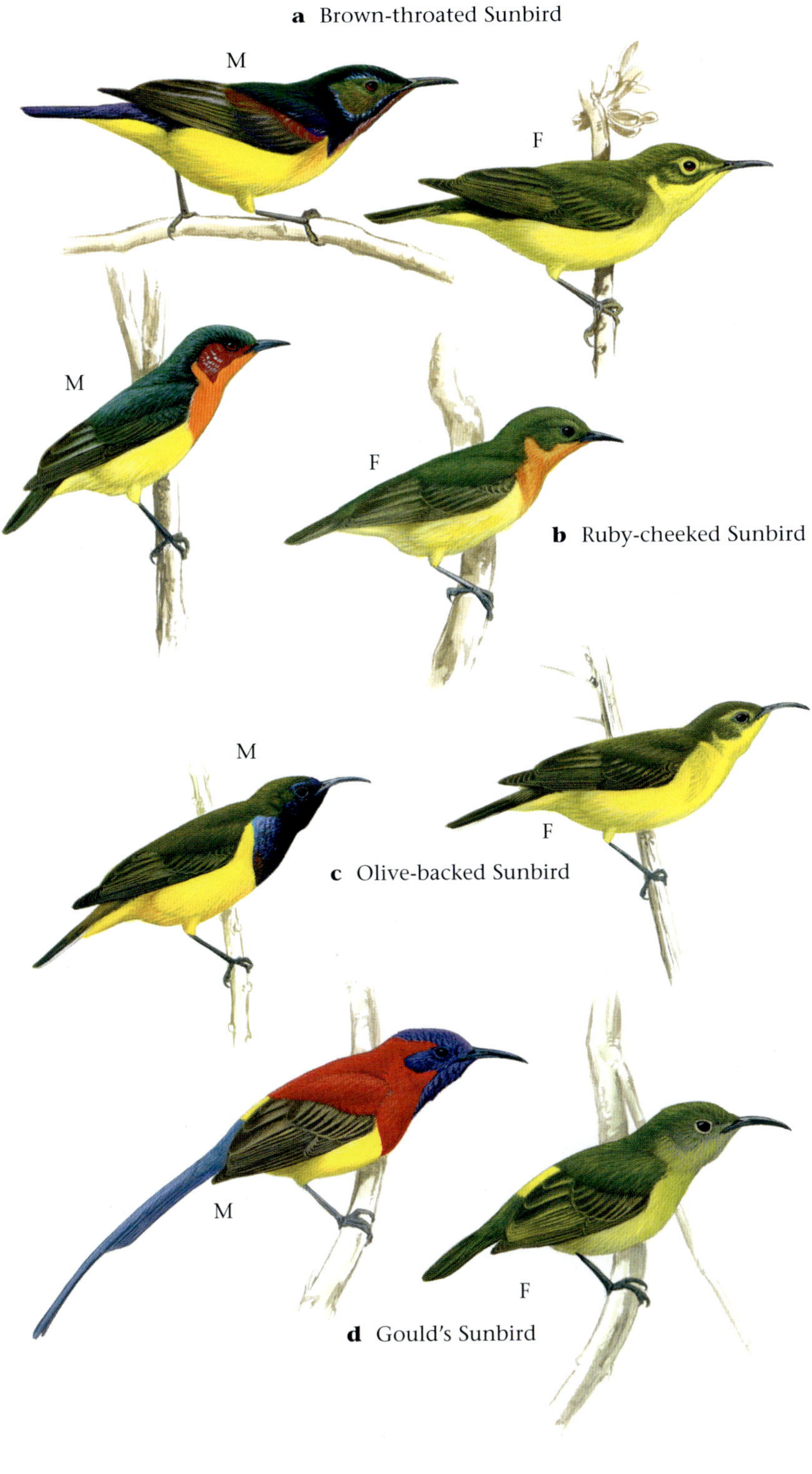

Plate 58

a Brown-throated Sunbird

b Ruby-cheeked Sunbird

c Olive-backed Sunbird

d Gould's Sunbird

Plate 59a
Little Spiderhunter
Arachnothera longirostra
ID: Small (15 cm, 6 in); upperparts olive-brown; underparts yellow with grayish white throat and short, white-tipped tail; long, curved bill.

HABITAT: Mid levels of dense forest, moist secondary forest, banana plantations, and forest edge of lowlands.

REGION: PT, SE, W, NE, FN

Plate 59b
Buff-bellied Flowerpecker
Dicaeum ignipectus
ID: Tiny (7 cm, 3 in); male upperparts metallic greenish black, underparts buff (with bright red patch on upper breast in populations of NE and FN) and black line down center of belly; female upperparts olive-brown, underparts buffy-brown.

HABITAT: Singly or pairs in open forests, orchards, and cultivated trees above 600 m (2000 ft) elevation; often found eating mistletoe berries high in treetops.

REGION: PT, SE, W, NE, FN

Plate 59c
Scarlet-backed Flowerpecker
Dicaeum cruentatum
ID: Tiny (7 cm, 3 in); male crown, back, and rump bright red; cheeks, wings, and tail black; underparts white; female upperparts gray-brown with red rump patch; underparts buff with gray sides.

HABITAT: Tops of trees in open forest, cultivated trees, forest edges, gardens, and city parks, from lowlands to 1200 m (4000 ft) elevation.

REGION: PT, CP, SE, W, NE, FN

Plate 59d
Crimson Sunbird
Aethopyga siparaja
ID: Small (10 cm, 4 in); male in breeding plumage with bright red throat and cheeks, dark red back, metallic violet crown and long tail, bright yellow patch on rump, and gray belly; female uniformly olive; male in non-breeding plumage like female but with red on throat and breast.

HABITAT: Singly foraging on flowers of bushes and trees in open forest, gardens, and scrub forest in lowlands. Clings acrobatically to branches for access to flower nectar and insects.

REGION: PT, SE, W, NE, FN

Plate 59e
Oriental White-eye
Zosterops palpebrosus
ID: Small (10 cm, 4 in); upperparts olive-yellow; distinct white eye-ring; underparts bright yellow with gray lower belly.

HABITAT: Pairs or flocks of 20 or more in a wide variety of open habitat, forest edges, plantations, gardens, and mangroves, from coast to 1800 m (6000 ft) elevation; often associated with mixed-species foraging flocks.

REGION: PT, CP, SE, W, NE, FN

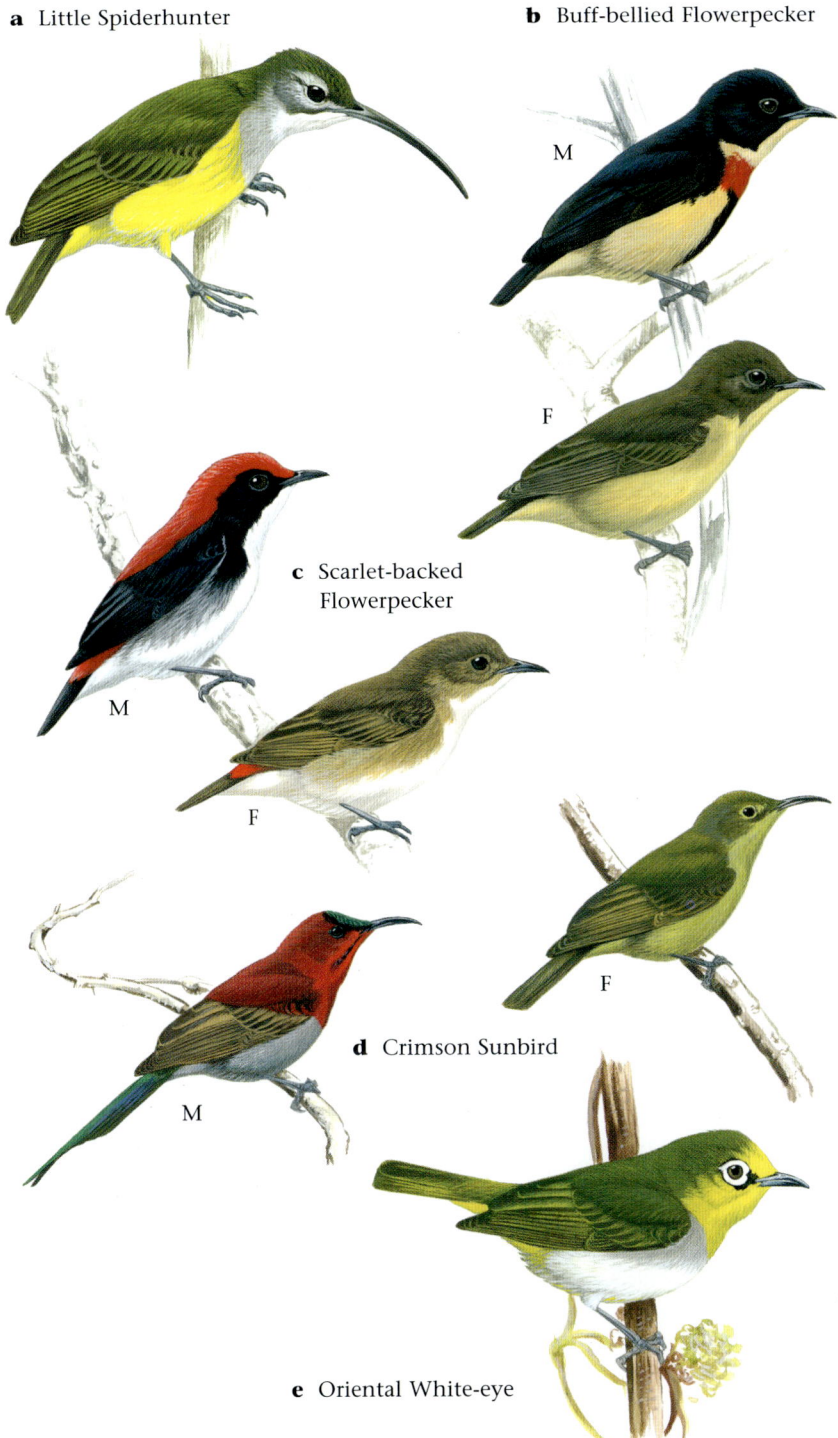

Plate 60 (See also: Sparrows, Munias, and Finches, p. 173)

Plate 60a
Scaly-breasted Munia
Lonchura punctulata
ID: Small (10 cm, 4 in); upperparts pale brown to tan; throat black, breast and sides pale brown spotted white, center of breast white.

HABITAT: Flocks, often large, feeding on the ground or in low bushes of grasslands, open scrub, gardens, and agricultural fields, from lowlands to 1500 m (5000 ft) elevation.

REGION: PT, CP, SE, W, NE, FN

Plate 60b
White-rumped Munia
Lonchura striata
ID: Small (10 cm, 4 in); dark brown with faint white streaks; belly and rump whitish; tail pointed.

HABITAT: Small flocks in scrubby forest, marshy grasslands, brush, open secondary forest, gardens, and roadside vegetation, from lowlands to 1500 m (5000 ft) elevation.

REGION: PT, CP, SE, W, NE, FN

Plate 60c
Eurasian Tree Sparrow
Passer montanus
ID: Small (15 cm, 6 in); brown back streaked black; brown cap and white cheeks; black throat; rest of underparts grayish white.

HABITAT: Flocks in villages and agricultural fields, from coast to 1800 m (6000 ft) elevation.

REGION: PT, CP, SE, W, NE, FN

Plate 60d
Plain-backed Sparrow
Passer flaveolus
ID: Medium-sized (15 cm, 6 in); male back and neck rusty, cheeks buffy, rump and breast buffy-gray, throat black; female unstreaked with upperparts brown and underparts buffy.

HABITAT: Lowland brushy areas, trees in agricultural fields, and near towns and villages.

REGION: PT, CP, SE, W, NE, FN

Plate 60e
Common Rosefinch
Carpodacus erythrinus
ID: Small (16 cm, 6 in); male all rosy pink; female brownish with dark-streaked breast.

HABITAT: Winter visitor in small flocks in open forests, cultivated fields, scrub, and bushes, from lowlands to 2200 m (7260 ft).

REGION: SE, W, NE, FN

Plate 60

a Scaly-breasted Munia
b White-rumped Munia
c Eurasian Tree Sparrow
d Plain-backed Sparrow
e Common Rosefinch

Plate 61 (*See also:* Treeshrews, Shrews, and Hedgehogs, p. 183; Flying Lemurs, p. 185)

Plate 61a
Common Treeshrew
Tupaia glis
ID: Like a small (body length 20 cm, 8 in) squirrel with small ears, a pointed nose, and a long bushy tail (18 cm, 7 in); various populations throughout the country vary from gray to rusty, with or without a light stripe on the shoulder. Some experts divide the northern and southern Thai populations of treeshrew into at least two different species.

HABITAT: Highly active during the daytime running rapidly, often in pairs, on the ground and into the lower branches of trees; secondary and open primary forest as well as gardens and plantations bordering forests, from lowlands to 600 m (2000 ft) elevation.

REGION: PT, CP, SE, W, NE, FN

Plate 61b
Malayan Flying Lemur
Cynocephalus variegatus
ID: Medium-sized (body length 36 cm; 1.2 ft); mottled gray and black; tail and legs attached together and included in the gliding membrane, which in flight has a "wingspan" of 70 cm (2.3 ft).

HABITAT: Nocturnal and arboreal in moist primary and tall secondary forests, and rubber plantations, from lowlands to 900 m (3000 ft) elevation.

REGION: PT, SE, W

Plate 61c
Moonrat
Echinosorex gymnurus
ID: Medium-sized (body length 38 cm, 1.2 ft) with long, naked tail (25 cm, 10 in); dark form is blackish overall with whitish mask and shoulders; pale form is whitish.

HABITAT: Nocturnal and solitary on floor of lowland moist forests, gardens, plantations, and mangroves. Its pungent ammonia-like smell often makes it obvious during the day, when it sleeps in underground burrows.

REGION: PT, CP, SE, W, NE, FN

Plate 61d
House Shrew
Crocidura murina
ID: Small (body length 13 cm, 5 in); upperparts blackish to brownish; underparts light gray; long thin tail (7 cm, 3 in) covered with long bristly hairs; long narrow snout.

HABITAT: Almost always associated with human habitations but occasionally in open forests.

REGION: PT, CP, SE, W, NE, FN

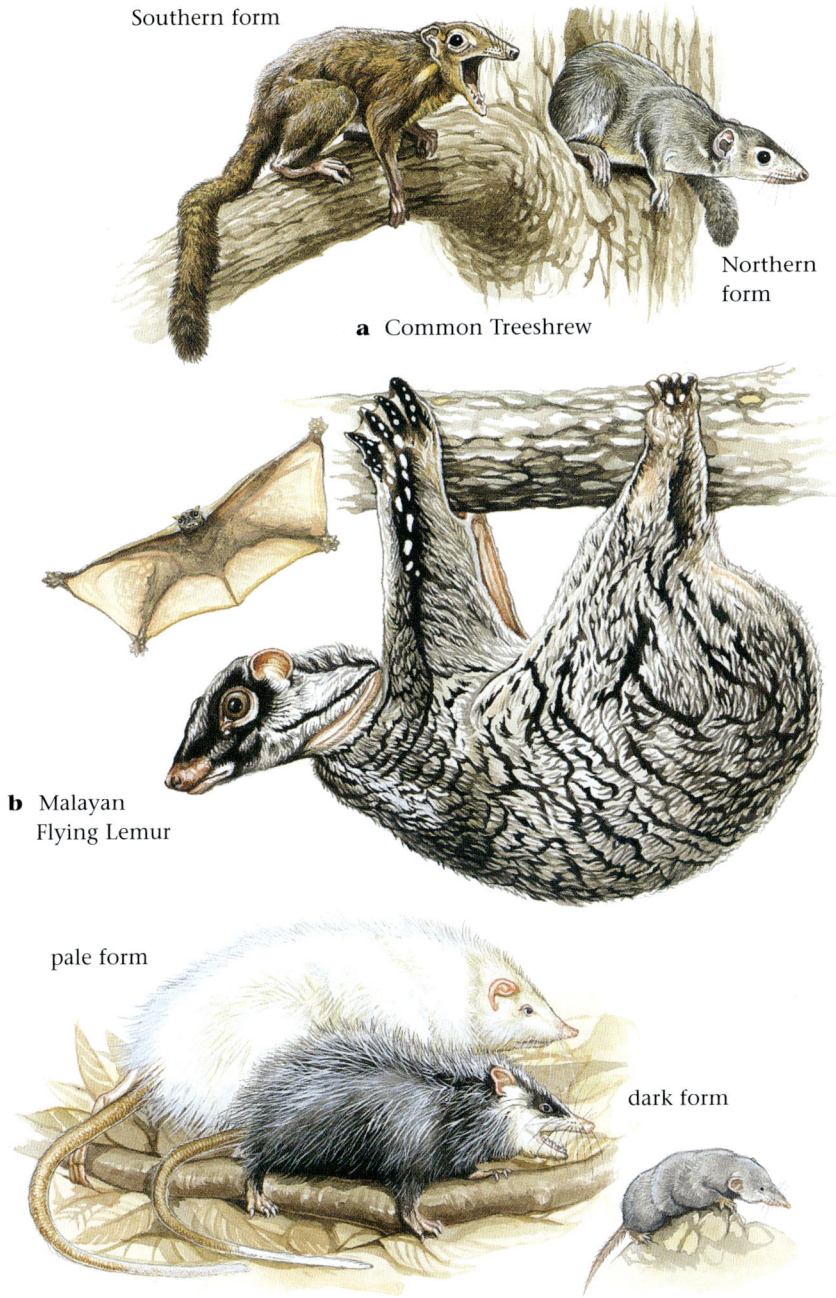

Plate 62 (See also: Bats, p. 185)

Plate 62a
Common Flying Fox
Pteropus vampyrus
ID: Largest bat in the world (body length 32 cm, 1 ft); black with rusty head.
HABITAT: Large roosting colonies in upper branches of open trees, mangroves, and palms in lowland coastal areas to 1300 m (4300 ft) elevation. At night feeds on fruits, often in orchards.

REGION: PT, CP, SE, W

Plate 62b
Kitti's Hog-nosed Bat
Craeseonycteris thonglongyai
ID: The smallest bat in the world (body length 3 cm, 1.2 in); upperparts brown to reddish brown or gray; underparts light gray.
HABITAT: Roosts in a few small limestone caves in open mixed deciduous forest at a single site near Sai Yoke, Kanchanaburi Province. Feeds at dusk on flying insects in mid levels of bamboo thickets and open forest.

REGION: W

Note: this species is endangered, IUCN Red List.

Plate 62c
Lesser Long-tongued Fruit Bat
Macroglossus minimus
ID: Tiny (body length 7 cm, 2.7 in); buffy brown with virtually no tail; long narrow snout.
HABITAT: Most common bat in coastal mangroves but also ranges up to 1000 m (3300 ft) elevation in open forests. Feeds primarily on small fruits.

REGION: PT, CP, SE

Plate 62d
Lyle's Flying Fox
Pteropus lyeli
ID: Medium-sized (body length 23 cm, 9 in); upperparts yellowish with a brown snout and black wings; underparts buffy with black lower belly; ears short.
HABITAT: Large roosting colonies in tall leafless trees in open country and mangroves. At night feeds on fruits, often in orchards.

REGION: PT, CP, SE

Plate 62e
Greater Short-nosed Fruit Bat
Cynopterus sphinx
ID: Medium-sized (body length 25 cm, 10 in); gray-brown with rusty collar.
HABITAT: Small groups roosting under palm fronds, roofs, and tall trees during the daytime. At night feeds on large fruits and nectar of night-blooming trees.

REGION: PT, CP, SE, W, NE, FN

Plate 62

a Common Flying Fox

b Kitti's Hog-nosed Bat

c Lesser Long-tongued Fruit Bat

d Lyle's Flying Fox

e Greater Short-nosed Fruit Bat

Plate 63 (*See also:* Bats, p. 185)

Plate 63a
Blyth's Tomb Bat
Taphozous saccolaimus
ID: Tiny (body length 9 cm, 3.5 in); brown with white spots on wings, conspicuous in flight; legs and tail hairless; pouch on throat.

HABITAT: Small to large colonies roosting in houses, hollow trees, and rock crevices in open forested areas of lowlands. At night, hunts flying insects over villages and open forests.

REGION: PT, W

Plate 63b
Long-winged Tomb Bat
Taphozous longimanus
ID: Tiny (body length 7 cm, 2.8 in); males reddish brown, females grayish, both with white spots; throat pouch of male naked; legs furred.

HABITAT: Roosts in small groups together under eaves of houses, in hollow trees, and rock crevices of lowlands. Commonly seen just before dusk hunting flying insects 30 m (100 ft) over the rooftops of Bangkok.

REGION: PT, CP, SE, W, NE, FN

Plate 63c
Greater Yellow Bat
Scotophilus heathi
ID: Small (body length 10 cm, 4 in); rusty body contrasting with dark brown wings; ears long and pointed.

HABITAT: Roosts in small groups under eaves of houses as well as in hollow trees of open agricultural areas. Feeds for a short period after dusk on flying insects.

REGION: CP, SE, W, NE, FN

Plate 63d
Wrinkle-lipped Bat
Tadarida plicata
ID: Tiny (body length 7 cm, 2.8 in); dark brown with long tail; face wrinkled; large rounded ears.

HABITAT: Huge colonies of 200,000 or more individuals roost together in limestone caves to emerge in a continuous, smoke-like cloud at dusk. A single colony can consume more than 35 million insects each night.

REGION: PT, CP, SE, W, NE, FN

Plate 63e
Greater Bent-winged Bat
(also called Common Bentwing Bat)
Miniopterus schreibersi
ID: Tiny (body length 7 cm, 2.7 in); dark brown with short, rounded ears and short snout; very long wings at rest are peculiarly folded so that the tip is bent up; long tail enclosed in a membrane extending between the legs.

HABITAT: Up to 100,000 individuals roost together during the day in caves. At night they emerge to feed on insects over lowland open forest.

REGION: PT, CP, SE, W, NE, FN

Plate 63

a Blyth's Tomb Bat

b Long-winged Tomb Bat

c Greater Yellow Bat

e Greater Bent-winged Bat

d Wrinkle-lipped Bat

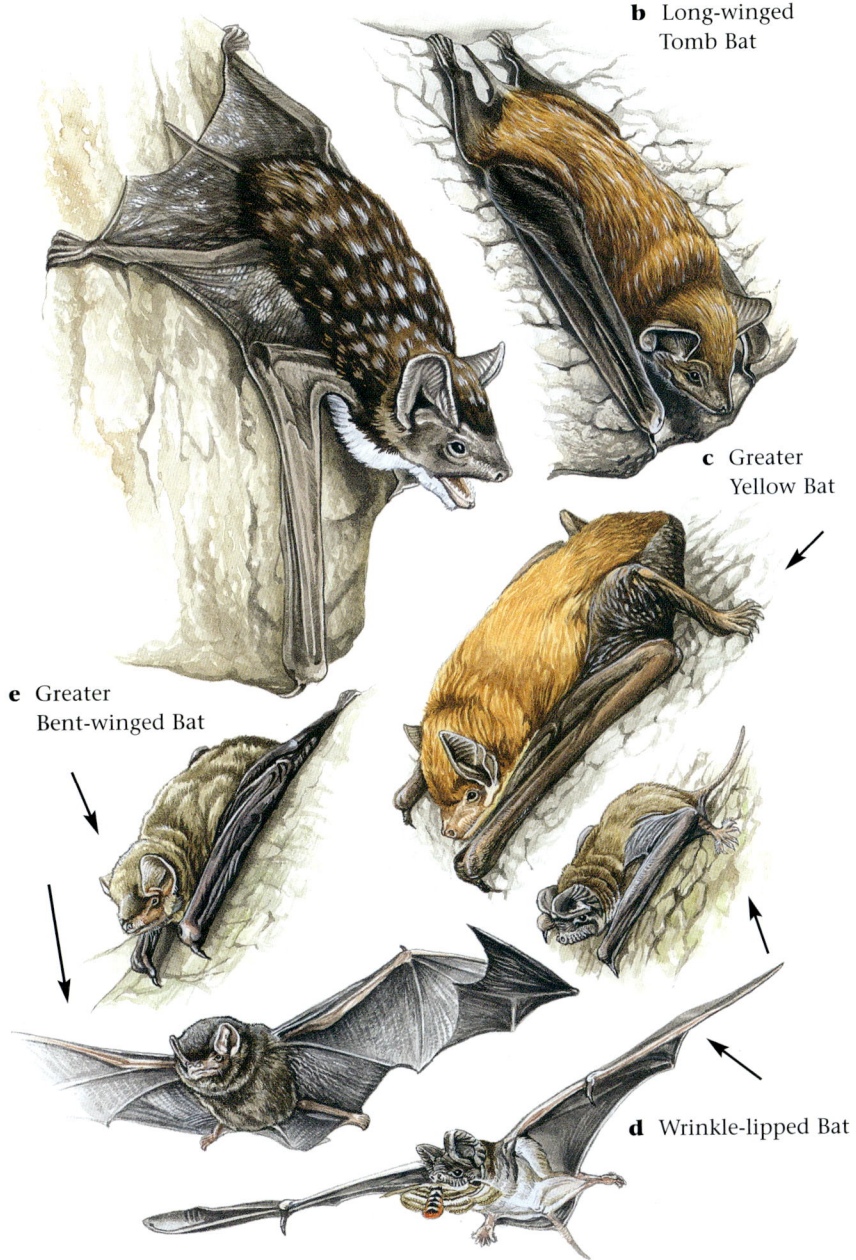

Plate 64 (See also: Primates, p. 189)

Plate 64a
Slow Loris
Nycticebus coucang
ID: Medium-sized (body length 35 cm, 1.2 ft); round-headed and round-eyed; color highly variable but generally buffy brown with dark brown stripe on back and top of head; sides of neck gray; face gray with white nose and black mask; tail short.

HABITAT: Solitary and nocturnal, walking slowly hand over hand along branches in moist primary and tall secondary forest of the lowlands. Eyes reflect brightly in light of a flashlight.

REGION: PT, CP, SE, W, NE, FN

Plate 64b
Pig-tailed Macaque
Macaca nemestrina
ID: Large (body length 52 cm, 1.7 ft); color highly variable from olive-brown to rusty; crown of head, back, and top of tail dark brown; long hairs on side of face form a fringe almost hiding the ears; tail less than half the length of the body and carried arched upward over the back.

HABITAT: Troops of 5 to 40 often feed on the ground in open lowland forest up to 1000 m (3300 ft) elevation. More arboreal in northern Thailand.

REGION: PT, SE, W, NE, FN

Plate 64c
Stump-tailed Macaque
Macaca arctoides
ID: Large (body length 56 cm, 1.8 ft); blackish to rusty with very long hair down the head and shoulders; bare patch on forehead; tail extremely short and nearly hairless.

HABITAT: Mainly terrestrial and often in large troops; found in moist forests in hills and mountains between 300 and 2000 m (1000 and 6600 ft) elevation.

REGION: PT, SE, W, NE, FN

Plate 64d
Rhesus Macaque
Macaca mulatta
ID: Large (body length 53 cm, 1.7 ft); grayish brown with rusty colored hips; tail a little more than half the length of the body.

HABITAT: Often in large troops of 50 or more; open forest and agricultural areas, regularly associated with human habitation.

REGION: W, NE, FN

Plate 64

a Slow Loris
b Pig-tailed Macaque
c Stump-tailed Macaque
d Rhesus Macaque

Plate 65 (See also: Primates, p. 189)

Plate 65a
Crab-eating Macaque
(also called Long-tailed Macaque)
Macaca fascicularis
ID: Large (52 cm, 1.7 ft); variable color from gray-brown to rusty; populations in forest tend to be darker than those in open coastal areas. Tail as long or longer than the body.

HABITAT: Large troops of up to 100 individuals primarily in mangrove and offshore island beaches, although they also occur in open primary and secondary forest up to 200 m (6600 ft) elevation. Regularly found around temples and human habitation.

REGION: PT, CP, SE, W

Plate 65b
Banded Langur
Presbytis melalophus
ID: Large (body length 53 cm, 1.7 ft; tail 78 cm, 2.6 ft); variable color from black to light brown, but the chest and belly are whitish with white extending on the inside of the legs to the ankles.

HABITAT: Troops of 5 to 6 in moist coastal forest and inland forest primarily below 600 m (2000 ft) elevation, but up to 2200 m (7260 ft) elevation where no other langur species are present. (The all-dark Silvered Langur, *Presbytis cristata,* has an all-dark face with no eye rings. It occurs primarily in coastal forest and mangroves.)

REGION: PT, W

Plate 65c
Dusky Langur
Presbytis obscura
ID: Large (body length 52 cm, 1.7 ft; tail 72 cm, 2.4 ft); highly variable in color from gray to brown, but the chest and forearms are generally the darkest part of the body, the back intermediate, and the hips, hind legs, and tail the lightest; the crown of the head is always lighter than the rest of the head, and the white spectacles around the eyes are conspicuous.

HABITAT: Small family groups often sitting quietly in tall trees of moist forest, from coastal islands to mountains, but most common above 600 m (2000 ft) elevation. (The rarer and much shier Phayre's Langur, *Presbytis phayrei,* has conspicuous bluish eye rings and snout. It is found in mountain forest and on limestone cliffs in northern Thailand.)

REGION: PT, W

Plate 65d
White-handed Gibbon
Hylobates lar
ID: Large (53 cm, 1.7 ft); white hands and ring around face; body either buffy white or dark brown.

HABITAT: Arboreal; small family groups in the tops of tall trees of a wide range of moist forest types; most obvious by their fantastical "whooping" chorus of calls given in the morning. (Adult females of the similar Pileated Gibbon, *Hylobates pileatus,* of southeastern Thailand are grayish white with a black cap; males are black. Their call notes are distinctly shortened and sound like a European ambulance siren. Along the Malaysian border, the Agile Gibbon, *Hylobates agilis,* is found only in southernmost Thailand. It looks like the White-handed Gibbon but has all dark hands.)

REGION: PT, W, NE, FN

Plate 65

a Crab-eating Macaque

b Banded Langur

c Dusky Langur

white form

black form

d White-handed Gibbon

Plate 66 (See also: Pangolins, p. 192; Rodents and Rabbits, p. 194)

Plate 66a
Malayan Pangolin
Manis javanica
ID: Large (body length 52 cm, 1.7 ft; tail 46 cm, 1.5 ft); brownish with distinctive scales, long front claws, and long prehensile tail. Head with small ears and long toothless snout.

HABITAT: Nocturnal and solitary in tall secondary and open primary forest of lowlands and low hills; most often seen crossing roads at night.

REGION: PT, CP, SE, W, NE, FN

Plate 66b
Siamese Hare
Lepus peguensis
ID: Medium-sized (body length 47 cm, 1.5 ft); upperparts dark brown with rusty neck; underparts white with rusty front legs; short tail white with black line; long ears brown with black tips.

HABITAT: Nocturnal in forest clearings and grassy areas; often associated with human activity.

REGION: CP, SE, W, NE, FN

Plate 66c
Black Giant Squirrel
Ratufa bicolor
ID: Medium-sized (body length 37 cm, 1.2 ft); upperparts black to dark brown; underparts buff to rusty; long (46 cm, 1.5 ft), bushy tail dark.

HABITAT: Solitary or in pairs high in the canopy of tall trees; sometimes noticed by the huge globular nest they construct of twigs and leaves high in the canopy; lowlands to 1200 m (4000 ft) elevation.

REGION: PT, SE, W, NE, FN

Plate 66d
Red Giant Flying Squirrel
Petaurista petaurista
ID: Medium-sized (body length 42 cm, 1.4 ft; tail 53 cm, 1.7 ft); color variable but primarily rusty with black tail tip, feet, and gliding membrane.

HABITAT: Mainly nocturnal but occasionally active during the daytime; glides from tall treetops in open forest, gardens, and plantations of lowlands up to 700 m (2310 ft) elevation. Several other species of large flying squirrels occur in Thailand but none of them has a black-tipped tail.

REGION: PT, CP, SE, W, NE, FN

Plate 66e
Red-cheeked Squirrel
Dremomys rufigenis
ID: Small (body length 19 cm, 8 in; tail 16 cm, 6 in); gray with rusty cheeks and underside of tail.

HABITAT: Solitary or in pairs near or on the ground in mountain forests above 900 m (3000 ft) elevation.

REGION: PT, W, NE, FN

Plate 67 (See also: Rodents, p. 194)

Plate 67a
Gray-bellied Squirrel
Callosciurus caniceps
ID: Medium-sized (body length 22 cm, 9 in; tail 23 cm, 9 in); upperparts gray to olive, underparts silvery gray; in almost all forms the black tail tip is distinctive.

HABITAT: Solitary or in pairs in trees or on the ground in a wide range of forest types, from plantations and secondary forest to open primary forest, gardens, and agricultural areas; lowlands to 1400 m (4700 ft) elevation.

REGION: PT, CP, SE, W, NE, FN

Plate 67b
Variable Squirrel
Callosciurus finlaysoni
ID: Medium-sized (body length 22 cm, 9 in); extremely variable in color from pure white to pure black to mixtures of color; long (23 cm, 9 in) bushy tail.

HABITAT: Arboreal in a wide range of forest types, from open secondary and plantations to closed primary forest.

REGION: CP, SE, W, NE, FN

Plate 67c
Striped Tree Squirrel
Tamiops macclellandi
ID: Small (body length 11 cm, 4 in; tail 11 cm, 4 in); brownish with broad buffy stripe high on each side and 5 alternating bands of black and chestnut along the back.

HABITAT: Solitary or in small family groups high in the canopy of tall trees from lowlands up to 2500 m (8250 ft) elevation. Most readily detected by their high-pitched, birdlike descending whistles.

REGION: PT, CP, SE, W, NE, FN

Plate 67d
Belly-banded Squirrel
Callosciurus flavimanus
ID: Medium-sized (body length 21 cm, 8 in; tail 20 cm, 8 in); upperparts brownish with a black rump in some populations; underparts rusty; tail whitish.

HABITAT: Arboreal; solitary or in small family groups in moist secondary and primary forest from lowlands to 1500 m (5000 ft) elevation.

REGION: PT, CP, W, NE, FN

Plate 67

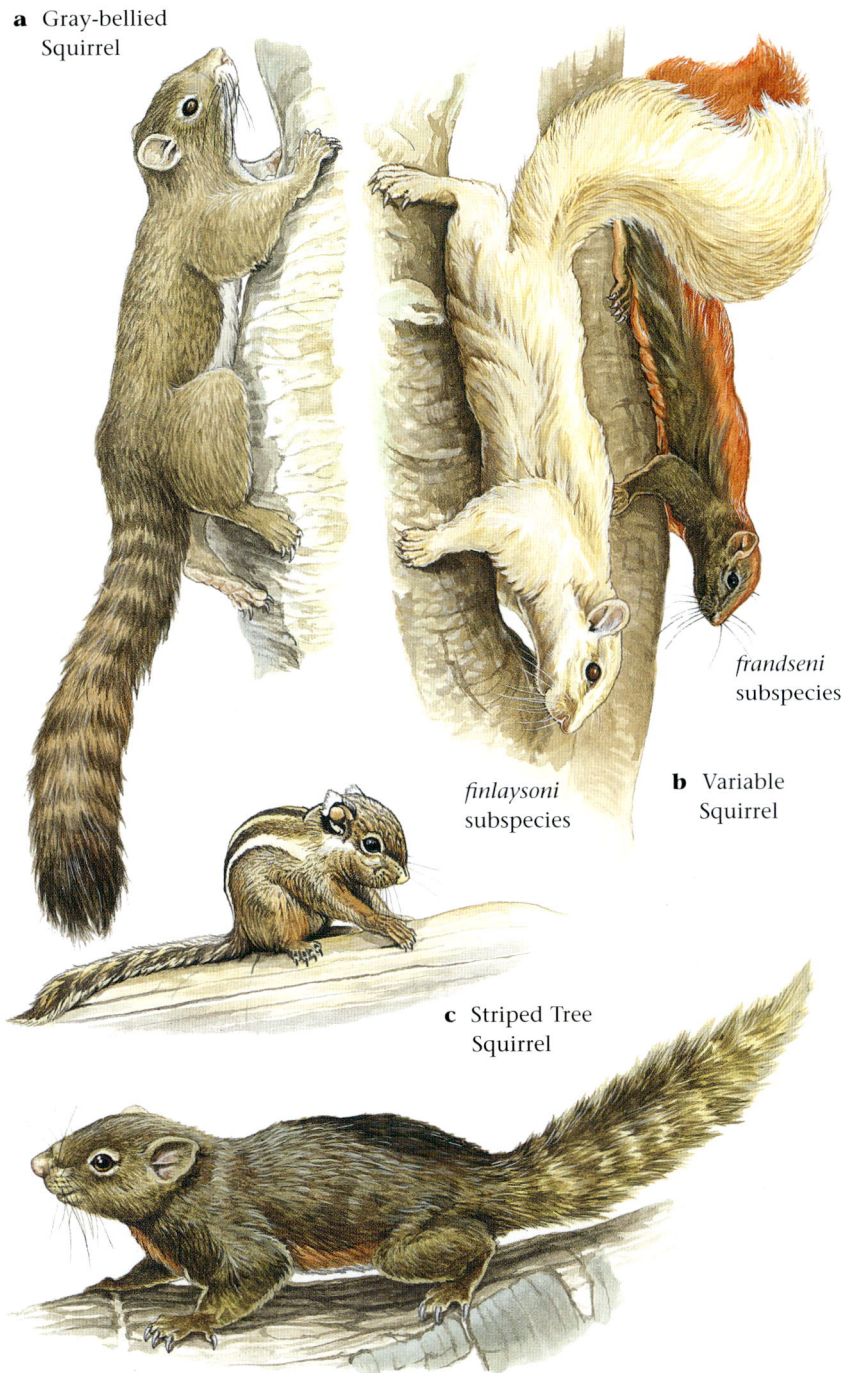

a Gray-bellied Squirrel

frandseni subspecies

finlaysoni subspecies

b Variable Squirrel

c Striped Tree Squirrel

d Belly-banded Squirrel

Plate 68 (See also: Rodents, p. 194)

Plate 68a
Malayan Porcupine
Hystrix brachyura
ID: Large (body length 68 cm, 2.2 ft); dark brown with short, dark spines on the front half of the body and long, whitish quills banded black protruding from the back half.

HABITAT: Mainly nocturnal; floor of primary and tall secondary forest from lowlands to 900 m (3000 ft) elevation. When frightened or challenged by danger, it rattles the hollow spines on the tail to make a distinctive noise. (Replaced north of peninsular Thailand by the similar Crestless Himalayan Porcupine, *Hystrix hodgsoni,* which ranges in forests from the lowlands to 1500 m (5000 ft) elevation.)

REGION: PT

Plate 68b
Bush-tailed Porcupine
Atherurus macrourus
ID: Medium-sized (body length 45 cm, 1.5 ft); long (18 cm, 7 in) scaly tail with bushy end; all brown with short pale-colored spines.

HABITAT: Nocturnal; family groups of 4 to 8 on floor of open primary and tall secondary forests in hilly country below 900 m (3000 ft) elevation.

REGION: PT, SE, CP, W, NE, FN

Plate 68c
Great Bandicoot
Bandicota indica
ID: Medium-sized (body length 28 cm, 11 in); upperparts blackish, underparts gray; long (24 cm, 9 in) naked black tail.

HABITAT: Primarily nocturnal; small family groups in burrows dug into fields, agricultural areas, marshes, and cane fields. Usually associated with human habitations and agricultural areas.

REGION: SE, CP, W, NE, FN

Plate 68d
Ryukyu Mouse
Mus caroli
ID: Tiny (body length 8 cm, 3 in); brownish gray with long naked tail, longer than body, that is black on top and grayish white on the bottom.

HABITAT: The common field mouse of agricultural areas in Thailand north of the peninsula.

REGION: SE, CP, W, NE, FN

Plate 68e
Yellow Rajah Rat
Rattus surifer
ID: Small (body length 18 cm, 7 in); upperparts yellowish orange with short spines, underparts white; long (18 cm, 7 in) naked tail is black with white tip.

HABITAT: Nocturnal and terrestrial on the floor of forests, grasslands, and rice paddies, from offshore islands to 1500 m (5000 ft) elevation. The common rat of wild habitats in Thailand. (Replaced in towns and cities by the familiar brown House, or Black, Rat, *Rattus rattus.*)

REGION: SE, CP, W, NE, FN

Plate 68

a Malayan Porcupine

b Bush-tailed Porcupine

c Great Bandicoot

d Ryukyu Mouse

e Yellow Rajah Rat

Plate 69 (See also: Carnivores, p. 197; Tapir, p. 203)

Plate 69a
Asiatic Jackal
Canis aureus
ID: Large (body length 68 cm, 2.2 ft); grayish brown with black saddle of hairs on back; bushy, fairly short (22 cm, 9 in) black-tipped tail; ears pointed.

HABITAT: Pairs active at night in a wide range of habitats from open fields to open forest floor. Its yelps and whines at dusk are more often heard than the animal is seen.

REGION: W, NE, FN

Plate 69b
Asian Wild Dog
Cuon alpinus
ID: Large (body length 85 cm, 2.8 ft); reddish color with dark tail and snout; ears rounded.

HABITAT: Packs of 4 to 8 hunting in remote areas of dense forest with clearings, primarily in mountainous areas.

REGION: PT, SE, CP, W, NE, FN

Plate 69c
Malayan Sun Bear
Helarctos malayanus
ID: Very large (body length 1.2 m, 4 ft) but the smallest bear in the world; covered with short black hair with white "U" on chest; ears small and rounded; snout gray.

HABITAT: Usually nocturnal but occasionally active during the daytime; on the ground or climbing trees in dense forests; its claw marks on trees are often the best indication of its presence. Occurs in remote forests from lowlands to 2300 m (7600 ft) elevation. (The larger [body length 1.4 m, 4.6 ft] Asiatic Black Bear, *Selenarctos thibetanus*, is rare in northern and western Thailand forests. It has long black hair, a white "V" on the chest, and long rounded ears.)

REGION: PT, SE, W, NE, FN

Plate 69d
Yellow-throated Marten
Martes flavigula
ID: Medium-sized (body length 43 cm, 1.4 ft); light brown except for dark brown feet, top of head, and long (33 cm, 1 ft) bushy tail; chest buffy-yellow.

HABITAT: Primarily diurnal; solitary or in pairs in a wide variety of habitats from 200 to 2500 m (660 to 8250 ft) elevation; hunts for small vertebrates by agilely climbing trees or running quickly across the ground.

REGION: PT, W, NE, FN

Plate 69e
Asian Tapir
Tapirus indicus
ID: Very large (2.3 m, 7.6 ft; 1 m, 3.3 ft tall at shoulder); black with white middle body and rump; young are dark with white stripes and spots.

HABITAT: Primarily nocturnal on floor of dense primary forest; often associated with forest streams and lakes, in which they submerge themselves for refuge from danger.

REGION: PT, W

Note: this species is endangered in parts of its range, CITES Appendix I listed.

Plate 69

a Asiatic Jackal

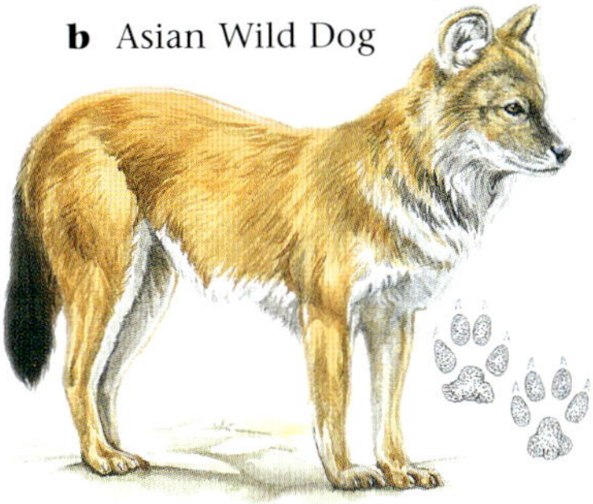

b Asian Wild Dog

c Malayan Sun Bear

d Yellow-throated Marten

e Asian Tapir

Plate 70a
Hog Badger
Arctonyx collaris
ID: Large (body length 1 m, 3.3 ft); buffy gray with black mask, white moustache and forehead; blackish legs, belly, and neck; long pig-like snout.
HABITAT: Nocturnal; solitary on forest floor from lowlands to 2500 m (8250 ft) elevation; sleeps during the day in deep burrows.

REGION: PT, W, NE, FN

Plate 70b
Smooth-coated Otter
Lutra perspicillata
ID: Large (body length 70 cm, 2.3 ft); sleek brown fur with long (42 cm, 1.4 ft) tail flattened on the underside; cheeks, throat, and entire upper chest creamy white. (The similar Common Otter, *Lutra lutra*, enters Thailand only in the northwest and is distinguished by its coarse fur, short "star-shaped" nose, and rounded tail tapering to a point.)
HABITAT: Small family groups in lowland rivers, reservoirs, lakes, and occasionally the ocean coast, especially in mangrove areas.

REGION: PT, CP, SE, W, NE, FN

Plate 70c
Small-clawed Otter
Aonyx cinerea
Large (body length 50 cm, 1.6 ft); grayish brown with whitish cheeks, mouth, and upper breast; short toes with small claws and little webbing; tail relatively short (30 cm, 1 ft) and rounded; the smallest otter in Thailand.
HABITAT: Small family groups in a wide variety of habitats with permanent water and trees, from mangrove lowlands to 1300 m (4300 ft) elevation. (The extremely rare Hairy-nosed Otter, *Lutra sumatrana*, has its nose completely covered by hairs; tail flattened; whitish face extends only to upper breast. Confined in Thailand to the peninsula and perhaps the extreme southeast.)

REGION: PT, CP, SE, W, NE, FN

Plate 70d
Small Indian Civet
Viverricula malaccensis
ID: Large (body length 59 cm, 1.9 ft); tan with black stripes and spots; legs and feet black; long (37 cm, 1.1 ft) tail tan with 6 to 7 narrow black rings; ears and legs relatively short.
HABITAT: Primarily nocturnal; solitary in long grass and forest scrub; often near rural human habitation; usually on the ground but often climbs low trees and shrubbery in the lowlands to 1000 m (3300 ft) elevation.

REGION: PT, CP, SE, W, NE, FN

Plate 70e
Large Indian Civet
Viverra zibetha
ID: Large (body length 80 cm, 2.6 ft); light brown with black stripes and spots; legs and feet dark brown; long (42 cm, 1.4 ft) tail dark brown with 4 or 5 narrow tan rings; ears and legs relatively long.
HABITAT: Primarily nocturnal; solitary in secondary forest often near rural human habitation; usually on the ground but often climbs low trees, in lowlands to 110 m (3300 ft) elevation. (The similar Large-spotted Civet, *Viverra megaspila*, has a black line running down the top of the tail so that none of the light tail rings is complete.)

REGION: PT, CP, SE, W, NE, FN

Plate 70

a Hog Badger

b Smooth-coated Otter

c Small-clawed Otter

d Small Indian Civet

e Large Indian Civet

Plate 71 (*See also:* Carnivores, p. 197)

Plate 71a
Common Palm Civet
Paradoxurus hermaphroditus
ID: Medium-sized (body length 45 cm, 1.5 ft); brownish gray with black snout, ears, legs, and face mask; three indistinct lines of black spots along each side; long tail about length of body, outer half black.

HABITAT: Nocturnal; floor and mid level branches of trees in secondary forest, plantations, and gardens of lowlands; often near human habitation.

REGION: PT, CP, SE, W, NE, FN

Plate 71b
Masked Palm Civet
Paguma larvata
ID: Large (body length 59 cm, 1.9 ft); brown with no stripes or spots on body; long thin tail about length of body and black-tipped; neck, ears, and legs dark brown; distinctive white mask on face over eyes and on snout.

HABITAT: Primarily nocturnal but occasionally active during daytime; usually in lower branches of trees in secondary forest plantations and gardens, but also often on the ground.

REGION: PT, CP, SE, W, NE, FN

Plate 71c
Binturong
Arctictis binturong
ID: Large (body length 79 cm, 2.6 ft); shaggy black fur with a long (67 cm, 2.2 ft), thickly-haired, prehensile tail; obvious tufts of hair on ear tips.

HABITAT: Active both day and night; primarily arboreal but sometimes seen on the ground lumbering slowly through the undergrowth; tall secondary and primary forest of lowlands to 1500 m (5000 ft) elevation.

REGION: PT, SE, W, NE, FN

Plate 71d
Javan Mongoose
Herpestes javanicus
ID: Medium-sized (body length 37 cm, 1.2 ft); brown grizzled black and white; tail long (27 cm, 11 in) and tapering to a tip, not bushy like that of the similar-appearing Common Treeshrew (Plate 61).

HABITAT: Solitary and active day and night in open forest, grasslands, and less commonly in moist primary forest clearings. Often seen bounding quickly across the road.

REGION: PT, CP, SE, W, NE, FN

Plate 71

olive form
gray form
a Common Palm Civet
b Masked Palm Civet
c Binturong
d Javan Mongoose

Plate 72a
Clouded Leopard
Neofelis nebulosa
ID: Large (body length 80 cm, 2.6 ft); pale to dark brown or grayish with huge black-bordered spots on its sides; long tail the length of the body is spotted black at the base, becoming black bands toward the tip. (The similarly colored and proportioned Marbled Cat, *Felis marmorata,* is a little more than half the size of the Clouded Leopard, and the large spots on its sides are more indistinct.)

HABITAT: Generally nocturnal; usually in upper tree branches of tall forest but regularly descends to move along the forest floor.

REGION: PT, SE, W, NE, FN

Note: this species is endangered in parts of its range, CITES Appendix I listed.

Plate 72b
Leopard Cat
Felis bengalensis
ID: Medium-sized (body length 48 cm, 1.6 ft); buffy colored with large black spots coalescing into stripes on the upper back and head; relatively long tail is more than half the length of the body and spotted its entire length.

HABITAT: Generally nocturnal; terrestrial over a wide range of habitats from agricultural fields to open primary forest; often around human habitation.

REGION: PT, CP, SE, W, NE, FN

Plate 72c
Leopard
Panthera pardus
ID: Very large (body length 1.2 m, 4 ft); buffy yellow with dark rosette spots but all-black individuals are regular, especially in southern Thailand; long tail almost the length of the body.

HABITAT: Solitary and active night and day in a wide range of habitats, from low scrub to primary forest; often hunts from trees but is also frequently on the ground.

REGION: PT, SE, W, NE, FN

Note: this species is endangered in parts of its range, CITES Appendix I listed.

Plate 72d
Tiger
Panthera tigris
ID: Very large (body length 2 m, 6.6 ft); large male can weigh 300 kg (660 lb); buffy yellow with black vertical stripes.

HABITAT: Active day or night over a wide range of remote habitats from savannah to primary forest.

REGION: PT, SE, W, NE, FN

Note: this species is endangered, CITES Appendix I and IUCN Red List.

Plate 72e
Fishing Cat
Felis viverrina
ID: Large (body length 75 cm, 3.3 ft); grayish brown with small black spots on the sides coalescing into short stripes on the upper back and head; relatively short gray tail is black tipped and only about one-third the length of the body.

HABITAT: Generally nocturnal; restricted to heavy vegetation along rivers, lakes, and reservoirs where they fish from the edge of the water by scooping prey from the water with their webbed feet and long claws.

REGION: CP, SE, W, NE, FN

Plate 72

a Clouded Leopard

b Leopard Cat

c Leopard

d Tiger

e Fishing Cat

Plate 73 (See also: Elephant and Rhinoceros, p. 203; Even-toed Ungulates, p. 201)

Plate 73a
Asian Elephant
Elephas maximus
ID: Huge (body length 5 m, 17 ft; height at shoulder 2.8 m, 9 ft); gray with long trunk and large ears.

HABITAT: Primarily nocturnal; females and young in herds of 5 to 20; males often solitary; tusks usually restricted to males; shaded forest and tall grass often near streams or lakes.

REGION: PT, SE, W, NE, FN

Note: this species is endangered, CITES Appendix I and IUCN Red List.

Plate 73b
Asian Two-horned Rhinoceros
(also called Sumatran Rhinoceros)
Dicerorhinus sumatrensis
ID: Very large (body length 2.5 m, 8 ft; height at the shoulder 1.3 m, 4 ft); buffy gray with long snout bearing one long horn at its end and another shorter one midway along its length.

HABITAT: Swamps and moist forests of the lowlands to steep mountain forests at 2000 m (6600 ft) elevation; fewer than 10 individuals remain in remote areas of Thailand along the Malaysian and Myanmar borders. (The larger Lesser One-horned Rhinoceros, or Javan Rhinocerous, *Rhinoceros sondaicus*, is extinct in Thailand, with fewer than 30 individuals remaining in Laos, Cambodia, and Java.)

REGION: PT, W, NE

Note: this species is endangered, CITES Appendix I and IUCN Red List.

Plate 73c
Gaur
Bos gaurus
ID: Very large (body length 2.8 m, 9 ft); heavily built with massive head, thick horns, and a prominent hump on shoulders; reddish to blackish with buffy-white legs.

HABITAT: Small herds of 5 to 15 in open forest and forest clearings above 300 m (1000 ft) elevation (lowlands below 200 m, 660 ft, in southernmost Peninsular Thailand); most active at night.

REGION: PT, SE, W, NE, FN

Note: this species is endangered, CITES Appendix I listed.

Plate 73d
Banteng
Bos javanicus
ID: Very large (body length 2 m, 6.6 ft); dark chestnut with white legs and a distinctive white rump patch; inconspicuous hump on shoulders.

HABITAT: Small herds of 10 to 30 in forested hilly country up to 2000 m (6600 ft) elevation.

REGION: PT, W, NE, FN

Note: this species is endangered, IUCN Red List.

Plate 73

a Asian Elephant

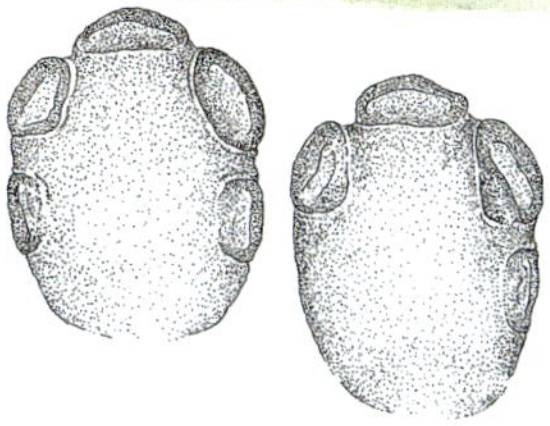

b Asian Two-horned Rhinoceros

c Gaur

d Banteng

Plate 74 (*See also:* Even-toed Ungulates, p. 201)

Plate 74a
Lesser Mouse Deer
Tragulus javanicus

ID: Medium-sized (body length 43 cm, 1.4 ft); stout body on extremely thin legs with arched, rusty brown back; three distinct white stripes on throat and chest.

HABITAT: Active both night and day; solitary on floor of lowland forest usually near water. (The similar Greater Mouse Deer, *Tragulus napu,* is larger (55 cm, 1.8 ft) and gray with dark and white stripes on throat and chest; it is confined in Thailand to the peninsula at elevations up to 1000 m (3300 ft).)

REGION: PT, SE, W, NE

Plate 74b
Common Barking Deer
Muntiacus muntjak

ID: Large (body length 1 m, 3.3 ft); reddish brown with dark face and legs; short spiked antlers arising from long furred bases.

HABITAT: Floor of a wide range of forest types; runs with head held low and often "barks" loudly when surprised.

REGION: PT, SE, W, NE, FN

Plate 74c
Sambar
Cervus unicolor

ID: Very large (body length 1.9 m, 6 ft; height at shoulder 1.5 m, 5 ft); coarse and shaggy hair yellowish gray; males in season (June to February) with large stout antlers; short bushy tail.

HABITAT: Solitary or in small groups on forested hillsides.

REGION: PT, CP, SE, W, NE, FN

Plate 74d
Serow
Capricornis sumatrensis

ID: Very large (body length 1.5 m, 5 ft); large headed, donkey-like ears, thick neck, and relatively short legs; highly variable color from black to rusty; legs in northern Thailand black, in southern Thailand rusty; short thick horns.

HABITAT: Solitary or in small family groups on steep limestone cliffs, from 200 to 2450 m (700 to 8000 ft) elevation, and steep coastal islands with dense vegetation.

REGION: PT, SE, NE, FN

Note: this species is endangered, CITES Appendix I.

Plate 74e
Wild Pig
Sus scrofa

ID: Very large (body length 1.4 m, 4.6 ft; males can exceed 225 kg, 500 lb); black mixed with rust and gray.

HABITAT: Crepuscular; herds in grassy forest clearings, open scrub, and secondary forest.

REGION: PT, CP, SE, W, NE, FN

Plate 74

a Lesser Mouse Deer

b Common Barking Deer

c Sambar

d Serow

e Wild Pig

Plate 75a
Irrawaddy Dolphin
Orcaella brevirostris
ID: Very large (body length 2.4 m, 8 ft); gray to slate-blue; small, rounded dorsal fin far back toward the tail; face bulbous and rounded with no snout.

HABITAT: Family groups in shallow, turbid coastal waters, mangrove swamps, and occasionally up large coastal rivers; does not jump from water; most easily noticed by noisy breathing when it "blows."

REGION: PT, SE, W

Plate 75b
Common Dolphin
Delphinus delphis
ID: Very large (body length 2.4 m, 8 ft); long beak, triangular dorsal fin gray; hourglass pattern of yellow and gray on sides.

HABITAT: Large, active schools with many individuals jumping from the water and often riding bow waves of vessels.

REGION: PT, CP, SE, W

Plate 75c
Bottle-nosed Dolphin
Tursiops truncatus
ID: Very large (body length 2.2 m, 7 ft); upperparts dark bluish gray; underparts grayish white; short beak and distinct dorsal fin hooked at tip. (The form off Thailand is given separate species status by some experts, Eastern Bottle-nosed Dolphin, *Tursiops aduncus,* but is considered only a geographical variant of *Tursiops truncatus* by most experts.)

HABITAT: Small groups actively jumping from water and riding bow waves of vessels.

REGION: PT, CP, SE, W

Plate 75d
Dugong
Dugong dugon
ID: Very large (body length 3 m, 10 ft); brownish gray with a broad, rounded head and no dorsal fin.

HABITAT: Rests by day in deep water; by night, feeds underwater in shallow coastal waters, grazing on green algae and other seaweeds, usually in areas of rocky outcroppings. Now limited in Thailand to 40 individuals at the mouth of the Trang River, on the west coast of the peninsula.

REGION: PT

Plate 75

a Irrawaddy Dolphin

b Common Dolphin

c Bottle-nosed Dolphin

d Dugong

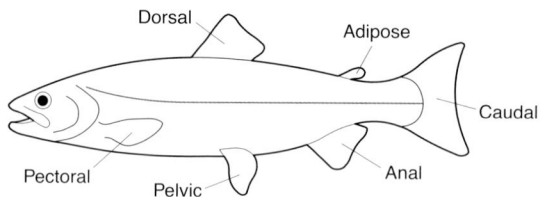

Figure 1 Typical fish form, showing position of fins.

Plate 76a
Threadfin Butterflyfish
Chaetodon auriga
This species is common in protected shallow reefs. It is one of the more omnivorous members of the family, feeding on algae, marine worms, small crustaceans, and even coral polyps. The background color is white in front and yellow toward the tail. Two series of dark stripes extend at right angles from each other and diagonally. A dark stripe extends through the eye, and there is a characteristic black spot toward the rear of the dorsal fin, from which extends a filament-like projection. (to 20 cm, 8 in)

Plate 76b
Speckled Butterflyfish
Chaetodon citrinellus
Also known as the Citron Butterflyfish, this relatively small species prefers shallow reefs in which there is relatively little coral growth. Look for somewhat irregular rows of small dark spots over a very pale yellow background. Also note the black eye-stripe. (to 11 cm, 4.3 in)

Plate 76c
Triangular Butterflyfish
Chaetodon triangulum
This Indian Ocean butterflyfish can be distinguished from its very similar sibling species (p. 212) in the Western Pacific (*Chaetodon baronessa*, variously called Triangular Butterflyfish, Eastern Triangular Butterflyfish, or Baroness Butterflyfish) by the larger patch of black on its tail. You will find it only where there are large patches of Acropora corals (Plate 102), upon which it exclusively feeds. (to 15 cm, 6 in)

Plate 76d
Lined Butterflyfish
Chaetodon lineolatus
The largest member of the family, this species prefers coral-rich areas, where it dines on polyps as well as anemones. It is white with thin vertical black lines, a prominent black eye-stripe, and a bright yellow posterior with a black swath. A pair of these beauties is a breathtaking sight. (to 30 cm, 12 in)

Plate 76e
Collared Butterflyfish
Chaetodon collare
This distinctive butterflyfish frequents coral-rich areas. Look for the prominent white band behind the eye. (to 16 cm, 6.3 in)

Plate 76f
Raccoon Butterflyfish
Chaetodon lunula
This species gets its common name from its black raccoon-like mask. The rest of the body is generally dusky greenish brown, tending toward yellow ventrally. Though monogamous, it is more likely to be found in small groups than are many other butterflyfish. (to 20 cm, 8 in)

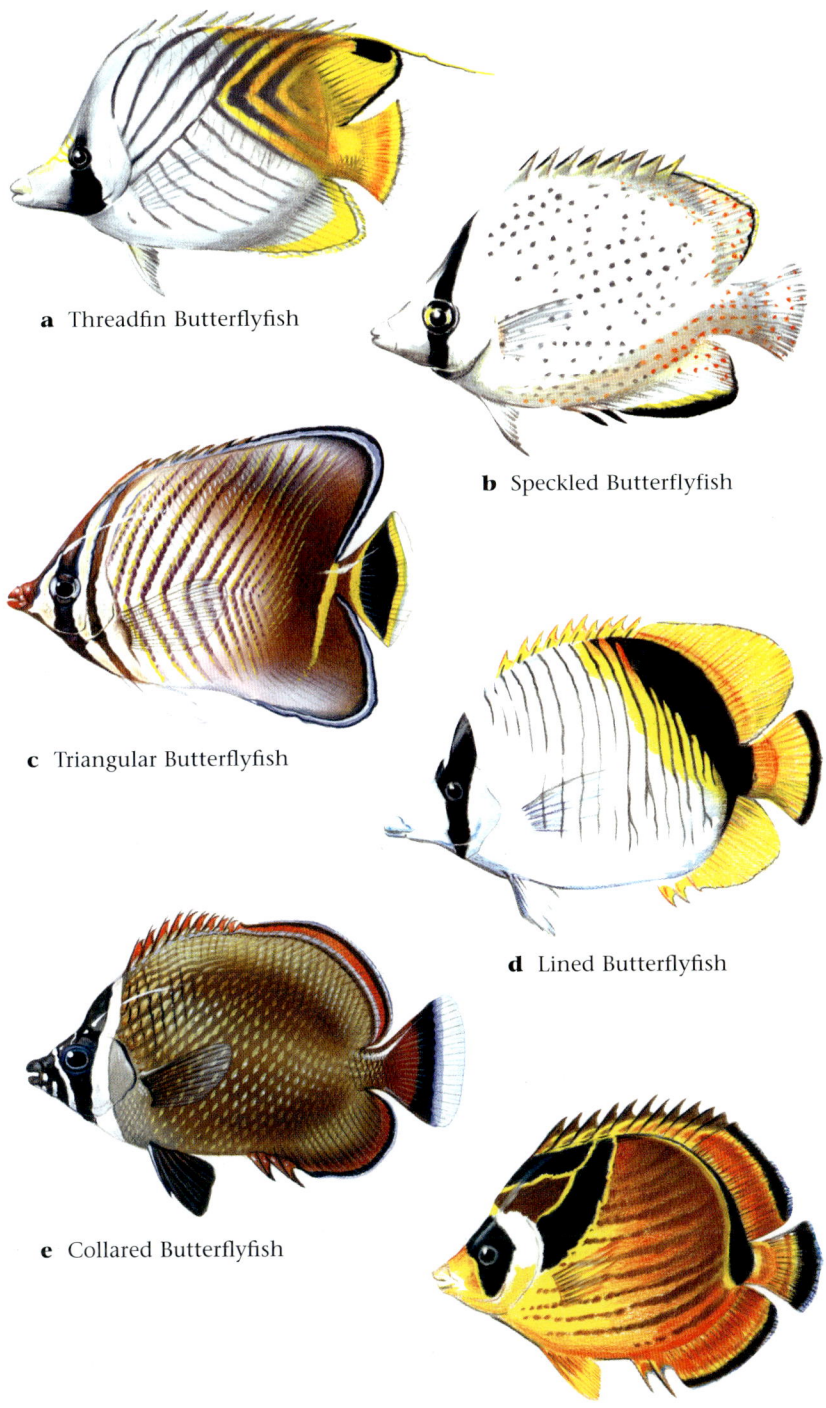

a Threadfin Butterflyfish

b Speckled Butterflyfish

c Triangular Butterflyfish

d Lined Butterflyfish

e Collared Butterflyfish

f Raccoon Butterflyfish

Plate 77a
Blackback Butterflyfish
Chaetodon melanotus
This species frequents areas with ample coral, its main food source. The body is white, with many thin, diagonal black bands. The fins and snout are bright yellow and a black stripe runs through the eyes. Note also the black band on the caudal peduncle (where the tail joins the body), by means of which this species can be distinguished from the very similar Spot-tail Butterflyfish (*Chaetodon ocellicaudus*), which has a black tail spot instead. (to 15 cm, 6 in)

Plate 77b
Meyer's Butterflyfish
Chaetodon meyeri
This is one of the more spectacular members of this family of eye-catching fishes. The body is bluish white with prominent oblique black bands. These bands continue through the yellow fins, and they are also outlined in yellow in the head region. It feeds primarily on coral polyps, so it prefers coral-rich areas. (to 18 cm, 7 in)

Plate 77c
Bluespot Butterflyfish
Chaetodon plebius
This butterflyfish can be distinguished from all others by the ovoid blue swatch on its upper body. Note also the black eye-stripe (outlined with blue) and black eye-spot near the tail. This species feeds primarily on coral polyps. (to 13 cm, 5 in)

Plate 77d
Chevroned Butterflyfish
Chaetodon trifascialis
This species is named for the chevron-shaped black lines over the white background color. Note also the black eye-stripe and black tail outlined with yellow. The dorsal and anal fins are also less rounded than in most butterflyfishes, giving it a distinctive profile. This species feeds solely on live coral; it maintains feeding territories around the more productive areas, which it ardently defends. (to 18 cm, 7 in)

Plate 77e
Indian Vagabond Butterflyfish
Chaetodon decussatus
This butterflyfish can be found on the Andaman Sea side of the peninsula; it prefers shallow, turbid water over coral rubble. It has chevron-shaped body markings resembling those of the Chevroned Butterflyfish (*Chaetodon trifascialis*), but look for the dusky dorsal and anal fins. (to 20 cm, 8 in)

Plate 77f
Peppered Butterflyfish
Chaetodon guttatissimus
Also called the Spotted Butterflyfish, this species is only found on the Andaman Sea side of the peninsula, where it frequents both lagoon and seaward reefs. (to 12 cm, 4.5 in)

Plate 77

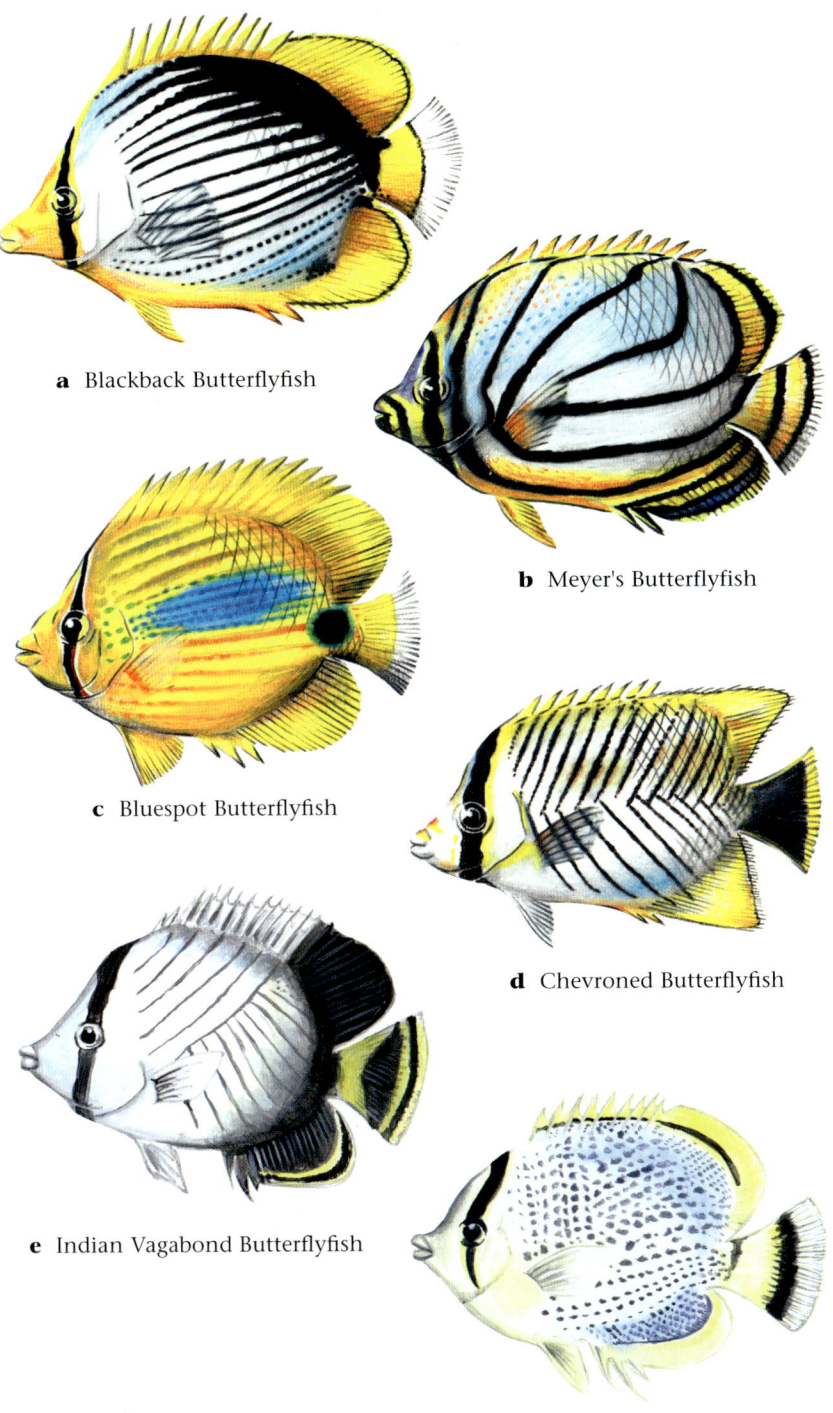

a Blackback Butterflyfish

b Meyer's Butterflyfish

c Bluespot Butterflyfish

d Chevroned Butterflyfish

e Indian Vagabond Butterflyfish

f Peppered Butterflyfish

Plate 78a
Redfin Butterflyfish
Chaetodon trifasciatus
This beauty, which is also known as the Oval Butterflyfish, can be found in pairs in protected coral-rich areas. The body is cream-colored with purplish, somewhat oblique horizontal stripes. A black bar, flanked by yellow, runs through the eyes. The common name derives from an orangish band near the rear of the anal fin. (to 15 cm, 6 in)

Plate 78b
Eibl's Anglefish
Centropyge eibli
This small angelfish is common in the Andaman Sea, especially in coral-rich rocky environments, where it dines primarily on filamentous algae. (to 15 cm, 6 in)

Plate 78c
Beaked Coralfish
Chelmon rostratus
This butterflyfish is common in shallow near-shore reefs. The background color is white but is transected by three orange bars, the rearmost of which has a prominent black spot near the base of the anal fin. Another, much thinner yellow-orange bar extends through the eye. Note also the forceps-like snout. (to 20 cm, 8 in)

Plate 78d
Forcepsfish
Forcipiger flavissimus
This distinctive butterflyfish uses its long snout to extract a variety of foodstuffs, including the tube-feet and pedicellaria (jaw-like appendages used for protection) of sea urchins and other echinoderms. The body is lemon yellow, while the head is black above and bluish white below. Note also the small black spot on the anal fin near the base of the tail. The Longnose Butterflyfish (*Forcipiger longirostris*) looks very similar but is much less common and can be distinguished by its much longer snout. (to 22 cm, 8.5 in)

Plate 78e
Longfin Bannerfish
Heniochus acuminatus
Bannerfish are named for their elongate dorsal fins. Of the several species that occur on the reef, this is the one with the longest banner. The body is white with two broad black bands. Note also the yellow on pectoral fins, tail fin, and the rear portion of the dorsal fin. (to 25 cm, 10 in)

Plate 78f
Three-spot Angelfish
Apolemichthys trimaculatus
This strikingly yellow angelfish prefers clear lagoons and seaward reefs with lots of ledges and vertical features. It dines on tunicates and sponges. Look for the distinctive blue lips and the black spot high on the head. (to to 25 cm, 10 in)

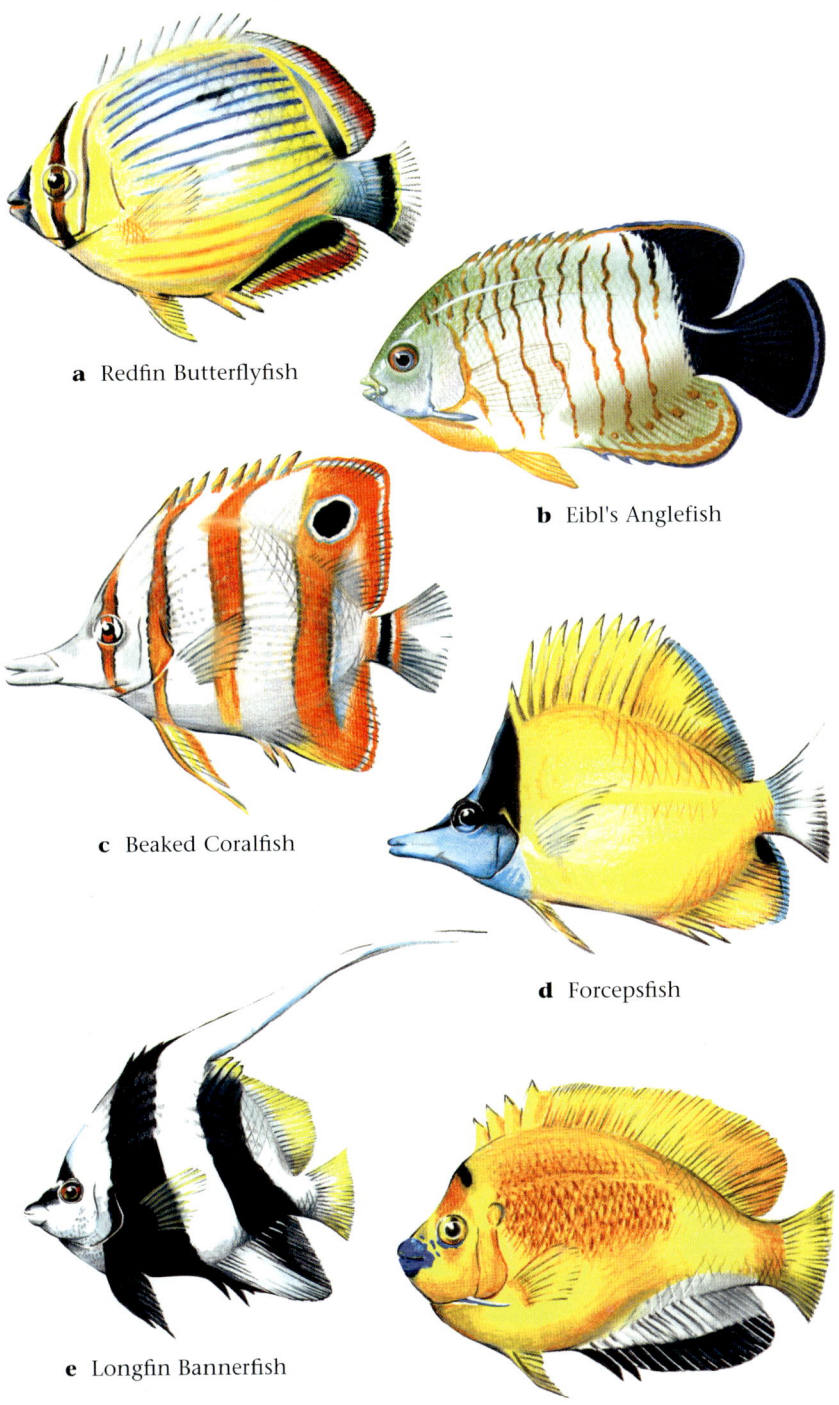

a Redfin Butterflyfish
b Eibl's Anglefish
c Beaked Coralfish
d Forcepsfish
e Longfin Bannerfish
f Three-spot Angelfish

Plate 79a
Golden-girdled Coralfish
Coradion chrysozonas
This species, also called the Orange-banded Coralfish, prefers the rocky or rubble areas of coastal reefs, where it dines on sponges. Look for the third wide, yellow body-bar with its distinctive black spot. (to 15 cm, 6 in)

Plate 79b
Emperor Angelfish
Pomacanthus imperator
This is one of the largest angelfishes and perhaps the most beautiful. It undergoes a striking color change during the transition from the juvenile state to adulthood. Juveniles are black with irregular blue and white lines. The adults cannot be confused with any other fish. This species prefers coral-rich areas, where it can be found near caves and overhangs. (to 38 cm, 15 in)

Plate 79c
Blue-ring Angelfish
Pomacanthus annularis
This very large angelfish is named for the light blue bands that adorn its body and fins. Typically found in pairs in or around caves and wrecks. (to 45 cm, 18 in)

Plate 79d
Yellowmask Angelfish
Pomacanthus xanthometapon
This species, also called the Blueface Angelfish, has a distinctive beard-like blue region around the cheeks and mouth, above and below which is the yellow mask. The tail is also yellow. Note also the black spot at the rear of the anal fin. Like 79b ands 79c (the previous two species), it feeds primarily on sponges. (to 38 cm, 15 in)

Plate 79e
Regal Angelfish
Pygoplites diacanthus
This beauty is a sponge-eater and prefers coral-rich clear-water environments in lagoons as well as seaward reefs. It can be identified by its distinctive body coloration, which consists of alternating bands of white, black, and gold. (to 26 cm, 10.5 in)

Plate 79f
Scissortail Sergeant
Abudefduf sexfasciatus
The sergeants are fairly drab-looking damselfishes with lots of personality, especially during the breeding season. This species closely resembles the Indo-Pacific Sergeant (*Abudefduf vaigiensis*), but can be distinguished from it by the distinct black stripes on each lobe of the caudal fin. It prefers coral-rich areas but feeds primarily on zooplankton and benthic (bottom-dwelling) algae. Often found high up in the water column in aggregations. (to 17 cm, 6.5 in)

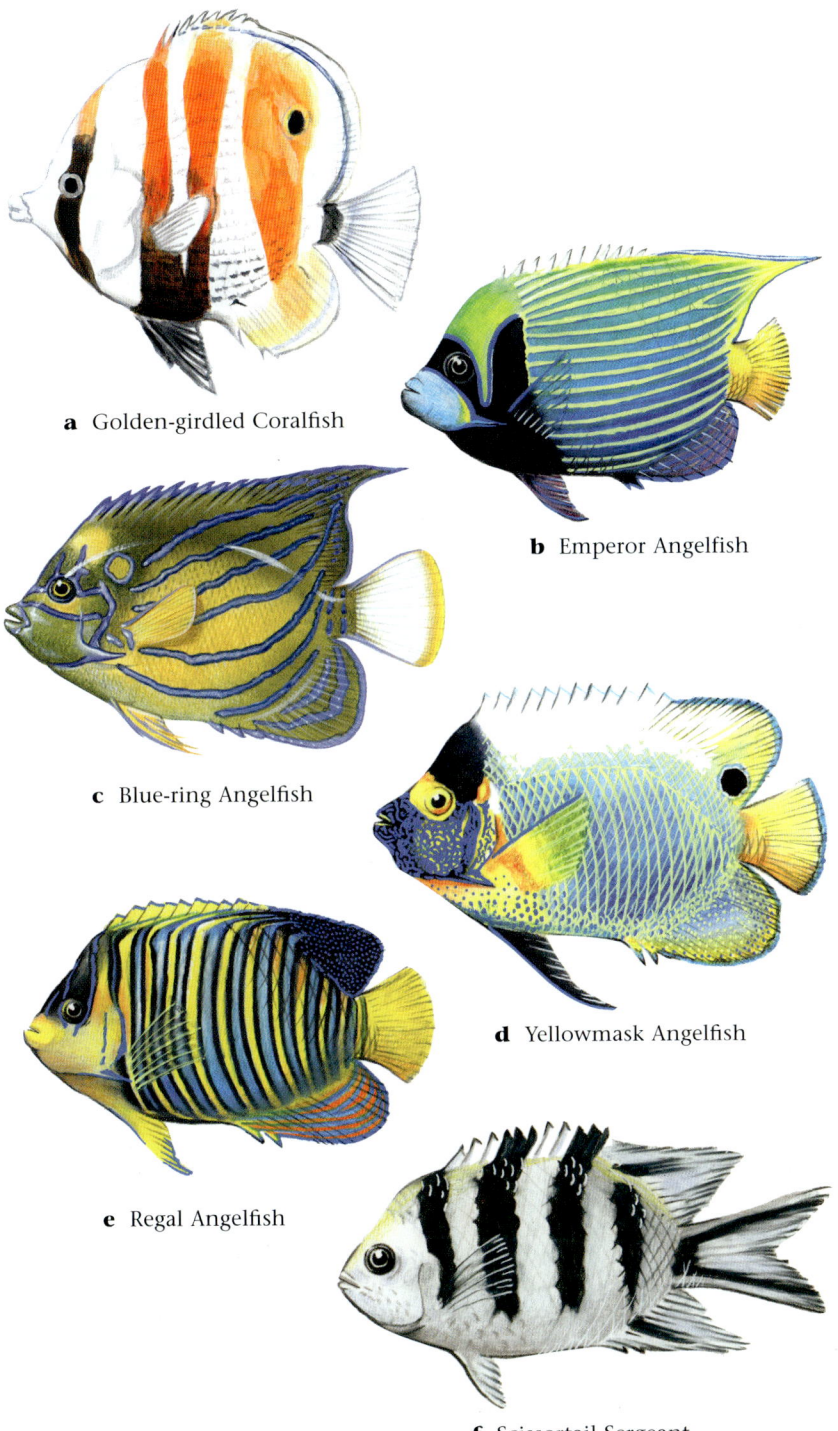

Plate 79

a Golden-girdled Coralfish
b Emperor Angelfish
c Blue-ring Angelfish
d Yellowmask Angelfish
e Regal Angelfish
f Scissortail Sergeant

Plate 80a
Bengal Sergeant
Abudefduf bengalensis
This highly territorial damselfish prefers inshore reefs and lagoons. (to 17 cm, 6.5 in)

Plate 80b
Western Gregory
Stegastes obreptus
This shallow-water damsel maintains patches of filamentous algae on dead coral (actually "weeding" the algae patches to keep other growth away), which provide much of its sustenance, and which they aggressively defend against interlopers. It is dark dusky brown all over. (to 15 cm, 6 in)

Plate 80c
Bluegreen Chromis
Chromis viridis
This damselfish forms large aggregations above branching corals, a dazzling sight. The body coloration is pale blue-green and appears iridescent in the right light. (to 9 cm, 3.5 in)

Plate 80d
Chocolate-dip Chromis
Chromis dimidiata
Also called the Two-tone Chromis, this damsel forms large aggregations above the reef tops. In Thailand, it is confined to the Andaman coast. Its common name derives from its coloration—brownish black in front and white in back. (to 9 cm, 3.5 in)

Plate 80e
Andaman Damselfish
Pomacentrus alleni
This attractive little damsel is confined to the Similan Islands. It can be distinguished from other small, blue-bodied, yellow-finned damsels by the black area at the bottom of the tail. It prefers areas of rubble and dead coral. (to 6 cm, 2.4 in)

Plate 80f
Gray Demoiselle
Chrysiptera glauca
This damsel prefers areas of moderate current or surge with plenty of rubble, usually on intertidal reef flats. It is grayish brown above and gray-white below. (to 11 cm, 4.25 in)

Plate 80

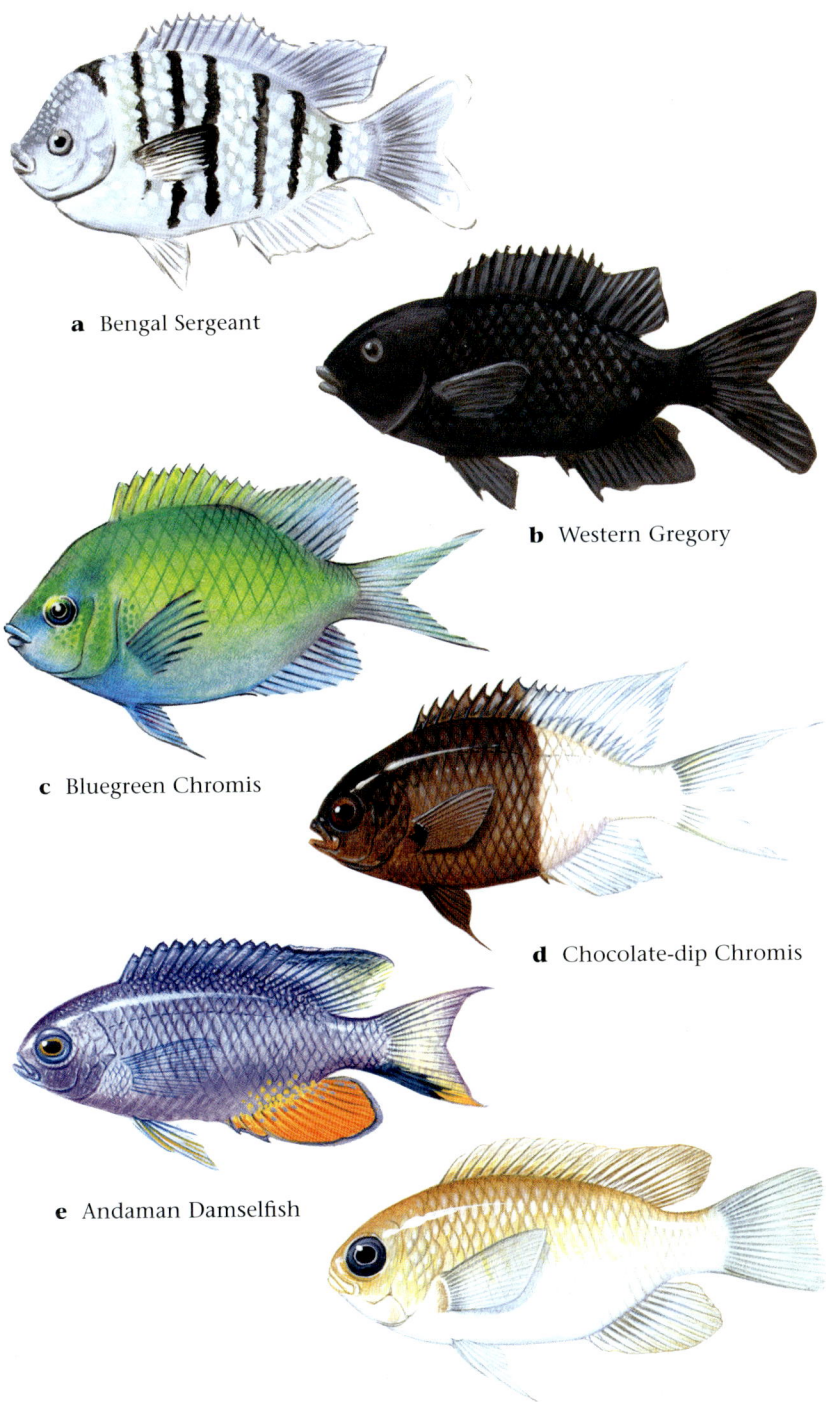

a Bengal Sergeant
b Western Gregory
c Bluegreen Chromis
d Chocolate-dip Chromis
e Andaman Damselfish
f Gray Demoiselle

Plate 81a
Ambon Damselfish
Pomacentrus amboinensis
Look for this damsel on sheltered reefs that border sandy areas, among branching coral, usually in small groups. The coloration is highly variable, but usually the belly is yellow. (to 10 cm, 4 in)

Plate 81b
Humbug Damselfish
Dascylus aruanus
You are most likely to find this handsome creature in groups of 10 to 50 over heads of Acropora corals, into which they will disappear if you approach too closely. The body is white with three broad vertical black bands, the front-most of which runs through the eyes. The Humbug Damsel and other members of the genus are known sex changers (female-to-male). (to 8.5 cm, 3.25 in)

Plate 81c
Indian Humbug
Dascyllus carneus
This engaging damsel replaces the closely related, similar-looking, and more broadly distributed Reticulated Humbug (*Dascyllus reticulatus*) in the Andaman Sea. It can be found in small groups among isolated heads of branching coral. (to 6 cm, 2.4 in)

Plate 81d
Three-spot Dascyllus
Dascyllus trimaculatus
This damsel often shares anemones with anemonefish; it can be found in both lagoons and seaward reefs. The body is charcoal-colored with black accents at the scale margins. The three spots, which are white, are easiest to see in the juveniles; the one on the head always disappears in adults. (to 13 cm, 5 in)

Plate 81e
Lemon Damsel
Pomacentrus mollucensis
Look for this damsel in clear-water areas among branching coral. It can be found in small groups actively seeking planktonic morsels, primarily small crustaceans. The body and fins are yellow, except for a black margin on the dorsal and anal fins. (to 7 cm, 3.75)

Plate 81f
Golden Damselfish
Amblyglyphidodon aureus
This damsel prefers steep outer reef slopes of moderate depth, where it feeds on zooplankton. Its coloration is a rich golden yellow throughout. (to 14 cm, 5.5 in)

Plate 81

a Ambon Damselfish

b Humbug Damselfish

c Indian Humbug

d Three-spot Dascyllus

e Lemon Damsel

f Golden Damselfish

Plate 82a
False Clownfish
(also called False Clown Anemonefish)
Amphiprion ocellaris
This delightful creature is always found in and around large anemones, especially, *Heteractis magnifica* and *Stichodactyla mertensii* (both Plate 101). The prominent white bands, outlined in black over a bright orange body, make it easy to identify. All anemonefish are monogamous male-to-female sex changers, which is why the largest member of the pair is the female. (to 11 cm, 4.25 in)

Plate 82b
Tomato Anemonefish
Amphiprion frenatus
This species associates exclusively (p. 213) with the anemone *Entacmaea quadricolor* (Plate 101). In Thailand it occurs only in the gulf. The body coloration is a rich brick-red, tending toward dusky brown near the back; a prominent white band runs behind the eye; the fins are orange. (to 14 cm, 5.5 in)

Plate 82c
Saddleback Anemonefish
Amphiprion polymnus
Look for this fish among the tentacles of the anemones *Heteractis* sp. and *Stichodactyla* sp. (p. 434). The body is dark brown, sometimes orangish-yellow toward the stomach, with a white band behind the eye and a white saddle on the back. In Thailand, this species occurs only in the Gulf. (to 13 cm, 5 in)

Plate 82d
Skunk Anemonefish
Amphiprion akallopisos
This species can be found with the anemones *Heteractis magnifica* and *Stichodactyla mertensii* (both Plate 101). It is pale orange with a white stripe running down the midline of the back. It is fairly common on the Andaman Sea side of the peninsula. (to 11 cm, 4.25 in)

Plate 82e
Spine-cheek Anemonefish
Premnas biaculeatus
Though it belongs to a completely different genus than the other so-called anemonefishes, this species too is intimately associated with anemones (p. 213). Females are larger than males in all anemonefishes but in this species the size difference is especially dramatic. The sexes also differ in coloration, the males being more deeply and brightly colored. The body coloration ranges from scarlet to reddish brown, with two or three vertical white bars. It associates primarily with the anemone *Entacmaea quadricolor* (Plate 101). (to 16 cm, 6.3 in)

Plate 82f
Longnose Hawkfish
Oxycirrhites typus
This hawkfish can be readily distinguished by its elongate forceps-like snout. Its background coloration is whitish, overlaid with reddish crosshatch markings. It can often be seen perched on the surface of soft corals and is more likely to move up into the water column than other hawkfishes. (to 13 cm, 5 in)

Plate 82

a False Clownfish

b Tomato Anemonefish

c Saddleback Anemonefish

d Skunk Anemonefish

e Spine-cheek Anemonefish

f Longnose Hawkfish

Plate 83a
Arc-eye Hawkfish
Paracirrhites arcatus
This hawkfish occurs in two color forms, one with a red background coloration and a prominent white band, the other a dark greenish brown. Both color varieties have a neon line arcing from below to above the eye. (to 14 cm, 5.5 in)

Plate 83b
Lyretail Hogfish
Bodianus anthoides
A denizen of dropoffs on seaward reefs, this species preys primarily on benthic (bottom-dwelling) invertebrates. The front end is brownish orange, the back half and tail are white, outlined in black, with irregular small black spots. (to 21 cm, 8.3 in)

Plate 83c
Spotted Wrasse
Anampses meleagrides
As in many wrasses, the males and females look markedly different, a phenomenon known as sexual dimorphism. Females are dark brown, almost black, with parallel rows of white spots, one on each body scale, and a bright yellow tail. Males are reddish brown with a bright orange tail adorned with blue spots. The head is covered with irregular blue lines and the stomach has rows of blue streaks. Note also the white crescent and blue band on the tail. (to 21 cm, 8.3 in)

Plate 83d
Indian Ocean Pin-striped Wrasse
Halichoeres vrolikii
This wrasse frequents shallow lagoons and reef channels, where coral areas are interspersed with sand. In Thailand it is confined to the Andaman Sea side of the peninsula. The body is green, with a number of thin red stripes; the head has curving blue and pink stripes. (to 13 cm, 5 in)

Plate 83e
Timor Wrasse
Halichoeres timorensis
Look for this wrasse in shallow coastal reefs. It has a white body with irregular red and pink markings; note also the distinctive red bands on the head. (to 14 cm, 5.5 in)

Plate 83f
Humphead Maori Wrasse
Cheilinus undulatus
All members of this genus are large by wrasse standards but this species, also called the Napolean Wrasse, is huge by any fish standards. It preys on a variety of benthic (bottom-dwelling) animals including sea urchins, mollusks, crabs, and other crustaceans. The common name comes from the prominent, bulbous protuberance on the head. Despite its immense size, it is quite shy. (to 2.3 m, 7.5 ft)

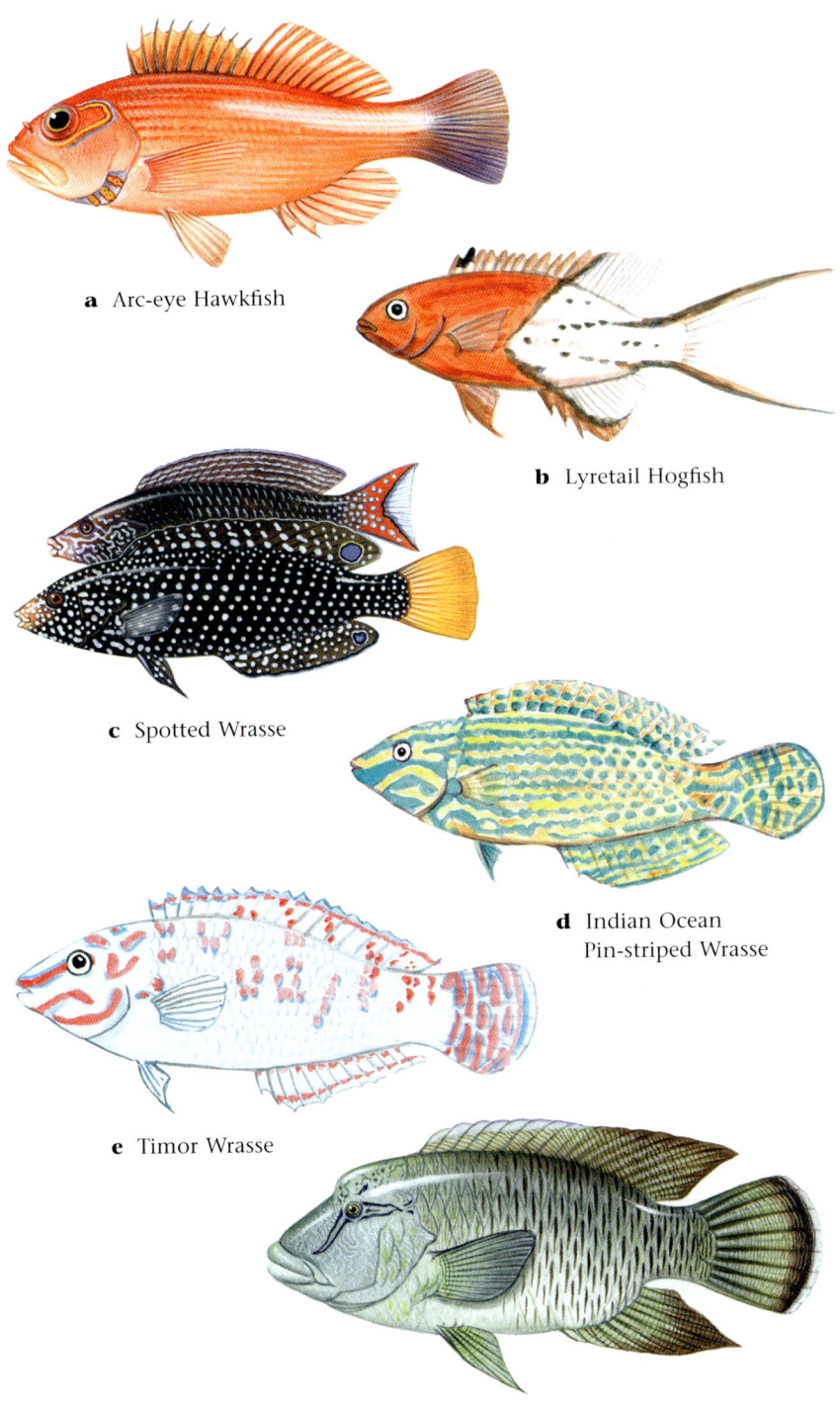

Plate 83

a Arc-eye Hawkfish

b Lyretail Hogfish

c Spotted Wrasse

d Indian Ocean Pin-striped Wrasse

e Timor Wrasse

f Humphead Maori Wrasse

Plate 84a
Argus Wrasse
Halichoeres argus
This wrasse frequents shallow coastal reefs and seagrass beds. A pinkish red checkerboard pattern overlays a green body coloration. The head is salmon-colored, with bright green markings. (to 11 cm, 4.25 in)

Plate 84b
Blue-sided Wrasse
Cirrhilabrus cyanopleura
An aggregating wrasse of seaward reefs and lagoons, where the water is clear, this species can be easily identified by its coloration. Note especially the blue area behind the head and the white belly region. (to 15 cm, 6 in)

Plate 84c
Ringwrasse
Hologymnosus annulatus
Ringwrasses have distinctive tapering snouts. Initial phase (mostly females; p. 213) fish of this species are a dusky olive brown, and the tail has a white region toward the tip. Terminal phase males are green with purplish red bars; the head is purplish with blue-green bands and the tail is blue with a green crescent toward its end. It feeds primarily on small fishes. (to 40 cm, 16 in)

Plate 84d
African Coris
Coris africana
This wrasse can be found in a variety of reef habitats, including sand and rubble areas. It feeds on hard-shelled invertebrates, including sea urchins. This wrasse can be found on the Andaman Sea side of the peninsula; the closely related and similar Yellowtail Coris (*Coris gaimard*) can be found in the Gulf. Its background coloration is olive green; a bright green band lies behind the pectoral fins. Note also the radiating light green bands on the head. The juveniles are reddish orange with white areas, outlined in black. (to 38 cm, 15 in)

Plate 84e
Bicolor Cleaner Wrasse
Labroides bicolor
Most members of this genus specialize as cleaners (p. 214), deriving their sustenance from the ectoparasites of larger fish. This species is less bound to a traditional cleaning station than are other cleaner wrasses. Females are gray with a black lateral stripe that becomes pale yellow as it approaches the tail. Males are black in the front half and yellow to white toward the tail. (to 14 cm, 5.5 in)

Plate 84f
Cleaner Wrasse
Labroides dimidiatus
This cleaner sticks close to traditional cleaning stations, at which its client fish assemble for its services. Females are black with a bright blue stripe on the back and head. Males are light blue, tending to pale yellow, with a black stripe running from the snout to the end of the tail. (to 11.5 cm, 4.5 in)

Plate 84

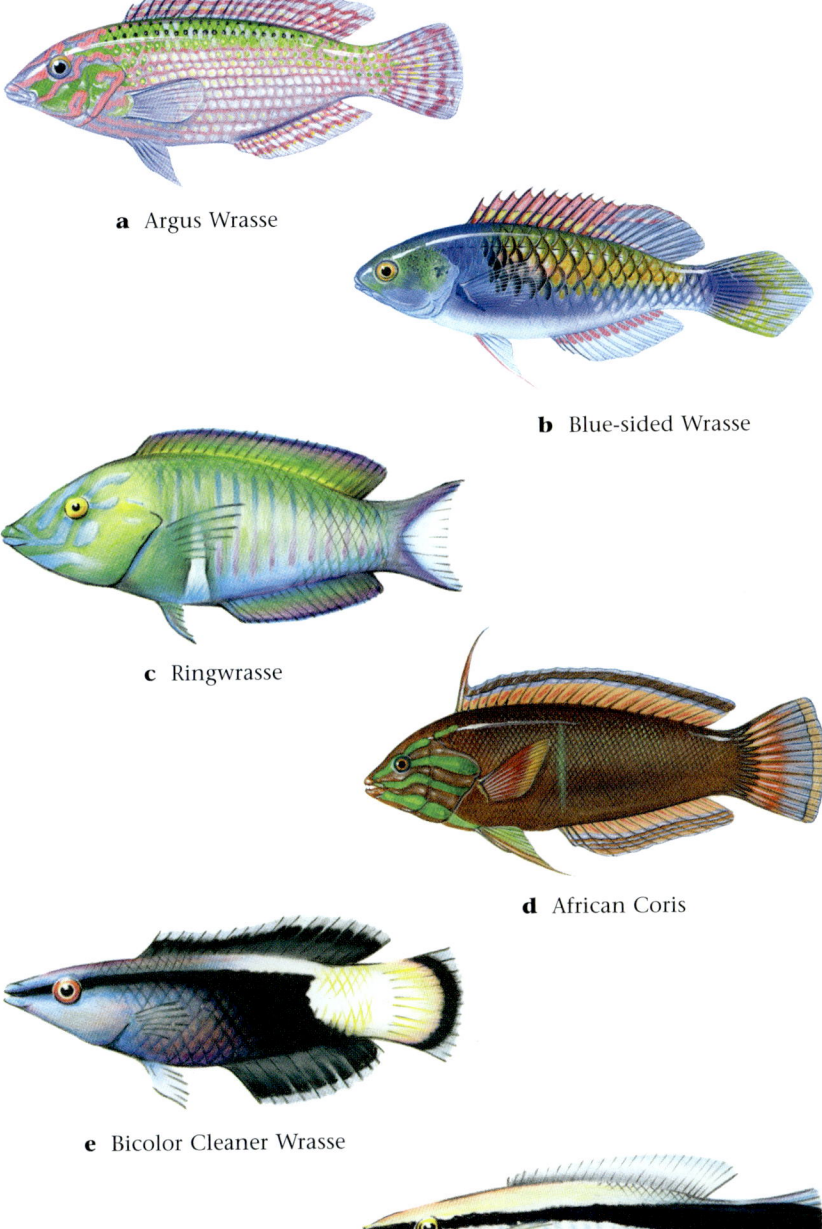

a Argus Wrasse

b Blue-sided Wrasse

c Ringwrasse

d African Coris

e Bicolor Cleaner Wrasse

f Cleaner Wrasse

Plate 85a
Indian Ocean Bird Wrasse
Gomphosus caeruleus
This distinctive wrasse prefers coral-rich environments. The proboscis-like mouth distinguishes it from other wrasses in the area. Look for it on the Andaman Sea side of the peninsula. (to 28 cm, 11 in)

Plate 85b
Rockmover Wrasse
Novaculichthys taeniourus
This wrasse gets its name from its habit of overturning and moving surprisingly large rocks in its quest for benthic (bottom-dwelling) invertebrates such as worms, urchins, mollusks, and crustaceans. All adults are dark brown with a white spot on each scale; the head is whitish gray with dark lines radiating from the eye; the tail is white in front and black at the back. Juveniles are uncanny mimics of drifting red algae. (to 30 cm, 12 in)

Plate 85c
Moon Wrasse
Thalassoma lunare
This very active wrasse can be found probing the upper portions of protected reefs for benthic (bottom-dwelling) invertebrates. The initial phase (p. 213) is green with vertical red dashes on each scale and irregular rose-colored bands on the head; there is also a rose band on each lobe of the tail. Terminal phase (male) is similar but more purplish blue throughout. (to 25 cm, 10 in)

Plate 85d
Sunset Wrasse
Thalassoma lutescens
This wrasse is most common in shallow-water environments, where it preys on benthic (bottom-dwelling) shrimp and crabs. The initial phase (male and female; p. 213) is greenish yellow with very faint reddish orange lines on the head; The terminal phase (male) has a rose pink coloration on the head with irregular curving green lines; behind the head the body is blue, tending to green toward the tail, which is yellow with a blue-edged rose band on each lobe. (to 25 cm, 10 in)

Plate 85e
Twotone Wrasse
Thalassoma amblycephalum
Most commonly observed over isolated coral heads and the uppermost portion of steeply-sloping reefs, this wrasse feeds primarily on zooplankton, especially larval crustaceans. Initial phase males (p. 213) and females are whitish with a wide stripe running the length of the body at the midline. Terminal phase males have a green head, behind which is a broad yellow saddle; the rest of the body is reddish with numerous thin green lines. (to 14 cm, 5.5 in)

Plate 85f
Bumphead Parrotfish
Bolbometapon muricatum
This is the largest parrotfish species on the reef, but it is wary and difficult to approach. Named for the bulbous protuberance on top of the head, it feeds on both algae and live coral. All adults (male and female) are greenish blue. Juveniles are greenish brown with five vertical arrays of small white spots. (to 1.2 m, 4 ft)

Plate 85

a Indian Ocean Bird Wrasse

b Rockmover Wrasse

c Moon Wrasse

d Sunset Wrasse

e Twotone Wrasse

f Bumphead Parrotfish

Plate 86a
Knothead Parrotfish
Chlorurus oedema
A shy, solitary parrotfish, this species frequents both coral and rocky reefs, where it feeds on algae. Its common name derives from the bulbous protuberance on the top of the head. The body is colored a dark dusky blue; look also for the yellow pectoral fins. (to 42 cm, 17 in)

Plate 86b
Stareye Parrotfish
Calatomus carolinus
This common parrotfish can be found in a variety of habitats, including seagrass beds. The initial phase (p. 213) is mottled pinkish gray and brown. The terminal phase males (p. 213) are blue-green with pink scale margins and irregular pink bands radiating from the eye. (to 50 cm, 20 in)

Plate 86c
Bicolor Parrotfish
Cetoscarus bicolor
Look for this parrotfish on upper reef slopes. The initial phase (p. 213) of this parrotfish is a dusky reddish brown with a pale back; the scales on the side of the body are black with white margins. Terminal phase males (p. 213) are green with pink scale margins; the head and front of body are covered with pink spots. The juveniles look like members of a completely different species: most of the body is white, as is the snout; an orange saddle covers most of the head. Note also the orange rimmed black area on the dorsal fin. (to 80 cm, 32 in)

Plate 86d
Indian Ocean Steephead Parrotfish
Scarus strongylocephalus
Confined to the Andaman Sea portion of Thailand, this species can be found in lagoons and seaward reefs. Females are yellow above and orange below, with prominent black lips. Males have steeply sloping heads with a pink region below the eye; most of the body is dark green with pink flecks; the chin area is a lighter shade of green. (to 70 cm, 28 in)

Plate 86e
Greenthroat Parrotfish
Scarus prasiognathus
Look for this parrotfish on the upper portion of dropoffs on outer reefs. Females are reddish brown throughout, with white flecks. Males can be distinguished from all other parrotfishes by the distinctive, irregularly shaped green area on the throat. (to 70 cm, 28 in)

Plate 86f
Yellowfin Parrotfish
Scarus flavipectoralis
This is a solitary parrotfish of deep lagoons and reefs channels. Females are brownish white, with a dark brown region on the upper half of the head. Males have purple heads transected by an irregular green stripe; the rest of the body is green. (to 30 cm, 12 in)

Plate 86

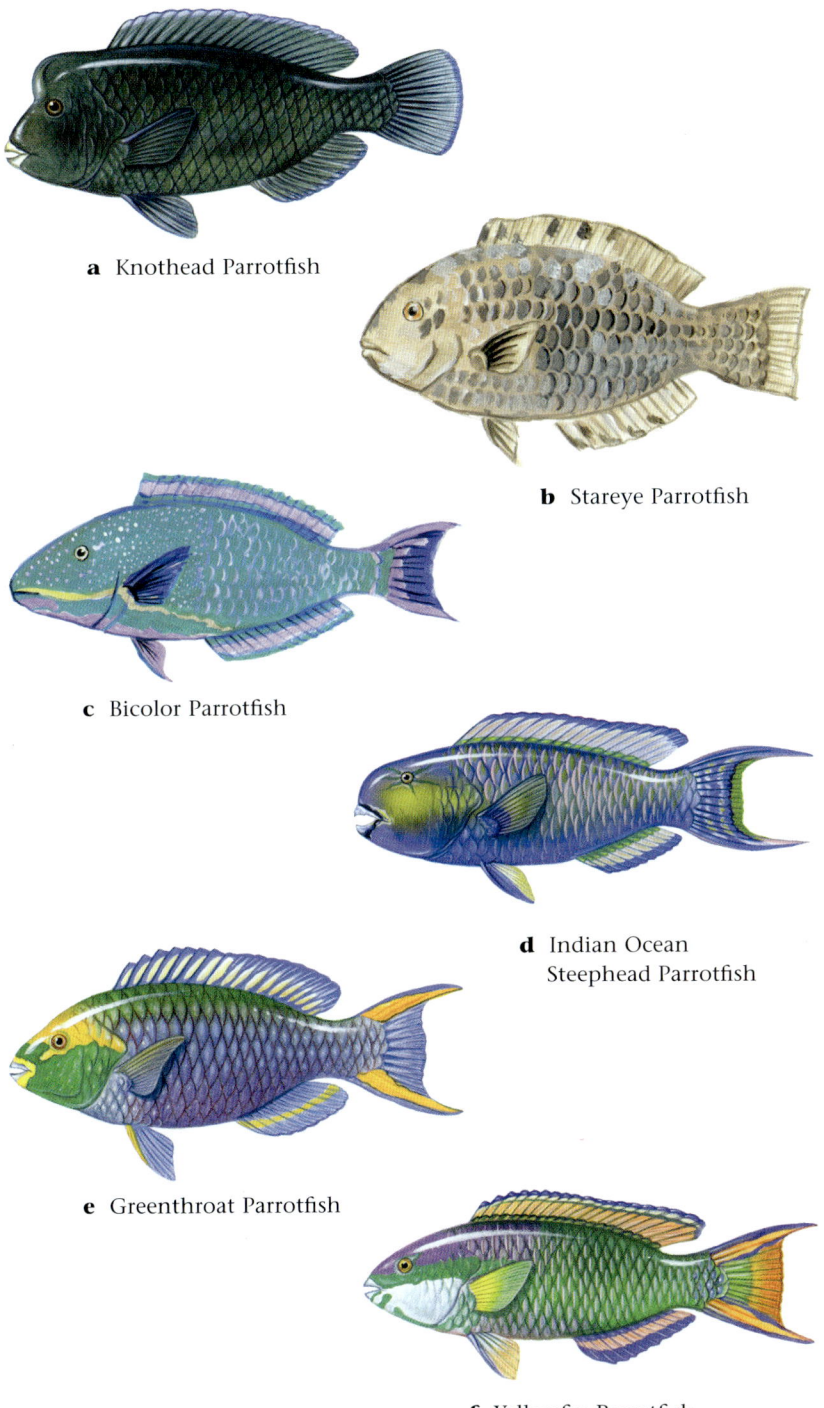

a Knothead Parrotfish

b Stareye Parrotfish

c Bicolor Parrotfish

d Indian Ocean Steephead Parrotfish

e Greenthroat Parrotfish

f Yellowfin Parrotfish

Plate 87a
Scalefin Anthias
Pseudanthias squamipinnis
This species is the most common member of this genus on shallow reefs. Males and females have markedly different coloration. Females are deep yellow throughout, while males are lavender to fuschia with magenta fins and a long projection from the front of the dorsal fin. This species, and probably other members of the genus, undergo socially regulated sex change. (to 15 cm, 6 in)

Plate 87b
Flame Anthias
Pseudanthias ignitis
This beauty can be found on outer reef slopes, near large coral heads. In the Thailand area, it is confined to the Similan Islands. Look for the band of bright red on the upper dorsal fin, as well as the distinctively two-toned tail. (to 8 cm, 3 in)

Plate 87c
Diadem Dottyback
Pseudochromis diadema
These tiny beauties can be found in small groups among corals and rocks on the reef slopes of the gulf region. The body is mostly an intense golden yellow, purple near the back. (to 6 cm, 2.5 in)

Plate 87d
Blue-barred Parrotfish
Scarus ghobban
Also called the Blue-chin Parrotfish, this species prefers lagoons with shallow reefs and sandy areas. The initial phase (p. 213) is yellowish to green with light blue areas. Terminal phase (males; p. 213) is mostly yellow, becoming green on top; the scale margins are salmon pink; there are two distinct blue bands on the chin. (to 75 cm, 30 in)

Plate 87e
Peacock Grouper
Cephalopholis argus
This is one of the more distinctively colored groupers. It can be found in coral-rich, clear-water areas where it feeds mainly on other fishes. Highly prized as a food fish, it has been implicated in ciguatera poisoning. Its coloration is olive-green to brown, with numerous dark-edged blue spots throughout; there are five or six pale bars on the rear half of the body. (to 40 cm, 16 in)

Plate 87f
Coral Hinde
Cephalopholis miniata
This beautiful grouper prefers coral-rich clear-water environments; it feeds mainly on small fishes but will also take an occasional crustacean. It is usually some shade of red, with numerous bright blue spots throughout. (to 41 cm, 16.5 in)

Plate 87

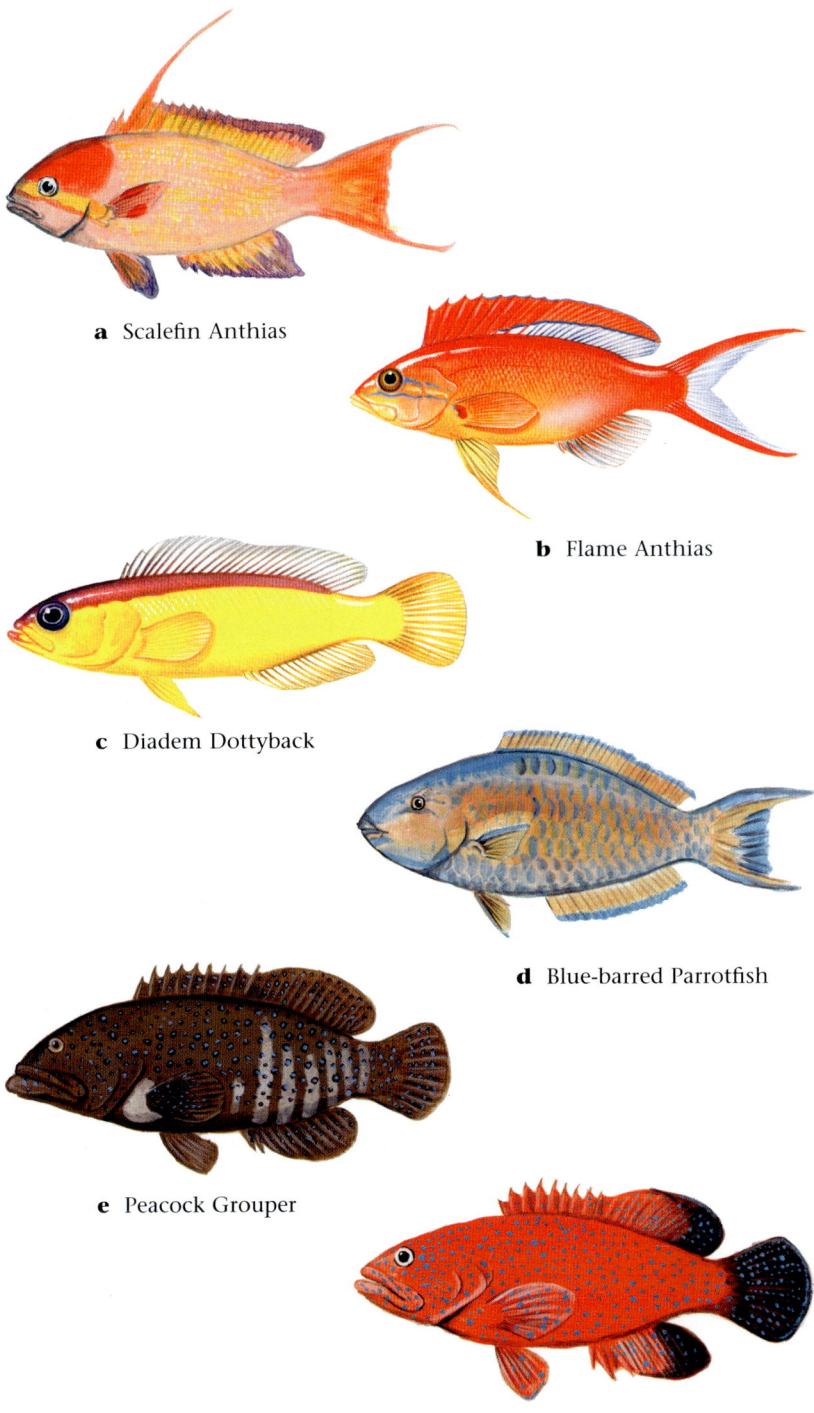

a Scalefin Anthias

b Flame Anthias

c Diadem Dottyback

d Blue-barred Parrotfish

e Peacock Grouper

f Coral Hinde

Plate 88a
Giant Grouper
Epinephelus lancelotus
This is the largest fish (to 400 kg, 880 lb) found on the reef itself. Look for it in caves and wrecks. It feeds on a variety of animals, but particularly spiny lobsters. The coloration is dark gray to brown, barred brown and yellow in juveniles. (to 270 cm, 8.8 ft).

Plate 88b
Blue-spotted Hinde
Cephalopholis cyanostigma
This grouper prefers protected areas of shallow coastal reefs and seagrass beds, where it feeds on crustaceans and fishes. The body is mottled brown with numerous blue spots. (to 35 cm, 14 in)

Plate 88c
Speckled Grouper
Epinephelus cyanopodus
This attractive grouper is most often seen near isolated coral heads on seaward reefs. Black speckles and small spots over a white background color make this species fairly easy to identify. (to 1 m, 3.3 ft)

Plate 88d
Malabar Grouper
Epinephelus malabaricus
A large predator of coastal reefs, this grouper feeds on fish and crustaceans. It has broad dark bands over a lighter brown background; the bands bifurcate toward the stomach. The number of black spots increases with age. (to 1.2 m, 4 ft)

Plate 88e
Coral Grouper
Epinephelus corallicola
This grouper prefers silty coastal reefs. In Thailand it is confined to the gulf region. Numerous dark spots cover the body, which is otherwise whitish to light brown. Note also the dark patch in the mid-back region. (to 50 cm)

Plate 88

a Giant Grouper

b Blue-spotted Hinde

c Speckled Grouper

d Malabar Grouper

e Coral Grouper

Plate 89a
Saddleback Coralgrouper
Plectropomus laevis
This large grouper is a highly prized food fish but it is one of the species most likely to be involved in ciguatera poisoning. It prefers coral-rich environments, particularly channels. It comes in two colorations; the light form is white with several broad brown bars and yellow fins; the dark form is reddish brown with numerous blue spots and less distinct bars. (to 1 m, 3.3 ft)

Plate 89b
Leopard Coralgrouper
Plectropomus leopardus
Also called the coral trout, this is another highly coveted food fish that can cause ciguatera poisoning,. It prefers coral-rich areas of lagoon reefs. The coloration is variable, ranging from tan to reddish brown, with many tiny blue spots. (to 75 cm, 30 in)

Plate 89c
Lyretail Grouper
Variola louti
Like members of genus Plectropomus (Plate 89a, b), this grouper, sometimes referred to as the Coronation Grouper or Coronation Trout, feeds primarily on reef fishes. It is good eating and has been implicated in ciguatera poisoning. It can be found in coral-rich portions of lagoon and seaward reefs. The tail has a distinctive lyre shape (as does the tail of the similar Lyretail Trout, *Variola albimarginata*). The coloration varies from red to brown, with numerous small blue, pink, or lavender spots. (to 80 cm, 32 in)

Plate 89d
Two-banded Soapfish
Diploprion bifasciatum
Look for this small grouper-like fish near caves and crevices. A broad black band over the mid-body region and a narrower black band through the eye are diagnostic. (to 25 cm, 10 in)

Plate 89e
Red Snapper
Lutjanus bohar
Snappers are among the prime offenders in ciguatera poisoning, and this voracious predator in particular is a frequent culprit. It is quite bold and will readily approach divers. Look for it on seaward and channel reefs, but it is especially common in atolls. It has a reddish tint throughout; smaller individuals have two white spots at the base of the dorsal fin. (to 75 cm, 30 in)

Plate 89f
Giant Trevally
Caranx ignobilis
Trevallys, or jacks (family Carangidae), are large predatory fishes of the midwater zone but can often be found on reef margins, especially near dropoffs on outer reefs. This species is one of the members of the family most likely to be found coursing over reef tops. It is silvery gray to black above and paler below. (to 1.7 m, 5.6 ft)

Plate 89

a Saddleback Coralgrouper

b Leopard Coralgrouper

c Lyretail Grouper

d Two-banded Soapfish

e Red Snapper

f Giant Trevally

Plate 90a
Blackspot Snapper
Lutjanus fulviflamma
This species is a common medium-sized snapper that can be found on fairly shallow reefs. It is gray brown with several yellow lateral stripes and yellow fins; there is a prominent black spot on each side. (to 35 cm, 14 in)

Plate 90b
Bengal Snapper
Lutjanus bengalensis
This snapper can be found alone or in small groups in a variety of reef habitats. It can be distinguished from several similar yellow, blue-striped snappers by the white belly area below the lowest blue stripe. (to 21 cm, 8.3 in)

Plate 90c
Lunar Fusilier
Caesio lunaris
Large schools of this planktivorous fish can be found on steep seaward reefs and dropoffs. It is silvery gray throughout, with characteristic black areas on its tail points. (to 30 cm, 12 in)

Plate 90d
Yellowtop Fusilier
Caesio xanthanota
This species is a mid-water fusilier of seaward reefs. In Thailand it is confined to the Andaman coast. The upper portion of the fish is yellow, as is the tail. (to 30 cm, 12 in)

Plate 90e
Red Emperor
Lutjanus sebae
This snapper prefers shallow, calm water such as lagoons, where there are coral patches surrounded by sandy areas. Adults are dark red to pink. Juveniles are white with three broad reddish brown bars, the frontmost of which runs through the eye. (to 60 cm, 24 in)

Plate 90f
Many-spotted Sweetlips
Plectorhinchus chaetodontoides
The term "sweetlips" is an apparent reference to the kissable-seeming (by fish standards at least) mouths of these fish. This species, also called the Harlequin Sweetlips, prefers coral-rich reefs in clear water. It is white with many brown spots. Juveniles, however, are light brown with large dark-edged white spots; this coloration mimics a toxic nudibranch (sea slug), and the imitation is reinforced by the seemingly spastic, whole-body movements. (to 60 cm, 24 in)

Plate 90

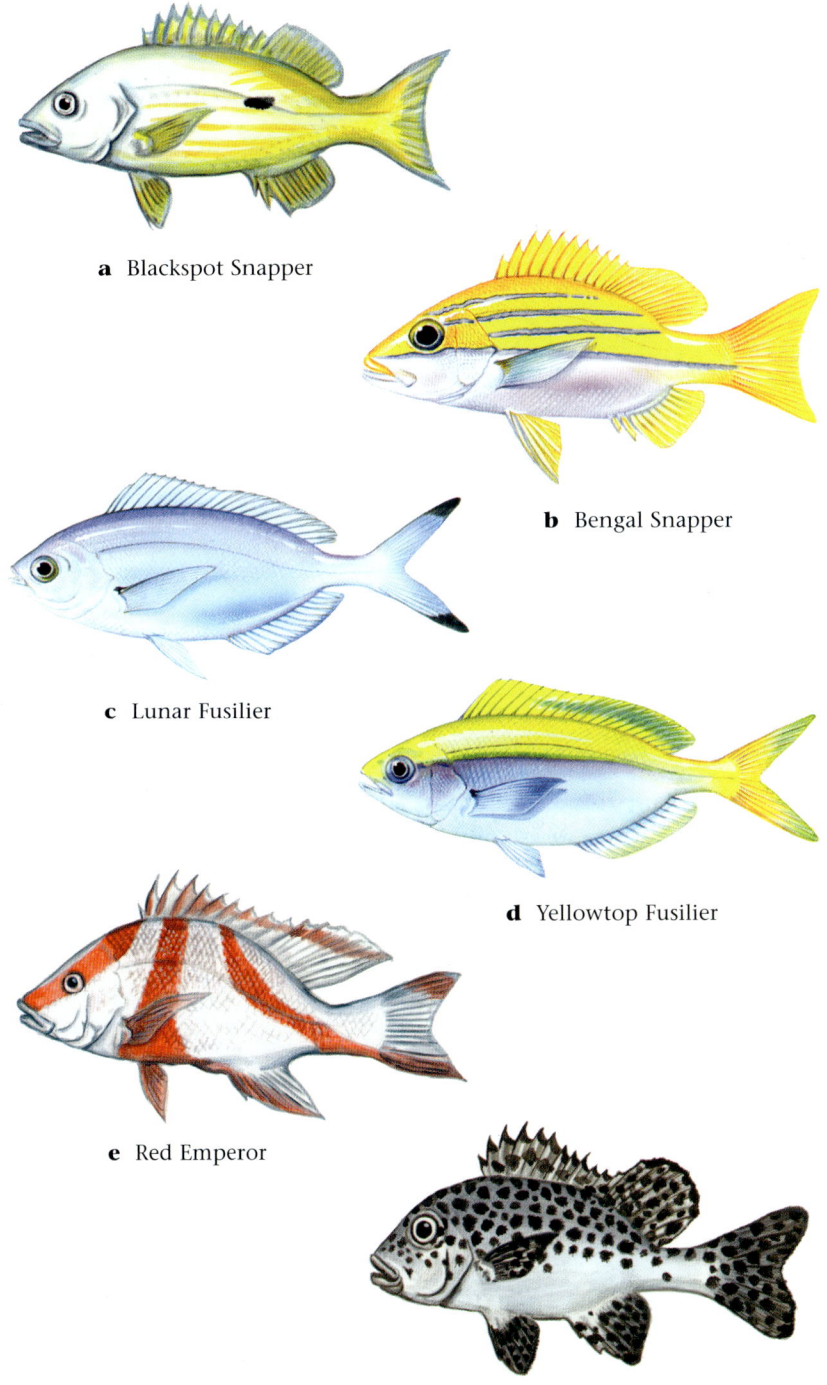

a Blackspot Snapper

b Bengal Snapper

c Lunar Fusilier

d Yellowtop Fusilier

e Red Emperor

f Many-spotted Sweetlips

Plate 91a
Yellowfin Goatfish
Mulloidichthys vanicolensis
Goatfishes (family Mullidae) can be readily recognized by their catfish-like barbels, chemosensory organs that allow them to taste their surroundings in their quest for benthic (bottom-dwelling) prey. Most are nocturnal but they can be found out in the open, often in groups, by day. This species is silvery white, with yellow fins and a yellow lateral stripe. (to 38 cm, 15 in)

Plate 91b
Goldsaddle Goatfish
Parupeneus cyclostomus
This goatfish differs from others in preying primarily on other fishes. It comes in two color varieties, a yellow form and a dark form. It is the dark form that has the golden saddle on the back near the base of the tail. (to 50 cm, 20 in)

Plate 91c
Indian Goatfish
Parupeneus indicus
Fairly common in lagoon and coastal reefs, where there is abundant sand or silt, this goatfish can best be identified by the black spot near the base of the tail and the larger yellow patch in the mid-back area. (to 35 cm, 14 in)

Plate 91d
Eared Blenny
Cirripectes auritus
This attractive blenny can be found in shallow seaward reefs on the Andaman coast. The front half of the body has a golden coloration; look for the black spot on the gill cover. (to 9 cm, 3.5 in)

Plate 91e
Mimic Blenny
Aspidontus taeniatus
This is one of the fang blennies, so called because of their impressive canines. This one mimics the Cleaner Wrasse (*Labroides dimidiatus*; Plate 84) in both coloration and behavior. It thereby is allowed to approach a client fish (p. 214), but instead of plucking ectoparasites off its surface, it takes a chunk of fin or flesh, the removal of which is much less appreciated. The body is elongate with a broad black stripe extending from the tail, which becomes narrower toward the nose; below the stripe its is white tending to bluish toward the tail. (to 11.5 cm, 4.5 in)

Plate 91f
Midas Blenny
Ecsenius midas
Named for the yellow coloration, this blenny schools with Scalefin Anthias (*Pseudanthias squamipinnis*; Plate 87), and is thought to be its mimic. There is also a second, dark blue color phase that does not associate with *Pseudanthias*. (to 13 cm, 5 in)

Plate 91

a Yellowfin Goatfish

b Goldsaddle Goatfish

c Indian Goatfish

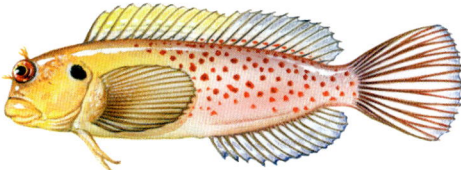

d Eared Blenny

e Mimic Blenny

f Midas Blenny

Plate 92a
Ornate Goby
Istigobius ornatus
A common goby of silty inner reefs, as well as mangroves, this species is white with black flecks and spots throughout. (to 11 cm, 4.25 in)

Plate 92b
Fire Dartfish
Nemateleotris magnifica
Dartfish, also called firefish or fire gobies, are closely related to the gobies but distinct enough to warrant their own family. This species is one of the most beautiful fishes in the ocean. The body is white in front, becoming purplish toward the tail. The elongate front portion of the dorsal fin is white to pale yellow and projects upward; the median fins (the dorsal, anal, and caudal fins) are red, becoming darker toward the tail. These fish are wary and never stray far from their burrow, into which they retreat at the slightest provocation. They are highly prized by aquarists. (to 8 cm, 3 in)

Plate 92c
Blackfin Dartfish
Ptereleotris evides
This striking fish can be found on exposed outer reef slopes, usually hovering in pairs over a hole. It can be easily identified by its coloration and shape. The front half is white, the rear half, including the second dorsal and anal fins, is black; the tail is black with a white center, outlined in red. (to 14 cm, 5.5 in)

Plate 92d
Ringtail Surgeonfish
Acanthurus blochii
You are more likely to find this surgeonfish grazing for algae over sandy areas than on the reef itself. It has a dark greenish body with bluish purple median fins (the dorsal, anal, and caudal fins) and a white swatch at the base of the tail. Note also the yellow area behind the eye. (to 50 cm, 20 in)

Plate 92e
Lieutenant Surgeonfish
Acanthurus tennenti
This surgeonfish frequents lagoon reefs as well as seaward reefs on the Andaman coast, where there are occasional sandy patches. It will graze the algae off the sand as well as the rocks. The face is light tan, the rest of the body a darker tan; note the blue outline of the tail spines and the dark marks behind the eye. (to 31 cm, 12 in)

Plate 92f
White-spotted Surgeonfish
Acanthurus guttatus
Look for this surgeonfish in the surge zone. It often forms small schools. The tailward portion of the body has white spots, while two vertical white stripes adorn the head region. This species is also more deep-bodied than most surgeonfishes. (to 38 cm, 15 in)

Plate 92

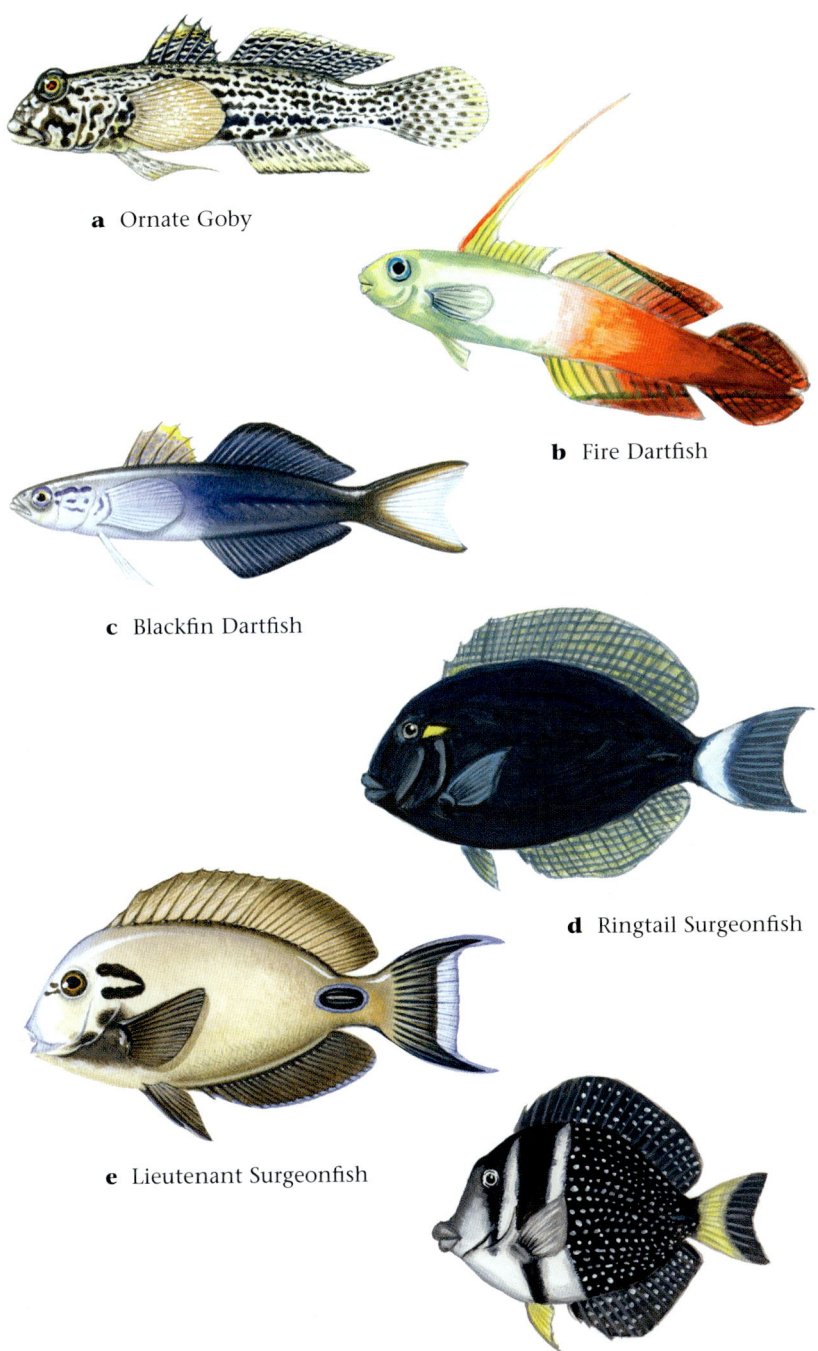

a Ornate Goby

b Fire Dartfish

c Blackfin Dartfish

d Ringtail Surgeonfish

e Lieutenant Surgeonfish

f White-spotted Surgeonfish

Plate 93a
Striped Surgeonfish
Acanthurus lineatus
This very aggressive and territorial surgeonfish lives on the outer edge of reefs that are most exposed to wave action. It is among the most strikingly colored members of the family. On the upper part of the body there are alternating yellow and black-edged blue bands; the belly area is lavender. (to 38 cm, 15 in)

Plate 93b
Brown Surgeonfish
Acanthurus nigrofuscus
This rather drab surgeonfish is quite common on shallow reefs. The body is tan with lavender tones; there are yellow spots on the head and black spots at the base of dorsal and anal fins near the tail. (to 21 cm, 8.3 in)

Plate 93c
Orangeband Surgeonfish
Acanthurus olivaceus
This surgeonfish, which is one of the more distinctively colored, can be found in sandy areas near reefs. Its body is tan in front and dark brown toward the tail; a striking orange patch, outlined in purple, extends from behind the eye. Juveniles are bright yellow. (to 35 cm, 14 in)

Plate 93d
Convict Surgeonfish
Acanthurus triostegus
This surgeonfish forms large aggregations that swarm over the reef, overwhelming, by their sheer numbers, the territorial damselfishes. The body is greenish gray with six vertical black bands. (to 26 cm, 10 in)

Plate 93e
Yellowfin Surgeonfish
Acanthurus xanthopterus
This is one of the largest surgeonfishes, often found in sandy areas far from coral reefs. The body is purplish gray; there is a yellowish area around the eye and on the pectoral fins. (to 56 cm, 22 in)

Plate 93f
Indian Ocean Mimic Surgeonfish
Acanthurus tristis
This surgeonfish frequents areas of the Andaman coast that provide a mixture of coral, rocks, and sand. Juveniles mimic Eibl's Angelfish (*Centropyge eibili*; Plate 78), but for reasons unknown. Adults closely resemble the Pacific's Mimic Surgeonfish (*Acanthurus pyroferus*), but can be distinguished by the white tail margin. (to 25 cm, 10 in)

Plate 93

a Striped Surgeonfish

b Brown Surgeonfish

c Orangeband Surgeonfish

d Convict Surgeonfish

e Yellowfin Surgeonfish

f Indian Ocean Mimic Surgeonfish

Plate 94a
Powder-blue Surgeonfish
Acanthurus leucosternon
This beauty can be found in aggegations, sometimes of immense size, over reef flats and seward reef slopes. The head is black, behind which is a white area; the rest of the body is blue; also look for the yellow dorsal fin and the black and white tail. (to 23 cm, 9 in)

Plate 94b
Orangespine Unicornfish
Naso lituratus
This fish, which seems like a caricature of artistic excess, is common in a variety of reef environments, including areas of sand or rubble, where it dines on leafy algae. There is no need to describe it; the illustration will suffice. (to 45 cm, 18 in)

Plate 94c
Humpnose Unicornfish
Naso tuberosus
One of the more bizarre-looking fish in the ocean, this species occurs in small groups over clearwater seaward reefs. It gets its name from the large bulbous protuberance on the nose; there is also a distinct hump on the upper back; the coloration is silvery gray. (to 60 cm, 24 in)

Plate 94d
Bluespine Unicornfish
Naso unicornis
This unicornifish is common in exposed areas with plenty of surge. It has the projections for which this group of surgeonfish derives its name. It feeds primarily on leafy algae such as Sargassum, and, somewhat surprisingly for such a large fish, it will enter very shallow water in search of it. It is named for its bright blue tail spines. (to 70 cm, 28 in)

Plate 94e
Moorish Idol
Zanclus cornutus
Perhaps the most extravagantly beautiful fish in the ocean, it cannot be mistaken for any other. It feeds primarily on sponges, over a wide range of depths and in a wide range of reef environments. (to 20 cm, 8 in)

Plate 94f
Coral Rabbitfish
Siganus corallinus
Rabbitfishes have venomous pelvic spines, which can inflict painful, but rarely fatal, injuries on the unwary human. This species frequents coral-rich environments. It is yellow with numerous blue dots over the entire body and head. The tail is forked. (to 28 cm, 11 in)

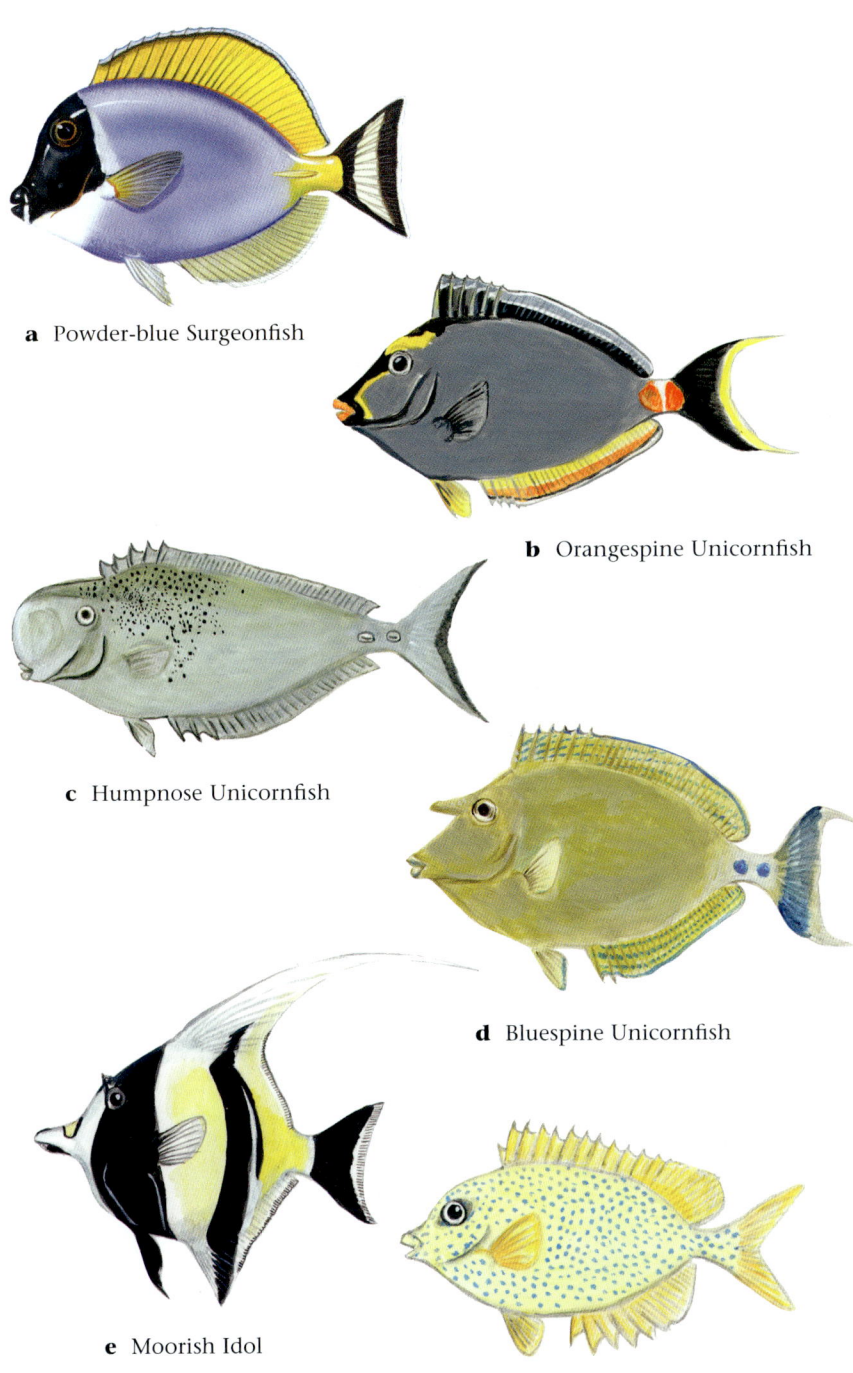

a Powder-blue Surgeonfish
b Orangespine Unicornfish
c Humpnose Unicornfish
d Bluespine Unicornfish
e Moorish Idol
f Coral Rabbitfish

Plate 95a
Magnificent Rabbitfish
Siganus magnificus
This species is endemic to the west coast of Thailand and the Similan Islands. It prefers protected open reef environments, and can be readily identified by its black snout. The rest of the body is white, with a large brown area. (to 23 cm, 9 in)

Plate 95b
Stellate Rabbitfish
Siganus stellatus
This distinctive rabbitfish can be found in clear seaward and lagoon reefs, usually in pairs. The white background coloration is covered with densely packed black spots; note also the yellow areas on the fins and head. (to 31 cm, 12.25 in)

Plate 95c
Orange-lined Triggerfish
Balistapus undulatus
Look for this trigger in coral-rich areas. It eats pretty much anything. The body, head, and fins are green with orange lines. (to 30 cm, 12 in)

Plate 95d
Titan Triggerfish
Balistoides viridescens
This is the largest triggerfish, so it is aptly named. Look for it in shallow reef environments. It is quite wary for its size, except when the female is guarding eggs; when so occupied, she is extremely aggressive and will deliver nasty bites to any intruder, including divers. The body is dusky brown to greenish; there is a dark band through the eye, as well as dark bands on the median fins (the dorsal, anal, and caudal fins). (to 75 cm, 30 in)

Plate 95e
Clown Triggerfish
Balistoides conspicillum
Also called Black Triggerfish, this is a spectacularly colored animal and highly sought by aquarists. It prefers outer reefs. The body is black with large white spots on the belly; there is a yellowish area on the back, a white band across the nose, and yellow margins below the dorsal and anal fins; note also the yellow mouth. (to 50 cm, 20 in)

Plate 95f
Indian Triggerfish
Melichthys indicus
Members of genus Melichthys, often called durgons, are more active swimmers than other triggerfishes. They flap their dorsal and anal fins to propel themselves through the water in coral-rich areas. Look for the white margin below the dorsal and anal fins, and at the end of the tail. (to 24 cm, 9.5 in)

Plate 95

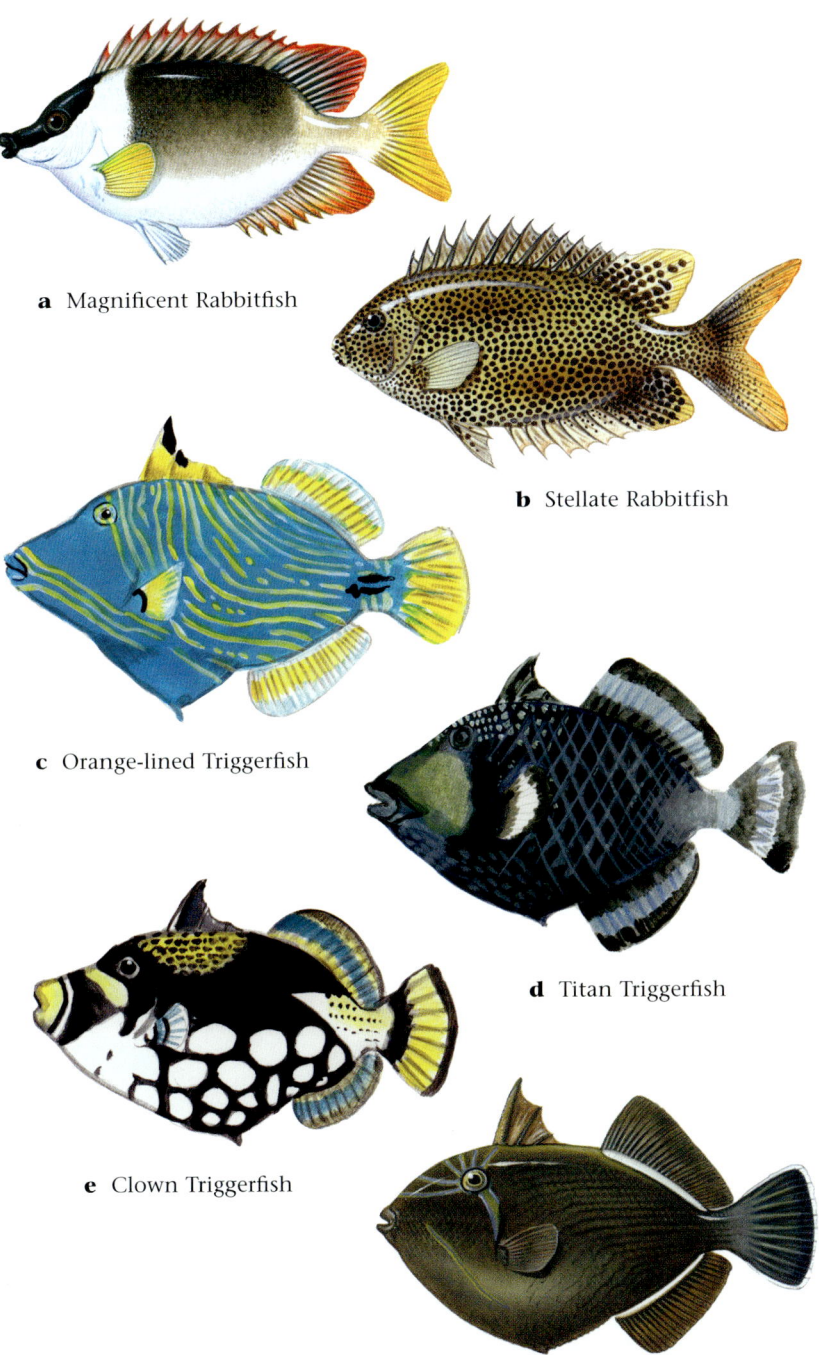

a Magnificent Rabbitfish

b Stellate Rabbitfish

c Orange-lined Triggerfish

d Titan Triggerfish

e Clown Triggerfish

f Indian Triggerfish

Plate 96a
Lagoon Triggerfish
Rhinecanthus aculeatus
Also called the Whitebanded Triggerfish, this species prefers reef flats in lagoons with sandy bottoms. The body is white with a large blackish region interrupted by four bluish white diagonal bands; there are thin blue lines around the eyes, a yellow area around the mouth, and a yellow line extending from the mouth. (to 25 cm, 10 in)

Plate 96b
Wedge-tail Triggerfish
Rhinecanthus rectangulus
Also called the Reef Triggerfish, this species likes outer reefs with lots of surge. The head and lower body are white with a broad, diagonal black band extending from the eye; above this band the body is tan; there is another triangle of black at the base of the tail. Note also the blue lines around the eye and the blue patch on the upper lip, as well as the triangular yellow lines over the tan area of upper body. (to 25 cm, 10 in)

Plate 96c
Blackbelly Picassofish
Rhinecanthus verrucosus
This triggerfish prefers protected reef areas; it is especially common in rubble areas and where coral is interspersed with seagrasses. Look for the distinctive black patch near the belly. (to 23 cm, 9 in)

Plate 96d
Longnose Filefish
Oxymonocanthus longirostris
You can find this species in clear-water areas of lagoon and seaward reefs, usually in pairs. It feeds on Acropora corals (Plate 102). The somewhat elongate body terminates in a tube-shaped mouth typical of coral-eaters. It is greenish blue with numerous orangish-yellow spots of varying size. (to 12 cm, 4.5 in)

Plate 96e
Mimic Filefish
Paraluteres prionurus
A denizen of clear-water coral reefs, this fish is a precise mimic of the poisonous Black-saddled Toby (*Canthigaster valentini*, Plate 97b). It can be distinguished primarily by its two dorsal fins, the frontmost of which is lacking in the toby. (to 10 cm, 4 in)

Plate 96f
Scrawled Filefish
Aluterus scriptus
Also called the Scribbled Filefish, this species is quite omnivorous, feeding on algae, anemones, hydrozoans, and gorgonians (soft corals), among other benthic (bottom-dwelling) items. The body is grayish green with irregular blue markings throughout, as well as small black spots. It has a rather droopy countenance. (to 75 cm, 30 in)

Plate 96

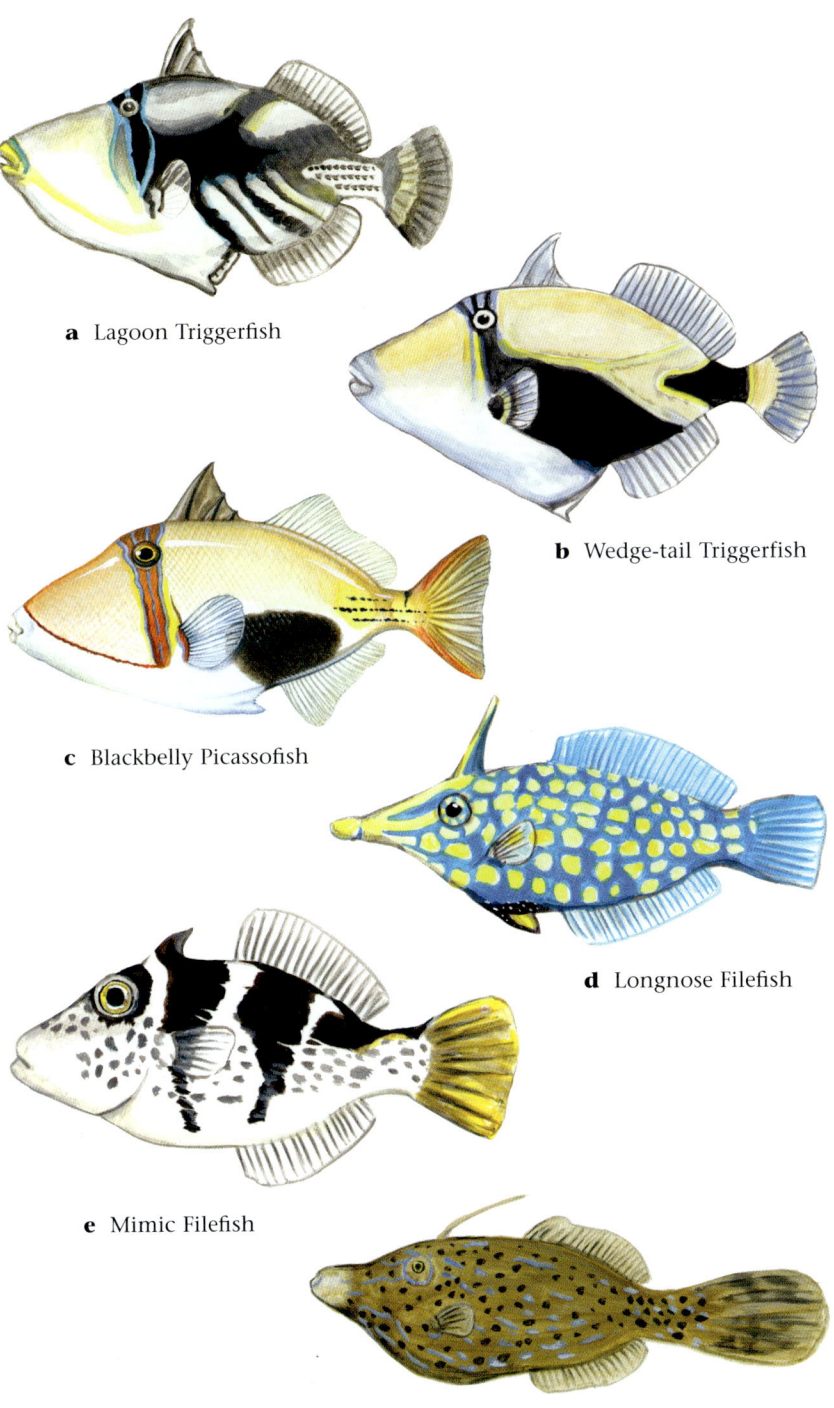

a Lagoon Triggerfish

b Wedge-tail Triggerfish

c Blackbelly Picassofish

d Longnose Filefish

e Mimic Filefish

f Scrawled Filefish

Plate 97a
Spotted Boxfish
Ostracion meleagris
This species is named for its box-like body shape. The sexes are very different. Females are black with numerous small white spots; males are black on top (with white spots) but blue elsewhere, with orangish brown spots. (to 18 cm, 7 in)

Plate 97b
Black-saddled Toby
Canthigaster valentini
This is the species mimicked by the Mimic Filefish (*Paraluteres prionurus*; Plate 96e). It is quite common in shallow-water coral reefs, much more so than the mimic. The body is white with a broad brown bar on the head and three more on the body; it also has small light brown spots distributed throughout most of the body, a yellow tail, and blue lines radiating from the eyes. (to 9 cm, 3.5 in)

Plate 97c
Bluestreak Cardinalfish
Apogon leptacanthus
Large groups of these fish can be found among the branching corals in sheltered lagoons. They feed on zooplankton, mostly at night. This species is stouter than most cardinalfishes; the body is whitish to tan above, with thin blue bands around the gill cover; note also the elongate front margin of the first dorsal fin, which is also blue. (to 6 cm, 2.4 in)

Plate 97d
Ringtail Cardinalfish
Apogon aureus
Look for this fish in sheltered reefs near deep crevices and caves. The upper body is yellowish, tending toward deep gold near the stomach. Note also the black band at the base of the tail. (to 12 cm, 4.5 in)

Plate 97e
Star Puffer
Arothron stellatus
This large puffer can be found in and around clear-water coral reefs, where it dines on hard-shelled benthic (bottom-dwelling) invertebrates. It is white with numerous small black spots throughout, except for the belly region. Juveniles are orange with black spots. (to 90 cm, 35 in)

Plate 97f
Porcupinefish
Diodon hystrix
Porcupinefish look like puffers with spines. This species frequents both coral and rocky reefs, where it dines on mollusks, urchins, and crabs. It is grayish brown, becoming white near the belly, with small black spots throughout. (to 70 cm, 28 in)

Plate 97

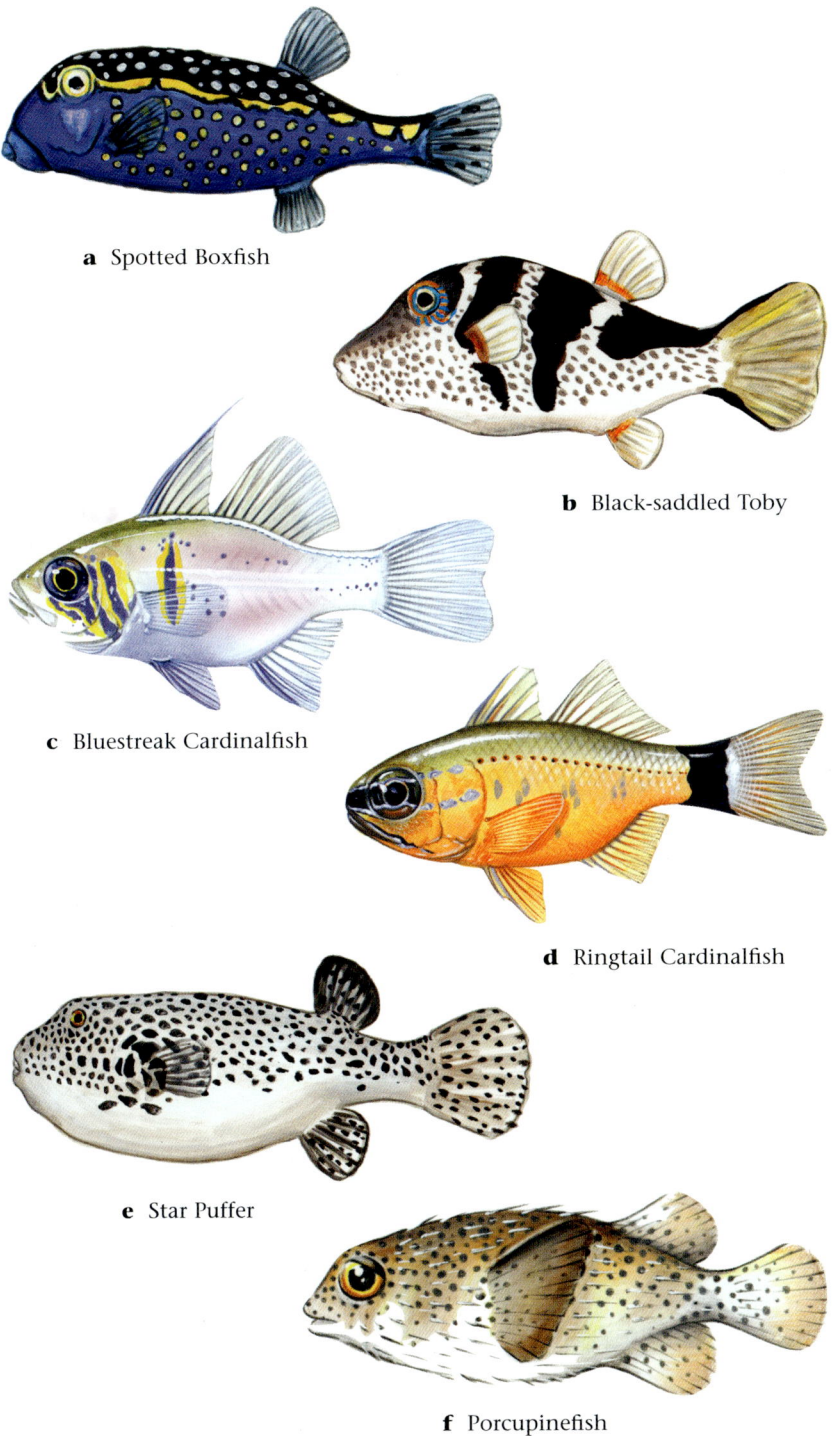

a Spotted Boxfish

b Black-saddled Toby

c Bluestreak Cardinalfish

d Ringtail Cardinalfish

e Star Puffer

f Porcupinefish

Plate 98a
Scarlet Soldierfish
Myripristis pralinia
Soliderfishes (and squirrelfishes, family Holocentridae) are large-eyed nocturnal animals that hang out in reef crevices and crannies by day. They feed on large zooplankton, especially larval crustaceans. This species can be found in loose groups near shelter. The body of this soldierfish is red, tending toward pink below. The pelvic fins are pink, but the rest are red. (to 20 cm, 8 in)

Plate 98b
Violet Soldierfish
Myripristis violacea
Look for this soldierfish in coral-rich areas. The body is whitish, with a distinctive violet sheen; the tips of the dorsal, anal, and tail fins are red. (to 20 cm, 8 in)

Plate 98c
Crown Squirrelfish
Sargocentron diadema
This is a common shallow-water reef fish. It is red with several white lateral stripes on the body; the dorsal fin is dark red to black. (to 13 cm, 5 in)

Plate 98d
Peppered Squirrelfish
Sargocentron punctatissimum
This species occurs in very shallow water, including tide pools. The body is silvery red with bluish highlights and narrow red stripes; the spiny dorsal fin is red with a white spot on each membrane segment. (to 13 cm, 5 in)

Plate 98e
Trumpetfish
Aulostomus chinensis
Also called the Painted Flutemouth, this odd-shaped predator uses stealth to approach its prey (small fish), sometimes even hiding behind larger fishes such as parrotfish. It also uses camouflage and can change color to match its surroundings. There are two color forms, brown and yellow. (to 80 cm, 32 in)

Plate 98f
Cornetfish
Fistularia commersonii
Also called the Smooth Flutemouth, this fish is similar to the Trumpetfish (Plate 98e) but much more slender. It is common on shallow reefs, where it is most active at night. (to 1.5 m, 4.9 ft)

Plate 98

a Scarlet Soldierfish

b Violet Soldierfish

c Crown Squirrelfish

d Peppered Squirrelfish

e Trumpetfish

f Cornetfish

Plate 99a
Indian Turkeyfish
Pterois miles
This extravagant beauty must be treated with respect because of its venomous spines. It hangs out under ledges by day, feeding at night on small fishes and crustaceans. It can be found on the Andaman coast; the closely related Red Firefish (*Pterois volitans*) occurs in the gulf; only an expert can distinguish the two. (to 38 cm, 15 in)

Plate 99b
Sawtooth Barracuda
Sphyraena putnamiae
This voracious predator occurs in large stationary schools by day, usually in heavy current. (to 87 cm, 34 in)

Plate 99c
Starry Moray
Echidna nebulosa
This smallish moray, also known as the Snowflake Moray, is more likely to be found out and about during daylight hours, actively swimming, than other morays. It is white with two rows of large black blotches. (to 70 cm, 28 in)

Plate 99d
Yellowmargin Moray
Gymnothorax flavimarginatus
This common moray is one of the most easily tamed, even to the point of taking food from a diver's hand. It is brown with yellow mottling. The yellow fin margins for which it is named can only be seen when it is out swimming. (to 1.2 m, 4 ft)

Plate 99e
Giant Moray
Gymnothorax javanicus
This is the largest Pacific moray and it occurs in a variety of reef habitats in shallow water. It is light brown with irregular darker brown spots. (to 2.2 m, 7.2 ft)

Plate 99f
Undulated Moray
Gymnothorax undulatus
This is one of the most common morays, and one of the most aggressive toward divers. The body is yellowish with dense, irregular dark brown blotches. (to 1 m, 3.3 ft)

Plate 99g
Whale Shark
Rhincodon typus
These gentle giants are generally pelagic (open-ocean) but at certain times of year, when the plankton is blooming, they can be found near shore, slowly cruising with their mouths agape. Aside from their large size, they can be readily distinguished from other sea creatures by their distinctive coloration of white spots over a dark background. (to 12 m, 39 ft)

Plate 99

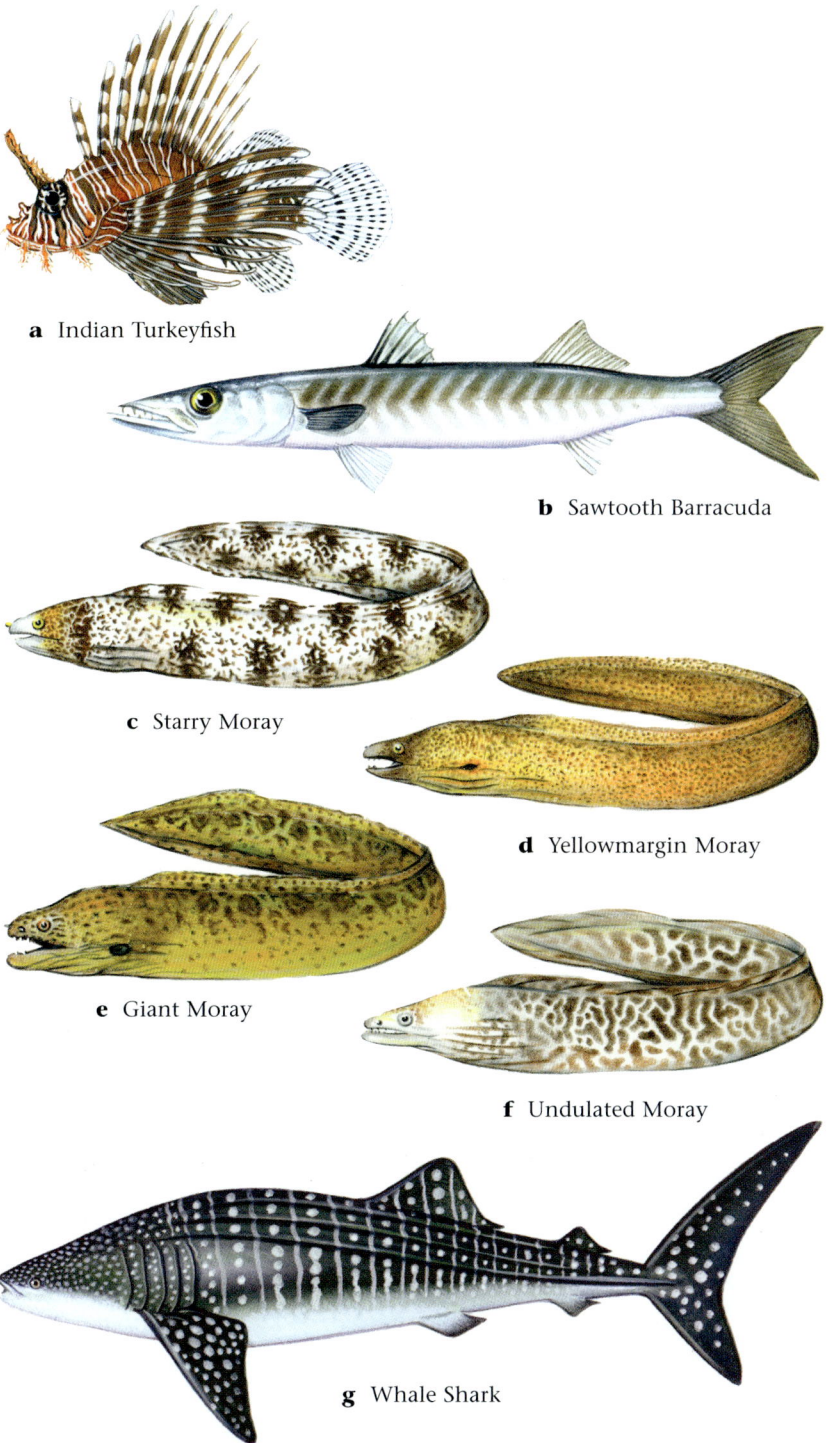

a Indian Turkeyfish

b Sawtooth Barracuda

c Starry Moray

d Yellowmargin Moray

e Giant Moray

f Undulated Moray

g Whale Shark

Plate 100a
Leopard Shark
Stegostoma fasciatum
This species, also called the Zebra Shark (because of its juvenile coloration), can be found resting by day on sandy areas, especially near reef channels. It feeds mostly on benthic (bottom-dwelling) invertebrates, especially mollusks, during the night. If you approach slowly, in a non-threatening manner, you can get quite close to one of these impressive creatures, but do not touch or otherwise molest them. (to 3.5 m, 11.5 ft)

Plate 100b
Gray Reef Shark
Carcharhinus amblyrhyncos
This requiem shark (family Carcharhinidae) is common on outer reef slopes, generally in shallower water than the Silvertip Sharks (*Carcharinus albimarginatus*). This shark is the most prone to adopt the hunch-backed threat posture when agitated. This threat should be heeded, as these sharks are potentially dangerous, and most attacks occur when divers approach too closely. The body is grayish brown, shading to white at the belly; the tail fin has a distinctive black trailing edge. (to 2.5 m, 8.2 ft)

Plate 100c
Blacktip Reef Shark
Carcharhinus melanopterus
This is one of the most common sharks on shallow reefs. It is timid, but has been known to bite the feet of waders. The snout is fairly short and rounded; the body is gray-brown above and white below. There is a distinct darker stripe extending into the white region, which runs from above the pectoral fin toward the tail. All of the fins have black near the tip, but the black area is especially pronounced on the first dorsal fin. (to 1.8 m, 5.9 ft)

Plate 100d
Whitetip Reef Shark
Triaenodon obesus
Though a bold and curious shark that often approaches divers, this species is considered harmless and has rarely been implicated in attacks. It is a nocturnal shallow-water shark that rests in caves and under ledges during the day. It is brownish above, tending toward yellowish white below; the tips of the dorsal fins and tail are white, but most noticeably on the first dorsal fin and upper tail fin. (to 2.1 m, 6.9 ft)

Plate 100e
Spotted Eagle Ray
Aetobatus narinari
Eagle rays are fairly common on inshore, shallow reefs. Like Manta Rays (Plate 100f), they have a penchant for leaping out of the water, for reasons not entirely clear. This species can be readily identified by the numerous white spots that cover its body. (to 2.5 m, 8.2 ft, wingtip to wingtip)

Plate 100f
Manta Ray
Manta biorostris
These gentle giants are among the largest of all fishes and among the most awe-inspiring ocean creatures. Aside from their size and graceful swimming movements, Mantas are famous for their spectacular leaps above the water surface. They are generally pelagic (open-ocean) but they are often encountered by divers near coral reefs. Aside from their huge size, they can be recognized by the distinctive flaps in front of the eyes. (to 6.7 m, 22 ft, wingtip to wingtip; to 1800+ kg, 4000+ lb)

Plate 100g
Blue-spotted Stingray
Taeniura lymma
There are a number of stingray species (family Dasyatidae) in the Thailand region. They are named for their tail spines, which can deliver an extremely painful wound. Stingrays generally prefer shallow water over sandy bottoms, so human waders should be cautious. This species is frequently encountered on coral reefs, resting under ledges. It can be identified by the prominent blue spots that cover the entire body. (to 2.4 m, 7.9 ft, wingtip to wingtip)

Plate 100

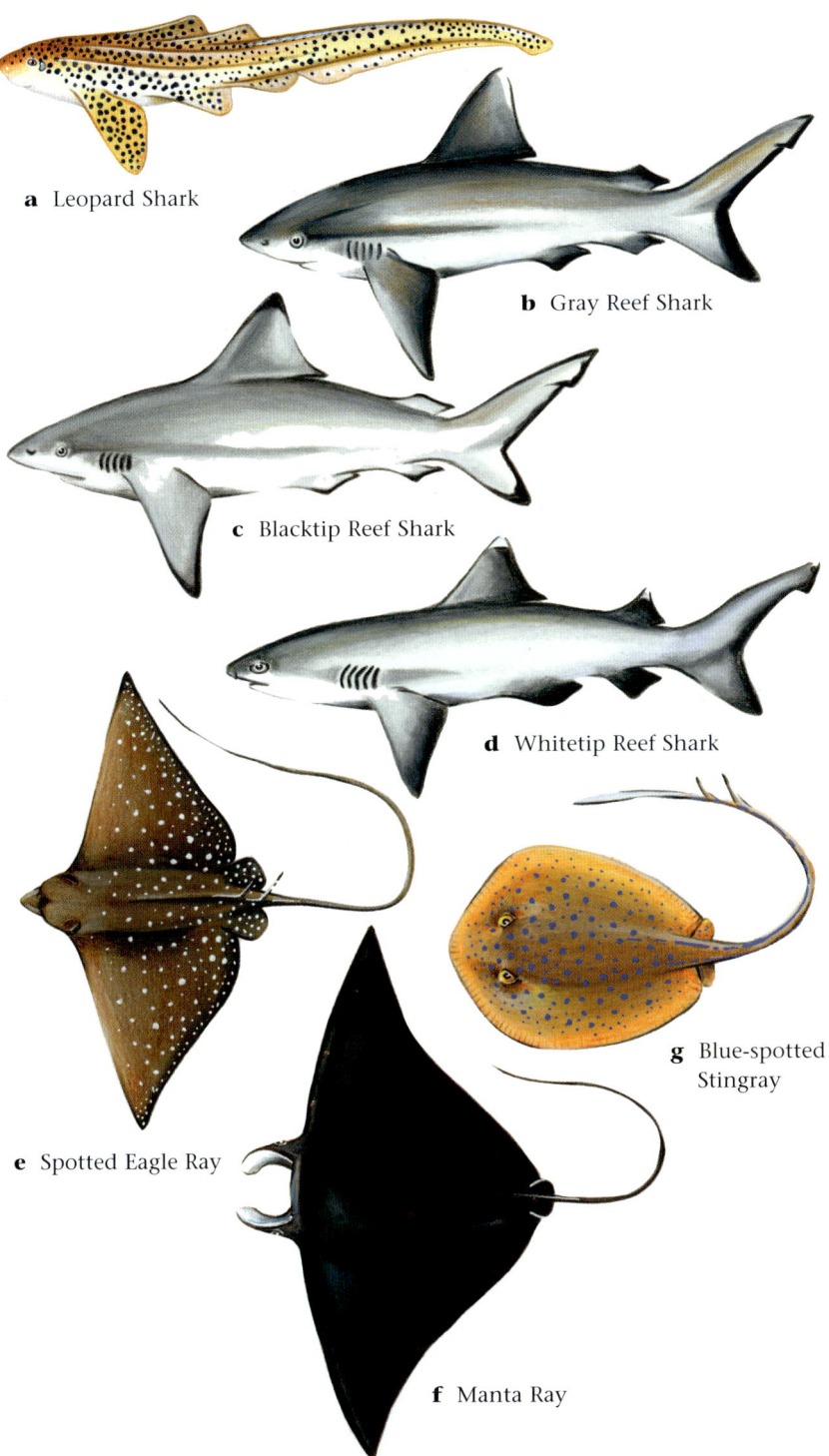

a Leopard Shark
b Gray Reef Shark
c Blacktip Reef Shark
d Whitetip Reef Shark
e Spotted Eagle Ray
f Manta Ray
g Blue-spotted Stingray

Plate 101a
Leucetta chagosensis
This strikingly colored sponge forms globular colonies. It can be found on reef slopes.

Plate 101b
Fire Coral
Millepora sp.
An encrusting, sometimes branching group of coral species that inflict very nasty, burning stings when touched. They can cause welts and swelling in sensitive people, although the effect is usually of short duration.

Plate 101c
Glomerate Tree Coral
Dendronephthya sp.
This gorgonian, or soft coral, forms attractive, prickly, rounded colonies. It is a favorite of underwater photographers.

Plate 101d
Sea Fan
Melithaea sp.
Sea fans form upright colonies in which their branches are are all in the same plane, or "dimension." Members of this genus form large colonies (1 to 2 m, 3.3 to 6.6 ft, in diameter); they are usually found on walls and steep reef slopes.

Plate 101e
Magnificent Sea Anemone
Heteractis magnifica
This large anemone is a favorite of anenomefishes and photographers alike. It prefers exposed areas with lots of current.

Plate 101f
Bulb Tentacle Anemone
Entacmaea quadricolor
The tentacles of this anemone are bulbous. It is a favorite of anemonefishes, but especially the Black Anemonefish (Amphiprion melanopus). Usually only the tentacles appear above the surface; the main part of the anemone lays hidden in crevices.

Plate 101g
Merten's Sea Anemone
Stichodactyla mertensi
Perhaps the world's largest anemone and a favorite of anemonefishes, this species can be distinguished by the convoluted disc margin.

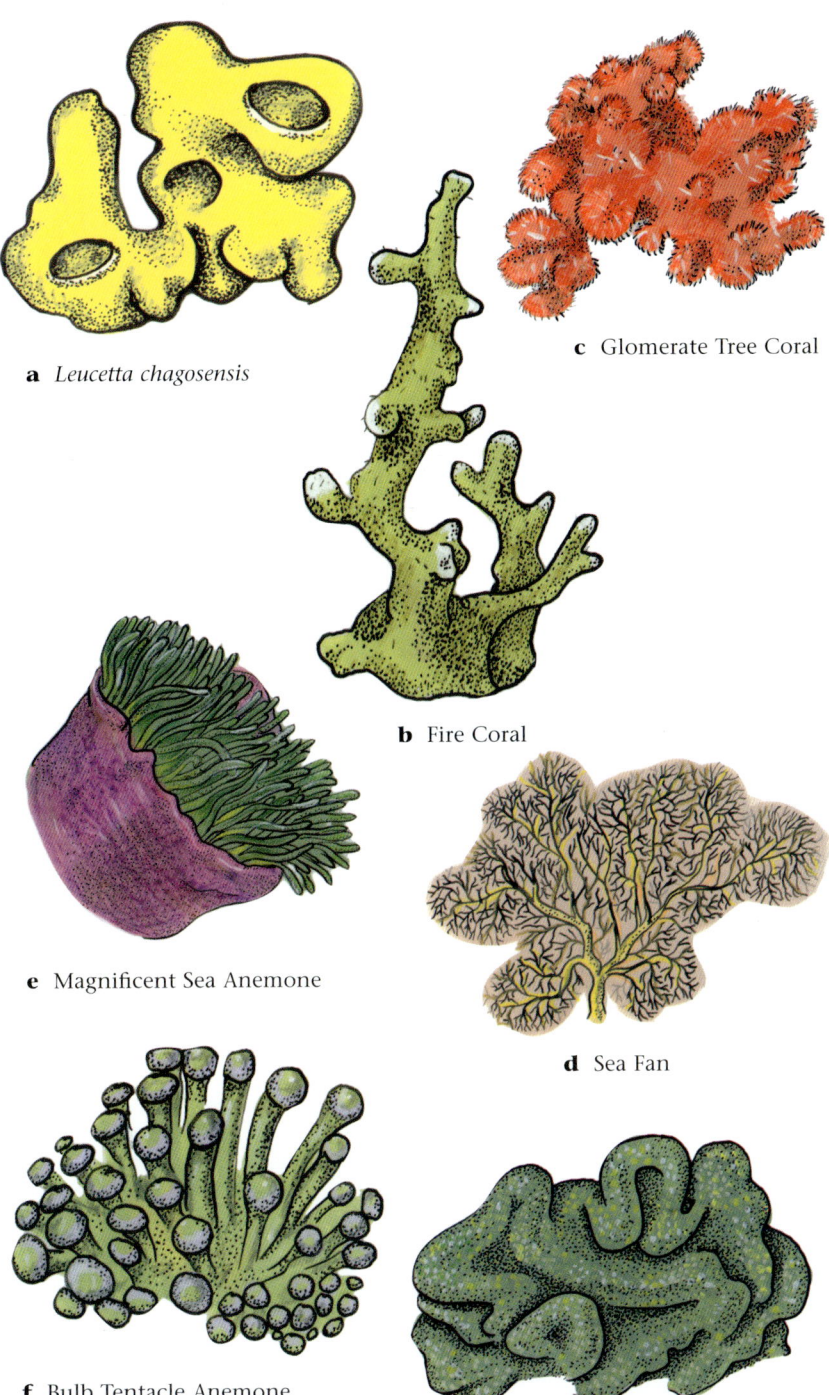

Plate 102

Plate 102a
Pocillopora eydouxi
This coral species prefers areas with lots of water movement. It forms round heads with compact branches of uniform size.

Plate 102b
Acropora gemmifera
Colonies of this coral form thick, conical branches with blunt tips. Look for it on reef flats or upper reef slopes. The color is variable, ranging from cream to bluish or pinkish.

Plate 102c
Acropora robusta
This common coral can be identified by the long vertical branches, especially toward the center of the colony. It is common where there is wave action. It is often has an intense green color, with pinkish or cream branch tips.

Plate 102d
Porites cf. Lobata
This mounding coral forms lumpy, shallow domes. It prefers calm waters and can be particularly abundant in lagoons.

Plate 102e
Fungia sp.
These mushroom-shaped, solitary corals have characteristic ridges radiating from the center. They are usually found on the substrate (sand or rubble) in turbid, shallow water.

Plate 102f
Brain Coral
Platygyra lamellina
Named for the cerebral-cortex-like surface invaginations, brain corals form circular dome-shaped colonies, sometimes of considerable size. The surface invaginations of this species are of uniform depth and width. Look for these on reef slopes in clear water.

Plate 102g
Plate Coral
Turbinaria reniformis
This coral forms characteristically flat, plate-like colonies, often in pure stands covering extensive portions of the reef surface. The color is usually yellow-green.

Plate 102

a *Pocillopora eydouxi*
b *Acropora gemmifera*
c *Acropora robusta*
d *Porites* cf. *Lobata*
e *Fungia* sp.
f Brain Coral
g Plate Coral

Plate 103

Plate 103a
Bushy Black Coral
Antipathes sp.
It's only black when its dead; living coral is brownish-orange. Antipathes is very plant-like in appearance—bushy and densely branched.

Plate 103b
Upside-Down Jellyfish
Cassiopea andromeda
Look for this jellyfish in calm water over sand. It hangs upside down in order to absorb the most sunlight for its symbiotic algae.

Plate 103c
Pseudoceros dimidiatus
The striking color of this flatworm suggests that, like nudibranchs (sea slugs), it is toxic. Color pattern varies, but the most common form has wide yellow stripes alternating with wide black stripes. Also look for the orange margin.

Plate 103d
Pherecardia striata
This species is a type of fireworm, which are known for their painful stings. It is covered with white hairy structures called setae, and if you get close enough you can see them—a series of thin pink and white stripes running longitudinally along the back.

Plate 103e
Christmas Tree Worm
Spirobranchus giganteus
This species is variable in color, but always has two spirals of tentacles; it lives in tubes on living coral.

Plate 103f
Horned Helmet
Cassia cornuta
This common helmet is also the largest. It feeds on echinoderms, including the notorious Crown-of-thorns (Plate 107). Look for it on sand inside the outer barrier reefs.

Plate 103g
Moon Snail
Polinices mammilla
The glossy shell is white and so is the animal inside. Moon Snails feed on other mollusks. They can be found on sand or on mudflats in shallow water.

Plate 103

a Bushy Black Coral

b Upside-Down Jellyfish

c *Pseudoceros dimidiatus*

d *Pherecardia striata*

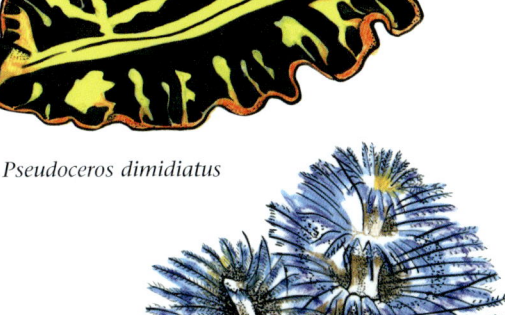
e Christmas Tree Worm

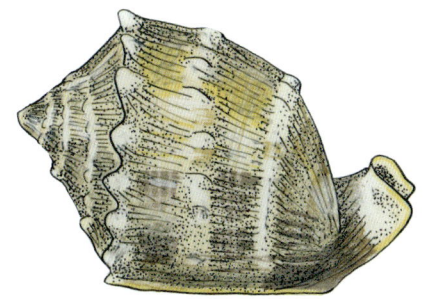
f Horned Helmet

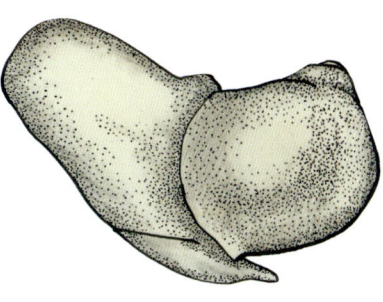
g Moon Snail

Plate 104a
Honey Cowrie
Cypraea helvola
A very common cowrie, this species is colored reddish brown with many white spots, and prefers shallow water.

Plate 104b
Mole Cowrie
Cypraea talpa
Look for this cowrie underneath coral heads; its shell is brown and gold banded and its mantle is black with many tiny white spots.

Plate 104c
Tiger Cowrie
Cypraea tigris
This species frequents a number of habitats but it is probably most common in coral rubble. It has a white shell with black spots. It is one of the larger cowries.

Plate 104d
Pacific Deer Cowrie
Cypraea vitellus
The shell of this cowrie is brown with white spots. The papillae (projections, or "bumps") on the mantle are particularly large.

Plate 104e
Triton's Trumpet
Charonia tritonis
This species is one of the largest sea snails and an important predator on the Crown-of-thorns (Plate 107). Look for it on sandy areas between reef patches.

Plate 104f
Coral Snail
Coralliophila neritoidea
Members of this genus prey on hard corals. Look for the shell's bright purple aperture.

Plate 104g
Pope's Miter
Mitra papalis
This large miter has orange spots on a cream-colored shell. Unlike most miters, this species prefers sandy habitats.

Plate 104

a Honey Cowrie
b Mole Cowrie
c Tiger Cowrie
d Pacific Deer Cowrie
e Triton's Trumpet
f Coral Snail
g Pope's Miter

Plate 105a
Marble Cone
Conus marmoreus
Like many cones, this species has many triangular markings, but it has a darker shell than most other members of the genus. Cones are predators and this one prefers to eat other cone snails.

Plate 105b
Textile Cone
Conus textile
A favorite among shell collectors, this species is extremely venomous. The venom, which it uses to kill small fish, can also kill humans. It is most common in coral rubble in shallow water.

Plate 105c
Sundial
Architectonica perspectiva
This beautiful gastropod (the largest group of mollusks, which includes the snails, limpets, slugs, whelks, conchs, and sea slugs) has a characteristic coiled form. It likes sandy areas in shallow water.

Plate 105d
Chelidonura hirudinina
This delicate little nudibranch (sea slug) rewards close inspection. It is blue-green with black lines forming a "T" on the head. It prefers shallow water over either sand or rocks.

Plate 105e
Elysia ornata
This sea slug (nudibranch) has a green body with orange and black margins.

Plate 105f
Umbraculum umbraculum
Look for this sea slug (nudibranch) in tide pools or shallow reefs. It is bright orange with round white papillae ("bumps") projecting from its back.

Plate 105g
Netted Olive
Oliva reticulara
This attractive sea snail preys on other gastropods (the largest group of mollusks, which includes the snails, limpets, slugs, whelks, conchs, and sea slugs). Look for the orange area near the front of the shell's aperture.

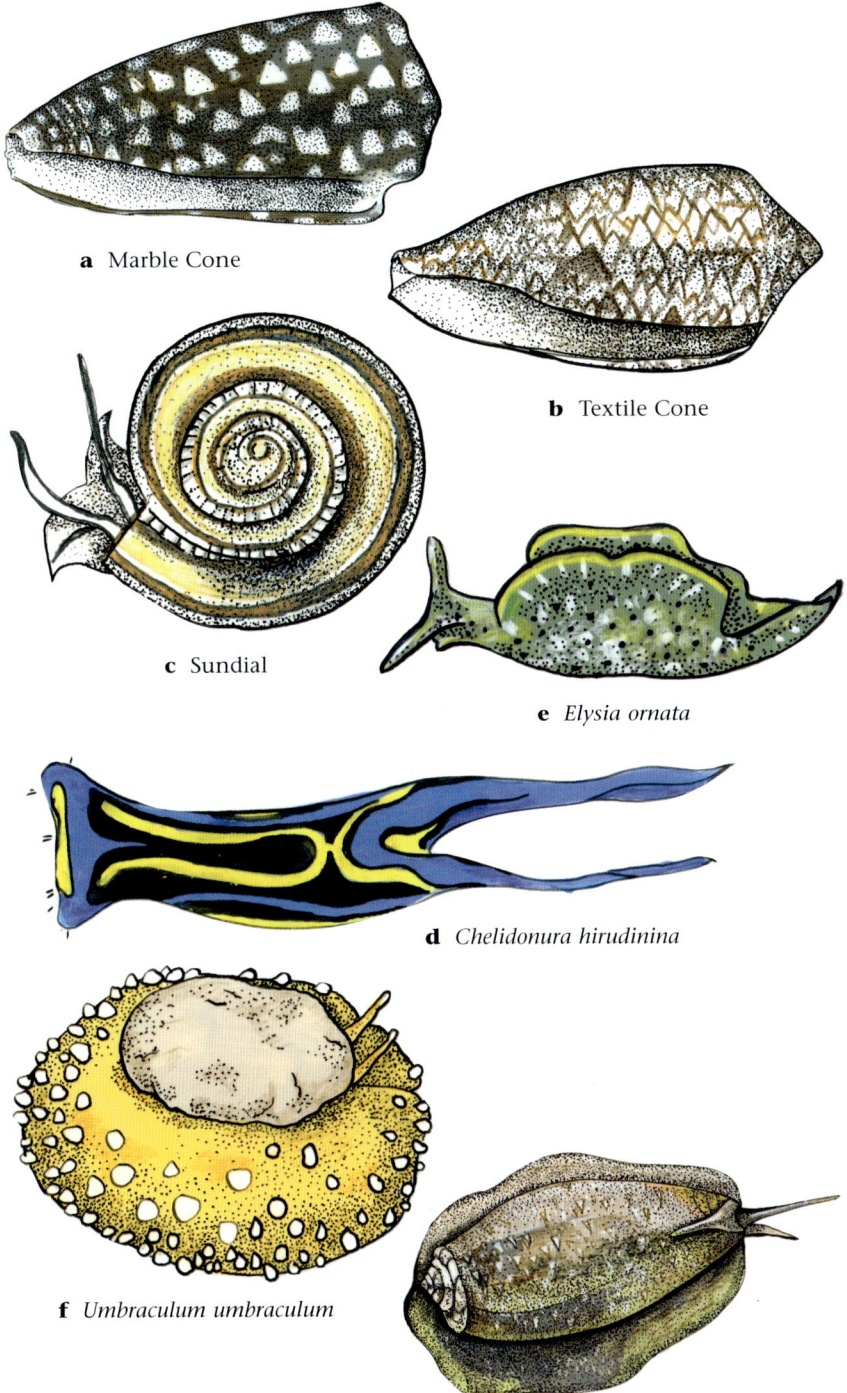

a Marble Cone
b Textile Cone
c Sundial
e *Elysia ornata*
d *Chelidonura hirudinina*
f *Umbraculum umbraculum*
g Netted Olive

Plate 106

Plate 106a
Berthella martensi
This sea slug (nudibranch) can literally come apart before your eyes. When disturbed, it sheds all or part of its mantle, which consists of three parts. The color is quite variable.

Plate 106b
Spanish Dancer
Hexabranchus sanguineus
This species is named for the undulating movements it makes while swimming through the water. It is the largest nudibranch (sea slug) in the world. It is always some shade of red.

Plate 106c
Phyllidiella pustulosa
This nudibranch (sea slug) has a black body with pink tubercles ("bumps") and is one of the most common species of nudibranch throughout the Indo-Pacific.

Plate 106d
Common Pearl Oyster
Pinctada margaritifera
This bivalve attaches to coral rubble and rocks. It can be recognized by the jagged teeth around the shell's aperture.

Plate 106e
Bigfin Reef Squid
Sepioteuthis lessoniana
This is the squid you are most likely to encounter on the reef, especially at its edges. The fins of this species extend much further down the mantle than in most squids. The color, as in most squids, is variable and changeable.

Plate 106f
Octopus cyanea
This is a relatively large octopus that is out and about during the day. It prefers relatively shallow water favored by snorkelers and scuba divers. Look for a black spot surrounded by a thin black ring at the base of the arm web.

Plate 106g
Giant Clam
Tridacna gigas
This is the largest of the giant clams (genus Tridacna), reaching a length of up to 1.3 m (4.3 ft), and the largest bivalve on Earth. Formerly common in offshore reefs, it is now rare over much of its range owing to overharvesting.

Plate 106

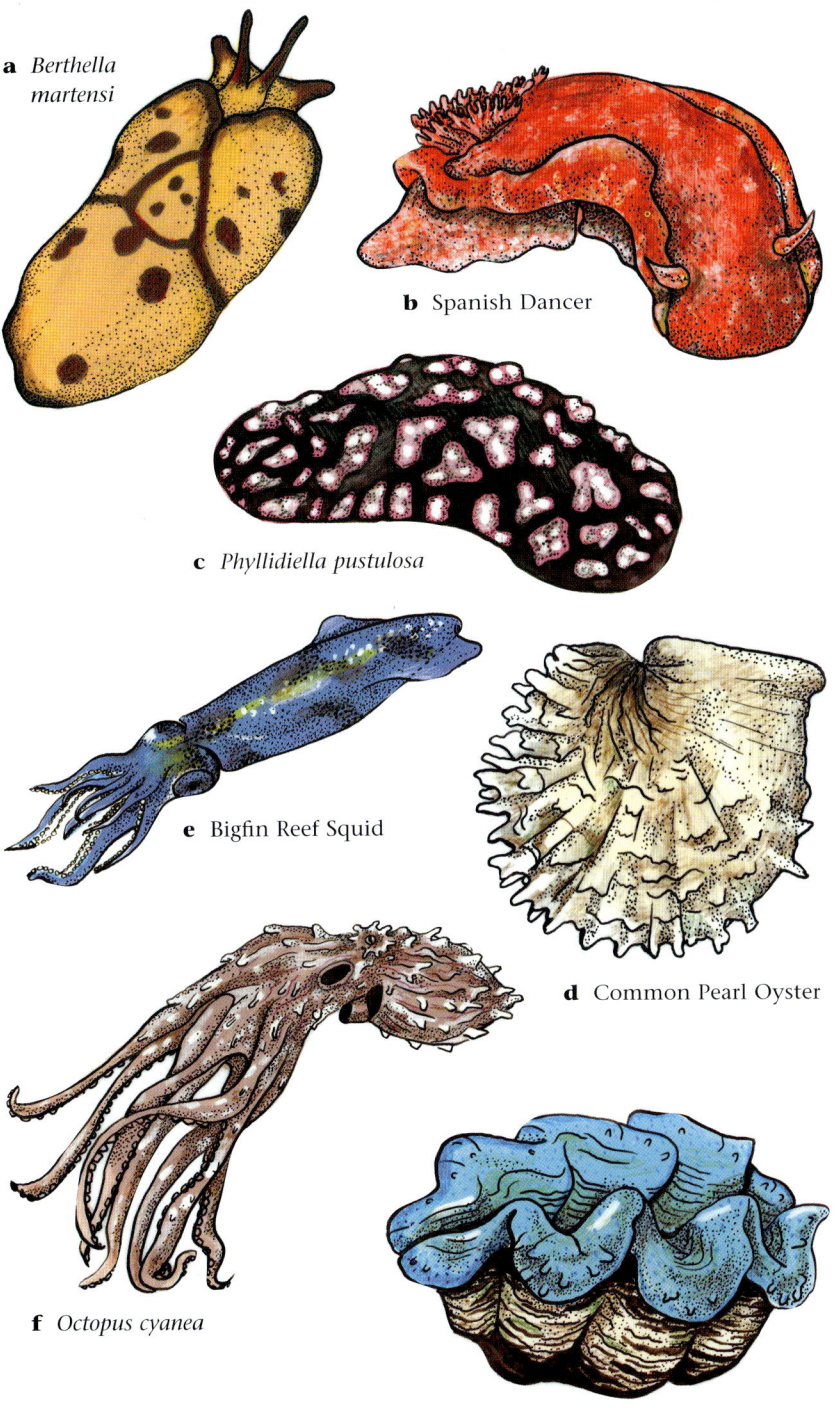

a *Berthella martensi*
b Spanish Dancer
c *Phyllidiella pustulosa*
e Bigfin Reef Squid
d Common Pearl Oyster
f *Octopus cyanea*
g Giant Clam

Plate 107a
Broadclub Cuttlefish
Sepia latimanus
This large cuttlefish is a quick (color) change artist. It is active during daylight on shallow reefs, where it can often be found in pairs. It can be quite curious.

Plate 107b
Bumblebee Shrimp
Gnathophyllum americanum
This blunt-headed shrimp usually has one large claw larger than the other, more so in males than females. Its body is white with black and brown bands.

Plate 107c
Odontodactylus scyllarus
This mantis shrimp is a real beauty. It has a bright green body, blue head and eyes, and bright red appendages. It prefers sand and rubble and feeds on a variety of other crustaceans, mollusks, and worms at night.

Plate 107d
Harlequin Shrimp
Hymenocera picta
This shrimp can be easily identified by its bold markings—red, burgundy, or purple spots on a white body. It preys on starfish, which it consumes from the tip of the arm toward the central mouth. In this way it keeps the starfish alive for an extended period so that the shrimp can dine at its leisure.

Plate 107e
Banded Coral Shrimp
Stenopus hispidus
Cleaner shrimp are often strikingly colored, ostensibly to attract clients to their cleaning stations (p. 214). This species has a thin body with red and white bands, extending to the claws. When a fish arrives at a cleaning station, the shrimp palpitates it with its antannae; this causes the fish to relax so that the shrimp can crawl all over its body, looking for ectoparasites.

Plate 107f
Linckia multiflora
This variably colored sea star is common on shallow reefs. It is usually mottled with red, blue, and yellow hues.

Plate 107g
Spiny Lobster
Panulirus pencillatus
This is the most common spiny lobster and can be readily identified by the white spots on the back of the carapace.

Plate 107h
Crown-of-thorns
Acanthaster planci
This notorious sea star is no longer considered quite the predatory demon it was once thought to be. But local population explosions of this species have resulted in the decimation of coral reefs. Its formidable spines make it easy to identify.

Plate 107

a Broadclub Cuttlefish

b Bumblebee Shrimp

c *Odontodactylus scyllarus*

d Harlequin Shrimp

e Banded Coral Shrimp

f *Linckia multiflora*

g Spiny Lobster

h Crown-of-thorns

Plate 108a
Ophiothrix nereidina
This brittle star has a green disc and long spines. It is active in shallow water.

Plate 108b
Echinothrix diadema
The spines of this sea urchin are closed at the tip and pointed. They are also densely packed. This species is more likely to be found out in the open than most urchins.

Plate 108c
Tripneustes gratilla
This is one of the more common sea urchins. It prefers calm, shallow water such as lagoons. It frequently covers itself with debris, presumably for camouflage. The color is quite variable, and the spines are arranged in distinct bands.

Plate 108d
Echinometra mathaei
This is a stout-spined sea urchin. The spines tend to be reddish, with a white ring around the base of each. It is found on very shallow reefs.

Plate 108e
Slate Pencil Urchin
Heterocentrotus mammillatus
The extremely thick, blunt spines are what distinguishes this sea urchin. The color is extremely variable. It prefers shallow reefs; look for it in the crevices.

Plate 108f
Bohadschia marmorata
This sea cucumber likes sandy habitats in shallow water. It is yellowish with wide brown bands. Note also the numerous thin papillae (projections, or "bumps") covering the upper body.

Plate 108g
Holothuria atra
This sausage-shaped sea cucumber is black, but it often covers itself with sand. One of the most common species, it sometimes forms aggregations in shallow sandy areas.

Plate 108h
Stichopus chloronotus
This sea cucumber prefers coral rubble and rocky areas. Its dark green body is adorned with long black papillae (projections, or "bumps") with orange tips.

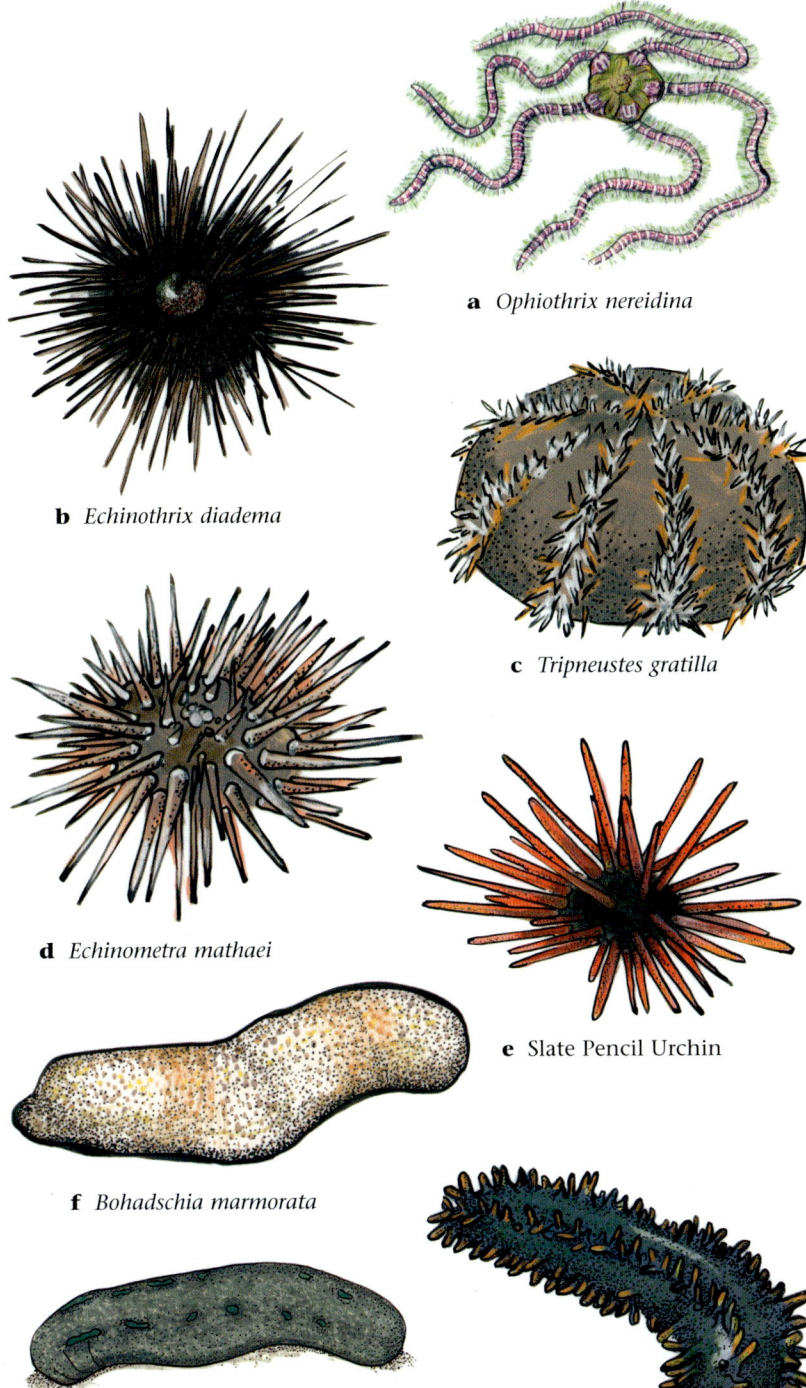

a *Ophiothrix nereidina*
b *Echinothrix diadema*
c *Tripneustes gratilla*
d *Echinometra mathaei*
e Slate Pencil Urchin
f *Bohadschia marmorata*
g *Holothuria atra*
h *Stichopus chloronotus*

SPECIES INDEX

Abudefduf bengalensis **80a**
Abudefduf sexfasciatus **79f**
Acanthaster planci **107h**
Acanthosaura crucigera 105, **16c**
Acanthurus blochii **92d**
Acanthurus guttatus **92f**
Acanthurus leucosternon **94a**
Acanthurus lineatus **93a**
Acanthurus nigrofuscus **93b**
Acanthurus olivaceus **93c**
Acanthurus tennenti **92e**
Acanthurus triostegus **93d**
Acanthurus tristis **93f**
Acanthurus xanthopterus **93e**
Accipiter badius 137, **26e**
Accipiter trivirgatus 137, **26d**
Acridotheres javanicus 171, **57d**
Acridotheres tristis 171, **56e**
Acropora gemmifera **102b**
Acropora robusta **102c**
Actias selene 70, **3c**
Actitis hypoleucos 133, **31d**
Aegithina tiphia 160, **46a**
Aethopyga gouldiae 173, **58d**
Aethopyga siparaja 173, **59d**
Aetobatus narinari **100e**
African Coris 213, **84d**
African Rock Python 112
Ahaetulla prasina 115, **22c**
Alcedo atthis **37b**
Aluterus scriptus **96f**
Amaurornis phoenicurus 128, **29a**
Amblyglyphidodon aureus **81f**
Ambon Damselfish **81a**
American Alligator 98
American Robin 168
Amolops larutensis 84, **10f**
Ampeliceps coronatus 171, **57e**
Amphiprion akallopisos **82d**
Amphiprion frenatus **82b**

Amphiprion ocellaris **82a**
Amphiprion polymnus **82c**
Anampses meleagrides **83c**
Ananas comosus 22, **Fig. 15c**
Anarcardium occidentale 22, **Fig. 14b**
Anas acuta 130, **25e**
Anas querquedula 130, **25c**
Anastomus oscitans 128, **23a**
Andaman Damselfish **80e**
Anisoptera sp. 17, **Fig. 4d**
Anoplolepis sp. 72, **6b**
Anoplophora longehirsuta 69, **2f**
Anorrhinus galeritus 151, **39e**
Anthracoceros albirostris 151, **39a**
Anthreptes malacensis 173, **58a**
Anthreptes singalensis 173, **58b**
Anthus rufulus 159, **45c**
Antipathes sp. **103a**
Antlion 66–67, **2a**
Aonyx cinerea 201, **70c**
Aplonis panayensis 171, **56c**
Apogon aureus **97d**
Apogon leptacanthus **97c**
Apolemichthys trimaculatus **78f**
Apus affinis 158, **44a**
Arachnothera longirostra 173, **59a**
Arborophila chloropus 135, **28a**
Arc–eye Hawkfish **83a**
Archaeoattacus edwardsii 70, **3b**
Architectonica perspectiva **105c**
Arctictis binturong 201, **71c**
Arctonyx collaris 201, **70a**
Ardea alba 126, **24f**
Ardea cinerea 126, **23c**
Ardea purpurea 126, **23d**
Ardeola bacchus 126, **24b**
Argus Wrasse **84a**
Argusianus argus 135, **28e**
Argyreia splendens 20, **Fig. 10c**
Arothron stellatus **97e**

Species Index

Artocarpus heterophylla 22, **Fig. 14e**
Artocarpus incisus 22, **Fig. 14d**
Asian Barred Owlet 144, **35a**
Asian Black Eagle 136
Asian Box Turtle 101, **13b**
Asian Brown Flycatcher 170, **54d**
Asian Brown Tortoise 100
Asian Dowitcher 133
Asian Elephant 45, 46, 183, 203–205, **73a**
Asian Fairy-bluebird 160, **46d**
Asian Glossy Starling 171, **56c**
Asian Golden Cat 199
Asian Openbill Stork 44, 120, 127, 128, **23a**
Asian Palm-Swift 158, **44b**
Asian Paradise Flycatcher 170, **55c**
Asian Pied Starling 171, **57a**
Asian Rat-Snake 96
Asian Rock Python 112
Asian Tapir 203–205, **69e**
Asian Two-horned (Sumatran) Rhinoceros 45, 46, 204–205, **73b**
Asian Weaver Ant 72, **6c**
Asian Wild Dog 198, 200, 201, **69b**
Asiatic Black Bear 198, 200
Asiatic Jackal 198, 201, **69a**
Asiatic Toad 83, **8a**
Aspidontus taeniatus **91e**
Athene brama 145, **35b**
Atherurus marourus 196, **68b**
Atrophaneura aristolochiae 70, **3d**
Aulostomus chinensis **98e**
Aviceda leuphotes 137, **26b**
Avicennia alba 21, **Fig. 12c**
Back-striped Weasel 200
Baer's Pochard 129
Balistapus undulatus **95c**
Balistoides conspicillum **95e**
Balistoides viridescens **95d**
Bambusa arundinacea 17, **Fig. 5c**
Banana 22, **Fig. 15b**
Banded Coral Shrimp **107e**
Banded Kingfisher 148, **37a**
Banded Krait 110, **19c**
Banded Langur 192, **65b**
Banded Ox-frog 85, 86, **11c**
Banded Rat-Snake 96, 114, 115, **21f**
Bandicota indica 197, **68c**
Band-tailed Rat-Snake. *See* Banded Rat-Snake.
Banteng 45, 201, 202, 203, **73d**
Bar-bellied Pitta 155
Barn Swallow 157, 158, **44d**
Barred Buttonquail 134, 135, **29b**
Bat Hawk 137
Batrachostomus javensis 146, **35c**
Bauhinia pulla 17, **Fig. 4a**
Beach Cycad 22, **Fig. 13c**
Beaked Coralfish **78c**
Beautiful Nuthatch 165
Belly-banded Squirrel 197, **67d**
Bengal Monitor 103, 105, **14d**
Bengal Sergeant 213, **80a**
Bengal Snapper **90b**
Berthella martensi **106a**
Bicolor Cleaner Wrasse **84e**
Bicolor Parrotfish **86c**
Bicolored Metallic Wood-boring Beetle 68, 69, **2e**
Bigfin Reef Squid **106e**
Big-headed Frog 84, **9c**
Big-headed Horned Frog 81, **7f**
Big-headed Turtle 101, **13e**
Big-lipped Burrowing Frog 86, **11b**
Binturong 201, **71c**
Black Baza 136, 137, **26b**
Black Bulbul 161, **47d**
Black Drongo 162, **48d**
Black Giant Squirrel 197, **66c**
Black Kite 137, **26c**
Black Mangrove 21, **Fig. 12c**
Black Rat 195
Black-and-red Broadbill 155
Black-and-yellow Broadbill 155, **43b**
Blackback Butterflyfish **77a**
Black-bellied Tern 131
Blackbelly Picassofish **96c**
Blackbird 168, 169
Black-capped Kingfisher 148, **37c**
Black-collared Starling 171, **57b**
Black-crested Bulbul 161, **47a**
Black-crowned Night-Heron 126, **23e**
Black-faced Spoonbill 128
Blackfin Dartfish **92c**
Black-naped Oriole 162, **48b**
Black-naped Tern 131
Black-necked Stork 128
Black-saddled Toby **97b**
Black-shouldered Kite 136, 137, **26a**

Blackspot Snapper **90a**
Black-throated Babbler 166
Black-throated Gliding Lizard 104, 105, **16d**
Black-throated Robin 169
Blacktip Reef Shark 216, **100c**
Black-webbed Gliding Treefrog 88, 89, 90, **12c**
Black-winged Stilt 131, 133, **31a**
Blood Python 111, 112
Blotched Spadefoot Frog 86, **11a**
Blue Crested Lizard 105, **16b**
Blue Krait 110, **19b**
Blue Magpie 164, **49b**
Blue Pitta 155, **43d**
Blue Rock Thrush 169, **54a**
Blue-barred Parrotfish **87d**
Blue-bearded Bee-eater 150, **38c**
Blue-eared Barbet 152, **40c**
Bluegreen Chromis **80c**
Blue-ring Angelfish **79c**
Blue-rumped Parrot 142
Blue-sided Wrasse **84b**
Bluespine Unicornfish 212, **94d**
Bluespot Butterflyfish **77c**
Blue-spotted Hinde **88b**
Blue-spotted Stingray 216, **100g**
Bluestreak Cardinalfish **97c**
Blue-tongued Skink 107
Blue-winged Leafbird 160, **46c**
Blyth's Hornbill 151
Blyth's Kingfisher 148
Blyth's Tomb Bat 189, **63a**
Bodianus anthoides **83b**
Bohadschia marmorata **108f**
Boiga dendrophila 96, 115, **22f**
Boiga multomaculata 115, **22e**
Bolbometapon muricatum **85f**
Bombax malabaricum 18, **Fig. 7c**
Bos gaurus 203, **73c**
Bos javanicus 203, **73d**
Bottle-nosed Dolphin 206, **75c**
Bowring's Supple Skink 107, **17d**
Brahminy Kite 136
Brain Coral 210, **102f**
Breadfruit 22, **Fig. 14d**
Broadclub Cuttlefish **107a**
Bronze-winged Jacana 127, 128, **29d**
Brow-antlered Deer 46, 203
Brown Fish-Owl 145, **35e**

Brown Hawk-Owl 145, **35d**
Brown Hornbill 150, 151, **39c**
Brown Shrike 171, **56b**
Brown Surgeonfish **93b**
Brown-chested Flycatcher 170
Brown-headed Gull 130, 131, **32b**
Brown-throated Sunbird 173, **58a**
Bubulcus ibis 126, **24e**
Buceros bicornis 53, 58, 151, **39b**
Buff-bellied Flowerpecker 173, **59b**
Bufo asper 83, **8b**
Bufo macrotis 83, **8c**
Bufo melanostictus 83, **8a**
Bufo parvus 83, **8d**
Bulb Tentacle Anemone **101f**
Bumblebee Shrimp **107b**
Bumphead Parrotfish **85f**
Bungarus candidus 110, **19b**
Bungarus fasciatus 110, **19c**
Burmese Python 111, 112
Burmese Sal 19, **Fig. 9a**
Bush-tailed Porcupine 194, 197, **68b**
Bushy Black Coral **103a**
Bushy-crested Hornbill 151, **39e**
Butea monosperma 18, **Fig. 8a**
Butterfly Lizard 104, 105, **16e**
Cacomantis merulinus 143, **34a**
Caesio lunaris **90c**
Caesio xanthonota **90d**
Calamus spp. 17, **Fig. 4c**
Calatomus carolinus **86b**
Calliophis maculiceps 110, **19a**
Callosciurus caniceps 197, **67a**
Callosciurus finlaysoni 197, **67b**
Callosciurus flavimanus 197, **67d**
Calloselasma rhodostoma 110, **18e**
Calluella guttulata 86, **11a**
Calotes mystaceus 105, **16b**
Calotes versicolor 105, **16a**
Canis aureus 201, **69a**
Canthigaster valentini **97b**
Capricornis sumatrensis 203, **74d**
Caprimulgus macrurus 146, **36d**
Caranx ignobilis **89f**
Carcharhinus amblyrhyncos **100b**
Carcharhinus melanopterus **100c**
Cardamom Slender-toed Gecko 103, **15f**
Carica papaya 22, **Fig. 15a**
Carpodacus erythrinus 174, **60e**

Species Index

Cascade Slender Leaf-litter Frog 81, **7d**
Cashew 22, 72, **Fig. 14b**
Cassia bakeriana 18, **Fig. 7d**
Cassia cornuta **103f**
Cassiopea andromeda **103b**
Castanopsis sp. 17, **Fig. 5d**
Casuarina equisetifolia 22, **Fig. 13a**
Catharsius molossus 69, **2d**
Cattle Egret 52, 125, 126, 202, **24e**
Celeus brachyurus 154, **41a**
Centropus sinensis 143, **34d**
Centropyge eibli **78b**
Cephalopholis argus **87e**
Cephalopholis cyanostigma **88b**
Cephalopholis miniata **87f**
Cerberus rynchops 115, **20b**
Cervus unicolor 203, **74c**
Cetoscarus bicolor **86c**
Chaen-daeng Lily 20, **Fig. 10d**
Chaetodon auriga **76a**
Chaetodon baronessa 212
Chaetodon citrinellus **76b**
Chaetodon collare 212, **76e**
Chaetodon decussatus **77e**
Chaetodon guttatissimus **77f**
Chaetodon lineolatus **76d**
Chaetodon lunula **76f**
Chaetodon melanotus **77a**
Chaetodon meyeri **77b**
Chaetodon plebius **77c**
Chaetodon reticulata 212
Chaetodon triangulum 212, **76c**
Chaetodon trifascialis **77d**
Chaetodon trifasciatus **78a**
Chalcophaps indica 140, **33c**
Charadrius dubius 133, **30b**
Charonia tritonis **104e**
Checkered Keelback 115, **20e**
Cheilinus undulatus **83f**
Chelidonura hirudinina **105d**
Chelmon rostratus **78c**
Chestnut-bellied Nuthatch 165, **50d**
Chestnut-crowned Warbler 167, **52f**
Chestnut-headed Bee-eater 150, **38b**
Chestnut-headed Partridge 122, 135
Chestnut-necklaced Partridge 135
Chevroned Butterflyfish **77d**
Chinese Crested-tern 122
Chinese Egret 126
Chinese Francolin 135, **28b**

Chinese Pond Heron 126, **24b**
Chirixalus vittatus 90, **12d**
Chlidonias hybridus 131, **32a**
Chloropsis aurifrons 160, **46b**
Chloropsis cochinchinensis 160, **46c**
Chlorurus oedema **86a**
Chocolate-dip Chromis **80d**
Christmas Tree Worm 211, **103e**
Chromis dimidiata **80d**
Chromis viridis **80c**
Chrysiptera glauca **80f**
Chrysopelea ornata 115, **22a**
Cicindela aurulenta 69, **2b**
Circus melanoleucos 137, **27d**
Cirrhilabrus cyanopleura **84b**
Cirripectes auritus **91d**
Cissa chinensis 164, **49c**
Cleaner Wrasse 211, 214, 215, **84f**
Clouded Leopard 200, 201, **72a**
Clown Triggerfish **95e**
Coconut Palm 22, **Fig. 15e**
Cocos nucifera 22, **Fig. 15e**
Collared Butterflyfish 212, **76e**
Collared Falconet 138, **27e**
Collared Kingfisher 148, **37d**
Colorado River Toad 83
Common Barking Deer 202, 203, **74b**
Common Cobra 110
Common Dolphin 206, **75b**
Common Flameback 154, **41b**
Common Flying Fox 186, 189, **62a**
Common Grass Yellow 70, **5a**
Common Iora 160, **46a**
Common Kingfisher 148, **37b**
Common Koel 143, **34b**
Common Mock Viper 115, **21b**
Common Moorhen 127, 128, **29c**
Common Myna 171, **56e**
Common Nawab 70, **5e**
Common Otter 198
Common Palm Civet 201, **71a**
Common Pearl Oyster **106d**
Common Rat-Snake 96
Common Raven 163, 164
Common Redshank 133, **30d**
Common Rose Swallowtail 70, **3d**
Common Rosefinch 174, **60e**
Common Sailor 70, **4c**
Common Sandpiper 133, **31d**
Common Starling 171

Common Treeshrew 183, 184, 185, **61a**
Common Wall Lizard 106
Conus marmoreus **105a**
Conus textile **105b**
Convict Surgeonfish **93d**
Copper-eared Frog 84, **10b**
Coppersmith Barbet 152, **40e**
Copsychus malabaricus 169, **53d**
Copsychus saularis 169, **53e**
Coracias benghalensis 150, **38a**
Coracina macei 159, **45e**
Coradion chrysozonas **79a**
Coral Grouper **88e**
Coral Hinde **87f**
Coral Rabbitfish 212, **94f**
Coral Snail **104f**
Coral Tree 18, **Fig. 7b**
Coral-billed Ground-cuckoo 143
Coralliophila neritoidea **104f**
Coris africana **84d**
Cork Tree 22, **Fig. 12d**
Cornetfish **98f**
Corvus macrorhynchos 164, **49a**
Corydon sumatranus 155, **43a**
Costus speciosus 16, **Fig. 3c**
Cosymbotus platyurus 103, **15a**
Cotton Pygmy-Goose 130, **25a**
Crab-eating Macaque 191, 192, **65a**
Craeseonycteris thonglongyai 189, **62b**
Crested Fireback 135
Crested Goshawk 137, **26d**
Crested Honey Buzzard 136
Crested Serpent-Eagle 136, 137, **27b**
Crested Treeswift 158, **44c**
Crimson Sunbird 173, **59d**
Crimson-winged Woodpecker 154, **42c**
Crocidura murina 185, **61d**
Crocodile Salamander 78, 79, **7a**
Crocodylus siamensis 99, **14c**
Cross-bearing Tree Lizard 105, **16c**
Crow Frog 84, **9e**
Crown Squirrelfish **98c**
Crown-of-Thorns 23, **107h**
Culicicapa ceylonensis 170, **55b**
Cuon alpinus 201, **69b**
Cuora amboinensis 101, **13b**
Curcuma sp. 16, **Fig. 3b**
Cycas litoralis 22, **Fig. 13c**
Cyclemys dentata 101, **13c**
Cylindrophis ruffus 113, **18b**

Cynocephalus variegatus 189, **61b**
Cynopterus sphinx 189, **62e**
Cyornis banyumas 170, **55d**
Cypraea helvola **104a**
Cypraea talpa **104b**
Cypraea tigris **104c**
Cypraea vitellus **104d**
Cypsiurus balasiensis 158, **44b**
Cyrtodactylus intermedius 103, **15f**
Cyrtodiopsis sp. 71, **6a**
Dark-flanked Stream Frog 84, **10d**
Dark-necked Tailorbird 167, **52c**
Dascyllus aruanus **81b**
Dascyllus carneus **81c**
Dascyllus reticulata 213
Dascyllus trimaculatus **81d**
Deignan's Babbler 158, 166
Delphinus delphis 206, **75b**
Dendrelaphis pictus 115, **22b**
Dendrocitta vagabunda 164, **49d**
Dendrocygna javanica 130, **25d**
Dendronephthya sp. **101c**
Dermochelys coriacea 101, **14b**
Dhole 198
Diadem Dottyback **87c**
Dicaeum cruentatum 173, **59c**
Dicaeum ignipectus 173, **59b**
Dicerorhinus sumatrensis 205, **73b**
Dicrurus hottentottus 162, **48c**
Dicrurus macrocercus 162, **48d**
Dicrurus paradiseus 162, **48a**
Dinopium javanense 154, **41b**
Diodon hystrix **97f**
Diploprion bifasciatum **89d**
Dipterocarpus costatus 17, **Fig. 5a**
Dipterocarpus obtusifolius 19, **Fig. 8b**
Dipterocarpus tuberculatus 19, **Fig. 8c**
Dixonius siamensis 103, **15e**
Dogania subplana 101, **13f**
Dog-faced Watersnake 115, **20b**
Dollarbird 149
Dracaena lourieri 20, **Fig. 10d**
Draco melanopogon 105, **16d**
Dremomys rufigenis 197, **66e**
Dryocopus javensis 154, **42a**
Ducula bicolor 140, **32d**
Dugong 43, 205–206, 208, **75d**
Dugong dugon 206, **75d**
Durian 22, **Fig. 14c**
Durio zibethinus 22, **Fig. 14c**

Dusky Broadbill 155, **43a**
Dusky Langur 192, **65c**
Dwarf Bush-frog 88, 89, 90, **12e**
Dwarf Toad 83, **8d**
Eared Blenny **91d**
Echidna nebulosa **99c**
Echinometra mathaei **108d**
Echinosorex gymnurus 185, **61c**
Echinothrix diadema **108b**
Ecsenius midas **91f**
Edible-nest Swiftlet 157
Egretta garzetta 126, **24c**
Egretta sacra 126, **24a**
Eibl's Angelfish 212, **78b**
Elanus caeruleus 137, **26a**
Elaphe prasina 115, **21d**
Elaphe taeniura ridleyi 115, **21e**
Eld's Deer 203
Elephas maximus 205, **73a**
Eliodoxa conferta 21, **Fig. 11a**
Elongated Tortoise 101, **13a**
Elysia ornata **105e**
Emerald Dove 140, **33c**
Emperor Angelfish 212, **79b**
Enhydris plumbea 115, **20a**
Enicurus schistaceus 169, **53c**
Entacmaea quadricolor **101f**
Epinephelus corallicola **88e**
Epinephelus cyanopodus **88c**
Epinephelus lancelotus **88a**
Epinephelus malabaricus **88d**
Eretmochelys imbricata 101, **14a**
Erpeton tentaculatum 115, **20d**
Erythrina sp. 18, **Fig. 7b**
Estuarine Crocodile 97, 98
Eudynamys scolopacea 143, **34b**
Eumyias thalassina 170, **55a**
Euphorbia sp. 20, **Fig. 8d**
Eurasian Kestrel 138, **27c**
Eurasian Tree-Sparrow 174, **60c**
Eurema hecabe 70, **5a**
European Starling 55, 171
Eurostopodus macrotis 146, **36c**
Eurylaimus ochromalus 155, **43b**
Evening Cicada 66, **1d**
Eye-browed Thrush 169, **54e**
Falco tinnunculus 138, **27c**
False Chestnut 17, **Fig. 5d**
False Clownfish 213, **82a**
False Gavial 97, 98

False Gharial *See* False Gavial.
Fan Palm 19, **Fig. 9c**
Felis bengalensis 201, **72b**
Felis viverrina 201, **72e**
Ficedula parva 170, **54c**
Ficus sp. 19, **Fig. 9d**
Field Frog 84, **9a**
Fig Tree 19, **Fig. 9d**
Fire Coral **101b**
Fire Dartfish **92b**
Fire-tailed Tree-skink 107, **17b**
Fishing Cat 201, **72e**
Fistularia commersonii **98f**
Fivebar Swordtail 70, **4e**
Flame Anthias 216, **87b**
Flame of the Forest 18, **Fig. 8a**
Flank-ridged Cascade Frog 84, **10f**
Flank-spotted Gliding Treefrog 88, **12b**
Flap-headed Stream Frog 84, **9f**
Flat-headed Cat 199, 200
Flat-tailed House Gecko 103, **15a**
Flyeater 167, **52a**
Forcepsfish **78d**
Forcipiger flavissimus **78d**
Francolinus pintadeanus 135, **28b**
Fungia sp. **102e**
Gallinula chloropus 128, **29c**
Gallus gallus 135, **28c**
Garden Fence Lizard 105, **16a**
Garganey 129, 130, **25c**
Garnet Pitta 155
Garrulax leucolophus 166, **51b**
Garrulax monileger 166, **51a**
Gaur 46, 125, 201, 203, **73c**
Gekko gecko 103, **15d**
Geopelia striata 140, **33a**
Gerygone sulphurea 167, **52a**
Giant Asian Dung Beetle 67, 69, **2d**
Giant Atlas Moth 70, **3b**
Giant Black Termite 65, 66, **6e**
Giant Clam **106g**
Giant Fiddler Beetle 67, 69, **2c**
Giant Grouper 215, **88a**
Giant Ibis 128
Giant Moray **99e**
Giant Nuthatch 165
Giant Pitta 155
Giant River Frog 84, **9d**
Giant Slippery Frog 84
Giant Trevally **89f**

Giant Wood Spider 73, 172, **1f**
Glareola maldivarum 133, **31e**
Glaucidium cuculoides 145, **35a**
Glomerate Tree Coral **101c**
Glyphoglossus molossus 86, **11b**
Gnathophyllum americanum **107b**
Golden Birdwing 70, **3a**
Golden Damselfish **81f**
Golden Oriole 162
Golden Tree-snake 113, 115, **22a**
Golden-crested Myna 171, **57e**
Golden-fronted Leafbird 160, **46b**
Golden-girdled Coralfish **79a**
Golden-spotted Tiger Beetle 67, 69, **2b**
Goldsaddle Goatfish **91b**
Gomphosus caeruleus **85a**
Goral 202, 203
Gould's Frogmouth 146
Gould's Sunbird 173, **58d**
Gracula religiosa 170, **57c**
Grasslands Earless Dragon 105
Gray Demoiselle **80f**
Gray Heron 126, **23c**
Gray Reef Shark 216, **100b**
Gray Wagtail 159, **45a**
Gray-bellied Squirrel 197, **67a**
Gray-breasted Prinia 167, **52e**
Gray-capped Woodpecker 154, **41d**
Gray-headed Canary Flycatcher 170, **55b**
Gray-headed Parrotbill 166, **52b**
Gray-headed Sea-eagle 136
Gray-sided Thrush 169
Great Argus 134, 135, **28e**
Great Bandicoot 197, **68c**
Great Barbet 152, **40a**
Great Crested Tern 131
Great Eared Nightjar 136, **36c**
Great Eggfly Butterfly 60, 70, **4a**
Great Egret 126, **24f**
Great Hornbill 53, 58, 151, **39b**
Great Orange Tip 70, **5b**
Great Slaty Woodpecker 154, **42b**
Greater Adjutant 122, 128
Greater Bent-winged Bat 189, **63e**
Greater Coucal 142, 143, **34d**
Greater Mouse Deer 201
Greater Racket-tailed Drongo 161, 162, **48a**
Greater Short-nosed Fruit Bat 189, **62e**

Greater Spotted Eagle 137
Greater Yellow Bat 189, **63c**
Greater Yellownape 154, **42d**
Green Bee-eater 150, **38e**
Green Boulder Frog 84, **10c**
Green Dragontail 70, **4b**
Green Imperial Pigeon 140
Green Magpie 164, **49c**
Green Marsh Frog 84, **10a**
Green Peafowl 135
Green Tree Racer 115, **21d**
Green-billed Malkoha 143, **34c**
Greenthroat Parrotfish **86e**
Gurney's Pitta 41, 122, 155, **43e**
Gymnothorax flavimarginatus **99d**
Gymnothorax javanicus **99e**
Gymnothorax undulatus **99f**
Gymnure 184
Hair-crested Drongo 162, **48c**
Hairy-nosed Otter 200
Halcyon chloris 148, **37d**
Halcyon pileata 148, **37c**
Halcyon smyrnensis 148, **37e**
Haliaeetus leucogaster 137, **27a**
Halichoeres argus **84a**
Halichoeres timorensis **83e**
Halichoeres vrolikii **83d**
Harlequin Shrimp **107d**
Harpactes erythrocephalus 147, **36b**
Harpactes oreskios 147, **36a**
Hawksbill Sea Turtle 101, **14a**
Heart-spotted Woodpecker 154, **41e**
Hebomoia glaucippe 70, **5b**
Helarctos malayanus 201, **69c**
Heliopais personata 128, **29e**
Helmeted Hornbill 151
Hemicircus canente 154, **41e**
Hemidactylus frenatus 103, **15b**
Hemiprocne coronata 158, **44c**
Heniochus acuminatus **78e**
Herpestes javanicus 201, **71d**
Heteractis magnifica **101e**
Heterocentrotus mammillatus **108e**
Hevea brasiliensis 22, 48, **Fig. 15d**
Hexabranchus sanguineus **106b**
Highland Morning Glory 20, **Fig. 10c**
Hill Bamboo 18, **Fig. 6c**
Hill Blue Flycatcher 170, **55d**
Hill Myna 171, **57c**
Hill Oak 17, **Fig. 6a**

Himantopus himantopus 133, **31a**
Hirsute Long-horned Beetle 68, 69, **2f**
Hirundo rustica 158, **44d**
Hirundo striolata 158, **44e**
Hog Badger 201, **70a**
Hologymnosus annulatus **84c**
Holothuria atra **108g**
Homalopsis buccata 115, **20c**
Honey Cowrie **104a**
Hopea sp. 17, **Fig. 5b**
Horned Helmet **103f**
House Crow 164
House Mouse 195
House Shrew 184, 185, **61d**
House Spider 72
House Swift 158, **44a**
House Wolf-Snake 115, **22d**
Humbug Damselfish 210, **81b**
Hume's Pheasant 135
Humphead Maori Wrasse **83f**
Humpnose Unicornfish **94c**
Hylobates lar 192, **65d**
Hymenocera picta **107d**
Hypolimnas bolina 70, **4a**
Hypsipetes madagascariensis 161, **47d**
Hystrix brachyura 197, **68a**
Ichthyophis kohtaoensis 81, **7b**
Imperial Eagle 137
Indian Goatfish **91c**
Indian Humbug 213, **81c**
Indian Ocean Bird Wrasse **85a**
Indian Ocean Mimic Surgeonfish **93f**
Indian Ocean Pin-striped Wrasse **83d**
Indian Ocean Steephead Parrotfish **86d**
Indian Python 112
Indian Roller 149, 150, **38a**
Indian Triggerfish **95f**
Indian Turkeyfish **99a**
Indian Vagabond Butterflyfish **77e**
Indo-Chinese Waterdragon 103, 105, **16f**
Indo-Chinese Rat-Snake 115
Indotestudo elongata 101, **13a**
Inornate Warbler 167, **52d**
Irena puella 160, **46d**
Ironwood 22, **Fig. 13a**
Irrawaddy Dolphin 206, **75a**
Istigobius ornatus **92a**
Ixobrychus sinensis 126, **24d**
Jackfruit 22, **Fig. 14e**

Javan Frogmouth 145, 146, **35c**
Javan Mongoose 198, 201, **71d**
Javan Rhinoceros 204
Jewel Narrow-mouthed Froglet 85, 86, **11e**
Jungle Cat 199
Kalophrynus interlineatus 86, **11f**
Kaloula pulchra 86, **11c**
Ketupa zeylonensis 145, **35e**
King Cobra 108, 109, 110, 111, 115, **19c**
Kitti's Hog-nosed Bat 45, 186, 189, **62b**
Knothead Parrotfish **86a**
Komodo Dragon 103, 105
Kouprey 203
Kuhl's Flying Gecko 102, 103, **15c**
Labroides bicolor **84e**
Labroides dimidiatus **84f**
Laced Woodpecker 154, **41c**
Lacedo pulchella 148, **37a**
Lagerstroemia speciosa 18, **Fig. 7a**
Lagoon Triggerfish **96a**
Lanius cristatus 171, **56b**
Lanius schach 171, **56a**
Large Cuckoo-shrike 159, **45e**
Large Frogmouth 146
Large Green Pigeon 140
Large Indian Civet 201, **70e**
Large Wren-babbler 166
Large-billed Crow 164, **49a**
Large-eared Toad 83, **8c**
Large-tailed Nightjar 146, **36d**
Larus brunnicephalus 131, **32b**
Leaf Insect 64, 65, **1c**
Leatherback Sea Turtle 43, 99, 101, **14b**
Leiolepis belliana 105, **16e**
Lemon Damsel **81e**
Leopard 46, 201, 202, **72c**
Leopard Cat 199, 201, **72b**
Leopard Coralgrouper **89b**
Leopard Shark 216, **100a**
Leptobrachium smithi 81, **7c**
Leptolalax pelodytoides 81, **7d**
Lepus peguensis 197, **66b**
Lesser Adjutant 128
Lesser Long-tongued Fruit Bat 187, 189, **62c**
Lesser Mouse Deer 203, **74a**
Lesser Necklaced Laughingthrush 166, **51a**
Lesser One-horned Rhinoceros 204

Lesser Whistling Duck 129, 130, **25d**
Leucetta chagosensis **101a**
Lichen Bush-frog 90, **12f**
Licuala sp. 19, **Fig. 9c**
Lieutenant Surgeonfish **92e**
Lime Swallowtail 70, **3e**
Linckia multiflora **107f**
Lineated Barbet 152, **40b**
Lined Butterflyfish **76d**
Lipinia vittigera 107, **17b**
Little Cormorant 124, 125, **23b**
Little Egret 125, 126, **24c**
Little Grebe 127, 128, **25b**
Little Ringed Plover 133, **30b**
Little Spiderhunter 173, **59a**
Lonchura punctulata 174, **60a**
Lonchura striata 174, **60b**
Longfin Bannerfish **78e**
Long-legged Katydid 65, **1b**
Longnose Butterflyfish 212
Longnose Filefish **96d**
Longnose Hawkfish **82f**
Long-tailed Broadbill 154, 155, **43c**
Long-tailed Grass Lizard 106, 107, **17a**
Long-tailed Shrike 170, 171, **56a**
Long-tailed Silk Moth 70, **3c**
Long-winged Tomb Bat 189, **63b**
Lophura nycthemera 135, **28d**
Loriculus vernalis 142, **33e**
Lunar Fusilier **90c**
Luscinia calliope 169, **53b**
Luscinia cyane 169, **53a**
Lutjanus bengalensis **90b**
Lutjanus bohar **89e**
Lutjanus fulviflamma **90a**
Lutjanus sebae **90e**
Lutra perspicillata 201, **70b**
Lycodon aulicus 115, **22d**
Lygosoma bowringii 107, **17d**
Lyle's Flying Fox 189, **62d**
Lyretail Grouper **89c**
Lyretail Hogfish **83b**
Mabuya macularia 107, **17e**
Mabuya multifasciata 107, **17f**
Macaca arctoides 192, **64c**
Macaca fascicularis 192, **65a**
Macaca mulatta 192, **64d**
Macaca nemestrina 192, **64b**
Macaranga 14, 17, 71, 72, **Fig. 3d**
Macaranga sp. 17, **Fig. 3d**

Macroglossus minimus 189, **62c**
Macrolyristes corporalis 65, **1b**
Macrotermes carbonarius 66, **6e**
Magnificent Rabbitfish 212, **95a**
Magnificent Sea Anemone **101e**
Magnolia 16, 18, **Fig. 6d**
Malabar Grouper **88d**
Malayan Flying Lemur 189, **61b**
Malayan Night-heron 125
Malayan Pangolin 193, **66a**
Malayan Peacock-pheasant 135
Malayan Pit-viper 108, 110, **18e**
Malayan Porcupine 197, **68a**
Malayan Sun Bear 198, 201, **69c**
Malayemys subtrijuga 101, **13d**
Malaysian Plover 133
Mangrove Cat-Snake 96, 113, 115, **22f**
Manis javanica 193, **66a**
Manta biorostris **100f**
Manta Ray 208, 216, **100f**
Many-lined Sun-skink 107, **17f**
Many-spotted Sweetlips **90f**
Marble Cone **105a**
Marbled Cat 199
Marbled Narrow-mouthed Frog 86, **11d**
Marine Toad 83
Marsh Puddle Frog 84, **8e**
Marsh Sandpiper 133, **31b**
Martes flavigula 201, **69d**
Masked Finfoot 127, 128, **29e**
Masked Palm Civet 201, **71b**
Megalaima australis 152, **40c**
Megalaima haemacephala 152, **40e**
Megalaima lineata 152, **40b**
Megalaima mystacophanos 152, **40d**
Megalaima virens 152, **40a**
Megaloxantha bicolor 69, **2e**
Meges virescens 70, **4b**
Megophrys carinensis 81, **7f**
Megophrys lateralis 81, **7e**
Melaleuca leucadendron 21, **Fig. 11b**
Melanochlora sultanea 165, **50b**
Melastoma normale 17, **Fig. 4b**
Melichthys indicus **95f**
Melithaea sp. **101d**
Merops leschenaulti 150, **38b**
Merops orientalis 150, **38e**
Merten's Sea Anemone **101g**
Metopidius indicus 128, **29d**
Meyer's Butterflyfish **77b**

Microhierax caerulescens 138, **27e**
Microhyla inornata 86, **11e**
Microhyla pulchra 86, **11d**
Midas Blenny 215, **91f**
Milky Stork 128
Millepora sp. **101b**
Milvus migrans 137, **26c**
Mimic Blenny 215, **91e**
Mimic Filefish **96e**
Miniopterus schreibersi 189, **63e**
Mitra papalis **104g**
Mole Cowrie **104b**
Monocellate Cobra 110, **19d**
Monticola solitarius 169, **54a**
Moon Snail **103g**
Moon Wrasse 214, **85c**
Moonrat 184, 185, **61c**
Moorish Idol 212, **94e**
Mormolyce phyllodes 69, **2c**
Motacilla cinerea 159, **45a**
Motacilla alba 159, **45b**
Mountain Horned Frog 81, **7e**
Muelleripicus pulverulentus 154, **42b**
Mueller's Blind Snake 111, 113, **18a**
Mulloidichthys vanicolensis **91a**
Muntiacus muntjak 203, **74b**
Mus caroli 197, **68d**
Musa sp. 22, **Fig. 15b**
Muscicapa dauurica 170, **54d**
Muscovy Duck 129
Myripristis pralinia **98a**
Myripristis violacea **98b**
Myrmeleon sp. 67, **2a**
Naja kaouthia 111, **19d**
Narrow-headed Softshell Turtle 101
Naso lituratus **94b**
Naso tuberosus **94c**
Naso unicornis **94d**
Nectarinia jugularis 173, **58c**
Neill's Rat 197
Nelumbo nucifera 21, **Fig. 11d**
Nemateleotris magnifica **92b**
Neofelis nebulosa 201, **72a**
Nephila sp. 73, **1f**
Neptis hylas 70, **4c**
Nettapus coromandelianus 130, **25a**
Netted Olive **105g**
Neurothemis sp. 64, **1a**
Nicobar Pigeon 140
Ninox scutulata 145, **35d**

Nordmann's Greenshank 122, 133
Northern Pintail 130, **25e**
Norway Rat 194–195
Novaculichthys taeniourus **85b**
Numenius phaeopus 133, **30e**
Nycticebus coucang 192, **64a**
Nycticorax nycticorax 126, **23e**
Nyctyornis amictus 150, **38d**
Nyctyornis athertoni 150, **38c**
Occidozyga lima 84, **8e**
Octopus cyanea **106f**
Odontodactylus scyllarus **107c**
Oecophylla smaragdina 72, **6c**
Oligodon taeniatus 115, **21c**
Oliva reticulara **105g**
Olive-backed Sunbird 172, **58c**
Ophiophagus hannah 111, **19e**
Ophiothrix nereidina **108a**
Orangeband Surgonfish **93c**
Orange-breasted Trogon 147, **36a**
Orange-eyed Leaf-litter Frog 81, **7c**
Orange-lined Triggerfish **95c**
Orangespine Unicornfish **94b**
Orcaella brevirostris 206, **75a**
Oriental Bullfrog 84, **9b**
Oriental Darter 124, 125
Oriental Magpie-Robin 168, 169, **53e**
Oriental Pied Hornbill 151, **39a**
Oriental Pratincole 132, 133, **31e**
Oriental Whip-snake 115, **22c**
Oriental White-eye 173, **59e**
Oriolus chinensis 162, **48b**
Ornate Goby **92a**
Orthotomus atrogularis 167, **52c**
Ostracion meleagris **97a**
Otter Civet 200
Oxycirrhites typus **82f**
Oxymonocanthus longirostris **96d**
Pacific Deer Cowrie **104d**
Pacific Golden Plover 133, **30c**
Pacific Reef-Egret 126, **24a**
Paddyfield Pipit 159, **45c**
Paguma larvata 201, **71b**
Painted Bronzeback 112, 115, **22b**
Painted Stork 128
Painted Terrapin 101
Pale-capped Pigeon 140
Pale-headed Woodpecker 153
Pandanus 22, **Fig. 13b**
Pandanus odoratissimus 22, **Fig. 13b**

Panthera pardus 201, **72c**
Panthera tigris 201, **72d**
Panulirus pencillatus **107g**
Papaya 22, **Fig. 15a**
Paper Bark 21, **Fig. 11b**
Papilio demoleus 70, **3e**
Paracirrhites arcatus **83a**
Paradoxornis gularis 166, **52b**
Paradoxurus hermaphroditus 201, **71a**
Paraluteres prionurus **96e**
Pareas margaritophorus 115, **21a**
Particolored Flying Squirrel 197
Parupeneus cyclostomus **91b**
Parupeneus indicus **91c**
Parus spilonotus 165, **50a**
Passenger Pigeon 139
Passer flaveolus 174, **60d**
Passer montanus 174, **60c**
Pathysa antiphates 70, **4e**
Peacock Grouper **87e**
Peacock Pansy 70, **4d**
Peacock Royal 70, **5d**
Pelamis platurus 111, **19f**
Pellorneum ruficeps 166, **51d**
Peninsular Dipterocarp 17, **Fig. 5b**
Peppered Butterflyfish **77f**
Peppered Squirrelfish **98d**
Peregrine Falcon 137
Pericrocotus flammeus 159, **45d**
Petaurista petaurista 197, **66d**
Phaenicophaeus tristis 143, **34c**
Phalacrocorax niger 125, **23b**
Pheasant-tailed Jacana 127
Pherecardia striata 211, **103d**
Philautus parvulus 90, **12e**
Phragmites Grass 21, **Fig. 11c**
Phragmites sp. 21, **Fig. 11c**
Phrynoglossus martensii 84, **8f**
Phu Kradung Gliding Treefrog 88
Phyllidiella pustulosa **106c**
Phyllium sp. 65, **1c**
Phylloscopus inornatus 167, **52d**
Physignathus cocincinus 105, **16f**
Picoides canicapillus 154, **41d**
Picumnus innominatus 154, **40f**
Picus flavinucha 154, **42d**
Picus puniceus 154, **42c**
Picus vittatus 154, **41c**
Pied Fantail 170, **55e**
Pied Harrier 136, 137, **27d**

Pied Imperial Pigeon 140, **32d**
Pied Kingfisher 147
Pig-tailed Macaque 192, **64b**
Pileated Gibbon 44, 192
Pinctada margaritifera **106d**
Pineapple 22, **Fig. 15c**
Pink Shower Tree 18, **Fig. 7d**
Pinus kesiya 20, **Fig. 10b**
Pinus merkusii 20, **Fig. 10a**
Pistia stratiotes 21, **Fig. 12a**
Pitta cyanea 155, **43d**
Pitta gurneyi 155, **43e**
Plain-backed Sparrow 174, **60d**
Plain-pouched Hornbill 151
Plaintive Cuckoo 143, **34a**
Plate Coral **102g**
Platygyra lamellina **102f**
Platysternon megacephalum 101, **13e**
Plectorhinchus chaetodontoides **90f**
Plectropomus laevis **89a**
Plectropomus leopardus **89b**
Pluvialis fulva 133, **30c**
Pnoepyga pusilla 166, **51f**
Pocillopora eydouxi **102a**
Polinices mammilla **103g**
Polypedates leucomystax 90, **12a**
Polyura athamas 70, **5e**
Pomacanthus annularis **79c**
Pomacanthus imperator **79b**
Pomacanthus xanthometapon **79d**
Pomacentrus alleni **80e**
Pomacentrus amboinensis **81a**
Pomacentrus moluccensis **81e**
Pomatorhinus schisticeps 166, **51e**
Pope's Miter **104g**
Porcupinefish 215, **97f**
Porites cf. *Lobata* **102d**
Powder-blue Surgeonfish 211, **94a**
Pratapa cippus 70, **5d**
Precis almana 70, **4d**
Prehensile-tailed Skink 107
Premnas biaculeatus **82e**
Presbytis melalophus 192, **65b**
Presbytis obscura 192, **65c**
Pride of India 18, **Fig. 7a**
Prinia hodgsonii 167, **52e**
Psammodynastes pulverulentus 115, **21b**
Psarisomus dalhousiae 155, **43c**
Pseudanthias ignitis **87b**
Pseudanthias squamipinnis **87a**

Species Index

Pseudoceros dimidiatus **103c**
Pseudochromis diadema **87c**
Psittacula alexandri 142, **33d**
Ptereleotris evides **92c**
Pterois miles **99a**
Pteropus lylei 189, **62d**
Pteropus vampyrus 189, **62a**
Pteruthius flaviscapis 166, **51c**
Ptilolaemus tickelli 151, **39c**
Ptyas mucosus 115, **21f**
Ptychozoon kuhlii 103, **15c**
Puff-faced Watersnake 115, **20c**
Puff-throated Babbler 166, **51d**
Purple Heron 126, **23d**
Pycnonotus aurigaster 161, **47c**
Pycnonotus blanfordi 161, **47e**
Pycnonotus jocosus 161, **47b**
Pycnonotus melanicterus 161, **47a**
Pygmy Wren-Babbler 166, **51f**
Pygoplites diacanthus **79e**
Python reticulatus 113, **18f**
Quercus sp. 17, 20, **Fig. 6a**
Raccoon Butterflyfish **76f**
Rachet-tailed Treepie 164
Rafflesia 14, 16, **Fig. 3a**
Rafflesia sp. 16, **Fig. 3a**
Rana blythi 84, **9d**
Rana chalconota 84, **10b**
Rana erythraea 84, **10a**
Rana glandulosa 84, **10e**
Rana hascheana 84, **9e**
Rana kuhlii 84, **9c**
Rana limnocharis 84, **9a**
Rana livida 84, **10c**
Rana nigrovittata 84, **10d**
Rana pileata 84, **9f**
Rana rugulosa 84, **9b**
Rattan Palm 15, 17, 225, **Fig. 4c**
Rattus surifer 197, **68e**
Ratufa bicolor 197, **66c**
Red Darter Dragonfly 64, **1a**
Red Emperor **90e**
Red Giant Flying Squirrel 197, **66d**
Red Junglefowl 135, **28c**
Red Mangrove 21, **Fig. 12b**
Red Silk Cotton Tree 18, **Fig. 7c**
Red Snapper **89e**
Red Turtle-Dove 140, **32e**
Red-bearded Bee-eater 149, 150, **38d**
Red-breasted Parakeet 142, **33d**

Red-cheeked Squirrel 197, **66e**
Red-crowned Barbet 152
Redfin Butterflyfish **78a**
Red-headed Trogon 146, 147, **36b**
Red-naped Trogon 137
Red-necked Keelback 115, **20f**
Red-rumped Squirrel 197
Red-stemmed Palm 21, **Fig. 11a**
Red-tailed Pipe Snake 111, 112, 113, **18b**
Red-throated Barbet 152, **40d**
Red-throated Flycatcher 170, **54c**
Red-wattled Lapwing 132, 133, **30a**
Red-whiskered Bulbul 161, **47b**
Redwing 168
Regal Angelfish **79e**
Reticulated Python 109, 111, 112, 113, **18f**
Reticulated Damselfish 213
Rhabdophis subminiatus 115, **20f**
Rhacophorus bipunctatus 90, **12b**
Rhacophorus nigropalmatus 90, **12c**
Rhesus Macaque 192, **64d**
Rhincodon typus **99g**
Rhinecanthus aculeatus **96a**
Rhinecanthus rectangulus **96b**
Rhinecanthus verrucosus **96c**
Rhinoceros Hornbill 151
Rhipidura javanica 170, **55e**
Rhizophora apiculata 21, **Fig. 12b**
Rhododendron 16, 17, **Fig. 6b**
Rhododendron spp. 17, **Fig. 6b**
Rhyticeros undulatus 151, **39d**
Ricefield Terrapin 101, **13d**
Ringtail Cardinalfish **97d**
Ringtail Surgeonfish **92d**
Ringwrasse **84c**
River Tern 131
River Terrapin 101
River Toad 83, **8b**
Riverine Bamboo 17, **Fig. 5c**
Robin 168
Rock Dove 139
Rockmover Wrasse 213, **85b**
Roseate Tern 131
Rough-sided Frog 84, **10e**
Rubber Tree 22, 48, 49, 223, **Fig. 15d**
Ruby-cheeked Sunbird 173, **58b**
Rufous Treepie 164, **49d**
Rufous Woodpecker 154, **41a**
Rufous-collared Kingfisher 148

Rufous-necked Hornbill 151
Russell's Viper 108
Ryukyu Mouse 197, **68d**
Saccharum officinarum 22, **Fig. 14a**
Sacred Lotus 21, **Fig. 11d**
Saddleback Anemonefish 213, **82c**
Saddleback Coralgrouper **89a**
Saltwater Crocodile 97
Sambar 45, 203, **74c**
Sargocentron diadema **98c**
Sargocentron punctatissimum **98d**
Sarus Crane 128
Sawtooth Barracuda **99b**
Saxicola torquata 169, **54b**
Scalefin Anthias 216, **87a**
Scaly-breasted Munia 174, **60a**
Scaly-breasted Partridge 135, **28a**
Scarlet Minivet 159, **45d**
Scarlet Soldierfish **98a**
Scarlet-backed Flowerpecker 173, **59c**
Scarus flavipectoralis **86f**
Scarus ghobban **87d**
Scarus prasiognathus **86e**
Scarus strongylocephalus **86d**
Schomburgk's Deer 203
Scissortail Sergeant **79f**
Scotophilus heathi 189, **63c**
Scrawled Filefish **96f**
Sea Fan **101d**
Sepia latimanus **107a**
Sepioteuthis lessoniana **106e**
Seicercus castaniceps 167, **52f**
Serow 46, 202, 203, **74d**
Shepherd Ant 72, **6b**
Shikra 137, **26e**
Shorea siamensis 19, **Fig. 9a**
Short-tailed Parrotbill 166
Siamese Crocodile 44, 45, 97, 98, 99, **14c**
Siamese Fireback 46, 135
Siamese Hare 195, 197, **66b**
Siamese Leaf-toed Gecko 103, **15e**
Siberian Blue Robin 169, **53a**
Siberian Rubythroat 169, **53b**
Siganus corallinus **94f**
Siganus magnificus **95a**
Siganus stellatus **95b**
Sikkim Rat 197
Silver Pheasant 134, 135, **28d**
Sitta castanea 165, **50d**

Sitta frontalis 165, **50c**
Skunk Anemonefish 213, **82d**
Slate Pencil Urchin **108e**
Slaty-backed Forktail 169, **53c**
Slow Loris 190, 191, 192, **64a**
Small Indian Civet 201, **70d**
Small-clawed Otter 199, 201, **70c**
Small-spotted Coral Snake 110, **19a**
Smooth-coated Otter 199, 200, 201, **70b**
Sonneratia caseolaris 22, **Fig. 12d**
Sooty-capped Babbler 166
Sooty-headed Bulbul 161, **47c**
Southern Stripe-tailed Racer 115, **21e**
Spanish Dancer 211, **106b**
Speckled Butterflyfish **76b**
Speckled Forest Skink 107, **17e**
Speckled Grouper **88c**
Speckled Piculet 154, **40f**
Sphenomorphus maculatus 107, **17c**
Sphyraena putnamiae **99b**
Spilornis cheela 137, **27b**
Spine-cheek Anemonefish **82e**
Spinifex Grass 22, **Fig. 13d**
Spinifex littoreus 22, **Fig. 13d**
Spiny Lobster **107g**
Spiny-tailed House Gecko 103, **15b**
Spirobranchus giganteus **103e**
Spoon-billed Sandpiper 133
Spot-billed Pelican 124, 125
Spotted Boxfish **97a**
Spotted Cat-Snake 115, **22e**
Spotted Dove 140, **33b**
Spotted Eagle Ray 216, **100e**
Spotted Owlet 143, 145, **35b**
Spotted Wrasse **83c**
Stalk-eyed Fly 71, **6a**
Star Puffer **97e**
Stareye Parrotfish **86b**
Starry Moray **99c**
Stegastes obreptus **80b**
Stegostoma fasciatum **100a**
Stellate Rabbitfish **95b**
Stenopus hispidus **107e**
Stichodactyla mertensi **101g**
Stichopus chloronotus **108h**
Stingless Bee 19, 72, **6d**
Stonechat 169, **54b**
Storm's Stork 122
Straits Melastome 17, **Fig. 4b**

Straw-headed Bulbul 161
Streak-eared Bulbul 161, **47e**
Stream Softshell Turtle 101, **13f**
Stream Terrapin 101, **13c**
Streamside Puddle Frog 84, **8f**
Streamside Skink 107, **17c**
Streptopelia chinensis 140, **33b**
Streptopelia tranquebarica 140, **32e**
Striated Heron 125
Striated Swallow 158, **44e**
Striped Bush-frog 88, 90, **12d**
Striped Kukri Snake 115, **21c**
Striped Sticky Frog 85, 86, **11f**
Striped Surgeonfish **93a**
Striped Tree Squirrel 197, **67c**
Striped Wren-babbler 166
Stump-tailed Macaque 192, **64c**
Sturnus contra 171, **57a**
Sturnus nigricollis 171, **57b**
Sturnus sinensis 171, **56d**
Sugar Cane 22, **Fig. 14a**
Sultan Tit 165, **50b**
Sunbeam Snake 111, 112, 113, **18c**
Sundial **105c**
Sunset Wrasse **85d**
Sus scrofa 203, **74e**
Tachybaptus ruficollis 128, **25b**
Tadarida plicata 189, **63d**
Taeniura lymma **100g**
Takydromus sexlineatus 107, **17a**
Talauma sp. 18, **Fig. 6d**
Tamiops macclellandi 197, **67c**
Taphozous longimanus 189, **63b**
Taphozous saccolaimus 189, **63a**
Tapirus indicus 205, **69e**
Teak 19, 22, 45, 167, **Fig. 9b**
Tectona grandis 19, 22, **Fig. 9b**
Tentacled Snake 114, 115, **20d**
Terpsiphone paradisi 170, **55c**
Textile Cone **105b**
Thai Bauhinia 17, **Fig. 4a**
Thalassoma amblycephalum **85e**
Thalassoma lunare **85c**
Thalassoma lutescens **85d**
The Wanderer 70, **5c**
Theloderma asperum 90, **12f**
Thick-billed Pigeon 140, **32c**
Threadfin Butterflyfish **76a**
Three-needled Pine 20, **Fig. 10b**
Three-spot Angelfish **78f**

Threespot Dascylus **81d**
Thyrostachys siamensis 18, **Fig. 6c**
Tiger 45, 46, 183, 199, 200, 201, 202, **72d**
Tiger Cowrie **104c**
Tiger Shark 213
Timor Wrasse **83e**
Titan Triggerfish 215, **95d**
Tockay Gecko 102, 103, **15d**
Tomato Anemonefish 213, **82b**
Tonic Ant 72
Tosena splendida 66, **1d**
Tragulus javanicus 203, **74a**
Treron curvirostra 140, **32c**
Triaenodon obesus **100d**
Triangular Butterflyfish 212, **76c**
Tridacna gigas **106g**
Trigona sp. 72, **6d**
Trimeresurus albolabris 110, **18d**
Tringa glareola 133, **31c**
Tringa stagnatilis 133, **31b**
Tringa totanus 133, **30d**
Tripneustes gratilla **108c**
Triton's Trumpet **104e**
Troides aeacus 70, **3a**
Tropical Dipterocarp 17, **Fig. 4d**
Trumpetfish **98e**
Tupaia glis 185, **61a**
Turbinaria reniformis **102g**
Turdus obscurus 169, **54e**
Turnix suscitator 134, **29b**
Tursiops truncatus **75c**
Two-banded Soapfish **89d**
Two-needled Pine 20, **Fig. 10a**
Twotone Wrasse **85e**
Tylototriton verrucosus 79, **7a**
Typhlops muelleri 113, **18a**
Umbraculum umbraculum **105f**
Undulated Moray **99f**
Upland Dipterocarp 17, **Fig. 5a**
Upside-Down Jellyfish **103b**
Urocissa erythrorhyncha 164, **49b**
Valeria valeria 70, **5c**
Vanellus indicus 133, **30a**
Varanus bengalensis 105, **14d**
Variable Squirrel 197, **67b**
Variola louti **89c**
Velvet-fronted Nuthatch 165, **50c**
Verditer Flycatcher 170, **55a**
Vernal Hanging Parrot 142, **33e**

Violet Soldierfish **98b**
Viverra zibetha 201, **70e**
Viverricula malaccensis 201, **70d**
Wallace's Hawk-eagle 137
Water Lettuce 21, **Fig. 12a**
Water Monitor 103, 105
Wedge-tail Triggerfish **96b**
Western Gregory 213, **80b**
Whale Shark 216, **99g**
Whimbrel 133, **30e**
Whiskered Tern 130, 131, **32a**
White Costus 16, **Fig. 3c**
White Wagtail 159, **45b**
White-bellied Sea-Eagle 136, 137, **27a**
White-bellied Woodpecker 154, **42a**
White-bellied Yuhina 166, **50e**
White-breasted Waterhen 127, 128, **29a**
White-browed Scimitar-Babbler 166, **51e**
White-browed Shrike-Babbler 166, **51c**
White-chested Babbler 166
White-crested Laughingthrush 166, **51b**
White-eyed River-Martin 55, 122, 158, 166
White-fronted Bee-eater 149
White-fronted Scops-owl 144
White-handed Gibbon 192, **65d**
White-lipped Pit-viper 110, **18d**
White-lipped Treefrog 88, 89, **12a**
White-rumped Munia 174, **60b**
White-rumped Shama 169, **53d**
White-rumped Vulture 122
White-shouldered Ibis 128
White-shouldered Starling 171, **56d**
White-spotted Slug-Snake 114, 115, **21a**
White-spotted Surgeonfish **92f**
White-throated Kingfisher 148, **37e**
Whitetip Reef Shark 216, **100d**
White-vented Myna 171, **57d**
White-winged Duck 129
Wild Ginger 16, **Fig. 3b**
Wild Pig 199, 201, 202, 203, **74e**
Wild Water Buffalo 203
Wood Sandpiper 133, **31c**
Woolly-necked Stork 128
Wreathed Hornbill 151, **39d**
Wrinkled Hornbill 151
Wrinkle-lipped Bat 187, 189, **63d**
Xenochrophis piscator 115, **20e**
Xenopeltis unicolor 113, **18c**

Yellow Bittern 126, **24d**
Yellow Rajah Rat 197, **68e**
Yellow-banded Caecilian 79, 81, **7b**
Yellow-bellied Sea Snake 108, 111, **19f**
Yellowbelly Watersnake 114, 115, **20a**
Yellow-cheeked Tit 165, **50a**
Yellowfin Goatfish **91a**
Yellowfin Parrotfish **86f**
Yellowfin Surgeonfish **93e**
Yellowmargin Moray **99d**
Yellowmask Angelfish **79d**
Yellow-throated Marten **69d**
Yellowtop Fusilier **90d**
Yuhina zantholeuca **50e**
Zanclus cornutus **94e**
Zebra Dove 140, **33a**
Zosterops palpebrosus 173, **59e**

GENERAL INDEX

Acanthuridae 211
Accipitridae 135
active searchers 95
agamid lizards 102, 103–105
Alcedinidae 147
alligators 94, 97, 98
altricial 55
amplexus 76, 82, 85, 89
anacondas 111
Anatidae 128
Andaman Sea 9, 23, 41, 43, 207, 208, 209, 211, 212, 213
anemonefishes 210, 213, 216
Angelfishes 212–213, 216
anhingas 124
antlions 66–67
ants 14, 17, 51, 61, 65, 71–72
Anura 75, 79
Apodidae 156
Arachnida 52, 61
Ardeidae 125
Arthropoda 59, 211
arthropods 52, 59, 61–63, 211. *See also* Chapter 5.
Artiodactyla 201
artiodactyls 201
babblers 123, 160, 165–166
baboons 190
badgers 198
baleen whales 206
Balistidae 215
Bangkok 4, 6, 9, 44, 112, 157
barbets 122, 151–152, 153
barrier reefs 23
Batrachostomidae 145
bats 19, 66, 102, 120, 136, 175, 176, 177, 180, 181, 182, 185–189
bears 197, 198, 199–200
bee-eaters 148–150
bees 15, 19, 71–72, 136, 148, 149

beetles 60, 61, 62, 67–69, 117
biodiversity 1, 90, 91, 116, 211
bioindicators 60
biological control 60, 71
biophilia 2
birdwings 70
bivalves 211
blennies 215
Blenniidae 215
blind snakes 111
boas 111, 112
boids 111
Bovidae 201
box turtles 99
broadbills 154–155
brown snakes 113
Bucerotidae 150
Buddhist philosophy 5–6, 101
buffalo 201
Bufonidae 82
bulbuls 160–161
bullfrogs 84
Burma Banks 208
burrowing frogs 86
bush-frogs 87, 88, 89
butterflies 19, 61, 62, 63, 69–70, 116, 117
butterflyfishes 210, 212, 213, 216
buttonquail 122, 128, 133–135
buttressed trees 14, 16
caecilians 75–76, 79–81, 109
caimans 97
Callitrichidae 190
Campephagidae 158
Canidae 53, 197
Capitonidae 151
Caprimulgidae 145
Carnivora 53, 197
carnivores 53, 55, 68, 181, 182, 197–201

cassava 22
caterpillars 62, 70, 143, 158
cats 83, 139, 144, 181, 197, 199–201, 202
cattle 28, 45, 52, 201, 202, 203
Caudata 75, 79
Cebidae 190
Central Plains 11, 12, 41, 44, 45, 48, 58, 125, 128, 131
cephalopods 211
Cercopithecidae 190, 191
Cervidae 201
Cerylidae 147
Cetacea 205
cetaceans 205–206
Chaetodontidae 212
Charadriidae 131
Charadriiformes 130, 131
Chevrotains 201
Chiang Dao 47, 166
Chiang Mai 4, 9, 11, 46, 47, 78
Chiroptera 186
Chloropseidae 159
cicadas 63, 66
Ciconiidae 127
CITES 56
civets 88, 187, 197–198, 200
cleaners 211, 214
cleaning stations 211, 214
climbers 14
cockroaches 64, 102, 188
coconuts 22
Coleoptera 67
colubrids 113–115
colugos 185
Columbidae 138
commensalisms 51, 52
competition 51
cone shells 211
Convention on International Trade in Endangered Species (CITES) 56
copperheads 108
Coraciidae 148
coral reefs 6, 22–23, 41, 43, 44, 209, 210
coral snakes 108
cormorants 124
corn 22, 37, 38, 98
Corvidae 159, 163
coucals 142–143

cowries 211
crabs 52, 59, 191, 199, 206, 211
crickets 64
crocodiles 93, 94, 97–99, 100
crocodilians 94, 97–99
crows 163–164
Crustacea 61, 211
crustaceans 61, 211
cryptic coloration 96, 102
cuckoos 123, 142–143, 167
cuckoo-shrikes 158–159
Cuculidae 142
cursorial 55
Cynocephalidae 185
damselfishes 210, 213, 216
damselflies 63–64
darters 124
decomposers 37, 38
deer 46, 183, 198, 199, 201, 202, 203
detritivores 55
dewlaps 95, 103
Dicaeidae 172
Dicruridae 161
Diodontidae 215
Diptera 70
Dipterocarp 12, 16, 17, 18, 19, 57, 178
Dipterocarpaceae 16
dogs 83, 197, 198, 199
Doi Ang Khang 47
Doi Inthanon 6, 9, 11, 47
Doi Inthanon National Park 47
Doi Suthep-Doi Pui National Park 46–47
dolphins 205–206
doves 138–140
dragonflies 63–64
dragons 103
drongos 123, 161–162, 202
dry deciduous dipterocarp forest 18–19, 57
ducks 124, 127, 128–130
eagles 135–137
echinoderms 211
ecotourism. See Chapter 1.
ecotravel 23, 40, 41. See also Chapter 1
egrets 44, 52, 125–126
Elapidae 108
elapids 108
Elephantidae 203
elephants 45, 125, 183, 203–205

General Index

emergents 12
endangered species 56
endemism 115–116
environmental threats 4–7
epiphytes 14–15, 16, 17, 51, 78
Erawan National Park 44–45
Erinaceidae 184
Eurylamidae 154
eutherians 181
evapotranspiration 38
fairy-bluebirds 159, 160
Falconidae 137
falcons 137–138
Fang 47
farms 22
Felidae 198
finches 173–174
flash coloration 90
flatworms 211
flies 61, 62, 70–71
flowerpeckers 171–173
flying dragons 102, 104
flying foxes 186, 189
flying geckos 102, 104
flying lemurs 185–189, 195
flying snakes 113
flying squirrels 194, 195
fossorial 55, 75, 85
foxes 53, 197
francolins 133, 134
Fringillidae 174
fringing reefs 23, 208, 209
frogmouths 145–146
frugivores 55, 121, 175, 176, 177, 191
fruit bats 187, 188, 189
galago 190
garter snakes 113
gastropods 211
gavials 97
geckos 101–103, 104, 106
geese 128, 129
Gekkonidae 101
genets 197, 198, 200
gestation 55
gibbons 190, 191, 192
gingers 14
gizzard 120, 139, 173
Glareolidae 132
gliding lizards 102, 104
gliding treefrogs 87, 89

goannas 103
goats 146, 201, 202, 203
goatsuckers 146
Gobeidae 214
gobies 214–216
gorgonians 210
granivores 55, 121
grass lizards 95, 106, 107
grasshoppers 64
green snakes 113
ground squirrels 194
ground-cuckoos 142–143
groupers 215–216
grubs 62, 64, 153, 165
Gulf of Thailand 9, 11, 23, 41, 44, 207, 208, 209, 212, 213
gulls 130–131
Gymnophiona 75, 79
Had Nai Yang National Park 43
hard corals 208, 210
Hat Jao Mai National Park 43
hawks 135–137, 146, 187
hedgehogs 183–184
Heliornithidae 127
helmets 211
Hemiprocnidae 156
herbivores 55, 71
herons 44, 125–126, 128
hill evergreen forest 16, 47, 57
Hirundinidae 156
Homoptera 66
hoofed mammals 201
hornbills 46, 65, 150–151
Huai Kha Khaeng Wildlife Sanctuary 45
Hydrophidae 108
Hylidae 84
Hylobatidae 191
Hymenoptera 71
Hystricidae 194
iguanas 103
indigenous species 53
insectivores 55, 121, 167, 176, 183, 185, 187
International Union for Conservation of Nature 3, 56
introduced species 55
invertebrates 21, 23, 52, 188, 208, 210
ioras 159–160
Irenidae 159

Isthmus of Kra 207, 208, 209, 212
IUCN Red List 56
jacanas 122, 127–128
Jacanidae 127
jackals 197
jays 121, 163
jumping spiders 63
Kaeng Krachan National Park 45, 99, 151, 164
Khao Ang Ru Nai Wildlife Sanctuary 44, 99
Khao Banthad Wildlife Sanctuary 43
Khao Kitchakut National Park 44
Khao Nor Chuchi Lowland Forest Project 41
Khao Phra Thaw Royal Wildlife and Forest Reserve 43
Khao Pra Bang Kram Wildlife Sanctuary 41
Khao Sam Roi Yot National Park 45
Khao Soi Dao Wildlife Sanctuary 44
Khao Sok National Park 41, 43
Khao Yai National Park 46, 183, 192
Khu Khut Waterbird Sanctuary 43
kingfishers 147–148
kites 135–137
Koh Chang National Marine Park 209
Koh Samui and Koh Ang Thong National Park 41, 209
Krabi 41, 126, 208
kraits 108, 109
Labridae 213
Lagamorpha 195
langurs 191
Laniidae 170
laterite 19, 38
latitudinal gradient in species diversity 116
leaf insects 64
leaf litter 12
leafbirds 159–160
leaf-litter toads 81
Lekagul, Dr. Boonsong 5
lemurs 116, 185–189, 190
Lepidoptera 69, 70
lianas 14
llimestone forest 19–20, 57
limpets 211
lizards 75, 78, 94–95, 96, 97, 100, 103–107. *See also* Chapter 5.

lobsters 61, 211
locusts 60
logging 5, 6, 7, 38, 205
lorises 190
Lorisidae 190
Lum Nam Pai and NAmtok Mae SUrin National Park 47
Lumphini Park 44
Mae Wong National Park 45
maggots 62
magpies 163–164
Malay Peninsula 9, 207, 208, 209
malkohas 142, 143
mambas 108
manatees 205, 206
mandrills 190
mangrove 11, 14, 19, 21–22, 43, 44, 45, 57
Manidae 192
marine arthropods 211
marine worms 211
marshes 11, 20–21, 44, 47, 57, 128
marsupials 180
Megophryidae 81
Mekong River 11, 47, 153
Melastomacea 14
melastomes 14
Meropidae 148
metamorphosis 62, 79
mice 194, 195, 196
Microhylidae 84
microhylids 85, 86
minivets 158, 159
minks 198
mixed-species foraging flock 123, 152, 160, 162, 164, 165, 167, 169
mollusks 211
mongooses 88, 197, 198, 200
monitor lizards 93, 103–105
monkeys 180, 182, 183, 189–191, 192
monks 6
monocultures 39
monogamy 62, 121, 132, 182, 188
monotremes 180
monsoon evergreen forest 16, 17, 43, 57
monsoons 9, 209
Motacillidae 158
moths 19, 69–70
mouse deer 201, 202, 203

General Index

munias 173–174
Muridae 194
Muscicapidae 169
Mustelidae 198
mutualisms 51, 52
Mycorrhizae 37, 39
Nam Nao National Park 46
narrow-mouthed frogs 84–86
native species 161. *See also* indigenous species.
Nectariniidae 171
nectarivores 55, 121
Neuroptera 66
New World monkeys 190
NGOs 5, 6, 7
nighthawks 146
nightjars 123, 145–146
non-passerines 121
nudibranchs 211
nuthatches 164–165
nymphs 62, 64, 65, 66
obligate mutualism 17, 51
octopuses 211
Odonata 63
odonates 63, 54
old growth forests 15
Old World flycatchers 169–170
Old World monkeys 182, 190, 191
Old World warblers 166–170
olives 211
omnivores 55, 163, 202
Oriental Region 9, 53, 81, 103, 159, 183
orioles 162–163
Oriolidae 161
Orthoptera 64
owls 123, 143–145
ox-frogs 85, 86
oysters 211
palms 14, 15, 16, 21
pangolins 192–193
parakeets 140, 141, 142
parasitism 51
Paridae 164
parotoid glands 82, 83
parrotfishes 214
parrots 140–142, 177, 178
partridges 133, 134
passeriformes 154
Passerines 121, 122
patch reefs 23

peacocks 133, 166
peafowl 133, 134
peahens 133
Pelicaniformes 124
pelicans 124–125
Peninsular Thailand 11, 41–43, 48, 58
perching birds 154, 156
Perissodactyla 203
Phasianidae 133
pheasants 53, 133–135
Pheromone 70, 109
Phu Hin Rong Kla National Park 46
Phu Khieo Wildlife Sanctuary 46
PHu Luang Royal Wildlife Sanctuary 46
Phuket 9, 41, 43, 208
Picidae 152
piculets 152, 153
pigeons 138–140
pigs 139, 178, 201, 202
pine forest 20, 57
pipe snakes 111, 113
pipits 158–159
piscivores 55, 147
pittas 154–155
Pittidae 154
pit-vipers 108
plankton 23, 81, 213,
plantations 19, 22, 43, 48, 49, 57
Ploceidae 173
plovers 131, 132
Podicipedidae 127
polyandry 55, 62, 121, 127, 134, 182
Polychaete worms 211
polygamy 55
polygyny 55, 62, 121, 134, 182, 188
Pomacanthidae 212
Pomacentridae 213
porcupinefishes 215
porcupines 194, 195, 196
Prajak, Phra 6
pratincoles 132
precocial 55
predation 51
prehensile 55
primates 189–192
proboscis monkeys 190
Prosimians 190
Psittacidae 140
puffers 215
Pycnonotidae 160

pythons 111–113
quail 133, 134
Queen Sirikit Botanical Gardens and Nature Educational Centre 43
rabbitfishes 212
rabbits 53, 194–197
Rafflesia 14, 16, 41
rails 127, 128
rainfall 9, 11, 16, 38, 65
Rallidae 127
range 53
Ranidae 83, 84
ranids 83, 84
rat snakes 113
rats 194, 195, 196, 197
rattan 15
rattlesnakes 108, 109
rays 216
rear-fanged snakes 113, 114
Recurvirostridae 131
Rhacophoridae 87
rhesus monkeys 190
rhinoceros 203–205
rice 4, 11, 20, 22, 44, 45, 57, 71, 196
River Kwai 45
Rodentia 194
rodents 194–197
rollers 148–150
rubber 22, 43, 47–49
Sai Yok National Park 45
salamanders 75, 77–79, 90
sand dollars 211
sandpipers 131, 132
Scaridae 214
Sciuridae 194
Scolopacidae 131
sea cow 205
sea cucumbers 211
sea fans 210
sea hares 211
sea slugs 211
sea snakes 108, 109, 110
sea stars 211
sea turtles 94, 99, 101
sea urchins 211, 215
sea whips 210
seals 205
Serranidae 215
sex changers 213, 216
sharks 52, 208, 209, 216

sheep 201, 203
shorebirds 131–133
shrews 180, 183–185
shrikes 170–171
shrimp 59, 61, 211
Siganidae 212
Similan Islands 208, 212, 216
Sirenia 205
sit-and-wait predators 95, 102, 106
Sittidae 164
skinks 105–107
skunks 198
slash-and-burn agriculture 38
slender toads 82
slugs 211
snails 211
snakes 94, 95, 96, 107–115
snout-vent lengths (SVLs) 57
soft corals 209, 210
Soricidae 183
soybeans 22
spadefoot toads 81
sparrows 173–174
spiders 52, 59, 61, 62, 63, 72–73
sponges 210, 212
squids 211
squirrels 177, 194, 195, 196, 197
starlings 138, 170–171
sticky frogs 85
stilts 131, 132
stoats 198
storks 127–128
Strigidae 143
Sturnidae 170
subtropical 53
Suidae 201
sunbirds 171–173
surgeonfishes 211–212
Surin and Similan Island National Marine Park 43, 208
Surin Islands 208
swallows 156–158
swallowtails 70
swamps 20–21, 57
swans 128, 129
swifts 156–158
Sylviidae 166
tadpoles 75
tail autotomy 106, 107
Tapiridae 203

General Index

tapirs 203–205
tarsiers 190
termitarium 65
termites 37, 51, 62, 65–66
terns 130–131
terrapins 99
terrestrial 55, 99
Tetradontidae 215
Thale Ban National Park 43, 66
Thale Sap Lagoons 43
Thaleh Noi Waterbird Sanctuary 43
Tha Ton 47
threatened species 56
thrushes 169–169
Thung Nai Naresuan Wildlife Sanctuary 45
Thung Salaeng Luang National Park 46
Timaliidae 165
tits 164–165
toothed whales 206
tortoises 94, 99
Tragulidae 201
Trang 43
tree squirrels 194, 196
treefrogs 87–90, 96
treepies 163
treeshrews 183–184
treeswifts 154, 156–158
triggerfishes 215
tritons 211
Trogonidae 146
trogons 123, 146–147
tropical evergreen forests 16, 177, 178
tropical mixed deciduous forest 18
true bugs 61
true frogs 83–84
true shrews 183–184
true toads 82–83
tsunami 41
tuataras 94
Tupaiidae 183
turbans 211
Turdidae 168
Turnicidae 134
turtles 94, 99–101
ungulates 201–203
Ursidae 197
venom 72, 95, 107, 108, 109, 110, 113
venomous snakes 96, 107–110
Viperidae 107
vipers 107, 108, 109
Viverridae 197
volutes 211
wagtails 158–159
wasps 15, 20, 71–72
Wat Asokoram 44
water moccasins 108
water snakes 133
weasels 197, 198, 200
weavers 173
whales 180, 205–206
whip snakes 113
white-eyes 171–173
wolf snakes 113
wolf spiders 63
wolverines 198
wolves 197
woodpeckers 123, 152–154
worm snakes 111
wrasses 211, 213–214
Zingiberaceae 14
Zostreopidae 172

Explanation of Symbols Used in the Plate Section

HABITAT SYMBOLS

- = Tropical evergreen forest

- = Monsoon evergreen forest

- = Hill evergreen forest

- = Mixed deciduous forest

- = Dry deciduous dipterocarp forest

- = Limestone forest

- = Pine forest

- = Forest edge and streamside. Some species typically are found along forest edges or near or along streams; these species prefer semi-open areas rather than dense, closed, interior parts of forests. Also included here: open woodlands, tree plantations, and shady gardens.

- = Pastureland, non-tree plantations, savannah (grassland with scattered trees and shrubs), gardens without shade trees, roadside. Species found in these habitats prefer very open areas.

- = Freshwater. For species typically found in or near lakes, streams, rivers, marshes, swamps, and wet rice paddies.

- = Saltwater/marine. For species found in or near the ocean, ocean beaches, or mangroves.

REGIONS (see Map 2, p. 42):

PT = Peninsular Thailand
SE = The Southeast
CP = The Central Plains
W = The West
NE = The Northeast
FN = The Far North